MACMILLAN

# DICTIONARY OF RELIGION

MACMILLAN

# DICTIONARY OF RELIGION

Michael Pye

M

First edition published 1994 by
THE MACMILLAN PRESS LTD,
London and Basingstoke

Associated companies in Auckland, Delhi, Dublin, Gaborone, Hamburg, Harare, Hong Kong, Johannesburg, Kuala Lumpur, Lagos, Manzini, Melbourne, Mexico City, Nairobi, New York, Singapore, Tokyo

A catalogue record for this book is available from The British Library.

ISBN 0-333-45409-X

Printed in Great Britain.

# Contents


| | |
|---|---|
| Editors | vii |
| Contributors | viii |
| Acknowledgements | xi |
| Using this Dictionary | xiii |
| DICTIONARY OF RELIGION | 1 |
| Bibliography | 303 |

# Editors

**General Editor**

Professor Michael Pye
Department of Religious Studies
Lancaster University

**Editorial Advisors**

*Judaism and Christianity*
Professor Peter Antes
University of Hannover, Germany

*Philosophy and Psychology of Religion*
Professor John Clayton
Lancaster University, UK

*Indian Religions*
Professor Klaus Klostermaier
University of Manitoba, Canada

*New Religions, Sociology of Religion*
Dr Kim Knott
University of Leeds, UK

*African Religions, Primal Religion*
Professor Thomas Lawson
University of Western Michigan, USA

*Classical and Hellenistic Religions*
Professor Luther Martin
University of Vermont, USA

*Islām*
Dr David Waines
Lancaster University, UK

# Contributors

Alderink, Larry
Concordia College
Moorhead
U S A

Amore, Roy
University of Windsor
Windsor
Canada

Antes, Peter
University of Hannover
Hannover
Germany

Byrt, Christopher
Marburg
Germany

Clayton, John
Lancaster University
Lancaster
England

David, Rosalie
Manchester University Museum
Manchester
England

Falk, Nancy Auer
Western Michigan University
Kalamazoo
U S A

Frank, Barbara
Institut für Völkerkunde und Afrikanistik
München
Germany

Girgensohn-Minker, Britta
University of Munich
München
Germany

Gothöni, René
University of Helsinki
Helsinki
Finland

Greschat, Hans-Jürgen
University of Marburg
Marburg
Germany

Hahn, Thomas
University of Heidelberg
Heidelberg
Germany

Heelas, Paul
Lancaster University
Lancaster
Englang

Hock, Klaus
München
Germany

Holm, Nils
Åbo Akademi
Åbo
Finland

Ibn Yusuf, Ya'qub
University of Manitoba
Winnipeg
Canada

Khan, Abrahim
University of Toronto
Toronto
Canada

Klostermaier, Klaus
University of Manitoba
Winnipeg
Canada

Knott, Kim
University of Leeds
Leeds
England

Lawson, E. Thomas
Western Michigan University
Kalamazoo
U S A

Martin, Luther
University of Vermont
Burlington
U S A

Milbank, John
University of Cambridge
Cambridge
England

Paper, Jordan
York University
North York
Canada

Pettersen, Alvvn
Corpus Christi College
Oxford
England

Phillips, Robert
Lehigh University
Bethlehem
U S A

Pye, Jocelyn
Cambridge
England

Pye, Michael
Lancaster University
Lancaster
England

Rudolph, Kurt
University of Marburg
Marburg
Germany

Schlang, S
Marburg
Germany

Schütt, Beate
Marburg
Germany

Seiwert, Hubert
University of Hannover
Hannover
Germany

Sharpe, Eric
University of Sydney
Sydney
Australia

Sherry, Patrick
Lancaster University
Lancaster
England

Siikala, Anna-Leena
University of Joensuu
Joensuu
Finland

Sonoda, Minoru
Kyoto University
Kyoto
Japan

Stegerhoff, Renate
University of Marburg
Marburg
Germany

Strenski, Ivan
University of California
Santa Barbara
U S A

Vasquez, Irene
Western Michigan University
Kalamazoo
USA

Waines, David
Lancaster University
Lancaster
England

Wiebe, Donald
University of Toronto
Toronto
Canada

Wyatt, Nicolas
Edinburgh University
Edinburgh
Scotland

# Acknowledgements

This dictionary is the result of teamwork by contributors from various countries who have all shown great care and patience. The editorial process itself has been somewhat complex. This is partly because it allowed, intentionally, for inductive contributions from a large number of provisional fields. In other words the list of headwords was not prescribed, but jointly created. Partly, also, it is because 'religions' and geographical or cultural 'areas' do not fall into symmetrical packages. For example, Buddhism, Christianity and Islām, cross many countries and continents. This gives rise to inconveniently dissimilar numbers of words! Moreover the various fields influence each other and are regarded by different specialists from various standpoints. This in turn has an effect on the reflective vocabulary used in studies of religion. Thus considerable editorial correlation, conflation and supplementation has been necessary.

This complex process makes it inappropriate to specify authorship for the individual entries, or even areas. Naturally, readers will recognize that in various cases a specialist has worked on a specific field; for example, that Dr. Barbara Frank has contributed specifically on *West* African religion, or that Dr. Rosalie David has contributed specifically on Egyptian religion. In wide areas such as Indian, Chinese or American religions, Israelite and Jewish religion, or philosophy of religion, there have been two or three leading contributors to the dictionary. Naturally, without the work of the many specialist contributors the dictionary could never have come into existence. However in other cases the correlations and editorial adjustments make such assignment less easy or even impossible. The editor therefore wishes to say that contributors should be credited with all the merit which the entries in their known fields of work display. At the same time they should not be blamed speculatively for any imperfections which may have crept in. To give another example, permission was obtained to draw material from the work *Basic Term of Shintō* published by the Shintō Committee for the *IXth* International Congress for the History of Religions (Tokyo 1958). The material has been freely selected and edited, so that any flaws are the responsibility of this editor. However the positive value of this source is most gratefully acknowledged.

The same principle applies in a broader sense to the editorial advisors, who are named separately. The field covered by the dictionary does not exactly divide up into the fields with which they are professionally identified. Thus there can be no assignment of responsibility, to them, for blemishes which may have arisen as a result of the overall editorial procedure. Nevertheless their perspicacious, yet discreet and kindly suggestions, have been of the greatest importance. They have provided solid assistance right up to publication.

Many of the contributors, and all the subject editors, are internationally well known as specialists in various aspects of the study of religion. I must ask them to excuse the simplicity of the format in which their names and places of work have been presented. This is partly to get over the fact that professional titles are set out very differently in various countries. Other contributors may be younger and less well known, but their work was similarly clearly and shrewdly presented. I am no less grateful to them. Several contributors, including busy and well established writers in the field, have provided a particularly large number of entries or have acted very speedily when it seemed especially urgent. It would embarrass them to be named specifically, but in these ways friendships are forged.

The editorial process itself was assisted not only by the editorial advisors, but also at various stages by Christopher Byrt, Roland Meyer, Beate Schütt and Renate Stegerhoff during their student days at Marburg. Extensive editorial assistance was also provided by my daughter Jocelyn Pye, especially at times of particular complexity.

Although the dictionary is internationally based, there is a slight clustering of contributors' names around the universities of Marburg and Lancaster. Each of these universities provides a fine, supportive and much appreciated context for studies in religion.

Michael Pye
Editor
Lancaster University, 1993

# Using this Dictionary

### *Alphabetic order*

The alphabetic order is determined without reference to spaces, hyphens and accents. The English definite article 'the' has been systematically avoided in headwords. The Arab prefix 'al-' occurs occasionally, but is ignored in the determination of the alphabetic order.

### *Cross References*

Cross-references to entries of related interest are shown in small capitals. The simple cross-reference in the form 'A *see* B' does *not* necessarily mean that A and B are identical; it merely means that at least some information about A, possibly indirect, may be found under B.

### *Romanization*

The romanization of foreign words, which are rather numerous, has followed modern practice in the various fields, as far as possible.

In general, the form given in the headword is to be preferred to the alternative forms given in brackets. For Chinese, the *pinyin* system has been given priority and the more traditional Wade-Giles forms are found in brackets. For Sanskrit, the customary diacritical marks are generally used, and anglicisms such as 'sh' (for ṣ or ś) have been avoided. Note that words derived from influential languages like Arabic and Sanskrit, for example in Indonesian or Punjabi, may have a slightly different form in these latter languages. For Buddhism, depending on the context, Sanskrit and Pāli equivalents are often given. This does not imply that the term has the same significance in the varying Buddhist literature of these two languages.

# A

**a**. The first letter of the Sanskrit alphabet, considered in esoteric Buddhism to embody the original, unproduced nature of all things, and hence used as a focus for meditation.

**Aaronic priesthood**. Named after Aaron, the brother of Moses, first in line of a priestly family in ancient Israel. Aaron's role was later seen as foreshadowing the priestly function of Christ, as in the *Epistle to the Hebrews*.

**abangan** (Javanese; Indonesian: 'the reds'). A term derived from the red complexion of corresponding WAYANG figures, designating the vast majority of Javanese who only nominally profess Islam and, contrary to the SANTRI, follow their own Javanese tradition (AGAMA KEJAWEN). (Geertz 1960a; Jay 1963, 1969; Koentjaraningrat 1971; Mulder 1983a).

**Abba** (Aramaic: 'Father'). The word used by Jesus when praying that he be spared crucifixion (*Mark* 14.36), and taken up by Paul as a direct address to God implying the sonship of man (*Romans* 8.15; *Galatians* 4.6).

**abbess**. The superior nun in convents observing the Benedictine rule, and in some others.

**abbot**. The superior, or 'father', of a monastic institution, elected by his peers but in some cases subordinate to the BISHOP.

**Abel.** *See* MANDAEANS.

**abhidhamma** (Pāli). The classical philosophy of Theravāda Buddhism on the ethics and philosophy of mind, elaborated in the third 'basket' of the Pāli Canon, the *Abhidhamma Piṭaka*. The Sanskrit equivalent, *Abhidharma Piṭaka*, designates comparable works of other schools of Buddhism, although the contents diverge significantly. *See also* TRIPIṬAKA.

**Abhidhamma Piṭaka**. *See* ABHIDHAMMA; TRIPIṬAKA.

**abhidharma**. *See* ABHIDHAMMA; TRIPIṬAKA.

**Abhidharma-Kośa**. *See* KUSHA-SHŪ.

**Abhidharma Piṭaka**. *See* ABHIDHAMMA; TRIPIṬAKA.

**àbìkú** (Yoruba). Malicious spirits who enter newborn children, who then will die in infancy. Belief in such spirits is current among the Yoruba of southwestern Nigeria (McClelland 1982).

**abjuration**. *See* OATH OF ABJURATION.

**Abode of the Blest** [Immortals' Realm]. A complex conception associated with ancient Chinese myths and the notion of paradise. Two concepts can be deduced, the first centring around Mount KUNLUN and the second centring on three geomythical locations off the North China coast, namely the imaginary islands Peng Lai, Fang Zhang and Ying Zhou. The islands were supposed to yield medicinal herbs that guaranteed immortality (*see* LONGEVITY).

**abrogation**. *See* AL-NASIKH WA'AL-MANSUKH.

**absolute**. Used either as substantive or modifier. As substantive, it refers to that which is unconditional, non-contingent without limitations, non-relative, perfect, ultimate. Hence, it signifies ultimate reality as contrasted with either appearance or whatever is limited or relative. Through certain 18th- and 19th-century European philosophical movements that rejected the Kantian idea of the limitation of human knowledge, it gained popularity as a synonym for Being, God or Reason. Schelling regarded philosophy as the science of the absolute. Hegel referred to the Absolute as the 'Idea which knows itself', and used it also as a modifier of Spirit. Thus in the *Encyclopaedia* Absolute Spirit is eternally generative. It frequently appears to qualify 'ego', 'truth', 'space', or 'idealism'. For example, Fichte refers to the absolute ego as the creator of all phenomena. In Hinduism the absolute is BRAHMAN which is one, real, without qualities and the ultimate principle of everything. With respect to 'philosophical' *Buddhism*, as for example in the MADHYAMIKA SCHOOL, the term should be used with caution because the relations between epistemology and ontology are differently conceived and cannot be understood without reference to the meditational function of Buddhist thought.

**absolution**. The pronouncement of the forgiveness of sins by a priest.

**abstinence**. Avoidance of particular kinds of food and drink or of sexual activity, either to maintain purity before a religious ceremony or as a personal discipline.

**Abuk**. The only well-known female manifestation of the divine creator-power *Jok* among the western Dinka, and sometimes the wife of *Deng*, presiding over the occupations of women (Lienhardt 1961).

**Abydos**. The burial place of early kings (*c.* 2700 BCE) and Egypt's major centre of pilgrimage where the mortuary temples of Sethos I (1300 BCE) and Ramesses II (1290 BCE) still stand. As the cult-centre of OSIRIS, Abydos was especially sacred (Calverley 1933).

**ācārya** (Sanskrit: 'master', 'one who leads the way'). A term used as honorific (e.g. Saṅkara *ācārya*) and as academic title (M.A. equivalent). In order to qualify for the title *ācārya* in VEDĀNTA, a person had to write commentaries on the *prasthāna trayī* (UPANIṢADS; BHAGAVADGĪTĀ; BRAHMASŪTRAS) and expound in these a coherent interpretation of the major points of Vedāntic doctrine.

**accidents**. In Christian SCHOLASTICISM, an accident is that which has no existence in itself, but only inheres in a SUBSTANCE, e.g. a colour. St Thomas Aquinas taught that in the MASS, although the accidents of the bread and wine remain, the substance become the body and blood of Christ (TRANSSUBSTANTIATION).

**accommodation**. A technical term in Western Christianity for the adapted interpretation of a biblical text or a specific detail of doctrine to special circumstances. *Compare* UPAYA.

**acolyte**. An assistant to a Christian priest, usually a lay person, whose task is to light and to carry candles and to hold ready the wine and the water used in celebrations of the MASS.

**acropolis**. An 'upper city' or strong point built on top of the highest point in an ancient city as a place of safety and worship. The most famous is the Acropolis of Athens, with its famous temples and the statue of ATHENA, visible throughout the city and from the sea. *See also* PANATHENAIA.

**Acts of the Apostles**. A work composed by Luke, author of the third Gospel, and intended by him to be a continuation illustrating the work of the Holy Spirit through the church.

**Acts of Peter and the Twelve Apostles**. *See* NAG HAMMADI.

**actual sin**. A specific, sinful act dependent on the will of the individual, as opposed to ORIGINAL SIN, the state of fallen humanity in which all human beings share.

**A.D.** *See* COMMON CALENDAR.

**Adad**. 'Thunderer': the title of the Semitic storm-god throughout the ancient Near East; in (Assyro-Babylonian) also Addu, and in (West-Semitic) Hadad, Haddu. *See also* BAAL; DAGAN; ENLIL: at times these gods are distinguished, and at others identified (Wyatt 1980).

**Adam**. A West Semitic word meaning 'man'; the First Man in biblical tradition, inhabitant of Paradise (EDEN), the 'gardener' (Wyatt 1988), archetype of the king, and, in the Judaeo-Christian tradition, the mythical ancestor of mankind. (Mowinckel 1948; Bentzen 1949; Brueggemann 1972).

**adan**. *See* ADONIS.

**Adapa**. A Mesopotamian tale of Adapa's (i.e. mankind's) wasted opportunity to gain immortality. When offered it under the symbols of bread and water his protecting deity EA tricks him into accepting oil and a garment, standing for death. Adapa is an equivalent for Adam, also standing for mankind in general, and the designation may be related.

**adat** (Indonesian, from the Arabic, *ʿāda*). In Bahasa Indonesia and many other languages of the Malay archipelago comprising 'custom', 'usage', 'practice', 'rule' etc. As a more general and broader notion, *adat* also includes the customary law of a country, a region, or an ethnic group. First coined by the Dutch scholar Snouck-Hurgronje (1893) and established by van Vollenhoven (1928), the Indonesian-Dutch term *adatrecht* ('*adat* law') was used to denote the juridical realm of *adat*; subsequently, the study of *adat* law became an independent academic discipline (*Adatrechtbundels*, 1910–), based on the discovery that for most Indonesian ethnic groups even including Muslims the observance of *adat* rules was far more important than that of the Islamic SHARĪʿA. Leaving aside some written local instructions (namely princely edicts in Java and Bali), *adat* law generally was transmitted by oral tradition. This caused the particularly fluent character of *adat* law, which is represented by different and numerous uncodified systems of regulations varying from region to region, some of them in overt contradiction to *sharīʿa* (Haar 1948; Holleman 1981). Though the term *adat* sometimes also is applied to any kind of customary law as distinguished from *sharīʿa* it is better to restrict it to the Malay archipelago.

**Addu**. *See* ADAD.

**ʿAdhān**. *See* MINARET.

**Ādi Granth** (Punjabi: 'First Book'). The chief scripture of the Sikhs. *See also* GURŪ GRANTH SĀHIB.

**ʿadl** (Arabic). Justice. In Islamic theology, the doctrine of God's justice, the implication of which is that man is free to act or not according to God's commands; he is thus responsible for his choice and will be accordingly punished or rewarded by God at the Day of Judgement.

**Adonai** (Hebrew: 'My Lord'). A common divine appellative (*Compare* Graeco-Phoenician ADONIS) increasingly used of YAHWEH in post-exilic Judaism. The term is used in Hebrew prayer in place of the TETRAGRAMMATON (yhwh), since pronunciation of the divine name is forbidden. The name 'Adonai' itself has taken on a sacred connotation, so that pious Jews avoid mentioning this too when not intentionally employing it in prayers and blessings.

**Adonia**. The youthful, dying Greek god mourned by his mother APHRODITE.

**Adonis**. The Greek divine name is a form of West Semitic ʿadan, ʿadon ('Lord') – a Canaanite title for gods and kings – derived from the (supposedly dying-and-rising) god of Byblus from *c*. 1000 BCE. Adonis was later known as a subordinate of Aphrodite. (Wagner 1967; 171–207; Istituto 1984). *Compare* ADONAI.

**adoptionism**. The view that the man Jesus was 'adopted' through grace into divine sonship, as opposed to the fully incarnational view that Christ as God became man. There is some evidence that this view was current in early Christianity. It is clearly illustrated by the story of Christ's BAPTISM by John the Baptist, in which the Holy Spirit descends upon him in the form of a dove and the voice of God is heard to say, 'You are my son in whom I am well pleased' (*Mark* 1.11).

**Adrianamitra**. *See* ZANAHARY

**advaita** (Sanskrit: non-duality). One of the ten systems of VEDĀNTA which in this case emphasizes radically the principle of nonduality. *Compare* MONISM; VIŚIṢṬĀDVAITA.

**Advaita Vedanta**. *See* BHAKTI; BRAHMAN; MADHVA; MOKSA.

**Advaitins**. *See* GURŪ; JIVANMUKTI.

**Advent** (from Latin *adventus*: 'coming'). The 'coming' of Christ, hence the name of the season covering the four Sundays before Christmas. In the Eastern churches the season of Advent begins in mid-November and is therefore longer.

**adventists**. A general name for various Christian sects which teach the imminent second coming of Christ. This was predicted for 1844 by William Miller in New York State, attracting many followers who later looked towards revised dates. The Seventh Day Adventists emerged as a distinct sect emphasizing belief in the second coming in combination with observance of Saturday (the seventh day) as Sabbath in line with biblical teaching.

**Advocate of the Devil**. *See* ADVOCATUS DIABOLI.

**advocatus diaboli** (Latin: 'Advocate of the devil'). An informal name for the 'promoter of the faith', who, in the Roman Catholic Church, critically questions the case made on behalf of a person proposed for BEATIFICATION or sainthood.

**advowson**. In English church law the right of appointment of a clergyman to a specific 'living' as a parish priest or in some other capacity.

**Aeneas**. The legendary founder of Rome (12th century BCE). A Trojan, mentioned in Homer's Iliad as fated to escape Troy's destruction. Later Greek tradition made him the founder of Rome, but it was for Hellenistic historiography and later Roman literature to develop the story fully, inserting the Alban king list between him and Romulus. *See also* ALBA LONGA; AENEID.

**Aeneid**. An epic poem about the legendary founder of Rome, AENEAS, composed by Publius Vergilius Maro (70–19 BCE), usually known as Virgil. Co-operating with AUGUSTAN RELIGION, he reworked various legendary traditions about early Rome to produce a chronological unity. An early collection of short poems by Virgil, the *Eclogues* (42–39 BCE), provides our earliest evidence for Augustus' imperial cult. *See also* ALBA LONGA.

**Aeon**. *See* AEON.

**aeon** (Greek). A Hellenistic concept of time and eternity (as a divinity, 'Aeon') which in gnosticism has come to refer to the levels or inhabitants of the PLEROMA. *See also* MITHRAISM.

**Aevum**. *See* MITHRAISM.

**Aesculapius**. The Roman variation of ASKLEPIOS, the Greek god of healing. The divinity was brought to Rome at the behest of the SIBYLLINE BOOKS after a plague in 293 BCE. This was probably the first time that the Romans imported a divinity directly from Greece rather than, as had hitherto been the case, from Greek colonies in south Italy.

**Aesir**. A race of gods in Germanic mythology led and fathered by ODIN. Their associations with strife and violence distinguished them from the other race of gods, the VANIR, with whom they were in conflict. Myth also tells us of a truce between the two races which resulted in the propagation of knowledge in various ways: in one version the omniscient Kvasir was created out of the saliva of all the gods; in another the wise Mimir's head was cut off by the Vanir and Odin was able to consult it for secret knowledge; finally a goddess of the Vanir, FREYJA, is said to have taught the Aesir the magic knowledge *seiðr*. *See also* THOR; LOKI; FRIGG; BALDER.

**Afa**. *See* IFÁ.

**affusion**. *See* ASPERSION.

**African Apostolic Church**. An independent African church founded in the early 1930s by John Maranke, a Shona Prophet in the former British Colony of Southern Rhodesia.

**African religion**. Since Africa is a vast continent which has known extremely diverse cultures and a multitude of languages and political forms the term 'African religion' can only be used with extreme caution. To achieve some precision, the religions of the coastal states north of the Sahara Desert, i.e. ancient Egyptian religion, various historic forms of Christianity and the currently dominant Islam, to name but the most salient, may be excluded from consideration here. South of the Sahara the documentable history of the continent has been fundamentally influenced by the colonial policies of European powers and the consequent independence movements, which, towards the end of the 20th century, remain incomplete. The religious history of Africa therefore revolves around the relations between the indigenously African belief and ritual systems, Christianity as promoted by the modern missionary movement stemming from Europe, and Islam regarded as an alternative to Christianity. In this context the social reaction to external pressures has led to a wide range of intermediate Christian movements and churches which are independent of European institutions (e.g. AFRICAN APOSTOLIC CHURCH; ALADURA; AMANAZARETHA; BROTHERHOOD OF THE CROSS AND THE STAR; HARRIST CHURCH; KIMBANGUIST CHURCH; KITAWALA; LUMPA CHURCH; MASOWE VAPOSTORI; SERAPHIM SOCIETY). Whereas the historical origins of both Christianity and Islam can be brought more or less clearly into focus, the older history of African religion, or religions, is far from clear. Hence attempts to point to a unity in African religion, whether made by external observers or by internal, African interpreters, have tended to focus on recurrent features thought to indicate a common or at least widespread structure. Such features include belief in a supreme being or HIGH GOD, who is, however, more or less remote from daily events; belief in other spiritual beings or forces active in the world of human experience; a clearly articulated ancestor cult and initiation system; ritual performances intended to maintain the equilibrium of society, of the means of livelihood, and of the cosmos as a whole; interaction with the supernatural world by means of spirit-possession or mediumship; and the use of manipulative magic. Such features are also characteristic of primal religion in a more general sense. Thus, the specific character of African religion lies rather, it may be argued, in the historically changing relationships between this primal pattern and the various forms of Christianity and Islam whose influence has spread over the whole continent. At the same time the inherent structural relationships between the various features mentioned above require further analysis, not only to provide a stable positive typology but also to account for the differences in the religious pattern of diverse African cultures. For general accounts of African religion see Smith 1961; Mbiti 1969; Lawson 1984.

**Afro-American religions**. Religious movements or systems based to a greater or lesser degree on elements of African culture but now functioning independently in the Americas. *See* CANDOMBLÉ; MACUMBA; MARIA LIONZA; SANTERÍA; RASTAFARIANISM; UMBANDA; VOODOO.

**Afro-critical approach**. An approach to the study of religion which entails the continuous revision of the way in which the subject is understood in the light of African perspectives on religion. *Compare* SINO-CRITICAL APPROACH; GENDER-CRITICAL APPROACH.

**agama Bali Hindu**. *See* AGAMA TIRTA.

**agama Islam santri** (Indonesian: '*santri* Islam religion'). A form of Javanese Islam, which is – contrary to its counterpart, AGAMA KEJAWEN – characterized by a more dogmatic, 'puritanical' orientation. In his studies of Javanese religion, Clifford Geertz presents Islam *santri* as a 'subvariant of the general Javanese religious system' (1960a: 6) alongside ABANGAN and PRIYAI variants, considering the latter the 'main line traditions' of Java (1973: 60), while regarding the former as a 'minority creed' (1973: 66) characterized by 'scripturalism' (1973: 65ff). Islam *santri* consists of 'a whole complex of social, charitable, and political Islamic organisations' (1960a: 6); basic beliefs (belief in god, the prophets, revealed books etc.; *see* ĪMĀM) as well as basic rituals (observance of the FIVE PILLARS, and of the Islamic calendrical celebrations etc.) are clearly determined by distinctive Islamic dogmas and rules – whether of 'orthodox' or 'modernist' provenance. Although Javanese Muslims themselves distinguish between *agama Islam santri* and *agama kejawen*, Islam *santri* is to a certain degree equally rooted in local Javanese traditions (Koentjaraningrat 1971; Jay 1969).

**agama kejawen** (Javanese; Indonesian: 'Javanese religion'). The totality of traditional Javanese religion and culture: *kejawen* (also *jawi*), as applied to the central Javanese regions around Surakarta and Yogyakarta, actually stands for 'Javanese-ism' (Geertz 1960a: 339). The origin of *agama kejawen* can be traced back to the 16th–18th centuries, when Islam finally penetrated the traditional centre of Hindu-Buddhistic civilization in Middle Java. Though Islam was adopted, elements of Islam, Hindu-Buddhism, and distinctive Javanese local traditions fused into what is now perceived as *agama kejawen*: a syncretistic variant of Islam, including religious thoughts and practices of various provenances. Alongside the belief in Allāh, Muḥammad and other prophets, a mystical, pantheistic view of life prevails (KEBATINAN), focused on the harmony of cosmic and social order; the cultic life is centred on ritual communal meals (SLAMETAN), often accompanied by WAYANG performances; ethics involve mutual assistance, avoidance of conflicts, and 'respect' in terms of 'recognition of superior rank by means of the appropriate etiquette' (Geertz 1961: 148). Contrary to AGAMA ISLAM SANTRI, *agama kejawen* generally represents the religion of PRIYAI and ABANGAN (Magnis-Suseno 1981; Mulder 1983a,b).

**āgamas** (Sanskrit). Scriptures, a term used in a general sense of all Hindu writing considered to be revealed, and in a more specific sense of the 28 scriptures of ŚAIVAS in South India (e.g. *Rauravāgama*) believed to contain *Śiva*'s own teaching.

**Āgama Sūtras** (from Sanskrit, *āgama*: 'a traditional teaching'). In Buddhism, the Sanskrit pre-Mahāyāna *sūtras* corresponding to the NIKĀYAS of the Pāli Canon.

**agama tirta** (Balinese, Indonesian: 'Religion of Holy Water'). The term usually applied by Balinese themselves to Balinese religion, which is commonly called *agama Bali Hindu*. As a recognized religion officially sanctioned by the Indonesian government (*see* PANCASILA), *agama Bali Hindu* grew out of a complex interplay of Hinduism, Buddhism and traditional Balinese religions; the more accurate term *agama tirta* (or *agama tirtha*) reflects the significance of consecrated, purifying water (*tirta*) flowing from Gunung Agung, the holy mountain in the northeast of Bali. Prepared by the PEDANDA reciting MANTRAS (sometimes also by or with the help of a PEMANGKU), holy water is part and parcel of the entire Balinese ritual life – in ceremonial cycles such as sacrifices to the gods, rituals for the dead, temple festivals, rites of passage, and so forth. 'It gives a feeling of unity with God, of regaining purity and strengthened physical and psychical power' (Hooykaas 1973: 11). (Hooykaas 1964, 1974, 1977; Swellengrebel 1960, 1969).

**agape** (Greek). A word used in the SEPTUAGINT and the NEW TESTAMENT to refer to love in a spiritually pure sense, in distinction from eros. It was earlier translated into English as 'charity', via Latin *caritas*, but the latter has now taken on a more practical, and occasionally more patronizing connotation. Additionally, an Agape is a 'love-feast', i.e. a communal, religious meal, as referred to in the New Testament and by some early Christian writers.

**agārasmā anagāriyan** (Pāli: 'from home to homelessness', 'renunciation'). In the Buddhist Pāli Canon (TRIPIṬAKA), an expression denoting the practice of becoming a wandering almsman. *See also* PRAVRAJYĀ.

**aggadah** (Hebrew). Legend. The broad category of non-legal materials found in the TALMUD and other rabbinic sources, particularly in collections of MIDRASH. Hence, as adjective, 'aggadic'.

**aggadic**. *See* AGGADAH.

**aggregates**. *See* SKANDHĀ.

**Aghā Khān**. *See* ISMĀʿĪLĪS.

**agni** (Sanskrit: 'fire'). Besides Indra, the most often invoked *deva* in the ṚGVEDA, of utmost importance in Vedic religion, whose central feature was the *yajña* in which organic substances were consumed (transformed) by fire into 'food for the gods'.

**agnosticism.** From Greek *a* + *gnostos* meaning 'not + know'). The view, distinguished from both THEISM and ATHEISM, that it is not possible to know what God is like or whether God exists. In its most general sense agnosticism is compatible with certain sorts of religious commitment, as for example in Nicholas Cusanus' *Of Learned Ignorance* (*De Docta Ignorantia*, 1440) and Henry Mansel's *The Limits of Religious Thought* (1858). In its more narrow sense, however, it almost always implies detachment from religious commitment. The term itself was coined by T.H. Huxley (1825–95) to express a suspension of belief in matters religious, an attitude which he regarded as more appropriate to the mentality of modern science. A number of well-known figures were attracted to agnosticism in the 19th century, including W.K. Clifford (1845–79), Charles Darwin (1809–82), John Stuart Mill (1807–73), Herbert Spencer (1820–1903) and Leslie Stephen (1832–1904). Interest was renewed in the 20th century through the rise of logical positivism. *See also* METHODOLOGICAL AGNOSTICISM.

**Agnus Dei** (Latin: 'Lamb of God'). A prayer sung after the consecration in the Latin mass asking for God's mercy and peace, named from the opening words.

**Agongyō**. Japanese name for the ĀGAMA SŪTRAS as preserved in the Chinese Buddhist Scriptures, regarded in East Asia as belonging to the HĪNAYĀNA school.

**ahiṁsā** (Sanskrit: 'non-killing'). One of the five (or ten) basic ethical commandments (*yamas* – *niyamas*) of Hinduism (from the time of the BHAGAVADGĪTĀ onwards), Buddhism and Jainism ('*ahiṁsā* is the foremost *dharma*'), universalized and made popular by Gāndhī as 'non-violence' in sociopolitical action.

**Ahl al-Bayt** (Arabic: 'the people of the house'). The descendants of the Prophet Muḥammad. Among SHĪ'A Muslims, the claim was that leadership of the Islamic community belonged exclusively to this group descended from ʿAlī ibn Abī Ṭālib (*d.* 661), the Prophet's cousin and son-in-law.

**Ahl al-Dhimma**. *See* DHIMMĪ.

**Ahl al-ḥall wål-ʿaqd**. *See* BAYʿA.

**Ahl al-Kitāb**. *See* PEOPLE OF THE BOOK.

**Ahl al-Sunna wåal-Jamāʿa** (Arabic: 'the people of established custom and the community'). The self-designation of the majority group of the Muslim community who are commonly called Sunnī. *See* SUNNA.

**Ahl-i Hadith** (Urdu). A late 19th-century, North Indian, puritanical Islamic movement which eschewed the conclusions of the medieval law schools and rooted itself in the injunctions of the QUR'ĀN and ḤADĪTH of the prophet Muḥammad (Robinson 1988; Metcalf 1982). *See also* DEOBAND SEMINARY.

**Aḥmadiya**. An Islamic reform movement founded in India by Mirza Ghulām Aḥmad (*c.*1835–1908). His claims that the QUR'ĀN foretold his coming and that he was both the MAHDĪ and the spirit of the Prophet Muḥammad placed his movement beyond the pale of Islām. He also claimed to be an avatar (incarnation) of Krishna. Disputes over these claims ultimately caused the movement to split: the main group of Aḥmad's followers, known as the Qadiani (a reference to his birthplace in the Punjab), pursues an activist missionary commitment in Europe and Africa; the more moderate branch, based in Lahore, retains links with the Islamic community. (Lavan 1974; Robinson 1988).

**ahu** (Polynesian). A religious shrine in Polynesia. Originally it was just a mound of earth or stone. On the Society Islands it developed into a raised stone platform which is a part of the ceremonial centres called MARAE, while on Easter Island this whole structure is termed *ahu*.

**Ahura Mazdā**. *See* ZOROASTRIANISM.

**aḥwāl** (Arabic; singular *ḥāl*). In SUFISM, steps or states of the soul. *See* MAQĀMĀT.

**aires** (New World Spanish). Mesoamerican term for noxious air-spirits, invisible aggressive entities that attach themselves to, or enter, the human body and cause illness. From the ordinary Spanish *aire* ('air', 'wind'), as in Buenos Aires. (Lopez Austin 1984).

**aisle**. The sections of a church building added on as wings (from French '*aile*') to the sides of the long, central area, or nave. An erroneous extension has led to the word being used to refer to the walkway between seats or pews, even in the central nave.

**Aitareya**. *See* UPANIṢADS.

**ajari** (Japanese). An eminent rank in Tendai and Shingon Buddhism (*see* TENDAI-SHŪ; SHINGON-SHŪ). The term derives from the Sanskrit *ācārya* meaning 'teacher' or 'master'.

**Akālī** (Punjabi: 'Follower of the immortal One'). A Warrior Sikh of the 18th or 19th century. The modern equivalent is NIHANG. *See also* AKĀLĪ DAL.

**Akālī Dal** (Punjabi: 'Army of the Followers of God'). A body of radical Sikhs formally established in 1920 though the AKĀLĪs had been active in military actions against the authorities since the 18th century. The Akālī Dal continues to be an important party in Punjabi politics. *See also* JATHĀ; MORCHA; NIHANG; KHĀLISTAN.

**Akāl takht** (Punjabi: 'Throne of the immortal One'). The supreme seat of Sikh authority at AMRITSAR.

**akh** (Egyptian). Shown as a tufted ibis, an indestructible force and part of the human personality.

**akhaṇḍ pāṭh** (Punjabi). An uninterrupted reading by Sikhs of the GURŪ GRANTH SĀHIB, often performed on special occasions such as festivals or anniversaries.

**Akhetaten**. *See* ATEN.

**ākhira** (Arabic). In Islām, the hereafter or afterlife when, following the resurrection (*yawm al-qiyāma*) and the last judgement (*yawm al-dīn*), the righteous will be separated from the damned respectively in heaven (*al-janna*) and hell (*jahannam*).

**akitu**. A periodic festival observed at several ancient Mesopotamian sites, involving the humiliation and rehabilitation of the king, the SACRED MARRIAGE, and the reading (and perhaps the dramatization) of the ENUMA ELISH. (Thureau-Dangin 1921; Pallis 1926; Frankfort 1948; Black 1981).

**Akṣar Puruṣottam Sanstha** (Sanskrit, Gujarati). A branch of the SWĀMINĀRĀYAṆ SAṂPRADĀYA founded in 1906 by Śastri Mahārāj which teaches that Swāmināṛāyaṇ appointed one of his close followers, Gunatītānand Swāmi, as his spiritual successor and as **akṣar**, the abode of God in the world (a role passed on through the lineage to each successive leader). This branch is the most flourishing within the tradition and is known in the West as the Swaminarayan Hindu Mission (Williams 1984).

**Akṣobhya**. A mythological Buddha, one of five who together make up the 'diamond world' of esoteric Buddhism. Akṣobhya Buddha's realm or PURE LAND is established in the east; *compare* that of AMITĀBHA, which is in the west.

**al-** (Arabic). Arabic definite article, disregarded in establishing alphabetic order of terms in this dictionary.

**Ala**. *See* MBARI.

**Aladura** (Yoruba: 'those who pray'). A religious movement within Nigeria which developed from 1920 onwards initially as a reform movement within the Anglican Church, emphasizing the importance of prayer. The 'praying ones' take many forms, one of which is the Church of the Seraphim. This form of Aladura was the consequence of a revelation in 1935 to Abiodun Akinsowon (*b* 1920) when, as a young woman of 15, she was viewing a Corpus Christi procession. In recounting her vision she tells how one of the angels represented in the procession followed her home, subjected her to tests, confirmed her status as the founder of a movement, and emphasized the importance of prayer, spiritual possession, and spiritual healing. This 'spiritualism' led to an attack both upon the Yoruba deities and to the standard forms of Yoruba medicine. One of its most basic ritual forms of expression is the large and highly visible procession through the streets of Nigerian cities meant to celebrate the original revelation. (Peel 1968).

**ālaya-vijñāna** (Sanskrit). Storehouse-consciousness. According to the Mahāyāna Buddhist *Laṇkāvatāra Sūtra* this deep consciousness is the underlying, indiscriminate matrix of all which is experienced. That which is experienced seems to be received from without into the storehouse-consciousness, but in reality it is the *ālaya-vijñāna* which contains the world whose separate, objective reality is an illusion caused by the will and the passions. The egoless recognition of the true state of affairs is achieved, according to the *Laṇkāvatāra Sūtra*, by a reversal of consciousness known as *parāvṛtti*. (Suzuki 1938). *See also* MANO-VIJÑĀNA; VIJÑĀNAVĀDA.

**alb**. A full-length white linen garment worn by Christian priests when celebrating the MASS.

**Alba Longa**. A legendary town on the Alban Mountain near Rome where AENEAS supposedly settled in preparation to the founding of Rome by his descendants. Roman tradition knew a series of Alban kings between Aeneas (12th century BCE) and Romulus (8th century BCE), the putative founder of Rome itself. *See also* QUIRINUS.

**Albigensians**. A name for the CATHARS in southern France, taken from the town Albi (Albigeois) in which they were based.

**Alexandrian theology**. An extremely influential school of early Christian theology based in Alexandria in northern Egypt, which was largely responsible for setting Christian doctrine in the context of Greek, especially Platonic, philosophy. The most eminent representatives were Clement and Origen.

**alienation**. A state of estrangement from someone else, from society in general or from oneself. The use of this concept in whatever context, whether psychological, sociological philosophical, etc., presupposes that separation and plurality are problematical and that harmony and unity are a normal state of social or psychological health and well-being. The notion became prominent in the 20th century with the rise of EXISTENTIALISM.

**Aligarh University**. An institution of higher education in Aligarh, Uttar Pradesh, India. It was founded in 1875 by Sir Sayyid Aḥmad Khān (*d* 1898) as a boys' school run on English lines, with instruction in that language. It was granted university status in 1920. Women have been enrolled since 1938. It possesses most of the faculties of a modern university: arts, science, technology, engineering and theology. Entrance has never been restricted to Muslims. It has upheld the long Islamic tradition of providing education for the needy.

**aliran** (Indonesian: 'streaming'). In Indonesia, an ideological, mainly religious, organization on a national level; in a narrower sense also a mystical movement (*see* KEBATINAN). (Geertz 1960a; Hadiwijono 1967; Mulder 1983a).

**aliyah** (Hebrew: 'ascent'). The ritual of being called up in the synagogue to recite the blessings for a section of the reading of the TORAH. Also, for a Jew to 'make aliyah' is to make a pilgrimage, or move, to the State of Israel.

**àljànnu.** *See* BÒRI.

**Allāh** (Arabic). In Islām, the name for God, as expressed in the essential Muslim credo, 'There is no God save Allāh'. The QUR'ĀN contains many epithets making up the 99 beautiful names of God; essentially, the stress is on God's unity (TAWḤĪD) and consequently the supreme, unforgivable sin is the association (*shirk*) of anything with Allāh. (Rahman 1980).

**Allāhu Akbar** (Arabic: 'Allāh is great(er)'). An expression of praise used in the Muslim's call to prayer (*see* MINARET), in the prayer itself, and on many other occasions in the Muslim's life.

**All-Ceylon Bhikkhu Congress**. The umbrella organization of all the branches of the YOUNG MEN'S BUDDHIST ASSOCIATION (YMBA) in Sri Lanka.

**allegory.** *See* PARABLE.

**alleluia**. An expression of praise from the Hebrew HALLELUJAH. Occurring in the Psalms and as a chant by saints in the *Book of Revelation*, it has found a place in Christian liturgy and hymns.

**almanac**. A yearbook containing calendrical and astrological information. Chinese almanacs, for example, are based on the traditional lunar calendar and the marking of time according to the system of ten 'HEAVENLY STEMS' or 'celestial stems' (*tiangan* [*t'ien-kan*]) and twelve 'terrestrial branches' (*dizhi* [*ti-chih*]). They contain information not only about the timing of the agricultural seasons and the various festivals, but also about lucky and unlucky days and different forms of prognostication and fortune-telling. The Chinese type of almanac is widespread in East Asia; special editions are sold by quite different religious institutions such as, in Japan, Buddhist temples and Shinto shrines. *See also* PRIMBON.

**almoner**. One who dispenses alms to the poor on behalf of a monarch.

**alms-round.** *See* PINDAPATA.

**aloha** (Hawaiian). Originally a sense of mutual receptivity determined by kinship, the concept of *aloha* now implies hospitality and deep affection shown to all and has thus become the standard proclamation of welcome in modern Hawaii.

**alpha and omega**. Letters equivalent to A and O, being the first and last in the Greek alphabet and therefore symbolizing totality or completeness, especially of God.

**altar**. The location for one of the more important acts of ancient religion, namely the killing and burning of an animal. In classical antiquity the altar was usually constructed from stone and situated in the open air at some distance to the east or at the entrance of the temple. Sacrifices to the gods and spirits of the earth were performed at hearths level with the ground or in pits dug into the ground. More widely, a raised area in the open air may be regarded as an altar if it is used for sacrifices or indeed for other offerings. Since in most cultures substitute offerings have come to take the place of living beings, the term has come to designate any raised place or table, whether outside or in a shrine, church or temple, upon which offerings are placed.

**Altar of Peace**. An immense Roman marble altar, dedicated 13 BCE and still visible in Rome. It displays prominent Romans in procession, AENEAS and Romulus. The precise iconography remains disputed. *See also* AUGUSTAN RELIGION; QUIRINUS.

**altomisayoq** (Quechua). The most powerful religious specialists in the high Andes. The term is hispanic Quechua and designates a person who celebrates the high *misa*, ceremonies for the APU, PACHAMAMA, the ancestors or other divinities. The *altomisayoq* is usually elected by the divinities through lightning, after which he is supposed to intercede between the sacred and the profane world, to help people to avert harm and evil and to improve life conditions. Other less powerful specialists are the *hampeq* and CURANDERO, who work usually with herbs to cure people from sickness. It is said that the BRUJO divines by black magic and the *pampamisayoq* divines by white magic, but neither can correspond directly with the deities. Divination is mostly practised by reading in coca leaves or in the entrails of guinea-pigs.

**aḷvārs**. A group of devotees of *Viṣṇu* from South India, who lived between the 6th and 12th centuries CE, and composed a large number of hymns which are still widely used both in popular and official worship by Śrīvaiṣṇavas.

**ʿAmal.** *See* IMĀN.

**amaNazaretha**. The Church of Nazareth, a religious movement in southern Africa, located predominantly in Zululand, which originated with a set of revelations to Isaiah Shembe and which, since his death, has been continued by his son Johannes. Regarded by some scholars as a heterodox form of Christianity, it is, in fact, as much a creative reformulation of long-standing Zulu religious symbols as it is a response to Christianity. Shembe built his first Church on top of a hill in Zululand, led an early pilgrimage to the Nhlangakazi Mountain in Natal and established there the amaNazaretha New Year festival. Shembe's revelation transformed a number of Zulu symbols associated with UMVELINQANGI, the remote God of the Sky, approachable only under very special conditions, into images that were closer to human spiritual life. He also continued to countenance many practices such as sorcery. The movement represents, therefore, a successful combination of Christian and African motifs integrated in powerful new ways. (Sundkler 1961).

**Amarapura Nikāya.** *See* NIKĀYA.

**Amarna.** *See* ATEN.

**Amaterasu Ōmikami**. The leading Japanese KAMI (deity), being both sun goddess and ancestral deity of the imperial house. According to early myth, Amaterasu showed human beings how to make food, clothing and dwellings, and was the source of all peace. She dispatched her grandson Ninigi no mikoto to unify the land and to have his descendants establish the imperial house. Ise no Jingū is dedicated to this goddess, and the *yata* mirror (*see* SANSHU NO SHINKI) which she bestowed is enshrined there. There are many shrines throughout Japan dedicated to Amaterasu Ōmikami, but the central one is Ise Jingū.

**amatsukami.** *See* KAMI.

**ambo**. A dais in early Christian churches used for liturgical readings of the scriptures.

**Ambrosian rite**. A form of the MASS traditional in Milan and ascribed to St Ambrose, which differs from the Roman rite in placing the offertory before the creed.

**Amduat.** *See* BOOK OF THE DEAD.

**amen**. The Hebrew expression of affirmation. Derived from the same root as EMUNAH ('faith'), 'amen' literally means 'it is trustworthy'. Reciting 'amen' after someone else has recited a blessing is considered in many instances as if one had recited the blessing oneself. The word is used both in Judaism and in Christianity.

**Amen-Re.** *See* AMUN, ATEN.

**Amenty**. The land of the dead, situated in the west, which the ancient Egyptians reached after their day of judgement.

**American Indian religions.** *See* NATIVE AMERICAN RELIGIONS.

**Amida.** *See* AMITĀBHA.

**Amidah** (Hebrew: 'standing'). The set of 19 benedictions (also known as the *Shmoneh Esrei* or '18'), which mark the high point of all Hebrew services. These are to be recited while standing, and without interruption.

**Amidakyō.** *See* JŌDO SANBUKYŌ.

**Amida sanzon** (Japanese). A group of three images with Amida Buddha at the centre, and the two bodhisattvas Kannon (AVALOKITEŚVARA) and Seishi (Mahāsthāmaprāpta) to his left and right hand respectively. Kannon represents compassion and Seishi (also known as Daiseishi) represents wisdom.

**Amitābha** (Sanskrit). A mythological Buddha who reigns over a PURE LAND in the western direction, where those who rely on the vows which he made while still a BODHISATTVA may be reborn, before attaining nirvāṇa for themselves. Of Indian origin, Amitābha Buddha has been popular throughout Mahāyāna Buddhism, and is central to the JŌDO and JŌDO SHINSHŪ traditions of Japan. The Chinese equivalent is A MI TO, the Japanese is Amida.

**A Mi To.** *See* AMITĀBHA.

**Amma**. Supreme God of the Dogon (Habbe in early reports) of Mali. According to Dogon cosmogony Amma existed before all things and is the ultimate source of the world, living beings and the ancestors of the Dogon (Griaule & Dieterlen 1965).

**amphictyony**. A league of adjacent communities based on a common shrine. As a sociological model it was derived from ancient Greek society and applied, first by Max Weber, to the relationship of Israelite tribes before the monarchy. However, this application is now discredited. (See Weber 1976; Noth 1930; Vaux 1971; Mayes 1977).

**Amrit** (Punjabi). Sweetened water; ceremony of initiation (also known as *Amrit Pāhul*) into the Sikh Order or KHĀLSĀ in which sweetened water is used.

**Amritdhārī** (Punjabi). A Sikh initiated into the KHĀLSĀ Order. *See also* AMRIT.

**Amritsar** (Punjabi). A city of the Indian Punjab, founded by Gurū Rām Dās (*see* TEN GURŪS) in which his son, Gurū Arjan, built the Harimandir, a place of worship and pilgrimage, on the site of which the Golden Temple now stands. Amritsar is also the site of the AKĀL TAKHT, established by Gurū Hargobind, the supreme seat of authority – both spiritual and temporal – for the Sikhs. *See also* JALLIĀNWĀLĀ BAGH; SINGH SABHĀ; KHĀLISTĀN; JATHĀ.

**Amset.** *See* CANOPIC JAR.

**amulet**. A small object carried on the person or kept in an appropriate individual place, giving the assurance of safety guaranteed by a supernatural power. *See also* WEDJAT EYE.

**Amun**. Originally one of the Ogdoad (Eight Gods) of the Egyptian city HERMOPOLIS, Amun ('The Hidden One') acquired a cult-centre at THEBES in the 12th Dynasty (1991–1786 BCE) (Wainwright 1934). When the Princes of Thebes seized the kingship in the 18th Dynasty (1567–1320 BCE), they elevated their local god Amun to become state-god of Egypt and her empire. He now incorporated the solar aspects of RE and thus was known as Amen-Re (Otto 1966). Lord of Thebes, King of Gods, Amun was worshipped with his wife MUT and son KHONSU in the Temple of KARNAK. He wore a plumed crown and his sacred animal was the ram. His supremacy was briefly undermined by the cult of the ATEN (*c.* 1575 BCE).

**An**. *See* ANU

**Anabaptists**. A general term for believers in rebaptism (Greek *ana* meaning 're-'). Anabaptists rejected infant baptism as non-scriptural and hence required rebaptism of believers on reaching adulthood. Anabaptism flourished in Germany, the Netherlands and Switzerland in the 16th century but was rejected by the influential church reformers Luther, Zwingli and Calvin. As regards the central matter of the baptism of adult believers, later Baptists have continued to make the same point. While the older Anabaptist groups were seriously persecuted, largely because they also posed utopian political alternatives, one group which has remained strong to this day, especially in North America, are the Mennonites, named after Menno Simons, who first led the movement in the northern Netherlands.

**anagārika** (Sanskrit, Pāli: 'homeless'). Originally an epithet of a Buddhist mendicant, now in Theravāda countries a celibate layman or laywoman observing the Ten Precepts and dedicating his or her life to Buddhism. The epithet took on a special significance through incorporation in the name Dharmapāla Anagārika (*see* BUDDHIST MODERNISM).

**anakephalaiosis.** *See* RECAPITULATION.

**anakok**. A shamanic personality among indigenous Greenlanders.

**Analects.** *See* LUN YU.

**analogia entis.** *See* ANALOGY.

**analogy**. A proportional similarity. In theology the term is used particularly of the relationship brtween human and DIVINE ATTRIBUTES, and of the way in which language used of the former may be applied in an extended sense to God. Thus, it is claimed that terms like 'love' and 'wisdom', which are learnt in everyday contexts, may be applied to God by analogy, because of some relationship (e.g. likeness and causation) between his perfections and human qualities. Thomas Aquinas claimed that analogical predication is midway between univocity and equivocation. His later followers classified different types of analogy, especially Analogy of Attribution (e.g. the various senses of 'healthy') and Analogy of Proper Proportionality (e.g. our knowledge, created beings, God's knowledge, His essence). They also spoke of the *analogia entis* ('analogy of being') underlying Thomistic metaphysics, a phrase not used by Aquinas himself, although he did specify that 'being' is an analogical term. (Burrell 1973).

**analytic philosophy**. The dominant philosophical movement in the English-speaking world since World War II, influenced especially by the work of Bertrand Russell and Ludwig Wittgenstein. Instead of building philosophical systems, it approaches individual philosophical issues by clarifying concepts and constructing rigorous arguments. Since it pays particular attention to analysing the language used, it is often referred to as 'linguistic philosophy'. Analytic philosophy has often been regarded as inimical to religion, in that the rigorous attempt to clarify the supposed meaning of religious assertions does not necessarily lead to positive results. On the other hand the discipline has also led to a renewed sense of the diversity of linguistic statements, and attempts to identify appropriate criteria for evaluating particular kinds of statements, including religious ones. (Flew & MacIntyre 1955).

**analytical psychology**. A school of depth psychology founded by the Swiss neurologist, Carl Gustav Jung. Central to it is its emphasis on the collective unconscious and the archetypes it contains. Humankind has, in other words, a common heritage of conceptions and patterns of behaviour given in and through birth. This heritage has over the course of history taken the form of myths, legends, rites, and images of different kinds. Of importance is the idea that behind all of these things lie common structures or ARCHETYPES like, for example, those of god – devil and mother – father. In Jungian theory, comparative research in the area of the study of religion plays an important role as do individual religious phenomena in general.

**Ānanda Mārga Yoga** (Hindi). Founded in India in 1955 by Ānandamūrtijī, but also with a presence in the West, a movement propounding a practical system of self-development based on the physical, mental and spiritual disciplines of yoga as taught by Patañjali. It combines an appreciation of the need for individual spirituality and a commitment to social welfare.

**Ananse** [Anansi]. Among the Akan of Ghana Ananse, 'Spider', a TRICKSTER character appearing in many fables, but also has divine qualities, among others as creator of man. He appears as a character in the stories of descendants of slaves in the West Indies. (Rattray 1930).

**Anat**. A Canaanite goddess worshipped from northern Syria to Egypt in the 2nd millennium BCE. Consort of BAAL. Like ANĀHITA, HATHOR and KALI, she embodied contradictory elements, being goddess both of fertility and destruction. Her mythology is given mainly in the BAAL CYCLE. Later Anat was fused with ASTARTE to become the ATARGATIS of Hellenistic times. Perhaps in origin an earth goddess, she appears in iconography with wings, weapons and the Egyptian Atef crown, indicating royal ideological associations. (Kapelrud 1969; Wyatt 1984).

**anātman** (Sanskrit: 'no self') [Pāli: *anatta*]. According to Buddhism there is no permanent, eternal and unchanging self (ĀTMAN). The psycho-physical being, which we usually call man, consists of five 'aggregates' (SKANDHA): body, feelings, perceptions, volitions and consciousness. In *Visuddhimagga* XVI the doctrine of no-self, one of the three fundamental characteristics of all phenomenal existence – the other two being suffering (DUḤKHA) and impermanence (ANITYA) – is explained as follows:

> Mere suffering exists, no sufferer is found.
> The deed is, but no doer of the deed is there.
> *Nirvāṇa* is, but not the man that enters it.
> The path is, but no traveller on it is seen.

**anatta.** *See* ANĀTMAN.

**ancestor cult**. Some form of ancestor cult has been widespread in many cultures and may be regarded as a normal constituent element of religious systems based on a natural community (*see* PRIMAL RELIGION). The precise form which an ancestor takes however is strongly characterized by other socio-political and ideological circumstances.

In China, for example, ancestor worship can be traced back at least till the Shang dynasty (*c.* 16th century – 1066 BCE). The evidence of oracle bones testifies that the deceased ancestors of the kings were thought of as powerful spirits who required offerings from their descendants. During the Zhou [Chou] dynasty (*c.* 1066–221 BCE) ancestor worship was the prerogative of the aristocracy, but in later times it was practised in all strata of the society. The practice of presenting offerings to the deceased ancestors is closely related to the belief in the soul (*hun* and *po*), which after death continues to exist for some time. If not provided with offerings the soul can become a vengeful ghost (*gui*), while an ancestor properly cared for will be a spirit which can bestow blessings to his descendants. The Confucianists advanced a more rational justification of ancestor worship, interpreting it as a continuation of the ritual respect which the children have to pay to their elders (*xiao*). Hence, ancestor worship came to be regarded as a fundamental ethical duty. *See also* MIZIMU.

**anchoress**. A female ANCHORITE.

**anchorite**. A person who lives entirely alone in prayer and mortification, i.e. as a hermit, or in a separate dwelling linked to a community of monks, thus being a COENOBITE. During the Middle Ages anchorites were ceremonially walled in by the bishop and an anchorite cell was occasionally linked to a parish church.

**ancilia** (Latin). Twelve archaic bronze shields kept in the sanctuary of MARS in the Roman Forum. Tradition remembered that one shield had fallen from the sky on 1 March and a divinely instructed blacksmith had made a further eleven. An aristocratic group, the Salii, used the shields in the yearly OCTOBER HORSE festival, which is probably one of the oldest in the Roman calendar.

**Andean religions**. Religions whose content, historical development and dynamics are determined by the unique ecological characteristics of the South American Andes mountain range. This range constitutes the backbone of the South American continent between the eastern coastal plain and the rain forest or savannas. The name 'Andes' is thought to be derived from the Quechua word *anti* ('east') or maybe *antasuyo* ('zone of metals'). (See Ossio 1973; Pease 1973). *See also* ALTOMISAYOQ; HUACA; INTI; CHICHA; PACHAMAMA.

**Andjety**. An early god of the mythological Egyptian King Busiris in the Delta; some of his features were absorbed by OSIRIS.

**angel**. A messenger of God, as referred to commonly in Jewish, Christian and Islamic writing. The Hebrew term *mal'ak* (translated into Greek as *angelos*' 'messenger') originally denoted any intermediary or ambassador, divine or human. In post-exilic Jewish thought, angels increasingly appear as supernatural, quasi-divine beings, evidently as survivals in a monotheistic context of ancient gods, operating both as celestial civil servants (in control of natural phenomena) or guardians of the nations, and as embodiments of the powers of evil in perpetual conflict with God, to be punished everlastingly at the end of history. The names of the chief angels (ARCHANGELS), Raphael, Gabriel, Uriel etc., show them to be hypostases of divine powers ('Healer of El', 'Warrior of El', 'Light [or king] of El'). (Kuhn 1948; Dion 1976).

**Angelus**. A church bell rung at 6 a.m., noon and 6 p.m., mostly in rural Catholic areas, calling the faithful to think of their salvation by reciting three Ave Marias. Each time a short sentence is added, recalling the greeting of the Angel Gabriel (hence the Latin name of the prayer, Angelus) to Mary, Mary's readiness to accept God's will and that the Word became flesh (*see also* CHRISTOLOGY).

**Angkor**. Extensive Khmer monuments in Kampuchea, including notably Angkor Wat and the Bayon, giving architectural expression to Indian-derived cosmology with both Hindu and Buddhist themes. According to Coedès the function of the buildings was largely the creation of impressive mausolea from the 9th to the 12th centuries CE (Coedès 1963).

**Angkor Wat.** *See* ANGKOR.

**Anglican Communion**. The various episcopal churches world-wide which perceive their unity as guaranteed by joint recognition of the see of Canterbury, England.

**Anglicanism**. The religious orientation of Christians who are members of the ANGLICAN COMMUNION, affirming the historic episcopate without acceptance of the primacy of Rome. Theologically an extremely wide range of belief is tolerated ranging from HIGH CHURCH Anglo-Catholicism to LOW CHURCH Evangelicalism and including a substantial body of non-partisan liberalism.

**Anglo-Catholicism**. A school of thought and liturgical practice within ANGLICANISM which emphasises sacramental worship and a high doctrine of the church as the locus for the exposition of scripture and doctrine. The term itself dates from 1838.

**Angra Mainyu**. *See* ZOROASTRIANISM.

**Angst** (German). A term common in existentialist writing, designating an undifferentiated sense of unease in the face of life's uncertainties. In this technical sense, unlike 'fear', *Angst* has no identifiable object. The term was at one time translated into English as 'dread', but since the popularization of psychoanalytic terminology, it is now normally rendered as 'anxiety'. *See also* EXISTENTIALISM.

**anicca**. *See* ANITYA.

**animism**. A term used by E.B. Tylor in his influential work *Primitive Culture* (1903), meaning belief in spiritual beings, and intended to describe a stage of prehistoric and primitive religion in which this belief is predominant. That the term is still widely used today may be regarded as a testimony to its simple appositeness. However, the developmental implications of Tylor's account are now not generally considered to be valid.

**anitya** (Sanskrit: 'impermanence') [Pāli; *anicca*]. A Buddhist term denoting the transitoriness of all psycho-physical phenomena of existence. *See also* ANĀTMAN.

**ankh**. The Egyptian hieroglyphic sign, in the form of a cross with a ring-shaped handle, representing life. It is frequently depicted in ritual and funerary scenes to convey the life-force.

**annihilationism**. In theism, the belief that at least some people will be neither saved nor damned, but will cease to exist after death or after the Last Judgement. In Buddhism, the view that all factors of existence (*dharma*) cease eternally; a view which however is rejected, along with the opposite view that all *dharmas* exist eternally (eternalism).

**anno domini** (AD) (Latin: 'in the year of the Lord'). A designation of the years of the Christian Era or Common Era (*see* COMMON CALENDAR).

**Annunciation**. The announcement to the Virgin Mary by the angel Gabriel that Christ had been conceived in her womb (*Luke* 1.26–38). The Annunciation of the Blessed Virgin Mary is celebrated as a feast day in Catholic countries.

**Anṣār.** *See* MUHĀJIRŪN.

**antaryāmin.** *See* PAÑCĀRATRA.

**ante-communion**. The section of eucharistic liturgy running as far as the prayer of intercession for the church but without the offering and consecration of bread and wine.

**anthem**. A choral composition, with or without organ accompaniment, usually based on a scriptural text, and sung, for example, in the context of the Morning or Evening Prayer services of the Church of England. The word derives from ANTIPHON.

**Antichrist**. An APOCALYPTIC opponent of Christ, and usurper of his position, expected to appear at the end of time for a final battle (which he will lose) but already identified with historical tyrants such as Caligula or Nero or even, by some Protestants, with the Pope. Specific reference to Antichrist occurs only marginally in the New Testament (in the Epistles of St John).

**antimension** (Greek). A cloth used to contain a RELIC or, on an altar, to represent a relic.

**antinomianism**. The view, apparently held by some early Christians, that if one is saved through grace it is superfluous to observe the moral law (Greek, *nomos*), or even religiously preferable not to do so. The Apostle Paul went to some trouble to avoid being identified with this line of thought (*Romans* 6.1ff). In spite of this, antinomianism reappeared in later centuries when emphasis has been laid on a present state of salvation transcending ordinary life, as occasionally among ANABAPTISTS in the 16th century.

**Antiochene theology**. A theological tradition based in Antioch, famous representatives being Paul (of Samosata), Chrysostom, Theodore (of Mopsuestia) and Nestorius. Though the teaching of these and others contains many variations, common threads may be seen in the historical exegesis of scripture (as opposed to the allegorical technique characteristic of ALEXANDRIAN THEOLOGY) and an emphasis on the oneness of God in the theology of the TRINITY.

**antiphon**. Liturgical music, such as psalms or canticles, sung in alternation between two choirs, i.e. antiphonally.

**antipope**. An alternative POPE set up in rivalry to the incumbent Bishop of Rome.

**anti-semitism**. Hatred of the Jewish people. Although Arab peoples are technically 'semites' as well, the term connotes hatred of Jews specifically. Though it is a modern term, anti-semitism has been a feature of much of Jewish history, frequently taking the form of paranoid conspiracy theories projected onto the Jewish people. *See also* HOLOCAUST.

**Anu**. The Assyro-Babylonian sky-god (equivalent to the Sumerian An), head of the pantheon and author of kingship. (Frankfort 1948: 231–8; Ringgren 1973: 52.55; Jacobsen 1976: 95–8)

**Anubis**. The jackal-headed Egyptian god of mummification and protector of cemeteries. Anubis is often shown in funerary scenes bending over the MUMMY and restoring it to life.

**Anuket**. An Egyptian goddess of the First Cataract area and Nubia, associated with KHNUM and shown wearing a feathered crown. She is known in Greek as Anukis.

**Anukis.** *See* ANUKET.

**Anunayaka.** *See* NĀYAKA.

**anuttara-saṃyak-saṃbodhi** (Sanskrit). 'Unsurpassed perfect enlightenment', an expression widely used in MAHĀYĀNA Buddhist texts.

**Aoi Matsuri**. An annual festival celebrated on 15 May at the two KAMO shrines in Kyōto, said to have originated during the reign of Emperor Kimmei in the 7th century as a festival of prayer for abundant grain harvests. The central rite is performed at night, away from the public gaze, to invite the divine spirit from the sacred mountain to the shrine. The public procession on the following morning of ox-drawn carts, horses with golden saddles, and participants in costumes with hollyhock flower (*aoi*) headdresses, sets out from the Kyōto Palace and makes its way toward the shrines. The festival is regarded as one of the three largest festivals in Japan.

**apacita.** *See* HUACA.

**Aphrodite**. Greek goddess of beauty and unabashed sexual desire and consummation; she was born from OURANOS' castrated genital when CRONOS threw it into the sea. *Compare* VENUS.

**Apis**. God of the ancient Egyptian city of Memphis, incarnate in sacred bulls; each of which was ultimately buried in the Serapeum at *Sakkara*. Apis was associated with PTAH-OSIRIS and RE.

**apocalypse** (from Greek, *apokalypsis*: 'uncovering', 'revelation'). An apocalyptic writing such as *The Apocalypse of John*, otherwise known as the *Book of Revelation*, being the last work in the New Testament. *See also* APOCALYPTIC.

**apocalyptic**. From APOCALYPSE, both as an adjective and as a noun referring to the literary genre. The earliest clearly apocalyptic writing is the biblical *Book of Daniel* (2nd century BCE). Other Jewish apocalyptic writings are the *Book of Enoch*, the *Apocalypse of Baruch*, the *Assumption of Moses*, the *Book of Jubilees*, and the *Testament of the Twelve Patriarchs*. In early Christianity the *Apocalypse of John* (i.e. the 'Book of Revelation') and the non-canonical *Apocalypse of Peter* are the most important examples, although apocalyptic elements are present in other works also, e.g. *Mark*, chapter 13, the so-called 'little apocalypse'. Apocalyptic writings are often pseudonymous, claiming the authority of a traditional figure, but at the same time concealing the true authorship, and heavily charged with obscure symbolism. This is because they reveal a cryptic message of hope to an oppressed minority who believe that, in an imminent climax, God will overturn the course of history in their favour. Thus apocalyptic is politically subversive, though it may be also interpreted as compensating for lack of real political results. Since apocalyptic represents a final dénouement of world events in mythical language it may be regarded as a form of ESCHATOLOGY. (For selected texts, see Charles 1913: vol. 3; Charlesworth 1983; Sparks 1984. For general studies see Koch 1972; Hanson 1975, 1983; Collins 1984).

**apocatastasis** (Greek). The doctrine, taught by Clement and Origen of Alexandria (*see* ALEXANDRIAN THEOLOGY), that all beings capable of moral decision, whether humans, angels or devils, will ultimately be brought to salvation. On this view there can be no eternal damnation. *See also* UNIVERSALISM.

**Apocrypha** (from Greek, *ta apokrypha*: 'the hidden things'). The name usually given to some 13 writings current in Hellenistic Judaism and included in the SEPTUAGINT but not in the HEBREW BIBLE. They were widely used and cited in the early church and are usually included in the Latin VULGATE. In the Eastern Orthodox churches those recognized as canonical scripture were eventually reduced to four, namely *Tobit, Judith, Ecclesiasticus* and the *Wisdom of Solomon*, and in Protestant churches the Apocrypha are not usually regarded as scripture. Nevertheless they provide very significant contextual material for the interpretation of the NEW TESTAMENT as well as direct evidence for Judaism in Hellenistic times. Catholic writers often refer to the Pseudepigrapha as apocrypha. *See also* CHENWEI.

**apocryphal writings**. A general designation for writings similar to those of the NEW TESTAMENT, i.e. gospels, epistles, acts and apocalypses, but regarded in the early church as being less reliable witnesses to what took place. Some such writings, e.g. the *Gospel According to the Hebrews* or the *Gospel of Peter*, may include authentic oral traditions going back to the life of Christ, but most are clearly secondary, emphasizing miraculous legends and particular theologies, e.g. DOCETISM or GNOSTICISM. *See also* APOCRYPHA.

**Apocryphon of John.** *See* NAG HAMMADI.

**Apollinarianism**. The teaching of Apollinarius (*c*.310–*c*.390) that, while man consists of body, soul and rational spirit, in Christ the divine LOGOS replaced the rational human spirit. A form of DOCETISM. (Kelly 1972.) *See also* TWO NATURES.

**Apollo**. The Greek god of music and balance, medicine and healing, prophecy and sanity, and light, clarity and rationality; son of ZEUS and Leto, he was worshipped in Delphi, the most famous Greek shrine, and is often called 'the most Greek of the Greek gods'. Apollo was introduced early to Rome via Etruria and Greek colonies. He always retained his Greek character, with emphasis on healing and prophecy, but he had a special role in AUGUSTAN RELIGION as a result of Augustus' victory over Mark Antony at the battle of Actium (31 BCE). *See also* MEKAL.

**Apologists**. The first generation of Christian thinkers who gave reasoned defences of Christianity, portraying it as politically harmless, and morally and culturally superior to Judaism and PAGANISM. Leading Apologists were Justin (Martyr), Clement of Alexandria, Origen (also of Alexandria). The term 'apologist' may be used of the representative of any faith who gives an argued defence of his position. (Chadwick 1966).

**Apophis**. An ancient Egyptian serpent and cloud-dragon. He was the traditional enemy of RE in his solar boat, against whom he waged daily battle.

**apostasy**. The abandoning of Christianity for error, which, like murder and fornication, initially was regarded as unpardonable in this life, and later as pardonable only after public PENANCE. *See also* GOLDEN CALF.

**apostle** (from Greek *apostolos*: 'one who is sent'). A designation for the 12 chief disciples called by Jesus. Of these Judas Iscariot was replaced, after his betrayal of Jesus and suicide, by Matthias. Paul regarded himself as an apostle on the basis of his conversion, and this was accepted by others. *See also* APOSTOLIC SUCCESSION.

**Apostles' Creed**. A CREED commonly used in western Christianity but not in the Eastern Orthodox churches. It was not in fact composed by the 12 Apostles, as legend later claimed.

**Apostolic Church of God**. *See* MASOWE VAPOSTORI.

**Apostolic Fathers**. Those Church Fathers (i.e. bishops and theologians of the early period) who still had the Apostolic time (i.e. the time when original Apostles of Christianity were still alive) in living memory. The designation is usually applied to Clement of Rome, Ignatius, Hermas, Polycarp, Papias and the otherwise unknown authors of the *Epistle of Barnabas*, the *Epistle to Diognetus, Two Clement* and the *Didache* (i.e. the Teaching) *of the Twelve Apostles*.

**apostolicity**. A characteristic of the true Christian church, according to the Nicene Creed which speaks of 'one, holy, catholic and apostolic church'. This is sometimes taken to mean 'in harmony with the teaching of the apostles' and sometimes to imply legitimation through the succession of consecrated bishops deriving ultimately from the first APOSTLES.

**Apostolic succession**. One of the criteria for judging the validity of consecration as a BISHOP in the Roman Catholic, Orthodox and Anglican churches. It implies the idea of an uninterrupted transmission of the power of ordination handed down from the APOSTLES to their successors and so on, down to the bishops of today, so that the spiritual authority of the episcopacy comes directly from that of the Apostles. Apostolicity may be defined therefore as unbroken continuity with the first Christian apostles in doctrine and tradition, exemplified and guarded by the succession of bishops.

**apotheosis**. The raising of a human being to divine status, usually accompanied by the development of a glorificatory cult.

**apotropaic**. Effective in warding off ill fortune. Thus an apotropaic ritual is one directed towards averting evil or calamity.

**Aprakos Gospel** (Greek). Biblical texts in liturgical order used in the ORTHODOX CHURCH.

**a priori.** *See* RELIGIOUS A PRIORI.

**apse**. The eastern end of a BASILICA, usually semicircular in shape and arranged to accommodate the seats of BISHOP and presbyters behind the altar.

**apu** (Quechua: 'sir', 'lord'). The spirits of the mountains as protectors of rural settlements and cities. In accordance with their varying power they are classified into four hierarchical groups. Thus the most important and powerful *apu* of the South Andean region in Peru is the Apu Ausangate. If not attended well the *apu* can punish their protégés with sickness, tempest or by diminishing the number of cattle. Religious specialists like the ALTOMISAYOQ can converse directly with the *apu* and intercede with them by performing rituals. The *apu* are thought to be assisted by vicuñas (undomesticated llamas), pumas and condors (an Andean species of vulture).

**ʿaqīda** (Arabic) 'Creed' in Islām. There is no supremely valid credal document in the Islamic tradition apart from the basic and simple profession of faith (SHAHĀDA) which proclaims the unity of ALLĀH (God) and the prophethood of Muḥammad.

**ʿArafāt.** A large plain near MECCA where Muslim pilgrims carry out the ceremony of *wuqūf*, standing in the presence of ALLĀH (God). This ceremony is at the heart of the pilgrimage rites.

**arahat.** *See* ARHAT.

**ārāma.** *See* VAS.

**ārāma(ya)** (Pāli, Sinhalese). A monastery or Buddhist temple. In the Pāli Canon (TRIPIṬAKA) the term denotes a monastic settlement that has been donated by the laity. In Sri Lanka the term is used as a synonym of VIHĀRA, but especially as part of the name of a monastery, for example, *Śrī Saddharmārāmaya*.

**aramitama.** *See* MI-TAMA.

**āraññavāsin** (Sinhalese: 'Forest-dwelling'). In Sri Lanka there is a traditional distinction between 'forest-dwelling' and 'village-dwelling' (GRĀMAVĀSIN) Buddhist monks. The forest-dwellers live in secluded forest caves or huts, devoting their time to meditation.

**āraññā-vihāra.** *See* VIHĀRA.

**aranya.** *See* ARANYAKAS.

**Āranyakas** (Sanskrit: 'forest-treatises'). A group of writings following the BRĀHMAṆAS, supposedly written by and for people who had entered the third stage of life (*araṇya*, 'forest-dweller'). These had no longer any ritual and social obligations but could devote themselves to meditation. Sometimes, as in the BṚHADĀRAYANKA-UPANIṢAD they are combined with the following UPANIṢAD.

**arca.** *See* PAÑCĀRATRA.

**arcane.** *See* ARCANUM.

**arcanum** (Latin). Secret. In post-classical Latin the term usually refers to the secrets (*arcana*) of alchemy. In classical Latin it occurs only as an adverb (*arcano*) and is used by Ovid to refer to the *sacra* (mysteries).

**archangel.** A chief ANGEL. Three named archangels in Christian tradition are Michael, Gabriel and Raphael. Two works of the APOCRYPHA, namely Tobit and Enoch, refer to seven archangels.

**archbishop.** The BISHOP of an especially important see, usually with jurisdiction over a larger ecclesiastical province.

**archdeacon.** A priest with special responsibility over a large area of a DIOCESE for the training and management of other priests.

**Archegos.** *See* MANICHAEISM.

**archetype.** A term used primarily in the analytical psychology of Carl Gustav Jung. Archetypes are instinctive patterns in the collective unconscious of humankind. Each individual shares, thus, through birth in a common heritage of experiential structures. Archetypes have through the course of history manifested themselves in the form of myths, tales, legends, pictorial representations, symbols (crosses, stars, MAṆḌALA etc.). Typical archetypes are, for example, man's image of woman (virgin and harlot) and of man (hero and liberator), of evil and good as well as of saviour and destroyer.

**archimandrite.** In the Eastern Orthodox churches, the religious superior of a group of monasteries or the holder of high ecclesiastical office below a BISHOP.

**archon** (Greek). A Greek political term which is used in gnostic texts to designate superhuman evil and tyrannical beings, especially the world ruler and creator (Gihus 1985).

**archpriest.** A priest to whom pre-eminence is assigned, notably in ritual and procedural contexts. In Christianity, although the title still occurs in the Roman Catholic and Orthodox Churches, it was more widespread during the 1st millennium, during which it was common for an archpriest to stand in for a BISHOP.

**arctic hysteria**. Various states of hysteria documented in Siberia. For example, among the Yakuts a form of hysteria appears from time to time which has the nature of an epidemic and is called a *menerik*. In addition, the initiatory sickness of SHAMANS has given rise to the theory of the nervous instability of arctic peoples. Åke Ohlmarks claimed that the basis of SHAMANISM is the psychopathological tendency of the shaman, arctic hysteria, which is caused by vitamin deficiencies in the arctic regions and is thus dependent at root on natural conditions. However, the scholars (Czaplick 1914; Ohlmarks 1939) who have linked shamanism with arctic hysteria have failed to consider the ecstatic cult systems of, for example, South America or Africa.

**Ardās** (Punjabi: 'petition'). A prayer recited at the end of Sikh rituals (McLeod 1984).

**Ares**. The Greek god of battle, son of ZEUS and Hera, passionate and violent and thus unlike the cunning and strategic ATHENA, who was also a deity of war. *Compare* MARS.

**aretology**. An oral or literary work celebrating the miraculous acts of a goddess or a god. *Compare* HAGIOGRAPHY.

**Argonauts.** *See* HERO(ES).

**arguments for the existence of God**. Although traditional arguments for the existence of God, for centuries regarded by many as compelling, are nowadays widely regarded as inconclusive, they continue to be instructive with respect to the meaning which may be attached to the concept of God in theistic contexts. At the same time, it has become evident that in so far as the arguments continue to have any force this would not necessarily be restricted to monotheistic contexts, hence the designation 'God' in the entries cross-referenced below should also be understood to include the concept 'gods'. See also COMMON CONSENT ARGUMENTS FOR THE EXISTENCE OF GOD; COSMOLOGICAL ARGUMENTS FOR THE EXISTENCE OF GOD; DESIGN ARGUMENTS FOR THE EXISTENCE OF GOD; MORAL ARGUMENTS FOR THE EXISTENCE OF GOD; ONTOLOGICAL ARGUMENTS FOR THE EXISTENCE OF GOD; PHYSICO-THEOLOGICAL ARGUMENTS FOR THE EXISTENCE OF GOD; TELEOLOGICAL ARGUMENTS FOR THE EXISTENCE OF GOD; RATIO ANSELMI.

**arhat** (Sanskrit: 'the worthy one') [Pāli: *arahat*]. An enlightened person, a Buddhist 'saint' who has surmounted the ten fetters, namely: (1) belief in a personality; (2) sceptical doubt; (3) attachment to rules and rituals; (4) craving for sensual pleasures; (5) ill will, antipathy; (6) craving for existence in the fine-material world; (7) craving for existence in the immaterial world; (8) conceit; (9) restlessness; (10) ignorance. Four stages are distinguished on the way to arhathood: (1) after having surmounted the first three fetters one is a 'stream-winner', which means that one attains NIRVĀṆA within a limited number of rebirths; (2) after having surmounted the fourth and the fifth fetter one is a 'once-returner', which means that one will be reborn only once more; (3) after having fully surmounted the first five fetters one is a 'non-returner', one who will not be reborn again but will attain NIRVĀṆA during a life in heaven; (4) after having surmounted all ten fetters one is an *arhat*, one who has attained *Nirvāṇa* in this life and will not be reborn again in any form.

**Arianism**. The teaching of Arius (4th century CE), who believed God to be absolutely single, and assumed the Saviour to be inferior, created to be God's instrument in the creation of the world. This teaching acquired a widespread following and was countered in the Nicene creed (325 CE), in particular by the phrases 'begotten not made' and 'of one substance [HOMOOUSIOS] with the Father'. (Kelly 1972: ch. 9).

**Aristotelianism**. The adoption and development of the ideas of Aristotle (348–322 BCE) by philosophers in the ancient world and by later thinkers, e.g. Muslim and Christian theologians in the Middle Ages. Unlike his master Plato, Aristotle regarded individual SUBSTANCES as the primary realities. Hence Aristotelianism concentrated especially on the relationship between substance and other categories, on matter and form, and on the four types of CAUSE. St Thomas Aquinas and his later followers developed Aristotle's METAPHYSICS of being in their teaching on ANALOGY, seeing God as 'pure act' and as the source of the being of other entities.

**ark**. A sacred box which in origin appears to have been the portable throne of a war-god (*1 Samuel* 4.1–11). In Israelite religion, the ark became the ark of the COVENANT with YAHWEH, containing the covenantal tablets. Although the English word 'ark' is derived from Latin *arca* ('chest') it is also used to refer to Noah's Ark, a covered vessel saving him, his family and representative animals from the flood (*see* FLOOD). (Vaux 1961, 1965: 297–302; Kraus 1966: 125–128; Campbell 1979; Ahlström 1984).

**Armant.** *See* MONT.

**Arminianism**. A theological position named after the influential Dutchman Jacobus Arminius (1560–1609), who resisted the Calvinist doctrine of PREDESTINATION. By contrast, he and others who took an Arminian position (later including John Wesley) asserted that salvation through Christ was open to all, and that its acceptance depended upon an act of free will. In the Netherlands a statement of this and related teachings, known as the Remonstrance, was published at Gouda in 1610. However, the theological debate was bedevilled by politics, for the Arminian party was suspected of being pro-Spanish; this led to condemnation at the Synod of Dort (1618–19) and to persecution as 'Remonstrants'.

**Arrhephoria**. Athenian nocturnal initiation festival in which two young girls who spent a year on the Acropolis weaving a robe for ATHENA descend to a shrine of Eros. It is probably connected to the myth in which the daughters of Cecrops, the mythical first king of Athens, fell to their deaths from the Acropolis after being frightened by snakes, thus signifying death to virginity.

**Arsaphes.** *See* HERISHEF.

**Artemis**. The daughter of ZEUS and Leto, the mistress of animals who nurses wild creatures and also guides hunters. She is also a virgin deity who is surrounded by NYMPHS and helps women in childbirth. *Compare* DIANA.

**artha** (Sanskrit: 'wealth'). One of the four aims of life (*puruṣārthas*) which a Hindu is to pursue as a householder (the others being KĀMA, DHARMA, MOKṢA). It also acquires the meaning 'statecraft' in texts like Kautilīya's *Ārthaśāstra*, 'wealth' being considered the pivot of the activity of a ruler on behalf of his country.

**arthaśāstra.** *See* ARTHA.

**Arunācala** (Sanskrit). The sacred mountain site of the ashram of the South Indian mystic Rāmaṇa Mahārṣī (1879–1950), whose teaching and practice was in the tradition of *advaita vedānta* and whose life was an inspiration to many Hindus and Christians in India (Sharma 1986).

**Arval Brethren**. A very ancient aristocratic Roman priestly college. Their most important ceremony was the May worship of the Dea Dia, about whom little is known. Many of the college's records are preserved, as are some of their cult songs, the oldest of which contains the first reference to the LARES.

**Āryā Samāj** (Hindi). Formed in the Punjab in 1985 by Dayānanda Saraswatī, a Hindu movement that looks back to the VEDAS as the source of Āryā ideology and culture, and eschews what it felt to be subsequent superstitious belief and practice, e.g. image worship and caste restrictions. (Dayānanda's teachings were set out in SATYĀRTHA PRAKĀŚA.) Dayānanda was concerned to slow the pace of conversion to other faiths by retraditionalization. This increasingly involved the movement in communalism and an alliance with ultra-orthodox groups (Jones 1976).

**Aryans.** *See* VṚṬA.

**Äsaḷla Perahära.** *See* DAḶADĀ MĀLIGĀVA.

**ascension**. A term usually restricted to the bodily ASSUMPTION of the resurrected Jesus Christ into the heavens as described in the Acts of the Apostles. Typologically however the ascension of Christ is comparable in a general sense to the 'assumption' of Elijah, of Mary, or of Muḥammad. The story of the ascension of Christ, which presages his return in a similar manner, may be seen as part of the step-by-step ESCHATOLOGY characteristic of the *Gospel of Luke* and the *Acts of the Apostles*. For the author it is clear that Jesus departed from the earth 40 days after his resurrection, and this view is faithfully reflected in church calendars which celebrate this event (Ascension Day) on the fifth Thursday after Easter.

**ascetical theology**. Systematic spiritual guidance in the Christian life with a view to the attainment of perfection with the assistance of divine grace. Moral theology, by contrast, in accordance with distinctions developed in the Middle Ages, is concerned with those right actions necessary to salvation, while the subject of mystical theology is unexpected divine action, which brings about exceptional spiritual blessings.

**aseity**. The quality of being *a se*, that is from or of oneself and not dependent on any other being. In Christian theology this quality distinguishes God from any other being.

**Asgard**. Realm of the gods in Germanic pre-Christian mythology.

**Ashʿarī** (Arabic). An early school of theology in Islām, named after Abū al-Ḥasan al-Ashʿarī (*d* 935). *See* KALĀM.

**Asherah**. A Semitic sun-goddess, worshipped from Mesopotamia to Egypt in the 2nd millennium, and in Palestine and south Arabia in the first. In Ugarit the Canaanite pantheon is commonly called 'the seventy sons of Asherah'. She is regarded as mother of the king in the royal cult. Paired with SHAPSH, she mothers the Venus deity in the Twin forms ASHTAR-ASTARTE and SHAHAR-SHALEM. (Patai 1965; Lipínski 1972; Day 1986).

**Ashkenazi** (Hebrew). In contrast to SEPHARDI, the designation for Jews from Germany, Poland, Russia, the Ukraine etc., and the Yiddish-speaking European tradition they represent.

**Ashtar**. An important West Semitic god, representing Venus and kingship, related to ASTARTE, and SHAHAR-SHALEM. (Gray 1949; Caqot 1959; Wyatt 1986a, b)

**Ashur**. The national god of Assyria and patron of Assyrian kings. His attributes are derived from older gods such as Anshar, ANU and ENLIL, being respectively primordial, sky and storm gods (Van Driel 1969).

**ʿĀshūrāʾ** (Arabic). The tenth day of the Islamic lunar month of AL-MUḤARRAM; the anniversary commemorating the martyrdom of the grandson of the Prophet Muḥammad.

**Ash Wednesday**. A day of PENANCE on which traditionally (i.e. during the Middle Ages) ashes were placed upon the heads of both clergy and lay people as a sign of penitence. Being the first day of LENT, it falls on the Wednesday in the seventh week before Easter Sunday, thus allowing 40 days of fasting (not counting Sundays).

**ashram.** *See* AŚRAMA.

**'as if' philosophy**. A development in philosophy (*see* KANTIANISM), initiated by Friedrich Carl Forberg (1770–1848) and extended by Hans Vaihinger (1852–1933), according to which we ought to act as if certain useful propositions in science, ethics and religion were true, even if they cannot be known to be true or – according to Vaihinger – even if they are known for certain to be factually false. The position is sometimes called 'fictionalism', though the term is possibly less accurately applied to Forberg than it is to Vaihinger, who used the word as descriptive of his own philosophical standpoint in his book *The Philosophy of 'as if'* (New York, 1924). Such fictionalism can be distinguished from PRAGMATISM, to which it shows some resemblance, in the following respect: according to pragmatism, some statement is held to be true if and only if it has practical use; but, according to fictionalism, some statement can have practical use even if it is known to be false. Among useful religious fictions, which – according to Vaihinger – are known to be false, are included the existence of God, the immortality of the soul, and the virgin birth. We are enjoined by him to embrace and act on such fictions 'as if' they were true, since we need them in order to cope with life in an indifferent and irrational universe.

**Asklepios**. Greek god of healing, famous for his temple at Epidauros, where people were healed through incubation (i.e. during their sleep). *Compare* AESCULAPIUS.

**al-Asmā' al-Ḥusnā** (Arabic). 'The most beautiful names (of Allāh).' According to Islamic tradition there are 99 such names (although more are known as well) and 'whosoever knows them shall enter Paradise'. Thus to meditate upon the names, with the aid of a rosary, is widely accepted (not, however, by purists such as the Wahhābis – *see* WAHHĀDIYA) as an act of pious devotion. The names are either found in or derived from the QUR'ĀN (see, for example, 59.22–4).

**asperges**. The name given to the Roman Catholic ceremony in which holy water is sprinkled over both altar and congregation before MASS to symbolize their purification. The name derives from the Latin text of Psalm 51.

**aspersion**. Baptism by sprinkling, performed only rarely in special medical circumstances. Aspersion is distinguished from the much more common practice of affusion, in which a small quantity of water is poured over the head of the person being baptized.

**āśrama** (Sanskrit). In its simple meaning, a 'place of work', i.e. a hermitage or monastery whose inmates live according to a specific rule and devote most of their time to spiritual exercises such as yoga. Most religions in India, including Christianity, have *āśramas* which are open to lay persons.

By extension the term also traditionally meant 'stage of life', as in the compound term *caturvarṇāśramadharma*. In the main tradition of Indian thought these are four: *brahmacarya* (studenthood, celibacy), *gṛhastya* (household or married life), *vānaprastya* (forest-dwelling life away from ordinary settlements) and *samnyāsa* (renunciation or homelessness). The student years are to be spent studying the Vedas and other subjects, while living a simple, celibate life under the guidance of a teacher. The householder years are the time for marrying, earning a living, raising a family, caring for older relatives and carrying out Hindu rituals for which one is responsible. The forest-dwelling stage is a time for meditation, penance and reflection on the transient nature of life, during which household responsibilities are handed over to the next generation. The fourth represents complete withdrawal from worldly responsibilities. The practice of the four *āśramas* was always restricted to the 'twice-born' Brahmin class. Even here it has always been regarded as an ideal scheme designed to integrate worldly and spiritual aspects of human life. In reality many have never entered the third stage, let alone the fourth.

**Assiut.** *See* WEPWAWET.

**assumption**. The drawing up into heaven of the body of a holy person, used particularly of the Virgin Mary, but also recounted in the cases of Elijah, Muḥammad and possibly of Moses (judging from the title of a largely lost work entitled *The Assumption of Moses*). From a comparative point of view the difference between assumption and ASCENSION is not at all clear, except that the latter is usually reserved for Jesus, implying divine initiative on his own part. In either case bodily remains are presumed not to remain on earth. Belief in the assumption of the Virgin Mary has been widespread in the Christian churches since the 7th century, but is rejected by Protestants as being entirely non-biblical. It was elevated into a formal doctrine of the Roman Catholic Church by Pope Pius XII in 1950.

**Astarte**. The goddess of love and war among the Canaanites, akin to ANAT, with whom she was fused by the first millennium BCE to form ATARGATIS. In the Old Testament she appears as Ashtarot (singular, not plural, as commonly supposed) and Ashtoret. In iconography she is armed, winged, wears the Egyptian Atef crown of Osiris, and commonly rides a horse (Wyatt 1984). Her name is the feminine form of ASHTAR, with whom she forms a twin pair as deities of the morning and evening stars (*see also* SHAHAR AND SHALEM). Astarte probably lies behind the designation 'Queen of Heaven'. Equivalents are West Semitic ʿaṯtartu and Akkadian *Ištar*.

**asuras** (Sanskrit: 'demons') In Vedic religion, counterparts to the DEVAS (*sura*). They are identified with whatever is hostile to the Āryans and defeating them is one of the major activities of Hindu deities.

**Atargatis**. A West Semitic goddess of the Hellenistic period, a fusion of ASTARTE and ANAT. She is the subject of Lucian's book *De dea Syria* (Attridge & Oden 1976).

**Aten**. An ancient Egyptian deity symbolized by the sun's disc and represented in this form, with rays ending in hands which bestowed bounty. Originally an aspect of the sun-god RE, towards the end of the 18th Dynasty (*c.* 1575 BCE), the Aten was elevated by Akhenaten to receive a form of monotheistic worship. This king started his reign as Amenophis IV, and the cult of Aten continued at THEBES alongside that of Amen-Re (Egypt's great state-god) and many other deities. However, Amenophis IV carried forward the policy started by his father, Amenophis III, and began to promote the Aten's cult to much greater lengths.

Changing his name to Akhenaten ('Servant of the Aten'), the king closed the temples of all other gods and disbanded their priesthoods. He moved the political and religious capital from Thebes to a virgin site mid-way between Memphis and Thebes. Known today as Tell el Amarna, this city was originally called Akhetaten. Here Akhenaten built great temples for the worship of the Aten, a number of royal palaces, and the offices and administrative headquarters of a capital city (Frankfort & Pendlebury 1933).

Akhenaten's worship of the Aten came close to monotheism. Symbolized by the sun's disc, the god was envisaged as an invisible life-force, a universal and loving deity, creator of foreign peoples as well as the Egyptians. His sole representative on earth was Akhenaten, and some scholars regard this 'revolution' as political as much as religious, with the king seeking to terminate the considerable power of the priesthoods, particularly that of Amen-Re, which had rivalled royal power during previous reigns.

These religious innovations inspired a new and distinctive art-form (sometimes known as 'Amarna Art'), which flourished briefly at Amarna and elsewhere (Davies 1903–8), and emphasized the joy and beauty of creation, nature, and plants and animals, but also represented the human figure almost as a caricature based, according to some scholars, on the supposed physical abnormalities of the king. However, since his body has never been discovered and his statues and art representations provide the only evidence for this theory, it cannot be proved conclusively.

Akhenaten lived at Amarna with his wife Nefertiti (who also played an important role in the Aten's cult) and their six daughters. With no direct male heir, at his death the throne passed consecutively to his two sons-in-law, Smenkhkare and Tutankhamun. Perhaps because there was no powerful son to continue his policy, but also because the Aten failed to attract a wide support beyond the royal court, this religious experiment failed and, under his successors, the court returned to Thebes. Akhetaten became a deserted city, and the multitude of old gods and their priesthoods were reinstated.

The tenets of Atenism, preserved in hymns inscribed in the courtiers' rock-cut tombs at Amarna, provide insight into the beliefs of this period and have much in common with *Psalm* 104 in the Bible.

**Atenism.** *See* ATEN.

**Athanasian Creed**. A CREED traditionally but unreliably attributed to Athanasius and probably dating from the late 4th or early 5th century CE. The text dwells on the themes of Trinity and Incarnation and contains damnatory anathemas of positions presumed to be heretical. It is also known by the opening words 'Quicunque vult' (i.e. 'Whosoever will' be saved . . .). *See also* TRINITY.

**Athar.** *See* ḤADĪTH.

**Atharvaveda**. The last and latest of the four Vedic *saṁhitās*, containing a great variety of hymns and spells, many of them of a magical nature, used as incantations, e.g. to rid a person from fever.

**atheism**. A view denying the existence of God. In recent years the term has come to be associated with philosophies that make no room for belief in a personal God or for the notion of transcendence in the interpretation of human existence, or the explanation of events and phenomena. In the 20th century Logical Positivism (*see* POSITIVISM) and Marxism have been primary examples of atheistic philosophies. *Compare* THEISM; AGNOSTICISM.

**Atheismusstreit** (German: 'dispute about atheism'). A controversy in Germany at the end of the 18th century over the alleged ATHEISM of Johann Gottlieb Fichte (1762–1814), which resulted in his being dismissed from the chair of philosophy at the University of Jena.

**Athena**. An armed, militant Greek goddess who was born from her father, ZEUS, and protected Athens; a virgin goddess who excels in political intelligence. *Compare* MINERVA.

**Athos**. Known in Greek as 'the holy mountain', Mount Athos is a Macedonian peninsula covered entirely with monastic settlements of the Greek Orthodox Church. Access is restricted to men.

**ātman** (Sanskrit: 'Self'). A central notion in VEDĀNTA from the UPANIṢADS onwards. The identification of the true self and the removal of all misidentifications is the core of the path of knowledge. This path is clearly delineated in some early Upaniṣads commented upon by later Vedāntācāryas and elaborated in their *Vedāntasūtrabhāṣyas*. Usually a four-step process is taught: *jāgarita sthāna – svapna – suṣupti – turīya*. In the waking state the Self is dispersed into the multitude of sense-objects perceived, alienated into identifying with the body. In dream a certain degree of freedom is reached, but states of terror and anxiety can occur in dreams as well as states of bliss and enjoyment. In deep sleep the Self is one with itself but not conscious of this. In the fourth state, a condition of pure awareness without a subject–object dichotomy and without the limitations of dream and deep sleep, the Self finds its true nature and perfect happiness. This state is identical with the realization of the *ātman*'s identity with BRAHMAN.

In Buddhism, *ātman* is an entity denied by the doctrine of ANĀTMAN.

**atonement**. The Day of Atonement is a Jewish day of fasting intended to cleanse the people of their sin and restore the right relationship with God. The appointed day is the tenth of the seventh month of the Jewish calender, and hence falls usually in October. In Christianity atonement is essentially a theological concept referring to reconciliation between man and God through the death of Christ understood sacrificially.

**Atrahasis**. A legendary hero of the Mesopotamian FLOOD-STORY who appears in the GILGAMESH EPIC as Utnapishtim. (Heidel 1946; Lambert & Millard 1969).

**atta.** *See* ĀTMAN.

**Attis**. A Phrygian deity which in late antiquity became a central figure in the MYSTERIES OF CYBELE (*magna mater*).

**atua** (Polynesian). Usually translated as 'god' but its meaning is much wider. It encompasses all sorts of spiritual beings ranging from personal creators to spiritual powers residing in material objects, and from ancestral spirits to malevolent demons.

**Atum**. A great creator-god, associated with the ancient Egyptian city Heliopolis. Atum's characteristics were eventually absorbed by RE. In mythology, Atum created himself.

**auditores.** *See* MANICHAEISM.

**Aufklärung** (German). The German term for the European ENLIGHTENMENT. In older books the word is sometimes translated as the 'ILLUMINATION'. *See also* HASKALAH.

**Augsburg Confession**. A statement of the faith of the German reformers Luther and Melanchthon which was drawn up for the consideration of the Emperor Charles V in 1530. It contained important teachings typical of LUTHERANISM, such as the doctrine of justification by faith, but also a list of Catholic practices considered undesirable, such as communion in one kind only and compulsory celibacy for the priesthood.

**augurs**. A Roman priestly college devoted to watching for signs, particularly those from birds, to determine the gods' opinion of a proposed action.

**augustale** (Latin). Priests of the Imperial cult in ancient Rome.

**Augustan religion**. The first Roman emperor Augustus (27 BCE – 14 CE) engaged in a religious revival to legitimate his power. He revived archaic festivals, rebuilt temples, began the imperial cult and encouraged authors to utilize supposedly ancient Roman mythology in their works. The revival received much acclaim from all orders of society, probably because many felt that disregard of Roman religion in the decades prior to Augustus had in part caused the ruinous Civil War. *See also* AENEID; METAMORPHOSES.

**Augustinianism**. Theology influenced by the work of St Augustine of Hippo (354–430). Like PLATONISM it teaches the primacy of form over matter – though for Augustine, God contains in himself the Forms or Ideas which are the archetypes of matter; and it regards the soul as a spiritual substance. It also teaches the primacy of faith over reason, for faith leads to understanding – indeed, divine illumination of the inner depths of the soul is necessary if we are to apprehend any truth and it does not subordinate the will to knowledge. Other characteristic positions of Augustinianism are that evil is a privation of good and so not an independent principle, and that human nature is flawed by ORIGINAL SIN as a result of the FALL, so that divine grace, which frees the will rather than limiting it, is necessary for salvation (to which only some are predestined). (Chadwick 1986).

**aum.** *See* OM.

**aumakua** (Hawaiian). Clan deities in precolonial Hawaii, usually animals or birds.

**Auroville.** *See* AUROBINDO ASHRAM.

**Authorized Version**. An English translation of the Bible, begun in 1607 at the behest of James I and hence known also as the 'King James Version', was first published in 1611 and quickly supplanted others to become the dominant translation of the Bible in English-speaking countries until the second half of the 20th century. The original publication included the APOCRYPHA, but this was often omitted in modern editions. Although concern for accurate theology was a dominant motive at the time when the translation was made, it was the power and richness of the language used which ensured its success. In practical church life it is now largely superseded by such translations as the Revised Standard Version, the New English Bible (of interdenominational Protestant provenance) and the Jerusalem Bible (of Catholic provenance). *See also* BIBLE.

**autocephalous church**. An autonomous regional church in the Orthodox communion, so named from the Greek *autos* ('self') and *kephalos* ('head').

**automatism**. Unintentional and often involuntary forms of behaviour such as automatic writing, speaking (GLOSSOLALIA) and dancing. Automatisms are often linked with the state of ECSTASY. Long preparation for it may have taken place, but when the process itself begins, the individual can no longer control him/herself. In religious contexts, automatisms have often been understood as having been brought on by higher powers, gods, or spirits. The product of the process in the form of a text or an utterance is deemed to be a divine statement or a prophecy from god to human beings.

**Avalokiteśvara**. A mythical BODHISATTVA in Mahāyāna Buddhism, especially known for his great compassion, and featuring in the LOTUS SUTRA and in the HEART SUTRA. Avalokiteśvara is known in China as Guanyin (old transcription Kuan-yin) and in Japanese as Kannon (old transcription Kwannon), and usually displays feminine traits in these countries, as also in Korea. For the Tibetan connection, *see* POTALAKA.

**āvāsa(ya)** (Pāli, Sinhalese). The residence of a Buddhist monk or monks. In the Pāli Canon (*Tipiṭaka*) the term denotes a monastic settlement built by the monks themselves. In Sri Lanka it refers to a monastery in which there is no building other than the living quarters for monks or nuns.

**avatāra** (Sanskrit: 'descent'). Used in Hinduism as a term to designate a manifestation of VIṢṆU in corporeal form. Most commonly known are the ten *avatāras* (*matsya* or fish, *kacchapa* or tortoise, *varāha* or boar, *narasinha* or man-lion, BUDDHA, RĀMA, Paraśurāma, Balarāma, KṚṢṆA, and the future Kalkin) but Hindu scriptures know also many others. In the PAÑCARĀTRA system AVATĀRAS are classified as *Vibhava*, a manifestation of Viṣṇu 'for the protection of the good and the destruction of the wicked', a line of thought also found in the BHAGAVADGĪTĀ. The idea of *avatāras* may have arisen in Hinduism under the influence of Buddhist thought (the appearances of *bodhisattvas* like MAITREYA at crucial junctures in history).

**Ave Maria** (Latin: 'Hail Mary'). A devotional recitation used mainly by Roman Catholics and composed of the sentences of the angel's greeting to Mary (*Luke* 1. 28), Elisabeth's praise of Mary (*Luke* 1. 42) and some additional invocations asking for Mary's intervention thanks to her rank close to her son who is the second person of the Trinity.

**Avīcī hell.** *See* HELL.

**Avesta.** *See* ZOROASTRIANISM.

**avidyā** (Sanskrit: 'ignorance'). The congenital condition of lacking wisdom and knowledge of the true nature of reality, leading to suffering and to rebirth. The UPANIṢADS claim to have found the path to *vidyā* ('knowledge') through which ignorance, suffering and rebirth come to an end.

**avodah** (Hebrew). Literally 'service' or 'work', especially the service and worship of God. The original *avodah* of Temple sacrifice was replaced by *avodat halev*, the 'service of the heart', that is, prayer.

**āya** (Arabic: 'sign'; plural, *ayāt*). In the QUR'ĀN the word means one of the manifest evidences of God's existence and power; by extension it is the name for a Qur'anic verse which constitutes such an evidence.

**ayahuasca**. A Native American hallucinogenic drink of the Amazonian region, made from the *Banisteropsis caopi* or related vines with the addition of other psychoactive plants, traditionally drunk in a communal ritual setting by hunter-warriors for divination etc. In *mestizo* (racially mixed) culture, it is now primarily used for healing.

**ayatollah.** *See* AYATULLĀH.

**Ayātullāh** (Arabic: 'Sign from God'). The title held by the highest dignitaries in the SHĪ'A religious hierarchy drawn from the ranks of outstanding mujtahids (*see* IJTIHĀD) who are considered qualified to give authoritative judgements in matters of faith and practice.

**Ayn Sof** (Hebrew). The kabbalistic term for the 'end-less' or 'infinite' aspect of God. The absolute and ultimate source of all creation, the Ayn Sof is the godhead beyond the SEFIROT. *See also* QLIPPOT.

**Azariqa.** *See* AL-IBADIYA.

**al-Azhar**. The famous centre for higher Islamic learning established in Cairo in the 10th century, and the oldest and most respected continuously operating institution of its kind in the world. The school attached to the al-Azhar mosque has instruction in the four main MADHHABS (law schools) of Sunnī Islām; in the 1960s its curriculum was reformed, adding a hospital and medical faculty among other non-traditional departments.

**Aztec calendar.** *See* TONALPOHUALI.

# B

**Ba** (Egyptian). In ancient Egypt, an aspect of the soul, represented as a human-headed bird; it retained a person's individuality after death.

**Baal**. A title ('Lord') given to various deities, but most commonly, at Ugarit, denoting the storm-god, also known as HADAD ('Thunderer'), and cognate with Mesopotamian ADAD. In the BAAL CYCLE of myths Baal fights and kills the sea (in Ugarit YAM, in Mesopotamia TIAMAT (*compare* also RAHAB and LEVIATHAN in the Old Testament). This myth is probably a COSMOGONY, though some authorities demur. After his victory over Sea, Baal is granted a palace-temple, but is immediately overwhelmed by Death (MOT), whom he subsequently conquers after his resurrection. This is the Canaanite type of the 'DYING-AND-RISING GOD', which is commonly interpreted along seasonal, agricultural lines (e.g. Gaster 1950; De Moor 1971), but is more complex than such simple allegorization allows. The Baal who appears frequently in the Old Testament as the epitome of false Canaanite cults may be the storm-god, but in some contexts (as in *Hosea*) is rather EL. (Kapelrud 1952; Zijl 1972; L'Heureux 1979; Grabbe 1976).

**Baal cycle**. A complex of myths from Ugarit, in six tablets, narrating conflicts between BAAL and YAM, BAAL and MOT, and the SACRED MARRIAGE with ANAT. (*See also* DRAGON.) (See Olmo Lete 1981: 79–235; Smith 1986. Text in Gibson 1978; De Moor 1987).

**babalawo.** *See* IFÁ.

**Bacchus.** *See* DIONYSIAN MYSTERIES.

**Bachwezi**. A spirit possession cult in the kingdoms of western Uganda. The Chwezi are mythical rulers who vanished mysteriously. There are said to be 19 important Chwezi spirit, partly or wholly personifications of certain elemental natural forces, and in the traditional cult each one of the localized social groups stood in a special relationship to one spirit and had its own initiated male or female priest or medium (Beattie 1966: 77f). Bachwezi is an official cult under control of the religious and secular establishment where the medium acts only as mouthpiece between the ancestors and the social group, whereas the so-called CULTS OF AFFLICTION centre on the possessed individuals themselves. In time of crisis mediatory spirit possession cults like Bachwezi can change into cults of affliction. (Baumann 1975c).

**Badarayana.** *See* BRAHMASŪTRA.

**Badb**. Irish Celtic war goddess who appears in the shape of a crow.

**Baisākhī** (Punjabi). A major Sikh festival instituted by Gurū Amar Dās in the 16th century and held at the time of the Punjabi new year. It is now associated particularly with the establishment of the KHĀLSĀ by Gurū Gobind Singh in 1699.

**Balarāma.** *See* AVATĀRA.

**Balder**. A figure of Germanic mythology, represented sometimes as a handsome and mild god and sometimes as a hero of divine parentage. He is a favourite of the gods and his death, brought about by LOKI in the PROSE EDDA and by a human rival, Hoder, in Saxo Grammaticus's account, is much lamented. According to the *Voluspá*, a poem of the EDDA, he returns from HEL after

RAGNAROK to inhabit the heaven of a new creation.

**Balian** (Balinese). A Balinese priest working especially in the medical field by applying various herbal remedies, but also by using trance techniques, consulting spirits, or muttering a MANTRA, and so forth (Hooykaas 1973).

**Balokole Revival**. A Ugandan revival movement inspired by (Simeoni Nsibandi) in the 1920s, which led in 1941 to a near schism within the Anglican Church of Uganda. In the longer term the Balokole movement has come to be seen as a constructive element within the church. ('*Balokole*' means 'saved people'.)

**Baltic religion**. The religion of the Latvians, the Lithuanians and the Old Prussians. The latter disappeared as a cultural unity by the 17th century, but the Latvians and Lithuanians have partly preserved the old religious beliefs despite formal Christianization in the 13th and 14th centuries respectively. These beliefs are closely linked with the agricultural life of the Baltic peoples, as is reflected in the function of many of the deities as guarantors of fertility, in the large proportion of the cultic festivals devoted to the success of the harvest, and in the idea of gods and goddesses living in the heavens as farmers. Sources for the study of Baltic religion consist mainly of commentaries by foreign conquerors and Christian missionaries, and a large body of folkloric material, notably the DAINAS.

**baṇa** (Sinhalese: 'preaching'). In Sri Lanka there are several types of Buddhist preaching, the most important of which are: *mataka baṇa* (preaching in the house of a dead man), *paṃsukūlē* (preaching at a funeral), *sāmānya baṇa* (preaching on *poya* (*uposatha*) days). In the principal monasteries there is a special building for the preaching which is called the 'preaching hall', *baṇa maḍuva* or *baṇa gedara*.

**Bao Pu Zi**. A Chinese text named after the pen-name of the author: 'The Master who embraces Simplicity', alias Ge Hong, a 4th-century scholar with a Confucian background and interests in Daoism. The text, ascribed to Ge Hong, is formally divided into two parts: the 'inner' chapters (20 chapters), and the 'outer' chapters (49 + 1 autobiographical chapters). Topics treated by Ge Hong include the use of talismans, recipes for concocting potent, life-prolonging elixirs, breathing exercises, regional folklore (not without a rational touch), the use of charms and talismans, and treatises on the nature of the *dao* (*see dao-de*). For translations of the more important 'inner' chapters see Ware 1966.

**baptism**. A rite symbolizing repentance and purification by water, commonly also, as in Christianity, initiation into the community of the saved. In early Christianity the baptism of grown-up converts was quickly accompanied by the baptism of children, the confession of belief being made on their behalf by godparents. The Baptist churches make a point of restricting baptism to those who have come of age and in some cases require total immersion of the baptisand, as opposed to a symbolic sprinkling. In Protestant churches baptism is regarded as one of the two sacraments initiated by Jesus Christ (the other being holy communion), while in the Catholic tradition it is one of the seven sacraments. In the major churches, including the Roman Catholic, baptism is considered valid, and hence efficacious as a vehicle of grace, if water is administered in the name of the Father, the Son and the Holy Spirit, whether the person performing it is ordained, lay or even unbaptized. Among the MANDAEANS baptism is an important adult rite. *See also* MYSTERIES OF CYBELE.

**baptism by blood**. The baptism of converts to Christianity deemed to have taken place by virtue of their martyrdom before they could be baptized normally with water.

**baqa'** (Arabic: 'remaining'). The SUFI expression for a state of mystical attainment beyond even extinction (FANA') in which the soul subsists eternally in ALLAH.

**Barabudur.** *See* BOROBUDUR.

**Baraita**. (Aramaic). Rabbinic commentaries from the Tannaitic period (*see* TANNAIM) that are ‘external’, that is, not included in the *Mishnah*.

**baraka.** *See* MANA.

**Barelwi Movement**. A conservative Islamic movement formed in North India by Aḥmad Riza Khān of Bareilly in the late 19th century. The movement affirmed, and gave legitimation to, current Sufi teaching, particularly the practices associated with pirs, sufi saints, and their shrines. (Robinson 1988; Metcalf 1982.) *See also* DEOBAND SEMINARY.

**Barmen declaration**. A declaration published in 1934 by the Confessing Church (bekennende Kirche) in Germany as opposed to the national church (Volkskirche), declaring the absolute primacy of the revelation of God through Jesus Christ over and against secondary sources or human additions. It was directed against the largely successful attempt by the Nazis to draw the Christian churches into their own ideological camp.

**bar mitzvah** (Hebrew: ‘son of commandment’). When a Jewish youth turns 13, he becomes subject to the obligation to perform the various commandments of the TORAH as they have been interpreted by the rabbis. Because of these obligations, he also becomes eligible to perform ritual functions on behalf of the community. To mark the occasion of becoming a *bar mitzvah*, it is customary for a youth to be given an ALIYAH, that is to read from the weekly portion of the Torah. Like others called up to recite an *aliyah*, the *bar mitzvah* will generally recite only the Hebrew benedictions for the Torah reading, and someone with special training will read from the Torah scroll itself. Following the Torah reading, however, it is customary for the *bar mitzvah* to read the more easily recited portion of the HAFTARAH. While every Jewish male may be technically considered a *bar mitzvah*, in common parlance the term has come to refer to a young man just becoming a *bar mitzvah*. A *bar mitzvah* has also come to mean the (often lavish) celebration which surrounds this event. *See also* BAT MITZVAH.

**bas mitzvah.** *See* BAT MITZVAH.

**Basnāyaka Nilamē.** *See* DĒVĀLĒ.

**basṭ** (Arabic). Expansion. A technical term of the SUFIS denoting one of the spiritual states (AḤWĀL) corresponding to the station or stage (MAQĀMĀT) of hope. It is contrasted with QABD (‘contraction’); the two terms are based upon the Qur’anic authority (2.245): ‘And Allāh contracts and expands.’ Expansion means a sense of joy and exaltation vouchsafed the mystic by ALLĀH.

**Bastet**. Egyptian cat-goddess, the peaceful and domestic version of SEKHMET, with a cult-centre at Bubastis. At death, sacred cats were mummified and buried in special cemeteries (Langton 1940–41).

**Batara Guru** (from Sanskrit: ‘Divine Teacher’). A god or a godlike hero in Indonesian traditional religions; in Java he is often identified with or representing an aspect of SHIVA (Stöhr & Zoetmulder 1965).

**Batara Kala** (from Sanskrit). A demon god, who is a central character in the WAYANG, sometimes presented as a son of BATARA GURU; originally perhaps representing the malicious aspect of SHIVA (Groenendael 1985).

**Bathara Guru.** *See* BATARA GURU.

**Bathara Kala.** *See* BATARA KALA.

**bāṭin** (Arabic: ‘hidden’, ‘concealed’). The esoteric aspect of a doctrine, teaching or of scripture in Islām which can be understood only through instruction from an authoritative teacher. The *bāṭin* is to be contrasted with the *ẓāhir*, or the evident, literal or exoteric meaning of doctrine and scripture.

**bat mitzvah** (Hebrew [Yiddish: *bas mitzvah*].) Traditionally, women were not subject to most of the ritual commandments obligating men, so that there was no female equivalent to becoming a BAR MITZVAH. In modern times, however, it was felt that a RITE OF PASSAGE marking entry into the religious community was needed for young women as well. As in the case of a *bar mitzvah*, a HAFTARAH is generally read by a young woman to mark the occasion of her *bat mitzvah*.

**Batō Kannon**. Horse-headed Kannon. In Japanese Buddhism, a representation of the bodhisattva Kannon (AVALOKITEŚVARA) with a horse's head or with a horse's head mounted in the crown of the image. While the ferocity of this image is connected with the idea that the horse tramples on evil, the Batō Kannon has popularly, and most frequently, been regarded as a protector of horses and cattle.

**bayʿa** (Arabic: 'rendering of allegiance'). In traditional Islām, the act by which certain persons (*ahl al-ḥall wa'l-ʿaqd*, 'those qualified to unbind and bind'), as representatives of the Muslim community appoint a Caliph or other ruler to govern over them. The oath of allegiance may also be rendered by others as well, acting either individually or collectively to acknowledge a head of the Islamic polity. With the abolition of the Caliphate in 1924, such practices are no longer performed.

**Bayon.** *See* ANGKOR.

**Bayram** (Turkish). A Muslim religious festival. *See also* ʿĪD; ʿĪD AL-AḌḤĀ; ʿĪD AL-FIṬR.

**bazma.** *See* OKLAD.

**B.C.** *See* COMMON CALENDAR.

**B.C.E.** *See* COMMON CALENDAR.

**Bear**. In Native American religions, a female spirit of regeneration, healing and nurture, connected with the EARTH MOTHER. In the western part of North America, the male grizzly bear can also symbolize warrior ferocity. *See also* SWEAT LODGE.

**beatification**. The first step towards CANONIZATION (declaration of sainthood) in the Roman Catholic church. The formal ecclesiastical process concludes with a papal statement declaring that the deceased person in question is in heaven.

**Beelzebub.** *See* BEELZEBUL.

**Beelzebul**. A Jewish designation for a demon, in the Hellenistic period, possibly as an equivalent to Satan; also occurs as Beelzebub. Derivations have been seen in the Ekronite (Philistine) god Beelzebub ('Lord of the fly' – probably a parody) in *2 Kings* 1.2ff. and the Aramaic *b$^{ec}$ el d$^{e}$baba* ('Lord of evil', 'evil one'). The best explanation is that of Gaston 1962, as 'Lord of the dwelling (*z$^{e}$-bul*), an Aramaic version (= Beʿelsamin) of the Olympian ZEUS (*see* MACCABAEAN CRISIS), head of the Phoenician pantheon. Since pagan gods were regarded as demons, their chief became the chief of demons in the Jewish view.

**Béghards**. A men's religious association probably formed in imitation of the BÉGUINES, but which fell into disrepute and, suffering attacks by the Inquisition, almost disappeared in the late Middle Ages. A reformed group of Béghards managed to continue until the French Revolution.

**Béguines**. An informal order of lay Catholic sisters dating from the 12th century in the Netherlands and Germany. Though not taking vows, the Béguines (named after the preacher Lambert le Bègue) gave their lives to the care of the poor, the sick and the aged. The loosely clustered dwelling-houses are known as *béguinages*. After suffering many vicissitudes some Béguines continue the tradition at Ghent in Belgium. *Compare* BÉGHARDS.

**Being**. Philosophy began in ancient Greece with the pre-socratics as an attempt to provide an ONTOLOGY, or to say what characterizes Being as such. Plato and the Neoplatonists spoke of the Good or the One as 'beyond Being', but the Christian thinkers Dionysius the Areopagite and Augustine (later followed by Aquinas) identified God with 'Being itself', thereby linking Christian theology with the Greek ontological enterprise, and at the same time denying the Platonic downgrading of ordinary ontological reality. Thomas Aquinas contended that finite being stood in an analogical relation to the infinite Godhead, thereby giving rise to the modern phrase 'analogy of Being' (Erich Przywara). Duns Scotus, by contrast, considered that the same meanings can be applied univocally, to both finite and infinite: the doctrine of the 'univocity of Being'. This difference of opinion has had multiple reverberations in later theology and philosophy.

**Being itself.** *See* BEING.

**Beit Din** (Hebrew 'house of law'). A Jewish religious court of law.

**Beit Haknesset** (Hebrew: 'house of congregation'). A synagogue.

**Beit Hamidrash** (Hebrew: 'house of interpretation'). A SYNAGOGUE, which might also serve as a place of informal study. A large synagogue may sometimes include a smaller Beit Hamidrash within itself.

**Beit Yosef.** *See* SHULHAN ARUKH.

**bekennende Kirche.** *See* BARMEN DECLARATION.

**Bektashi** (Turkish). A Turkish ṢŪFĪ brotherhood, the legendary patron of which, Hajji Bektash, probably lived in Anatolia around the mid-13th century, although the order only gained its final form some three centuries later. Its heterodox aspects, a fusion of SHĪ'A and ISMĀ'ĪLĪ tendencies, rites suggesting confession and the Eucharist, and the participation of unveiled women, may be later accretions.

**Belial** (Hebrew: 'Worthlessness'). An embodiment of evil, analogous to SATAN, appearing in (probably) abstract form in *Nahum* 1.11, 2.1 and *Psalm* 18.4 (= *2 Samuel* 22.5), where it represents the nether world. In APOCALYPTIC writings it is personified as a prince among Demons, like Satan and BEELZEBUL, a rival for man's loyalty (e.g. *Martyrdom of Isaiah* 2.4, *T. Benj.* 6.1, 7. 1ff, *T. Jud.* 25.3, *T. Naph.* 2.6).

**Bema festival** (from Greek *bema*, 'tribune', 'throne', 'raised place'). A commemoration of the death of Mani, founder of MANICHAEISM, in March 276. During the festival an image of Mani was revered in a raised place. The festival corresponds calendrically to the Jewish PASSOVER and Christian EASTER.

**ben** (Hebrew). A standard form of a proper name, meaning 'son of' (one's father's name), also occurring as *bar*. The feminine form is *bat*.

**Benedictus**. The second part of the SANCTUS, which is usually sung separately after the consecration in musically composed masses. The text is 'Blessed [*benedictus*] is he who comes in the name of the Lord' (*Matthew* 21.9).

**benefice.** *See* SIMONY.

**Benzaiten**. The Japanese designation for Sarasvatī, a popular Indian goddess conveyed to Japan in the context of Buddhism. She is notable for eloquence, music and protection from disasters and is revered especially on the 11th day of the month. (*See* ENNICHI).

**berdache**. A term of French origin often used in Native American religions for transvestites of either sex. Such individuals, who may or may not be homosexual, were usually considered holy and to have sacred powers.

**bersih desa** (Indonesian: 'cleansing of the village'). A Javanese festival performed as a communal SLAMETAN to cleanse the village from evil spirits (Geertz 1960a; H. Geertz 1967).

**Bes**. Grotesque dwarf god (sometimes lion-headed) of ancient Egypt, associated with the home, marriage, childbirth and music; protector against crocodiles and venomous bites.

**beserkers**. Members of a Germanic warrior cult who lived together in a separate community. In battle they reached a state of ecstasy, said to be inspired by ODIN, during which they were completely determined by the function of killing and themselves became invulnerable to attack.

**Bhagavadgītā** (Sanskrit: 'Song of the Lord'). An epic poem of great religious depth and literary beauty, part of the *Bhīṣmaparvan* in the MAHĀBHĀRATA, recording the dialogue between Arjuna and *Kṛṣṇa* on the eve of the Mahābhārata war. Its *c.*700 *Ślokas* (stanzas), divided into 18 chapters, present the gist of theistic Hinduism. Available in many translations and studies by numerous scholars, the *Bhagavadgītā* is the most popular and most widely known of all Hindu scriptures. Mahātma Gāndhī called it his 'Mother' and used to speak frequently on it.

**Bhāgavan.** *See* BHAGAVATISM.

**Bhagavat** (Sanskrit: 'Lord', 'Blessed One'). The early followers addressed Gautama BUDDHA as *Bhagavat*.

**Bhāgavata Puranas.** *See* SRŪTI, VIṢNU.

**Bhāgavatam.** *See* KṚṢṆA, PURĀṆAS.

**Bhāgavatism.** The form of Hinduism in which *bhagavan* ('the Lord') usually identified with VIṢṆU/KṚṢṆA is prominent. It originated probably already in pre-Buddhist times, was eclipsed for over a thousand years by BUDDHISM and JAINISM, whose teachings reject the notion of a lord (creator, maintainer, destroyer of the word) and became prominent from the 5th century onwards. The BHAKTI-movement both in South and North India greatly strengthened Bhāgavatism and a number of large SAṀPRADĀYAS developed within it.

**bhajan** (Hindī: 'hymn'). A hymn sung individually or collectively in praise of a deity (usually VIṢṆU or one of his AVATĀRAS), one of the most popular forms of worship in North India, often going on for many hours. A very large number of such hymns is available in print (some translations), composed often by highly respected ĀCĀRYAS.

**bhakta.** *See* SAKSATKARA.

**bhaktas.** *See* VIṢṆU.

**bhakti** (Sanskrit: 'devotion' – either from the root *bhañj-* ('to separate') or from the root *bhaj-* ('to worship'). A devotional practice that characterizes the most popular form of Indian religions. It is centred on the worship of a personal deity and considers love and service the essential elements of *sādhana*. Its beginnings may be found already in some hymns in the ṚGVEDA, expressing Indrabhakti or Varuṇabhakti. Its full development took place under the influence of the non-āryan indigenous populations and found its expression in the Epics and PURĀṆAS, the Saṁhitās and the ĀGAMAS, including a great deal of hymnal literature. Its doctrinal elements have been articulated in the *Bhaktisūtra* by Śāṇḍilya and the *Bhaktidarśana* of Nārada. It also received philosophical and theological elaboration in the systems of RĀMĀNUJA (VIŚIṢṬĀDVAITA Vedānta), MADHVA (Dvaita Vedānta) Vallabha (Śuddhādvaita Vedānta) and others. Between the 6th and the 14th centuries CE saint-singers spread the devotion to VIṢṆU, KṚṢṆA, RĀMA, ŚIVA, Devī through their songs and their preachings, which are even now immensely popular in India.

**Bhaktidarśana.** *See* BHAKTI.

**Bhaktimarga.** *See* BHAKTIYOGA.

**Bhaktisūtra.** *See* BHAKTI.

**Bhaktiyoga** [Bhaktimārga]. The path and practice of devotion that is the religion of the majority of today's Hindus. It is difficult to provide figures because of the lack of specific statistics, but it is safe to say that more than 500 million Hindus are *bhaktas*. That makes *bhaktiyoga* one of the major religions of the world, subdivided into numerous denominations such as Kṛṣṇa-bhaktas,Rāma-bhaktas,Śiva-bhaktas, Devībhaktas etc. *Bhaktiyoga* includes the worship of God in a bodily form in the shape of an icon or MŪRTI, the listening to recitations from bhakti-scriptures, such as the *Rāmāyaṇa*, the PURĀṆAS, the hymns of great saints, the singing of the praises of God.

**Bharata Yuddha.** *See* BRATAYUDA.

**bhāvanā** (Sanskrit, Pāli: 'calling into existence', 'development of the mind'). Buddhist meditation, one of the Ten Good Deeds. There are two kinds of *bhāvanā*, namely, one aiming at development of tranquillity (*samatha-bhāvanā*), i.e. concentration (SAMĀDHI), and the other aiming at development of insight (*vipaśyanā-bhāvanā*; Pāli: *vipassanā-bhāvanā*), i.e. PAÑÑĀ ('wisdom'), a practice cultivated especially by forest-dwelling (ĀRAÑÑAVĀSIN) monks in Burma, Sri Lanka and Thailand.

**bhikkhu.** *See* BHIKṢU.

**bhikkhūṇī.** *See* BHIKṢŪṆĪ.

**bhikṣu** (Sanskrit) [Pāli: *bhikku*: 'beggar']. A Buddhist monk with higher ordination (UPASAMPAD).

**bhikṣuṇī** (Sanskrit) [Pāli: *bhikkunī*]. Buddhist nun with higher ordination (UPASAMPAD).

**Bible**. The Bible (meaning 'book') consists for Christians of the Old Testament, first known to non-Jewish Christians in its Greek translation (the SEPTUAGINT) and the New Testament, also written in Greek. The Old and New Testaments have usually been understood in the Christian churches in the light of each other and hence as constituting a single and conclusive revelation. In the early church only Marcion and his followers (*see* MARCIONISM) diverged from this position. Other disputes within the church were waged on the basis of the same Bible, although the choice of proof-texts and the widely used allegorical method left much use for theological differences. The works of the NEW TESTAMENT were first selected from among a wider range of writings on the basis of their presumed apostolic origin, although direct proof of this is no longer possible and in several cases is historically unlikely. The APOCRYPHA, which is sometimes printed in the Bible between the Old and New Testaments, consists of late Jewish works which have been considered edifying but not an essential part of the record of revelation. Since the New Testament is not regarded as holy scripture in the Jewish faith the term 'Hebrew Bible' has come into informal use to refer to the OLD TESTAMENT alone from a Jewish point of view. This is indeed appropriate in that it is the original Hebrew text which is widely used in Jewish worship, rather than the Septuagint or other translations. The world 'bible' is also used loosely to refer to the sacred writings of various other religions, but this should be avoided since it tends to obscure the specific qualities and functions of sacred writings in different religions.

**Bhismaparvan.** *See* BHAGAVADGĪTA.

**bidʿa** (Arabic). In Islām, it stands as the opposite of *Sunna* (*see* ḤADĪTH), meaning innovation; any view, thing, or action the like of which had not been practised or approved of by the Prophet Muḥammad and was thus deemed an illegitimate novelty.

**bidental**. An Etruscan tradition followed by the Romans. When lightning struck, the presumed fragments of the bolt were collected and buried in the bidental, which acquired sacred status in consequence.

**bilima**. Local guardian-spirits of social units in northern Zaire: a familiar concept in West Africa, but rare among Bantu-speaking people, where spirits of the dead are more important (Baumann 1975c).

**binah.** *See* HABAD.

**binitarianism**. The view, in the context of Christian theology, that there are only two persons, not three, in the godhead. Binitarianism usually ignores or denies the HOLY SPIRIT.

**binou.** *See* BINU.

**binu** [binou]. Immortal ancestors of the Dogon of Mali, who lived in mythical time before death came into the world (Dieterlen 1941).

**bishop**. The highest form of ordination in those churches, notably the Roman Catholic Church, which lay stress on the APOSTOLIC SUCCESSION, believed to be guaranteed and transmitted through the consecration of bishops. In administrative terms a bishop, with his insignia of crook and mitre, is normally responsible for the visible unity of the church in a DIOCESE, in which task he may be assisted by a suffragan bishop. The earliest clear statements about the special role of bishops in the church are to be found in the writings of Ignatius (2nd century CE).

**bismillāh** (Arabic: 'In the name of Allāh). The shortened form of the phrase *bismillāh* *al-Raḥmān al-Raḥīm*, 'In the name of Allāh, the Compassionate, the Merciful' with which all but one of the SŪRAS or chapters of the QUR'ĀN commence. Used by Muslims as an invocation of divine blessing, accompanying both solemn acts and activities of daily life such as eating or letter writing.

**Bison**. The major manifestation of the EARTH MOTHER in North American Plains cultures, as well as a culture hero (provider of the SACRED PIPE) in Lakota (Siouan) culture. The bull bison represents warrior ferocity and male fertility.

**black canons**. A nickname for Augustinian (or 'Austin') canons, a monastic order restricted to ordained priests following the Rule of St Augustine. The name arose from the black habits worn.

**Black Muslims**. A religious-political movement of Black Americans whose objective is to heighten the socio-economic position and moral consciousness of non-Whites in the United States against the dominant white culture. Founded in Detroit by W.D. Fard before his disappearance in 1934, his work was furthered by his closest disciple Elijah Muḥammad (*d* 1975), who claimed that God had come to the USA in the person of Fard and appointed him prophet. Worship includes readings from both the QUR'ĀN and Bible. Alcohol, tobacco and drugs are strictly forbidden, and heavy emphasis is placed upon the individual's dignity, including that of women. The Black power activist Malcolm X (assassinated 1965) was Elijah's deputy until they parted company following the former's pilgrimage to Mecca.

**Black Stone.** *See* KA'BA.

**black theology**. Theology devised by black theologians to express the meaning of the Christian faith in terms of the history and the needs of black people.

**blessing.** *See* BRAKHA.

**bodai** (Japanese). Enlightenment; from Sanskrit *bodhi*.

**bodhi** (Sanskrit, Pāli). Awakening, enlightenment, especially in Buddhism. A distinction is made between a 'supreme enlightenment' (*samyaksambodhi*), ascribed to Gautama BUDDHA only, an 'individual enlightenment' (*pratyekabodhi*), the enlightenment of a hermit who does not teach others, and the 'enlightenment of a disciple' (*śrāvakabodhi*). (*See also* PRATYEKABUDDHA; ŚRĀVAKABUDDHA.) Moreover, the term *bodhi* denotes the pipal tree (*ficus religiosa*) under which Gautama Buddha attained enlightenment while meditating. After his enlightenment the tree became known as the *bodhi* tree.

**Bodhi Leaves.** *See* BUDDHIST PUBLICATION SOCIETY.

**bodhisattva** (Sanskrit; Pāli: *bodhisatta*). A being who has vowed to attain supreme enlightenment, and, especially in MAHĀYĀNA Buddhism, to lead all other sentient beings along the same path. In the Pāli Canon and its commentaries the epithet is applied to Prince Siddhārtha only, referring to the life he led in former existences before becoming the Buddha, stories of such existences being collected particularly in the JĀTAKA. According to Buddhist mythology in general a *bodhisattva* dwells in the Tuṣita Heaven, waiting for an appropriate moment to be reborn on earth as a Buddha-to-be. In Mahāyāna Buddhism the term takes on a wider range of meaning as numerous spiritually advanced *bodhisattvas*, of mythical character, are specifically named (e.g. AVALOKITEŚVARA; KṢITIGARBHA, Samantabhadra) and are regarded as saviour figures in a complex Buddhist soteriology.

**Bogomils** (Bulgarian). A dualistic Christian church founded in the Balkans in the 10th century by the Bulgarian priest Bogomil ('Mercy of God'), which lasted for a few centuries, its influence at times extending as far as northern Italy (Patarenes) and southern France (Cathars). It was based on the older 'heresy' of the Paulicians (*see* PAULICIANISM) and maintained a modified version of GNOSTIC and Manichaeist ideas.

**bon.** *See* O-BON.

**Bonten**. The Japanese designation for the Indian creator god Brahmadeva, who became known in Japan during the introduction of Buddhism. In some places Bonten is revered in a Shintō context and all connection with Buddhism or with India has been lost.

**Book of Amduat.** *See* BOOK OF THE DEAD.

**Book of Changes.** *See* YI CHING.

**Book of the Dead**. By the time of the New Kingdom of ancient Egypt 1567–1085 BCE), a number of 'books', of which the Book of the Dead is best known, were included amongst the funerary goods placed in tombs (Allen 1960). Derived from the royal PYRAMID TEXTS, these books incorporated spells and hymns to assist the deceased in attaining the afterlife. They were either represented in tomb wall-scenes or placed in the tomb as papyrus rolls written in HIEROGLYPHS, or in hieratic or demotic script, and illustrated with colourful vignettes. The Book of Amduat ('What is in the Underworld') sought to assist the deceased on his night-time journey through the underworld, where, simulating the sun-god's own nightly journey, he combated evils and demons.

**Book of John.** *See* MANDAEANS.

**Book of Kells**. A decorated manuscript of the Gospels, regarded as one of the finest of its kind, written at the monastery of Kells, Ireland, probably in the 8th century.

**Book of Thomas.** *See* NAG HAMMADI.

**Books of Discipline.** *See* VINAYA.

**Booths.** *See* SUKKOT.

**bori** [bòri] (Hausa). A cult of spirit possession among Muslim as well as non-Muslim Hausa in Niger and Nigeria and in the Hausa diaspora in West and North Africa, occurring also among some neighbouring peoples. The cult of the spirits (*iskoki* or *àljànnu*) is slightly different in the non-Muslim and Muslim context. Among Muslims the mediums are mainly women and their aim is to control and placate the spirits, who cause diseases. (Tremearne 1914; Greenberg 1946; Besmer 1983).

**Borobudur**. A Buddhist monument or CANDI in Central Java, erected between 780 and 850 under the Shailendra dynasty (750–856), then the centre of MAHĀYĀNA-Buddhism in the Malay archipelago. In accordance with ancient Javanese tradition, Borobudur is constructed as a terraced sanctuary: the lowest six, square stages consist of galleries decorated with reliefs, ornaments, sculptures of Dhyāna-Buddhas and BODHISATTVAS. The next three, circular terraces are furnished with 72 bell-shaped perforated STŪPAS, each one enclosing the sculpture of a meditating Buddha. The whole is crowned by the main *stūpa* on the tenth stage. While there exist numerous theories on the purpose and meaning of Borobudur – one stressing its symbolic representation of Buddhist cosmology, another interpreting the entire structure as an image of Mount MERU, yet another suspecting influences of ancestor worship – it is reasonably certain that the edifice is constructed in the form of a giant MANDALA. (Stöhr & Zoetmulder 1965; Kempers 1973; Dumarcay 1978).

**bosatsu** (Japanese). The usual Japanese word for BODHISATTVA, frequently occurring in the names of Buddhist divinities such as Kannon Bosatsu and Jizō Bosatsu.

**botánica** (New World Spanish). A store or shop which sells religious paraphernalia, candles, herbs, icons etc. for use by practitioners of SANTERÍA (Gonzalez-Wippler 1973).

**Bragi**. Germanic god of poetry.

**Brahmā**. One of the Great Gods of Hinduism, around whom a major religion with its proper mythology and ritual developed. Its origin goes back to Vedic times. In competition with VAIṢṆAVISM and ŚAIVISM Brahmānism lost most of its followers. In the 'ecumenical' Hindu *trimūrti*, Brahmā, ŚIVA and VIṢṆU form the divine triad, within which he is assigned the function of creation. There are only a few active Brahmā-temples left in India today, but there is a large literature (e.g. *Brahmā*-PURĀṆAS).

**brahmācarya.** *See* ĀŚRAMA.

**Brahmā Kumārī Movement**. Literally, 'Daughters of Brahmā'. This movement was founded in the late 1930s by Dādā Lekhrāj in Sind. Largely a women's movement, it focuses on meditation on Śiv Bābā and communication from him via a woman medium to the membership. It has a complex philosophical and cosmological framework which is taught through literature and a range of visual forms. The headquarters is at Mount Abu in Rajasthan (Babb 1986).

**Brahmadeva.** *See* BONTEN.

**brahman** (usually derived from the Sanskrit root *bṛh*: 'to grow', 'to increase'). The designation (neuter gender) of the Supreme Principle and a key concept in VEDĀNTA. Theistic forms of Vedānta identify *brahman* with VIṢṆU, ŚIVA or Devī respectively; non-theistic forms (Advaita Vedānta) place *brahman* above the 'Lords' as ultimate principle of everything, itself unchanging and inactive. Some UPANIṢADS distinguish between a *brahman saguṇa* (with qualities) and a *brahman nirguṇa* (without qualities) – a distinction which Śaṅkara utilizes to establish his concept of *brahman*'s identity with ĀTMAN.

**brahmaṇas** (Sanskrit: 'that which/who belongs to *brahman*'). Either a class of scriptures (following the *samhitās*) or a class of people (the highest caste, brahmins). The former contain the explanation of the ritual to be followed in Vedic YAJÑAS together with some mythological materials which are often the earliest versions of the major myths associated with later Hinduism. The latter are the hereditary custodians of BRAHMAN, the sacred word and teaching, who considered themselves superior to all other humans by virtue of being born into the brahmin caste.

**brahman nirguṇa.** *See* BRAHMAN.

**brahman saguna.** *See* BRAHMAN.

***Brahmasūtra*** [*Vedāntasūtra*]. A compilation of 550 extremely short aphorisms, purporting systematically to represent the teachings of the UPANIṢADS. (It does, however, draw its material largely from one major Upaniṣad, the Chāṇḍogya.) The existing *Brahmasūtra* ascribed to Bādārāyaṇa (*c*.300 BCE) had been preceded by other similar works, which have not been preserved. The *Brahmasūtra* became the central text of the VEDĀNTA system; each ĀCĀRYA had to write a lengthy commentary on it, which constituted the major work to be studied by the followers of the particular school of Vedanta. Several of these *brahmasūtrabhāṣyas* have been translated into English as well.

**Brahmasūtrabhasyas.** *See* BRAHMASŪTRA.

**Brāhmo Samāj** (Bengali). A Hindu reform movement founded in Bengal by Rām Mohan Roy in 1828 (then known as the Brāhmo Sabha). Roy taught a universalistic theism and condemned what he saw as the later accretions of the Hindu religious tradition, particularly 'idol-worship'. Roy and later leaders, Debendranath Tagore and Keshub Chandra Sen, in addition to their relationship to Hinduism, were influenced by the Christian presence in Bengal, particularly by the theology and social teachings of the *Unitarians* (*see* UNITARIANISM). The Samāj, despite undergoing schism, grew in popularity and influence in India for a century (Kopf 1979). *See also* NAVĀ VIDHĀN; ŚANTINIKETAN.

**brakha** (Hebrew) [Yiddish: *brokheh*]. A blessing. The recitation of blessings is a central feature of Jewish ritual and prayer. The usual formula is as follows: 'Blessed are You O Lord our God, king of the universe, who has sanctified us by Your commandments and commanded us . . . [for example] . . . to light the candle of Sabbath.' Also, a general word for 'blessing'. Thus, 'It's a *brokheh*' would mean 'It's a sign of grace'.

**Bratayuda** [*Bharata Yuddha*]. A Javanese translation of parts of the MAHĀBHĀRATA, and an important cycle of the WAYANG repertoire. In a narrower sense the term also designates the last great war at the end of the MAHĀBHĀRATA (Stöhr & Zoetmulder 1965; Brandon 1970).

**Breastplate of Saint Patrick**. A hymn, originally in Irish, and plausibly ascribed to St Patrick, calling on the Trinity, heavenly powers and Christ for protection against evil.

**Brethren of the Common Life**. A devotional association with clergy and lay members founded in the Netherlands by Geert de Grote (1340–84), which continued in existence until the 17th century. The emphasis was put on spirituality in ordinary occupations.

**breviary**. A book containing the forms of service, psalms and scriptural readings for the daily liturgical practice required of Roman Catholic priests and some non-ordained monks.

**Bṛhadāranyaka Upaniṣad**. The longest and one of the oldest UPANIṢADS. It deals with a great many different issues and combines the ĀRAṆYAKA following the *Śatapatha Brāhmaṇa* with an Upaniṣad. It has been commented upon by Śaṅkara in the 8th century as well as by other writers.

**Brigantia.** *See* BRIGIT.

**Brigit**. Irish Celtic goddess of poetry, metalwork and medicine. In England she was called Brigantia, and the Gaulish goddess Caesar called MINERVA, whose Celtic name is not known, was probably her equivalent.

**bris.** *See* BRIT.

**brit** (Hebrew) [Yiddish: *bris*]. Covenant. A *brit mila* is the ritual of CIRCUMCISION of a Jewish male baby eight days old, acknowledging his entrance into the COVENANT of Israel.

**broad church**. The popular name for a tradition of Anglican churchmanship taking a liberal position between the HIGH CHURCH (tending towards Catholicism) and the LOW CHURCH (of evangelical tendency).

**brokheh.** *See* BRAKHA.

**Brotherhood of the Cross and the Star**. A new religious movement in Nigeria which stresses that death is an illusion. The 'mystery of death' is a passage from physical existence through a morally conditioned rebirth into a physical existence (Mbou 1988).

**brujo** (New World Spanish). Medicine-man, male witch, the feminine form being *bruja*. The brujo is more commonly associated with black magic than the benevolent curandero/CURANDERA. See *also* ALTOMISAYOQ.

**Buddha** (Sanskrit, Pāli). 'One who has awakened', usually translated 'enlightened' (BODHI): a Buddhist term metaphorically denoting the change in consciousness that leads to a release (NIRVĀṆA) from this world of perpetual rebirths (SAṂSĀRA). The term is generally used as an honorific title for the historical founder of Buddhism, the Indian nobleman whose forename was Siddhārtha ('Aim Attained'), but who commonly was known as Gautama (Pāli, Gotama) or as *Śākyamuni* ('the sage of the Śākya tribe') of the KṢATRIYA (warrior) caste. His followers addressed him as BHAGAVAT ('Lord', 'Blessed One'), but he referred to himself with the enigmatic epithet TATHĀGATA ('thus progressed').

*Buddha* is also an appellative term denoting both the infinite series of buddhas who rediscover and teach the Doctrine (DHARMA), and the idea of a buddhahood, according to which there is in every human being a buddha-nature waiting to be discovered. In principle, therefore, everyone can attain enlightenment, buddhahood.

**Buddha Jayanti** (Sinhalese). The 2,500th anniversary of Buddhism, celebrated in 1956.

**buddhakṣetra.** *See* PURE LAND.

**buddhanusmṛti.** *See* NENBUTSU.

**Buddha-sāsana.** *See* SĀSANA.

**Buddhism**. Originally an Indian religion founded some 2,500 years ago by the nobleman Siddhārtha Gautama, later known as BUDDHA or preferably 'the Buddha'. It is now one of the three great 'world religions', the other two being Christianity and Islām.

**Buddhist modernism**. A 19th- and 20th-century movement in Theravāda Buddhist countries that aims at reforming Buddhism by settling up with the influence of the European culture.

An outstanding Sinhalese leader of the

Buddhist modernist movement at the turn of the century was Dharmapāla Anagārika (1864–1933). Originally his name was Don David Hevāvitārāne, but after having joined the Buddhist Theosophical Society he adopted the name ANAGĀRIKA ('the homeless one') Dharmapāla ('the guardian of the doctrine'), which later proved to provide a role model for Buddhist this-worldly asceticism. Most of his adult life he spent in India running the Mahā Bodhi Society which he founded. He also represented Buddhism in 1893 at the World Parliament on Religions in Chicago.

Another outstanding leader of Buddhist modernism was the Indian Dr Bhimrao Ramji Ambedkar (1891–1956), an Indian leader reviving Buddhism in India. As his family belonged to the Mahar caste, one of the many groups of 'Untouchables', he spent all his life fighting for the human rights of the repressed castes in India. In 1950 he formally became a Buddhist.

**Buddhist Publication Society**. Founded in 1958 by Nyanaponika Mahāthera in cooperation with two Sinhalese lay Buddhists, the publishing house, located in Kandy, Sri Lanka, publishes two well-known series, *The Wheel* and *Bodhi Leaves*, and monographs. Nyanaponika Mahāthera is a western Buddhist monk, who was born as Siegmund Feniger in 1901 in Germany. A pupil of Nyanatiloka Mahāthera, he was ordained in 1936 in Sri Lanka, and since 1952 has lived in the Forest Hermitage in Kandy, from where he has led the Buddhist Publication Society.

**Buddhist Theosophical Society**. A society founded by Colonel Olcott in 1880 in Ceylon.

**Budi Setia** (Javanese; Indonesian: 'Faithful Mind'). A mystical movement founded in 1947 in Java, being a kind of 'high-thinking religious discussion group' (Geertz 1960a: 339) influenced by theosophical doctrines.

**bugaku** (Japanese). Ceremonial dancing accompanied by music. *See also* GAGAKU.

**bukkyō** (Japanese). Buddhism; the teaching (*kyō*) of the Buddha (Butsu). Compare the term *butsudō* ('the way of the Buddha'), which was earlier in more common use.

**bull** (from Latin, *bulla*: 'seal'). An edict issued by the Pope and confirmed by his seal.

**bundle.** *See* SACRED BUNDLE.

**Bundu.** *See* SANDE.

**Buphonia.** *See* DIPOLIEIA.

**bunrei.** *See* GO-BUNREI.

**Busiris.** *See* OSIRIS.

**Buto.** *See* WADJET.

**butsudō.** *See* BUKKYŌ.

**Buzan-ha**. One of the branches of Shingon Buddhism (*see* SHINGON-SHŪ), the other main branch being the CHIZAN-HA.

**Bwiti**. A male secret society in Gabon, closely connected with the ancestral cult, but partly changed into a national movement based on traditional beliefs (Fernandez 1982).

# C

**Cabirians**. *See* MYSTERY RELIGIONS.

**Cadi**. *See* QĀḌI.

**caesaropapism**. A political arrangement in which ecclesiastical matters, including doctrinal questions, are under the control of the temporal monarch. The position of the late Byzantine emperors was so described by others.

**caitya** [cetiya] (Sanskrit). A tumulus or mound of remembrance and veneration. Originally referring to shrines dedicated to various 'spirits' (YAKṢA), the term came to be used as synonymous with STŪPA, although the *caitya* does not contain relics. Also occurs as *cetiya*.

**cakkavatti**. *See* CAKRAVARTIN.

**cakra** (Sanskrit: 'circle'). (1) A discus-like weapon, found as one of the emblems of VIṢṆU. (2) The universe: a universal ruler is called a *cakravartin*. (3) The symbol for a teaching which is complete and universal: thus the Buddhists use the *dharma (dhamma)-cakra* as an emblem of Buddha's teaching. (4) The term has been used by the Tantrics to denote psycho-physical centres in the body (usually six are mentioned) through which ŚAKTI ('energy') passes and to which certain conditions of mind and body are ascribed. (5) The 'circle of initiates' assembling for tantric worship.

**cakravartin** (Sanskrit: 'one who sets the wheel rolling') [Pāli: *cakkavatti*]. In Buddhism, a righteous world ruler.

**calendricity**. A fundamental characteristic of many religious systems which are conceived in terms of an annual round of events and/or a complex cycle of years. A particularly elaborate example was the ancient Mesoamerican calendar round, consisting of a 52-year sequence of two permutating cycles, the 260-day ritual calendar (*tonalpohualli*) and the 365-day solar or 'vague' year of 18 named months of 20 days each plus an added interval of five unlucky days (UAYEB). The completion of a perfect cycle of years was compared to the binding of a bundle and was called *nexiuhilpiliztli*. Drawn as a circle divided into four parts of 13 years, each part was associated with a cardinal direction juxtaposing time and space; a great solemn feast was held to celebrate this occasion. For the Maya calendar *see also* KATUN; LONG COUNT; SHORT COUNT. For classical antiquity *see* HORAE; MENOLOGIA; FASTI; FERIAE. For East Asia, especially Japan, *see* NENJŪGYŌJI.

**Caliph**. *See* KHALĪFA.

**Calumet**. From the medieval French word for 'reed', a common western term for the SACRED PIPE. Also (confusingly) a particular ritual using wands, a particular pipe shape, pipes made from red stones, or all sacred pipes.

**Calvary**. The place of Christ's crucifixion. Also, an iconographic representation of Christ's crucifixion, for example on a small hill, sometimes approached by the stations of the cross, i.e. the points marking Christ's progress to the place of crucifixion. Such a 'calvary' is used for devotional practices.

**Calvinism**. A theological position based on the teaching of John (Jean) Calvin (1509–64) especially as set out in his *Institutes of the Christian Religion*. Themes which have attracted most debate follow from his emphasis on the absolute sovereignty of God. This led organizationally to the subordination of politics to religion, as practised for a while at Geneva. In doctrine it led to the teaching on double PREDESTINATION, that is, both of the saved and of the damned. Calvinism has been influential in its broad outlines on many protestant churches, especially in the Netherlands and in Scotland (PRESBYTERIANISM).

**Cambridge Platonists**. Several philosophical theologians in 17th-century Cambridge who viewed the indwelling of God in the human mind as the guarantee of a reasoned assessment of both revealed and NATURAL THEOLOGY.

**Camenae**. Native Roman water NYMPHS, documented since the 3rd century BCE and identified with the Greek Muses. The identification was never complete, and Roman poets often developed elaborate conceits based upon the differences.

**Canaanite religion**. The ancient religious beliefs and practice of Syria and Palestine, excluding ISRAEL and JUDAH (except pejoratively of tendencies rejected by biblical writers). Sources of information are UGARIT and its literature for the 2nd millennium BCE; the OLD TESTAMENT for the early first millennium (generally deliberately misrepresented and therefore to be handled with circumspection); Philo of Byblos (fragments preserved in Eusebius' *Praeparatio Evangelica*); and Lucian (*De dea syria*) for the Hellenistic and early Christian periods. From the first millennium BCE the term 'Phoenician' is commonly used instead of Canaanite. In spite of a wealth of material, we are ill-informed about much of the theory and practice of Canaanite cults. Animal sacrifices, sexual rites (the so-called SACRED MARRIAGE) and dramatized myths probably characterized temple-worship, and the ROYAL CULT was important in national centres. The structure of local pantheons is imperfectly understood, but EL is the chief deity in most places.

**candi** (Indonesian). Pre-Islamic sanctuaries, originally designating a place or an object of divine manifestation, today commonly applied in Indonesia to ancient monuments of every kind, e.g. BOROBUDUR. (Stöhr & Zoetmulder; Kempers 1979).

**Candomblé**. An Afro-American religion which originated among the Yoruba slaves from Nigeria and is now practised mainly in northern Brazil. OLÓRUN, the creator of all being, is not revered directly but relations with him are mediated by the ORISHAS, who speak through mediums in the context of ecstatic cults.

**canon**. A rule or list, in particular a list of scriptures regarded as authoritative (the sacred canon) or a set of ecclesiastical rules (canon law). As an ecclesiastical title it refers to a member of clergy on the regular staff of a cathedral.

**canon law**. *See* CANON.

**canonization**. The declaration of a Christian church that a person who has previously died and been beatified (*see* BEATIFICATION) is a SAINT, i.e. someone who is particularly close to God and therefore thought to be able to speak to God on behalf of an ordinary person. The process of canonization is essentially an ecclesiastical procedure for which various conditions must be fulfilled, e.g. the occurrence of miracles. The Catholic and Orthodox Churches have different registers of saints. In the Anglican communion the formal ecclesiastical status of saints has fallen away, and hence no new saints can be proclaimed. In Protestant churches the idea that saints can intervene on behalf of others is usually rejected on the grounds that all Christians enjoy an immediate relationship to God in Christ.

**canopic jar**. The name given by Egyptologists to jars, four to a set, used to contain the viscera of the dead. Their lids represented the Four Sons of HORUS (Amset, Hapi, Duamutef and Qebehsenuf), who guarded and protected the viscera.

**Cappadocian Fathers**. Three Church Fathers from Cappadocia in Asia Minor – Basil of Caesarea, Gregory of Nazianzus and Gregory of Nyssa – who were influential in the theological debates of the 4th century culminating in the rejection of ARIANISM in 381 at the COUNCIL OF CONSTANTINOPLE.

**Capuchins**. A reforming branch of Franciscan monks so named because of their pointed hoods (*capuche*). The order was founded in 1529 to restore the ideals of St Francis and was particularly active during the COUNTER-REFORMATION.

**cardinal virtues**. Prudence, temperance, fortitude and justice, being virtues adopted by Christian theologians from Greek philosophy, juxtaposed with the 'theological virtues', that is the virtues characteristic of the religious life, namely faith, hope and charity (meaning love).

**caritas**. *See* AGAPE.

**Caroline Divines**. Anglican theologians active during the reigns of Charles I (1625–49) and Charles II (1660–85) who espoused a HIGH CHURCH position.

**Carpocratians**. *See* GNOSTICISM.

**Carthusians**. Monks following an extremely austere rule in an order founded by Bruno in 1084 at 'la Grande Chartreuse' in eastern France.

**carya**. *See* ŚAIVA SIDDHANTA.

**Caryatids**. The 'maidens of Caryae', a city near Sparta where young women danced at the annual festival of ARTEMIS; their attitudes and postures were represented in sculpture, the most famous of which are in the Erechthion, a sanctuary built on the Athenian Acropolis.

**caste**. A hereditary, hierarchical social group sanctioned by religious belief. The early Portuguese traders in India used the word *casta* to describe the hereditary divisions of Indian society. The word derives from Latin *castus*, meaning 'chaste', and was used in the sense of 'unmixed'. That is, a caste puts limits on the ways in which its members mix with other groups.

Caste is a strong characteristic of Indian society and has also spread beyond India through migration. Three characteristics of castes in India, according to Bouglé, are the *division of labour* along group lines, the practice of *separation restrictions*, and the idea that each group falls somewhere on a *hierarchy of status*.

Many Indian castes are named after the occupation of their members, although this may be more traditional than actual. Thus, one might belong to the toddy tapper caste, but not actually work as a tapper of toddy palms. The hereditary nature of caste is reflected in the most common Indian term for caste, *jāti*, which literally means 'birth'. The term *varṇa* refers to the four broad social classes (BRAHMAN, KṢATRIYA, *Vaiśya, Sūdra), each of which encompasses numerous jātis*.

The *jajmāni* system, an intricate network of patrons and clients, is a characteristic of Indian society and caste relationships. The religious background is reflected in the word patron (*jajmān*), which derives from the Sanskrit term for the (upper class) householder who hires a brahman priest to conduct a sacrificial ritual. Many castes receive fixed payments, in money or goods, in return for services to a patron. Just as the caste is hereditary, so too is the *jajmāni* relationship between a certain family and the priest or workers who serve it.

Caste is primarily a system of social organization, but it enjoys religious sanction. In the Vedic hymn to Puruṣa the four *varṇa* are said to emerge from the body of the sacrificed Primal Person. The brahmans have used this as divine authority for the nature and hierarchy of the system of four *varṇa* and the thousands of (post-vedic) caste subdivisions. The doctrine of KARMA and rebirth are also tied to caste by brahmans, for one is said to be reborn into the caste status that befits one's level of purity, as per past deeds.

Most Hindu writings glorifying caste and *varṇa* laws are conceived from a brahman point of view; but from a lower caste standpoint the system is exploitative, especially for the large number of groups considered as 'untouchable' or 'outcaste'. Both British laws and Hindu reformers such as Gandhi sought to end untouchability, and Indian law now forbids such discrimination; however, the status of many castes is still a miserable one in rural areas.

Some scholars use the term caste for rigid social hierarchies outside South Asia, such as the Afro-Americans of the southern United States, or the stratifications of South Africa. (Dumont 1980; Klass 1980).

**casuistry**. The discussion of how general moral principles are to be applied to particular cases. Because over-subtle reasoning can be used to justify moral laxity, the term has acquired pejorative connotations.

**catacomb**. A subterranean Christian cemetery arranged in tiered galleries with tombs set into the sides. The most famous are in Rome, where they were used as sanctuaries during persecution periods.

**catechism**. Instruction leading to Christian baptism, or to confirmation after infant baptism, and by extension the designation of a short manual of essential doctrines, as in Martin Luther's Short Catechism (*Kleiner Katechismus*).

**catechumens**. Those who are under instruction preparatory to baptism, so called (in Greek *katechoumenoi*) in the early Christian church.

**categorical imperative**. The term used by Kant for the universal moral law which is binding in every circumstance upon all rational beings. The term was used first in his book *The Foundations of the Metaphysics of Morals* (1785b), where it is given in at least two forms: (1) 'Act only according to that maxim by which you can at the same time will that it should become a universal law' and (2) 'Act so that you treat humanity, whether in your own person or in that of another, always as an end and never merely as a means.' The categorical imperative is the supreme limiting condition upon one's freedom as a rational being. It is in Kant's philosophy the basis for any adequate account of moral experience, the explanation of which is said to require us to postulate the existence of God (*see* MORAL ARGUMENTS FOR EXISTENCE OF GOD), the freedom of the will, and the IMMORTALITY of the soul (*see* SELF).

**Cathars**. Members of a Church with many Christian features but, like that of the BOGOMILS, with roots in PAULICIANISM, MANICHAEISM and GNOSTICISM. The belief system was strongly characterized by a DUALISM of spirit and matter. Ordinary believers were religiously dependent on 'the pure' (*cathari*), who went to great lengths to provide their ministrations during times of persecution. The main centres, in the 12th to 14th centuries CE, were in the south of France (especially Albi and Toulouse), but the Cathars were ruthlessly suppressed through a crusade and by means of the INQUISITION initiated by the POPE Innocent III. (Lambert 1977; Duvernoy 1979).

**catholic**. As occurring in the major creeds of Christianity the term means 'universal' or 'world-wide', and is therefore so used in various churches, most obviously in the very name of the Roman Catholic Church. The same word is also frequently used to refer just to this latter, in which case, to avoid confusion, a capital letter is to be preferred.

**Catholicism**. That form of Christianity which recognizes the supreme authority of the POPE, normally resident in Rome. Catholicism took on distinctive form as a result of two major schisms, one with the Eastern Orthodox Churches in 1054 CE and one within the western church at the time of the Protestant Reformation.

**caturvarnasramadharma**. *See* ĀŚRAMA.

**C.E.** *See* COMMON CALENDAR.

**Cecrops**. *See* ARRHEPHORIA.

**cella** (Latin). A small room; the room in a Roman temple containing the divine image; in Christian contexts, a hermit's hut or a monk's room (cell).

**Celtic Church**. The Christian church as occurring in the British Isles from the 3rd to the 6th centuries. It remained independent of Rome until the Synod of Whitby in 664.

**Celtic religion**. The collective term for the religious beliefs and practices of the Celtic tribes whose first historical mention places them in the central Europe of the La Tène period in the 5th century BCE, and who had settled in Britain, Gaul, Spain, Italy and Asia Minor (Galatia) by the 3rd century BCE. The main evidence for the religion is supplied by the predominantly literary sources from Britain, the inscriptions and images from Gaul and accounts of Greek and Roman authors. The various information sometimes coincides; at others it differs or is contradictory. A vast number of gods are known by name, varying greatly from region to region, but their precise functions can often only be guessed, and a unified 'pantheon' of Celtic gods cannot be distinguished. Nevertheless, in his *De Bello Gallico* Julius Caesar claims that the deities worshipped in Gaul corresponded to the five Roman deities MERCURY, APOLLO, MARS, JUPITER and MINERVA, in that order of importance, and after the Roman invasion the names of some Celtic goddesses and gods were indeed given in inscriptions as epithets of the Roman deities, or vice versa. Common characteristics of Celtic religious beliefs are the importance of topographical connections and animal attributes in the identity of the deities, the frequency of earth and fertility goddesses and the authority of the DRUIDS.

**cenote** (Maya). A cavity in the limestone area of Yucatan where bedrock has collapsed, exposing the water table. A major source of water in the Yucatan peninsula, and consequently a locus for ritual activity. (Adams 1977; Fariss 1984).

**Centhini**. *See* SERAT CENTINI.

**ceque**. In ancient Peru, a centralistic net of imaginary lines that copied geographically the socio-economic system of the Inca Empire. On the *ceque* lines were located approximately 400 sacred places (HUACA). The central point of the net was Cuzco. The town of Cuzco and the Cuzco region were divided through the *ceques* into four quarters, the Chinchaysuyu in the north, the Antisuyu in the east, the Collasuyu in the south and the Cuntisuyu in the west. From this quadripartition derives the term TAWANTINSUVU (world of the four quarters), which is used synonymously for the Inca Empire. The four quarters were divided into two halves, the north-east half was Hanan-Cuzco (upper part) and the south-west half was the Hurin-Cuzco (lower part). The dualism of the two mutually attracting poles plays a central role in Andean cosmology.

The sites located on the *ceque* were assigned to particular social groups such as *ayllu* and *panaca*, and the four quarters corresponded to four different marriage classes. Integrated in these bipartite and quadripartite structures was another system of tripartition specifying special kinship relations.

**Ceres** (Latin *ceres*: 'corn'). The Roman divinity of corn, publicly worshipped principally by plebeians, and later identified with the Greek DEMETER. Her initial character was native Roman and she had particular connections with TELLUS. At one of her major festivals, the Cerialia (19 April), flaming torches were tied to the tails of foxes, which were then let loose in the Circus Maximus. There may be a connection between Ceres and ROBIGUS.

**Cerialia**. *See* CERES.

**certainty**. The term refers generally to the presumed indubitability of particular truths, especially in logic and mathematics. Hence, its applicability is primarily to relational statements or propositions. Those statements admitting of certainty are based on either claims of reason or immediate sense experience. Some connection exists, therefore, between certainty and knowledge in so far as whatever a person knows he is also certain of. But between certainty and truth a distinction is required, since it might be said of a statement that it is certainly true or certainly false, but not falsely certain. Hence the terms 'certainty' and 'truth' have different functions. The term is likely to occur in discussions over statements based primarily on religious experience or over utterances by mystics. Care should therefore be taken to distinguish between certainty in a philosophical sense, as outlined above, and certainty in a psychological sense (*see* CERTITUDE), which may be attached to beliefs which are false.

**certitude**. Psychological certainty, that is the firmness with which the mind holds to any proposition, as opposed to philosophical or, in particular, logical certainty. Whereas logical certainty either obtains, or not, psychological certainty may be more or less justified or even be quite unjustified. In religion, certitude may be felt with respect to religious beliefs or presumed truths of revelation, especially when these are considered to be based on direct religious experience. In this context it should be noted that as a matter of general observation psychological certainty, or certitude, may *increase* in proportion to the undemonstrability of the beliefs held. *See also* CERTAINTY.

**cetiya**. *See* CAITYA.

**Chalcedon**. *See* COUNCIL OF CHALCEDON.

**chalice**. The goblet used for the wine in the liturgy of the EUCHARIST or MASS.

**Chan** (Chinese; Japanese: *Zen*; Sanskrit: DHYANA). One of the main buddhist streams of thought, much influenced by DAOISM. Chinese Chan developed during the 4th century, stressing that the mind (which is BUDDHA-NATURE) should not be moulded into a conceptualized, analytical form of a cognitive tool; rather, the Chan teachers stressed spontaneous enlightenment and undifferentiated 'pure' wisdom.

Famous Chinese Chan masters were of Indian origin: Buddhabhadra and Buddhasanta (both 4th century). Native Chinese masters that propounded the teaching were Dao An (312–85) and Hui Yuan (334–416). With the arrival of the Indian (or possibly Persian) monk Bodhidharma in China (520 or, disputable, 526 CE) starts the count of the Chan patriarchs in China. Today Chan still forms one of the most influential schools of Buddhism in China, with a vast number of active temples and monasteries under the Chan priests' administrative control.

In Japan Chan is known as ZEN.

**ch'an**. *See* CHAN.

**Chandogya Upaniṣad**. *See* TAT TVAM ASI, UPANIṢAD.

**Changó** [Shangó, Xangó]. The Yoruba god of lightning and fire, in character strong, wild, unpredictable and easily angered. The MACUMBA associate him with St Jerome; in the SANTERÍA he is identified with St Barbara.

**chantry**. Specially funded performances of the MASS, usually provided for by bequest, in favour of the soul of the benefactor or other named persons. In the Middle Ages such services were often provided by a chantry priest, who thereby made his living in a chantry chapel set aside for the purpose.

**chapter house**. The building in a cathedral complex set aside for meetings of the chapter, i.e. the administrative assembly responsible for cathedral affairs.

**Charybdis**. The whirlpool of Greek epic, near the straits of Messina and opposite the lair of the monster Scylla. To sail between Scylla and Charybdis is to be in danger from both, for the one drove ships into the other.

**Chenghuang** [Ch'eng-huang]. A Chinese divinity whose name means literally '(God of) Ramparts and Ditches', usually translated as 'City God'. Its origin can be traced back to antiquity but the designation Chenghuang first appeared in the 3rd century. During the Tang and Song dynasties his cult became very common and virtually every Chinese city had its Chenghuang temple. The City God played an important role in the official state cult, being regarded as a spiritual counterpart of the human magistrate. As such he supervised the various local gods (TUDI) and spirits. In cases of misfortune, like drought or excessive rain, the living magistrate prayed to his spiritual colleague. The annual festivals of the City God were usually occasions for processions and other forms of entertainment.

**chen jen**. *See* ZHEN REN.

**Chenwei** [Ch'an-wei]. A type of literature which flourished during the Chinese Han dynasty (206 BCE – 220 CE). Originally *Chen* signifies writings of prognostication, while the *Wei* (or *wei shu*) are apocryphal Confucian scriptures that seek to interpret the hidden meaning of the classical books. They were particularly influential among the New Text School (*Jinwen Jing Xue/Chinwen Ching Hsüeh*) of Han Confucianism, which added cosmological and mystifying speculations to the Confucian tradition. After the decline of the school during the later Han (25–220) most of the *Chenwei* scriptures disappeared. According to A. Seidel the apocrypha as 'prognostic texts originated in the concern for the definition, the delimitation, as well as the confirmation of imperial authority . . . and proliferated under an emperor who based his divine legitimation on their prophecies' (Seidel 1983: 307–8). So far only one full-scale study of this difficult but important genre of literature exists: see Dull 1966.

**Cherubim Society**. *See* SERAPHIM SOCIETY.

**chi**. *See* IKENGA, CHUKWU.

**ch'i**. *See* QI.

**chicha** (New World Spanish). Maize beer, often used as an offering or consumed in ritual contexts throughout the Andean region (Kauffman Doig 1986).

**Chilam Balam**. Colonial texts written in Maya and transcribed into Spanish. Approximately a dozen are known but more are assumed to exist in oral and/or written form. Based on the SHORT COUNT, they contain myth, chronicle, prophecy, medicine, astrology, ritual, procedures and other materials. *Chilam* (or *chilan*) refers to a class of priests who read the texts to interpret the will of the gods. According to Landa, the term means 'he who is the mouth'. *Balam* is the name of a family, signifying 'jaguar' or 'sorceror'; but it is also the name of the most renowned of the *chilanes* prior to Contact. Although there is some evidence of Christian influence, the texts constitute a major source of ethnohistoric data on the Maya. (Barrera Vasquez & Rendon 1948).

**Chineke**. *See* CHUKWU.

**Chinese Classics**. *See* WU JING.

**Chinese religion**. The origins of Chinese religion have to be sought well before the times of Confucius in the rituals of the Shang and Zhou (Chou) dynasties. After Qin Shi Huangdi (Ch'in Shih Huang-ti) had united the empire in 221 BCE an imperial state cult was established which continued many of the rituals of the former state of Qin (Ch'in). The first emperors of the Han dynasty (206 BCE – 220 CE) followed the example of the Qin, but under Confucian influence the state cult was gradually reorganized, making Heaven (*Tian*) and Earth (*Di*) its principal objects of worship. From the Han period onwards Chinese religion has been dominated by the three major traditions: CONFUCIANISM, DAOISM (Taoism) and BUDDHISM, the last being introduced via Central Asia. Entering by the same route CHRISTIANITY (as Nestorianism), MANICHAEISM and ISLAM have all enjoyed a significant history in China. Of these, Islam continues to be especially important in north-west China, while Christianity has a certain presence in various regions as a result of later missions. Confucianism, Daoism and Buddhism have interacted with each other in very complex ways, and many attempts at synthesis have been made. Hence they are often described, jointly, as the 'three teachings'. Much of the popular religion of China, revolving around the needs of family life and the demands of the calendar, does not distinguish clearly between these traditions. There have also been many dissenting sects, usually regarded as problematic by the state (Overmyer 1976). For brief introductions to Chinese religion see Thompson 1969; Overmyer 1986. For a classic account concentrating on the ancestor system and popular practices of all kinds see De Groot 1892–1910. For a sociologically oriented account see Yang 1967 and for a history of ideas approach see Fung 1952 and de Bary 1960. For studies of Chinese religion in modern Taiwan, continuing many pre-revolutionary features, see Wolf 1974 and Seiwert 1985.

**Ching-t'u**. *See* PURE LAND.

**chinju no kami** (Japanese). A god (KAMI) protecting a specific geographical area. In Shinto a person who settles or builds in a new place either performs a *jichinsai*, a celebration in honour of the spirit already dwelling in the place, or invites a deity from elsewhere to dwell in and protect the location. *Chinju no kami* are presumed to be present in imperial residences, large mansions, Buddhist temples, and in the territories and castles of aristocratic families, and have come gradually to be worshipped as local community *kami*, with which they are sometimes identified.

**Chishtiyya**. A ṢŪFĪ brotherhood, founded by Mu ʿīn al-Dīn Muḥammad (*d* 1236), which became widely disseminated throughout India. Vocal music is used in their religious services and members are recognized by their ochre-coloured vestments.

**chisungu**. A widespread type of individual female initiation into adulthood in Zambia, with elaborate public ritual (Richard 1956).

**Chi ukwu**. *See* CHUKWU.

**chiwara**. *See* TYIWARA.

**Chizan-ha**. One of the branches of Shingon Buddhism (*see* SHINGON-SHŪ), the other main branch being the BUZAN-HA.

**chokushi** (Japanese). An imperial messenger dispatched to convey the greetings of the Japanese emperor on the occasion of a shrine festival, for example to the three great festivals at Ise Jingū.

**chrism**. Consecrated oil made of a mixture of olive and balsam, used in the Catholic and Orthodox churches as an accessory in various rites of a consecratory character, notably BAPTISM, CONFIRMATION and ORDINATION.

**Christadelphians**. A sect founded in America by John Thomas in 1848 in secession from the DISCIPLES OF CHRIST. Belief centres on the salvation of those who love God to an unending life in this world, while those who fail to love him will simply die for ever. BAPTISM by immersion is practised. Church organization is congregational without an ordained ministry. The followers of the English-born Thomas have also been known as Thomasites.

**Christian Ashram Movement**. A movement that has developed during the 20th century and has focused around an attempt to indigenize Christianity in India. The broad movement includes Protestant, Syrian Orthodox and Catholic ashrams or communities. Some of these are oriented towards the Gandhian ideal of social service whereas others, particularly the Catholic ashrams, place an emphasis on the paths of devotion and spiritual knowledge. The best-known ashram is of this second type, the Catholic Saccidānanda Ashram at Śantivanam of which Bede Griffiths was gurū. The movement is represented by two organizations, the Inter Ashram Fellowship and the Ashram Aikiya. (Ralston 1987).

**Christian Socialism**. A school of thought in the Church of England which was vigorous in the 1850s, expressing a determined social conscience and seeking to raise the self-consciousness of working people in both religious and political terms. Key figures were F.D. Maurice and C. Kingsley.

**christology**. The theory of the nature of Christ. In PATRISTICS the term refers to the fraught question as to how Christ could be at once human and divine (*see* ARIANISM; COUNCIL OF CHALCEDON; COUNCIL OF NICAEA; HOMOIOUSIOS; HOMOOUSIOS; INCARNATION; MONOPHYSITISM; MONOTHELETISM; TWO NATURES). In New Testament studies, as in later theology, it refers more generally to the way in which Christ, including the 'work' of Christ, is understood.

**Chronicles**. The Books *1 and 2 Chronicles*, together with *Ezra* and *Nehemiah*, contained in the Hebrew Bible, constitute a 3rd-century BCE summary of Judaean history from creation to the time of the second temple. Increasingly polemical, it champions the nationalistic and exclusivist interests of its day (Noth 1981).

**Chronos**. *See* ORPHIC MYSTERIES.

**chthonic deities**. Deities who live in the earth (from the Greek: *chthon*), the opposite of heavenly or OLYMPIAN GODS; the recipients of sacrifice and honour and of increasing attention as humans approach death. Examples of Greek chthonic deities are DEMETER, HADES and DIONYSOS. The term is nowadays freely used in contexts other than ancient Greece, e.g. to characterize African deities associated with the earth rather than the sky.

**ch'üan chen**. *See* QUAN ZHEN.

**Chuang-Tzu**. *See* ZHUANG ZI.

**chūgen** (Japanese). A Japanese seasonal feast of Daoist origin on the 15th day of the seventh month. Theoretically all the gods gather on this day to report on the activities of humankind. In modern Japan it is mainly marked as a season of present-giving towards those to whom one is obligated.

**Chukwu** (from *Chi ukwu*: 'great god') [Chineke]. The supreme creator God of the Igbo (Ibo) of Nigeria (Arinze 1970).

**Chung-lun**. *See* MĀDHYAMIKA.

**Chunqiu** [*Chu'un-ch'iu*] (Chinese: 'Spring and Autumn Annals'). A chronicle of the ancient Chinese state of Lu, covering the years 722–484 BCE. According to tradition it was written or edited by Confucius and contains his appraisal of past rulers. There are three classical commentaries, called *Zuo zhuan* [*Tso chuan*], *Guliang zhuan* [*Ku-liang chuang*] and *Gongyang zhuan* [*Kung-yang chuan*]. The *Chunqiu* with its commentaries is part of the Confucian canon (WU JING: 'Five Scriptures').

**church**. The community of Christians, whether understood ecumenically (in the sense of world-wide) or as a specific local gathering. From the latter arises the use of the same word for a building of Christian worship. Although the word 'church' and congnate terms like the German *Kirche* are derived from the Greek *kuriakon*, apparently first used for buildings 'of the Lord', it also translates the older New Testament term *ekklesia* ('assembly'). Thus, the spiritual concept takes precedence over buildings. By extension 'church' is sometimes used in other religions, e.g. Buddhism in America, both for an overall organization and for its religious buildings. However, such usage obscures the theological complexity of the term in most Christian contexts.

**Church Army**. An organization of the Church of England devoted to welfare work, especially in the context of urban deprivation. It was founded in 1882 by W. Carlisle, who played a leading role in it until his death in 1942. The idea of such an 'Army' was clearly modelled on the SALVATION ARMY, but the Church Army sought to work within ecclesiastical structures.

**Church Commissioners**. A large body consisting of the bishops of the Church of England and various appointed persons, whose duty is to manage the finances of that church.

**churching of women**. A rite in the Roman Catholic and Anglican churches which offers thanks after childbirth. Though said to have originated in the Jewish 'Purification' rite (*Leviticus* 12.6) and commonly believed to ensure ritual purification, the liturgical forms themselves concentrate entirely on thanksgiving.

**Church of England**. The established church in England, dating, as some would say, from the declaration of ecclesiastical independence by Henry VIII, but on its own view at least from the papal mission to England under Augustine in 597, if not indeed from the origins of the CELTIC CHURCH. The Church of England assumes the validity of its own ordinations to the priesthood by virtue of the unbroken apostolic succession in the EPISCOPACY. *See also* ANGLICAN COMMUNION; ANGLICANISM.

**Church of Jesus Christ of Latter-Day Saints**. *See* MORMONISM.

**Chūron**. *See* MĀDHYAMIKA.

**circumambulation**. Ritual walk round a holy site or object, or round a revered person. Common in Indian religious contexts, the Sanskrit term is *pradakṣiṇā*; however, the practice has spread widely in Asia, not least because of the influence of Buddhism, and thus may also be observed elsewhere. Since the respectful feature of the practice is to keep the right-hand side of the body directed towards the object of reverence, the circulation takes place in a clockwise direction. *See also* KA'BAH.

**circumincessio**. *See* PERICHORESIS.

**circumcision**. The removal of foreskin; a widespread RITE OF PASSAGE in the ancient world. Practised in ancient Israel as a marital rite (*Genesis* 34), during the EXILE it was transposed into an infant rite denoting membership of the COVENANT community (*Genesis* 17; *Exodus* 24.24–6). (Schur 1937; Isaac 1964; Vaux 1965: 46–8; Fox 1974).

**Cistercian Order**. A strict order of Benedictine monks founded in 1098, emphasizing remote seclusion, simplicity of liturgy and manual labour.

**cloud of unknowing**. A characteristic expression from a mystical writing of the same name, whose provenance is 14th-century England but of unknown authorship. The text indicates that God is hidden from rational human endeavour by a cloud of unknowing and that access to God is therefore only possible through an act of love.

**coca** (New World Spanish). The leaves of the coca bush (*Erythroxylum coca*), grown on the eastern slopes of the Andes in Colombia, Peru and Bolivia, are used in the production of cocaine but also play a traditional role in ANDEAN RELIGION since pre-conquest times. In particular they are used both in offerings (*see* APU; PACHAMAMA) and by healers (*see* CURANDERA; ALTOMISAYOQ) as a basis for divination. The stimulatory effects of the leaves when chewed are also used to combat lack of energy at great heights and hunger pangs, and a coca tea preparation is used medicinally against altitude sickness and stomach upsets.

**Codex Sinaiticus**. One of the most important ancient manuscripts, probably dating from the 4th century, of the Christian Bible in Greek. As well as the Old and New Testaments the manuscript contains the *Epistle of Barnabus*. Discovered in a monastery on Mount Sinai, the codex is now held in the British Museum.

**Codex Vaticanus**. An important 4th-century manuscript of the Christian Bible in Greek held in the Vatican Library.

**coenobite**. One who shares in the common life of a monastery or convent, subject to religious vows.

**Coffin Texts**. Magical spells inscribed on coffins (particularly non-royal) during the Middle Kingdom of ancient Egypt (1991–1786 BCE), designed to protect the deceased and ensure his safe passage to the afterlife. They are derived from the PYRAMID TEXTS (Faulkner 1973–8).

**collective unconscious**. A central term in the analytical psychology of Carl Gustav Jung, referring to the common heritage of thought, action and conceptual material which is given to human beings in and through birth. The structures included in this are called ARCHETYPES, an example of which is the mother-archetype. Religion was primarily seen by Jung as a construction of archetypal structures.

**common calendar**. While the system of counting years in general use in western and many other countries begins from the presumed birth of Jesus Christ, its use in a pluralist society has led to its being called the common calendar. In this perspective, and to avoid the tacit Christianization of history, the abbreviations BCE and CE are preferred to BC and AD. BCE refers to 'Before the Common Era' or 'Before the Christian Era', whereas BC refers to 'Before Christ'. CE refers to the 'Common Era' whereas AD refers to '*Anno Domini*' (Latin: 'Year of our Lord').

**common consent arguments for the existence of God**. A group of informal proofs from the alleged universality of belief in the existence of God. Examples of this type of argument can be found in the writings of medieval Indian thinkers such as Udayana (11th century) as well as in classical Western philosophers (e.g. Cicero and Seneca) and Christian theologians (e.g. John Calvin and Richard Hooker). Such arguments invite the response of Pierre Bayle (1647–1706): 'neither general tradition nor the unvarying consent of the whole of humankind can place any injunction upon truth'. *See also* ARGUMENTS FOR THE EXISTENCE OF GOD.

**communicatio idiomatum** (Latin). A patristic teaching which asserted the sharing of the creaturely flesh in the names and properties of the divine LOGOS, and the divine Logos or Son's sharing in those of the flesh, without any loss or detriment to either. The teaching became current in the 4th century CE. *See also* TOME OF LEO.

**compadrazgo** (New World Spanish). In Latin America, godparenthood, ritual kinship ties betwen godparents and natural parents, often established around a child's ritual change of status, i.e. baptism, confirmation, or marriage. Thus two sets of relationships are involved, between sets of adults, and between godparents and godchild. The specific terms are as follows: *mad-*

*rina* (godmother), *padrino* (godfather), *ahijada* (female godchild), *ahijado* (male godchild); godparents and parents refer to each other as *comadre* (female) or *compadre* (male). After this relationship is formally established (often, but not necessarily, in a Christian church) FIESTAS are celebrated, gifts exchanged, a new very formal behaviour pattern ensues between *comadres* and *compadres*, and a formal yet often affectionate relationship evolves between godparent and godchild.

Non-sacramental types of godparenthood also exist, and include the blessing of persons and objects to mark stages of life-cycle development, aid during illness, or to ensure well-being. Blessed items may be ritual paraphernalia, edifices, homes, animals, seeds, tools, machines etc. Godparenthood brings into play an extensive range of positive practical, emotional and spiritual relationships that bind households and communities together, reinforcing the value of harmony over competition or dissent. (*See* Ingham 1986).

**comparative religion**. This frequently used phrase usually implies the comparative *study* of religion which, as understood in the West, may be said to have begun in the ancient world. Greek and Roman travellers, soldiers and officials compared the divinities they encountered abroad with those familiar to them at home, often giving them Greek or Roman names. Coupled with this was a trend toward the intellectual criticism of popular religion which began with Xenophanes in the 6th century BCE (but *see* especially EUHEMERISM), and reached an early high-point in the work of the Stoics, especially Cicero. This line of thought emphasized the resemblances, rather than differences, between local religious traditions. The Judaeo-Christian tendency did the opposite, emphasizing a unique revelation to one people of one true God, and condemning other deities as either useless 'idols' or dangerous 'demons'. Neither the Old nor the New Testament denied that these deities exist; but both forbade entering into relations with them. The Indian tradition was more like the Graeco-Roman, combining a philosophical reflection on oneness and a recognition of competitive diversity on the devotional level. Further east, in China and adjacent cultures, comparative reflection on religion took place particularly in the context of THREE TEACHINGS thought.

The rediscovery of classical Graeco-Roman literature during the Renaissance, however, added a fresh body of written evidence, and a new flexibility in interpretation. In the same period the great voyages of discovery revealed much new material, especially from Asia. China and Japan, then India began to be not only goals for colonial and missionary expansion but also objects of both scholarly and popular curiosity. Scriptures and philosophical treatises were translated, at this stage chiefly from Chinese into Latin, and parallels were noted between Confucian philosophy and the Deism which developed in Europe in the 17th century and became an intellectual orthodoxy in the 18th. The first notable translation of a Hindu scripture into a modern European language took place in 1785, with the appearance of Wilkins's translation of the *Bhagavadgita*.

By the end of the 18th century, western scholars had accumulated a large growing body of evidence about the religions of the world, as may be seen from such huge works as William Hurd's *A New Universal History of the Religious Rites, Ceremonies, and Customs of the Whole World* (1788). Some of the information was invaluable, much of it inaccurate; but there was no adequate theory to hold it together, once the theological explanation had been abandoned. The Deists' 'natural religion' theory could account only for that which seemed worthy of recognition, leaving other features unexplained except in terms of FETISHISM or fear of the unknown (Hume 1976).

In the 19th century the comparative study of religion took on a shape which is still influential today. There was a vast influx of new material by way of the developing sciences of archaelogy, philology, anthropology and folklore (all of them understood as branches of history). Following Bonaparte's Egyptian expedition of 1798–1800, and the Mesopotamian discoveries of Rich, Botta, Layard and others, hieroglyphs and cuneiform scripts were deciphered. The dependence of Sanskrit, Greek, Latin and the Germanic and Celtic languages on a common Indo-European source was demonstrated. Editions and translations of sacred scriptures multiplied, culminating in the 50-

volume *Sacred Books of the East* edited by Friedrich Max Müller in the last years of the century. Müller saw the history of religion as a movement away from a pure and lofty 'perception of the infinite' and toward a decadent obsession with the intrigues of mythology. In the end he lost out to anthropologists such as Andrew Lang, for whom mythology, like folklore, could be summed up as a 'study of survivals'. Müller's achievements were less in the realm of theory than in Indology, and in helping to make fashionable a study which once had been merely eccentric.

However, evolutionist theory, following the publication of Charles Darwin's *Origin of Species* (1859), had other implications for comparative religion. Just as man had evolved from something other than man, so religion was presumed to have evolved out of something which was not quite religion. The prehistory of religion could not be studied directly; it could on the other hand be inferred, it was thought, from the beliefs and practices of surviving 'primitive' peoples – notably the Aborigines of Australia. The publication in 1871 of E.B. Tylor's *Primitive Culture* marked the introduction of the term ANIMISM – the belief in spiritual beings – to describe this level of prehistoric and primitive religion. Also of importance was the work of Andrew Lang in drawing attention to a belief in 'high gods' – creators and lawgivers, not necessarily worshipped – at relatively undeveloped levels of human culture.

Although not completed until well on into the 20th century, the most notable achievement of 19th-century comparative religion in the English language was J.G. Frazer's multi-volume work THE GOLDEN BOUGH. This brought together classical scholarship, ethnology and folklore, emphasized the primacy of ritual over belief, distinguished religion from MAGIC, and highlighted kingship. Later scholarship has often disagreed with Frazer: it has been unable to ignore him.

Before this came about, however, seminal works had been published by Freud on the subconscious, Durkheim on TOTEMISM, and Schmidt on primal monotheism (*Urmonotheismus*). After the disruption of belief in the capacities of human reason to sustain an orderly society the post-war years saw a growing tendency to emphasize the non-rational aspect of religion. This may be seen, for example, in the immense influence of Rudolph Otto's *The Idea of the Holy*. In the revolt against what came to be called 'historicism', the psychology of religion went through a period of popularity and great interest was shown in MYSTICISM.

In the 1920s the main sociological issue was the role of heredity and environment in shaping human belief and behaviour, a well-known work in this regard being Margaret Mead's *Coming of Age in Samoa* (1928). In historical discussion the main controversy was between a hitherto dominant unilinear evolutionism and a 'diffusionist' theory which saw first Egypt, and later Mesopotamia, as the source from which dominant religious and cultural impulses had spread (*compare* DIFFUSIONISM). The 'pan-Egyptian' theories of Grafton Elliot Smith and W.J. Perry were never widely accepted. However, they led indirectly to a school of thought usually labelled 'myth and ritual', which emphasized the performative character of MYTH, especially myths of creation, their ritual setting, and the role of the king in carrying them out. There were two MYTH AND RITUAL schools, one in Britain, led by S.H. Hooke (a disciple of Perry) and A.M. Hocart, the other in Scandinavia, led by G. Widengren and I. Engell.

The so-called PHENOMENOLOGY OF RELIGION which emerged in the inter-war years, its chief spokesman being the Dutch scholar G. van der Leeuw, was another attempt to escape from the treatment of religion in purely historical terms. It functioned cross-culturally, dealing with the significance of specific 'phenomena' (e.g. prayer, sacrifice, purification) in the world of religion as a whole. This led to the composition of comparative compendia of religious phenomena which continued to be published after the Second World War. The sheer mass of theoretically available material has discouraged the production of such works in recent years, and there has been a strong tendency to concentrate on selected themes for comparative study, even, for example, in the expansive writings of Mircea Eliade.

**competence theorizing about religion**. A recently advanced method for the cognitive study of religion that employs some of the strategies of generative linguistics and which uses as data for its analysis the judgements that ritual participants make about the form of their religion. (Lawson & McCauley 1990).

**Compidalia**. A Roman movable feast of late December to early January, offered to the LARES in their capacity as guardians of the crossroads. The festival caused considerable political unrest in the later Republic.

**Compostela**. A pilgrimage centre in northwest Spain focused on the legendary burial site of St James (Sant Iago), and therefore also known as Santiago de Compostela.

**concordat**. An agreement or treaty concluded between a state or government and the HOLY SEE, represented by the POPE himself or by a NUNTIO.

**concupiscence**. In Christian theology, any desire of the lower faculties of human nature not brought under the control of the rational faculties.

**Confessing church**. *See* BARMEN DECLARATION.

**confessional**. A separate place in Roman Catholic churches, often in the form of a wooden cubicle, where the faithful enter individually to meet the priest seated behind a partition. To him they confess their sins and from him they receive remission and forgiveness in the name of God. *See also* PENANCE.

**confessor**. A member of the Christian church who has faithfully survived official persecution. During the persecutions under the Roman Empire a confessor acquired the privilege of forgiving those who had lapsed.

**confirmation**. A Christian rite of initiation complementary to BAPTISM in which the gift of the Holy Spirit is conveyed through the laying on of hands. Theological opinion has varied about its precise relationship to BAPTISM, the extent to which it requires adult commitment and whether it is a SACRAMENT.

**Confucianism**. The Western designation for the intellectual tradition which in Chinese is called *Rujia* [*Ju-chia*] or 'School of the Literati'. The school was founded by Confucius (551–479 BCE), hence its Western name, and became the official doctrine of the Chinese state during the former Han dynasty (206 BCE – 23 CE). While its philosophical and religious vigour was overshadowed by Buddhism and Taoism during the 1st millennium CE, Confucianism still remained the ideological foundation of the Chinese social and political system, and Confucian moral values and rules of conduct came to permeate all strata of the Chinese society. During the Song (Sung) dynasty (960–1279) the movement of Neo-Confucianism marked a revival of Confucian philosophical thinking. Since then Confucianism dominated Chinese intellectual life till the end of the empire in 1911. In the 20th century Confucianism has been criticized, both in the Republic and in the People's Republic of China, but Confucian social and moral values are still deeply rooted in Chinese society. The influence of Confucian thinking is not confined to China but extends to all East Asian countries, including Japan, Korea and Vietnam.

The teachings of Confucius are transmitted in the LUN YU (often translated as *Analects*), a collection of his sayings written down by his disciples. In the main it is a moral and political philosophy focusing on the question how the order of society can be established. Confucius advocated following the way of the sage kings of antiquity and regarded himself as the transmitter of their teachings. In his view the order of society depends on the moral qualification of the ruler, who has to be a JUNZI (*chün-tzu*) or superior man. He cultivates the virtue of human-heartness (REN [*jen*]) by observing the LI (rules of propriety).

There are different opinions about whether Confucianism is to be regarded as a religion or not. Although Confucius himself and other early Confucian thinkers like Mencius (Meng Zi [Meng-tzu] *c*.372–289 BCE) and Xun Zi [Hsün-tzu] (*c*.313–238 BCE) did not talk much about religious matters, the Confucian tradition embraced many traditional notions and practices with strong religious connotations. Thus, in the field of ethics the central virtue of filial piety (XIAO [*hsiao*]) demanded not only to serve the parents while they are alive, but also to pay respect to them after they have deceased. In this way ancestor worship was an essential part of the Confucian rules of propriety (LI). Likewise, in the field of political thinking the position of the emperor was intimately related with cosmological concepts regarding him as the intermediary between Heaven (*tian* [*t'ien*]) and men. The official state cult, which included offerings to Heaven and Earth by the emperor, can be regarded, therefore, as a Confucianist institution.

The religious coloration of Confucian thinking became especially marked during the former Han dynasty, when Dong Zhongshu [Tung Chung-shu] (*c.* 179–104 BCE) developed an eclectic system which explained the human world as part of the cosmic order governed by Heaven. Cosmological speculations of this kind gave way to the widespread belief in omina and prognostication, which to a lesser degree continued also in later times. In the main, however, Confucian thinking after the Former Han tended to be more or less agnostic and even critical towards popular religious beliefs, while at the same time maintaining such institutions as ancestor worship and the state cult. The strong position of Confucianism vis-à-vis BUDDHISM and DAOISM is reflected in the fact that the official state examinations required a thoroughgoing knowledge of the Confucian Classics (WU JING). (Fung 1952; de Bary 1960; D.H. Smith 1973; Dawson 1981). *See also* NEO-CONFUCIANISM.

**Congregationalism**. The belief that authority in the Church lies within each and every single gathered congregation, among whose members Christ is present, a viewpoint first advanced in the works of the Englishman Robert Browne (*c.*1550–1633). Accordingly, the wider unions of such churches have an advisory, co-ordinating function.

**consacranei**. *See* MITHRAISM.

**Conservative Judaism**. The movement which began in Germany and was established in the United States at the beginning of the 20th century by rabbis who objected to the neglect of HALAKHAH by REFORM JUDAISM. Conservative Judaism interprets Jewish law as an 'organic' process which should reflect both continuity and change. The movement has focused much of its attention on reconciling modern historical scholarship with traditional Jewish study.

**consistory**. A court for the enactment or administration of church law. The term is used in various churches. In the Roman Catholic Church it consists of the cardinals with the Pope and is of particular importance for diplomatic protocol and in the canonization of new saints.

**consubstantiation**. The doctrine held by Martin Luther and others that the bread and wine of the EUCHARIST remain in substance themselves while at the same time becoming the substance of the body and blood of Christ. *Contrast* TRANSUBSTANTIATION.

**conversion**. To turn about or to change directions. In religious contexts, the term usually implies that one religious path is dropped in favour of another: the Christian adopts the Jewish faith; the Hindu becomes a Buddhist; or the Protestant becomes a Catholic. In the older literature on the psychology of religion it has commonly referred to adolescent conversion from religious indifference into the warm espousal of Christian faith (e.g. Starbuck 1901). It can also imply the abandonment of a religious way of life.

The process of conversion can be sudden and dramatic or gradual and almost imperceptible, though in either case the result entails significant kinds of change. The liberal Christian who joins a fundamentalist congregation, for instance, acquires a new self-understanding, new doctrinal beliefs, and a new life-style informed by a new ethic (Ammermann 1987; Hunter 1987). Western converts to monastic eastern paths, or to new religious movements, such as the Church of Scientology, enter environments where life is very different from that in the mainstream of the dominant culture (Wallis 1977). Members of small-scale societies who become attracted to Christianity are often required to give up practices which are normally expected within their societies, because those practices are – from their newly adopted stand-point – regarded as 'heathen' (Lewis 1988).

A wide variety of theories have been put forward to explain the process of 'conversion', with much of the most interesting research having been focused on new religious movements in the contemporary west. What, for instance, induces well-educated, middle-class people in their twenties and thirties to abandon an established way of life in order to join movements which teach reincarnation or practise magic and 'channelling'? Common answers to such a question range from 'brain-washing' (much favoured in the popular press, but adopted by few academic researchers in the area), through 'dissatisfaction' theories which stress the role played by emotional distress or feelings of disquiet, to 'substitution' theories which seek to show that converts tend to adopt a new religious path which enables them to pursue their prior interests by a new means. See Thomas Robbins 1988 for a summary and critical assessment of such theories.

**copal** [copalli] (Nahuatl). An aromatic resin used primarily in Aztec culture as an incense. There are numerous varieties, most deriving from the genus *Bursera*, a tree or shrub with small flowers, used also in medicines for various illnesses (Ruiz de Alarcon 1984).

**copalli**. *See* COPAL.

**Coptic Church**. One of the most ancient Christian churches, still existing as a minority in Egypt, Coptic remaining as a liturgical language only. The Coptic Church became detached from the major churches after the COUNCIL OF CHALCEDON (451 CE) at which MONOPHYSITISM was condemned.

**corn mother**. A major manifestation of the EARTH MOTHER in Native American religions, corn (i.e. maize) being the basic subsistence crop and thus the symbol of Earth's nourishment of humans. In many Native American cultures corn serves as the central metaphor of human birth and other phases of life and death.

**Corpus Christi** (Latin: 'body of Christ'). A Catholic festival falling on the Thursday after Trinity Sunday to celebrate the foundation of the EUCHARIST. Typical services include a procession bearing the 'HOST'.

**Corpus Hermeticum**. *See* HERMETIC WRITINGS.

**Cosmogonic**. *See* COSMOGONY.

**cosmogony**. The emergence or creation of the world, described in mythical or theological terms. Although in a broad sense all cosmogonies are comparable to each other and a normal feature of any mythological tradition, the details of the creation story frequently imply a claim to political legitimacy. Thus, Egyptian creation myths described an original place of creation, usually an island emerging from the waters of chaos. The most important featured HELIOPOLIS as the site of creation; here the Great Ennead (nine gods) made the world and life out of darkness and chaos. ATUM or RE, the first god, created himself. Thereafter his offspring SHU and TEFNUT produced GEB (earth) and NUT (sky) who in turn became the parents of OSIRIS, ISIS, NEPHTHYS and SETH. HORUS, son of Osiris and Isis, headed the lesser Ennead. However, a rival Egyptian cosmogony emphasized Memphis as the place of creation and its patron god, PTAH, as the creator. At Hermepolis another myth featured that city's god Thoth, and its Ogdoad (eight gods), while at KARNAK the Theban cosmogony promoted the claim of Amun as the first creator god. Similarly the Hebrew creation myths, though drawing elements from other cultures of the ancient Near East, leads eventually through genealogies into the story of Israel and its special place in the world. The same may be said of traditional Japanese cosmogony to which the Tenno (Emperor) system is linked. Although such political legitimation is almost always in evidence the explanatory (aetiological) motive of cosmogonic myth should not be entirely discounted, and it is in this light that specific geographical colouring, e.g. creation as the creations of islands, is to be understood. *See also* BAAL CYCLE; ENUMA ELISH; COSMOLOGY; CREATION; MYTH.

**cosmological arguments for the existence of God**. The name first given by Kant (1724–1804) to a varied group of speculative attempts to reason from the non-self-explanatory character of the universe to a Supreme Being whose existence is said to be self-explanatory. Such proofs may incorporate some general facts about the world (e.g. that some things are in motion), but their force as proofs often depends more on reasoning of an *a priori* kind. Such arguments form a continuum with other speculative proofs for God (or gods): when empirical detail is expanded, they tend toward design arguments; but when more *a priori* considerations dominate, they may tend more toward some ontological arguments (*see* DESIGN ARGUMENTS FOR THE EXISTENCE OF GOD; ONTOLOGICAL ARGUMENTS FOR THE EXISTENCE OF GOD). One explanation for this continuum could be Kant's observation that the cosmological proof is itself built on the ontological and is also foundation for the teleological proof. Cosmological arguments are among the historically most persistent and culturally most distributed proofs for the existence of God (or gods). It has both supporters (Śaṅkara, Udayana, Madhva, Gaṅgeśa) and critics (e.g. Rāmānuja) within Indian thought, as well as within Western traditions since at least the time of Plato and Aristotle. Muslims, Jews and Christians alike have found that such proofs can be adapted to serve their individualized theistic requirements. Within Western traditions, three distinct but historically intertwined cosmological arguments have proved influential. Representative of the first type, which derives ultimately from Aristotle, is the style of argument preferred by the likes of al-Fārābi [Latin: Abunaser] (870–950), Moses ben Maimon [Latin: Maimonides] (1135–1204) and Thomas Aquinas (*c.*1224–74). Such proofs stress the *causal dependency* of the world on God as 'first cause' or 'prime mover' and are compatible with the universe's being eternal and uncreated (as, e.g., Aristotle had held and even Thomas Aquinas allowed was not an issue that could be settled by reason apart from revelation). Not so the second type of cosmological argument (sometimes called 'the Kalām argument'; see Craig 1979, 1980), whose leading exponent was the Persian al-Ghazālī (*c.*1058–1111). His preferred proof was built, not on merely causal dependency, but on the *temporal contingency* or originatedness of the universe. Ghazālī repudiated the more Aristotelian argument, which had been widely used by Muslim philosophers, because it was incompatible with the Qur'anic doctrine of creation and because it implied a sub-Islamic concept of God. (Davidson 1987.) Finally, Leibniz (1646–1716) argues for the existence of God from the fact that something exists and from the principle that there must be a rational basis or a *sufficient reason* for there being something and not nothing. That basis cannot be something in the world (since each thing is itself contingent and in need of some reason sufficient to explain its own existence), nor can it be the world conceived as a whole (since the sum of all things is no less contingent than is each thing considered separately). From this he infers that the sufficient reason for there being something and not nothing must exist outside the totality of things that make up the universe as a whole; it must be a 'necessary being' or a being which contains within itself the sufficient reason of its own existence; such a being is what is meant by 'God', whose existence – according to Leibniz – is thereby proved. Each of these three types of cosmological argument has attracted extensive criticism, but each continues to have contemporary defenders. (Mackie 1982; Craig 1979; Swinburne 1979; Rowe 1975; Meynell 1982). *See also* ARGUMENTS FOR THE EXISTENCE OF GOD.

**cosmology** (from Greek, *kosmos*: 'world', 'universe'). A view, picture or map of the cosmos couched in mythical or theological language, with the emphasis on its structure rather than its origin or genesis (*see* COSMOGONY). Thus in traditional Jewish belief, Jerusalem was at the centre of the world (identified as the Garden of Eden) which reached out to the deserts and sea at the end (*see* YAM SUF), the entire saucer-like structure dividing a sphere of air above and underworld below. The waters of chaos surrounded the whole structure as in a womb. For essays on the cosmologies of various ancient cultures see Blacker & Loewe 1975. *See also* OMPHALOS.

**council**. A formal meeting of bishops and other representatives of regionally distinct Christian churches to regulate doctrine or discipline. *See also* ECUMENICAL COUNCILS. For Buddhist Councils, *see* SAṂGĪTI.

**Council of Chalcedon**. The fourth of the seven ECUMENICAL COUNCILS, held in 451 to condemn Eutychianism, a form of MONOPHYSITISM taught by Eutyches (*c.*378–454), but in effect largely settling, or at least freezing politically, the long-standing disputes over CHRISTOLOGY and the nature of the

TRINITY. The Council defined Christ as one person in TWO NATURES (rather than one nature as in monophysitism), divine and human, 'unconfusedly, unchangeably, indivisible and inseparable'. It also allowed the description of Mary as THEOTOKOS. The normative documents were doctrinal letters by Cyril of Alexandria and *Tome* of Pope Leo of Rome (*see* TOME OF LEO). (Kelly 1972: ch.12).

**Council of Constantinople**. The second ECUMENICAL COUNCIL (381), which ratified the christology of the COUNCIL OF NICEA and, against APOLLINARIANISM, asserted Christ's full humanity. Two further ecumenical councils in Constantinople dealt with writings favourable to NESTORIANISM (553) and MONOTHELITISM (680–81).

**Council of Ephesus**. *See* THEOTOKOS.

**Council of Nicaea**. The first ECUMENICAL COUNCIL (325), which sought to assert, against ARIANISM, the Son's full divinity, that is his being of one and the same substance (HOMOOUSIOS) with the father. The seventh Ecumenical Council was also held in Nicaea (787) to clarify the role of icons in the Church (*see* ICONOCLAST CONTROVERSY).

**Council of Trent**. *See* TRIDENTINE THEOLOGY.

**Counter-Reformation**. A pan-European religious revival restating the claims of the Catholic Church over against those of the Lutheran and Reformed persuasion. A strong role was played by the Society of Jesus (Jesuits), founded in 1540, which also initiated missionary activity in Asia and the Americas.

**covenant**. An important biblical motif and the central metaphor of Judaism. It is understood that Israel is bound to God for all generations, by a 'legal' covenant whose terms were revealed to Moses on Mount SINAI in the form of the TORAH. Though supposedly modelled on old near-eastern forms (Mendenhall 1954), the Sinai covenant itself is evidently an exilic tradition (Nicholson 1973). Thus, it is best construed as a metaphor for the relationship between Yahweh and Israel developed as a message of hope in exile; each broken covenant (*Genesis* 1; *Exodus* 32) being renewed (*Genesis* 9; *Exodus* 34). See also BRIT (Hebrew), for which 'covenant' is the English translation. (Beyerlin 1961; McCarthy 1965; Nicholson 1973).

**Covenanters**. Members of the Scottish Presbyterian associations sworn to defend the integrity of Scottish reformed Christianity in the 17th and 18th centuries.

**Coyote**. In many western Native American religions, a TRICKSTER or culture hero and the subject of many humorous traditional Native stories, as well as modern Euro-American ones.

**creatio ex nihilo**. *See* CREATION.

**creation**. The origination of the world through the action of God, especially as understood in Jewish and Christian theology. The HEBREW BIBLE contains two accounts of creation. The first (*Genesis* 1.1–2.4a), though in its present form based on the motif of the divine word as creative, derives from the Canaanite myth of the deity killing a dragon, a myth which survives intact elsewhere (e.g. *Psalms* 74 and 89, and *Exodus* 15). *Genesis* 2.4b–25, on the other hand, derives from agricultural and related cultic imagery. In neither case is creation represented as taking place out of nothing, for an already present chaos is described as being arranged by God into a structured cosmos. In Christian theology Origen (185–254) argued that God is eternally creative and that there are therefore always pre-existent, created souls. Athanasius (*c*.296–373) thought, like the biblical myths but also like Plato (*c*.427–342 BCE) that the world was fashioned from pre-existent, chaotic matter, thus not asserting God to be the sole source of everything. Augustine (354–436), however, asserted *creatio ex nihilo* (creation out of nothing), creation being an absolutely free and unnecessary act of God, mysterious and without analogy. God therefore is not identified with the world, though he can be known through it; both matter and spirit are good, being sustained by one single God;

man, made in the image of God, is responsible for the welfare of creation. Since the time of Augustine, creation *ex nihilo* has become the normal Christian doctrine of creation. It is also believed by Muslims. The original creation myths of Jewish and Christian tradition have many parallels in other cultures and are a specific example of COSMOGONY.

**creationism**. The doctrine that human souls are new creations by God which are implanted at conception or birth in human bodies. *Contrast* TRADUCIANISM.

**credo**. *See* CREED.

**credo ut intelligam** (Latin: 'I believe so that I may understand'). Anselm's famous phrase, which indicates that knowledge follows from faith and not vice versa.

**creed**. A short statement of faith in the Christian church, originally recited in particular by baptismal candidates. These creeds varied verbally in different localities, but certain forms were standardized in the context of the ECUMENICAL COUNCILS in order to finalize doctrinal agreements. The most important of these, still used regularly in eucharistic liturgy, are the Apostles' Creed and the Nicene Creed, the latter containing important christological and trinitarian formulations (*see* COUNCIL OF NICAEA). The Latin text of the Nicene Creed is the third piece of music (i.e. the *credo*, meaning 'I believe') in traditional MASS compositions.

**Cronos**. A Greek TITAN deity who destroyed his father and repressed the OLYMPIAN GODS, of whom he and RHEA are the parents.

**crook**. *See* BISHOP.

**crosier**. A bishop's staff or crook.

**crucifix**. A cross in wood, metal etc., bearing an image of the crucified Christ. The crucifix is widely used, especially on altars, in the Roman Catholic and Lutheran churches. In the Orthodox churches the figure of Christ is not three-dimensional. In most Protestant churches the cross stands bare as a symbol of crucifixion to avoid the making of an image (held to contravene the second of the TEN COMMANDMENTS).

**crypt**. An architectural space beneath a church, especially under the sanctuary, frequently used as a mausoleum.

**cuius regio eius religio** (Latin: 'of whom the government, of him the religion'). The principle that the ruler of a particular territory should determine whether it should be Catholic or Protestant, put into operation in the German Empire at the Peace of Augsburg (1555).

**cults of affliction**. Cults, usually centred on mediums, which are activated at times of crisis or disaster. *See* for example, in Africa, PEPO; MIRA-MIRA; YEBOLA; ZAR.

**curandera** (New World Spanish). A healer, medicine woman (or man: *curandero*), who employs a wide range of techniques and materials from the pre-Contact periods, Colonial-era influences of Europe, Africa and Asia, and contemporary modern medicine and practices. Healing knowledge and practices are invariably intertwined with a specific religious cosmology and cognitive system (Marcos 1987). *See also* ALTOMISAYOQ.

**curandero**. *See* CURANDERA.

**Cur deus homo** (Latin: 'Why did God become man?'). A work on the atonement written by Anselm (1033–1109), turning away from the idea that Christ was crucified as a ransom demanded by Satan and setting forth the merciful initiative of God to achieve justice.

**Curia**. The central administrative body of the Roman Catholic Church, which acts under the authority of the Pope.

**Cybele**. *See* MYSTERIES OF CYBELE.

**Cyclopes**. Sons of Greek divinities OURANOS and GAIA who had but one eye set in the middle of their foreheads. They were craftsmen who made weapons for ZEUS' battle against the TITANS.

**Cyclops**. The savage one-eyed giant of Homer's epic THE ILIAD who roasted and ate two of Odysseus' companions before Odysseus blinded him to escape; connected in legend with the islands of Sicily.

# D

**Da**. 'Serpent', the moving, and hence also life-giving force in any living being, including gods (VODU) among the Fon of Dahomey (Republic of Benin). The concept of Da has given rise to different private and public serpent cults (Herskovits 1933).

**daat**. *See* HABAD.

**Da Dong Zhen Jing**. One of the numerous 'revealed' texts of DAOISM. Located in a prominent place of the great collection of Daoist scriptures (the DAOZANG) as the first scripture of the first greater partition, it is said to have first surfaced in public (after a long period of secret transmission) in the year 364 CE. The text represents one of the most sacred scriptures of the SHANG QING SECT of Daoism. Different versions are or were known, many of them lost. The one in question is 39 sections (6 chapters) long and contains incantations of various gods of the Daoist pantheon. As I. Robinet convincingly shows (Robinet 1983) the scripture does not stand alone, but is linked to other texts of the *daozang*, and also involved ritual practices.

**Daedalus**. The perfect mythic craftsman who invented the plumb-line, axe, saw and glue and whose sculptures were lifelike. After helping the Cretan queen enjoy an affair with a friend of POSEIDON, he made wings that enabled him to fly to Sicily, but his son Icarus flew too near the sun, and the heat melted his wings.

**dāgaba** (Sinhalese). A relic-container. *See also* STŪPA.

**Dagan**. A storm-god of the early 2nd millennium BCE, worshipped from Mesopotamia (where he is identified with ENLIL) to Palestine. A Philistine cult of Dagan (Dagon) survived into the Hellenistic period. Also regarded as a fertility deity, he has strong underworld associations. (Schmökel 1928; Montalbano 1951; Wyatt 1980).

**Dagda**. Celtic god who appears in Irish mythology and to whom are attributed various functions including god of knowledge and poetry, 'All-father', sky god and earth god. His cauldron, which is said to hold enough to feed the whole of mankind, suggests he is a guarantor of fertility. He is also shown with a huge club on wheels, a blow from one end of which is said to kill, while the other end brings the dead back to life. His name has been translated as 'good god' (*dago-devos*) or 'good hand' (*dag-dae*).

**dahr** (Arabic). Time. In the poetry of the Arabs of pre-Islamic times, an impersonal, arbitrary force which was the most powerful in affecting human destiny. In the Islamic world-view, this force was negated and replaced by the all-powerful Creator, ALLĀH.

**daibutsu** (Japanese). Great Buddha. There are two famous *daibutsu* in Japan, one in the ancient capital of Nara representing Locana Buddha and one in Kamakura representing Amida Buddha (*see* AMITĀBHA). The latter now stands in the open air since the building in which it was housed was destroyed by fire.

**Daichidoron**. *See* TA-CHIH-TU-LUN.

**ḍaʿīf** (Arabic: 'weak'). In the classification of Prophetic tradition (ḤADĪTH) in Islām, reports which are least acceptable owing to a serious defect in its chain of authority (ISNĀD).

**Daijizaiten**. The Japanese name for Maheśvara (i.e. Great Śiva), an Indian creator god who occurs in Buddhist iconography.

**daimon** (Greek). A class of spiritual beings or semi-definable powers lower than deities but nevertheless influential in the affairs of humans, frequently dangerously so. The word has come into widespread use in contexts other than ancient Greece to denote malevolent superhuman powers. The English form is DEMON.

**Daimuryōjukyō**. *See* JŌDO SANBUKYŌ.

**dainas** (Latvian). Traditional songs sung by the Baltic peoples at the different stages of their life (birth, death and marriage) and the different stages of the agricultural year. These were seen as the essential aspects of human existence and were also at the centre of Baltic religious beliefs, and therefore the *dainas* which accompanied them are a major religious expression of the Baltic peoples.

**Dainichi**. *See* VAIROCANA.

**Dainichikyō**. The Japanese name for the Mahāvairocana Sūtra, the most important sutra of Shingon Buddhism (*see* SHINGON-SHŪ).

**Dainichi Nyorai**. The Japanese name for the mythical Buddha Mahāvairocana Tathāgata, who is the central object of reverence in Shingon Buddhism (*see* SHINGON-SHŪ), being regarded as a visualized symbol of the ultimate truth from which all Buddhas and bodhisattvas proceed. (Dai-nichi means 'great sun'.)

**Daisekiji**. The head temple of the Japanese Buddhist sect NICHIREN-SHŌSHŪ. Although founded in the 13th century, Daisekiji has taken on great importance in the 20th century as the devotional focus of the SŌKA GAKKAI.

**Daitokuji**. One of the most important Zen Buddhist temples in Kyōto, Japan, standing in the Rinzai tradition (*see* RINZAI-SHŪ) and known especially for its association with the teaching of the tea ceremony by Rikyū.

**Daizōkyō**. Japanese designation for the comprehensive collection of Buddhist writings as extant in their Chinese versions; also known as Issaikyō. This collection, consisting of many volumes (originally scrolls), contains both pre-Mahāyāna and MAHĀYĀNA works with many overlapping texts and many which were first composed in China rather than India. Japanese Buddhist schools usually focus on one or more selected sūtras out of this vast collection.

**al-Dajjāl** (Arabic: 'the Deceiver'). In Islām, the anti-Christ, the false Messiah, whose appearance on earth will foretell the end of the world.

**Daḷadā Māligāva** (Sinhalese: 'Palace of the Tooth Relic'). The Tooth Temple in Kandy, Sri Lanka, where, according to the Sinhalese Buddhists, one of the Buddha's teeth is kept. Once a year the tooth is taken in procession (*perahära*) inside its casket on the back of the largest available elephant. This takes place on the ten nights leading to the full moon of the Sinhalese month of Äsaḷa (in August) and on the day itself, hence the name *Äsaḷa Perahära*, Sri Lanka's most famous tourist attraction. The lay administrator of the Tooth Temple is called *Diyavadana Nilamē*.

**Dalai Lama**. The Grand Lama of the Yellow Hat or DGE LUGS PA Buddhist order of Tibet who was also, until 1959, the temporal ruler of the country. 'Dalai' is a western rendering of *Ta-le* ('ocean'), probably implying 'ocean of wisdom' (Snellgrove & Richardson 1980: 184). The succession to the office of Dalai Lama is by search for a suitable boy child who is regarded as a reincarnation of the previously deceased office holder. While this is expressed in religious terms political considerations have often played a role, as for example in the selection of a Mongolian successor in 1588.

**dalang** (Javanese; Indonesian). A puppeteer in the Javanese shadow-play (WAYANG); as story-teller, director, producer and so on also key figure in other *wayang* genres (Groenendael 1985).

**Damdamī takṣal** (Punjabi). A Sikh revivalist movement founded in the 18th century by Bābā Deep Singh. Its main concerns are to maintain the KHĀLSĀ tradition and hasten Sikh independence. Bhindranwale was appointed leader in 1977. (Tully & Jacob 1985).

**dāna** (Sanskrit, Pāli: 'giving'). Almsgiving, the first of the Ten Good Deeds. The term may refer specifically to a monk's meal.

**dance of death**. A theme in medieval and later art in which Death in personified form leads the living to their graves in a grotesque dance. The macabre juxtaposition of people in various conditions of life with their common end (hence the French term *danse macabre*) is meant as a religious warning.

**dane**. *See* PINKAMA.

**dano** (New World Spanish). Harm, damage, injury, physical illness; often associated with AIRES and SUSTO (Ingham 1986).

**danse macabre**. *See* DANCE OF DEATH.

**Danu**. *See* TUATHA DÉ DANANN.

**dao-de** (Chinese). Numerous attempts have been made to translate these ancient Chinese philosophical terms; for *dao* (or *tao*): 'the Way' (its basic meaning), 'Ultimate Reality', 'civilizing power', 'Principle of Order', 'Natural Law' etc.; for *de* (or *te*) 'Virtue', also 'Power' (or manifestation thereof), 'magical potency' etc. Taken together this compound term encapsulates the key issues of DAOISM. The world as consisting of heaven, earth and man is interdependent, the underlying order or regulative principle not yet ethically qualified. By exerting *de* as a controlling energy (later *de* acquires a moral connotation), man (or, to be more precise, the *dao*-'ist', i.e. anybody who could establish a balancing communication between heaven, earth and man) was able to support the primordial cosmic principle that the word *dao* came to mean in the scripture DAODE JING. On the different meanings of *dao* and *de* see Kaltenmark 1969, esp. pp. 22–8.

**Dao De Jing**. Literally, the 'Classic of the Dao and De' (*see* DAO-DE); a very important Chinese text in 81 chapters dating back probably to the 3rd century BCE. Although it only consists of roughly 5,000 words the influence of this basic text cannot be underestimated. Generally regarded as the basic text of DAOISM, it discusses such metaphysical questions as the decline of the world, the *dao* as the basic principle that generates the living, the sagely attitudes beyond the usual emotional attitudes displayed in everyday life. However, questions of government, basic military strategies and economic issues are also treated. The chapters are rhymed throughout. Two quite different versions of the *Dao De Jing* exist: (1) the text discovered as late as 1972 in a grave in southern China, named the 'Mawang Dui text variant' after the excavation site and dating back to the 4th century BCE (*see* Henricks 1979); and (2) the text that was transmitted and commented on by a certain Wang Bi, which until the 1972 excavations was considered to be the original. Translations of both versions into European languages possibly amount to a hundred works. For text variant (2) see the translation by Lin Yu Tang 1948; for text variant (1) see Henricks 1979.

**Daoism** [Taoism]. Derived from the Chinese word *dao* (*see* DAO-DE) and supplemented with the western suffix 'ism' (designating a doctrine, a school of thought etc.), the term 'Daoism' has been a 'source of perplexity' for many western and eastern scholars (Sivin 1978; also Creel 1970). It is indeed not an easy term to explain, since it comprises a number of very different and highly complex ideas, abstractions and practices. We may start out analysing what Daoism stands for by looking at the scriptures that are called 'Daoist'. The first and most influential scripture of Daoism is doubtless the DAO DE JING. Said to have been written by the sage-philosopher Lao Zi (Lao Tzu), the text dates back to at least the 3rd century BCE. Another text of almost equal importance (philosophically speaking) is the book ZHUANG ZI, compiled in parts around the same era, with later interpolations. What these two books have in common (besides the formal aspects that they are rhymed and possibly date from about the same period) are the discussions of key philosophical issues that are somewhat connected with the word *dao*: epistemological problems, on the quality of things and human emotions, on culture, on the introspection of mysticism, on nature, on morality and the individual, on 'non-action' (*see* WU WEI) and, very importantly, on language (its function and its limits).

All these treatments of the above-mentioned issues (and other topics) are included in the two texts *Dao De Jing* and *Zhuang Zi*. What makes these texts explicitly 'Daoist' is the constant use of the word *dao* in connection with the discussion of nature, human insight and the mystic experience of this *dao* (or the union with *dao*). That other, so-called Confucian texts also use the word *dao* makes the problem even more complicated. Nevertheless, it is the metaphysical substratum in the *Dao De Jing* and the flowery neglect of duty and obligations to society in the *Zhuang Zi* that mark these texts as outstanding, 'unorthodox and heterodox' (Confucian wording) – in short, Daoist. That early Daoism also deals with military and political issues is often overlooked, but should not go unmentioned here.

Besides these two early scriptures there exists a vast number of texts that are of a more religious than philosophical nature. Some of them are important for the study of scientific history in China (medicine, mineralogy, geology, geography, astrology etc.), while others are a conglomerate of very cryptic descriptions of the heavens, the body, the *dao* and its manifestations. Many of these scriptures (compiled in the DAOZANG) have the following characteristics in common: they are 'revealed' texts (that is, they are by origin attributed to some god or deity); they deal with something that might be called 'physical felicity', but usually is termed LONGEVITY or immortality; they include prayers and charms, incantations and talismans, as means to cope with and to control the numinous powers that roam the world.

This second magico-religious class of texts stems from a tradition that is at least as old as the philosophical reflections gathered in the *Dao De Jing* and the *Zhuang Zi*. That does not mean that the texts are just as old, but it implies that shamanistic practices as a religion of nature (with socially integrative aims, besides the exorcist aspects) forms one (if not the most important) foundation for this magico-religious tendency that later, in the 2nd century CE, became institutionalized as the first 'Daoist' congregation (*see* TIANSHI DAO; SHANG GING DAO; QUAN ZHEN SECT). What added a new impetus to the latter versions of Daoism was the strife for longevity (*chang sheng*), which was sought after with alchemical means (*see* NEIDAN), either on an individual basis or in the form of elixirs as a special service to the leaders of society (the emperor, for example). Thus, the history of Daoism has two principal undercurrents: a striving for the 'natural way' (*see* ZIRAN] as a method of governing one's own destiny and that of others (which makes it a political issue), including all sorts of speculative philosophy on the topics listed above; and a striving for 'life', the vitalist tendency to attain longevity, if not immortality. This positive attitude, connected with an early adoption of such Confucian ideals as humanity, filial piety and righteousness, contradicts the usual judgement that Daoism is a nihilistic movement with anarchic elements. Daoists (and their forerunners) were in fact much concerned about 'worldly affairs', and frequently engaged in supporting emperors or legitimizing benevolent rulership in general.

**Daozang**. A vast collection of scriptures originating from the Chinese Daoist (Taoist) tradition (*see* DAOISM). The collection can be viewed as the counterpart to the Buddhist TRIPITAKA. It is divided into seven parts, three major and four lesser divisions. The Daozang as it has been transmitted to our days includes altogether 1,487 works in 1,120 fascicles (older versions ran up to 5,000 independent works, of which many are now lost). Included are almost all the relevant texts of Daoism, compiled during the years 1436–50 (printed in 1477), and supplemented in 1607. Works of the Daozang treated in this dictionary are: BAO PU ZI; DAO DE JING (more than 60 versions); ZHUANG ZI; DA DONG ZHEN JING; BI CHUAN ZHENGYANG; ZHENREN LINGBAO BIFA; LIE XIAN CHUAN; WU ZHEN PIAN; HUAN TING JING; WU YUE ZHEN XING TU; LI JIAO SHIWU LUN; LINGBAO WUFU JING. For the continuation of the Daozang, comprising later scriptures, see the entry on the DAO ZANG JIAYAO. From the late 1970s until 1986 an international study group checked, dated and analysed all the works of the Daozang; the results are expected to be published shortly.

**Daozang Jiyao**. A supplement to the Great Collection of Daoist (*see* DAOISM) writings, the DAOZANG. The Daozang Jiyao of the 1906 printing contains 292 sorts of Daoist and other works (numerous travelogues to holy sites, cosmological charts with explanations etc.) in 28 parts. Around 170 works are also included in the Daozang, while many of the rest of the texts originate from the latter Qing Dynasty (1644–1911). Especially interesting are the texts written and compiled by the Daoists of Sichuan Province, one of the former cradles of Daoism. The Daozang Jiyao was reprinted in 1987–8 in Chengdu (province of Sichuan, West China), using the old pear-tree woodblocks of the 'Two-Immortals-Monastery'. This version (called the *Er Xian An Daozang Jiyao*) even contains texts from the Chinese republican period (1911–49), augmenting the number of texts to a total of 306.

**dār al-ḥarb**. (Arabic). Abode of war. *See* DĀR AL-ISLĀM.

**Dār al-Islām** (Arabic). 'Abode of Islam' where the ordinances of Islam are established under rule of a Muslim sovereign. This is contrasted with *dār al-ḥarb*, the abode of war, which, in Islamic constitutional law, is a potential *dār al-Islām* whether achieved by conquest or conversion. A somewhat intermediate case is the *dār al-ṣulḥ*, the abode of agreement, a territory in tributary relationship with Islam.

**dār al-ṣulḥ** (Arabic). Abode of agreement. *See* DĀR AL-ISLĀM.

**dār al-ʿulūm**. 'House of Sciences.' A Muslim institution of higher learning (*see also* DEOBAND SEMINARY), established in Cairo in 1872 by ʿAlī Pasha Mubārak (*d* 1893), the Egyptian statesman and intellectual. Its original aim was to introduce students of the AL-AZHAR to modern branches of learning equipping them to teach in the new Egyptian schools. In 1946 it became a faculty of Cairo University and the leading Muslim teachers' training college; women have been enrolled since 1953 and so have ordinary high school graduates.

**Darul Islām**. An Islamic movement aiming at establishing an Islamic state in Indonesia by force. Uprisings under the banner of Darul Islam ('territory', 'house of Islam') began in 1950 in West Java and followed by revolts in North Sumatra and South Sulawesi, were finally defeated in 1966. (Boland 1982; Dijk 1981).

**Darwīsh** [Dervish] (Arabic). A common name for ṢŪFĪS of any persuasion, but often used in special reference to wandering Sufi mendicants (QALANDARIYA) who belonged to no established brotherhood.

**Dasam Granth** (Punjabi: 'Book of the Tenth (Gurū)'). A book held to contain the teachings of Gurū Gobind Singh, compiled by a disciple after the Guru's death. In addition to probable autobiographical material and poetry by the Gurū (some of which remains important in contemporary Sikh practice), it contains many popular legendary stories, some of which focus on the god Krishna.

**dawla** (Arabic). In Islamic usage, the term for government, or the domain of politics as distinct from DĪN, religion. Islamic tradition, however, tends to obscure the difference between the two, fusing both the spiritual proper and temporal, both being embraced by God's dominion. In modern usage, *dawla* is the word for the secular 'state'.

***Da Xue*** [Ta-hsüeh] (Chinese: 'The Great Learning'). A short Confucian scripture, originally a chapter of the LI JI [*Li Chi*] which was given special prominence by the Song dynasty Neo-Confucians. It deals with the ordering of society through individual self-cultivation. The *Da Xue* is one of the Four Books (SI SHU), the basic Confucian writings selected by the Neo-Confucians.

**Day of Atonement**. *See* ATONEMENT.

**dāyaka(ya)** (Pāli, Sinhalese: 'donor'). A Buddhist lay supporter of a monastery.

**deacon**. The lowest rank of ordination in the Roman Catholic and Episcopal Churches (below priest and BISHOP), conferring the authority to perform all priestly functions except the consecration during the EUCHARIST or MASS.

**Dead Sea Scrolls**. Numerous, mainly fragmentary manuscripts of biblical texts but also of other previously unknown religious writings, found near the Dead Sea between 1947 and 1956. The manuscripts, in Hebrew and Aramaic, are thought to have belonged to a Jewish religious community which existed at QUMRAN, the place of discovery, until 70 CE. Apart from the importance of the find for the textual history of the Hebrew Bible, two works relating to the community itself are of particular interest, namely *The War of the Sons of Light against the Sons of Darkness* and *The Manual of Discipline*. (Vermes 1968, 1977).

**Decalogue** (from Greek, *Hoi deka logoi*: 'the ten commandments'). The TEN COMMANDMENTS.

**Deer Mother**. An aspect of the Earth Mother in many Native American religions, representing the animal relations who offer themselves to humans for nourishment, the deer being the primary hunted animal outside of the Plains.

**deesis** (Greek). The section of an ICONOSTASIS bearing ICONS of saints and angels.

**deconstruction**. In linguistics, an analytic operation whereby one shows how meaning is generated in the grammatical construction of a sentence or larger linguistic unit. The term has been given additional overtones and wider currency through its employment in the writings of Jacques Derrida and Paul de Man. For Derrida, deconstruction implies a demystification, in that he contends that any apparently meaningful linguistic unit, however large or small, only achieves its effect of meaning by disguising its self-construction. It does this in two main ways: first, by concealing that it can equally mean the opposite of what it appears to mean; second, by hiding the arbitrariness of its own claim to stand as a 'total' and self-sufficient unit. The conception of the first way indicates the strong link of deconstruction with Hegelian dialectics: since meanings are constructed through the interaction of differences which negate each other as opposites, every assertion unavoidably entails its own refutation. The conception of the second appeals to the manner in which meaning is generated by the play of linguistic signs. As words only point to other words, no collection of words can ever be truly complete. The establishing of a definite meaning is endlessly 'deferred', and any claimed experience of a direct encounter with a 'present' determinate meaning is a suppression of this necessary deferral. (Derrida 1976). *See also* DIFFERENCE; POSTSTRUCTURALISM.

**Defender of the Faith**. A title carried by British monarchs as titular heads of the CHURCH OF ENGLAND. It was first bestowed on Henry VIII by Pope Leo X in 1521 for his defence of the doctrine that the sacraments are seven in number. The abbreviation 'Fid. Def.' arises from the Latin form of the title, *Fidei Defensor*.

**deism**. Belief in a single God who is known through natural reason without appeal to revelation, and who does not intervene in the world which he has created. Many 17th- and 18th-century thinkers such as Lord Herbert of Cherbury and Voltaire are regarded as deists, though it is sometimes difficult to draw a line between them and other thinkers of the time such as John Locke, who sought to give a rational defence of Christianity.

**deity**. A divinity, goddess, or god. These synonymous words are not usually used in explicit religious contexts and imply the distanced, objective designation of a being presumed by others to be of godly quality.

**Deivas**. *See* DIEVS.

**Delphi**. The most famous sacred place in ancient Greece, it included a stadium, a theatre of DIONYSOS, a temple of APOLLO where ORACLES were uttered by a priestess on matters political and public, a temple of ATHENA, and a spring of GAIA; more generally, it was known as the centre of political, moral, athletic, dramatic and religious excellence.

**Demeter**. The daughter of CRONOS and RHEA, and thus sister of ZEUS, a Greek mother-goddess known for her gifts of grain and happiness in the after life and as the mother of PERSEPHONE. *Compare* CERES. *See also* ELEUSINIAN MYSTERIES.

**demiurge** (Greek: 'craftsman'). A platonist term for the creator. In GNOSTICISM the demiurge is given derogatory names such as Jaldabaoth or Sahlas ('Fool'), and is identified with the Jewish god. *See also* KAGGEN.

**democratized shamanism**. A term which has been applied to some Native American religions in which the purpose of an initial vision quest lies in the individual's gaining of one or more guardian spirits, considered essential for human life. *Compare* SHAMANISM; VISION QUEST.

**demon**. A malevolent superhuman power. The term comes from the Greek DAIMON, but may be used appropriately in many other cultural contexts.

**Dendera**. The capital city of the 6th Nome (district) of Upper Egypt; centre of the worship of HATHOR, whose impressive temple (1st century BCE) still stands. It is known in Greek as Tentyra.

**Deng**. One of the many manifestations of JOK; an important Dinka **divinity** (southern Sudan), rain god and 'ancestor and protector of the Dinka' (Lienhardt 1961: 90f).

**Deoband Seminary**. Located in Uttar Pradesh, India, the seminary (or *dār al-ʿulūm*, 'House of Sciences' as it is known) was founded by Ḥajji Muḥammad ʿAbid Husayn and Mawlawi Muḥammad Qāsim who was appointed in first principal in 1867. It has since attained an acknowledged place among the best-known Muslim religious institutions of instruction, where the teaching of Quran'ic commentary (TAFSĪR), Prophetic tradition (ḤADĪTH), law (FIQH), theology (KALĀM) and philosophy are offered following the tradition established by the reforming spirit of Shāh Wali Allāh (*d* 1762) of Dehli. The seminary's aim to produce graduates of sound religious character who could assume positions of leadership in the community implicitly meant that some would adopt political postures as well; the staff remained in India following the formation of Pakistan as a Muslim state in 1947, suspicious of the political motives of its founder, Muḥammad ʿAlī Jinnah (*d* 1948). (Robinson 1988, Metcalf 1982).

**Dep**. *See* WADJET.

**dependent origination**. *See* PRATĪTYA-SAMUTPĀDA.

**dependent variable**. A factor in a social system, the specific significance of which varies in accordance with other factors which are presumed to be determinative. It is debatable, and a matter for investigation in particular cases, whether religion as a sociocultural factor is dependent on other factors (e.g. economic ones) or whether it is an independent variable which itself has an effect on economic activity.

**Derwish** *See* DARWĪSH.

**design arguments for the existence of God**. A standard designation for any theistic proof attempting to argue analogically from evidence of regularity and purpose in the world to the existence of an intelligent being who is responsible for the orderly goal-directedness of the universe considered as a whole. Some examples, also called 'physico-theological arguments' (Kant), emphasize orderliness; others, also called 'teleological arguments', stress adaptiveness of particular things to specific purposes within the universe. Design arguments are possibly the oldest, most persistent and most widespread types of proof for the existence of God (or gods). They are prevalent in Indian philosophy (e.g. Śaṃ kara and Madhva amongst Vedānta systems, Udayana and Gaṅgeśa within the Nyāya-Vaiśeṣika tradition) as well as in both ancient and modern Western philosophy. Anticipated by the pre-socratics (e.g. Anaximander, Heraclitus, Anaxagoras) and made explicit by Socrates (Xenophon, *Memorabilia*), such arguments were employed to good effect by Plato (*Laws*) and Aristotle (*On Philosophy* – now lost – as cited in Cicero, *On the Nature of the Gods*). They became favourite arguments amongst the Stoics (Dragona-Monachou, 1976). Arguments from design are implicit in the Hebrew Bible (Psalm 19) and in the Apocrypha (*Wisdom of Solomon* 13), as well as in the Qur'an (*sūra* 2). Within rabbinical tradition, an argument from design was offered as an informal proof in a *midrash* by Rabbi Akiba: 'Just as a house makes known the builder and a garment makes known the weaver and a door makes known the carpenter, so the world makes known the Holy One, Blessed be He, Who created it.' (*Sefer Ha-aggada*) Arguments from design flourished in medieval Christianity, both Eastern and Western, having gained approval by John of Damascus (*On the Orthodox Faith*) and Thomas Aquinas (*Summa theologiae*; *Summa contra gentiles*) alike. Such arguments are capable of being expressed in terms of either mechanical or organic models. Mechanical versions experienced widespread popularity in and after the work of Leibniz and Newton, not least amongst the deists (*compare* DEISM). Robert Boyle was apparently the first to use the analogy between the workings of the universe and those of a clock, even though this analogy is more popularly associated with William Paley's *Natural Theology*. Organic versions of the argument, regularly used alongside mechanical ones (see Paley and, before him, Leonardus Lessius, *On the Providence of God and the Immortality of the Soul*), have been thought by many to have been made untenable by the discoveries of Darwin (e.g. Dawkins 1986). Significant critics of arguments from design have included the 11th-century Vedānta philosopher Rāmānuja (see his commentary on the *Brahmā-Sūtra*), and – belatedly – the 18th-century European philosophers David Hume (*Dialogues concerning Natural Religion*) and Immanuel Kant (*Critique of Pure Reason*). Recent proponents of arguments from design include Richard Swinburne (Swinburne 1977). *See also* ARGUMENTS FOR THE EXISTENCE OF GOD.

**determinism**. The theory that all events, including human actions, are determined by their CAUSES, so that we are not free (in the sense of being able to act in more than one way in the same situation).

**deus ex machina** (Latin: 'God out of the machine [i.e. any artificial contrivance for performing work]'). A common characterization for any attempt artificially to introduce 'God' as an explanatory hypothesis to supplement or correct existing scientific knowledge in order to solve the inherent deficiencies of a theory or explanation (*see* GOD OF THE GAPS). The phrase was originally used in reference to the custom at the critical moment in Greek tragedies of bringing God on stage from somewhere out of sight (*ex machina*) in order to resolve the apparently insoluble difficulties of the plot.

**deus otiosus** (Latin). A deity, usually in a polytheistic frame of reference, who has no apparent function and who is therefore presumed to be, or to have become, otiose or redundant as far as the arrangements of life are concerned. *See*, for example, MULUNGU; EL; NUM-TUREM.

**deus sive natura** (Latin: 'God or nature'). A phrase used by and commonly associated with Baruch Spinoza (1632–97) to suggest that it does not matter whether one calls the ABSOLUTE 'God' or 'Nature', since in either case the same infinite substance is being named. This position is often termed (mainly by its opponents) PANTHEISM.

**Deutero-Isaiah**. A designation of an anonymous figure of the Jewish Exile, the author of *Isaiah* 40–55 (probably including the SERVANT SONGS). Perhaps the high-point in creative theology in early Judaism, he declares liberation for the exiles in Babylon in a powerful mélange of cosmogonic and redemptive themes, pointing to a new Exodus which will eclipse the old, asserting uncompromisingly the monotheistic nature of YAHWEH, whom he identifies (possibly for the first time – see Barker 1987: 170f.) with the Canaanite EL. (Stuehlmuller 1970; Blenkinsopp 1988). *See also* TRITO-ISAIAH.

**Deuteronomic School**. A group in ISRAEL who championed the exclusive cult of *Yahweh* in the 8th century BCE (compiling early parts of *Deuteronomy*). The influence of the school spread to JUDAH after the destruction of Samaria.

**Deuteronomistic History**. The influence of the DEUTERONOMIC SCHOOL in JUDAH after 721 BCE culminated in a history written in Josiah's reign (*c*.620–609 BCE) representing him as a second David. A second edition written *c*.560 BCE sets the whole history in an exilic perspective, with national destruction regarded as the inexorable outcome of national sin, the final form being the book of *Deuteronomy* as a thematic programme. (Noth 1981; Nelson 1981; Friedman 1981: 1–43; Provan 1988).

**deva**. *See* AGNI.

**deva** (Sanskrit). A type of celestial being in Indian mythology. Sometimes specific beings such as Brahmā are described as devas, but at other times such large numbers are referred to that they lose all individuality. In Buddhist mythology devas frequently play the role of mediators or prompters, but like humans and other living beings they are subject to rebirth. *Compare* DEWATA.

**dēvālē** (Sinhalese: 'shrine'). In Sri Lanka a Buddhist shrine to a god or gods. The chief priest of a *dēvālē* is called *Basnāyaka Nilamē*.

**devas**. *See* ASURAS, ṚGVEDA.

**Devi**. *See* BRAHMAN, PURANAS, ŚAKTI.

**Devi-bhakti**. *See* ŚAKTISM.

**devotio moderna** (Latin: 'modern devotion'). A general term, referring to a broad movement to deepen religious life among priests and laity outside the religious orders in the late Middle Ages, centring on the Netherlands. A famous representative work was *The Imitation of Christ* by Thomas à Kempis. *See also* BRETHREN OF THE COMMON LIFE.

**Dewaruci**. A Javanese goddess, a prominent character in a poem of the same name reflecting old-Javanese mysticism, the most famous story of the WAYANG repertoire (Soebardi 1975).

**dewata** (Indonesian, from Sanskrit, *deva*: 'goddess'). In Indonesian traditional religions a lower order of gods, often female deities or godlike beings (Stöhr & Zoetmulder 1965). *Compare* DEVA.

**Dewi Sri**. An Indian-derived spirit or goddess of rice integrated into Javanese traditional beliefs, 'favouring both human procreation and agricultural fertility' (Akkeren 1970: 13). (Geertz 1960a; Stöhr 1976).

**dGe lugs pa**. A major school of Tibetan Buddhism founded on the basis of the reformed teaching of Tsong kha pa (1357–1419) and supported massively in the 17th century by the political rulers of Mongolia. The dGe lugs pa is commonly referred to in English as the Yellow Hat Sect, and the traditional school from which it was distinguished became known as the Red Hat Sect.

**Dhamma**. *See* DHARMA.

**dhanb**. *See* KHATĪA.

**Dharma** (Sanskrit: 'bearer', 'law', 'condition', 'phenomenon', 'thing') [Pāli: *Dhamma*]. In Brahmanism, the natural law of the universe. *Dharma*, depending on context, has many different meanings, all based on the root-meaning of dhr=to bear, to sustain. In a religious context it means doctrine, in a legal context law, in a grammatical context a characteristic of a word, in a sectarian context the peculiar customs of a sect etc. In Buddhism, the conditioned dependencies (PRATĪTYA-SAMUT-PĀDA) and regularities of the phenomena in the universe; indicating the ultimate constituent parts when spelled (in English) with a lower-case initial letter. With a capital letter (*Dharma*), the term generally denotes the Buddhist teaching, according to which all the phenomena of the conditioned world, both bodily and mental, are impermanent (ANITYA), without any separate enduring self or soul (ĀTMAN) and liable to suffering and unease (DUḤKHA). In *Saṃyutta-nikāya* (XXII 15:1) this is explained as follows: 'Body, O monks, is impermanent. What is impermanent that is liable to suffering. What is suffering that is void of the self. What is void of the self that is not mine, I am not it, it is not my self.' The occasion when Gautama BUDDHA taught for the first time is known in the canonical scriptures as the 'First Turning of the Wheel of Dharma' (*Dharmacakrapravartana*).

**dharma-cakra**. *See* CAKRA.

**Dharmacakrapravartana**. *See* DHARMA, FOUR NOBLE TRUTHS.

**dharmakāya**. *See* TRIKĀYA.

**dhawq** (Arabic: 'taste', 'foretaste'). A term much used by Muslim mystics, the ṢŪFĪS, to denote the endurance and directness of Heart-knowledge as opposed to mind-knowledge or sense-knowledge. This inner 'taste' escapes the constraints of space, time and other earthly conditions.

**dhikr** (Arabic). The ṢŪFĪ ceremony of worship, of a different nature in each order, the principal element being the remembrance (*dhikr*), by repetition, of the name of ALLĀH.

**dhimmī** (Arabic). In Islām, a 'protected person'; collectively referred to as *ahl al-dhimma*, members of other scriptural or revealed religions (e.g. Christians and Jews) to whom the Muslim community extended its protection in return for their acknowledgement of Islām's dominion over them.

**dhyāna** (Sanskrit: 'meditation') [Pāli: *jhāna*] A Buddhist term denoting both meditation exercises on concentrating the mind and states attained by those exercises. The term occurs in Chinese as CHAN and in Japanese as ZEN.

**Di**. *See* SHE AND TUDI.

**diaconikon** (Greek). That part of a Greek Orthodox church which lies to the right of the sanctuary, but behind the ICONOSTASIS, and in which the deacons are responsible for the sacramental vessels and liturgical books required for services. The equivalent in western churches is the SACRISTY.

**dialectic**. Originally, dialectic argument was a form of discourse for the logical development of an idea through questions and answers. Some medieval Muslim and Christian scholars employed the technique in a formal way to articulate and defend their respective theological positions against opponents. In the 19th century, however, Hegel (*see* HEGELIANISM) identifies it as a method of human thinking about reality, originating with Heraclitus and Zeno. According to this method, reason, in its attempt to reach the highest truth, posits a thesis which in turn generates its own antithesis; from the tension between these two there emerges as a further step in the dialectic a synthesis that reconciles them. European thinkers such as Kierkegaard and Marx, in reaction to Hegel's thought, employed the same method as a corrective in their interpretations of human existence and history, thus increasing the prominence of the term as indicative of a style for representing and articulating thought about reality. Among neo-Reformed theologians influenced by Kierkegaard, the term gained further prominence as a way through which the contradictions and tensions of human existence are preserved in the interpretation of the human predicament. In Asia, although the term itself is not traditional, the adversative style of argument, as an instrument in the elucidatism of truth, has been widely current, especially in Buddhist contexts, whether in MĀDHYAMIKA philosophy or in ritualized form in the training of Tibetan Buddhist monks.

**dialectical theology**. A type of theology initiated by Swiss theologian Karl Barth which seeks to formulate the meaning of Christian faith by a critical juxtaposition of 'the Word of God', i.e. revelation, and human efforts to apprehend the divine. Dialectical theology may be distinguished from fundamentalism in that the method is turned on the literal text of the Bible itself. In general, however, NATURAL THEOLOGY is rejected.

**Diamond Maṇḍala**. *See* MAṆḌALA.

**Diana**. An early Roman forest divinity, later associated with the Greek ARTEMIS. Her temple on the Aventine Hill was an important political centre in archaic Rome.

**Diancecht**. Celtic doctor-god who in Irish mythology was said to possess the magic spring which brought back to life those who fell in battle.

**diaspora** (Greek). The Jewish communities of the dispersion. The earliest recorded deportation of people from Palestine (Israel) took place *c.*721 BCE, under Assyrian attacks. Deportations to Babylon (the EXILE) took place from Judah in 597, 586 (following the destruction of the Jerusalem temple) and 582 BCE. The ELEPHANTINE community in Upper Egypt may date from the 7th century. While some exiles returned to Judah following Cyrus' conquest of Babylon, many remained, and there were continued deportations and slave-trading under Persian, Greek and Roman rule (M. Smith 1987, 53, 179). After the Babylonian Exile the second major disaster leading to a dispersion of Jewish population was the destruction of the second Temple at Jerusalem in 70 CE. Thus, the overseas population, from Italy to Iran, probably always outnumbered the domestic population and this had profound implications for developments in belief and practice. (Ackroyd 1968; Oded 1977: 480–88).

**Diatessaron**. A single harmonized narrative of the gospels originally composed by the apologist Tatian in the 2nd century CE, probably in Greek, but apart from a tiny papyrus fragment now only known in Arabic and Latin translations.

**Didache**. A very early, possibly 1st century, Christian work on church practice and morals, the full title being *The Teaching* (*didache*) *of the Lord through the Twelve Apostles*. *See also* APOSTOLIC FATHERS

**Didascalia Apostolorum**. A work on church practice and discipline, purporting to be the 'teachings of the apostles'. It probably dates from the 3rd century CE, was originally written in Greek but is now only extant in Syriac and, fragmentarily, in Latin. *See also* DIDACHE.

**Didyma**. The location of a temple of APOLLO near Miletus in Asia Minor, where a priestess uttered ORACLES and a pan-Hellenic festival was held each year.

**Dies irae** (Latin: 'the day of wrath'). A portion of the liturgical MASS for the dead in western Christianity, which takes its name from its opening words.

**Dieva Deli**. *See* SAULES MEITA.

**Dievas**. *See* DIEVS.

**Dievs**. Baltic sky god and creator. He is believed to live the life of a wealthy farmer on the mountain of heaven, occasionally riding down to earth on one of his many horses to assure agricultural prosperity on earth by actively participating in the work of the farmers. He is also one of the deities who determine human fate (*see* LAIMA). Dievs is his Latvian name; the Lithuanian equivalent is *Dievas*, the old Prussian *Deivas*, from the common Indoeuropean root *diēu*, 'the heavens'.

**difference**. A key term for poststructuralist thinkers such as Deleuze, Lyotard and Derrida. Its prominence derives from two sources. First, the linguistics of Ferdinand de Saussure, who claimed that language is a formal system of relations, in which words only signify because of their positional difference from other words, not by virtue of any inherent relation to a referential content (Saussure 1985). Second, the philosophies of Henri Bergson (Bergson 1911) and Martin Heidegger, which by foregrounding temporality and creative change, called into question the traditional western ontological subordination of difference to the categorical classification of 'identities'. In the case of Gilles Deleuze (who appeals to earlier forebears, such as the Plato of *The Sophist*, Duns Scotus, Spinoza and Kant) the positive assertion of difference is opposed not just to any totalizing inventory of Being, but also to Hegelian dialectics, in which the 'negative' moment of differential distinction turns out to be merely a ruse of the ultimately self-identical (Deleuze 1990a,b). *See also* EXTERIORITY; NIHILISM; POSTSTRUCTURALISM; REPETITION.

**diffusionism**. The theory that culture, and hence religion as an aspect of culture, derived from a particular cradle of civilization such as Egypt (*compare* PAN-EGYPTIANISM) or Mesopotamia, and spread from there to other regions of the world. While there has evidently been a significant diffusion of leading religious ideas from several important centres of civilization such as China, India and the Ancient Near East, modern knowledge does not permit a comprehensive, integrated, diffusionist theory of the history of religions along a single line of development.

**Dīgha Nikāya.** *See* NIKĀYA.

**dīn**. *See* (Arabic). The term used in Islām for religion in general; the domain of divine prescriptions concerning acts of worship and everything involved in the spiritual life. According to various contexts or etymologies, *dīn* signifies obligation, direction, submission and retribution, all senses overlapping when God (ALLĀH) is the referent.

For example, the equivalence of *dīn* and ISLĀM is seen in the Qur'ānic verse, 'This day I have perfected your religion [*dīn*] and completed my favour to you and chosen as your religion *al-islām* [submission to Allāh].' (5.3) *See also* DAWLA; DUNYĀ; ĀKHIRA; YAWM AL-DĪN.

**diocese**. The area of jurisdiction of a BISHOP.

**Dionysia**. *See* DIONYSIAN MYSTERIES.

**Dionysian mysteries** The Greek god DIONYSOS (in his capacity as god of wine also known as Bacchus) has an ambivalent character which is difficult to reconcile with the rest of the Pantheon gods. Festivals in his honour held in spring and autumn (Dionysia) included processions parading a large wooden phallus and cultic performances in which the origins of drama are to be perceived. Festivals taking place at night in the countryside during which participants wore special costumes, danced to flute music and waved staffs garlanded with ivy and wine leaves, drank wine and ate raw game, may be regarded as falling into the category of mystery religions. In the ecstatic climax the participants experienced Dionysos taking possession of them, leading to prophesying and speaking in tongues. The unusual activities of the Dionysos festivals, above all the egalitarian participation of women, children and slaves, brought them ridicule and criticism (Euripides, Aeschylos, Livy). In Rome their appearance met initially with strong resistance, and in 186 BCE they were officially prohibited. However, the only frescos believed to represent various stages of the mysteries are of later date in the Villa Item at Pompey. The community of Dionysos worshippers formed a kind of church with a priesthood (including women and children), sacred writings, social aspirations and a firm belief in life after death. The latter is indicated by the objects buried with corpses, although the influence of Orphism (*see* ORPHIC MYSTERIES) should not be overlooked here (Nilsson 1985).

**Dionysos**. Ancient Greek god of wine and intoxication and thus ECSTASY, the son of ZEUS and Semele, a mortal mother, and the one who gives joy and pleasure to human beings. *See also* DIONYSIAN MYSTERIES.

**Dioscuri**. Castor and Polydeuces, heavenly and heroic twins, loved by ZEUS, whose exploits are recounted in myth and poetry.

**di-polar theism**. *See* PANENTHEISM; PROCESS PHILOSOPHY/THEOLOGY.

**Dipolieia**. An Athenian festival consisting of a civic procession, offering sacrificial grain, and the group slaying of an ox, followed by a ceremonial meal, and thus marking a connection between agriculture, SACRIFICE and social institutions.

**Disciples of Christ**. A major Protestant church organization in the United States and Canada founded in 1812 in Bethany, Virginia, by Irish-born Alexander Campbell. Campbell founded Bethany College in 1840 and was a prolific religious writer.

**dispensation**. A relaxation of ecclesiastical law on the authority of the Pope, mainly applied in matters of clerical discipline and marital arrangements.

**Dispersion of the Jews**. *See* DIASPORA.

**divination**. The identification of hidden reasons for personal or social problems, or of the likely outcome of events, by means of special techniques such as throwing bones (Africa), by interpreting the cracks caused by heat in tortoise shells (China), or by 'reading' the livers and entrails of sacrificial victims (Ancient Near East). *See also* IFA; YURUG; OMPHALOMANCY; ORACLE; AUGURS; HARUSPICES; ALTOMISAYOQ; AYAHUASCA. At an earlier period of the English language 'divination' also meant 'making into a god', but it is less confusing to refer to this as 'deification'.

**divine**. A word which has been used confusingly both as an adjective, meaning godly, and as a noun, referring to a clergyman, as in the expression 'an Anglican divine'.

**Divine Life Society**. An organization formed in 1937 by Swāmi Śivānanda in Rishikesh. Renowned for the stress it places on *nām saṇkīrtan*, singing the names of God, it has become popular both in India and amongst diaspora Hindus in Africa. (Mangalvadi 1977).

**Divine Light Mission**. Although Śrī Hans Jī Mahārāj first taught meditation on the Divine Light and Holy Name in the 1930s in the Lahore region, the main period of growth and institutionalization of this movement in India and the West followed the enlightenment in 1966 of his son, Balyogeshwar, later known as 'Gurū Mahārāj Jī', who became the spiritual focus of the movement. The movement's meditation is known as 'knowledge'. (Mangalvadi 1977).

**divinity**. Either the quality of being divine (that is being God, or being a god or goddess) or a synonym for DEITY.

**Diyavadana Nilame**. *See* DAḶADĀ MĀLIGĀVA.

**djed pillar**. An ancient Egyptian sign, perhaps originally representing a tree or post, but later associated with the concepts of stability and the resurrection of OSIRIS.

**docetism** (from Greek, *dokein*: 'to seem'). In Christian theology, the view that Christ merely seemed to be a man of flesh and blood and that his sufferings and death were illusory. This view, assuming a DUALISM of divine spirit and earthly matter, and often linked with GNOSTICISM, was attacked by Christian theologians from the 2nd century onwards. The latter stressed the radical incarnation of Christ in the world, thus laying the foundations of the CHRISTOLOGY eventually accepted as orthodox.

Transferred to another context, the term has been used more recently to refer to a similar teaching found mainly in MAHAYANA Buddhist texts such as the LOTUS SUTRA and the LALITAVISTARA, but also in the non-Mahayana MAHAVASTU. According to this, the birth and subsequent life of the Buddha was a transcendental contrivance, not subject to the rigours of ordinary existence, and played out for the benefit of mankind.

**dòdànni**. *See* DÒDO.

**dodem**. *See* TOTEM.

**dòdo** (Hausa; plural, *dòdànni*). Monster, evil spirit. In the non-Hausa, non-Muslim areas of northern Nigeria the word is used for a type of men's cult in which masquerades, voice disguisers or musical instruments are used to represent a spiritual being.

**Dodona**. The location of an ORACLE of ZEUS in northern Greece, focusing on oak trees and birds, where petitioners sought advice on personal matters by writing their requests on lead tablets.

**dogma**. An established article or statement of faith. In the Roman Catholic Church such a statement is believed to be without error if it has been declared EX CATHEDRA by the POPE.

**Dome of the Rock**. The famous mosque in Jerusalem erected in 691 CE over a rock from which Muslims believe the Prophet Muḥammad ascended to heaven (*see* MIR'ĀJ). It is a symbol, too, that Jerusalem was from early times regarded by Muslims as a sacred place, third behind MECCA and MADINA.

**dominus vobiscum** (Latin: 'The Lord be with you [plural]'). A very ancient liturgical greeting with the response *et cum spiritu tuo* ('and with your spirit').

**Donar**. *See* THOR.

**Donation of Constantine**. A document forged in the 8th or 9th centuries purporting to give the Roman POPE (specifically Sylvester I, 314–335) authority over almost the whole known church, not only in Rome and other parts of Italy, but in particular over historic centres of the eastern church such as Antioch, Jerusalem, Alexandria and Constantinople. It was widely influential in the Middle Ages but proven to be spurious in the 15th century.

**Donatism**. A 4th-century North African schism named after the bishop Donatus, which demanded a pure church of MARTYRS and not one which was compromised with the Roman state in time of persecution. The Donatist Church was vigorously criticized by Catholic theologians (including St Augustine) until it finally disappeared in the 8th century.

**dongtian** (Chinese: 'palace-heaven'). Sacred sites distributed throughout China, most of them constituting real caves. There are ten 'major' grottoes and 36 'minor' ones. They are associated with holy mountains and 'immortals' (SHENXIAN) of the Daoist (*see* DAOISM) pantheon of gods. Often only Daoist scriptures were stored in and recovered from those caverns. The 'major' dongtian and some of the 'minor' ones are thought to be linked together underground, forming a sacred network that disseminates QI (odem or pneuma) as a lifegiving element. Dongtian are also related to Chinese concepts of paradise: the world *behind the cave* belongs to an ageless, peaceful society untouched by external wars or internal strife – a theme often alluded to in Chinese medieval utopist literature.

**dōsojin** (Japanese). KAMI of roads and borders. Stone representations of these deities are often found at village borders, mountain passes, crossroads and bridges. *Dōsojin* are believed to protect not only villages from pestilent spirits coming from outside, but also travellers on the road and others in 'transitional' stages. For this reason, the *dōsojin* are sometimes also thought of as a god of children or of easy childbirth.

**double procession**. *See* FILIOQUE.

**doubt**. The opposite of certitude. While modern philosophy, beginning with Descartes, has adopted methodological doubt rather than genuine scepticism as a technique for achieving truth, modern Christianity under Kierkegaard's influence contends that doubt in philosophy cannot be overcome intellectually. It is a form of sickness or mark of the universal human situation which requires the courage of faith. Faith does not remove doubt but takes it as an element into itself. Hence Christian faith requires that some doubt be present at all times. This understanding of doubt as a pathos-filled concern about one's own existence is clearly different from the doubt of the sceptics, who simply doubted in the sense of withholding assent by an act of the will.

**Doukhobours**. A dissenting Russian sect which developed in the 18th century and whose members were banished to Siberia and later (1841) to Transcaucasia. In 1895 a further forced exile on account of their pacifism led many of them to Cyprus and to Canada. They are noted for attempts to set up a separate, ideal Christian community which does not necessarily co-operate with secular authorities. The belief system is notable for emphasizing that God is a principle combining memory, reason and will, dwelling in all and to the highest degree in Jesus Christ.

**doxology** (from Greek, *doxa*: 'glory'). A hymn of glory such as the *Gloria in excelsis deo* . . . ('Glory be to God on high . . .') or the short appendix to psalms in Christian usage beginning 'Glory be to the Father, and to the Son, and to the Holy Ghost . . .'

**Dragon Gate Sect**. *See* QUAN ZHEN SECT

**Dragon King**. In China the dragon is usually regarded as a beneficent being producing rain and representing the fecundating principle in nature. Dragons were imagined as living in lakes and rivers or in the sea. They were worshipped under the name of *Long Wang* [*Lung Wang*] or 'Dragon King'. The dragon is the emblem of the Chinese emperor. Under the influence of Buddhism the idea of harmful dragon-spirits or dragon-demons inhabiting the mountains was also introduced into China.

**drash** (Hebrew). An interpretation of the TORAH.

**dread**. *See* ANGST; NUMINOUS.

**dreydel** (Yiddish). A top inscribed with Hebrew letters on each of its four sides, used by children during the festival of *Ḥanukkah*.

**druid**. Celtic priest who seems to have occupied a position of considerable social power. He led sacrificial, prophetic and other religious ceremonies, was called upon to pass judgement in conflicts and cases of criminal offence and practised herbal medicine connected with magic. The knowledge required for these activities together with religious teaching, including that of the immortality of the soul and its rebirth in a new body, was passed on orally. According to Caesar (in *De Bellico Gallico*), the druids in Gaul held an annual meeting under a single head druid. In Irish texts there is also evidence for a head druid, who advised the king and played a decisive role in the religious divinatory ceremonies held to choose new kings. The theory that the druids were a pre-Celtic institution has not been proved. The word is usually explained as meaning 'very wise' (from the emphatic prefix *dru-* and *uid*, to see or know), although it has also been connected with the Greek *drus* ('oak').

**Drush**. *See* PARDES.

**Druze** [Druse]. A community found today in the mountainous region of Lebanon, southern Syria and northern Israel which originated as an offshoot of a radical SHĪʿA Muslim sect, the ISMĀʿĪLĪS in the 11th century. They do not observe the Islamic injunction to fast nor perform the pilgrimage and they hold to the idea of transmigration of souls, all of which places them outside the mainstream Islamic community. (Makarim 1974).

**dryad**. The spirit of a tree. *Compare* NYMPH.

**dualism**. Any system of religious or philosophical thought which distinguishes sharply between two fundamental principles in terms of which the world is interpreted, typically spirit and matter, good and evil, light and darkness. It is possible to differentiate different kinds of dualism, although these may merge into each in particular historical cases. Thus radical dualism, as in Platonism, some forms of Buddhism, and Manichaeism, assumes two independent original principles. Qualified dualism presupposes one ultimate, original principle out of which in some way a second principle (matter) arose; Gnosticism and some Platonic schools are examples of this. Dialectical or ethical dualism posits two original principles regarded as good and evil or eternal and transient respectively which meet and mingle in a cosmological process. This is met with in Indian, Orphic and Platonic thought. In eschatological dualism the polarity is between two opposing ages in cosmic time, of which one will ultimately prove victorious. This is typical of Zoroastrianism, Manichaeism, Gnosticism, and Jewish and Christian APOCALYPTIC. Finally one may speak of 'pro-cosmic' and 'anti-cosmic' dualism. In the former the cosmos itself is regarded as good, but the evil (material) principle enters the good (spiritual) principle from without, as in Zoroastrianism; whereas in the latter the world, body and matter are defined by the evil principle, that is, good and evil are identified with spirit and with body or matter respectively, as in Gnosticism, Manichaeism and the teaching of the Bogomils and Cathars. Dualistic world-views continue to be influential in science and fiction and also in the ideological articulation of human conflict. In a more general sense 'dual' world-views are present in many mythic traditions, especially in the context of cosmogony and in explanation of the duality of the sexes or the relation between life and death. *Contrast* MONISM.

**Duamutef**. *See* CANOPICJAR

**duḥkha** (Sanskrit: 'unease: [either bodily or mental]') [Pāli: *dukka*]. *Duḥkha* is used as a generic term for 'suffering' in Sanskrit and is also employed by Hindu philosophical systems such as Sāṁkhya to denote 'evil' from which salvation is sought by means of insight or action As a Buddhist term, usually translated 'suffering', it denotes one of the three fundamental characteristics of all phenomenal existence – the other two being impermanence (ANITYA) and no self (ANĀTMAN) – and the first of the FOUR NOBLE TRUTHS: everything is liable to suffering (*duḥkha*).

**dukkha**. *See* DUḤKHA.

**dukun** (Indonesian). In Bahasa Indonesia, as in many other languages of the Malay archipelago, a term designating a person capable of healing, magical practices, divination etc. (Geertz 1960a; Utrecht 1975).

**Dumuzi**. The Sumerian prototype of TAMMUZ.

**Dun-Huang** [Tun-Huang]. A site in northwestern China where caves excavated in modern times have revealed large numbers of paintings and texts, mainly Buddhist.

**dunyā** (Arabic: 'this world'). In Islamic usage, the domain of material life as distinct from the spiritual (DĪN) and, as the opposite correlative of ĀKHIRA (the hereafter).

**Durgā**. One of the names of the Hindu Goddess, alluding to her terrible form in which she killed the buffalo-headed demon. To commemorate this feat *Śāktas* celebrate each year Durgā-pūjā, a string of festivals, which is the major festive season in Bengal. At this occasion images of Durgā are displayed in homes and in public places which are decorated and carried in procession through the streets at the end of the festive season. During Durgāpūjā the *Devī Māhātmyam*, the story of Devī-mahiṣa-asuramardiṇī is being recited. Durgā-pūjā is also the time when married daughters return for an extended visit to their families.

**Durgā-Pūjā**. *See* DURGA.

**dying-and-rising god**. Supposedly vegetation-deities especially in the ancient Near East whose death and resurrection echoes the agricultural year. In no case is this proven. *See also* BAAL; TAMMUZ; ADONIS; ESHMUN.

# E

**Ea**. The Assyro-Babylonian god of fresh water (equivalent to the Sumerian Enki), a fertility god, who saves ATRAHASIS from the FLOOD (Jacobsen 1976: 110–120). *See also* ADAPA.

**Eagle**. In Native American religions, a spirit that often represents either FATHER SUN or the THUNDERBIRDS. In some cultures, Eagle functions as the eyes of Sun. There are many elaborate rituals surrounding Eagle, and eagle feathers are a major ritual accessory, used both as fans and as pendants from other ritual artefacts.

**Earth Mother**. The idea of the earth as mother is widespread, clear examples being found in Native American religions, where the Earth Mother is commonly regarded as the female, cosmic, generative and spiritual force which symbolizes creation, regeneration, nourishment and nurture. Her manifestations include CORN, BEAR, Deer and Bison. In Inuit (Eskimo) religion, the Sea Mother has a similar function. *See also* PACHAMAMA; SWEAT LODGE.

**Easter**. The most important festival in the Christian year, celebrating the resurrection of Jesus Christ, and falling on a Sunday between 21 March and 25 April. Easter is preceded by Holy Week and Lent. *See also* QUINQUAGESIMA.

**Ebionites**. An early Jewish Christian community which, though the documentation is slight, appears to have held to an adoptionist CHRISTOLOGY, emphasizing the descent of the Holy Spirit to Jesus at his baptism rather than supernatural intervention at his birth. *See also* ADOPTIONISM.

**Ebisu**. A KAMI (Shintō deity) worshipped as the protector of basic livelihoods and believed to impart happiness and prosperity, in the city market as the god of merchants and in rural areas as the god of the ricefields. Ebisu belief originated in fishing villages, where he was believed to be the god of abundant catches.

**ecclesiology** (from Greek, *ekklesia*: 'church'). The study or theory of the church. The term is used both with reference to churches as buildings and to the church as a theological concept.

**eclecticism**. The selection of elements from various sources and their juxtaposition in one system of philosophical or religious thought.

**ecstasy**. A change in one's state of consciousness under which an individual is shielded from normal influences from his/her surroundings and instead lives out an intense inner life, which often brings with it strong mystical experiences. Ecstasy can be found in all religions but is cultivated particularly by SHAMANS and by mystics of different kinds (*see* MYSTICISM). Special schools and directions exist in which ecstasy is considered to be a high objective which one should pursue in different ways – through meditation, intensive reading, mortification, dance etc. The methods by which the state of ecstasy is achieved can be analysed psychologically from the perspective of hypnosis or more generally from the viewpoints of the different theories which discuss intensive influence on a human being.

The word 'ecstasy' itself comes from a Greek word meaning the act of moving oneself from one place to another. Most often the movement of the ego from the body to another location is meant. Another term which lies close to the heart of the meaning of ecstasy is 'trance'. Explanations for ecstasy have been sought in, for example, the fields of psychobiology, neurology, depth psychology and social psychology (Holm 1982b). *See also* HITLAHAVUT.

**Ecumenical Council**. A council attended by representatives of the whole church, whose consensus decisions were called 'ecumenical', from the Greek *oikuméne* ('the whole inhabited (earth)'). Their decisions were viewed as normative. Ecumenical Councils recognized by both the Catholic and Orthodox churches were held in Nicaea (325 and 787), Constantinople (381, 553, and 680–1), Ephesus (431) and Chalcedon (451). *See also* COUNCIL OF NICAEA; COUNCIL OF CONSTANTINOPLE; COUNCIL OF CHALCEDON; ARIANISM.

**Ecumenical Movement**. The movement towards unity between the various Christian churches generally considered to have begun at an interdenominational meeting in 1910 known as the Edinburgh Missionary Conference, and currently focused in the World Council of Churches with its headquarters in Geneva. The older spelling 'Oecumenical' reflects the derivation from the Greek term *oikuméne* (see above). *See also* ECUMENICAL COUNCIL.

**Edda**. A collection of anonymous Icelandic poems recorded in the 13th century about the figures and events of Germanic mythology.

**Eden**. The Garden of Paradise in the biblical account of creation and fall of man in *Genesis* 2–3. Although it is often identified with Mesopotamian *edinu* ('riverine plain'), a derivation from *eden* ('delight') symbolizing 'Promised Land' and Jerusalem is more likely. ADAM tilling the garden may be seen as a figure of the king's cultic duties (Wyatt 1988). (Humbert 1940; Och 1988).

**Edfu**. The capital city of the 2nd Nome (district) of Upper Egypt, with a well-preserved temple of HORUS (consort of HATHOR), built between 237 and 57 BCE.

**Edit of Nantes**. *See* HUGUENOTS.

**Edicts of Aśoka**. Aśoka was the third ruler (ruled *c*.269–*c*.230 BCE) in a line of Mauryan Emperors who established the first pan-Indian empire through military conquest. Converted to Buddhism, Aśoka sent monks to all the outlying regions and border countries round India to teach Buddhist *Dharma*, with ambassadors going as far as Egypt and Macedonia. His own son Mahinda was sent to Sri Lanka (Ceylon), as narrated in the Sinhalese chronicle *Mahāvaṃsa*. Aśoka's influence on Buddhism can be studied particularly from the numerous edicts, which were inscribed on stone columns and on rocks, 30 of which have been preserved.

**Edjo**. *See* WADJET.

**Edshu**. *See* ESHU.

**efficacious grace**. A term in Roman Catholic theology indicating assistance from God (grace) to which co-operative assent is given by the human will such that a spiritual effect is in fact brought about.

**Egbe Serafu**. *See* SERAPHIM SOCIETY.

**Egbo**. The name generally applied (in English) in the Crossriver area of Nigeria and the Cameroons (especially among the Efik and Ekoi) to graded men's associations which were formerly very powerful. The term is probably derived from *ekpo* ('the dead') in Crossriver languages. A leading symbol of the cult is the leopard, *ekpe* among the Efik group of the Ibibio people. The latter name (*ekpe*) is applied to similar associations among the Ekoi and the Crossriver Igbo. (Talbot 1969).

**Egúngún**. A masquerade cult of the dead among the Yoruba of southwestern Nigeria. The Egúngún, who performs a dance, is costumed and masked to represent his embodiment of the spirit of a deceased person who is visiting his descendants (Awolalu 1979).

**Egyptian religion**. The history of ancient Egyptian religion falls into the following main periods: Old Kingdom (*c*.3100–2200 BCE), Middle Kingdom (*c*.1991–1786 or, more widely defined, *c*.2134–1660) the New Kingdom (1567–1085) and subsequent dynasties largely under foreign rule. Particularly important sources for knowledge of religious belief and ritual for these periods are the PYRAMID TEXTS, the COFFIN TEXTS and the BOOK OF THE DEAD, respectively. Archaeological evidence in the form of the PYRAMIDS, other tombs (*see* MASTABA TOMB; NECROPOLIS) and temples (*see* ISLAND OF CREATION) is also of great significance, as too is the ancient Egyptian reliance on writing (*see* HIEROGLYPHS) as opposed to oral tradition.

Egyptian religion was dominated politically by the notion of power as expressed in the massive architecture of mausolea and temples alike; geographically and cosmologically by the south–north course of the Nile and the east–west progression of the sun from one bank to the other in mainly clear skies; and popularly by the progressive extension or 'democratization' of arrangements for the afterlife and welfare of the dead, especially in association with the OSIRIS myth. In general conceptions of divinity were polytheistic (but *see* ATEN) and frequently THEREOMORPHIC.

The 'liberation' of Egypt from Persian rule by the Greek Alexander 'the Great' led to the establishment of the Ptolemy dynasty (323–30 BCE). This led to a certain amount of Hellenistic influence, visible in late temple architecture, while Egyptian deities such as ISIS and OSIRIS became popular in the wider Hellenistic world. Later the old Egyptian religion was displaced by COPTIC CHRISTIANITY and by ISLĀM (both religions leaving their mark, for example, on the great temple site of LUXOR), only to be rediscovered by the European romantic imagination and ultimately to be refunctionalized as a mass tourist attraction in today's largely Islamic Egypt. *See also especially* COSMOGONY; MUMMY; WISDOM LITERATURE.

**Eight Gods**. *See* COSMOGONY.

**Eightfold Path**. *See* FOUR NOBLE TRUTHS, SAMĀDHI.

**Eight Precepts** *See* ŚĪLA, TEN PRECEPTS.

**Eileithya**. The ancient Greek goddess of birth.

**EIS**. A philosophical system developed by Polish atheist philosopher Andrzej Nowicki (*b* 1919), incorporating erganthropy (E), incontrology (I) and spaciocentrism (S). See various articles in the Polish journal for the science of religion *Euhemer*.

**eklektes**. *See* ELECTI; MANICHAEISM.

**ekpo**. *See* EGBO.

**El**. A generic term for deity throughout the Semitic world (also occurring as *ilu*), and evidently the designation of an ancient high god in Mesopotamia. In Ugarit the generic use is continued (f. *ilt*: 'goddess'), but it also designates the chief god of the pantheon (Ilu, commonly written El).

El was an ancient moon-god, husband of the sun-goddess ASHERAH, and father of the lesser deities of the pantheon. Some scholars have supposed that he was deposed, and remained merely as a *deus otiosus* (Pope 1955, 1977; Oldenburg 1969) but he undoubtedly remained in active control of the world through his agents (Parker 1977; Peterson & Woodward 1977; L'Heureux 1979).

As a Hebrew designation, El (plural: *Elim*) is a generic biblical term for divinity, occurring for example in El-Elyon, 'God-Most-High'. *See also* ELOHIM.

El is to be discerned behind YAHWEH (Cross 1973: 73; Wyatt 1979a), who may have developed from a local form of this widely recognized deity (Wyatt 1983).

**electi** (Latin: 'chosen ones'). A designation of the Manichaean priestly class as distinguished from the laity, known as *auditores* ('hearers') or catechumens (Greek: *katechumenoi*). The Greek equivalent for *electi* is *eklektes*. *Compare* MANICHAEISM.

**election**. Ancient societies commonly represented human beings as 'children' of their god(s). In the Hebrew Bible the election or choice of the people of Israel for this status is an important metaphor of the relationship with YAHWEH (*Deuteronomy* 32.8–9; *Hosea* 11.1). The corollary is that judgement is passed on disobedience (*Amos* 3.1, 4.4–12; *Deuteronomy passim*).

**Elegba**. *See* ESHU.

**El-Elyon**. *See* EL.

**Eleousa** (Greek). A type of ICON emphasizing tenderness between Mary and the infant Jesus and anticipation of the compassion felt by Mary at the crucifixion.

**Elephantine**. Island at Aswan in Upper Egypt, home of a Jewish mercenary garrison, perhaps from the 7th century BCE. They had a temple, destroyed in the late 5th century, and the cult was apparently polytheistic (Porten 1968). *See also* COSMOGONY.

**Eleusinian mysteries**. The oldest and best known of the secret cults of the Greeks, probably developed from a pre-Hellenistic tribal cult with initiation rites and agrarian religiosity. There is evidence of prehistoric habitation of Eleusis, but it was not until its incorporation into Athens in the 7th century that the cult took on panhellenic significance, which under the Roman emperors (some of whom were initiated) extended as far as Rome. The cult came to an end when it was destroyed in 395 CE by the Gothic king Alarich.

The mythical background to the mysteries is provided by the story of DEMETER and Kore (or Persephone), who as mother and daughter exemplify the experience of loss, or death, pain, quest and recovery, in other words the fate of life. The rituals took place every year, the 'Lesser Mysteries' in spring and the 'Greater Mysteries' in autumn from 16–20 September, and consisted of sacrifices, bathing, fasting and processions. The central event was the nocturnal ceremony accessible only to the initiated (*Epoptes*). Details of this ceremony are uncertain and difficult to explain, but it is known that dramatic performances of the adventures of the two goddesses, including their reunion after Kore's abduction by Hades, served to strengthen the believers' faith in a life after death (i.e. after entering the earth).

Platonic, stoic and gnostic interpretations of the rites began in early antiquity and have contributed towards establishing their 'timeless' substance. (Bianchi 1976; Burkert 1987).

**Eleusis**. *See* ELEUSINIAN MYSTERIES.

**elima**. *See* MANA.

**elixir**. According to the Indian linguist and chemist Mahdihassan (*Journal of the University of Bombay*, 20, 1951) a word of Chinese origin. In Daoist tradition (*see* DAOISM) it was refined and concocted according to special recipes incorporating cinnabar, base metals, minerals, numinous mushrooms etc. Elixirs were the result of *waidan* (Daoist alchemy: *see* NEIDAN) practices of Daoist adepts that sought to attain LONGEVITY for themselves or for sponsors of these costly procedures (often Chinese emperors).

**Elkesaism**. Jewish-Christian baptismal sect with dualistic (gnostic) traits, founded by the Prophet Elkasai (Elchasaios, Elxai, i.e. 'hidden power of God'), who appeared about 100 CE in Syria. The sect spread to Rome (*c*.220) and also to Mesopotamia, where Mani was familiar with it during childhood (*c*.220–40).

**Elohim**. Derived from the common Semitic term *ilu* (Hebrew EL, and thus a term for deity; while plural in form, it usually denotes YAHWEH in the Hebrew Bible. On the documentary hypothesis of biblical criticism it was used before the revelation of the divine name in *Exodus* 3 and 6 (Murtonen 1952). The name Elohim stands in contrast to the TETRAGRAMMATON, which was the specific divine name revealed to Moses and the people of Israel. The rabbis equated the former with the aspect of divine justice, and the latter with divine mercy.

**Elysian fields**. *See* ELYSIUM.

**Elysium**. A mythical location at the horizon (Greek: *elysion*), where humans specially beloved by the gods could spend a happy afterlife rather than suffer oblivion, the common lot of humanity. Hence arises the term 'Elysian fields', a place of pleasure. *Contrast* HADES.

**ema** (Japanese). Votive tablets presented at Shintō shrines and many Buddhist temples in Japan. *Ema* were originally pictures of horses (as the name implies) hung before a deity as a substitute for offerings of live horses. Variety in the form and style of the paintings gradually increased, and the works of famous artists began to appear. In modern times innumerable *ema* are offered, representing the hopes and wishes of shrine visitors.

**emanationism**. The doctrine that everything flows from a single, transcendent, supreme, ineffable and absolute Reality.

Akin to PANENTHEISM, which sees in everything an element of the divine, it appears full blown in the writings of Plotinus, which exerted significant influence on medieval Christian, Muslim and Jewish philosophers. Religious emanationism purports, according to gnostic systems, that the material world is the product of an emanation which is evil. In that respect it stands in contrast with the (originally biblical) idea of creation *ex nihilo* (out of nothing) according to which all of God's work is good. *See also* GNOSTICISM; NEO-PLATONISM.

**Ember Days**. Twelve days of fasting or abstinence traditional to western Christianity and associated with prayers for the ordained priesthood. Ember Days are observed in groups of three, falling approximately in the four seasons of the year; this has been taken to suggest a pre-Christian origin.

**Emma-ō**. *See* YAMA.

**empiricism**. The philosophical thesis that all knowledge of matters of fact is based on experience, in contrast to PLATONISM and other philosophies which allow for innate knowledge. Most traditional empiricists equated experience with sense experience, a position which seems to preclude any direct religious knowledge, though allowing for an inferential knowledge of God through NATURAL THEOLOGY. While there may be a sense in which experience does not require to be identified solely with sense-experience, the extension of the term to this wider range of meaning is certainly problematic. *See also* RELIGIOUS EXPERIENCE.

**emunah** (Hebrew). Faith. The Jewish notion of *emunah* is not so much an intellectual belief in the existence of God (which is anyway taken for granted), but a feeling of 'trust' in relationship to God. *Compare* AMEN.

**en**. *See* ENNICHI.

**encyclical**. A letter of the POPE addressed to the whole of the Roman Catholic Church and dealing, normally, with questions of faith or conduct. It is usually referred to by the opening words in Latin. Although the authority of an encyclical is very high it does not in itself fall under the principle of papal INFALLIBILITY except in so far as specific statements are so designated EX CATHEDRA. It is therefore acceptable for Catholic believers to reject the Pope's position on particular points in an encyclical if valid arguments can be advanced to the contrary.

**Enkai** [Ngai]. A dualistically conceived supreme being among the Maasai and some neighbouring peoples in Kenya and Tanzania. The name of this celestial god is connected with the sky – 'black (benevolent) Ngai' – and with rain – 'red (malevolent) Ngai' (Fokken 1916).

**Enlightenment**. An extremely important period in modern European history and thought, comparable in impact to the Renaissance and the Reformation, and falling approximately between 1650 and 1800 CE. During this period there were many thinkers who felt that their minds were being illumined in a significant new way by critical reason (in German *Vernunft*), which was therefore elevated to being the supreme arbiter on all questions of importance. The following reasons may be adduced for this: (a) reaction to the emphasis on faith characteristic of the Reformation; (b) disillusion with religion as a factor in the strife of the Thirty Years War, and (c) the success of reason in pushing forward the boundaries of mathematics and natural sciences which encouraged Descartes to attempt to put metaphysics on the same footing. Nearly all forms of human activity – politics (especially Church-State relations), economics and social structures – were subjected to rational examination and found in many respects to be wanting. The extreme form of this in practical politics culminated in the French Revolution of 1789, in which religion was disestablished and reason symbolically enthroned in its place. Religion in particular, being the traditional locus of authority, was subjected to analysis by critical reason in a sustained philosophical process which in many ways has continued to the present day.

The outstanding figures here were David Hume (a seminal work being his *Dialogues concerning Natural Religion*) and Immanuel Kant (key works being his *Critique of Natural Reason* and *Critique of Practical Reason*). Other important figures were, in Germany, Reimarus, Lessing and Herder, and in France, Rousseau, Diderot and Voltaire. Some Enlightenment thinkers were inimical to religion (e.g. Voltaire) and some were favourably inclined (e.g. Kant and Lessing), but they shared the basic assumption that reason rather then the mere acceptance of dogmatic authority or supernatural miracle should be the arbiter in such questions. Also important in the Enlightenment was the recognition that the specific forms of religion are historically and culturally conditioned, which further undermined the claims of dogmatic authority. *See also* AUFKLÄRUNG; DEISM; GALLICANISM; HASKALAH' ILLUMINATION; KAJO; WOLFENBÜTTEL FRAGMENTS.

**Enlil** (Sumerian: 'Lord Wind'). An Assyro-Babylonian storm-god (*see also* ADAD, DAGAN), a fertility and royal deity also known as instigator of the flood (Lambert & Millard 1969; Jacobsen 1976: 98–104).

**ennichi** (Japanese). A day (*nichi*) on which a special relation (*en*) is believed to obtain between a specific buddha, *bodhisattva* or *kami* (deity) and his devotees. Examples are: Amida Buddha, 15th of each month; Kannon Bosatsu, 18th of the month. Devotees often make a point of visiting the appropriate temple or shrine on this day of connection in order to gain MERIT and other benefits.

**Enoch**. The legendary figure of *Genesis* 4.17f. and 5.18–24 became the type of the seer in the Hellenistic period, ascending to heaven, being initiated into royal mysteries, and being given information of the eschatological divine-messianic triumph. Three recensions of Enochic literature survive – *1 Enoch* (Ethiopic), *2 Enoch* (Slavonic) and *3 Enoch* (Hebrew). This reflects important non-rabbinic Jewish currents of thought, and lies behind many New Testament issues. (Alexander 1977; Knibb 1978; Collins 1978; Suter 1979; Black *et al* 1985; Barker 1987, 1988). *See also* APOCALYPTIC; PSEUDEPIGRAPHA.

**Enosh**. *See* MANDAEANS.

**Enryakuji**. The headquarters of the Japanese Tendai school of Buddhism (*see* TENDAI-SHŪ) founded in 785 CE by Saichō. Located on Mount Hiei near Kyōto, the numerous monks were known to descend on this former Japanese captial city with armed attacks. Much of the temple complex was razed in 1571 by the warlord Oda Nobunaga.

**ens realissimum** (Latin: 'the most real being'). A characterization of God, as Absolute Being, possessing all possible perfections. In Kant's critical philosophy, the phrase is allowed as legitimate if it designates a 'transcendental ideal', i.e. the concept of primordial, highest, most perfect being; but it becomes illicit if the ideal is hypostatized, i.e. if we think that some *object* must correspond to that *concept*. 'We are left entirely without knowledge as to the existence of a being of such outstanding preëminence.' (*Critique of Pure Reason*, B607) Such a being, according to Kant, is 'a mere fiction'. *See also* 'AS IF' PHILOSOPHY.

**Enuma Elish**. The Assyro-Babylonian creation myth. Drawing on Sumerian and perhaps Amorite sources, it recounts the theogony, the fight between MARDUK and TIAMAT, the creation of the world and man. It ends with a hymn reciting Marduk's titles. (*See also* AKITU.) (See Langdon 1923; Labat 1935; Heidel 1942; Jacobsen 1968, 1976: 167–91; Black 1981.Text in Pritchard 1969: 60–72, 501–3.) *Ashur* was the parallel deity involved in Assyrian versions (Van Driel 1969: 162–65).

**Epic of Gilgamesh**. Gilgamesh was a legendary king of Uruk, a city on the Euphrates. A number of poems, legends and folktales grew up round him, culminating in the heroic epic tale preserved on twelve tablets in the library of Ashurbanipal in Nineveh. This Assyrian version may be supplemented, where damaged, by survivals in Old Babylonian, Hittite and Sumerian.

Gilgamesh ('cultured man') behaves antisocially: his libido knows no bounds. A 'wild man', Enkidu, is made to tame him. Enkidu is tamed (made cultured) by a temple harlot, comes to Uruk, challenges Gilgamesh and wrestles with him. Gilgamesh wins the match, the two become fast friends; they journey to the Cedar Forest in north-west Syria, where they kill the guardian, Humbaba (or Huwawa). Ishtar attempts to seduce Gilgamesh, who rejects her. She demands the 'Bull of Heaven' to punish his temerity, but the friends kill it, Enkidu throwing its right thigh (= genitals?) in her face. The gods decree that Enkidu must die. Lamenting him, Gilgamesh sets out to find immortality. He hears of Utnapishtim, hero of the flood, and seeks him out across the sea. Utnapishtim recounts the FLOOD STORY, telling him of a plant of rejuvenation. Returning home, Gilgamesh finds the plant, but a snake steals it while he is bathing.

The story explores the restraints imposed by culture, the nature of sexuality and friendship, the balance between piety and environmental exploitation, and the problem of mortality. (*See* Heidel 1946; Thorbjørnsrud 1983. Text in Pritchard 1969: 72–99, 503–7).

**Epiphany** (from Greek, *epiphania*: 'manifestation'). The day marking the manifestation of Christ at his baptism in the river Jordan, and hence linked in Orthodox churches with the blessing of baptismal water. In western Christianity Epiphany became identified with the legend of the showing of Jesus to the three magi or wise men and is celebrated on 6 January.

**epiqores** (Hebrew; from Greek, *epikoureios*: 'Epicurean', 'a follower of Epicurus'). A heretic, especially a materialist who makes light of religious values. *Epiqorsut* ('*epiqores*-ism') means 'irreverence' and 'heresy'.

**Epiqorsut**. *See* EPIQORES.

**episcopacy**. An organizational form of the Christian church based on bishops, usually thought to be consecrated in a continuous line of succession (*see* APOSTOLIC SUCCESSION). The term derives from the Greek *episkopos*, translated into English as 'bishop'. While *episkopos* in the New Testament is practically synonymous with 'presbyter' (*presbuteros*), 'the' bishop of a particular place soon came to be regarded as the focus of church unity, as in the epistles of Ignatius (*c*.35–107 CE).

**episkopos**. *See* EPISCOPACY

**Epistle of Barnabas**. *See* APOSTOLIC FATHERS, CODEX SINAITICUS.

**Epistle to Diognetus**. *See* APOSTOLIC FATHERS.

**Epona**. Celtic goddess represented riding a horse, often accompanied by another horse which she feeds. She also holds attributes such as a horn of plenty, a bowl and fruits and is therefore interpreted as a fertility goddess. When her cult was carried to Italy her function shifted to that of patron of riding and cavalry.

**Epoptes**. *See* ELEUSINIAN MYSTERIES.

**Eranos**. The name of a series of congresses dealing with various aspects of religion, symbolism, MYTHOLOGY etc., with significant participation by representatives of various cultures. The proceedings of these conferences are found in the regularly published *Eranos Yearbook*.

**erastianism**. The teaching of the Swiss Thomas Erastus (1524–83), who argued, against radical versions of Calvinist theocracy, that it was the state which should be the arbiter not only of civil matters but also of ecclesiastical ones. This position was adopted by the Englishman R. Hooker in his influential work *Ecclesiastical Polity* (1594) and has influenced English church legislation ever since. Originally intended to reduce the dangers of arbitrary religious rule in a state committed to a single faith, even modified erastianism is nowadays regarded by some as a limitation on the freedom of the established church (of England) by a state which has become secular and pluralist.

**Ereshkigal**. The Sumerian goddess of the Underworld (equivalent to the Babylonian Allatu), the consort of NERGAL.

**Eretz Yisrael** (Hebrew). The Land of Israel.

**Ériú.** *See* MEDB.

**Eros**. The force of attraction between people and between deities, as well a Greek deity, often pictured as an old figure or as a baby with bow and arrow which smites people; his force was feared as well as appreciated, for it could destroy propriety. *See also* AGAPE.

**eschatological**. *See* ESCHATOLOGY.

**eschatology** (from Greek, *eschaton*: 'the end'). A religious conception of what will happen in 'the end', such as a final judgement of humankind or a restoration of a state of primal well-being. The word was coined in the context of Christian theology, where ideas about 'the end' centre on the ushering in of the kingdom of God, i.e. God's rule, which being already set in motion by the life of Christ is variously understood as 'realized' or at least 'inaugurated' eschatology. Such conceptions assume a corporate outcome for humankind and therefore the use of the word to refer to the destiny of individual 'souls' after death should be regarded as secondary.

**Eshmun**. A Phoenician healing god of the first millennium. God of Sidon. The name was probably used epithetically, meaning 'healer' of an older god of uncertain identity (Lipínski 1973).

**Eshu** [Esù, Edshu, Elegba]. TRICKSTER god of the Yoruba of Nigeria. As a god of chance he is linked to IFA divination and is a messenger between men and gods as a bearer of sacrifice. Eshu also occurs in various Afro-American religions, e.g. as a trickster figure communicating between the ORISHA of the SANTERÍA and humankind and is thus a symbol of balance. At the same time he can be associated with the devil, and in the CHUMBANDA religion he is regarded as the king of black magic. (Wescott 1962).

**Esna**. An ancient town with a partially excavated temple dedicated to KHNUM, built and decorated from *c.*300 BCE to 3rd century CE. It is known in Greek as Latopolis.

**essence**. In Latin (*essentia*) or Latin-derived philosophical parlance this term has been used to mean that which belongs to a SUBSTANCE (a self-subsisting thing) by nature, and which cannot be taken away from it without totally altering its character. In the field of Christian theology it is associated with a quest for the 'identity' of Christianity within liberal Protestantism, or an attempt to define an indispensable minimum that characterizes Christian faith, apart from supposed superfluities such as inessential dogma, or affirmation of certain non-provable historical occurrences (Harnack 1986). The nature of this quest for a historically perceived essence (German: *Wesen*) was analysed by Ernst Troeltsch (Morgan & Pye 1977). The task of identifying the nature of *a* specific religion should be distinguished from attempts to define the 'essence' of religion in general, especially as the latter not uncommonly blurs the identity of specific religions. *See also* BEING: ESSENTIALISM.

**essence of religion**. *See* ESSENCE.

**Essenes**. A Jewish sect appearing in the mid-2nd century BCE, scattered throughout rural Palestine; also identified by most scholars with the QUMRAN community. Their founder, the 'Teacher of Righteousness' (i.e. legitimate teacher [of TORAH]) was perhaps a disappointed claimant to the High Priesthood. Of millenarian tendencies, they produced the DEAD SEA SCROLLS, and contributed to the APOCALYPTIC tradition. The sect was presumably destroyed *c.*73 CE at the end of the Jewish War. (Hengel 1974: i/218–47; Schürer 1979, 555–90). *See also* ḤASIDIM.

**essentialism**. Any philosophical or theological doctrine which makes a hard and fast distinction between what is 'substantial', necessary for a thing to be the kind of thing it is, and what is merely 'accidental'. It is sometimes used to characterize certain supposedly 'Augustinian' strains in medieval theology which advocate an intellectual-spiritual approach to God via the 'reduction' of the existential diversity of beings to formal essences directly intuited by the mind. This may be contrasted with the theology of Thomas Aquinas, who associated God himself with the 'existential' (though he did not use this term) as follows. He claimed that created and material beings fully possess their proper essences, although these are only 'in potential' to Being, which is fully and properly possessed by God alone. From the ultimate perspective of the order pertaining between creator and creation, certain 'accidents' such as superadded grace can be seen as belonging as 'properly' to creatures as to their intrinsic essences. Thus the doctrine of creation tends to prevent essentialism in Aquinas. *See also* BEING; ESSENCE.

**Èṣù**. *See* ESHU.

**Esus**. Gaulish Celtic god of unclear function, depicted hitting a tree and connected with sacrifices involving people hanging from trees.

**Eternalism**. *See* ANNIHILATIONISM.

**eternal life**. The notion of eternal life appears to be primarily associated with the Christian religion, within which there are two dominant interpretations. One sees eternal life as an everlasting life that begins here and now with faith in Christ. The other regards it as beginning after death in the resurrection of the body. The classical Greek idea of the immortality of the soul was easily incorporated by early Christian theologians into the idea of eternal life.

**eternal recurrence**. A belief that the world – that is, any and every event in the world – will repeat itself infinitely. Such a notion is to be found in early Greek thought and is intertwined with cyclical views of history and notions of periodicity in nature. Although similar views can be found in other cultural traditions, it has become particularly well known in the West in the work of the 19th-century philosopher Friedrich Nietzsche (1844–1900), who regarded the notion of infinity as self-contradictory. Because of this he concluded that a finite universe involving only a finite variety of material configurations implied the necessity of the endless repetition of those configurations.

**ethics**. In its classical sense, ethics is linked to Greek *ethos* and implies that questions of proper moral conduct are inseparable from participation in a particular cultural environment and the defining of social roles necessary to its functioning. In modern times ethics has come to mean a field of critical enquiry and debate into moral questions, with subareas such as medical ethics. The relations between religion and ethics have been most diverse, ranging between unquestioning acceptance and radical criticism of current thinking or practice; or, in other contexts, the total equation of religion and ethics (as social role) and the conscious disregard of ethics as secondary in relation to the religious quest. *See also* EUTHYPHRO DILEMMA; MORALITY.

**Ethiopian churches**. A group of African churches located in both western and southern Africa, Christian in origin and intent but in fact independent and separatist, with an important element of traditional African practices included in their social arrangements. The biblical image of Ethiopia provides an important organizing metaphor for their self-understanding. These churches should not be confused with the Ethiopian Church of Ethiopia itself, which is at least as old as the 4th century CE.

**Eucharist**. A common name for the Christian service of Holy Communion or MASS deriving from the Greek verb *eucharizein* ('to give thanks'), used in the words of inauguration. The liturgical structure of the Eucharist has varied considerably in detail, but the main elements have remained constant (*see* MASS). These consist of (a) the 'liturgy of the Word', consisting of hymns of praise including the traditional Gloria, readings from Old and New Testaments and a sermon, and (b) the 'liturgy of the sacrament', consisting of the consecration and distribution of the elements of bread and wine which symbolize (according to various theories such as, in the Roman Catholic Church, TRANSSUBSTANTIATION) the body and the blood of Christ offered in sacrifice. The word 'Eucharist' may also be used to refer only to the second of these two parts.

**Euhemerism**. The theory, so named in honour of Euhemerus (4th century BCE), that mythical accounts of the lives and deeds of gods and goddesses arose in reminiscence of real people.

**Euthyphro Dilemma**. The question asked in Plato's *Euthyphro*: 'Is the holy loved by the gods because it is holy, or is it holy because it is loved by the gods?', raising the issue of the relationship between ethics and religion. This question has arisen in various forms down to the present day.

**evangelical**. Pertaining to the Gospel (Greek, *euangelion*; Latin, *evangelium*). Thus an 'evangelical saying' is a saying attributed to Jesus in one of the four Gospels of the New Testament. *See also* EVANGELICALISM; EVANGELISM.

**evangelicalism**. A standpoint within Protestant Christianity which emphasizes the message of the Gospel as opposed to secondary theological reflection. *See also* EVANGELICAL.

**evangelism**. The spreading of the Gospel (Greek, *euangelion*; Latin, *evangelium*).

**evocatio** (Latin). A ritual by which the Romans hastened the fall of a besieged city by persuading its gods to depart.

**ewige Wiederkehr**. *See* ETERNAL RECURRENCE.

**ex cathedra** (Latin: 'from the chair'). A statement by the POPE on matters of faith or moral conduct promulgated as a final decision on the issue and believed to be free from any possibility of misinterpretation or error. *See also* INFALLIBILITY.

**Exclusive Brethren**. *See* PLYMOUTH BRETHREN.

**excommunication**. The most severe punishment in the Roman Catholic Church, namely the declaration that a person is excluded from the Church because of moral fault or erroneous teaching for as long as this persists. Excommunication is less practised today than in former times. Thus in the past marriage irregularities often led to excommunication whereas currently a temporary exclusion from Holy Communion as a warning is more frequent.

**Exegesis on the Soul**. *See* NAG HAMMADI.

**Exile**. The experience of royal, aristocratic, priestly and other groups in Judahite society deported by the Babylonians following attacks on Jerusalem in 597 BCE (King Jehoiakin deported), 587–6 (temple sacked) and 582 (accounts *2 Kings* 24–25, *2 Chronicles* 36; *see also Jeremiah* 52). The end of the Exile is conventionally dated *c.* 538, following Cyrus' capture of Babylon, though the 'return' of exilic descendants was spasmodic and protracted. The Exile was the single most important event in the formation of Judaism; an experience which obliged a complete reassessment of cultic, theological and national traditions, completing the transformation of a traditional national polytheistic cult into MONOTHEISM. All older traditions were now edited into their present biblical forms, reflecting the exilic perspective. (Ackroyd 1968; Friedman 1981; M. Smith 1987: 75–82) *See also* DEUTERONOMISTIC HISTORY; PRIESTLY WORK; DEUTERO-ISAIAH; DIASPORA.

**existence**. A quality ascribed to that which is, which stands out, and is contrasted with the idea of ESSENCE. The term occurs in discussion regarding whether the idea of perfection with respect to Being (God) implies its existence. In that context, the ONTOLOGICAL ARGUMENT crystallizes the problematic character of the use of the term in our language, and as an issue in contemporary philosophy of religion. Anselm's argument, the source spawning the contemporary debate, suggests in at least one of its versions that the idea of God as perfect BEING logically implies the idea of necessary existence. According to the style of thinking known as EXISTENTIALISM, existence takes priority over ESSENCE and is not a correlate of it. Thus, in the writings of Kierkegaard and existentialist thinkers, the term has come to refer to modes in which humans live their lives or situate themselves in the world. To depict the human situation as a lived experience these thinkers depicted certain modes – melancholy, anxiety, despair, guilt, and faith – which fall roughly in aesthetic, ethical or religious categories.

**existentialism**. A term apparently coined by Karl Jaspers, and used as an umbrella to cover a disparate group of philosophies centred variously on the nature and problems of human 'existence'. Known in Germany also as *Existenzphilosophie*, and in France as *philosophie existentielle* or *philosophie de l'existence*, existentialism flourished mainly in the second quarter of the 20th century. However, it should be understood as a pervasive 'mood' rather than a united movement or 'school' of thought. There is no set of common doctrines among its leading proponents; indeed, not all of them would even accept the description 'existentialist'. There are nonetheless some recurring themes running through their writings: (1) a contempt for most 'academic' or university philosophy as over-technical, pedantic and irrelevant to the human condition; (2) a preoccupation with anxieties (ANGST) concerning human finitude, the ever-present threat of death and the possibility of ultimate meaninglessness; (3) human nature conceived as undetermined and unfinished; (4) human life characterized as a series of ambiguous possibilities, among which one chooses in order 'to become what one is'; (5) a focus on the individual and the decisions faced in 'the moment'; (6) repudiation of the claims of any 'system' or of any 'ideology', whether political or metaphysical or religious. Leading thinkers associated with existentialism have included Rainer Maria Rilke (1875–1926), Martin Buber (1878–1965), Franz Kafka (1883–1924), Karl Jaspers (1883–1969), Rudolf Bultmann (1884–1976), Paul Tillich (1886–1965), Gabriel Marcel (1889–1973), Martin Heidegger (1889–1976), Jean-Paul Sartre (1905–80), Maurice Merleau-Ponty (1908–61). Its most important precursors in the 19th century were Søren Kierkegaard (1813–55), Fyodor Dostoevsky (1821–81), and Friedrich Nietzsche (1844–1900). (Soloman 1972; Macquarrie 1973).

**Exodus**. The Journey of Israel from EGYPT to Palestine under Moses, narrated in *Exodus*, *Numbers* and *Deuteronomy*. The legend has been used typologically of later liberations (e.g. from EXILE) and has been a major theme in biblical interpretation ever since down to the preaching, for example, of Martin Luther King in the American Civil Rights movement. *See also* MOSES; YAM SUF.

**ex opere operato** (Latin). A technical term in Roman Catholic theology which indicates that the power to operate the consecration (*See* MASS) is dependent on the consecrative act of an ordained priest and not on his personal worth.

**exorcism**. The driving out of evil spirits or demons which are believed to have possessed human beings, through intense prayer, incantations and sometimes physically disturbing rituals. While belief in the efficacy of the ritual may help to release afflicted persons from their suffering, the carrying out of the ritual itself tends to confirm belief in the demon possession. For this reason the practice of exorcism in modern times has been a matter of some controversy.

**exteriority**. The term is particularly associated with the POSTSTRUCTURALISM of Gilles Deleuze and J.-F. Lyotard, but it can also have an application to the work of Wittgenstein. Deleuze and Lyotard are anxious to deny all 'inwardness', both in the sense of any objective essence or 'thing in itself' apart from external manifestation, and in the sense of a subjective inwardness proper to the human subject. All subjectivity is a construct of language or else a manifestation of the unpredictable creative energies of bodies and sign-systems working in conjunction. It is therefore visible, 'on the surface' and open to public inspection. *See also* ESSENCE.

**extreme unction**. A Christian sacrament, consisting of prayer and anointment with oil, intended to comfort the critically sick and to free him or her from sins. Also known as 'holy unction'. *See also* UNCTION.

**extrinsic religion**. A term introduced by the American psychologist Gordon W. Allport to indicate an immature religious orientation in which religion becomes a means to achieve secondary ends (Allport 1950). An example of this is going to church to obtain prestige in a certain place or setting. *Contrast* INTRINSIC RELIGION.

# F

**Fa**. *See* IFÀ.

**faith** (Irish). Celtic seer and administrator of sacrifices. In Gaul *vates*.

**Fall**. Term commonly used in the interpretation of the expulsion from EDEN in *Genesis* 2–3 (Wyatt 1986a: 428f). ADAM may be seen as a royal figure, his expulsion denoting exile, as he becomes a figure of human alienation from God. Barker (1987: 233ff) takes the narrative to be a late derivative of *Ezekiel* 28. This suggests it is a human parallel to myths of falling ANGELS. Later references to heavenly *and* earthly Edens (e.g. *2 Enoch* 8.4ff, *Jubilees* 4.23ff) support this link. Christian teaching presents the Fall as the distancing of humankind from the state of original innocence and happiness intended by God the Creator; humankind is thus in need of salvation to make good this state of affairs. (Tennant 1903; Humbert 1940; Soggin 1975: 88–111). *See also* ORIGINAL SIN.

**False Decretals**. A large number of documents forged in 9th-century France, purporting to be letters of early popes, and used to bolster papal authority. The documents were influential throughout the Middle Ages, but exposed in the 16th century.

**falsification**. The process of showing that something is false. Karl Popper argued that statements and explanations are scientific if they are open to potential falsification (Popper 1959). Anthony Flew questioned the logical status of many theological statements because they are seemingly not open to potential falsification (Flew 1955). *Contrast* VERIFICATION.

**famadihana** (Malagasy). Turning of the corpse, a burial ceremony of the Merina people of Madagascar. Among the varied burial customs of Madagascar a common feature is the separation of the skeleton from the decaying soft parts of the body. The clean bones are placed in the ancestral tomb, mixed with bones of the ancestors. The dead person is then believed to be at rest and to have become one with the ancestors. During the ceremony of *famadihana* the body is taken from the tomb, the bones washed and re-wrapped in a new shroud of red silk, the *lamba-mena*. The skeleton is then nursed, caressed, danced with, taken around the village with music, singing and dancing, and shown the changes in the village since the death occurred. This festival, with great rejoicing and feasting, is thought to bring approval and blessing from the ancestors (Mack 1986).

**fanā'** (Arabic: 'extinction'). A ṢŪFĪ expression for the loss of personality and identity in the mystic's union with ALLĀH.

**Fanany** (Malagasy). A myth found in different variations from north-eastern Africa and the Interlacustrine kingdoms to Zimbabwe, the kingdom of Kongo (Loango), and Madagascar. It is essentially concerned with sacral kingship and the idea of reincarnation into animals. Fanany is based on the belief that the human soul is split into a 'shadow-soul' which becomes an ancestral spirit after death (*see* MIZIMU) and a 'body-soul' which contains 'life' and is bound to the body fluids. After the death of a noble personage his cadaverous fluids are transformed into a maggot, the maggot changes into a snake and the snake into a leopard or a lion, both royal animals. (Hirschberg 1967).

**fang-bien**. *See* HŌBEN, UPĀYA.

**fang-pien**. *See* HŌBEN, UPĀYA.

**fang shi** (Chinese: 'recipe masters'). So-called 'magician-druggists'. In China during the Qin (221–206 BCE) and Han (206 BCE – 220 CE) these magicians were influential at court. They specialized in drugs and herbs that were said to extend the ordinary lifespan. *Fang shi* also claimed to have direct dealings with IMMORTALS dwelling in the various ABODES OF THE BLEST. Whoever wanted to become an immortal had to undergo a rigid purification programme. Powers attributed to the ZHEN REN (the 'Realized Man' were transferred to the immortals (like invisibility, LONGEVITY etc.). Thus *fang shi* are considered the originators of the ancient Chinese immortality cult. Likewise, they are the forerunners of the later on more organized Daoist priests (*see* DAOISM).

**fang shih**. *See* FANG SHI.

**faqír** (Arabic; plural *fuqarā'*). A term meaning 'poor' but which can refer to either physical or spiritual need. Muslim mystics (ṢŪFĪS) give themselves this name. The origin of the term is the verse in the QUR'ĀN [35:15]: 'You are the poor of Allāh, but He is self-sufficient.' In the Arab world, the term is applied to a mendicant DARWĪSH, while in western languages the term has been extended to cover Indian ascetics and yogis.

**Fara'idī**. A Muslim 'purification' movement founded in Bengal, India, by Hajji Shariat Allāh in the early 19th century. The movement was characterized by an anti-British programme, socio-economic reform directed against rich landlords in favour of the peasants and workers and purification of Islām from Hindu ideas and the excesses of SUFISM. His son Dudhu Miyan (*d* 1864) succeeded his father and the movement still has its adherents to this day (Ahmad 1969).

**farḍ** [also farīḍa] (Arabic). Something that has been made obligatory; a religious duty or obligation; a synonym of *wājib*. Islamic law distinguishes between an individual duty (*farḍ ʿayn*) such as each of the FIVE PILLARS (prayer, fasting etc.) and collective duty (*farḍ kifāya*), the fulfilment of which, for example funeral prayers, by a sufficient number of individuals excuses others from doing so.

**Faro**. Among the Bambara (Bamana) and neighbouring peoples in Mali the 'lord of water', an androgynous deity worshipped through sacrifices along the river Niger, manifested also in rain, rainbow, thunder and lightning. In Bambara myth he completes the work of the Creator God. (Zahan 1974; Dieterlen 1951).

**fa-shih** (Chinese). A term of respect for a Buddhist teacher, 'Master of the Dharma'.

**fast**. Abstinence from food, a widespread practice in many religions, either to maintain physical purity before a religious act or as a form of self-discipline and asceticism. The extreme form is fasting to death, as for example at the end of a Jain ascetic. *See also* RAMAḌĀN; VISION QUEST.

**fasti** (Latin). Ancient Roman religious calendars, many of which are preserved in inscriptions. Their listings of festivals (*feriae*) varied depending on the town which produced them. The ancient Romans wrote commentaries on them, which have strongly influenced all subsequent scholarship. Ovid's *Fasti* devotes one book to each month of the Roman religious calendar; this was incomplete at the time of his death, and only the first six books survive, but they constitute a prime source of information about Roman religion. For Ovid *see also* METAMORPHOSES.

**fate** (from Latin *fatum*: 'the decreed'). According to widespread belief in antiquity the major events of a person's life were predetermined by the gods or divine force. Fate should be distinguished from 'fortune' (from Latin *fortuna*), which means luck, good or bad. Fate was believed to determine such matters as the time, place and social level of one's birth, one's personal character, the choice of a spouse, the number and gender of one's children, one's general welfare in life, and especially the time and manner of one's death.

Since humans do not normally know their fate, the desire to gain such knowledge is the basis for oracles and astrology. Sometimes it was thought to be possible to avoid one's fate, by taking refuge in a temple for instance, but generally it is unavoidable. Thus Oedipus unwittingly slew his father and married his mother, just as the oracle at DELPHI had foretold. Some polytheistic religions think of fate as ruling even the gods, but a more typical view is that the gods (e.g. Zeus in the *Iliad*) choose not to intervene in fated matters. (For fate in Greek thought see Greene 1944.)

Fate can be personified (e.g. the three Greek *Moirai*), or be an impersonal cosmic force (Indian *daivam*: 'the divine'). In the Indian context, one's destiny is also determined by previous deeds of positive or negative moral value (KARMA). In monotheistic religions fate is regarded as subordinate to the will of God. Among the Ibo of Nigeria it is held that one's fate is determined each year when a guardian angel blindly picks one's destiny bundle. However and whenever it is laid down, the concept of fate and its parallels provide humans with an explanation for the seeming absurdities and inequities of their existence. *See also* DIVINATION.

**Father Sky**. *See* FATHER SUN.

**Father Sun**. In Native American religions, the major male celestial spirit, essentially the same as Father Sky. The path of Sun (east to west) represents the path of life, and his movement (clockwise) is the general direction of ritual in most cultures. *See also* SWEAT LODGE.

**fātiḥa** (Arabic: 'opening'). The short opening SŪRA or chapter of the Muslims' sacred text, the QUR'ĀN. An introductory prayer, it proclaims the lordship of ALLĀH over all creation and the worshippers' dedication to seeking guidance solely in accordance with His will. The *sura* holds a place of special reverence for Muslims, indispensable in the performance of the daily prayer-ritual (ṢALĀT) and as an invocation for the sick and deceased.

**Fatima**. A pilgrimage centre in central Portugal which achieved fame as the result of visions of Mary experienced by three children, one of whom later, as a Carmelite nun, wrote two normative accounts. In the last of the five visions Mary named herself as 'Our Lady of the Rosary'. While consequent devotions have therefore focused on the recitation of the rosary, as well as on 'the immaculate heart' of Mary, interest was also held by the mysterious 'secret' vouchsafed to the nun Lucia Santos. Pope John Paul II ascribed his narrow escape from death by assassination to 'Our Lady of Fatima', thereby contributing still further to the popularity of the pilgrimage.

**fatwā** (Arabic; plural, *fatāwā*). In Islām, a formal legal opinion issued by a *muftī* in response to a query on a point of religious law from a Muslim, whether a governor or a member of the public. The opinion is advisory only and does not bind a judge's (*gādī*) final decision.

**Faunus**. A Roman forest divinity especially devoted to herdsmen. Faunus sometimes gave oracles, especially by means of incubation (i.e. during sleep), and was often dangerous to passers-by.

**feng (s.)**. *See* FENG (SACRIFICE).

**Feng Shan** (Chinese). *Feng* and *Shan* were two important sacrifices in the Chinese imperial state cult. The *Feng* (literally, 'bestowal') sacrifice was offered to Heaven (TIAN) on the top of Taishan Mountain, while the *Shan* sacrifice addresses the Earth (*Di*) and is offered on a lower hill south of the same mountain. Both rituals have to be performed by the emperor in person. The *Feng* sacrifices were performed on a regular basis (i.e. every four years) by emperor Wu (140–86 BCE) and still flourished under the Tang dynasty empress Wu, who performed the ceremonies on Mt. Song (in 695), the holy mountain of the centre (*see* WU YUE). They were regarded as highly prestigious because the ritual expressed the conviction that the empire had reached an exemplary state of peace and prosperity. Many emperors declined, therefore, to perform the *Feng* and *Shan* sacrifices, although they were occasionally repeated during the Tang and Song dynasties. The sinologist E. Chavannes has speculated that the purpose of the rites was not only the legitimation of power, but also the longing for (the bestowal of) LONGEVITY and happiness (Chavannes 1910).

**fengshui** [feng-shui] (Chinese: 'winds and water'). Usually called 'geomancy' in English writings. The theory and practice of *fengshui* deals with the influences of terrestrial and celestial elements on a given site, especially human dwellings and graves. It is based on traditional Chinese cosmology, the theories of FIVE ELEMENTS and YIN-YANG. (Feuchtwang 1974; Skinner 1982).

**Fenrir**. *See* LOKI, TYR.

**feriae** (Latin). Roman religious festivals, recorded in the *Fasti* (*see* FASTI). Some took place on fixed dates, others were movable. They determined the auspiciousness or inauspiciousness of the days on which they took place, and the preceding and subsequent days. Since Roman political officials determined the placing of the movable feasts, there existed the possibility of impeding the flow of public business to political advantage, although it remains uncertain how often this actually happened.

**festival**. An extremely wide term indicating a joyous communal occasion frequently with a religious focus. In the classical world, for example, festivals were times for both social activities and worship of the gods, usually consisting of a procession to the temple where sacrifice and prayer were offered, athletic contests and communal meals. *See also* FIESTA; MATSURI.

**Festival of Weeks**. An early summer harvest festival in ancient Israel, connected by *Exodus* 19.1 to the revelatory events at SINAI (*Exodus* 19–34). (Kraus 1966: 55–61; Vaux 1965: 493–5)

**fetiales**. Archaic Roman priests in charge of treaties and declarations of war. Their rituals were elaborate, but appear less frequently from the late Republic onwards.

**fetish**. A term formerly used to refer to a cultic object but now used, mainly pejoratively, to indicate something to which one is irrationally and obstinately attached. As a descriptive term it must be regarded as inexact. *Compare* FETISHISM; TSAFI.

**fetishism**. A term apparently first used by De Brosses (1760) to account for forms of religion which were considered insufficiently noble to be part of the 'natural religion' common to humanity as perceived by the Deists (*see* DEISM). The term is now considered to be inappropriate and misleading. *Compare* FETISH.

**fictionalism**. *See* 'AS IF' PHILOSOPHY.

**ficus religiosa.** *See* BODHI.

**Fidel Defensor**. *See* DEFENDER OF THE FAITH.

**fideism**. The conviction that fundamental religious beliefs depend primarily on faith, not on argument. The term is often used pejoratively, to suggest irrationality.

**fiesta** (Spanish). A festival, feast, holiday or merry celebration, either completely secular or in conjunction with religious events.

**fikr** (Arabic). Meditation, an essential element in the ṢŪFĪ spiritual path as an accompaniment to DHIKR.

**filial piety**. *See* XIAO.

**filidh** (Irish). Celtic seer and poet.

**filioque** (Latin: 'and from the Son'). The belief, dating from Augustine (354–430), that the Holy Spirit proceeds from the Father 'and from the Son', the Son's capacity to bestow the Spirit yet being derived from the Father. The phrase was first added to the original text of the Nicene Creed in the western church in 589, but has always been rejected by the Orthodox Church as representing poor Trinitarian theology.

**fiqh** (Arabic: 'knowledge', 'understanding'). Islamic jurisprudence, the science of finding specific rules of law from the sources (or roots, *uṣūl*) such as the QUR'ĀN and the Prophet tradition (ḤADĪTH).

**first cause**. *See* COSMOLOGICAL ARGUMENTS FOR THE EXISTENCE OF GOD(S).

**first fruits**. Offerings of food, from hunting, gathering or agriculture, given to a god or gods at festivals with gratitude and in hope of continued economic welfare.

**five aggregates**. *See* SKANDHĀ.

**Five Bushels of Rice Sect**. *See* TIANSHI DAO.

**Five Classics**. *See* WU JING.

**five constants**. *See* WU CHANG.

**five elements**. The Chinese theory of five vital agents [*Wu Xing*) that constitute the material world – wood, fire, earth, metal and water. Each component is associated (1) with a certain time of year, (2) with a certain organ in the body, (3) with a colour, (4) with one of the five directions (centre being the fifth). Since one element 'conquers' the next, like one season is followed by another, a cyclical, dynamic notion is born that explains the inner working of the earth, indeed of the whole universe. The idea of cyclical stress laid on what was at one time the dominant element (which does not become dominantly active until the cycle catches up with it again) was only partially accepted. Not only are at least four different 'series' of elements known from the classical Chinese sources (the one given above is the one most widely known) but in the book ZHUANG ZI (*Chuang Tzu*) every element is perceived as being in an immediate and spontaneous 'state of action' (Zhuang Zi chap. 2), without temporarily dominating over the other four (Tsung-Tung Chang 1983: 61–2).

The notion of the five constituents is closely connected to the YIN-YANG idea, i.e. all elements have a rising and a falling tendency. Growth and decline thus constitute the vital criteria for the cyclical properties of the elements. The *wu xing* theory, despite the severe criticisms of such early philosophers as ZHUANG ZI and Xün Zi (283–238 BCE) – 'the . . . theory is eccentric, obscure and without any sound explanations' – forms one of the theoretical foundations of Chinese medicine seeking to cope with internal disorders.

**Five Emperors**. *See* WU DI.

**Five Ks**. The five symbols worn by Sikhs, the PAÑJ KAKKE.

**Five Pillars**. The basic ritual components of the Muslims' faith (the SHAHĀDA), together with four essential ritual acts of the Islamic religion, namely, prayer (ṢALĀT), fasting (SAWM), alms-giving (ZAKĀT) and pilgrimage (ḤĀJJ).

**Five Precepts**. *See* ŚILA, TEN PRECEPTS.

**five relationships**. *See* WU LUN.

**five sacred mountains**. *See* WU YUE.

**five virtues**. *See* WU CHANG.

**Five Ways**. The proofs or 'ways' used by Thomas Aquinas (1225–74) in his *Summa Theologiae* to show that God exists: (1) from change or motion (*ex parte motus*), (2) from the nature of causation (*ex ratione causae efficientis*), (3) from possibility and necessity (*ex possibili et necessario*), (4) from the gradation of qualities in things (*ex gradibus qui in rebus*), and (5) from the orderliness and guidedness of things (*ex gubernatione rerum*). All five 'ways' are from CAUSALITY, as analysed by Aristotle in book Δ of the *Metaphysics*. *See also* COSMOLOGICAL ARGUMENTS FOR THE EXISTENCE OF GOD; DESIGN ARGUMENTS FOR THE EXISTENCE OF GOD.

**flagellant**. *See* FLAGELLATION.

**flagellation**. Ritual flogging carried out as a penance for sins with the compliance of the penitent, and sometimes self-inflicted. Persons taking part are called flagellants.

**flamen** (Latin; plural, *flamines*). A member of a Roman priesthood which, apart from the FLAMEN DIALIS, remained secular. There were three major flamens and twelve minor, together forming the pontifical college. Whether a divinity possessed a flamen provides a way to determine the antiquity of a cult. *See also* PONTIFEX MAXIMUS.

**flamen dialis** (Latin). The Roman high priest of JUPITER. A very archaic office, surrounded by many taboos, which lapsed in the late Republic and was revived by Augustus. *See also* AUGUSTAN RELIGION; FLAMENS.

**flamines**. *See* FLAMEN.

**flood myth**. In various forms of the flood myth, probably diffused from a common Mesopotamian origin, human sin leads to world-destruction, one man (Atrahasis, Utnapishtim, Noah) and wife or family surviving in boat. (See Lambert & Millard 1969; Heidel 1946. Texts in Pritchard 1969: 42–4, 93–6, 104–6; *Genesis* 6–9; Attridge & Oden 1976).

The biblical flood-story, a conflation of two accounts, is related to the Babylonian and other ancient versions. Its distinctive nature lies in its implicit application of the theme to the exilic experience; the ensuing covenant between God and Noah (*Genesis* 9) renewing the broken one of *Genesis* 1 (Clines 1978: 73–6, 98).

**Fomorians**. Evil spirits in Irish mythology, adversaries of the Celtic gods.

**foundationalism**. The view that we rationally justify our beliefs by tracing them back to basic, self-evident ones. Some have attacked THEISM because it does not seem to be so justifiable; others have argued that it too is a foundational belief.

**Fortuna**. The archaic Roman goddess of 'increase', later identified with the Greek goddess of fortune, TYCHE. She had an elaborate temple at Praenaste and a special cult for women as *Fortuna muliebris* (6 July).

**four**. In virtually all Native American religions, the most pervasive and most holy number. Rituals in their entirety and in their elements tend to be repeated four times. The sacred is referred to in sequences of four (e.g. FOUR WINDS) or its multiples.

**Four Directions**. North, south, east and west: entirely relative, conventional concepts, which, however, in many contexts play an important role in the structuring of the cosmos, particularly in association with the zenith and the nadir (representing earth and sky respectively). In Native American religions they are referred to as the FOUR WINDS. *See also* TEN DIRECTIONS, and (for pre-Columbian Peru) TAWATINSUYU.

**Four Fruits**. In Buddhism, the fruits of leading the homeless life under monastic discipline, namely becoming a 'stream-winner', a 'once-returner', a 'non-returner' or an *arhat*. (*See* ARHAT for further details.)

**Four Noble Truths**. The Doctrine which Gautama Buddha expounded in his first sermon, known as the 'First Turning of the Wheel of Dharma' (*Dharmacakrapravartana*). It has been summarized as follows: (1) Everything is suffering (*duḥkha*), (2) The origin of suffering is desire (*tṛṣṇā*), (3) By 'blowing out' desire there is an end to suffering (*nirvāṇa*), (4) The path to *nirvāṇa* is eightfold: right view, right resolve, right speech, right action, right livelihood, right effort, right mindfulness and right concentration.

**Four spirits**. *See* MI-TAMA.

**Four Winds**. In Native American religions, the cosmos is understood to be composed of spiritual powers. The most powerful of these are the Four Winds, symbolizing the four cardinal directions, in association with Sky (the zenith) and Earth (the nadir).

**Four Worlds**. *See* OLAM, PARDES.

**fraction**. The ritual breaking of the bread in the eucharistic liturgy of various Christian churches, modelled on Christ's own action at the Last Supper, and recalling the recognition of the risen Christ 'in the breaking of the bread' when he met with disciples on the road to Emmaus (*Gospel According to Luke*).

**fratres**. *See* MITHRAISM.

**free will**. The idea that a person is capable of making decisions that are not determined by antecedent conditions. Controversy over it has given rise to a cluster of problems that are due mainly to an incompatibility between sets of beliefs. In religion, however, the discussion focuses on whether a person is able to will and change his/her ultimate destiny. In that respect it occurs in debates about PREDESTINATION and about human responsibility for actions leading to evil in the world. The Muslim and Christian traditions, in particular, wrestled with free will as a problem. It is treated in the writings of both al-Ashʿari and Calvin, representative figures in the history of the two traditions.

**Freyja**. Germanic goddess of love and fertility belonging to the VANIR; daughter of NJORD and sister of FREYR. Freyja was believed to give help in marriage, childbirth and love. She is said to have taught *seiðr* (*see also* AESIR), the magic used by the VǪLVA for divination and both helpful and harmful spells.

**Freyr**. The most prominent Germanic fertility god at the end of the pre-Christian period. He is the son of NJORD and together with his sister FREYJA the main representative of the VANIR, the race of gods connected with peace and prosperity. A probable cult event was Freyr's autumn journey through the land to bless the harvest; as in the cult of NERTHUS, an image of the god was taken round in a wagon to attend his worshippers' feasts and be consulted via his priestess. Symbols connected with Freyr are the horse, the boar (for protection) and the ship (used in funeral ceremonies). Freyr's temples stood near fertile fields, and no weapons were allowed inside them.

**Friends**. *See* SOCIETY OF FRIENDS.

**Frigg**. Germanic goddess connected with love and childbirth. As ODIN's wife, or in her German form Frija (the wife of Odin's German equivalent, Wodan), she is the mother goddess of the AESIR. Friday takes its name from her.

**Frija**. *See* FRIGG.

**fuda**. *See* O-FUDA.

**Fudō Myōō**. The Japanese name for Ācāla ('Immovable'), Myōō meaning 'Bright King'. Fudō is widespread iconographically, especially in Shingon Buddhism (*see* SHINGON-SHŪ), and is usually shown on the background of roaring flames. This is because he represents the ferocious aspect of DAINICHI NYORAI and is able to destroy evil with his sword and bind the wicked with his curled rope.

**Fugen Bosatsu**. The Japanese name for the bodhisattva Samantabhadra, who stands for great compassion, and is often linked to Mañjuśrī, who stands for great wisdom.

**fuji**. *See* FULUAN.

**Fukko Shintō**. Restoration Shintō. A school of thought represented by Kada no Azumamaro (1669–1736), Kamo no Mabuchi (1697–1769), Motoori Norinaga (1730–1801) and Hirata Atsutane (1776–1843). While other Shintō schools also sought to rediscover ancient, natural Shintō, they often relied on Buddhist or Confucian ways of thought, and therefore produced Buddhistic or Confucianistic theories about Shintō. The Fukko Shintō scholars began with a painstaking study of ancient philology in their attempt to elucidate the mentality of the ancient Japanese and thus to discover the essence of Shintō.

**fuluan** [fu-luan fuji, fu-chi] (Chinese). A Chinese method of divination, comparable to what is known in the West as 'spirit writing' or 'automatic writing'. Usually a wooden stick is held by one or two mediums and then moves on a table covered with sand thereby writing characters. In this way messages from the spiritual world are transmitted to mankind. The practice became very popular in China in the 19th and 20th centuries, but revelations by automatic writing were received by Daoists as early as the 4th century.

**Furies**. In ancient Greece, demanding and vengeful spirits born after CRONOS castrated OURANOS. They were offended by crimes against ties of family and kinship but could become kindly spirits.

**Fu Xi** [Fu Hsi]. A figure in Chinese mythology regarded as the ancestor of the human race. He married his sister NÜ WA, who gave birth to men. According to tradition, he invented the art of braiding nets and fishing. He is also attributed with the invention of the Eight Trigrams (*Ba Gua*), making use of the *Hetu* ('River Chart').

# G

**Gabriel** [Arabic: *Jabrā'īl*, *Jibrīl*]. The best known of the archangels in Islām who brought the orders of God (ALLĀH) to the prophet Muḥammad, thus revealing the divine mysteries to him, in the form of revelations which make up the Muslims' scripture, the QUR'ĀN.

**gagaku** (Japanese). Ceremonial court music and dancing, preserved from antiquity in the music department of the imperial household and at certain shrines and temples. Gagaku music, which is of continental origin, is performed on reed and percussion instruments. A performance of instrumental music without dancing is *kangen* while a dance performance with musical accompaniment is BUGAKU.

**Gaia** [Ge]. Ancient Greek earth goddess to whom libations were poured; she and OURANOS are parents of the OLYMPIAN GODS. *See also* ORPHIC MYSTERIES.

**gaki** (Japanese). Hungry ghosts; the Japanese equivalent of Sanskrit PRETA. One of the states of existence into which rebirth is possible according to Buddhist teaching.

**Gallican Rite**. *See* GALLICANISM, MOZARABIC RITE.

**Gallicanism**. A church-political tradition in France which sought relative independence from the authority of the papacy. It took precise form in the four Gallican Articles adopted by bishops and deputies under Louis XIV in 1682. These denied any authority of the pope over the monarchy, asserted the precedence of general councils (specifically the Council of Constance, 1414–18) over the pope, claimed validity for the traditions of the ancient Gallican Church (which had had its own Gallican Rite for the mass), and declared that papal decisions taken alone were subject to revision. Although these articles lost their official standing again in 1693, Gallicanism remained robust until the post-Napoleonic restoration of the monarchy. Thereafter the tendency to promote the authority of the papacy beyond the Alps, known as ultramontanism, gained the upper hand, and may be said to have asserted itself triumphantly at the Vatican Council of 1869–70, particularly with the declaration of papal INFALLIBILITY. At the same time most questions of 'temporal' interference, such as the possibility of the deposition of the monarch by ecclesiastical ruling, have lost their relevance.

**galut** (Hebrew) [Yiddish: *goles*]. Exile; diaspora. *Galut* describes the alienation experienced by the Jewish people outside the Land of Israel.

**Gaṇeśa** [Gaṇapati]. 'Lord of the celestial armies', usually represented with a pot-belly and an elephant-head. Considered to be the son of ŚIVA and Pārvatī, whom Śiva in a fit of rage decapitated and, not being able to find his human head, provided with an elephant head. Also supposed to have been the scribe of Vyāsa, noting down the VEDAS and the MAHĀBHĀRATA with the PURĀṆAS. The patron-deity of students, scholars and business people. His yearly festival, *Gaṇeśa caturthī*, is celebrated with especial solemnity in Mahārāṣṭra, where it was used by G.B. Tilak during the early time of the

Indian Freedom movement to mount protests against the British.

**garbagṛham**. *See* LIṆGAM.

**garbhadhātu**. *See* RYŌBU MANDARA.

**gateless barrier**. *See* WU MEN KUAN.

**Gāthās**. *See* ZOROASTRIANISM.

**Gauḍīya Vaiṣṇava Math** (Bengali). A movement formed in 1886 in Bengal by Bhaktivinoda Thākura based on devotion to Kṛṣṇa through veneration of Caitanya Mahāprabhu (1486–1533), who was seen by followers as an AVATĀRA of Kṛṣṇa.

**Gaunab**. Apart from TSUI-GOAB and HEITSI-EIBIB the most powerful character in Hottentot and Bushman religion; the greatly feared master of the dead (Schapera 1930).

**Ge**. *See* GAIA.

**Geb**. An ancient Egyptian earth-god, husband of NUT, son of SHU (air) and TEFNUT (moisture). He was revered at HELIOPOLIS.

**Gebirah**. The cultic office of dowager or chief queen in JUDAH, and an 'ideological replica' of ASHERAH (Ahlström 1963:76; Molin 1954; Andreasen 1983).

**Gẹ̀lẹ̀dẹ̀**. A masquerade cult to placate witches and worship deities connected with witchcraft among the southwestern group of Yoruba in Nigeria (Drewal 1983).

**Gemara** (Hebrew). The portion of the TALMUD which comments upon and is the 'completion' of the MISHNAH. The term is used colloquially to refer to the Talmud as a whole.

**gender-critical approach**. The reconception of the study of religion in terms which do justice to the function of gender in religion and in reflection on religion. The approach builds on feminist insights regarding the androcentric character of supposedly 'neutral' treatments of religion, but does not advocate any specific form of feminist ideology. The term was apparently coined by Randi Warne and was current in 1989 (Warne 1990). *Compare* AFRO-CRITICAL APPROACH; SINO-CRITICAL APPROACH.

**genealogy**. In a special sense, going beyond the ordinary meaning of 'heredity derivation', the term derives from Nietzsche's *Genealogy of Morals*, in which he sought to show that 'morality', meaning especially Platonic and Christian morality, was a contingent historical invention. The enterprise of 'genealogy' has recently been resumed by Michel Foucault and others, with the similar aim of disclosing the construction within time of things we take as timeless realities, such as madness, or sexuality. For Foucault, as for Nietzsche, genealogy is a strategy of 'suspicion' (often likewise focusing on the western and Christian heritage) because the disguised construction of such ahistorical entities is regarded as a ruse of power. While Foucault distinguishes material control over human bodies from the production of scientific truth, he considers that the 'power' involved in the first instance is usually enabled by the 'knowledge' involved in the second. Inversely, the arbitrariness which reigns in the field of knowledge is normally both invested and defused through a definite material deployment in the exercise of power. *See also* NIHILISM.

**generation**. The generation of the Son, i.e. Christ, implying the Father's eternal communication of being to the Son, who is thus distinguished from the Father who is unbegotten and the spirit who 'proceeds' from the Father. *See also* FILIOQUE.

**Genesia**. A festival of the dead when Athenians remembered their war dead and honoured the city for which they died, followed by festivals marking the beginning of the agricultural and social year, and celebrating a new crop of soldiers and citizens.

**Geneva Bible**. An English translation of the BIBLE published in Geneva in 1560, with Calvinist annotations, and the first to enumerate the text in 'verses', thus allowing easier use of proof-texts in doctrinal discussion. The translation was particularly influential in the further development of the Protestant Reformation in subsequent decades. *Compare* AUTHORIZED VERSION.

**genius** (Latin). The ancient Roman concept of 'soul'. Sometimes identified with a LAR, the genius was held to be immortal, although its precise status remained a subject of debate. In later western usage, an effective spirit of special quality.

**genuflexion**. The brief adoption of a half-kneeling position, by bending one knee (Latin; *genus*), as a sign of reverence in Catholic and some other churches.

**ghost dance**. A Native American religious movement, based on the visions of the Paiute, Wovoka, that spread among Plains tribes between 1870 and 1890. The ghost dance was particularly prominent in 1890 under the inspired leadership of the Paiute Indian Jack Wilson, who had a vision of a new world, and who taught that performing the ghost dance would inaugurate it. However, it was inspired by a number of Native American leaders and therefore took a number of forms; in each case there is a continuity between the new form and an earlier form, for example the round-dance. The new form constitutes a reinterpretation and is given not only new religious meaning but also new political meaning. The movement sought the disappearance of Euro-Americans and the reappearance of the bison (becoming virtually extinct due to US policy) and the many dead (due to epidemics and warfare with the US military), through a universal cataclysm instigated, in part, by a ritual dance. Brutally suppressed by the US military, it lost many of its adherents following the massacre at Wounded Knee, although it continues among a small number of Lakota (Sioux).

**Ghusl**. *See* TAHĀRA.

**giānī** (Punjabi). One who possesses knowledge, a Sikh theologian or scholar.

**Gilgamesh**. *See* EPIC OF GILGAMESH.

**gilgul** (Hebrew). The Kabbalistic doctrine of the 'cycling' of souls, that is, reincarnation.

**Ginnungagap**. In Germanic pre-Christian mythology, a land of nothingness before creation which lay between a land of cold and darkness, Niflheim, and a land of heat and light, Muspell. Creation took place when cold and heat met in Ginnungagap (*see* MIDGARD).

**Ginza** (Aramaic: 'treasure'). The major work of the Mandaeans, also called 'the great book' (*sidra rabba*). Translated into German by Mark Lidzbarski in 1925.

**Gion**. A term of Hindu-Buddhistic origin referring to the deities (chiefly Susanoo no mikoto) enshrined in the Yasaka shrine in Kyōto, and worshipped for their ability to cast out evil. The term is also popularly used as a name for the shrine itself and its branch shrines throughout Japan.

**Gion Matsuri**. An annual festival celebrated from 17 to 24 July at the Yasaka Jinja in Kyōto. Said to have originated during the reign of Emperor Seiwa (reigned 858–76) as a festival to guard against pestilence. Today the processions of *yamaboko* (festival floats) pulled through the city on the first and last days are the highlights of the festival. These floats, displaying dolls, sculptures created by famous artists, and even imported Gobelin tapestries, are valued as cultural treasures. The festival is regarded as one of the three great festivals of Japan.

**Gitagovinda**. *See* RADHĀ.

**Glooscap** [Kluscap]. The Micmac (north-eastern North America) culture-hero or TRICKSTER. *See also* NANABUSH.

**Gloria**. The traditional hymn that occurs as the second piece in musical compositions of the EUCHARIST or MASS. The name derives from the opening line, *Gloria in excelsis Deo* ('Glory be to God on high').

**Glossolalia**. Coined from Greek to mean 'speaking in tongues', in Christianity the term refers confusingly to two different things. First, it refers to the miraculous ability of the first Christian apostles, as narrated in *Acts 2*, to be understood in different languages through the power of the Holy Spirit. Second, it refers to the practice of speaking excitedly in unknown language, thought to be prophetic but in need of interpretation. This phenomenon was criticized by Paul (*1 Corinthians* 14), but continues to occur in modern times during prayer meetings where ecstatic reliance on the power of the Holy Spirit is paramount. Glossolalia in this second sense occurs in a large number of other religions: shamans and witch-doctors speak in tongues when in a state of ecstasy. This is understood to be the language of spirits.

**gnosis** (Greek). Knowledge. The term is widely used in the German-speaking world to refer to GNOSTICISM.

**gnostic**. *See* GNOSTICISM.

**gnosticism**. A religious movement of late antiquity which regarded material existence as the imperfect creation of an inferior god (*demiurge*) and strove for the release of the human self or spirit (*pneuma*) from the body and its return to the divine realm of light. The self is seen as a spark of this light which is trapped in the darkness of the material world; it can be liberated after death through the possession of a certain secret knowledge (Greek: *gnosis*). This knowledge is revealed by a saviour who acts in the name of the highest and sole benevolent god and is given various names: Seth, Shem, Heres, Christ, Zostrianos, or alternatively appears as an anonymous 'call'. The required lifestyle was ascetic; the claim that it could also be libertinarian has not been proved by original sources. Gnosticism is a typical product of Hellenistic syncretism and contains Greek, Jewish, Iranian and Christian elements. There were various tendencies or schools such as the Simonians (Simon Magus), the Carpocratians (Carpocrates), the Sethians (Seth), the Ophites or NAASSENES; the most influential and systematized form was the Christian gnosticism of the 2nd/3rd centuries CE (in its narrow sense, 'gnosticism' refers specifically to this form), which included the schools of Basilides (around 130) and Valentinus (*see* VALENTINIANISM). MANICHAISM is also based on gnostic concepts. The early Christian church was partially influenced by gnosticism but finally, with its unified, 'apostolic' teaching, succeeded in declaring it a heresy. Until the discovery of the NAG HAMMADI texts in 1945 the only source of information was the polemical literature of Christian heresiologists. A form of gnosticism still survives in the religion of the MANDAEANS of Iraq and Iran. (Jonas 1962; Rudolph 1984; Foerster 1974).

**go-bunrei** (Japanese). A divided or apportioned spirit. When a new branch of an already existing Shintō shrine is established, the spirit of the deity of the former shrine is divided, and a portion enshrined in the new location. While the original deity is not considered in any way lessened by this procedure, the newly formed branch spirit is generally thought of as inferior in stature to the original. *Bunrei* refers both to the act of dividing and to the newly formed branch spirit.

**god**. A term of Germanic origin designating the transcendent object or objects of religious devotion and worship. In the context of monotheism, God, often conceived of as male, is written with a capital letter as being a proper noun. In the context of polytheism 'god' designates a class of beings (i.e. gods and goddesses) who usually have their own specific names. Thus, in Greek mythology the gods are beings distinguished by their immortality from humans who are mortal, demons or spirits who are less powerful, and heroes who were elevated from human to divine status and therefore received worship. In view of the widely varying nature and status of transcendent or supernatural beings in various cultures, care should be taken over the extension of the terms 'God' and 'gods' into contexts in which they have no substantial history. For example, in the context of Buddhism it is preferable to speak of BODHISATTVAS, DEVAS etc. *See also* ARGUMENTS FOR THE EXISTENCE OF GOD; ATHEISM; AGNOSTICISM; DEISM; HENOTHEISM; PANENTHEISM; PANTHEISM; THEISM; DEITY.

**goddess**. A female divinity or deity (*compare* GOD). In most religious contexts goddesses and gods are of comparable importance and it is not unusual for the supreme deity to be thought of as female, e.g. Amaterasu, the Japanese sun-goddess.

**Godianism**. A Nigerian religious movement founded in 1962 on the basis of a nationalist organization called National Church dating from 1948. Although the National Church espoused an anti-white stance in the context of the Nigerian independence movement,

Godianism preaches the universal brotherhood of mankind. (Onunwa 1989).

**God of the gaps**. A pejorative phrase referring to the use of 'God' as an explanatory hypothesis to plug the current holes in existing scientific explanations; also called DEUS EX MACHINA. As science itself gradually fills the holes in our understanding of the world, Dietrich Bonhoeffer (1906–45) and others have observed, the need for 'God' in this sense recedes until God is 'pushed out of the universe' altogether: ' "God" as a working hypothesis, as a stop-gap for our embarrassments, has become superfluous.' (Bonhoeffer 1971: 381).

**godparent**. A person (i.e. a godfather or a godmother) who stands as proxy for a child in the Christian rite of the baptism of infants, making promises on the child's behalf and accepting responsibility for the child's spiritual upbringing. *See also* COMPADRAZGO.

**gohei** (Japanese). Cut and folded white paper strips; commonly attached to a *shimenawa* (a dividing rope hung before a Shintō shrine) indicating separation and purity.

**Goibniu**. Irish Celtic god of smiths said to possess the ale of immortality. In Wales he is called Govannon.

**Golden Bough**. An extremely influential multi-volume work created by 'arm-chair' anthropologist T.G. Frazer in the heyday of 19th-century comparative religion, and finally completed in 1915. The work brought together classical scholarship, ethnology and folklore, emphasized the primacy of ritual over belief, distinguished religion from magic, and highlighted kingship. Although it has been extremely influential, not least on popular thinking about religion, Frazer's work is now mainly of historical interest; he contributed to the now widespread recognition that religious studies must take account of anthropological data and theory.

**Golden Calf**. The effigy made by the Israelites while MOSES was on Mount SINAI (*Exodus* 32). The episode is undoubtedly a literary echo of JEROBOAM'S REFORM (*1 Kings* 12.26–33) and is to be construed in that context. It sets the theme of apostasy at the heart of the COVENANT narrative. (Bailey 1971; Sasson 1973; Motzki 1975; Vermeylen 1985).

**Golden Fleece**. *See* HERO(ES).

**Golden Temple**. *See* AMRITSAR.

**golem** (Hebrew: 'clod'). An earthen robot sustained by the consciousness of its maker. The best-known golem, according to legend, was the one fashioned by the famous Kabbalist Rabbi Judah Loew of Prague.

**goles**. *See* GALUT.

**goma ceremony**. A ceremony, frequently carried out in Tendai and Shingon Buddhism (*see* TENDAI-SHŪ; SHINGON-SHŪ), in which wooden sticks are burned to the accompaniment of sutra recitation. Since the sticks bear brief statements of the prayers and wishes of the people the goma ceremony represents the burning of the passions of this world. The Japanese word *goma* is derived, via Chinese, from the Sanskrit *homa*, the ceremony being Indian (non-Buddhist) in origin.

**gongen** (Japanese). An avatar or manifestation of a buddha or bodhisattva, often in the form of another deity or a human being.

**gongūji**. *See* GUJI.

**gongyō** (Japanese). The chanting of Buddhist sutras.

**gopi**. *See* KṚṢṆA.

**gopis**. *See* RĀDHĀ.

**go-ryō** (Japanese). Furious spirits, among the Shintō KAMI. The vengeful spirits (*on-ryō*) of those who had died a tragic death or had been viciously executed used to be specially enshrined as *go-ryō*, when fears arose that they might cause disasters such as storm, drought or plague. Rituals held for their corporate pacification are *go-ryō-e*, and are mostly held as summer festivals.

**go-shintai** (Japanese). An object such as a mirror, special stone(s) or metal object(s) with which the presence of a SHINTŌ deity (KAMI) is associated, shintai literally meaning the 'body of the kami'. Since the *go-shintai* is wrapped up and kept in the inaccessible main shrine (*honden*) its precise nature is usually unknown. In some instances the *go-shintai* is nothing less than a mountain, known as a *shintaizan*, lying behind the shrine.

**Gospel of Philip**. *See* NAG HAMMADI.

**Gospel of Thomas**. *See* NAG HAMMADI.

**Gospel of Truth**. *See* NAG HAMMADI.

**Govannon**. *See* GOIBNIU.

**goy** (Hebrew). The Hebrew term for a 'nation', be it Israel or any other. In Yiddish, however, the term has come to mean a specifically non-Jewish person, and the plural form *goyim* means non-Jews in general.

**Graces**. Daughters of ZEUS who personified the joy and well-being of nature and who were considered to be present at divine and human marriages in ancient Greece.

**grail**. *See* HOLY GRAIL.

**grāmavāsin** (Sinhalese: 'village-dwelling'). In Sri Lanka there is a traditional distinction between 'forest-dwelling' (ĀRAÑÑAVĀSIN) and 'village-dwelling' Buddhist monks. The village-dwellers live in close and frequent contact with the laity and the secular authorities as well as taking care of various ceremonies, feasts and rituals.

**Grandfather/Grandmother**. A collective designation in Native American religions for spirits understood to be relatives. The spirits may also be spoken to individually. *Compare* GRANDMOTHER MOON.

**Grandmother Moon**. The major female celestial spirit in Native American religions. She is closely related to menstrual rituals and female spiritual power.

**granicero** (New World Spanish). A weather-worker (from *granizo*: 'hail'), a conjurer of clouds, a person who survives being struck by lightning and is then obligated to serve the weather spirits. Though especially gifted in controlling bad weather and curing AIRE illnesses, he can also use his gift for evil. In Central Mexico the *granicero* seeks visions through the use of OLOLIUHQUI. (Ingham 1986).

**Granth**. *See* GURŪ GRANTH SĀHIB.

**granthī** (Punjabi). A reader of the GURŪ GRANTH SĀHIB who is often also responsible for the care of the GURDWĀRĀ, a Sikh place of worship.

**great doubt**. In Zen Buddhism, fundamental doubt or great doubt, which drives a person to the limits of ordinary, discriminating consciousness, after which a new freedom is enjoyed. A stage in Zen Buddhist experience.

**Great Ennead**. *See* COSMOGONY.

**Great Mother**. *See* METER.

**Great Renunciation**. *See* RENUNCIATION.

**Great Spirit**. In Native American religions, the spirits may be collectively referred to by terms which are frequently translated as the 'Great Spirit'. In more recent times, the term may be used for a HIGH GOD, and, under Christian influence, may be replaced by the term 'Creator'. *See also* MANITOU.

**greegree** [gree gree, gri-gri]. In western areas of West Africa a charm or amulet; also refers to the SANDE association. The word is of unknown origin but is used in local French and English as well as in some African languages (Hair 1967).

**Gregorian Chant**. The musical form of the Latin MASS ascribed to Gregory I (Pope from 590 to 604) current throughout western Christianity until the Reformation, and thereafter mainly in the Roman Catholic Church until the Second Vatican Council (1962–5). Grout defines it as follows: 'Gregorian Chant consists of single-line melody sung to Latin words by unaccompanied men's voices, in a flexible rhythm articulated by means other than regular accentuation, in a scale system different from our major or minor; and it has an impersonal, objective, other-worldly quality in which sensuous beauty and emotional appeal are largely subordinate to expression of the religious content of the text.' (Grout 1973: 36).

**gṛhastya**. *See* ĀŚRAMA.

**gri gri**. *See* GREEGREE.

**Guadalupe**. The short name for the Virgin Mary of Guadalupe, Mexico City, popularly regarded as the Queen of Mexico and the Empress of the Americas.

**Guan Di** (Chinese: 'Emperor Guan') [Kuan Ti, Guan Gong, Kuan Kung]. A popular Chinese deity, sometimes called the Chinese God of War. This designation is misleading, however, because he is worshipped not only as a martial hero but also as a patron saint of literature, commerce and sworn brotherhoods. Like many popular Chinese gods he is a deified historical personage, i.e. Guan Yu, a famous general of the 3rd century.

**Guanyin**. *See* AVALOKITEŚVARA.

**guardian angel**. According to some Christian beliefs, especially among Roman Catholics, a specific angel is assigned to individual persons to accompany them through life and protect them from harm and from wrongdoing, and is hence known as a guardian angel. It has sometimes been believed that Satan too has assigned a devil to accompany individuals on their path and to strengthen their innate inclination towards wrongdoing. In the Middle Ages there was sometimes speculation about the number of guardian angels or accompanying devils per person.

**gui** [kuei] (Chinese). In Chinese religion, usually a malignant spirit who can cause all possible kinds of misfortune. In this sense it can be translated as 'demon' or 'evil spirit'. More specifically *gui* are the spirits of human beings that for some reason have not entered the underworld but haunt among the living. They belong to the sphere of YIN; as such they are opposed to SHEN. The *gui* may be propitiated by offerings or exorcised.

**guji** (Japanese). The head priest of a Shintō shrine. His deputy is a *gongūji*.

**Gungnir**. *See* ODIN.

**gunungan** (Indonesian). A leaf-shaped, triangular symbol of MERU, used in WAYANG performances for different purposes such as announcing the beginning, pauses and the end of a play (Stutterheim 1926; Groenendael 1985).

**gurbānī** (Punjabi). The verses or 'utterances' of the Sikh spiritual teachers of which the GURŪ GRANTH SĀHIB is composed.

**gurdwārā** [Gurdvārā] (Punjabi: 'door of the Gurū'). A place of worship where the Sikh scripture is installed. Originally, Sikhs gathered in buildings known as *dharamśālā* which subsequently became known as *gurdwārā* as they were felt, through the presence of gathered Sikhs and later the Sikh scripture (GURŪ GRANTH SĀHIB), to contain the mystic presence of the Gurū or God (*see* TEN GURŪS). In addition to the area for worship in which regular rituals, festivals and life cycle rites (SAṄSKĀR) are performed, there is a *laṅgar* or communal kitchen in which food is prepared and shared. Another common feature of *gurdwārās* is the NIŚAÑ SĀHIB. (Cole and Sambhi 1978).

**Gurmat** (Punjabi). The teachings of the gurūs; the Sikh belief system. *See also* TEN GURŪS; GURŪ GRANTH SĀHIB; KHĀLSĀ.

**Gurmukh** (Punjabi). A Sikh who follows the GURŪ's Word (ŚABD).

**Gurmukhī** (Punjabi). The script of the GURŪ GRANTH SĀHIB, used for writing modern Punjabi.

**gurpurb** (Punjabi). Anniversaries of events in the lives of the Sikh Gurūs (*see* TEN GURŪS), particularly the birthdays of Gurū Nānak and Gurū Gobind Singh, often commemorated in the GURDWĀRĀ with an AKHAṆḌ PAṬH.

**gurū/guru**. A term used in various Indian languages to mean a teacher of great spiritual authority towards whom a sense of personal submission is felt.

**Gurū Granth Sāhib** (Punjabi). The principal scripture of the Sikhs, also known as ĀDI GRANTH. As its name implies, it is a revered book or anthology containing the words of the TEN GURŪS. At the time of the death of Gobind Singh, in 1708, the last of the ten Gurūs, it was instituted as the ultimate spiritual authority and accepted as the repository of the 'utterances of the Gurū' or GURBĀNĪ. This text includes verses by the ninth Gurū in addition to those contained in an earlier work, compiled in 1604 by the fifth Gurū, Arjan. The earlier work contained verses by the first five Gurūs and several North Indian poets (SANT tradition), Kabīr, Ravidās, Nāmdev and Sheikh Farīd.

It is divided into 31 parts based on the Indian musical modes, *rāga*, and has 1,430 pages. It is written in GURMUKHĪ script, which is now used for modern Punjabi. The introductory section contains verses used in daily prayer (*see* JAPJI), and the book as a whole, which is placed in all Sikh temples (GURDWĀRĀ), is used in rites and festivals (SAṄSKĀR, AKHAṆḌ PAṬH, BAISĀKHĪ; *see also* HUKAM). Its poetic content focuses primarily on the human quest to attain the ultimate relationship with the one Gurū or God (SAHAJ). (For discussions on Sikh texts as sources for study see Juergensmeyer & Barrier 1979; Cole & Sambhi 1978; Cole 1984b; McLeod 1984.)

**Gurū Nanak**. *See* SANT TRADITION.

**gutuater**. Celtic priest. It is not known to what extent the gutuater is to be distinguished from the DRUID, but the derivation of the word from the Irish *guth* ('voice') suggests the particular function of invocation of the gods.

# H

**Ḥabad**. An anagram of '*ḥokhmah*' ('wisdom'), *binah* ('understanding') and *daat* ('knowledge'), the uppermost triad of the ten SEFIROT. Also, the proper name of the Lubavitcher School of ḤASIDISM, founded by Reb Shneur Zalman of Liadi.

**Hachiman**. Generally, the deified Japanese Emperor Ōjin together with his mother Empress Jingū and his wife Himegami. They were first enshrined in the Usa Hachiman Shrine in Ōita Prefecture and later in many Hachiman shrines throughout Japan. Historically worshipped by the military class as a god (KAMI) of war, Hachiman has now become a more general object of devotion.

**Hadad**. *See* ADAD.

**ḥadath** (Arabic). Minor ritual impurity in Islām. *See also* ṬAHĀRA.

**ḥadd** (Arabic; plural, *ḥudūd*). In the QUR'ĀN, the limits or the commands and prohibitions laid down by ALLĀH (God). Hence in Islamic law, the term is used for the unalterable punishments prescribed by canon, for example, stoning or scourging for falsely accusing (*qadhf*) a married woman of adultery.

**Haddu**. *See* ADAD.

**Hades**. A son of CRONOS and RHEA and brother of ZEUS and POSEIDON, Hades became ruler of the underground realm of the dead when the three brothers drew lots after they had deposed CRONOS. Thus Hades becomes the name of the abode where departed souls spend a dreary existence. *Contrast* ELYSIUM.

**ḥadīth** (Arabic). In Islamic tradition a report relating especially the words, deeds and views of the Prophet Muḥammad, or those of his Companions and other early prominent Muslims (more properly designated *athar*). The ḥadīth, which have survived in major collections from the 9th and 10th centuries CE, notably those of al-Bukhārī (*d* 870) and Muslim (*d* 875), constitute the Prophet's *Sunna*, or exemplary and normative practice, which forms a source of the law (SHARĪ'A) second only to that of the QUR'ĀN.

**ḥāfiẓ** (Arabic). Literally 'preserver'. One who memorizes the text of the QUR'ĀN.

**Haftarah** (Hebrew). The 'additional' portion, usually taken from the Hebrew Prophets, which corresponds to the weekly TORAH reading recited in the SYNAGOGUE. The reading of a Haftarah was originally instituted at a time of persecution of the Jews, when public reading of the Torah was forbidden. It is easier to read the Haftarah, because the section is shorter, and because it is read from a book containing vowel and cantillation marks not included in the scroll from which the Torah is read. (Cantillation marks indicate how a text is to be intoned.)

**Haggadah**. Literally, the 'telling' of the story of the Exodus of Israel from Egypt. A book of commentaries, blessings and prayers recited by Jews at a Passover SEDER.

**Hagia Sophia**. The name of the huge Byzantine cathedral at Constantinople (now Istanbul) which was forcibly turned into a mosque at the fall of that city to the Ottomans in 1453 and is now a museum. The name, being Greek, means Sacred (*hagia*) Wisdom (*Sophia*) and referred to the Wisdom of God.

**hagiography**. The life-story of a saint (Greek, *hagios*), or the practice of writing such works. In particular hagiography is regarded as the painstaking compilation of a saint's life-story in such a way as to bring out not only his or her saintly qualities but also miraculous incidents. As a result a hagiographical narrative is often regarded as one which fictitiously heightens the supernatural features of a saint's experience and activity. Accordingly, *hagiology* is the detailed study of such legends, usually by an admirer of the genre, and *hagiolatry* is the idolatrous worship of saints, who in Catholic teaching are supposed to be venerated but not worshipped. *Compare* ARETOLOGY.

**hagiolatry**. *See* HAGIOGRAPHY.

**hagiology**. *See* HAGIOGRAPHY.

**haiden** (Japanese). Hall of worship standing to the fore of a Shintō shrine.

**Hail Mary**. The name given to a short prayer which begins with these words (in Latin, AVE MARIA) and based in part on the salutation of Mary by the Angel Gabriel and by Elizabeth (*Luke*, chapter 1). The text runs as follows: 'Hail Mary, full of grace, the Lord is with thee. Blessed art thou among women, and blessed is the fruit of thy womb, Jesus. Holy Mary, Mother of God, pray for us sinners, now and in the hour of our death.' The saying of a number of Hail Marys is often used as a form of PENANCE in the Roman Catholic Church.

**ḥājj** (Arabic). The Muslim pilgrimage to MECCA, one of the FIVE PILLARS of their faith, enjoined upon every adult Muslim, of either sex, to be performed at least once in a lifetime provided one is able to do so. The pilgrimage is fixed for certain days in the first half of the month Dhū 'l-Ḥijja, the last of the Muslim lunar year. The pilgrim wears a special, ritually clean garment (*iḥrām*) and avoids certain taboos during the period of the *Ḥājj*. The end of the pilgrimage is celebrated by the Feast of the Sacrifice ('Īd al-Aḍḥā). The pilgrim is accorded the special prestige of the honourary title of *Ḥājj* or *Ḥājjī* (for men) and *Ḥājja* (for women). (*See* article 'Hadjdj', *Encyclopedia of Islam*.)

**ḥakham** (Hebrew; plural, *ḥakhmim*). A wise man or a sage.

**halakhah** (Hebrew). The 'path' or way of life described by rabbinic law. As an adjective: halakhic.

**ḥallah** (Hebrew). Traditional Jewish SABBATH bread, from which a portion of dough is 'separated' and burned in memory of the destruction of the Temple in Jerusalem. It is customary for *ḥallah* to be an egg bread, made of several strands twisted together.

**Hallel** (Hebrew). A special service of 'praise', containing Psalms 113–18, recited on Jewish holy days.

**Hallelujah** (Hebrew: 'praise God'). A jubilant expression found in the Jewish Psalms which has hence come into widespread Christian usage. *See also* ALLELUIA.

**hallucination**. Experiences, impressions or perceptions which do not correspond to any outer stimuli as in the case of perceptions of normal sight, hearing or feeling. They occur in normal individuals in the form of dreams, in the process of falling asleep, and in the form of daydreams (so-called hypnagogical pictures). Hallucinations may occur in conjunction with the taking of hallucinatory drugs (such as LSD) and may also be associated with certain mental disturbances such as schizophrenia. Many visions of a religious character can be interpreted as being hallucinatory or illusory.

**halo**. A bright ring or disc around the head of a holy person depicted iconographically. Halo derives from Greek *halos*, meaning such a disc, but the Latin-derived term *nimbus* ('a cloud') is sometimes used with the same meaning as halo in the context of ICONOGRAPHY.

**Haloa**. An Athenian winter festival marked by a feast of food and ribald humour, including pastries resembling male and female genital organs to celebrate the sexual potential in society and in nature.

**Hanafi**. *See* MADHHAB.

**hampeq**. *See* ALTOMISAYOQ.

**hanaqpacha** (Quechua). The upper world which can be reached after life, where God and other deities are thought to exist. The counterpart to *hanaqpacha* is *ukhupacha*, which means underworld. The entrance to this part of the world is through rivers or lakes. This explains the importance of water-places to the Andean people. The *ukhupacha* is inhabited by tiny people and animals who have the capability of shamans. The profane world in between these two worlds is *kaypacha*, this world. The Quechua people use the same word *pacha* to indicate space and time as two inseparable aspects of the cosmos. *See* PACHAMAMA.

**Ḥanbalī**. *See* MADHHAB

**Ḥanif**. *See* MECCA

**Hannya Shingyō**. *See* HEART SUTRA

**Ḥanukkah** (Hebrew). The festival of the 'rededication' of the Holy Temple in Jerusalem, after the successful Ḥasmonean revolt against the Syrian Greeks in 165 BCE. The celebration of Ḥanukkah traditionally involves the lighting of a special eight-branched MENORAH, as well as playing games of chance with a DREYDEL.

**haoma**. *See* ZOROASTRIANISM.

**Hapi**. An ancient Egyptian god of the Nile, often represented in hermaphrodite form. He was one of the Four Sons of HORUS, demigods who protected the deceased's viscera. *See also* CANOPIC JAR.

**ḥaqīqa** (Arabic). Literally, in its plural form (*haqā'iq*), 'realities', a term used among ṢŪFĪS for the attributes of ALLĀH that are to be distinguished from his essence.

**ḥaqq** (Arabic: 'truth', 'reality'). Used as a designation of ALLĀH or ultimate reality, especially by ṢŪFĪS.

**hara** (Māori). Wrong-doing in the form of ritual transgressions or of breaking a TAPU. It is followed by sickness or even death.

**harae** (Japanese). Traditional pronunciation for HARAI, Shintō purification ceremony.

**harai** (Japanese). Shintō purification ceremonies in which prayers are offered for the removal of all sin, pollution and misfortune. The body and mind are purified and restored to a condition worthy of approaching the god (KAMI). The origin of *harae* is described in the Kojiki myth of the god Izanagi no mikoto, who is said to have washed in order to remove pollution after visiting the land of the dead (YOMI). *Harae* is performed at the beginning of all religious ceremonies and whenever a specified need arises. (In ancient times, two types of *harae*, called *yoshi-harae* and *ashi-harae* [literally, 'purification of good' and 'purification of evil'], seem to have been performed, but the meaning of the two terms is not clear.) The Ōharae (great purification) is a major ceremony performed at the end of June and December of each year and on other special occasions.

**Harakhte**. A hawk-headed god of HELIOPOLIS, associated with RE. A form of HORUS (literally, 'Horus of the Horizon').

**ḥaram** (Arabic). Sanctuary or sacred enclave. Few Islamic monuments count as sanctuaries, apart from MECCA, MADINA and Jerusalem and certain towns in Iraq (e.g. Najaf) and Iran (e.g. Mashhad) which SHĪʿA Muslims regard as such. The MOSQUE is not regarded as a sanctuary by Muslims.

**ḥārām** (Arabic). Forbidden. *See* SHARĪʿA.

**Ḥaramain**. *See* MECCA.

**Hare Krishna Movement**. Known also as the International Society for Krishna Consciousness (ISKCON), this movement was founded in New York in the mid-1960s by Bhaktivedānta Swāmi Prabhupāda, a *sannyāsī* of the GAUḌIYA VAIṢṆAVA MATH. Like this earlier movement, it focuses on devotion to Kṛṣṇa through veneration of Caitanya. It has a number of temples in India but the majority of its members are migrant Hindus or Western converts. (Mangalvadi 1977; Knott 1986).

**Harimandir** (Punjabi). A place of Sikh worship and pilgrimage at AMRITSAR on the site where the Golden Temple now stands. Also known as Darbār Sāhib.

**Haroeris**. *See* KOM OMBO.

**Harpocrates**. *See* ISIS CULT.

**Harrist Church**. An independent African church located in the Ivory Coast, and founded by William Harris (1850–1929), a Liberian. Harris, like Abiodun Akinsowon (*see* 'ALADURA') claimed a visitation from the Angel Gabriel, who instructed him to preach the healing message of Christ and a political message about improving the conditions of African life. The church is now well established in the Ivory Coast and has led to the development of other religious movements in neighbouring countries (Haliburton 1971).

**haruspices** (Latin). Etruscan diviners devoted to interpreting entrails, omens and lightning. Their methods were generally continued in Roman religion.

**ḥasan** (Arabic: 'good', 'beautiful'). In Islām, Prophetic traditions (ḤADĪTH) which are in the middle category, acceptable but not perfectly sound. *See also* SAḤĪḤ; ḌAʿĪF.

**ḥasid** (Hebrew; plural, *ḥasidim*). Literally, a person of 'generosity', 'loving kindness', or great devotion. In the Ḥasidic movement (*See* ḤASIDISM) the term came to mean a member of that movement, especially the 'disciple' of a certain Ḥasidic Rebbe. According to Hengel (1974: i/175ff) these 'Righteous Ones' had already formed a sect in the Maccabaean period, from whom derived the ESSENES (possibly a Greek formation on *ḥasid*), the PHARISEES and ideas associated with APOCALYPSE. However these views have been questioned in Davies 1977.

**Ḥasidism** (from Hebrew, *ḥasidut*). Although the term was used by earlier pietistic movements, Ḥasidism generally refers to the popular movement of mystical revival which swept through the Jewish communities of Galicia and much of Eastern Europe in the latter half of the 18th century. Founded by Rabbi Israel Baal Shem Tov, and given shape by his disciple, Rabbi Dov Baer the Maggid of Mezerich, Ḥasidism gave rise in a very short time to a great many charismatic rabbis, known as tzaddiqim (*See* TZADDIQ), who represented a rich variety of spiritual types. Ḥasidism reshaped Kabbalistic doctrines, giving them a psychological interpretation and a folksy expression which made them accessible to the Jewish masses instead of only the scholarly and ascetic élite. The movement was vigorously opposed by the Mitnaggdim, who feared that the spread of mystical ideas would bring back the chaos that had accompanied false messiahs like Shabbtai Tzvi and Jacob Frank in previous generations. The decline of Ḥasidism which had already begun at the beginning of the 19th century, was caused mainly by the complacency of its own leaders, and the inroads made by the HASKALAH or secular Enlightenment. While remnants of a number of Ḥasidic sects survive into our day, only the Ḥabad movement of Lubavitcher Ḥasidism continues to attract a large following. In a less organized way, the Ḥasidic teachings of Reb Nahman of Bratzlav – who died in 1810, leaving no successor – continue to exert an influence on the contemporary scene.

**hasina** (Malagasy). An extra-human force in Madagascar; every soul becomes more or less *hasina* after death, according to the previous social status (Schomerus-Gernböck 1975).

**hasina**. *See* MANA.

**Haskalah** (Hebrew). The Jewish movement of secular 'Enlightenment' which flourished in 19th-century Europe. Encouraged by the egalitarian spirit represented by the French revolution, the *maskilim* ('enlightened') urged their fellow Jews to set aside the traditional religious practices and beliefs which separated them from the world around them, and to pursue studies and pursuits which would relate them to the secular world.

**Hasmoneans**. A Jewish dynasty. After a protracted war following the MACCABAEAN REVOLT, independence from Seleucid rule was attained in 142 BCE under Simon Hasmon, who established a dynasty which lasted until the Roman annexation of 63 BCE.

**hathayoga**. *See* YOGA.

**Hathor**. An ancient Egyptian cow-goddess of love, beauty and dancing, worshipped particularly in Sinai and at LUXOR and DENDERA. She was the wife of HORUS the Elder and mother of Ihy.

**hatsumōde** (Japanese). A visit to a Shintō shrine at the beginning of the year to pray for happiness and divine protection. The term is also used at Buddhist temples in Japan which draw large numbers of visitors at New Year.

**Havdalah** (Hebrew). A special service marking the 'separation' between the SABBATH and the rest of the week, recited after the evening prayers at the conclusion of the Sabbath. This brief but moving service involves blessings recited over a cup of wine, a box of spices and the light of a twisted candle.

**ḥaver** (Hebrew). A friend. Also, a member of a KIBBUTZ.

**ḥavurah** (Hebrew; plural *ḥavurot*). An informal closely knit 'fellowship' of friends, who gather for prayer, celebration and study. The *ḥavurah* movement arose in the United States in the late 1960s, among Jews who felt alienated by large Jewish institutions. Although originally a non-sectarian movement, some SYNAGOGUES in recent years have sponsored the formation of small *ḥavurot* among their membership.

**Hawaiki**. According to most central and eastern Polynesian traditions, the mythical home from which the ancestors originally came and to which the spirits of the dead return. It is also the name originally given to the largest of the Hawaiian islands by Polynesian settlers.

**ḥazzan** (Hebrew). A cantor, chosen to lead Jewish communal prayers because of his voice and/or his piety. The *ḥazzan* is not a priest; according to Jewish law, any Jewish male may serve as a *ḥazzan*. Yet a *ḥazzan* is needed to lead the congregation when prayers requiring a quorum of a MINYAN are recited.

**Heart Scarab**. *See* SCARAB.

**Heart Sūtra**. A short Mahāyāna Buddhist sutra stating the teaching of PRAJÑĀPĀRAMITĀ and widely used in ritual contexts because of its brevity and its concluding mantra (Conze 1958).

**heaven**. The mythically conceived abode of God, where he is enthroned. Jewish tradition sometimes referred to seven heavens, suggested by the sun, moon and five planets. The Garden of Eden has been located in the third heaven (*2 Enoch* 8.4ff) and Adam has been thought to be in Paradise there (*Apocalypse of Moses* 37.5, 40.2). New Testament views of heaven, which are entirely unsystematic, are a continuation of such ideas (*Luke* 23.43; *2 Corinthians* 12.2). In Indian and Buddhist cosmology there is also a plurality of heavens, largely understood as the abode of Brahma and other heavenly beings such as devas or as a place of temporary existence for a bodhisattva who will be reborn as a buddha (the Tusita Heaven). In classical Chinese thought Heaven (*tian* [*t' ien*]) represents a principle of cosmic order and authority and is not a place of abode.

**Heavenly Stems**. The Ten Heavenly Stems (*tiangan [t'ien-kan*]) and Twelve Terrestrial Branches (*dizhi* [*ti-chih*]) are a traditional Chinese system for marking the time. In combination they account for a cycle of 60 units, e.g. years, months, days or hours. For example: the first year is marked by a combination of two characters, the symbol of the first of the Ten Heavenly Stems and the symbol of the first of the Twelve Terrestrial Branches. The second year is composed of the second Stem and the second Branch and so on. After a cycle of ten Stems is completed it starts again with the first one, now being combined with the eleventh of the Branches and so on. In this way a complete cycle consists of 60 years. The system of the Ten Heavenly Branches and Twelve Terrestrial Branches has great significance in traditional Chinese cosmological and historical speculations and is widely used in astrology and geomancy (FENGSHUI). *See also* ALMANAC.

**Hebat**. A Hurrian fertility goddess, consort of TESHUB (Laroche 1948).

**Hecate**. The ancient Greek virgin goddess of pathways and journeys.

**ḥeder** (Yiddish: 'a room'). An Eastern European Jewish elementary school, frequently a one-room schoolhouse.

**hedonism** (from Greek *hedone*: 'pleasure'). A world-view according to which the maximization of pleasure should be the main principle of regulating action.

**Hegelianism**. In Europe, a philosophical school shaped by Hegel's thinking at the beginning of the 1820s. It was influential in the development of Protestant theology and philosophy of religion. The school was distinguished for its use of a method of analysis which requires the positing of a thesis that then generated its own antithesis, with the tension between the two resulting in a synthesis. The method, which was believed to triumph over the contradictions of historical concreteness, delineated a system which accounted for all aspects of reality and culminated with a final category called Absolute Spirit. Through the period 1830–41, it led to conflicts over certain theological issues, especially survival after death, attributes of Christ, and the idea of God. The influence of this school assisted in the emergence of Marxism and existentialism.

**Heilsgeschichte** (German: 'Salvation history'). The history, or story in history, of the salvific action of God for the benefit of humankind.

**heimarmene** (Greek). Fate, destiny; from Heraclitus onwards the Greek term for the law of the cosmos, and in the *Stoa* the inescapable fate of gods and human beings. The MYSTERY RELIGIONS, GNOSTICISM and Christianity promised salvation from heimarmene through ritual, knowledge and faith.

**Heimdall**. Germanic god, probably one of the VANIR. He was the watchman of ASGARD, said to blow his horn to warn the gods of the immanence of RAGNAROK.

**Heitsi-Eibib**. A mythological 'national hero' of the Hottentots and benevolent TRICKSTER (*see* KAGGEN). Countless heaps of stone in Cape Province and Kalahari are considered as his graves (Hirschberg 1975: 402).

**Heket**. An ancient Egyptian frog-headed goddess, with a centre at Antinopolis. Associated with KHNUM, she was a protective goddess of childbirth.

**Hekiganroku**. The Japanese title of the Chinese work (*Pi-yen-lu*), being a collection of one hundred kōan completed in 1125 and later regarded as one of the most important texts of Ch'an or Zen Buddhism.

**Hel**. In Germanic mythology both the name of the goddess of the underworld and the term used to refer to the underworld itself. According to the PROSE EDDA Hel is the daughter of LOKI, and ODIN gave her charge of the nine worlds of the dead in the land of cold and darkness, Niflheim.

***Heliand***. A 9th-century epic poem which presents Christ and his Apostles after the manner of an Anglo-Saxon lord with his vassals, thus conveying an impression of Christian virtues in the language of the time.

**Heliopolis** (Greek: 'city of the sun'). The Greek name for the ancient Egyptian city of Iwnw, centre of the solar cult where, according to Heliopolitan mythology, creation had occurred.

**Helios** (Greek: 'sun'). The ancient Greek god of the sun.

**hell**. A place of punishment after death for the wicked, from which there is no further escape. In the main theistic religions the notion developed from the ancient Jewish conception of Sheol, a shadowy underworld for all the departed, apparently modified by recollections of cultic human sacrifice from the valley of Hinnom (*Ge Hinnom*, giving Greek *Gehenna*). In Buddhist teaching the various hells, which together amount to one of the possible states of rebirth, are in principle states of existence in which bad karma is worked off, usually while suffering terrible torments. In this sense they are more comparable to the purgatory of Catholic tradition, where souls are purged of their sins in preparation for going to heaven later. However, the worst hell of all in Buddhist teaching (the Avici hell) is supposed to inflict interminable suffering from which one can only be saved by the intervention of a bodhisattva. *See also* HADES.

**Hellenistic Judaism**. In the Jewish context, Hellenism implies the influence of Greek, and especially Hellenistic, culture on theology, due to the Ptolemaic and Seleucid occupations of Palestine, and the influence of Jewish literature from Alexandria. (Tcherikover 1961; Hengel 1974; Schürer 1979: 1–183).

**Hellenistic religions**. Varying religions of the Hellenistic period, which may be classified as (a) piety, or traditional Hellenic (Greek) practices that established and maintained right relationship to the cosmic order, including the social order; (b) the Greco-Roman mystery cults; and (c) the various gnostic traditions of late antiquity. These diverse religious expressions were constituents of a coherent religious system informed by an expanded image of space due to the conquests of Alexander the Great, the resulting ideal of imperial internationalism and the widening of cultural and intellectual horizons, especially by influences from the East and Egypt. This spatial expanse was given systematic structure by the cosmological revolution that occurred during the 3rd century BCE, later named the Ptolemaic revolution after the astronomical compendium of Ptolemy (2nd century CE). A period of Hellenistic religious history beginning with these new conditions for knowledge in the late 4th century BCE concludes with the official dominance of Christianity by the late 4th century CE (Martin 1987).

**Helvetic Confessions**. Two theological statements, issued in 1536 and 1566 respectively, being based largely on the ideas of Zwingli and in the second case also of Calvin, which won acceptance in Protestant Switzerland.

**henotheism**. Belief that only one god saves or is to be worshipped, although other gods may exist.

**henoticon** (Greek). A theological formula (482 CE) which attempted to mediate between MONOPHYSITISM and Nicene theology (*see* COUNCIL OF NICAEA) by omitting mention of the TWO NATURES in Christ.

**Hephaistos**. The son of ZEUS and HERA and husband of APHRODITE, the Greek deity of the fire and forge, often portrayed with a powerful torso but crippled feet. *Compare* VULCAN.

**Hera**. A daughter of CRONOS and RHEA, and sister and wife of ZEUS. In ancient Greece she was queen of the gods and protector of marriage, often complaining about her husband's infidelity.

**Heracleopolis**. *See* HERISHEF.

**Herakles**. In ancient Greece, a legendary human HERO, son of the divine ZEUS and the mortal Alcmene, who performed 'twelve labours' and eventually became divine. Herakles is known in Latin and hence in English as Hercules. *See also* MELGART.

**Heres**. *See* GNOSTICISM.

**heresy**. In the Christian church, the conscious, wilful choosing (from Greek *haíresis*: 'choice') of doctrine held to be contrary to APOSTOLIC teaching. Most of those deemed to be heretics from the standpoint of victorious orthodoxy thought of themselves as true Christians. Hence the term 'heresy' cannot be used in the history of religions without adopting an *a priori* partisan standpoint.

**Herishef**. An ancient Egyptian deity of Heracleopolis who protected foreigners; shown with a ram's head. He is known in Greek as Arsaphes.

**hermaphrodite**. A being displaying the characteristics of both the female and male sex.

**hermeneutical vortex**. The inescapable whirlpool down which those depart who agonize too greatly over difficulties of interpretation.

**hermeneutic circle**. The hermeneutic principle, associated in particular with Friedrich Schleiermacher, that one should interpret the whole in terms of the parts, and the parts in terms of the whole. It has been given a wider, ontological sense by Martin Heidegger and Hans-Georg Gadamer. For these thinkers the circle embraces a temporally or spatially distant text and its present interpreter, allowing a mutual illumination to take place between the perspectives of the text and the interpreter's own cultural assumptions. This circular to-and-fro, or 'fusion of horizons', is permitted by the common horizon of possible human meaning which is projected by all human beings upon Being itself. The later Heidegger, however, rejected the hermeneutic circle as too humanistic, preferring to speak of the endlessly *different* 'occurrence' of Being in succeeding historical epochs. *See also* DIFFERENCE; HERMENEUTICS.

**hermeneutics** (from Greek, *hermēneutikos*: 'of interpretation'). The science of interpretation of texts, or of other cultural artefacts (and sometimes, even, of natural processes). Such a science was already mooted by Aristotle, but was not systematically developed until the 18th century, in connection with a Protestant need to find criteria for the correct reading of the Bible. A need for such criteria was felt by Protestants rather than Catholics, because in the latter case the developing ecclesial tradition – which had at its heart the explication of the infinite allegorical riches of the Bible, but was here guided only by precedent and the creative promptings of the Spirit – was regarded as authoritative, rather than the Bible taken alone.

Since the work of Schleiermacher, which may be regarded as a watershed, hermeneutics has evolved from a branch of theology into a general human science. At the hands of Martin Heidegger, Hans-Georg Gadamer and Paul Ricoeur it has further developed into 'hermeneutic philosophy', for which the fundamental characteristic of all Being is its openness to interpretation, which is in principle never complete. However, the Protestant inheritance still tends to tie hermeneutics to notions of a self-interpreting totality (whether a text or a supposedly universal 'human' condition) and of a conversation between a distant text and an interpreting subject standing outside it. Beginning with the later Heidegger himself, postmodernist thinkers have tended to reject both notions, and this has thrown the hermeneutic enterprise into disfavour among some, including certain theologians. *See also* HERMENEUTIC CIRCLE; TEXT.

**Hermes**. The son of ZEUS and Maia; the perpetually young Greek deity who bears messages between gods and humans and also between humans. He is symbolized by the pile of stones that marked the boundaries of cities and travel between them. *Compare* MERCURY; THOTH.

**Hermetic writings**. A collection of theosophic, occult writings of the 2nd–4th centuries CE, which claim to be a revelation of the 'thrice-powerful' Hermes (Hermes Trismegistos). They are written in the form of dialogues and propagate in devotional manner the hellenistic (Platonist), gnostic, Jewish and Egyptian concepts of rebirth and the deliverance of the soul (*nous*) from the material world. Until the Renaissance, when they were studied with new interest, they were considered to be Platonic writings (Nock & Festugiere 1945).

**Hermopolis**. The capital of the 15th Nome (district) of Upper Egypt, and cult-centre of THOTH, where, according to Hermopolitan mythology, creation had occurred.

**heroes**. A class of Greek demigods, such as HERAKLES (Hercules) and THESEUS, who performed great deeds while alive. Also notable is Jason, the leader of the Argonauts and hero of the search for the Golden Fleece. Heroes were honoured with burial in a special grave (*heroon*) and continued to influence humans after they had died.

**Hestia**. A daughter of ZEUS and HERA, the ancient Greek goddess of home and hearth. *Compare* VESTA.

**hesychasm**. A system of meditation and asceticism, including breathing exercises and the repetition of the Jesus prayer ('Lord Jesus Christ, son of God, have mercy on me'), first developed by monks of Mount ATHOS. The purpose of these practices was to bring about visions of light, understood to be the energy of God (as opposed to his essence), implying theologically that knowledge of God is available through inward illumination (as opposed to revelation mediated by the church). Systematically stated by Philotheus Kokkinus, and further defended by Gregory Palamas, hesychasm became a subject of intense controversy in the 14th century and was widely seen as a distinctive feature of the Orthodox churches.

**Hetu and Luoshu** [*Ho-t'u* and *Lo-shu*] (Chinese: 'Chart [which came out] of the [Yellow] River'; 'River Chart' and 'Book [which came out] of the [river] Luo'). Two mysterious Chinese scriptures which seem to have been first mentioned in the YI JING and the SHU JING. They gained prominence during the Former Han dynasty (206 BCE – 23 CE) as part of the apocryphical *Chenwei* literature. According to one tradition the *Hetu* was carried by a dragon-horse which came out of the Yellow River and was used by Fu Xi to draw the Eight Trigrams. In this way it became the origin of the *Yi Jing*. The *Luoshu* is said to have been written on the back of a divine tortoise which appeared in the river Luo. It was used by Yu to organize the empire in nine parts. There are, however, many other explanations. Confucian scholars of different times attempted to reconstruct both drawings, but no agreement was reached.

**hetu-pratyaya** (Sanskrit). Cause and condition. The confluence of internal causality and external conditioning which gives rise to particular situations of human existence, according to Buddhist teaching.

**Hevajra Tantra**. *See* SA SKYA PA.

**hexagram**. *See* YIJING.

**Hexapla** (Greek: 'sixfold'). An edition of the Old Testament in six columns, giving the Hebrew text, a Greek transliteration of the Hebrew, and four Greek translations, compiled by the Alexandrian Origen (*c*.185 – *c*.254).

**hierarchy**. Holy order or holy rule, especially as guaranteed through a system of stratified offices. Thus in the Roman Catholic Church 'hierarchy' denotes the whole pattern of ranked membership from the lay person up to the POPE. 'The' hierarchy refers more commonly to the ordained ranks, of which there are in principle three (*see* ORDINATION). In practice further differentiations made for the purposes of administration have led to the institution of many others such as DEAN, ARCHDEACON, suffragan BISHOP, ARCHBISHOP and CARDINAL (*see also* DIOCESE; PATRIARCH; POPE). While the hierarchy appears to most believers to be a simple, God-given and authoritative structure, which ensures the validity and efficacy of religious practice, the historical variations, for example in the mode of election or appointment of bishops, have been quite striking.

**hieroglyphs**. The writing of ancient Egypt, incorporating ideograms (picture signs) and phonograms (sound signs). Cursive forms of hieroglyphs, known as hieratic and demotic, came into use for everyday writing purposes, but the older forms of hieroglyphs were retained for religious and formal texts.

**hieroi logoi**. *See* ORPHIC MYSTERIES.

**Higan**. The three-day period at the spring and autumn equinoxes during which Buddhist memorial services (*Higan-e*) are held for the dead.

**Higan-e**. *See* HIGAN.

**Higashi Honganji**. *See* HONGANJI.

**high church**. The name given to a loosely defined movement or party in the Church of England which stresses the continuity of this church with historic Christianity by emphasizing the apostolic succession and the sacramental ministry. The term itself arose in the late 17th century, when many high churchmen linked these views to the concept of the divine right of kings and support for the Stuarts. In changed political circumstances, however, the high church tradition was given a new lease of life by the 19th-century 'Oxford Movement' led by theologians Keble, Pusey and Newman.

**high gods**. The realization by Europeans that many apparently polytheistic religious systems, especially in Africa, included a celestial 'High God' holding sway above lesser divinities and spirits caused considerable interest in the 19th century in that it seemed to provide a point of contact for the Christian teaching of God. It also spurred speculation that there might have been a generally current ancient, or original monotheism (URMONOTHEISMUS) in Africa and elsewhere. More thorough research and reflection have made clear, however, that the innumerable variations do not permit such a simple conclusion. For various supreme beings and powers, some only of which fit into such a picture, *see* AMMA; CHUKWU; EL; GREAT SPIRIT; JOK; KAGGEN; KALUNGA; KIUMBI; KWOTH; LEZA; MANITOU; MULUNGU; MVIDYE; MWARI; NZAMBI; OLORUN; OURANOS; RUHANGA; U-MVELIQUANGI; U-NKHULUN-KHULU; U-TIXO; WAKAN; WAQA.

**High Holidays**. *See* ROSH HASHANNAH.

**high places**. Religious sites condemned by biblical writers (e.g. *1 Kings* 15.14). Their nature is uncertain, but they may have been tumuli where ancestral cults were observed for ancestors invoked as deities (*1 Samuel* 28.3–25, where, in v. 13, Samuel is called '*Elohim*', 'a god'). (Barrick 1975; Grintz 1977).

**Hijra** (Arabic). The migration of Muḥammad from MECCA to MEDINA in the year 632 CE, the event from which the Muslim era is computed in lunar years to give the *Anno Hegirae*.

**himatsuri** (Japanese). A Japanese festival centring around fire. Most are winter festivals held to pray for the restoration of the power of the sun. Some, such as that held at Yoshida-machi at the foot of Mount Fuji, are held with a view to divining the good or ill fortune of the coming year. The significance of fire in religious ceremonies is great. It is considered to be sacred, to have the power to destroy evil, and is used as a sign of the descent of a deity.

**Hīnayāna** (Sanskrit: 'the lesser vehicle'). A Mahāyāna term collectively denoting all early forms and schools of Buddhism, of which only THERAVĀDA now survives. Essentially a term of scorn, it should be avoided except in quotations, or in statements expressing the polemical Mahāyāna standpoint.

**Hinduism**. A modern term used to refer collectively to various traditions of Indian religion in which the Vedas and various subsequent texts are regarded as authoritative. *See also* INDIAN RELIGIONS.

**historicism**. A positivistic emphasis on the real events of particular history, elevated into a principle of thought and set over against some other guiding principle such as rationalism. *Compare* HISTORICITY.

**historicity**. The quality of an event's having taken place or of a person's having existed in real history. The historicity of several important religious figures has been questioned (Confucius, Lao Tse, the Buddha, Jesus, Mohammed), mainly by negative critics of the religions in question. In fact there is no serious historical doubt about the existence of any of these. It is quite a different question when it comes to particular events in their lives, since the formation of religious tradition typically involves a high degree of ARETOLOGY or HAGIOGRAPHY. Thus, the critical questioning of the historicity of particular events in religious contexts has justifiably become a common feature of thought about religion. Some religious people feel threatened by such questioning; others simply disregard it. It is sometimes argued that because of the nature of their teaching some religions, such as Buddhism, are less affected by critical questions about historicity than are others, such as Christianity or Islām. *Compare* HISTORICISM.

**hitbodedut** (Hebrew). 'Aloneness' and heart-felt conversation with God. A form of meditation taught by Rebbe Nahman of Bratzlav.

**hitlahavut** (Hebrew: 'flaming adoration'). The Ḥasidic term (*See* ḤASIDISM) for ecstasy or enthusiasm.

**Hittite religion**. An amalgam of Indo-European, ancient Anatolian and Hurrian religions in Asia Minor. (The Hittite Kingdom was founded in the 14th century BCE). (Dussaud 1945: 333–53; Cavaignac 1950; MacQueen 1986).

**hōben** (Japanese). An expedient or contrivance, especially, in Buddhist contexts, an expedient or provisional teaching intended to lead living beings into the full truth. The term is equivalent to Chinese *fang bien*. *Compare* Sanskrit UPĀYA (means) and UPĀYAKAUŚALYA (skilfulness in means).

**hogon**. *See* LÉBÉ.

**Hokekyō** [Hokkekyō]. Generally used Japanese name for the LOTUS SŪTRA.

**hokhmah**. *See* HABAD.

**Hokkekyō**. *See* HOKEKYŌ.

**Holocaust**. The extermination of some 6 million Jews by Nazi Germany in World War II, as part of the Nazi plan for the extermination of all Jews as a 'final solution to the Jewish problem'. Literally, the Greek-derived English term 'holocaust' means a 'whole sacrifice'; it is derived from a category of biblical sacrifices which were not to be partly eaten and enjoyed, but entirely consumed.

**holy**. As synonymous with 'sacred', the holy is the opposite of the profane. In primal religion the holy is that which is set apart from daily life, being unpredictably powerful, whether in a benign or threatening sense. Behaviour related to the holy is therefore directed towards maintaining the fragile stability of life by avoiding the transgression of boundaries (*see* TAPU) and harnessing the power for human benefit. This fundamental conception has radically influenced all complex religious developments in the most diverse cultures. In soteriological religious systems the holiness of the saviour figure or of God, in spite of any wrathful aspect, is usually understood in an overwhelmingly positive and ultimately non-dangerous sense. It thus becomes that quality of great goodness in which the believer aspires to participate. *Compare* NUMINOUS.

**Holy Communion**. *See* EUCHARIST.

**Holy Family**. The collective name for Jesus (as a child), Mary and Joseph, as celebrated specifically in the Roman Catholic Church since 1921 on the first Sunday after Epiphany.

**Holy Grail**. The cup or the flat dish (grail meaning 'dish' or 'bowl', from Old French) used at the Last Supper of Christ with his disciples and in medieval legend thought still to contain some of Christ's blood caught up by Joseph of Arimathaea. Appearing in French medieval tales, the legend was taken up in the stories of King Arthur. For those who were worthy and could find it, the Holy Grail was supposed to be of great mystical value, offering an ultimate and exclusive form of Holy Communion.

**Holy Land**. The Land of ISRAEL. The designation was first assigned to Palestine in the Middle Ages, partly in connection with the Crusades, to indicate the place where the sacred events of Christian history took place. In recent times the country has once again been claimed by the majority of Jews as the Promised Land of the Abrahamic COVENANT. *See also* ZIONISM.

**Holy See**. The episcopal seat of the Bishop of Rome, who is at the same time the POPE or supreme pontiff of the Roman Catholic Church.

**holy shroud**. *See* SHROUD OF TURIN.

**Holy Spirit**. The third person, with the Father and the Son, in the Christian conception of the TRINITY. In spite of his importance in the New Testament the Holy Spirit was relatively neglected in the early period of Christianity. The doctrine became problematical in the 2nd century, when the charismatic movement known as MONTANISM raised the question of distinguishing true and false operations of the Holy Spirit. In the theology of the influential Alexandrian theologian Origen (*c*185–*c*.254) the activity of the Spirit was restricted to the church alongside that of the Logos in all creation. The 4th-century 'Macedonians' (named after Macedonius, bishop of Constantinople) denied the Spirit's full divinity. However, the COUNCIL OF CONSTANTINOPLE (381) condemned Macedonianism, and the western church accepted the formula of three coequal persons in one Godhead. *See also* FILIOQUE.

**Holy Unction**. *See* EXTREME UNCTION, UNCTION.

**Holy Week**. The week in the Christian year which commemorates the passion (i.e. the suffering), death and resurrection of Christ, beginning with his triumphal entry into Jerusalem on Palm Sunday and including Maundy Thursday (commemorating Jesus' washing of his disciples' feet), Good Friday, Holy Saturday and Easter Sunday.

**homoios** (Greek: 'similar'). The word used by the Arians in repudiation of HOMOIOUSIOS and HOMOOUSIOS, the attempt to retain solely biblical language to describe the distinction between God the Father and God the Son. *See* ARIANISM.

**homoiousios** (Greek: 'of similar substance'). An anti-ARIAN term used by those dissatisfied with the SABELLIAN overtones of HOMOOUSIOS and wishing to allow distinction within the Trinity.

**homoousios** (Greek: 'of the same substance'). The term used in the Nicene Creed (COUNCIL OF NICAEA, 325) to counter the Arian (*see* ARIANISM) teaching of the subordination of the Son to Father. It was thought by some to imply a lack of difference between the persons of the Trinity (SABELLIANISM) and was therefore rejected in favour of HOMOIOUSIOS. However it is *homoousios* ('the *homoousion*') which is established in the Nicene Creed.

**honden** (Japanese). Inner sanctuary of a Shintō shrine, standing behind the HAIDEN or hall of worship.

**hongan** (Japanese). The 'original vow' of Amida (AMITĀBHA) Buddha, according to which all beings who sincerely trust in him may be reborn in his realm or PURE LAND.

**Honganji**. Temple of the Original Vow (HONGAN). Two temples in Kyōto, Japan, bear this name, the western and the eastern (Nishihonganji and Higashihonganji), being the head temples of the two leading sects of Shin Buddhism (JŌDO SHINSHŪ).

**hongū** (Japanese). The central Shintō shrine housing a particular deity as opposed to secondary buildings either nearby or elsewhere.

**honji**. *See* HONJI-SUIJAKU.

**honji-suijaku** (Japanese). Originally a Buddhist term referring to the Buddha's nature as a metaphysical being (*honji*) and the historical figure, Śākyamuni, described as a 'trace' (*suijaku*), the theory was used in Japan to explain the relation between Shintō gods and Buddhas; the Buddhas were regarded as the *honji*, and the Shintō gods as their incarnations or *suijaku*. In the early Nara period (646–794) the *honji* were regarded as more important than the *suijaku*, but in the Kamakura period (1185–1382) Shintoists also proposed the opposite theory, namely that the Shintō gods were the *honji* and the Buddhas the *suijaku*. In modern times, since the devotion to Shinto and Buddhist divinities has been to some extent been drawn apart again, there is little interest in debating which are ontologically prior.

**honsha** (Japanese). A Shintō shrine building dedicated to the principal deity of a shrine.

**Horae**. In ancient Greece, three daughters of ZEUS and Themis, representing spring, summer and winter. They had the ability to make plants and crops grow and bloom.

**Horagalles**. The thunder god of the Saami (Lapps). The name Horagalles has been connected to the Scandinavian THOR. (Holmberg 1915; Karsten 1955; Hultkrantz 1962).

**Horon**. The Canaanite god of war, death and healing, worshipped in Syria and Egypt in the 2nd millennium BCE (Caquot 1979–80).

**Horus**. An ancient Egyptian deity with many forms: god of the sky, protector of the king (who was Horus incarnate), son of Osiris and Isis who fought Seth to avenge Osiris' death. Horus is often shown as falcon-headed (Mercer 1942). *See also* CANOPIC JAR; EDFU.

**hossu** (Japanese). A whisk used to flick mosquitoes away, carried ceremonially by Zen masters.

**Host**. The bread (or wafers) consecrated as the body of Christ during a MASS. As such, whether it is consumed by those present or kept as a 'reserved sacrament', it is regarded in Roman Catholic and some other churches as an object of veneration. *See also* MASS; MONSTRANCE; PYX; TABERNACLE.

**Hou Tu** [Hou T'u] (Chinese: 'Sovereign Earth'). In Chinese antiquity a designation for the deity Earth as the counterpart of

Heaven (TIAN). In popular religion Hou Tu is worshipped as the goddess of the Earth.

**Hsiang Er Chu**. *See* XIANG ER ZHU.

**Hsiang-erh chu**. *See* XIANG ER ZHU.

**hsiao**. *See* XIAO.

**hsien jen**. *See* XIAN REN.

**hsien-ren**. *See* IMMORTALS.

**Hsi Wang Mu**. *See* XI WANG MU.

**hsoon** (Burmese). The ritual giving of food to Buddhist monks. *See also* DĀNA.

**huaca** [waca] (New World Spanish). Possibly a Spanish translation of a Quechua term referring to the 'holy' in general and to the entire supernatural world including unusual geographical features (stones, hills, lakes), heavenly bodies and astronomical phenomena, shrines, tombs, religious paraphernalia, mummies, icons, and the Inca ruler as a representation of a living god (Kauffman Doig 1986). The meaning of *huaca* as sacred position or site is of special importance. According to their position on the CEQUE lines, their meaning and importance varies. Some of the *huacas* were thought of as petrified supernatural beings, others were located in rocks, springs or other extraordinary places. *Huacas* were the visible marks of the sacred landscape and veneration took place for various reasons. For protection during a journey a special type of *huaca* – the *apacita* – were venerated; these were piles of stones to which the travellers often added more stones. *Huacas* that were movable images venerated by peoples conquered by the Incas were brought to Cuzco and there integrated in the Inca pantheon. Most of the *huacas* were thereafter destroyed by the Spaniards; but the cult of the *huacas* resisted the 'expulsion of idolatry' much longer than the more official elements of Inca religion. (Rowe 1975; Gonzalez 1989).

**huaca**. *See* CEQUE.

**hua hu ching**. *See* HUA HU JING.

**Hua Hu Jing** (Chinese). Originally a Daoist scripture (*see* DAOISM) in one fascicle expounding the idea that the Daoist philosopher Lao Tse (Laozi), when leaving China, went west (actually south-west) to become (the) Buddha in India. Thus BUDDHISM is perceived as a Chinese invention. One version bears the longer title *Lao Zi Hua Hu Jing*. The one-fascicle version was allegedly written during the Western Jin dynasty (266–315), but later versions ran up to ten fascicles (then termed *Xi Cheng Hua Hu Jing*). The book was banned frequently for its polemical content, but resurfaced with astonishing verve in other forms. It is usually associated with disagreements between Buddhists and Daoists at Chinese court debates on religious matters. This, however, might only be true for the *Xi Cheng* (and/or the Lao Tse) version of the *Hua Hu Jing*. The *Hua Hu* (*Miao*) *Jing* discovered by Aurel Stein at Dun-Huang (full title of the six-page text: *Taishang Lingbao Laozi Huahu Miao Jing*; Stein ms. no. 2081) treats Daoism and Buddhism as interlocking doctrines, using concepts of both religions. Here Lao Tse is not mentioned as the one who travels west to convert the 'barbarians', but as a certain 'Celestial Worthy'. The Stein ms. *Hua Hu Jing* was tentatively dated as a 6th-century text.

**Huang Di** [Huang Ti]. The 'Yellow Emperor', a legendary figure in Chinese history. In the *Record of the Historian* (*Shi Ji*) of Sima Qian [Ssu-ma Ch'ien] (2nd/1st century BCE) he appears at the beginning of Chinese history as the first emperor and successor of SHEN NONG. By the time of the Zhou dynasty (*c*.1066–221 BCE), however, Huang Di had also become the name of a deity, being one of the WU DI ('Five Emperors'). During the Former Han dynasty (206 BCE – 23 CE) Huang Di was integrated into the Daoist HUANG-LAO tradition, where he is considered as an ideal emperor who gained immortality.

**Huang-Lao Doctrine**. An ancient Chinese teaching relating to the art of 'true rulership'. According to this teaching the great 'Yellow Emperor', a mythological sage of political acumen, pacified the Chinese empire by employing teachings laid down by the sage-philosopher Lao Tse (Laozi) in his DAO DE JING. This Daoist (*see* DAOISM) art of ruling consists of non-action (or non-intervention; *see* WU WEI), i.e. let things have their way according to their true innate nature. In this context Lao Tse was regarded as the supreme government advisor, while the sage Emperor Huang Di was his model student, hence the expression Huang-Lao Doctrine. The doctrine was influential in China already in the 4th century BCE, and entered court politics of the united Han empire (210 BCE – 225 CE) during the reign of emperor Wen Di (179–155 BCE) Chinese historians of religion link the Huang-Lao doctrine to the Daoist teachings of immortality (*see* LONGEVITY), which results in a problematic extension of Huang-Lao thought at least until the Tang dynasty (618–908 CE).

**Huang-T'ing-ching**. *See* HUANG TING JING

**Huang Ting Jing** (Chinese: 'Yellow Court Scripture'). A Chinese text supposedly dating back to the 2nd century CE. The full title of the 'confused and cryptic' work (Welch 1957) is *Tai Shang Huang Ting Nei / Wai Yu Jing*. The dates of the book are unclear: the *Huang Ting Nei Jing* (=inner chapters) were compiled some time before the middle of the 4th century CE, while the *Huang Ting Wai Jing* (=outer chapters) are supposed to date from the late Tang dynasty (618–906 CE). The scripture develops the idea of a central generative executive organ in the human body, i.e. the Yellow Court. The location is populated by gods with administrative functions. Thus, the meditative visualization of the gods (in action) serves as a guarantee for their well-being and consequently also one's own. The 'Yellow Court' text belongs to an important scriptural tradition of DAOISM. A systematization of its contents is given in the DA DONG ZHEN JING.

**huehuetl** (Nahuatl). An upright Aztec drum resembling a modern-day conga drum, played with the hands, used to accompany ritual songs, i.e. *Cantares mexicanos*, often played together with the TEPONAZTLI (Haly 1986).

**Huguenots**. French Protestants in the tradition of Calvinism, 'Huguenots' being a nickname of uncertain derivation which came into use shortly after their formal organization in 1559 at the Synod of Paris. Tension with the dominant Catholic Church reached a peak with the Massacre of St Bartholemew in 1572 when thousands of Protestants were put to death in Paris and other places. The Edict of Nantes (1598) granted freedom of worship, but this was revoked in 1685, whereupon more than a quarter of a million fled to various Protestant lands. In France restrictions were endured for more than another century before legal recognition was achieved in 1802.

**hukam** (Punjabi: 'command'). In Sikhism, the verses of the GURŪ GRANTH SĀHIB read during worship and selected by opening the book at random. The term is derived from Arabic.

**humanism**. A world-view which focuses on human possibilities and achievements, in modern times commonly implying a rejection of religious belief. As an organized movement, humanism has in turn sometimes been regarded as an alternative to religious belief which itself provides a perspective of meaning and requires commitment. At the same time some modern religious attitudes may be described as humanist in that human experience, need and potential are placed at the centre of concern while religious belief is relativized.

**Hume's Fork**. The distinction made by David Hume (1711–76) between logically necessary propositions and those dealing with 'matters of fact and real existence'.

**Ḥunafā**. *See* MECCA.

**hundun** [hun-tun] (Chinese). The primordial chaos that produced the world through spontaneous separation. While the theme in its mythological form is not very prominent in classical Chinese literature, the idea of an undifferentiated primordial state which through the interaction of YIN and YANG generated the myriad things can be related to the cosmological theories of DAOISM and is associated with the idea of the *dao* (*See* DAODE).

**hungry ghost**. *See* GAKI; PRETA.

**hun-po** (Chinese). The Chinese concept of the soul. In fact, several souls are supposed to exist and influence one's lifespan: three *hun*-souls and seven *po*-souls. According to the YUN QI QI JIAN (chap. 54) the first of the *hun*-souls belongs to the 'media' earth, the second to the FIVE ELEMENTS, and the third is associated with the 'media' heaven. In contrast to these are the seven *po* souls, each of which has its own appellation. They are taken as the source of evil deeds, lust, slander etc. Consequently, the Daoist (*see* DAOISM) is eager to control these souls, which may cause physical or mental disorder, when not properly dealt with. In case of death the seven *po*-souls disperse (mostly as evil spirits), but the three *hun*-souls are said to stay within the remains of the body, transformed into positive QI ('breath').

**ḥuppah** (Hebrew). A wedding 'canopy', traditionally suspended from four poles, each of which is held by someone supporting it. It is also a symbolic term for marriage itself.

**Hurrian religion**. The scantily attested religion of people scattered throughout the ancient Near East (see Imparati 1964), apparently containing elements borrowed from Mesopotamian, Hittite and Syrian culture. (Dussaud 1945: 333–53; Laroche 1948, 1968a,b).

**Hussites**. Supporters of the Czech reformer John Huss (Jan Hus, *c*.1369–1415). Hus, influenced by the works of English reformer Wycliffe, came into conflict with the papacy, appealed to the Council of Constance (1414), and ultimately to the authority of Jesus alone, but was burned at the stake for heresy. The Hussite church which thereby came into existence has maintained its tradition in Czechoslovakia down to the present day.

**hyle**. *See* MANICHAEISM.

**Hymn to Demeter**. A Greek poem which belongs to the 'Homeric Hymns', an ancient collection of 33 hymns to Greek deities of various origin and ages. The Hymn to Demeter tells the story of the two Eleusian goddesses Demeter and Persephone (Kore), and is one of the most important documents of the myth of the ELEUSINIAN MYSTERIES (6th century BCE). (Hesiod 1964).

**hypnotic suggestion**. An influence on a person which occurs in the absence of critical, logical thought. The individual is not able to comprehend and integrate the information in his mind, but rather can be led into experiences and actions which he does not personally stand for. Hypnotic suggestion has been used in many religious and political contexts to influence people in a particular direction.

**hypostasis** (Greek). A classical Greek word in general use signifying either that which identifies something as belonging to a class (i.e. its essential being) or a particular embodiment of certain qualities (i.e. an individual being). In Patristic theology it was eventually accepted as signifying the latter, equivalent to 'person' in the Latin formulation 'three persons in one substance'. In the context of christology it referred to the individuality of Christ, i.e. one hypostasis combining TWO NATURES, or one hypostasis with ONE nature (MONOPHYSITISM). In later, more general use, a hypostasis is a personification or an objectification of a divine quality such as wisdom or justice.

**hypostyle hall**. *See* ISLAND OF CREATION.

# I

**ʿibādāt** (Arabic). Those religious duties which Muslims owe to ALLAH (God) such as ritual purity, fasting and pilgrimage. *See also* FIVE PILLARS; MUʿĀMALĀT.

**al-ʿIbādiya**. One of the main branches descended from the early Muslim sect of KHĀRIJĪS of the 7th–10th centuries, originating in Basra (Iraq) with communities spreading across the medieval Muslim world, but present today mainly in Uman, East Africa, Libya and Algeria. As moderate Khārijīs they differed from extremists (like the Azāriqa) in holding that a non-Muslim was an infidel (KĀFIR) but not a polytheist; hence, the infidel's life was not forfeit. Politically they do not believe in the necessity for a strictly religious headship of the community.

**Ibéji** (Yoruba). Twins and wooden images of twins. Among the Yoruba of Nigeria twins are considered to have supernatural powers. The images of twin children must be treated like their living counterparts, and if one twin dies his image must keep the living one company.

**ibis**. *See* AKH.

**Iblīs**. In Islām, the personal name for the Devil, found in the QUR'ĀN (2.57) associated with the story of creation; he is referred to as *al-Shayṭān*, SATAN, in the story of temptation of Adam in Paradise (2.36).

**ichinen sanzen** (Japanese). The teaching that in one thought (*ichinen*) three thousand (*sanzen*) realms of existence are comprehended or contained. This is a central concept in Tendai (*see* TENDAI-SHŪ) and Nichirenite Buddhism (*see* NICHIREN-SHŪ; NICHIREN-SHŌSHŪ) based on the LOTUS SŪTRA.

**I Ching**. *See* YI JING.

**icon**. A sacred image painted on wood, which, because it is regarded as partaking of the reality which it represents, is considered worthy of veneration in itself. Icons portray SAINTS, especially martyrs, apostles, Mary and the child Jesus, Christ in majesty, the Trinity, and biblical themes such as the ascension of Elijah or the last judgement. Many icons are related to particular cities because of miraculous interventions by the figures portrayed, e.g. Demetrios of Thessaloniki or the Virgin of Kazan. First known in COPTIC CHRISTIANITY, the use of icons is characteristic of, and in the strict sense restricted to the Byzantine and related ORTHODOX CHURCHES such as the Russian. In spite of strict iconographic rules, an astonishing range of artistic treatment has arisen on account of national and regional stylistic developments and the incorporation of local saints. As a result, major collections of icons are now housed in art galleries rather than churches. The underlying intention of an icon, however, whose artists for centuries remained nameless, is not artistic but religious, and its true place is therefore not in a gallery but mounted on the ICONOSTASIS of an Orthodox church, on a separate stand in the nave of the church where it can be kissed by believers on entry, or in the icon corner of an Orthodox family home.

**iconoclasm**. The destruction of sacred images, especially ICONS, and thus metaphorically an attack on cherished beliefs or symbols. *See* ICON; ICONOCLAST CONTROVERSY.

**Iconoclast Controversy**. A controversy set in motion by Byzantine Emperor Leo III, who prohibited all image worship and issued edicts against the use of ICONS in 726 and 729. Complicated by political power struggles the controversy raged for over a century. During its course the theological position of icons for the ORTHODOX CHURCH was clarified at the Second Council of Nicaea, convened in 787 by the Empress Irene. In answer to the objection that the images of the divine were tantamount to idolatry, the position adopted was that icons may be venerated in so far as they provide mediation to the divine reality on which they themselves depend.

**iconography**. The detailed description and analysis of religious images. Though it incorporates the Greek word ICON (*eikon*), the term iconography may be employed with respect to any religious culture and is even used to refer to the religious art of ISLĀM, in which images of the divine are strictly prohibited.

**iconostasis** (from Greek, *eikonostasis*). The dividing wall between nave and sanctuary in ORTHODOX CHURCHES, usually with a central and two side entrances and panels for ICONS. The main icons depict Christ as Saviour, Mary as Mother of God, The Last Supper, the four Evangelists, archangels and saints.

**ʿīd** (Arabic). The general term in Islām for religious festival. The Turkish equivalent is *bayram*.

**ʿĪd al-Aḍḥā** (Arabic). The Muslim Feast of the Sacrifice, marking the end of the rites of pilgrimage. Pilgrims make their sacrifice at Mīna (near MECCA) while Muslims who have not made the pilgrimage, sacrifice in their respective locales. The sacrifice is in commemoration of Ibrāhīm's (Abraham's) willingness to offer his son. *See also* ḤĀJJ.

**ʿĪd al-Fiṭr** (Arabic). The Muslim festival of the breaking of the fast, celebrated on the first day of the month following RAMAḌĀN. It is a time of festive rejoicing, visits and exchange of presents; the obligatory payment of alms, the *zakāt al-fiṭr*, is due at this time (Grunebaum 1976).

**idealism**. Various philosophical positions which give priority to mind over matter, found typically, if most diversely, in the thought of Plato, Berkeley, Kant and Hegel. Through Platonic philosophy and in modern times through Hegel's writings, the doctrine regarding the ontological nature of reality as ideal rather than material came to have considerable influence on the development of western Christian thought. Idealism may be contrasted with MATERIALISM, as when for example Hegel's thought is contrasted with that of Marx. In the east, Hindu and Buddhist religious traditions also produced equivalents to idealism, the former allowing for both personal and impersonal idealism, the latter for strictly impersonal idealism (VIJÑĀNAVĀDA). *See also* PLATONISM; NEOPLATONISM; HEGELIANISM.

**Ifá** (Yoruba). A system of divination among the Yoruba and Edo of Benin in Nigeria and descendants of slaves in Cuba and Brazil. It is also practiced by the Fon of the Dahomey kingdom under the name Fa and by the Ewe of Togo under the name Afa. Similar systems, although less elaborate in their manner of interpretation, occur among other peoples of the region. Ifá refers not only to the technique of divination but also to the god of divination and wisdom, otherwise called Orunmila. In the technique of divination a set of 16 palm nuts is manipulated or a chain (*opele*) with eight half seed shells is cast to obtain the figures (*odu*), which are interpreted by the diviner (*babalawo*). There are 16 basic *odu*, which, combined with each other, make up 256 derivative figures. The *odu* are considered to be gods (ORISHA). Each of the *odu* can be interpreted through a number of verses and legends belonging to it. Thus a vast amount of sacred poetry is central to the cult of Ifá and must be known by its priests (*babalawo*), who derive from it the advice they give to their clients. In this way Ifá provides moral guidance and support and its advice is sought by the followers of any Yoruba god for all kinds of problems as well as on regular occasions. (Abimbola 1976; Bascom 1969; Maupoil 1943; Surgy 1981).

**Iḥrām**. *See* ḤĀJJ.

**IHS**. An abbreviation of the name of Jesus as written in Greek, consisting of the first three letters written in capitals. In western Christianity the second letter has been widely misinterpreted as the letter 'h' rather than the long 'e' which it represents in Greek.

**Ihy**. *See* HATHOR.

**ijmāʿ** (Arabic: 'consensus'). In Islamic jurisprudence, one of the roots of the law (SHARĪʿA), subordinate to the QURʾĀN and the Prophetic tradition (ḤADĪTH). In mainstream or SUNNĪ Islām, it refers to the agreement of opinion on matters of law by all those qualified to make such judgements. It was based upon the prophetic tradition that 'My community will never agree upon error.' Among SHĪʿA Muslims, *ijmāʿ* was rejected and substituted by the views of the authorative IMĀM.

**ijtihād** (Arabic). In Islām, the action of forming an opinion either in a legal case or as to a rule of law. One who performs such action in the interpretation of the faith is a *mujtahid*. In Sunnī legal tradition, *mujtahids* of the first rank were the founders of the four legal schools (MADHHAB) who had possessed a peculiar right and knowledge to work out all questions from the law's foundations, the QURʾĀN and Prophetic tradition (ḤADĪTH) and whose judgements should be followed by others; subsequent generations of canon lawyers were more strictly regarded as *muqallids*, or 'imitators' of the founders. In SHĪʿA Islam, the *mujtahid* is regarded as spokesman of the twelfth or Hidden IMĀM, and thus is seen to be freer to criticize the actions of the temporal authorities than his Sunnī counterpart.

**ikenga**. A personal, wooden, carved shrine connected with a personified life force, *chi*, the cult of which aims at personal accomplishment and success. Similar cults exist among neighbouring peoples of southern Nigeria (the Igala, the Edo and the Ijaw) (Boston 1977).

**al-Ikhwān al-Muslimūn**. The Muslim Brethren. A politico-religious movement founded in Egypt in 1928 by Ḥasan al-Banna (*d* 1949) who was its first Supreme Guide (al-Murshid al-ʿĀmm). The period 1936–52 marked their most intense activity: they preached against imperialism, both 'external' in the form of continued British interference in Egypt's affairs and 'internal' in the shape of corrupt parliamentary parties representing narrow political interests and their allies among the traditional religious leadership of the AL-AZHAR mosque. The Brethren founded schools and mosques for the moral and religious instruction of men and women, and hospitals and dispensaries for health care especially in rural areas. Commercial and industrial enterprises with worker share participation gained support for their cause in the cities. Their support of Palestinian Arabs against the Zionists helped spread their ideas in Syria, Jordan and Lebanon. Acts of violence from an armed wing of the movement caused their proscription under President Nasser, 1954–70, and the execution of a leading theorist Sayyid Qutb in 1966. More recently their reentry into Egyptian political life has been restrained, their objective nevertheless remaining the establishment of an authentic Muslim state (Enayat 1982).

**Iliad**. Homer's epic poem recounting the battle of the Greeks against Ilion or Troy as the deeds of HEROES influenced by gods.

**Illapa**. *See* INCA.

**illumination**. The enlightenment of the SOUL by divine grace; an important concept in AUGUSTINIANISM.

**Illumination**. The European, and in particular the French ENLIGHTENMENT, so called because its leading lights were referred to as *les lumières*, and the period as a whole as *le siècle des lumières*, i.e. the century of the Illuminators.

**illuminative path**. *See* VIA UNITIVA.

**illusion**. A perceptual experience in which outer stimuli (often light or sound) occur but result in mistaken interpretation or misconceptions. This is often because subjective factors, desires and needs influence our interpretation of stimuli. Many visions of a religious nature can be characterized as illusory, in this precise sense.

**ʿilm al-kalām** (Arabic). In Islām, the term for dialectical theology. *See also* KALĀM.

**Ilmu Sejati**. Literally, 'True Science'; an informally organized mystical movement (KEBATINAN in Indonesian), taking as its main theme 'a cabalistic reinterpretation of the five pillars of Islām as well as of various other threads from Javanese tradition' (Geertz 1960a: 339).

**imagines** (Latin). Wax masks of departed aristocratic Romans kept by their descendants, treated as objects of family cult, and carried in funeral processions. *See also* GENIUS; LARES.

**imago dei** (Latin: 'image of God'). A technical term in western Christian theology, referring to the teaching that 'man' was made in the image of God, as stated in *Genesis* 1.26f. Theologians have usually regarded this view of the nature of humankind as the presupposition for salvation, but there have been different views regarding the extent to which the imago was obscured by the FALL.

**imām** (Arabic: 'leader'). In the Islamic tradition: (1) a prayer leader in a MOSQUE; (2) the title given to learned and respected men such as the founders of schools of law and certain theologians; (3) the head of the Muslim community, virtually equivalent to Caliph (KHALĪFA); (4) the charismatic leaders of the SHĪʿA whom, as sinless and infallible members of the family of ʿAlī, God has designated the legitimate spiritual and temporal successors of the Prophet Muḥammad. Since the spiritual occultation of the twelfth Imām in the 9th century the Shīʿa await his return to establish a reign of peace and justice on earth.

**imāma** [imāmah] (Arabic: 'leadership'). In Islām, Sunnīs hold that the leader of the community must be chosen from the Quraysh, the tribe into which the Prophet Muḥammad was born; the SHĪʿA, on the other hand, hold that he must be from Muḥammad's descendants (AHL AL-BAYT) each of whom was believed to have been designated by ALLĀH (God) and who was the locus of a divine spark of wisdom passed on through Muḥammad.

**īmān** (Arabic). The term for 'faith' in Islām, a believer being called *mu'min*. Faith as generally conceived comprised three elements, intention or conviction (*niyya*), verbal profession (*qawl*) and the performance of works (*ʿamal*), although theologians differed as to their relative importance and proportion; likewise they debated whether faith was constant or could increase or decrease.

**Imana**. The supreme being in Ruanda/Burundi, quite similar to the Nilotic JOK, but never directly addressed in prayer or sacrifice (Maquet 1954: 166f).

**Imhotep**. The architect and vizier of King Zoser (*c*.2686 BCE). Imhotep was responsible for the design and execution of the Step Pyramid at SAKKARA, the world's first major stone building. However, the Egyptians revered him as a physician, and he was later deified and worshipped as a god of medicine. The Greeks finally equated Imhotep (known in Greek as Imouthes) with their own god of medicine, ASKLEPIOS; his statues (all dating from the later historical periods) show him as a man holding a papyrus roll. Such deification was rare, and only a few kings and sages received the honour of divine cults.

**Immaculate Conception**. A teaching of the Roman Catholic Church according to which the Virgin Mary was born free from any taint of ORIGINAL SIN in a state of perfection, and apart from her son Jesus is therefore unique among human beings in this respect. This teaching was declared a DOGMA of the faith by an EX CATHEDRA declaration of Pope Pius IX in 1864 and is liturgically commemorated on 8 December each year.

**immanence**. Indwelling, particularly with reference to God's presence in the world. *Compare* TRANSCENDENCE.

**Immanuel**. A title accorded to an unborn child (Hezekiah?) in *Isaiah* 7.14, and subsequently interpreted messianically. (Hammarshaimb 1949; Lindblom 1959; Wyatt 1985a; 45).

**immortality**. The continuing existence of human beings, or of parts or aspects of them, after death. A common version of belief in immortality is that the SOUL alone survives. Some Eastern religions, e.g. Jainism, teach that the soul is then reincarnated in another body. Christianity and some other religions teach that the whole person will be resurrected, with a glorified and incorruptible body. We find a 'mixed' view in some thinkers, e.g. St Gregory of Nyssa (d. 394) and St Thomas Aquinas (d. 1274), namely that the soul alone survives death, but that it is reunited with a body at the Last Judgement (Hick 1976). *See also* ETERNAL LIFE.

**immortals**. Daoist (*see* DAOISM) 'fairies' or 'genii' that have, through certain methods of alchemy or meditation, transgressed into the realm of 'no-death'. Immortals abstain from the 'Five Grains' (i.e. they do not eat wheat, rice, and similar coarse foods), but feed on dew, 'pure breath' (*see* QI; TAI XI) and ride on dragons or the clouds. From a number of Daoist scriptures dealing with hagiographical materials of immortals (Chinese, *shenxian* or *xianren*) two graded systems of immortals can be deduced: the first system of three grades distinguishes between Heavenly Immortals, Earthly Immortals and Corps-liberated Immortals (i.e. Daoists of attainment who have died and whose body is transformed after burial); the second system comprises nine (3 x 3) varieties, hierarchically structured. High-ranking immortals entered in this dictionary are XI WANG MU and Huang Di (*see* HUANG-LAO DOCTRINE). A 'Realized Man' (*see* ZHEN REN) according to the nine-grade system holds rank six. Some of the Immortals are employed by heavenly authorities to help and assist on earth persons of virtue. As such the theme of the immortals has generated a notable output in the fields of Chinese literature, painting and sculpture.

**Imouthes**. *See* IMHOTEP.

**impassibility**. A theological term denoting God's characteristic of not being affected by any events and not being subject to change. *Contrast* PATRIPASSIANISM.

**imprimatur** (Latin: 'it may be printed'). A term used at the front of a work dealing with theology or morals to indicate that the work has been authorized as not conflicting with the teaching of the Roman Catholic Church. A related authorization is *nihil obstat*, meaning that nothing stands in the way of publication.

**Inanna**. A Sumerian fertility goddess, the planet Venus. She is identified with the Babylonian ISHTAR.

**Inari**. A Shintō deity (KAMI) of rice cultivation and the five grains, designated in the Shintō classics as Uka-no-mitama-no-kami. The *kami* is enshrined in the extensive Fushimi Inari Taisha near Kyōto and many other Inari shrines, many of which are quite small. Characteristic of Inari shrines are the bright red entrance gates (*torii*) which may, as votive offerings, form long tunnels, and stone or clay images of the fox, regarded as the messenger of Inari. Inari shrines today are the focus of prayers not only for success in agriculture but also in industry and commerce.

**inaugurated eschatology**. *See* ESCHATOLOGY.

**Inca**. The title of the kings of the Inca dynasty in ancient Peru (*c.*1400–1532). The sun was the highest deity after the creator divinity VIRACOCHA and the personal ancester of the Incas, which is why they were called *inti churin* ('son of the sun'), which already includes the legitimation for sovereignty. The cult of the sun played a central role, e.g. in the construction of the temple of the sun (Corincancha) or in feasts like Inti Raymi (solstice feast on 24 June). Other important celestial divinities were the moon, the stars, the rainbow and lightning (Illapa). It is notable that Inca rule did not destroy the local deities of conquered peoples. These deities were integrated in the Inca pantheon mostly as HUACA. The images were brought to the capital Cuzco, which cemented the ties between the periphery and the capital. The Inca Empire had its widest extension under Huayna Capac (1493–1527) and reached from today's central Chile over Bolivia, Peru and parts of Ecuador to the river Ancasmaya in Columbia (*see* CEQUE). Many Inca temples are still visible, especially in and around Cuzco, built in a highly developed architectural style (Rowe 1975).

**incarnation**. Most commonly, this term refers to the Christian teaching that God was born into the world as a human being of flesh and blood with attendant physical awareness, in particular, of physical suffering (*contrast* DOCETISM). The word derives from Latin *incarnare* ('to enflesh'), the credal phrase *incarnatus est* ('he was made flesh') being of decisive influence.

More widely, however, the teaching that God/s take earthly (usually human) form in order to achieve some purpose in the affairs of humankind occurs in several religious traditions. Incarnation is sometimes understood to be repeated as occasion requires, as in common Hindu doctrine, and sometimes to occur once for all, as in Christian doctrine. However often they may be thought to occur, incarnations in most religious traditions are surrounded by mystery and fantastic stories. Though apparently in one sense 'empirical', merely witnessing the event may not be sufficient to 'see' it as an incarnation; a special, spiritual insight may be required. This element is central to the accounts given both in the Gospel of John in the Christian scriptures (see Bultmann, 1971, 232f and *passim*) and in the Sanskrit classic the *Bhagavad Gītā*, in which the Lord Kṛṣṇa gives Arjuna a 'celestial eye' so that he can see Krishna 'as he is' (§11).

The Christian doctrine of incarnation was gradually made more precise as a result of controversies within the early church. Thus Athanasius (*c.*296–373) insisted, against GNOSTICISM, on the possibility in principle of spirit being properly involved in matter, and that God the creator could be incarnate in a part of his creation. In agreement with this, theologians sought to exclude an overemphasis, in God become man, of either divinity (*compare* APOLLINARIANISM; MONOPHYSITISM) or humanity (*compare* ARIANISM). Alexandrian theology stressed the divine LOGOS ('word') who became human, union lying in the Logos as the subject in both natures. Antiochian theology emphasized the manhood assumed by the Son, the unity with divinity being maintained largely through his human moral effort. The COUNCIL OF CHALCEDON (451) affirmed one person in two natures, a permanent union of godhead and manhood, the integrity of each being unharmed (*compare* TOME OF LEO). This statement excluded teachings thought to be erroneous, but without explaining the process of incarnation in more detail (Kelly 1972). The doctrine itself has therefore remained controversial, especially within modern Protestant Christianity, where it has frequently been reinterpreted or even rejected altogether. For an analysis of one theologian's case against incarnationalism, see Coakley 1988. (See also Bultmann 1971.)

**Indian religions**. A term referring collectively to the various strands of Hinduism (the Hinduism of the Vedas, of the Upaniṣads, and of the Bhakti movements, together with many local cults loosely connected with these), and to such other traditions as JAINISM, BUDDHISM and SIKHISM. ISLĀM, ZOROASTRIANISM and CHRISTIANITY, though firmly established in India, are not usually regarded as Indian religions *per se*. In the 19th and 20th centuries a large number of new religious movements have been established in India, many within the broad compass of the Hindu tradition, others linked to Christianity, Sikhism, Islām or Buddhism. These include movements which focus on reform, revitalization, retraditionalization, religious fundamentalism or syncretism. Most movements are both 'new' and 'not new', being novel in some ways, perhaps in belief, practice or organization, yet developing within the context of established traditions (Sarma 1973; French & Sharma 1981; Mangalvadi 1977; Babb 1986; Sharma 1986; Robinson 1988). *See also* BRĀHMO SAMĀJ; NAVĀ VIDHĀN; PRĀRTHANA SAMĀJ; ĀRYĀ SAMĀJ; ŚANTINIKETAN; THEOSOPHICAL SOCIETY; RĀMAKRISHNA MISSION; RĀMAKRISHNA SĀRADĀ MATH; SWĀMINĀRĀYAN SAMPRADĀYA; INTEGRAL YOGA; SATYĀGRAHA; VIŚVA HINDU PARIṢAD; HARE KRISHNA MOVEMENT; CHRISTIAN ASHRAM MOVEMENT; NĀMDHĀRĪ MOVEMENT; NIRANKĀRĪ MOVEMENT; RAVIDĀSĪ MOVEMENT; RADHĀSOAMĪ MOVEMENT; DIVINE LIGHT MISSION; RAJNEESH MOVEMENT; TRANSCENDENTAL MEDITATION; ĀNANDA MĀRGA YOGA; BRAHMĀ KUMĀRĪ MOVEMENT; SĀĪ BĀBĀ MOVEMENT; DIVINE LIFE SOCIETY; DEOBAND; AHL-I HADITH; BARELWI MOVEMENT; AHMADIYYA MOVEMENT; ISLAMIC MODERNIST MOVEMENT (INDIA); JAMA'AT-I ISLAMI; TABLIGHI JAMA' AT.

**indigites** (Latin). A category of minor Roman divinities, held by some to be the first Roman divinities. Little was certain about them even in antiquity. *See also* NUMEN.

**individuation**. A term used in the analytical psychology of Carl Gustav Jung to refer to a person's life-long maturation process. The ultimate aim of this process is the realization of Self, the high ideal in which the concept of God is contained. This journey is complicated, and different for the two sexes. The archetypal structures which one embodies throughout life and which should be dealt with in some way are, among others, persona (the outer mask of the individual), the shadow (the repressed dark and evil sides of human nature), anima (man's image of woman) and animus (woman's image of man), and finally 'the great mother' and 'the magician'. Expressions for the archetypal structures of the individuation process (*see* ARCHETYPES) have been found in religious pictorial art and literature.

**Indonesian religions**. The religious history of Indonesia is extremely complex since indigenous traditions have been joined by various importations, notably Buddhism, Hinduism and Islām. *See also* AGAMA ISLAM SANTRI; AGAMA KEJAWEN; AGAMA TIRTA; SLAMETAN.

**Indra**. *See* VṚTA, VIṢṆU.

**Indrabhakti**. *See* BHAKTI.

**indulgence**. In Roman Catholic teaching, the remission of temporal punishment for sin which would otherwise be endured in PURGATORY. An indulgence is usually granted with respect to the penitent performance of a specific devotion, e.g. the saying of a number of prayers such as the PATER NOSTER (Our Father . . .) or the AVE MARIA (Hail Mary . . .). In the late Middle Ages indulgences were granted in exchange for money and controversy over this 'sale' of indulgences was one of the triggers of the Protestant Reformation. *See also* PLENARY INDULGENCE.

**infallibility**. In Roman Catholic teaching, the POPE's incapability of erring while making an EX CATHEDRA pronouncement on faith or morals. The principle of infallibility was itself proclaimed by Pope Pius IX in 1870.

**inga** (Japanese). Cause (*in*) and effect (*ka*), i.e. the law of KARMA in Buddhist teaching.

**ingō** (Japanese). Cause (*in*) and KARMA (*gō*). The combination of primary and secondary causality in Buddhist teaching. *Compare* INGA; INNEN.

**initia**. *See* MYSTERY RELIGIONS

**Inkarrío** (from *Inca* + Spanish *rey* ('King')). A mythic figure in ancient Peru with different aspects. Some myths describe him together with Qollarrí as creators of the divinities. (The sources disagree whether Qollarrí is the sister or the wife of Inkarrí.) They are culture heroes teaching man how to cultivate potatoes and women how to cultivate vegetables and how to weave. Apart from this Inkarrí plays a messianic role in that myths say he will grow in the subsoil out of the decapitated and buried head of the last Inca ruler Atahualpa. Eventually he will be reborn with a magnificent body to renew the world and to restore the cosmic order. (Pease 1973; Ossio 1973).

**Inkosi Yezulu**. Zulu name for god of the sky, also known as Inkosi Yaphezulu.

**innen** (Japanese). Cause (*in*) and condition (*en*), i.e. HETU-PRATYAYA, in Buddhist teaching. *Compare* INGA; INGŌ; JŪNI INNEN.

**inner alchemy**. *See* NEIDAN.

**Innere Mission**. The German name for missionary activity, taking both evangelical and social or charitable forms, directed towards the home society in which a church is established.

**Inquisition**. A general name given to ecclesiastical courts and papal appointees for the identification and prosecution of heresy. From the 13th century onwards the medieval western church co-operated with secular authorities in this activity, ruthlessly extirpating those of other beliefs such as the CATHARS and also seeking to eradicate 'witchcraft'. The Spanish Inquisition (dating from 1479 to 1820) was directly under the control of the monarchy, though enjoying the approval of the papacy, and was used against Muslims, Jews and Protestants to ensure the ideological homogeneity of Spain.

**International Association for the History of Religions (IAHR).** An umbrella organization founded in 1950 to further scholarship in the history of religions and related fields. The central focus is a series of quinquennial congresses which, in a looser organizational perspective, goes back to 1900 (Paris). For recent proceedings and detailed information see McKenzie and Pye 1979 (Lancaster Congress 1975), Slater and Wiebe 1983 (Winnipeg Congress 1980) and Hayes 1986 (Sydney Congress 1985). The XVI Congress was held in Rome 1990 and the XVII is due to take place in Mexico City in 1995. Further information on the activities of the IAHR may be found in the scholarly journal of the association entitled *Numen* (*compare* NUMEN) or in the news bulletin distributed regularly to its affiliated associations. In recent years regional conferences have been sponsored by one or other of the national affiliates for the history (or study) of religion, notably in Turku (1973), Warsaw (1979), Groningen (1989), Beijing (1992) and Harare (1992), and special conferences have also been held, focusing on particular points of concern (Marburg 1988, see Pye 1989 and Tyloch 1990). Current strategy envisages efforts to increase awareness of the intercultural dimension of the study of religion, while maintaining its integrity as a discipline which is itself religiously neutral.

**International Society for Krishna Consciousness** (ISKCON). *See* HARE KRISHNA MOVEMENT.

**Inter-Religious League.** *See* RELIGIÖSER MENSCHHEITSBUND.

**Inti.** The sun, the incarnate form of masculine creative force associated with fertility and rain, gold, and the person of the royal ruler, the INCA (Kauffman Doig 1986).

**intrinsic religion.** A term introduced by the American psychologist Gordon W. Allport to indicate a mature religious attitude in which the religion's ethical and moral demands become an end in their own right (Allport 1950). A person with an intrinsic religious orientation does not use religion in order to achieve secondary gains. *Contrast* EXTRINSIC RELIGION.

**Io.** According to an esoteric Māori tradition, the creator of the world now living in the twelfth and uppermost heaven, separated from anything else because of his extreme TAPU. This tradition was virtually unknown to the public until it was disclosed by two Māori priests at a meeting in the 1860s and published by S. Percy Smith 50 years later (Smith 1913–15). From the historian's point of view it is still open to question whether this is an authentic Māori tradition or the result of European contact. But as it was made public in a time of growing tensions between Maori and white settlers it definitely served the purpose of proving that Māori religion was equivalent to Christianity. Most Māori people today believe that Io was known to their ancestors and that he is identical with the Christian god.

**Irwolsŏngshin.** Korean gods of the sun, moon and stars.

**Iśa.** *See* UPANIṢADS.

**ʿIsā.** The Islamic name for Jesus. In the QUR'ĀN 4.171, he is referred to as *al-Masīḥ* (Messiah) ʿIsā, son of Maryam. *See also* KALĀM.

**ISKCON.** *See* HARE KRISHNA MOVEMENT.

**Ise Jingū.** The Grand Shrine of Ise, the largest and most revered shrine in Japan, composed of the Kōtai Jingū (Naikū) and the Toyouke Daijingū (Gekū), plus their respective subordinate shrines. The imperial ancestress and sun-goddess Amaterasu Ōmikami is enshrined in the Naikū, and the god Toyouke Ōmikami in the Gekū. According to legend, the Naikū was founded in the year 5 CE, during the reign of Emperor Suinin (legendary reign 29 BCE to 70 CE), and the Gekū in 478, during the reign of Emperor Yūryaku (reigned 456–79). The deity of the Naikū, Amaterasu Ōmikami, is symbolized by the yata mirror, one of the three imperial regalia (the others being the sword and the jewel, *see* SANSHU NO SHINKI). The custom of rebuilding the shrine every 20 years (*see* SHIKINEN SENGŪ) was prescribed by Emperor Temmu (reigned 673–86) and first carried out by Empress Jitō (reigned 686–9). The Grand Shrine of Ise may be regarded as the spiritual centre of all shrines in the country and the leading focus of the Shintō religion. There is evidence of widespread popular devotion to the shrine, such as mass pilgrimages called *okagemairi* (especially in the Edo period 1600–1868) and the enshrinement of amulets (*taima*) from the shrine on family altars.

**Ise kō**. A confraternity dedicated to the worship of ISE JINGŪ. Such confraternities are generally based on a village unit, sponsoring religious meetings several times a year, and sending representative pilgrims chosen from its membership to worship at the shrine.

**Isenheim Altar**. An altar dating from 1514 in the church of the Antonite monastery at Isenheim, Alsace. The central shrine contains carved figures of St Anthony, Augustine and Jerome, while the folding wings bear paintings by Matthias Grünewald (1475–1528). Themes depicted are (inner doors) annunciation and resurrection and (outer doors) crucifixion and patron saints of the sick, Sebastian and Anthony (Strieder 1966). It is now in the museum of Uterlinden at Colmar, Alsace.

**Ise Shintō**. A school of Shintō thought established by priests of the Grand Shrine of Ise (ISE JINGŪ) in medieval times containing Buddhist elements to which Daoist (Taoist) elements were added. It was held that purity and honesty are the highest virtues and that these virtues should be acquired through religious experience.

**Ishtar**. The Assyro-Babylonian goddess of love and war. Originally a god (*compare* West Semitic ASHTAR, ASTARTE), she changes sex when assimilated to the Sumerian INANNA, goddess of the planet Venus. Priestesses impersonated her in SACRED MARRIAGE rites with kings. Myths and hymns celebrate her marriage with TAMMUZ (Sumerian DUMUZI). The myth of her descent into the nether world (texts Pritchard 1969: 52–7, 106–9) is important for Mesopotamian ideas about death. (Barrelet 1955; Kramer 1969; Jacobsen 1976: 135–43; Heimpel 1982; Wolkstein & Kramer 1984; Vanstiphout 1984).

**Isia**. *See* ISIS CULT.

**Isis**. The wife and sister of OSIRIS, mother of HORUS and patroness of magicians, this ancient Egyptian goddess features in the Osiris myth and eventually came to be worshipped throughout the Roman Empire.

**Isis Cult**. The ancient Egyptian goddess ISIS ('Throne') was incorporated into the myth of OSIRIS to become sister and wife of the Egyptian Shepherd God Osiris, and bore a son, Horus (Harpocrates). From the 3rd century BCE Hellenistic influence identified Isis with DEMETER and made her the central figure of a mystery religion which, together with Serapis, spread over most of the ancient Mediterranean world and left archaeological traces in the Roman provinces (Gaul, Spain, Britain, the Rhine area, Pannonia). Despite considerable resistance from the Senate, from the 2nd century BCE the Isis Cult also established itself in Rome; later emperors (Caligula and Caracalla) had temples built for it. Signs of the cult coming to an end are not visible until the 5th century CE. Numerous hymns (aretologies) sing of Isis as the goddess of heaven and the universe who overcomes fate (HEIMARMENE) and suffering, brings cultural progress, protects sailors and grants eternal life. She is depicted with the horns of a cow and a moon disc and resembles APHRODITE and TYCHE. The Isis festivals (Isia) were celebrated in Rome from 26 October to 3 November. The mysteries themselves, of which Apuleius gives a detailed account in his *Metamorphoses* (Book II), consisted of ablutions, fasting, the wearing of white robes and initiation into the most sacred part of the temple, a representation of the journey to heaven, at the end of which the believer becomes a symbolic sun god (SOL) and thus escapes the fate of birth and death. This is a combination of ancient Egyptian and Greek elements. (Griffiths 1976; Leclant & Clerk 1972–4).

**iskoki**. *See* BÒRI.

**Islām**. As the name of the faith of Muslims, Islām means active and voluntary submission to the will of God (ALLĀH); a Muslim therefore is one who, in thus submitting himself, acknowledges that God's will encompasses all the facets of human activity as expressed in the religious law (SHARĪ'A). 'Islām' also refers, in an extended sense, to the whole of Muslim civilization, for general accounts of which see for example Hodgson 1974; Rodinson 1974; Savory 1976; Stowasser 1987.

**Islamic Modernist Movement** (India). Though not formally institutionalized, this movement developed in India from the second half of the 19th century. The modernist position, initially expressed by Sayyid Aḥmad Khān and later by Muḥammad Iqbāl and Fazlur Raḥmān, explored the relationship between revelation in the QUR'ĀN and the ever-changing historical context of its interpretation. (Robinson 1988; Ahmad 1967).

**Island of Creation**. In general, three types of temple may be distinguished in ancient Egyptian religion: solar temples specifically designed for the sun-god's cult, cultus temples for the worship of other specific gods and mortuary temples for the worship of gods and the royal ancestors (dead, deified kings). Cultus and mortuary temples first developed from the reed hut-shrines of predynastic villages (before 3100 BCE); built of massive stone in the Pharaonic and Graeco-Roman periods, they preserved the same forms and basic architectural features over the millennia (Nelson 1944).

Each temple was regarded as the 'Island of Creation' where, according to the Building Texts in the Temple of *Edfu*, creation had occurred; the wall-scenes and plant-form columns and capitals magically re-created this potent landscape. The temple was also the 'House of God' where the god's needs were met through the rituals performed by the priests (as the king's delegates), both on a daily basis (washing, clothing and feeding the divine statue) and at the great festivals held at regular intervals, when the god's statue was paraded outside the temple.

Houses, tombs and temples were all designed on the same basic plan, to provide reception areas and private chambers for the occupant. Rectangular in shape to provide processional routes, each cultus temple consisted of the same units – the pylon (a massive gateway) led into unroofed forecourts which gave access to hypostyle halls (where the roof was supported by columns); the sanctuary opened off these. There were also storerooms for the god's possessions, and between the temple building and the enclosure wall of the whole complex there were butchering and food preparation areas, magazines to store the temple revenue, and a sacred lake where the priests performed daily ablutions and washed the god's utensils. The priests, 'servants of the god', performed their ritual duties on a part-time and rotational basis; they also held positions as lawyers, doctors and scribes in the community. They had no pastoral duties but served the god through the liturgy and the rituals. Wall-scenes in the temples preserve information about these rites; in the cultus temples, certain areas were devoted to the daily rituals for the god, whereas in the mortuary temples, additional areas were included for the ritual to the royal ancestors. This followed after the god's ritual, when the food offered up thrice daily to the god's statue reverted to the altar of the deified kings (David 1981). Finally, this food reverted from the kings' altar and was apportioned among the priests as their payment. The solar temples, probably derived from a different origin, had some unique features. In all temples, the basis of the ritual was the concept of barter. In return for regular attention, the god promised eternal life and everlasting victory to the king, who, theoretically, alone performed the rituals in every temple, and prosperity and fertility for Egypt. The temples were never centres of community worship; indeed, the populace were never permitted beyond the forecourts. However, they were a major economic force and employer; they also had an additional role as centres of higher education and learning. Some temples acquired a reputation as a place of healing and became the focus of medical training.

For specific temples see ABYDOS; EDFU; ESNA; KARNAK; KOM OMBO; LUXOR; PHILAE; THEBES.

**Ismā'īlī** (Arabic). Historically, an offshoot of the SHĪ'A tradition in Islām, whose adherents held that Ismā'īl, son of the sixth IMĀM, should have been the designated seventh *imām*. Hence they are also referred to as 'Seveners'. A radical group, politically active from Egypt to Iran between the 10th and 13th centuries, they survive today in generally prosperous business communities in India, Iran, Syria and East Africa whose *imāms* bear the title of Aghā Khān (Daftary 1990).

**isnād** (Arabic). The chain of transmitters of a tradition (ḤADĪTH) reported from the Prophet Muḥammad, his companions or other prominent early Muslims which constitutes its authority, the subject matter of which is called the *matn*.

**Isrā'**. *See* MI'RĀJ.

**Israel**. The name of the people descended from Abraham, Isaac and Jacob (which includes the descendants of others who have joined them). After he wrestled with the angel (*Genesis* 32.29) Jacob was renamed 'Israel', meaning 'one who wrestles with God and men and prevails'. The 12 sons of Jacob are believed to have originated the 12 tribes of Israel. When, in the period of Kings, the northern tribes under the kingship of Saul split from the southern Kingdom of JUDAH, they called themselves the Kingdom of Israel. Under King David Israel was reunited with Judah, but seceded again under Jeroboam I and was annexed by Assyria *c.*721 BCE (Danell 1946; Block 1984). When a Jewish political state was established in 1948, it was named 'Israel'. Whereas the term 'Israelite' means a member of the people of Israel, an 'Israeli' is a citizen of the modern Jewish State.

**Israelite religion**. Local developments of Canaanite cults in ISRAEL and JUDAH, accompanying the establishment of a state under Saul and David. YAHWEH was the national god under the united monarchy. After the division he remained god of Judah, but his position in Israel was problematic (*see* JEROBOAM'S REFORM). A clear development towards MONOTHEISM took place from the 7th-century BCE onwards under the influence of PROPHECY and the YAHWEH-ALONE PARTY. (Kraus 1966; Rowley 1967; Vriezen 1967).

**Issaikyō**. *See* DAIZŌKYŌ.

**Istiṣlāḥ**. *See* ISTIḤSĀN.

**istihsān** (Arabic: 'to consider good'). In Islamic law, this and *istislāḥ* ('to deem expedient') are methods of reasoning connected with analogy (QIYĀS) in which the former is the legist's adoption of a course, or judgement, which he considers better than one suggested by an analogy with a fixed, legal provision; the latter is doing the same for the sake of the general benefit to the community.

**Īśvara** (Sanskrit: 'the Lord'). A title of God, implying creatorship, maintenance of the world, providence and divine grace for believers. *See also* BRAHMAN.

**iśvarakṛṣṇa**. *See* SĀMKHYA.

**Ithnā ʿAshariya**. *See* TWELVER SHĪ'A.

**Iwuw**. *See* HELIOPOLIS.

**Izanagi and Izanami** [Izanagi no mikoto and Izanami no mikoto]. The first wedded couple in the age of the Shintō gods (KAMI). They gave birth to the terrestrial regions, mountains, rivers, seas, plants, animals and men, and became the gods of the earth and of all things on earth. Izanami died giving birth to the God of Fire and became a goddess in the land of the dead (YOMI). Izanagi went to visit her there but broke a taboo and was forced to depart. Having come in contact with pollution, he feared that misfortune would result, and so went to a river and purified himself. He is thus regarded as the founder of the practice of HARAE. The three most important deities born to Izanagi at his purification were Amaterasu Ōmikami, Susanoo no mikoto and Tsukiyomi no mikoto.

**Izumo Taisha**. The Grand Shrine of Izumo, one of the biggest and oldest Shintō shrines, located at Izumo in Shimane Prefecture, and often compared with ISE JINGŪ in its nationwide popularity. It enshrines Ōkuninushi no kami, the heir of Susanoo no kami as the head of the gods of the earth, the tutelary deities of the various regions of Japan. The chief priest is even now the distant offspring of the ancient priest-lords of the region. The rituals carried out at Izumo have retained a notably archaic form, and the shrine is noted for its fine wooden architecture and massive twisted rope (SHIMENAWA), symbolic of entry to a holy place. Visitors frequent the shrine especially to pray for fortune and successful marital arrangements.

# J

**Jade Emperor**. *See* YUHUANG.

**jagrita**. *See* OM OR AUM.

**Jah**. RASTAFARIAN term for God.

**Jahannam**. *See* ĀKHIRA

**Jāhiliya** (Arabic). The name given in post-Islamic times to the period of 'ignorance or barbarism' which preceded the mission of the Prophet Muḥammad (*c.* 610–32), whose proclamation of ISLĀM, the worship of one God, stood in sharp contrast with the ethics and worship associated with idolatry.

**jajman**. *See* CASTE.

**jajmani**. *See* CASTE.

**Jaldabaoth**. *See* DEMIURGE.

**Jalliānwālā Bagh** (Punjabi). The site of the massacre in AMRITSAR led by General Dyer in 1919 in which 379 Sikh civilians were killed.

**Jamaa** (Swahili: 'family'). A religious movement begun by the Franciscan missionary Placide Tempels (*b* 1906) within the Roman Catholic Church in Zaire, but which has since developed into an independent institution because of the attraction of its ideas and because of falling into disfavour with the Catholic hierarchy. Jamaa places a central emphasis upon the family.

**Jamāʿat al-Muslimīn** (Arabic). Society of Muslims, the correct name for a small underground radical organization which became widely known in Egypt as Takfīr wa'l Hijra, led by Shukrī Muṣṭafa, who was executed in 1977 along with others of the group for the kidnapping and murder of a former Egyptian minister of religious endowments. The group's religio-political doctrine declared that Egyptian society had lapsed into pre-Islamic barbarism (JĀHILIYA) which had to be violently destroyed in order to erect a genuine Muslim society upon its ruins (Kepel 1985).

**Jamāʿat-i-Islāmi** (Urdu). A Muslim reform movement founded in 1941 by Mawlana Abū al-ʿAlā al-Mawdūdi (*d* 1979) in pre-partition India. His programme, similar to that of the Muslim Brethren (AL-IKHWĀN AL-MUSLIMŪN) in Egypt, was to install a vigorous sense of service to the community in education, social action and propagation of the faith. From 1932, al-Mawdūdi published the widely respected Urdu journal *Tarjumān al-Qur'ān*. He held that the whole order of life and society was revealed in the QUR'ĀN and Prophetic tradition (ḤADĪTH), hence his views were essentially anti-nationalistic and pan-Islamic. Thus, politically he initially argued against the creation of Pakistan; unable, however, to ignore the fact of its creation he moved there and continued to call for an authentic Islamic state under the sovereignty of the SHARĪʿA. (Piscatori 1983; Robinson 1988).

**janāba** (Arabic). Major ritual impurity in Islām. *See also* ṬAHĀRA.

**Janam Sākhīs** (Punjabi). Anecdotal stories of the life of the first Sikh teacher, Gurū Nānak. These hagiographic accounts describe episodes in his childhood, travels and later period of religious teaching in the Punjab. There are a number of different collections (McLeod 1968, 1980; Harbans Singh 1969) containing varying accounts, all chronologically organized. They are written in Punjabi prose and are well suited to oral transmission, hence their continued popularity.

**Janna**. *See* ĀKHIRA.

**Jansenism**. The theological position ascribed to Cornelius Jansen (1585–1638), particularly on the basis of his posthumously published work *Augustinus*, and condemned as heretical by Pope Innocent X in 1653. The Jansenist position, which had many supporters in France and in the Netherlands, was a subtly argued version of the theology of Augustine which emphasized the irresistibility of divine grace in a a manner verging on determinism.

**Janus**. A Roman god, popularly depicted as two-faced, and connected with doors and beginnings. His archaic origins, however, lie with bridges.

**japa**. *See* NĀMA.

**Japjī** (Punjabi). The poem by Gurū Nānak with which the GURŪ GRANTH SĀHIB opens. The Japji is recited each morning by devout Sikhs.

**jātaka** (Sanskrit, Pāli). A genre of Buddhist literature describing the previous lives of Gautama BUDDHA. *See also* TRIPIṬAKA.

**jathā** (Punjabi). A Sikh military unit, composed of volunteers, first organized in the 18th century but still formed in times of need. A recent example is Bhindranwale Jathā, the Sikh revivalist group calling for state autonomy for Sikhs, which under the leadership of Sant Jarnail Singh Bhindranwale fortified itself in the Golden Temple in AMRITSAR in 1984. Many of the group were killed when the Indian Government sent in troops in 'Operation Bluestar'. *See also* KHĀLISTAN; AKĀLĪ DAL; DAMDAMĪ TAKṢAL.

**jati**. *See* CASTE.

**Jehovah**. *See* YAHWEH.

**jawi**. *See* AGAMA KEJAWEN.

**Jehovah's Witnesses**. *See* WATCHTOWER BIBLE AND TRACT SOCIETY.

**Jen**. *See* REN.

**Jeroboam's Reform**. Religious policies undertaken by Jeroboam I on the secession of ISRAEL from JUDAH (*1 Kings* 12). A bull deity was worshipped through GOLDEN CALF images for which various interpretations are offered, the most probable being that it was a representation of EL in accordance with *Hosea* 8.6 (*NEB*). (Debus 1967; Aberbach & Smolar 1967; Dus 1968; Donner 1973; Motzki 1975).

**Jerusalem**. Interpreted in Hebrew as the 'city of peace', the ancient city of Jerusalem came to represent the national sovereignty of ISRAEL ever since it was first conquered by King David. The first allusion to Jerusalem in the Bible is in *Genesis* 14.18, where Abraham is blessed by Melchizedek, 'King of Salem'. According to tradition, the site of Solomon's Temple is Mount Moriah, where Abraham offered his son Isaac as a sacrifice. Solomon's Temple completed the work of David, making Jerusalem the cultic and political capital of the first Jewish Commonwealth. It has been, ever since, the symbol of corporate Jewish identity. The destruction of the First Temple in 587 BCE and of the Second Temple in 70 CE served to dramatize the importance of Jerusalem even more strongly in the Jewish consciousness: 'If I forget thee, O Jerusalem, may my tongue cleave to the roof of my mouth' (*Psalms* 137.6). The celebration of Jerusalem in the *Book of Psalms* led to an idealized notion in Judaism of a 'heavenly Jerusalem' corresponding to the 'earthly Jerusalem', a theme which also found many echoes in Christian thought. Various post-exilic Hebrew prophets expressed a vision of Jerusalem to be restored in the future, both physically and spiritually. For OMPHALOS symbolism see Terrien 1970; in general Metzger 1970; Jeremias 1971; Roberts 1973; Ollenburger 1987.

**Jesuits**. *See* COUNTER REFORMATION.

**Jew**. A member of the people of ISRAEL, especially a follower of their religion. The origins of the name Jew go back to the tribe of JUDAH, when the Hebrew, *Yehudi*, meant a citizen of the state of Judah (*2 Kings* 16.6, 25.25; *Jeremiah* 32.12 etc.). After the Assyrians conquered the northern Kingdom Israel in 721 BCE, the southern Kingdom of Judea survived, for a time; since then, the remaining people of Israel have been associated, with Judea, or Judah. After the EXILE the term sometimes had a confessional sense, e.g. in the books of *Nehemiah* and *Esther*. In modern usage 'Judaism' refers to the religion of the people of Israel. The adjective 'Jewish' describes a follower of the religion of Israel, a member of the people of Israel, or anything which pertains to Judaism.

**Jewish War**. A war of attempted liberation against the Romans running from 66 to 70 CE with a last suicidal defence at MASADA in 73 CE. The decisive conclusion was the sack of Jerusalem in 70 CE and the destruction of the temple. Large numbers of Jews were enslaved, and many Jewish religious groupings ceased to exist. (Schürer 1973: 484–513; Smallwood 1976: 293–330).

**jhāna**. *See* DHYĀNA.

**Ji**. *See* SHE.

**Jidai Matsuri**. Festival of the Ages. An annual festival celebrated on 22 October at the Heian Grand Shrine in Kyōto which enshrines the founder of Kyōto, Emperor Kammu. The procession that makes its way through the city in a pageant of historical characters dressed in period costumes represents the 1,000-year history of Kyōto as the capital of Japan.

**jihād** (Arabic: 'struggle'). In several Qur'ānic contexts (eg. 9.73, 25.52), striving against unbelievers who rejected the true way of God (ALLĀH). Although the word's primary sense does not include actual warfare, *jihād* in Islām came to mean 'holy war', either against the infidel or in defence of the Muslim community. It also bears the sense of a spiritual struggle against one's evil inclinations.

**Jing tu**. *See* PURE LAND.

**Jingikan**. The Department of Divinities, an ancient government office in charge of Shintō worship. The Taihō code, established in 701, stipulated that the Daijōkan, in charge of political affairs and local administration, be the highest government office, and that the Jingikan be on a level equal with it. Whereas the Daijōkan was established in imitation of the government system of Tang China, giving the Jingikan the same rank was a unique Japanese development. The Jingikan was responsible for all matters related to the worship of the gods (KAMI). In 1868, the first year of the Meiji Period, the Jingikan was re-established in accordance with the prevailing ideal of *saisei-itchi* ('the union of worship and government'); in August 1871 it became the Jingishō, and in March 1872 it became the Kyōbushō (Ministry of Religious Education).

**jingū**. *See* JINJA.

**Jingū taima**. An amulet distributed by the Grand Shrine of Ise (ISE JINGŪ).

**jinja** (Japanese). A Shintō shrine. There are reckoned to be some 80,000 Shintō shrines in Japan ranging from tiny village shrines to majestic wooden buildings such as Izumo Taisha and ISE JINGŪ. The terms *taisha* ('grand shrine') and *jingū* ('divine palace') occur only in the names of especially important shrines. A typical shrine consists of several buildings. The largest is usually the HAIDEN, before which or in which prayers and ceremonies are held. Behind the HAIDEN, and not entered by the public is the smaller, and higher HONDEN, in which the deity (KAMI) is presumed to reside. A visit to a shrine includes, minimally, purification at the entrance by rinsing hands and mouth with water, and a sequence of (usually) two bows, two handclaps (*kashiwade*), and a bow. *See also* SHINTŌ.

**Jinja Honchō**. Association of Shintō Shrines, organized when Shintō was disestablished as a result of the Occupation order issued in 1945. Shintō in this nationally coordinated form, independent of the state, is called Jinja (Shrine) Shintō. It is a free association of shrines in which the Grand Shrine of Ise is given a religious precedence.

**Jinjakyoku**. Bureau of Shrine Affairs. The government bureau under the Japanese Ministry of Home Affairs (Naimushō) which, until 1940, dealt with the administration of shrines and the Shinto priesthood. After the abolition of the Kyobushō (Ministry of Religious Education) in 1877, Shinto affairs had been administered by the Shajikyoku, a Naimushō bureau that dealt with both Shinto and Buddhist affairs. In April 1900 the Shajikyoku was replaced by two new agencies, the Jinjakyoku for Shinto and the Shūkyōkyoku for all other religions in the Ministry of Education. Later, when the Naimushō was reorganized, the Jinja-kyoku became the highest ranked of the five Ministerial bureaus. From 1940 until 1946 it was replaced by the Jingiin and in 1946 Shinto was reorganized in a disestablished form. *See* SHRINE SHINTŌ.

**Jinja Shintō**. *See* SHINTŌ.

**Ji-shū**. A Japanese Buddhist sect in the PURE LAND tradition inaugurated in 1276 by Ippen (1239–89), who wandered about the country preaching that one should recite the NENBUTSU at every possible moment in case death was imminent.

**jīva** (Sanskrit). The individual 'soul' or life-principle, usually considered immortal but in need of liberation through the practices of particular schools of Hinduism.

**jivanmukti** (Sanskrit). Liberation while still in a body, assumed to be possible by the Advaitins and some other schools of Hinduism, suggesting that regardless of what such a person might do or omit to do, he or she would not be bereft of ultimate bliss.

**jivātman**. *See* MĀDHVA.

**Jizō**. The Japanese name (derived from the Chinese *Dì-zàng*) for the bodhisattva Kṣitigarbha. In Japan this extremely popular bodhisattva is believed to be especially responsible for the care of deceased children or infants, and in recent times millions of votive statues or figurines of Jizō have been sponsored on the occasion of interrupted pregnancies.

**jñānamārga** (Sanskrit: 'path of knowledge'). One of the three traditional 'paths' of Hinduism, the other two being Karmamārga, path of works and BHAKTIMĀRGA, path of devotion. It takes the UPANIṢADS as its scriptural basis and has been systematically developed in the various systems of VEDĀNTA.

**jñānayoga**. *See* YOGA.

**Jōdo**. *See* PURE LAND.

**Jōdo Sanbukyō**. The collective name for the three Chinese sūtras recognized in Japan as normative in PURE LAND Buddhism, namely the *Daimuryōjukyō* (of which the Sanskrit original is the Larger *Sukhāvativyūha Sūtra*), the *Kanmuryōjukyō* (no Sanskrit original) and the *Amidakyō* (of which the Sanskrit original is the Smaller *Sukhāvativyūha Sūtra*).

**Jōdo Shinshū**. (Often abbreviated to Shinshū.) The radical form of PURE LAND Buddhism based on the teaching of the Japanese monk Shinran (1173–1262), a disciple of Hōnen (*see* JŌDO-SHŪ). Shinran's teaching emphasized the consistent removal of all possible forms of self-reliance, even on the practice of repeating the NENBUTSU. His leading work is the *Kyōgyōshinshō*, but a succint collection of his sayings is found in the *Tannishō*, which is widely read in Japan. Most of the numerous adherents of Jōdo Shinshū give allegiance to one of two major temples in Kyōto, Japan, namely the Nishi Honganji (headquarters of the Honganji Sect) and the Higashi Honganji (headquarters of the Ōtani Sect). The literal meaning of Jōdo Shinshū is 'True Sect [*Shinshū*] of the Pure Land [*Jō-do*]'. *See also* AMITĀBHA.

**Jōdo-shū**. The PURE LAND Sect, a Japanese Buddhist sect based on the teaching of Hōnen (1133–1212), who emphasized reliance on the saving power of the Buddha Amida (AMITĀBHA) and the practice of calling on this buddha by name (*see* NENBUTSU). *See also* JŌDO SHINSHŪ.

**Jōdo Wasan**. *See* WASAN.

**Jok**. Ultra-human power among most of the peoples (Shilluk, Dinka, Acholi) speaking Western Nilotic languages in southern Sudan and Uganda. Jok is regarded as having created heaven, earth and mankind; he is still alive and responsible for maintaining his rules. It is characteristic of him that he is split up into different manifestations with special names and functions. Jok is the essence of every being, and the supreme being, 'The Greatest Jok', is life-force itself. The concept of Jok is as different from POLYTHEISM, however, as it is from the Polynesian MANA (which, in contrast to Jok, can be manipulated). Jok and his manifestations can be approached in ritual, but these rituals and ancestral rituals are strictly distinguished (Baumann 1936).

**josephine marriage**. *See* VIRGIN BIRTH.

**Josiah's Reform**. The enforced centralization and 'purification' of the cult of YAHWEH *c*.621 BCE. It may have been motivated by discovery of the book of DEUTERONOMY, if indeed the latter was not written for the purpose (Oded 1977).

**Judah**. One of the twelve tribes of ISRAEL, with a complex political relationship to the other tribes leading to two kingdoms, Israel in the north and Judah (including the tribe of Benjamin) in the south. These kingdoms were united under David but separated again later. The term 'Israel' was commonly applied also to Judah from the 8th century onwards. The pre-exilic Judahites became the post-exilic Jews (*see* EXILE), both being called *Yehudim* in Hebrew. Thus, Israel gave its name to the Jewish people as a nation and Judah provided the designation for its individual members.

**Judaism**. The religion and way of life of Jews. Many Jewish estimates trace Judaism back to the legendary figure of Abraham, who is regarded as a historical person. More realistically, it can be traced to the influence of Ezra in imposing conformity to TORAH (see books of *Ezra* and *Nehemiah*) in the 5th or 4th century BCE. From the EXILE onwards, a distinction can increasingly be made between the old Judahite cult of YAHWEH, which was essentially ethnic and territorial in a Canaanite mould, and more absolutist and exclusivist conceptions independent of this geographical and political context. Judaism was never monolithic. Its many inner tensions resulted in different sects. (M. Smith 1987; Fackenheim 1987; Fishbane 1987; Cohen and Mendes-Flohr 1987; de Lange 1987, Solomon 1991). *See also* JEW; ESSENES; ḤASIDIM; MITZVAH; PHARISEES; SADDUCEES; SAMARITANS.

**ju ju** (West African Pidgin English). Magic, FETISH. The term is often indiscriminately used for any cult, ritual, ritual object or deity in traditional West African religion, and hence has no precise value for descriptive purposes.

**Jung Codex**. A manuscript held at the Jung Institute in Zürich, thought to date from the 4th century CE and consisting of four texts including the well known *Gospel of Truth*. It is of importance as a modern discovery providing primary information about GNOSTICISM.

**juni innen** (Japanese). The Buddhist concept of the twelve causes and conditions, i.e. PRATĪTYA-SAMUTPĀDA. *Compare* INNEN.

**Juno**. An ancient Italian divinity later identified with the Greek HERA, but without the latter's extensive mythologies. Juno particularly favoured women, and later became an important goddess of the state.

**junpai** (Japanese). A pilgrimage following a definite course linking a series of sacred places, usually Buddhist temples. Famous routes include 88 temples on Japan's fourth largest island, Shikoku, and various routes linking 33 temples dedicated to Kannonsama (i.e. the bodhisattva AVALOKITEŚVARA).

**junzi** [chün-tzu] (Chinese). A term that originally meant 'nobleman', but which is used by Confucius to signify a person who has accomplished the moral cultivation of his personality. It is often translated as 'superior man'.

**Jupiter**. The Roman sky god whose name is etymologically equivalent to the Greek ZEUS. He was associated with the Ides of every month and was the recipient of numerous cults, but never received the extensive mythological treatment of his Greek counterpart. With JUNO and MINERVA he formed part of the Etruscan Capitoline triad. As *Jupiter Optimus Maximus* (Jupiter the Best and Greatest) his popularity remained high in the later Roman Empire. *See also* FLAMEN DIALIS.

# K

**ka**. In ancient Egypt, an aspect of the soul, represented as a pair of uplifted arms. The ka (Spirit or double) was born with each individual; it survived death and required food and drink. Originally, this was presented by the deceased's relatives, or by a ka-priest who, with his descendants, was employed in perpetuity for this task and paid from the dead man's estate. However, as a countermeasure to human fallibility, tomb wall-scenes depicted the presentation of this meal which was believed to 'come alive' to ensure a magical and eternal food supply. The ka received the food through the MUMMY, but if this were destroyed, a portrait-statue, positioned in a *serdab* (a cell-like chamber in the tomb), could act as a substitute for the deceased.

**Kaʿba** (Arabic). The cubical stone building in the centre of the sacred area of MECCA which Muslims call the House of God. Into the wall of its eastern corner is found the Black Stone which pilgrims touch or kiss in their ritual circumambulation (*tawāf*) of the building. In pre-Islamic times it was a shrine for idol-worshippers, later cleansed by the Prophet Muḥammad. *See also* ḤAJJ.

**kaʿbah**. *See* KAʿBA.

**kabāʾir**. (Arabic: singular, *kabīr*). In Islām, heavy sins. *See also* KHAṬĪA.

**Kabbalah** (Hebrew). Literally, a 'received' tradition or spiritual transmission, thus the general term for the Jewish mystical tradition. The influential scholar Gershom Scholem has described Kabbalah mainly in terms of a speculative system concerning the nature of the divine, distinguished by letter and number symbolism, and by the doctrines of the Four Worlds and the Ten SEFIROT. Its principal application was in the practice of mystical intentions which, accompanying the performance of mitzvot, or commandments (*see* MITZVAH), were aimed at influencing the divine (Scholem 1946). This view has recently been challenged, or rather broadened, by Moshe Idel, who draws attention not only to theosophical Kabbalah but to a stream of prophetic Kabbalah concerned with the ecstatic experience of mystical union (Idel 1988). The former approach might be said to be rooted in the Ma'aseh Bereshit ('Workings of Creation'), and the later in the Ma'aseh Merkavah ('Workings of the Chariot'), two kinds of Kabbalistic literature originating in the Talmudic period. The classical period of Kabbalah, when its major works were published, was in the 12th and 13th centuries. Rabbi Isaac Luria and his followers in 16th-century Safed, and the Ḥasidic Masters of the 18th and early 19th centuries, represent significant developments of Kabbalah.

**Kabbalat Shabbat** (Hebrew). The Friday evening service of 'receiving the Sabbath', symbolically conceived of as a bride or queen. The Friday evening liturgy revolves around imagery identifying the Sabbath with the SHEKHINAH, a feminine characterization of the immanence of God. Much of it originated in 16th-century Safed, where Kabbalists would dress in white and go out to an apple orchard to welcome in the Sabbath.

**kabbalistic**. *See* KABBALAH.

**Kabir**. *See* SANT TRADITION.

**Kacchapa**. *See* AVATĀRA.

**Kaddish** [Qaddish]. A well-known Aramaic prayer of 'sanctification', which praises God's majesty and looks forward to the establishment of God's kingdom among all ISRAEL. There is a Kaddish prayer which is recited in memory of the dead, but the

Kaddish is also recited as a kind of punctuation, marking transitions at various points in the Hebrew liturgy. The Kaddish is one of the Hebrew prayers which requires a quorum of a MINYAN in order to be recited.

**kadi**. *See* QĀDĪ.

**kāfir** (Arabic: plural *kāfirūn*). Originally meaning 'ungrateful to ALLĀH (God)', in Islām it is the term used to designate an infidel, or unbeliever who, in the QUR'ĀN, is threatened with punishment in hell (JAHANNAM). It is therefore the opposite of Muslim and Mu'min. *See* also ISLĀM; IMĀN.

**Kaggen**. A characteristic mythical personality among the Khoisan-speaking peoples of southern Africa; originally a TRICKSTER (a bush-spirit of ambivalent character), comparable to the ANANSE spider-trickster of West Africa. The KhamSan identify him with the *Mantis religiosa*, a kind of praying locust who is believed to have once belonged to the 'men of the early race'. They give him the attributes of a DEMIURGE and deified hero and a rich legendary cycle has developed around him. Mostly he is malevolent, having 'got spoilt' through many battles (Bleek 1923). But other Bushmen, the San of Lesotho, see Kaggen as supreme being and creator, lord over life and death, sun and rain, who is worshipped in cult (Hirschberg 1975).

**kagura** (Japanese). A performance of Japanese music and dance whose origin is attributed to a performance by the heavenly gods to persuade Amaterasu Ōmikami, the Sun Goddess, to come out of the cave where she had hidden herself. Thus the performance serves to pacify, console and give pleasure to a deity. The tradition of the *kagura* preserved at the imperial court is particularly ancient. At shrines *kagura* is mostly performed by female shrine officiants (*miko*). There is also a popular form of kagura called *satokagura* which is performed for local deities. The developed *kagura* tradition includes dance dramas portraying numerous scenes from Shintō mythology.

**kagura-den** (Japanese). Building for the performance of KAGURA. Originally *kagura* was performed in the open area in front of a shrine; the development of a stage parallels that of the theatrical arts such as *nō* and *kabuki*.

**Kaivalya**. *See* PURĀṆAS.

**kajō** (Japanese: 'superseding'). A term used by Tominaga Nakamoto (1715–46) to indicate the common tendency on the part of religious leaders to bring out a new variation in the teaching which they transmit, thereby establishing a special claim to authority. This idea, which occurs in both of his extant works, amounts to a theory of religious tradition based on the position of historical criticism.

**Kakashi-Kakulu**. Mythical old woman who assists the supreme being (MVIDYE) in creation; frequently found character in African myths (Baumann 1936).

**kalām** (Arabic). Literally, 'speech' or 'word'. In Islām, both the QUR'ĀN and Jesus (ʿIsā) are referred to as Kalām Allāh, the word of God. In the expression *ʿIlm al-kalām*, the science of disputation, the word refers to the activity of producing rational arguments for the elucidation and support of religious doctrines, and hence loosely, 'dialectical theology'. A practioner was called a *mutakallim*. The first major exponents of the method in Islām were the Muʿtazilī of the late 8th to 10th centuries, who were attacked in turn by another school of *kalām*, the Ashʿarī with later refinements by the Māturīdī school from the tenth century onwards. Theology played a less important role historically in Islām than jurisprudence and Muslim modernists tend more towards pragmatic reform than theological debate. (Rahman 1979; Watt 1973).

**Kālī** (Sanskrit: the black one). Often used as synonymous with DURGĀ, a name of the Hindu Goddess, connoting her terrible aspect. She is propitiated through blood-sacrifices (humans and animals), and is supposed to cause epidemics and other catastrophes if not properly worshipped. The city of Calcutta derives its name from Kālī-ghāta, i.e. Kālī's steps to the river.

**Kalishata**. *See* KĀLI.

**Kaliyuga** (Sanskrit: 'the age of strife', from *kali* ('strife', 'quarrel') and *yuga*, one of the four divisions of a *kalpa* ('world age')). The least desirable and lowest of all ages. It is supposed to have begun with the MAHĀBHĀRATA war (*c*.1400 BCE) and to last for another 30,000 years or so, during which the human condition would constantly deteriorate.

**Kalpa**. *See* KĀLIYUGA.

**Kalunga**. In Angola and Zaire the supreme being with dominant chthonic, or earth-related, and manistic or power-bearing aspects; partly a counterpart of NZAMBI or MVIDYE as the ruler of the underworld or alternatively used as the name of the underworld (Baumann 1975a).

**kami** (Japanese). Spirituals beings regarded as objects of worship in Shintō. Numerous etymological theories exist regarding the origins of the word, but none is entirely satisfactory. A leading modern view suggests that kami originally meant something like 'hidden source'. The influential Shintō scholar Motoori Norinaga (1730–1801) interpreted the word as an appellation for all beings which possess extraordinary ability or virtue, and which were awesome and worthy of reverence. He pointed out that the word was used not only for good beings, but also for evil ones. The deities in Shintō are regarded as numerous, and, indeed, as constantly increasing in numbers, as is expressed in the term *yaoyorozu no kami* ('ever-increasing myriad deities'). These deities make up a single whole however united in peace and harmony. *Kami* may include everything from the divine spirits who realized the production of heaven and earth, the great ancestors of men, to all the specific things in the universe including plants, rocks, birds, beasts and fish. These beings are divided into heavenly and earthly *kami*; heavenly deities (*amatsukami*) have their home in heaven (Takama no Hara), while earthly deities (*kunitsukami*) live on the earth. Originally the heavenly deities were thought to be noble and the earthly deities base, but this distinction is not now clearly upheld.

**kamidana** (Japanese). Household altar (literally, 'god-shelf') in the home of a Shintō believer. The *kamidana* usually houses a rectangular paper or wooden amulet known as *o-fuda*, brought from a major shrine in the region, and prayers and food are offered each morning and evening.

**kamma**. *See* KARMA.

**kan**. *See* KARMA.

**Kanda Matsuri**. An annual festival celebrated on 15 May at the Kanda Shrine in Tokyo. During the Edo period (1600–1868) this festival was celebrated in autumn and co-ordinated with the Hie Shrine festival (*see* SANNŌ MATSURI). The procession with portable shrines and floats combined with a spirit of community rivalry produced an extremely showy festival.

**Kane**. *See* TANE.

**Kanmuryōjukyō**. *See* JŌDO SANBUKYŌ.

**Kannon**. *See* AVALOKITEŚVARA.

**kannushi** (Japanese). A Shintō priest. Now a general designation, it originally referred to the head priest of a shrine or someone who, after strict abstinence, had qualified to serve as a medium for a deity.

**kangshinmu**. *See* MUDANG.

**kapu** (Hawaiian). A traditional prohibition system of the Hawaiian islands, abolished in a radical policy decision by King Kamehameha II in 1819, at the instigation of his mother Kaahumanu, widow of Kamehameha I. *See also* TAPU (=taboo), of which *kapu* is the Hawaiian equivalent.

**karah praśād** (Punjabi). A sweet food made from semolina, ghee and sugar, shared at the end of Sikh worship, which signifies that social differences, particularly CASTE, are of no importance in Sikh teaching and practice.

**karakia** (Māori). Traditional Māori incantations, words of power, necessary for all ritual performances. In modern Māori language the term also denotes Christian prayers and services.

**karma** (Sanskrit: 'action', 'deed') [Pāli: *kamma*]. In Indian religions generally, *karma* designates both the action and the psychological/spiritual residue of that action which determines the future life of a person. Religious disciplines are designed to neutralize *karma* and to lead to MOKṢA/MUKTI.

**Karma**. *See* CASTE; PUNARJANMA.

**Karmamarga**. *See* JÑĀNAMARGA.

**Karmayoga**. *See* YOGA.

**Karnak**. A great temple complex at the ancient Egyptian city of THEBES, dedicated to AMUN (Amen-Re), MUT and KHONSU, built from the 18th Dynasty (1567–1320 BCE) onwards, around the original 12th Dynasty shrine (1991–1786 BCE) (Chicago University 1936).

**Karneia**. In ancient Greece, a Dorian festival of military life, including dancing, sacrifices, and athletic competition. It was sacred to APOLLO.

**karuṇā** (Sanskrit). Compassion; a quality ascribed to a bodhisattva in MAHĀYĀNA Buddhism.

**kasb** (Arabic: 'acquisition'). A doctrine expounded by the Muslim theologian Abū al-Ḥasan al-Ashʿarī (*d* 935) with regard to the problem of man's responsibility for his actions. Al-Ashʿarī taught that all acts are performed by ALLĀH's (God's) immediate initiative but once performed man acquires (*kasb, iktisāb*) them. Thus men are responsible for their acts and will accordingly be punished or rewarded for them by Allāh.

**Kashiwade**. *See* JINJA.

**Kasuga**. Four deities enshrined at Kasuga Shrine in Nara. Originally they were the clan (*see* KAMI and UJIGAMI) of the Fujiwara family, but they later became a focus of common devotion to which branch shrines were established locally. The Kasuga Matsuri is regarded as a major festival in Japan; the shrine is also known for the beauty of its architecture and grounds, as well as for its herds of tame deer.

**Kataragama**. The most important deity of the Tamil Hindus of Sri Lanka. Although the principal Kataragama shrine located in the extreme south-east corner of Sri Lanka is primarily for Hindus, it has since ancient times been a place of Buddhist pilgrimage also. Nowadays the annual Kataragama festivals held in July–August draw people from all of Sri Lanka's main religious groups – mainly Buddhists and Hindus, but also Muslims and Christians – and the festival at Kataragama has become the most important event in the religious calendar, attracting more pilgrims than the *Äsaḷa Perahära* of the Tooth Temple in Kandy.

**katcina** (Hopi). Deities of the Hopi people (southwestern North America) when they appear in ceremonies; that is, humans who are wearing appropriate masks and costumes become the deities. Also dolls which function as mnemonic devices for children to learn the appearances of the different *katcina*.

**kaṭhina** (Sanskrit, Pāli: 'raw cotton', 'robe-giving'). In Buddhism, the ceremonial act in which a group of laymen hand over a robe (or robes) to a particular monastery. In Sri Lanka the ceremony, which is held in early November, is known as *kaṭhina pinkama*, i.e. the act of MERIT of giving a robe.

**katholikentag**. *See* KIRCHENTAG.

**katikāvata** (Sinhalese: 'special rule'). A book of regulations that lays down the principles of application of the original Buddhist monastic rules (PRĀTIMOKṢA). The first *katikāvata* was promulgated during the 12th century, but of particular importance is the edition by King Kīrti Śrī Rājasiṃha (King of Kandy, Ceylon, 1747–82), because it remains the foundation of the one in use today. The revival of Buddhist monasticism in Sri Lanka during the second half of the 18th century and the re-introduction of the new higher ordination tradition from Thailand (Siam) in 1753, was primarily the result of the friendly relationship between Kīrti Śrī Rājasiṃha and the last *Sangharāja* ('King of Sangha') Välivițiyē Saraṇankara (1698–1778).

**katun** (Maya). A period of 7,200 days – nearly 20 years in the Maya LONG COUNT calendar, used 1250–1520 CE as an abbreviated notation system for longer dates used during the Maya Classic period (200–900 CE). (Adams 1977). *See also* SHORT COUNT.

**Kaur** (Punjabi: 'Princess'). A name taken by all female members of the Sikh KHĀLSĀ.

**Kausitaki**. *See* UPANIṢADS.

**kavvanah** (Hebrew; plural *kavvanot*). Intention. Heightened consciousness brought to Jewish prayer and the performance of *mitzvot*, or commandments (*see* MITZVAH). *Kavvanot* are the specific kabbalistic meditations which may accompany ritual and liturgy.

**Kawruh Beja**. Literally, 'Knowledge of the True Good Fortune'; an intellectualistic mystical movement centred in Java. Its speculative dogmatics are based on a 'phenomenological analysis of experience' (Geertz 1960a: 339).

**Kawruh Kasunyatan**. Literally, 'Knowledge of the Highest Reality'; a mystical movement (KEBATINAN) founded in 1925 in Surakarta (Indonesia), which emphasizes practice to the relative exclusion of speculative theory (Geertz 1960a: 339f).

**kāya**. *See* TRIKĀYA.

**kaypacha**. *See* HANAQPACHA.

**kebatinan** (Indonesian, from Javanese (originally Arabic) *bāṭin*: 'inner', 'interior', 'hidden', 'mysterious'). Generally, the practice of Javanese mysticism as it is apparent in different ALIRAN, among them large movements such as PAGUYUBAN NGESTI TUNGGAL, SAPTA DARMA, SUSILA BUDI DARMA, or PAGUYUBAN SUMARAH. *Kebatinan* in terms of 'individual articulation' also means 'the cult of the inner man' (Mulder 1983b: 265), aiming at organizing the whole life to 'the inner realm of human experience' (Geertz 1960a: 232). Beyond that, *kebatinan* in a wider sense also implies 'a style of life that is not necessarily mystically expressed' (Mulder 1983a: 26). It may even refer to 'Javaneseness' by 'glorification of and the belief in the Javanese cultural heritage' (Mulder 1983a: 26), stressing the distinctive Javanese origin of *kebatinan* (AGAMA KEJAWEN). Generally, *kebatinan* claims to lead man to harmony or ultimately unity with the underlying reality on which all life in its cosmic and social order is based. This can be achieved through ascetism or meditation, but also through metaphysical speculation or other practices under the guidance of a charismatic leader. (Hadiwijono 1967; Magnis-Suseno 1981).

**kegare** (Japanese). An important Shintō term meaning 'pollution', which is regarded as inauspicious, the source of unhappiness and evil, and as an impediment to religious ceremonies. Pollution is removed by avoiding participation in religious matters and social life for a certain period of time, and by performing ceremonies of exorcism or purification (*see* HARAE). Until the Middle Ages the death of humans and domestic animals, childbirth, menstruation, eating meat and sickness were all regarded as sources of pollution. Today more emphasis is placed on mental or spiritual pollution.

**Kena**. *See* UPANIṢADS.

**Kenites**. Migrant metalworkers named after Cain in ancient Palestine. The 'Kenite hypothesis' argues that YAHWEH was originally a Kenite god. (Rowley 1950: 149ff; Vaux 1969: 28–32, 1978: 28–32).

**kenotic theology**. A kenotic theology, or CHRISTOLOGY, is one which emphasizes the self-emptying activity of God in INCARNATION, that is, the renunciation of omnipotence and omniscience by God the Son in order to take on the limitations of manhood. The term arises from the Greek verb used to refer to this in *Philippians* 2.7.

**Keret**. A Legendary king and hero of Ugaritic epic. Bereft of wife and children, he wages war, wins a new wife and has fresh children, but by impiety and stupidity he is reduced to his original condition. The tale of Keret may be regarded as a critique of ROYAL IDEOLOGY. (See Bernhardt 1955–6; Gray 1964; Merrill 1968; Parker 1977; Olmo Lete 1981: 240–323. Text in Gibson 1978; de Moor 1987.)

**keris**. *See* KRIS.

**keśdhārī** (Punjabi). A SIKH who keeps the hair uncut. *See also* AMRITDHĀRĪ; SAHAJDHĀRĪ.

**Ketubah** (Hebrew). A Jewish marriage contract. The lettering and embellishment of marriage contracts became a major form of Jewish art.

**Khalīfa** (Arabic: 'successor'). The title of rulers of the Islamic community who succeeded the Prophet Muḥammad. As a religious/political title it was formally abolished in 1924 by the first President of the Turkish Republic, Kemal Ataturk. The word is also used for the favourite disciple of a ṢŪFĪ SHAYKH, upon whom the leader's spiritual authority will devolve when he dies (Kennedy 1986).

**Khālistān** (Urdu, Punjabi: 'Land of the Pure'). Sikh homeland. Recent calls for an independent state for Sikhs have been voiced since 1946 by the AKĀLĪ DAL. Such demands were intensified at the time of the AMRITSAR tragedy in 1984 (*see* JATHĀ). Sikh opinion is divided on the issue of Khālistān (Shackle 1984).

**Khālsā** (Punjabi). A Sikh institution or order established with the initiation of five Sikhs (PAÑJ PYĀRE) at the BAISĀKHĪ gathering of 1699 by the tenth Gurū, Gobind Singh. The term, which means 'pure' but relates also to land held under royal control, is indicative of the loyal commitment of Sikhs to the teachings of the Gurūs. Membership of the Khālsā requires obedience to a code of conduct (*see* RAHIT NĀMĀ) and maintenance of a set of symbols (PAÑJ KAKKE), and is ideally marked by initiation (AMRIT). Sikhs are often distinguished by their degree of commitment to these features (*see* KEŚDHĀRĪ, SAHAJDHĀRĪ, AMRITDHĀRĪ). Theologically, Khālsā Sikhs hold to a belief both in one God (*see* TEN GURŪS) and in meditation on his name (*see* NĀM; WAHEGURU).

**khandhā**. *See* SKANDHĀ.

**khanqah**. (Persian). In Iran, an endowed foundation governed by a SHAYKH provided for the maintenance of ṢŪFĪS. In some respects they were similar to medieval European monasteries except that there was no specific rule to govern the order.

**Khārijī**. An early Islamic sect of the 7th to 10th centuries with strict puritanical views which broke with the majority by insisting that leadership of the community must be determined by unrestricted election and that sinners were apostates. More moderate and intellectualist groups survived the activist phase and are found today in the communities of 'IBĀDIYA.

**khaṭīa** (Arabic). Synonymous with *dhanb*, the two general terms in Islām for sin, defined as a deliberate act. While there is no concept of original sin in Islām, human nature is considered to be innately weak and subject to temptation and disobedience. The gravest of all sins is to deny the unity of ALLĀH (God) which is unforgivable. Otherwise Allāh is All Forgiving (Qur'ān 7.155) and one who forgives sins totally (39.53), although He also remains free to spare or punish the sinner (3.129). There was a distinction between light (*ṣaghā'ir*) and heavy (*kabā'ir*) sins, but debate as to what constituted the graver kind, some early schools holding that these latter led to eternal damnation.

**Khepri**. A form of the sun-god in ancient Egypt represented as a SCARAB (dung-beetle), symbolizing the rising sun and the concept of 'coming into being'.

**Khlysts**. Members of a Russian sect known for FLAGELLATION.

**Khnum**. The ram-headed, ancient Egyptian creator god of the Cataract region, protector of the sources of the Nile. He fashioned mankind on a potter's wheel.

**Khonsu**. An ancient Egyptian moon-god, son of AMUN and MUT. Khonsu was worshipped with these deities at KARNAK (THEBES).

**al-Khulafā' al-Rāshidūn**. *See* RIGHTLY GUIDED CALIPHS.

**Khuṭba** (Arabic). The address or sermon following Friday congregational prayers in the MOSQUE.

**kibbutz** (Hebrew). A 'collective' Jewish community, usually a farm, established by settlers of the modern State of ISRAEL. Land, as well as most property and child-rearing, is shared collectively in kibbutz life.

**Kimbanguist Church**. An independent African church with over 4 million members in Zaire and neighbouring countries, founded by Simon Kimbangu (1889–1951) in the early 20th century. Kimbangu named his church The Church of Jesus Christ on earth through the Prophet Simon Kimbangu. Kimbangu was perceived as a charismatic figure with profound healing powers by his followers, and as a political threat by the Belgian Colonial functionaries to such an extent that he was imprisoned for 30 years until his death in 1951. His imprisonment spurred the movement onward to become such a powerful religious presence in Africa that it was admitted to the WORLD COUNCIL OF CHURCHES in 1969. Its successful establishment testifies to the creativity of both Christianity and the so-called 'traditional' religions, both of which here demonstrated their ability to develop in novel directions in fertile situations (Martin 1975).

**kin** (Maya). Sun, the single day unit in Maya calendar (Coe 1980).

**Kirche**. *See* CHURCH.

**Kirchentag** (German). In Germany, an assembly of church representatives for wide-ranging, public discussion of religious and social issues, organized by Protestant churches. The Roman Catholic equivalent is KATHOLIKENTAG.

**kīrtan**. (From Sanscrit *kīrtanam* meaning 'praise', 'eulogy'). This term is used in all North Indian languages to mean singing of devotional poetry, usually by groups of devotees, a fairly universal practice of Hindus, Sikhs and Christians in India. It was popularized as *nēgara-kīrtan*, public singing and dancing in the streets by Caitanya and his followers. In Sikhism the devotional songs are generally from the GURŪ GRANTH SĀHIB, often to a musical accompaniment, commonly known as *sabd-kirtan*.

**Kitawala**. A powerful African religious movement which developed in the early 20th century in the context of the WATCH TOWER BIBLE AND TRACT SOCIETY and which continues to flourish in various African countries today. One of its key themes is a new age of peace, prosperity and independence.

**Kitche Manitou**. *See* MANITOU.

**Kiumbi**. The supreme being in northern East Africa who is continously 'creating' (*-mbi*); a celestial god without ancestral character (Baumann 1936: 44).

**kiva**. In Pueblo religions (southwestern North America), a round underground structure for rituals that symbolizes the fundamental emergence myth and continues the original habitation structures of many centuries previous.

**kiyai** (Javanese, Indonesian). A Javanese form of address for an Islamic scholar, usually headteacher of a PESANTREN, 'roughly comparable to the Mid-Eastern 'ulamā' (Geertz 1960a: 134). (Geertz 1960b; Binder 1960; Steenbrinck 1974; Dhofier 1980). *See also* KIYAYI; KYAI.

**Kluscap**. *See* GLOOSCAP.

**Knights Templar**. *See* TEMPLARS.

**kōan** (Japanese). Traditional questions, with their answers, first developed in China and used as subjects of teaching and meditation in Zen Buddhism generally.

**Kōgakkan**. *See* JINGŪ KŌGAKKAN.

**Kogo Shūi**. A work presented by Imbe Hironari to Japanese Emperor Heizei in 807, containing much ancient material on Shintō practice, important shrines such as Ise and Atsuta and the relation between the Nakatomi and the Imbe clan.

**Kohen** (Hebrew). A descendant of the family of Aaron; a Jew from the family of Temple priests. The name continues in the anglicized forms Cohen, Cohn.

**Kokka Shintō**. *See* STATE SHINTŌ.

**kokua** (Hawaiian). Freely given helpfulness: a traditional Hawaiian value. The term currently implies cheerful co-operation, as in the phrase 'please *kokua*' used in public morality requests against smoking, litter and so on.

**kokubunji** (Japanese). Buddhist temples established in each of the ancient provinces of Japan, from 741 onwards, in order to pray for the welfare of the state.

***Kojiki***. A Japanese classic based on oral traditions, compiled in 712. It relates myths, legends and historical accounts centring around the imperial court, from the 'age of the gods' until the reign of Empress Suiko (reigned 593–623). Shintō thought has developed largely through the interpretation of *Kojiki* mythology. The work contains much detail on ceremonies, customs, taboos, magical practices and divination practices of ancient Japan.

**Kol Nidre** (Aramaic: 'all my vows'). The stirring opening prayer recited on the eve of YOM KIPPUR, popularly believed to have been written during the Spanish Inquisition, when Jews were forced to (pretend to) convert to Christianity. In the Kol Nidre one asks to be absolved of all one's vows, promises and oaths.

**Kom Ombo**. A Nome (district) capital in ancient Egypt, with the remains of a unique double temple dedicated to *Sobek* and the falcon-headed Haroeris, built in the Graeco-Roman period (*c.*300 BCE – 2nd century CE).

**kongōkai**. *See* MAṆḌALA, RYŌBU MANDARA.

**Kore**. *See* ELEUSINIAN MYSTERIES.

**Koran**. *See* QUR'ĀN

**Koshar**. An artificer god who appears in the BAAL CYCLE. Entrusted with the task of building the sea-god's temple-palace, instead he helps BAAL overcome the latter and then builds Baal's palace. The west semitic form is Kataru: both represent a semitized form of the Egyptian PTAH.

**kosher** (Yiddish; from Hebrew, *kasher*). 'Proper' and permissible food. The Jewish laws of keeping *kosher* (Hebrew, *kashrut*) involve the prohibition against certain kinds of food (such as pork and shellfish), the correct method of slaughter, as well as the separation of foods and utensils relating to dairy and to meat.

**Kraton** (Javanese; Indonesian). A walled palace city, symbolic representation of the universe, former politico-religious centre in the Javanese states (Heine-Geldern 1963; Anderson 1972).

**kris** (Indonesian). A dagger with an undulated sheath, to which magical powers are attributed; nowadays mainly used on ceremonial occasions. The *kris* is well known all over South-East Asia, especially in Java and Bali (Anderson 1972; Frey 1986).

**Kriya**. *See* ŚAIVA SIDDHANTA.

**Kronos**. *See* ORPHIC MYSTERIES.

**kṛpā** (Sanskrit: 'grace'). A key term in the vocabulary of theistic VEDĀNTA, which insists that a person cannot gain MOKṢA either through his or her own actions or through knowledge alone but through God's grace.

**Kṛṣṇa**. 'The black one', also called Śyāma, one of the 'full' AVATĀRAS of VIṢṆU, the most widely worshipped deity in India, believed to be the manifestation of VIṢṆU himself on earth. His teaching is contained in the BHAGAVADGĪTĀ. The most important PURPĀṆA associated with Kṛṣṇa is the *Bhāgavatam*, providing a detailed account of Kṛṣṇa's birth, childhood and youth in Brāja (the district of Mathurā, Vrindaban, Govardhāna) and his exploits with the *gopīs* ('milkmaids'). His birthday, *Kṛṣṇajanmāṣṭamī*, is celebrated as public holiday all over India.

**kṣatriya** (Sanskrit: 'ruling'). The rulers and warriors, the second CASTE in rank of the four Hindu social classes.

**Kshatriya.** *See* CASTE.

**Kṣitigarbha**. A BODHISATTVA in MAHĀYĀNA Buddhism who is believed to enter hell to rescue and guide lost spirits. *See also* JIZŌ.

**Ku**. *See* TU.

**Kūkās** (Punjabi). *See* NĀMDHĀRĪ MOVEMENT.

**Kulturkampf** (German). Cultural struggle between the Church and the State. Originally the term was used for the tensions created by the Prussian State in its attempt to reduce the influence of the Roman Catholic Church during the years 1872–87.

**Kumano**. *See* SENDATSU.

**Kunitsukami.** *See* KAMI.

**Kunlun**. A mythological mountain believed to be in the western confines of China. A vast mountain range there is today called Kunlun, but we have no way of knowing whether this was the place where the Han (Chinese) emperor Wu Di (140–87 BCE) sought the advice of the 'Queen Mother of the West' (XI WANG MU) on government principles and other vital matters. Kunlun figures prominently in Chinese cosmological thinking. As a macrocosmic entity Kunlun is the starting point of an eschatological process aimed at world renewal. With its primordial QI force administered by the various strata of IMMORTALS (genii) on the mountain, Kunlun is also thought to act as the navel of a microcosmic human body, radiating forth life-spending energy.

**k'un lun**. *See* KUNLUN.

**Kusha-shū.** The Kusha 'sect' of Japanese Buddhism, based on the teaching of the *Abhidharma-kośa*. Although this teaching was introduced at an early time it never became a major religious organization.

**kut** (Korean). A general term for Korean shamanist rituals usually including music and dance. *See also* MUDANG.

**Kuttāb**. *See* MAKTAB.

**Kuzari**. A work by the Jewish poet and philosopher Yehudah Halevi in 12th-century Spain, retelling the story of the conversion of the Kingdom of the Khazars to Judaism in the 8th century CE. Halevi describes the choice of the King of the Khazars to convert to Judaism, rather than Christianity or Islam, on the basis of the arguments he hears from representatives of all three religions.

**Kvasir**. *See* AESIR.

**kwatz!** An exclamation used in ZEN Buddhism to express a forceful perception of reality which cannot be expressed in words.

**Kwoth**. The spiritual supreme being the Nuer in the southern Sudan, power in the sky and everywhere, comparable to JOK; Kwoth can be approached, but not manipulated, by prayer or sacrifice (Evans-Pritchard 1956).

**Kyai**. *See* KIYAI.

**kyaung** (Burmese: 'school') the most common Burmese term for a monastic settlement, since the monastery was the school for the children of the village.

**Kyōgyōshinshō**. *See* JŌDO SHINSHŪ.

**Kyōha Shintō**. *See* SECT SHINTŌ.

**Kyrie** (Greek). Abbreviated designation of a traditional ovation in Greek which in full (*kyrie eleison*) means 'Lord have mercy'. Current in both the eastern and western liturgies it was eventually set to music as the first piece in the MASS as a musical composition.

**kyrie eleison**. *See* KYRIE.

# L

**L**. *See* SYNOPTIC GOSPELS.

**labyrinth**. A building designed and constructed by Daedalus on Minoan Crete with intricate corridors in which the MINOTAUR could hide and from which no one could escape. Eventually the problem was solved by the hero Theseus, who tied a ball of string at the entrance and unravelled it as he advanced within, thus later being able to retrace his steps by following the thread. In wider English usage, a powerful symbol of the apparently hopeless search for a reliable thread of meaning and hence salvation.

**Laestadianism**. A revivalist Christian movement which began in northern Sweden in the 19th century, being named after Lars Levi Laestadius (1800–61). The movement became especially strong in Finland and is centred, at its strongest and most conservative, in the Oulu area. It emphasizes personal conversion and militates against alcohol abuse. However, it also plays an important social role in providing a focus of loyalty for the sparse population of northern Finland. More recently, under the name Central Union of Finnish Quietist Societies (Suomen rauhanyhdistysten keskusyhdistys) it has extended its influence to the major towns of southern Finland.

**Laima**. Baltic goddess of fortune; also the word for material fortune. Laima sets a child's fate at birth, chooses husbands and decides the moment of death, as well as being called on by individuals for help in various situations. Her companion is *Nelaime* ('Misfortune'). Folklore describes her discussions about particular strokes of fate with the sky god DIEVS, which invariably lead to differences of opinion, Laima insisting on the more difficult fate though at the same time lamenting it. She is also a fertility goddess, appearing as a sower to guarantee successful grain harvest, and a protector of cattle.

**Lakṣmī** [Śrī]. 'Good Fortune', 'Wealth', considered to be the spouse of VIṢṆU and inseparably connected with him.

**Lamaism**. A 19th-century term commonly used for that form of Buddhist culture typical of Tibet and Mongolia, in which the head of state is also the supreme spiritual leader (*see* DALAI LAMA; PANCHEN LAMA), supported by a large number of Buddhist clergy. 'Lāma' ('superior one') is a term of respect used to designate a Buddhist monk. The justification for the use of the term 'Lamaism' lay in that it pointed correctly to the dominance of the monks in traditional Tibetan society. However, it corresponds neither to the Tibeto-Mongolian Buddhist consciousness nor to current political conditions, and hence is usually avoided by specialists today.

**laṅgar** (Punjabi). A communal kitchen in a Sikh GURDWĀRĀ.

**Laṅkāvatāra Sūtra**. An important early Mahāyāna Buddhist sūtra containing the first extended, though unsystematic statement of the 'consciousness-only' school of thought. (For the text see Suzuki 1968.) *See also* ĀLAYA-VIJÑĀNA; VIJÑĀNAVĀDA.

**Lao Tzu**. *See* LAOZI.

**lar familiares.** *See* LAR(ES).

**Lares** (Latin; singular, *lar*). Minor Roman gods, perhaps originally either one of the INDIGITES or a deified ancestor. Subject of many cults, of which that of the hearth (*lar familiaris*) and COMPITALIA were the most famous. The lares are sometimes combined with PENATES. *See also* ARVAL BRETHREN.

**al-Lat**. *See* 'DAUGHTERS' OF ALLAH.

**Lateran Councils**. Ecclesiastical councils convened at the Lateran Palace at Rome, and which have contributed significantly to the definition of Roman Catholicism not only doctrinally but also in terms of church order. The fourth, for example, held in 1215, formally introduced the term TRANSSUBSTANTIATION, but also made provisions about the organization of dioceses and religious orders.

**latitudinarianism**. A scornful term applied to Church of England clergymen, especially in the 17th century, who adopted a liberal view of doctrinal and liturgical questions.

**Latopolis**. *See* ESNA.

**Latter-Day Saints.** *See* MORMONISM.

**Lauds.** *See* VESPERS.

**laukika.** *See* LOKOTTARA.

**lawḥ maḥfūẓ** (Arabic: 'preserved tablet'). In Islām, the tablet kept in heaven from which the revelations vouchsafed the Prophet Muḥammad by ALLĀH (God) were taken (Qur'ān, 85.22).

**Laylat al-Qadar** (Arabic). Night of Power. *See* RAMAḌĀN.

**lebaran**. *See* RIYAYA.

**Lébé**. A mythical ancestor of the Dogon of Mali, who after his death came back to life in the form of a snake. His priest is the *hogon*, the senior elder of any one group who exercises highest authority in its ritual and social life (Dieterlen 1941).

**lectionary**. A book containing portions of scripture which are designated to be read aloud at services of Holy Communion or Mass and at Matins and Evensong. The readings (or 'pericopes') are selected because of their relevance to the sequence of the church year and are therefore taken out of their context in the original biblical works.

**lectisternium**. A symbolic Roman banquet to which gods were invited and represented by statues. It was often sponsored in times of crisis.

**Legalism**. The common Western name for a Chinese school of political philosophy (*fajia* [*fa-chia*], 'school of law') which flourished during the 4th and 3rd centuries BCE and reached its maximum influence during the Qin [Ch'in] dynasty (221–206 BCE). Its most important thinkers were Shang Yang (*d* 338 BCE) and Han Fei Zi [Han Fei-tzu] (*d* 233 BCE).

The main concern of Legalist philosophy is how to strengthen the state, both internally and externally. Unlike the Confucians (*see* CONFUCIANISM), who advocated government by moral virtue, the Legalists maintained that the state should be ruled by statutary law. The laws should be enacted according to the circumstances and enforced ruthlessly by harsh punishments. In this way the economic and military strength of the state could be secured and the position of the ruler safeguarded.

The rational policies of the Legalists were applied by the ruler of the state of Qin [Ch'in], who succeeded in overthrowing all competing states, thus establishing for the first time a unified Chinese empire in 221 BCE. After the collapse of the short-lived Qin dynasty, legalist philosophy was sharply criticized by the Confucians, who finally dominated the political thinking of the Chinese empire. However, many of the institutions implemented by the Qin dynasty continued to exist throughout Chinese history and despite the Confucian ideology the actual policy of the Chinese state often relied on Legalist principles.

**Legba**. TRICKSTER god of the Ewe of Togo and the Fon of the Republic of Benin. He is similar to ESHU or Elegba of the Yoruba of Nigeria (Pelton 1980).

**lelembut** (Javanese; Indonesian: 'ethereal ones'). A group of invisible possessing spirits causing sickness or death, if the possessed is not treated by a DUKUN (Geertz 1960a).

**Lemuria**. A Roman festival held on 9, 11, 13 May to appease dangerous ghosts (*lemures*). The head of the household utilized APO-

TROPAIC rituals in the dead of night. *See also* PARENTALIA.

**Lent**. The period of fasting or abstinence observed by Christians of various churches in the 40 days before Easter, not counting Sundays, beginning with Ash Wednesday. The 40 days correspond to the 40 days during which Jesus is said to have fasted, and to have been tempted, in the desert. Historically the way of counting the 40 days has varied, as too have the precise rules for fasting. In modern times the fasting has been reduced to almost token forms of abstinence. Churches which observe Lent usually do not perform marriages during this period.

**Ler** [Lir]. Celtic sea god in Irish mythology. His Welsh equivalent is Llyr.

**Lesser Ennead**. *See* COSMOGONY.

**Letter of Peter to Philip**. *See* NAG HAMMADI.

**Levite**. A Jew descended from the tribe of Levi, who served the apparatus of Temple sacrifice.

**Leza**. The supreme being in Zambia and Malawi, comparable to MULUNGU and KALUNGA, and closely associated with rain (Baumann 1975c).

**Li** (Chinese). (1) Propriety, one of the five cardinal virtues of CONFUCIANISM (*Wu Chang*). Its meaning is very broad, ranging from religious ritual to social etiquette. Generally, *Li* is the correct behaviour in a given situation. *Li* regulates social relationships (WU LUN) as well as the relations between men and gods or spirits. *See also* LI BU; CI JI.

(2) A key term in the Neo-Confucian philosophy of Zhu Xi (1130–1300), usually translated as 'principle' or 'reason'. All things have their own *li*, or principle, which defines their nature, while their actual physical form depends on the *qi* [*ch'i*], or material force. The *li* of particular things are aspects of the *li* of the universe, which is called *tian li* [*t'ien-li*] ('Principle of Heaven or Nature') or TAIJI [*t'ai-chi*] ('Supreme Ultimate'). In the metaphysical system of the *Li Xue* ('Study of Li'), a school of Neo-Confucianism, *li* is seen not only as the ground of the natural order of the physical world, but also as the foundation of moral principles and the social order.

These two meanings of *li* are written with different characters in Chinese script.

**libation**. The pouring of wine, oil, honey or water on to the ground. In ancient Greek religion this was an action performed for the dead who reside in the underground realm of Hades, and who may still influence the living, or for the gods who dwell in the earth.

**Liber**. An ancient Italian fertility divinity later identified with the Greek DIONYSOS. With his partner Libera he had an early connection with CERES on the Aventine Hill (one of the seven hills of Rome).

**Libera**. *See* LIBER.

**Li Bu** [Li Pu] (Chinese). The Ministry of Rites, which was first established during the Northern Zhou dynasty (557–581) and continued to exist until the end of the Chinese empire in 1911. It supervised not only all kinds of religious rituals and the Buddhist and Taoist clergy, but was also responsible for court protocol, and hence dealings with foreign envoys and diplomatic relations.

**Li-chiao shih-wu lun**. *See* LI JIAO SHIWU LUN.

**Lie-hsien-ch'uan**. *See* LIE XIAN CHUAN.

**Lie Xian Chuan**. Daoist (*see* DAOISM) hagiographical work compiled presumably during the 3rd or 4th century by one or several persons using the name of Liu Xiang, a historical personage of much earlier times. The work records and appraises the deeds of 72 so-called IMMORTALS. The relatively short work of only two chapters served as a model for later Daoist works on former saints and immortals. The DAOZANG version of the Lie Xian Chuan lists the 72 immortals, while the YUN QI QI JIAN version (chapter 108) only has entries on 48. (For a translation of the complete version see Kaltenmark 1953.)

**Li Ji** [*Li Chi*] (Chinese). One of the Five Classics (WU JING) of the Confucian canon, whose title is usually translated as 'Book of Ritual'. According to tradition it was collected by Dai Sheng during the Former Han dynasty (206 BCE – 23 CE), hence it is also called *Xiao Dai Li Ji* [*Hsiao Tai Li Chi*]

('Record of Ritual of the younger Dai'). It contains material which goes back to the third-generation disciples of Confucius and elucidates many of the philosophical, moral and ritual concepts of classical CONFUCIANISM.

**Li Jiao Shiwu Lun**. An important scripture of the Daoist (*see* DAOISM) QUAN ZHEN SECT, possibly dating from the hands of the founder Wang Zhe (*fl.* 11th century). The text is grouped into three sections, each comprising five 'discussions' (together 15 = *shiwu lun*). The first section deals with basic meditational practices, the art of travelling, studying etc. The second section treats such topics as related to NEIDAN (inner alchemy) theories. And the final part of five discussions deals with the concepts of becoming immortal (*see* LONGEVITY). One of the concepts breaking new ground for the Daoist adepts is the notion of leading one's life within a monastic compound, celibate and subjected to rather rigid regulations similar to the Buddhist monastic code. The *Li Jiao Shiwu Lun* is incorporated in the great collection of Daoist works, the DAOZANG, under the complete title *Chong Yang Li jiao shiwu lun*, in 1 juan.

**likundu** (Lingala). A substance of evil power, found as malformed intestinal parts in the corpse of suspected witches: this concept is prevalent under different names from the frontier of the southern Sudan through northern Zaire to Cameroun and Gabon (Baumann 1928). Witches with this substance are the extremes among the persons with inherited or acquired evil powers (*see* NDOKI). The Azande, who live on the Nile–Congo divide, believe that this substance can be inherited by children from their parents. Men and women can be witches; they 'perform no rite, utter no spell, and possess no medicine. An act of witchcraft is a psychic act' (Evans-Pritchard 1937: 21). They are consistently anti-social and do damage by their very existence, sometimes completely unconsciously; the cause is mostly greediness, envy, or wrath.

**līlā** (Sanskrit: 'play'). A term used to describe the activity of the Creator creating the visible universe and specifically of KṚṢṆA playfully 'redeeming' souls. In the former context it refers to the incomprehensible nature of things, the apparent contradiction between creation and destruction, life and death, abundance and deprivation. ŚIVA's cosmic dance of creation is called *līlā*, too. In the Kṛṣṇa context, his *līlā* is seen in the relationship to the GOPĪs of Vṛṇḍāvan, his teasing and tricking, his dancing with them and disappearing from them. The theatrical re-enactment of scenes from the life of Kṛṣṇa is called *rasa-līlā*, from the life of RĀMA *Rāma-līlā*, connoting a participation in the redemptive activities of these AVĀTARAS. *Rasa-līlās* and *Rāma-līlās* are still very popular in Indian villages, towns and cities.

**limbo**. According to Roman Catholic tradition a special hell-like realm reserved for children who died very young and were therefore not baptized. The belief used to be current that since they were not freed through BAPTISM from ORIGINAL SIN, the bliss of heaven was not accessible to them. Nowadays, however, reference to limbo is very rare in Catholic writings and may be regarded as characteristic of a very conservative theological standpoint.

**liminality**. Limen (margin) was first used as a category by Van Gennep to indicate the middle of the three phases which are comprised by the 'rites of passage'. Characteristic for the liminal phase is the ambiguous situation for the 'passenger' or 'liminar' because he had already left his familiar situation but had not yet reached the future status. The concept was taken up again by Victor Turner, who used the term 'liminality' to denote a social, and ritual, status 'between the positions assigned and arrayed by law, custom, convention, and ceremonial' (Turner 1969: 95).

**limpia** (New World Spanish). A common ritual cleansing where healers sweep the patient's entire body with a bundle of aromatic plants made into a brush capable of absorbing the sickness. Afterwards the brush is destroyed by burning (Marcos 1987).

**Lin-chi-tsung**. A major school of CHAN Buddhism in China based on the teaching (commenced 854 CE) of Lin-chi (Japanese: Rinzai). *See also* RINZAIROKU; RINZAI-SHŪ.

**Liṅgam** (Sanskrit: 'sign'). The emblem of Śiva which usually occupies the most sacred place in the *garbagṛha* of a Śiva temple. Its association with phallus-worship and its prehistoric origin are beyond doubt; however, this does not appear to be a motif in most of today's Śaivites' minds, who practice a Śivabhakti very much like the Viṣṇubhakti of the VAIṢṆAVAS. The *liṅgam* is usually placed in the centre of the *yoni*, the female counterpart.

**Liṅgāyats**. A sect of ŚAIVISM, characterized by their custom to constantly wear a small replica of a Śiva-liṅga on a necklace. They are concentrated in the state of Karṇātaka, where they also exert a major influence on state politics. They are reformist, having arisen as a result of the activities of Basava (12th century), who worked for the abolition of certain practices. They are also called Vīra-Śaivas or 'heroic' Śaivas. Their *pañcācāra*, the 'fivefold way', prescribes daily worship of the *liṅga*, a moral and active life, amity towards fellow Liṅgāyats, humility and active struggle against those who despise ŚIVA or treat his devotees ill.

**Lingbao Wufu Jing**. An important revelatory text belonging to the Ling-bao sect of DAOISM. It is dated back to the 4th century CE (but might include older materials) and existed then in two versions. Primarily dealing with the spiritual properties of the Five Talismans (*wu fu*), the text (in three chapters) was perceived as a potent dispelling agent of such hazards as mountain spirits, the notorious hungry ghosts, wolves or sickness. The complicated strategy involved in generating the talismans' potencies goes back to the ancient Chinese belief in the cyclical Five Elements (*see* WU XING). Along with the Five Element theory the Five Monarchs of antiquity are cut off from their historic manifestations and now reign supreme over the Five Elements (or 'Five Phases') through their accumulated 'power of virtue' (Bokenkamp 1983).

**Lingpao-wu-fu-ching**. *See* LINGBAO WUFU JING.

**linguistic philosophy**. *See* ANALYTIC PHILOSOPHY.

**Lir**. *See* LER.

**Lisa**. *See* MAWU.

**litany**. A special type of Christian prayer consisting of short sentences expressing hopes and supplications. These are read or sung by an officiant and followed by a repetitive formula on the part of the people.

**liturgical movement**. The informal designation of a trend in the Roman Catholic and Anglican Churches in the 20th century to renew liturgical practice, especially with regard to the MASS OF EUCHARIST, and in a manner which encourages greater participation by the laity.

**liturgy**. A general term used to designate the whole procedure of ritual actions and prayers used in religious services, in particular in the context of the Jewish and Christian traditions.

**living**; *See* ADVOWSON; SIMONY.

**Living Gospel**. A writing composed by Mani (216–276/7), now preserved only in the form of quotations, but probably conceived as an alternative to the Christian Gospels. *See also* MANICHAEISM.

**Llyr**. *See* LER.

**loa**. The divinities or powers of the VOODOO pantheon which display correspondences similar to those of the ORISHAS of the SANTERÍA.

**logocentrism**. A term used by Jacques Derrida to denote what he regards as western fixation upon theoretical reason, in connection with an overestimation of the significance of the spoken word. According to Derrida, the direct presence of voices in speech is easily allied to the notion of a direct 'presence' of things spoken about, whereas written texts, which persist through time as 'records', are allied to historical absence. This absence, however, is also to be understood as an ontological absence which pertains to significance and action as such:

explications and consequences are always already begun or, as Derrida puts it, there is a 'supplement at the origin'. This original absence, however, has been concealed from view in western culture by its privileging of speech over writing, initially through the replacement of pictographs by 'arbitrary' written marks representing alphabetic sounds. When written marks stand for momentarily 'present' sounds, it is easy to further suppose that all language stands for 'present' entities, which reason can mirror. This 'logocentrism' disguises the historicity and indeterminability of linguistic practice which is best described as 'writing'. (Derrida 1976) *See also* DECONSTRUCTION.

**Logos** (Greek). 'Word', as in the sentence 'And the word became flesh' (*John* 1.14). Justin Martyr (*c*.100–*c*.165) understood the Logos as the eternal pre-existent mind of God, which perfectly expressed God's being and was completely disclosed in Jesus. Clement of Alexandria (150–215) saw Logos as the source of all truth, whenever found; thus for him Plato, Moses and Christ were not wholly incompatible. Later some thinkers emphasized the remote incomprehensibility of God and subordinated the Logos to him (ARIANISM). Others however identified God and Logos so closely as to drift towards MONARCHIANISM. All 'logos' theology sees the principle of divine reason running through creation. Mankind, made in the image of God, is believed to share in this divine reason. At the FALL he turns away from divine reason, sinking to irrationality; but through the incarnation divine reason restores rationality to mankind (Stead 1977).

**Loki**. A god in Germanic mythology who in the hostilities between the gods and the giants plays the part of a TRICKSTER, using his cunning and magic power both for and against the gods. He is also known as a slanderer. Often his exploits are merely mischievous, but he is also shown as an evil enemy of his own race, the AESIR. According to the PROSE EDDA his offspring include ODIN's much valued horse Sleipnir, but also the monsters Fenrir the wolf, the MIDGARD SERPENT and HEL, the goddess of the underworld. He is said to be responsible for the death of BALDER, for which he is bound by the gods until RAGNAROK, when he fights on the side of the giants against the gods.

**lokottara** (Sanskrit: 'superworldly'). In Buddhism there is a dichotomy *laukika/lokottara*. *Lokottara* refers to that which has to do with *nirvāṇa*, i.e. beyond the round of rebirths (*saṃsāra*), whereas *laukika* denotes things of the world, within the round of rebirths. Therefore, in spiritual matters the laity seek help from the Buddhist monks and the ŚĀSANA, because they teach how to attain *nirvāṇa*, which is beyond this world, but in mundane affairs they seek help from the gods, because the gods are considered to function within the sphere of the round of rebirths, i.e. *saṃsāra*. A special teaching identified with the MAHĀSAṂGHIKA School describes the Buddha as being in principle superworldly (*lokottara*), appearing in this world for the sake of giving his teaching, but not being subject to its constraints.

**lolo** (Malagasy). Spirits of the dead in Madagascar where the ancestral cult forms a very important part of religion (Schomerus-Gernböck 1975: 804f).

**long count**. A hierarchy of calendrical units in the Classic Maya period (200–900 CE). The units are progressively larger according to the vigesimal system; each unit has a specially designated glyph: 1 KIN = 1 day; 1 uinal = 20 days; 1 tun = 360 days; 1 KATUN = 7,200 days (about 20 years); 1 baktun = 144,000 days (about 400 years) (Adams 1977). *See also* SHORT COUNT.

**longevity**. A term frequently used in the context of Daoism, corresponding to Chinese *chang sheng* ('long life') and an important goal for the Daoist adept (*see* DAOISM) who positively wishes to remain alive forever. This can be achieved through the concocting of life-prolonging ELIXIRS. The term 'long life' is already mentioned in the DAO DE JING (chap. 7): 'Whereby heaven and earth are able to endure and . . . to last, is through their not living for themselves. Thereby they are able to live long.' This means that through an unreflected, spontaneous (*see* ZIRAN) way of life, supported by either NEIDAN or 'real alchemy' practices, the lifespan can be prolonged until the desired final state of immortality has been reached. While longevity does not imply any duties except the responsibility to care for one's own well-being, immortality carries with it a series of moral obligations that have to be fulfilled by the immortal (*see* ABODE OF THE BLEST), the first principle being the duty to help mankind and administer the heavens above.

**longhouse religion**. A continuing 18th-century revitalization of Iroquoian religion (northeast North America) developed after the visions of Ganeodiyo (Handsome Lake) (Wallace 1969).

**Longmen Sect**. *See* QUAN ZHEN SECT.

**Lord's Day Observance Society**. *See* SABBATARIANISM.

**Lono**. *See* RONGO.

**Lotus Sūtra**. An important sūtra in MAHĀYĀNA Buddhism, compiled in phases up to about 100 CE. It teaches that the forms taken by Buddhist doctrine are provisional only and are provided in accordance with the abilities of its recipients. Even the life-story of the Buddha is said to be a teaching device (*see* UPĀYA), including his entry into nirvāṇa, so that instead of having lived for 80 years he is presented as existing indefinitely as a superhuman being. Later chapters refer to various BODHISATTVAS revered in East Asia, notably Avalokiteśvara. The sūtra is of special importance in T'ien T'ai and Nichirenite Buddhism. The Sanskrit name of the sūtra is *Saddharmapuṇḍarīka Sūtra*, but it is frequently met with under the Japanese title *Myōhōrengekyō*.

**Lourdes**. A PILGRIMAGE centre in southern France developed after visions of the Virgin Mary experienced by Bernadette Soubirous in 1858. Lourdes receives about 3,000,000 visitors a year, mainly from Catholic communities in Europe, including many invalids who pray for healing.

**love feast**. *See* AGAPE.

**low church**. The name loosely applied to those in the Church of England who have emphasized the doctrines of the protestant reformation, in particular the primacy of scripture. 'Low churchmen' were first so designated in the 18th century by contrast with those associated with the HIGH CHURCH view. Thus, the low church view typically does not set a high value on bishops as guarantors of the tradition nor on a priestly function of the ordained ministry.

**Low Sunday**. The Sunday after EASTER, thought to be so named because Easter itself is regarded as the most important feast of the Christian year.

**Lubavitcher School**. *See* ḤABAD, ḤASIDISM.

**Lucifer** (Latin: 'light-bearer'). A name first used in the VULGATE for the King of Babylon (*Isaiah* 14.12), and then, because of an identification made in the *Gospel of Luke* (10.18), taken to refer to the devil.

**ludi** (Latin). Roman games, of which over 40 are known, which had the worship of various divinities as their origins. Most were founded in the Republic.

**Lug**. A widely worshipped Celtic god with the epithets 'skilled in many crafts' (*samildánach*) and 'the long-armed' (*lámfada*). In Irish mythology, although related to the FOMORIANS, he assisted their enemies the TUATHA DÉ DANANN in the legendary battle of Mag Tured with his magic and battle skills. Gaulish representations of the God associate him with the raven. The Irish festival Lughnasa which took place on 1 August is connected with Lug (perhaps 'marriage of Lug'). It involved the veneration of the burial mound of a female deity and was the traditional date on which marriages were arranged. On the same date there was a major festival in the capital of Gaul, Lugdunum or the 'fort of Lug'. Lug was possibly the deity, or the most prominent of a number of deities, whose worship caused Caesar to state that 'MERCURY' was the main god of the Gauls.

**Lughnasa**. *See* LUG.

**lumières**. *See* ILLUMINATION.

**Lumpa Church**. An independent African church founded by Alice Lenshina in Zambia in 1953 after experiencing a vision about a new form of religious practice, but which was suppressed by the Zambian government in 1964.

**Lun Yu** [*Lun Yü*]. A Confucian text which contains the sayings and conversations of Confucius as collected by his disciples. In English it is often called 'Analects'. It is part of the Four Books (SI SHU), the basic Confucian writings selected by the Neo-Confucians.

**Lupercalia**. An Italian festival on 15 February which centred on nearly naked youths running through the Roman streets. Its origins are obscure, but seem to be related both to fertility and to wolves. *See also* LUSTRATION.

**Lustration**. A Roman purification ceremony conducted every five years (*lustrum*) by the censors. It was probably related to the LUPERCALIA.

**Lutheranism**. The teachings associated with Martin Luther (1483–1546), who successfully launched the far-reaching Reformation in Germany with repercussions in many other countries. The most important single doctrine was that of justification by faith alone, that is, the belief that man's relationship with God, marred by sin, can be set right only through faith in and reliance on God's saving action through Jesus Christ. From this flowed many implications for the understanding of the church, the priesthood (now understood as the priesthood of all believers), and all aspects of religious practice. Greatly influential was Luther's insistence on reading and interpreting the Bible without reference to ecclesiastical authority, to which end he prepared a German translation which was of immense cultural significance. Lutheranism has established itself widely in Scandinavia and in North America. *See also* HUSSITES; CALVINISM.

**Luxor**. The ancient Egyptian temple of Luxor (the 'Southern Harem'), built mainly by Amenophis III (*c*.1400 BCE) and Rameses II (*c*.1290 BCE), and dedicated to AMUN, MUT and KHONSU.

# M

**M.** *See* SYNOPTIC GOSPELS.

**ma'aseh** (Hebrew; plural, *ma'asiyot*). A notable 'deed'. Also, a Jewish folk tale.

**Ma'aseh Bereshit.** *See* KABBALAH.

**Ma'aseh Merkavah.** *See* KABBALAH.

**Maat.** The ancient Egyptian goddess of truth and justice; more abstractly, the principle of the equilibrium of the universe. Maat was represented as a woman wearing a single plume on her head. She symbolized the divine order established at the creation, and all beings, including the king, were subject to her control. Lawyers held priesthoods of Maat and the king, as Chief Justice, was her high-priest. Maat is represented at the Day of Judgement in the form of the feather; this is weighed against the deceased's heart in the Balance of Truth. The opposite of Maat was Chaos, which the Egyptians feared and hated.

**Maccabaean Revolt.** The military reaction of Jews under Mattathias Hasmon and sons (particularly Judas Maccabaeus ['the Hammer']) to the proscription of Judaism by Antiochus Epiphanes and the rededication of the temple at Jerusalem to ZEUS in 167 BC. The crisis turned into a protracted national war of liberation, leading eventually to the Hasmonean dynasty (*see* HASMONEANS). (Schürer 1973: 125–99; Schäfer 1977: 585–96).

**Maccabees.** The name of a Jewish family, several members of which were prominent in fighting for the independence of Judaea from Syria in the 2nd century BCE, and thus for the integrity of Judaism as a national religion. By extension it is the name given to four books of Jewish history and thought, included in the Apocrypha, focused on the period of the Maccabaean wars, and authored variously between 100 BCE and 70 CE.

**Macedonianism.** *See* HOLY SPIRIT.

**Macha.** The name of three different Celtic goddesses of Irish mythology, or of one goddess combining three distinct functions – prophetess, war goddess and fertility goddess.

**Macumba.** An Afro-American religion of Southern Brazil with African roots among the Yoruba of Nigeria. *See also* UMBANDA.

**madhhab** (Arabic; plural, *madhāhib*). Literally, 'way'. It is used in Islām to refer to the accepted schools of religious law in the majority Sunnī Islām. The four most important, historically and in the present day, are the Hanafī, Mālikī, Shāfiʿī and Ḥanbalī. Differences between the schools are slight, permitting modern reformers to borrow standpoints from other schools than their own. The SHĪʿA, who have their own body of law, do not vary greatly from the Sunnī schools.

**Madhva-saṁpradāya** [Brahmā-saṁpradāya]. One of the four recognized major sects of VAIṢṆAVISM, with its major seat in Uḍipī, whose occupancy changes every 12 years. It was formed by the followers of Madhva (1197–1276), representative of Dvaita Vedānta, who insisted on permanent differences (*bheda*) (between BRAHMAN and *jīvātman*, etc.) in contrast to Advaita Vedānta. He combined devotion to *Viṣṇu* with Vedāntic thought and wrote a large number of works to express his standpoint. The members of the Madhva-saṁpradāya used to burn the emblems of VIṢṆU into their bodies to demonstrate their being 'slaves of

Viṣṇu' (*Viṣṇudāsa*). Organizationally, so as to have an affiliation with one of the four recognized SAMPRADĀYAS, some later sects such as the Caitanya *saṁpradāya*, have been grouped into the Madhva-saṁpradāya, despite considerable differences in theory and practice.

**Mādhyamaka**. *See* MĀDHYAMIKA.

**Mādhyamika**. The Mādhyamika School (also known as Mādhyamaka) arose through the systematic teaching of Nāgārjuna (fl. *c*.200 CE) on the basis of PRAJÑĀPĀRAMITĀ Sūtras of MAHĀYĀNA Buddhism. Nagārjuna is thus not the 'founder' of Mahāyana Buddhism, as is sometimes erroneously presented, since it already existed. From the 2nd century onwards the school diverged into two traditions, following the *svātantrika* teaching of Bhāvaviveka and the *prāsaṅgika* teaching of Buddhapalita respectively. The latter, more radical form of Mādhyamika teaching was energetically espoused by Candrakīrti, who, in his commentary (Prasannapadā) on famous verses of Nāgārjuna known as the *Middle Stanzas*, argued that the positions of opponents in religious debate should be demolished on the basis of their own inherent logical weakness and not on the basis of a position advanced by the exponent of Mādhyamika himself. Only thus could the true middle (*mādhya*) path be pursued. In China the school was effectively adopted thanks to the translations by Kumārajīva and indigenous Chinese commentaries such as the Chung-lun (Japanese: Chūron), on which, together with two others the Chinese Three Treatise (San-lun; Japanese: Sanron) School was based.

**Madina**. [Medina] In pre-Islamic times, known as Yathrib, this central Arabian oasis became called Madinat al-Nabī, city of the Prophet (Muḥammad), where he and his followers established base after leaving Mecca in 622. It became centre of the new Muslim commonwealth and, after the Prophet's death, capital of the new Arab caliphate until 661. It remained a centre of scholarship and piety devoted in particular to the study of the law and prophetic traditions (*see* ḤADĪTH).

**Madonna**. A term of respect for the Virgin Mary, equivalent to 'Our Lady'. Also, a statue or painting of the Virgin Mary.

**madrasa** (Arabic). An institution of higher religious learning in traditional Islamic education. Founded as state institutions from the 11th century onwards, teachers granted successful students certificates of qualification to teach the texts they had studied. They did not, however, displace the MOSQUE as an educational institution, although over the past century the *madrasas* have been increasingly replaced by universities and colleges with more modern programmes and methods of instruction.

**Mag Tured**. *See* TUATHA DÉ DANANN, NUADA, LUG.

**Magadha**. A kingdom in ancient India ruled, at the time of the BUDDHA, by King Bimbisāra and then by his son Ajātasattu. The language spoken by the Buddha is presumed to have been Magadhi.

**Māgadhi**. *See* MĀGADHA.

**Magen David** (Hebrew: 'shield of David'). The six-pointed 'Jewish star'. This symbol was first associated with the Jewish people only in the 17th and 18th centuries. Only in modern times has it become a symbol of Judaism, and of modern Israel (Scholem 1971).

**maggid** (Yiddish). A popular 'preacher' who is not necessarily ordained as a RABBI.

**Magna Mater**. *See* MYSTERIES OF CYBELE.

**Magnificat** (Latin). The hymn of praise uttered by Mary the mother of Jesus according to the *Gospel of Luke* (1.46–55) on being recognized by her cousin Elizabeth as the mother of the expected messiah. The name is the first word in Latin, meaning 'does magnify' as in the opening 'My soul does magnify the Lord'.

**mahabba** (Arabic). Love. *See* MA'RIFA.

**Mahābhārata** (Sanskrit: 'The Great Epic'). Originally a story of the war between two related clans, the Kauravas and the Pāṇḍavas, for the hegemony of North India (Indraprāṣṭa, near today's Delhi, was the capital). Through addition of vast masses of literature it became a kind of encyclopedia of Indian culture and religion. It is the largest such work in world literature; the Critical Edition produced by the Bhandarkar Oriental Research Institute between 1933 and 1966 comprises 21 large volumes of text and six volumes of indexes. In spite of its age and its large size it has remained popular throughout the ages, as a recent TV and stage adaptation of some parts of it indicate.

**Maha Bodhi Society**. A Society founded by Anagārika Dharmapāla in 1891 in Ceylon, with the aim of winning back for Buddhists ownership of the Bodh Gayā site, the spot where Buddha attained his Great Enlightenment, *Mahā Bodhi*.

**mahākalpa** (Sanskrit). An extremely long cosmic period. According to Buddhist mythology, the inconceivably wide universe consists of innumerable globular world-systems, each of which contains thousands of worlds that dissolve and evolve successively for all eternity. One large world-system is considered to last for a cosmic period called a *mahākalpa*. A mahākalpa consists of 100 years of Brahmā. Each year of Brahmā consists of 360 days-and-nights of Brahmā. Each day-and-night of Brahmā is a *kalpa*, which consists of 2000 *Mahāyugas*. A Mahāyuga consists of 4 320 000 human years.

**Mahānāyaka**. *See* NĀYAKA.

**Mahāpurānas**. *See* PURĀṆAS.

**Mahāsaṃghika** (Sanskrit: '(those) of the larger community'). In the 3rd century BCE a schism arose among the Buddhists which divided them into two groups or schools: the Sthaviravādins, those faithful to the tradition of the Elders (Sthavira) and the literal keeping of the VINAYA rules and regulations, and the Mahāsaṃghikas ('the majority'), who adopted a more liberal and interpretative attitude regarding the *vinaya*. Of the main schools of today, Theravāda is a tradition derived from the Sthaviravāda group whereas the Mahāsaṃghika is often regarded, in a general sense, as providing a basis for the development of Mahāyāna Buddhism (but *see also* SARVĀSTIVĀDA).

**Mahā Saṭipatthāna Sutta**. *See* SAṬIPATTHĀNA.

**Mahāsthāmaprapta**. *See* AMIDA SANZON.

**mahāthera** (Pāli: 'great elder', 'venerable senior monk'). A Buddhist monk (BHIKṢU) with more than twenty years of monkhood from the day of his higher ordination (UPASAṂPAD). *See also* THERA.

**mahāvākyas** (Sanskrit: 'Great Saying') four brief texts from the UPANIṢADS which summarize the purport of the VEDĀNTA and have become the focus of major controversies between various schools of VEDĀNTA (TAT TVAM ASI, 'That art thou'; *ayam ātman brahman*, 'This self is the BRAHMAN', etc.).

**Mahāvairocana**. *See* DAINICHI NYORAI, VAIROCANA.

**Mahāvaṃṣa**. *See* EDICTS OF AŚOKA.

**Mahāvihāra**. The first Sinhalese Buddhist monastery, established in the royal pavilion of the Mahāmegha park during the reign of King Devānaṃpiyatissa (*c*.250–210 BCE), a contemporary and friend of the Indian Emperor Aśoka. During the reign of King Vaṭṭagāmaṇī Abhaya (89–77 BCE) monks of the Mahāvihāra monastery wrote down the Pāli Canon (TRIPIṬAKA) on palm-leaves with commentaries.

**Mahāyāna** (Sanskrit: 'Great Vehicle'). One of the two major schools of Buddhism. In Mahāyāna texts it is opposed to Hīnayāna Buddhism, a collective and pejorative term for all those schools which preceded the rise of the Mahāyāna. The latter appeared around the 1st century CE, or perhaps shortly before, spreading to the whole of Central and East Asia and to parts of South-east Asia. Mahāyāna includes the two major schools MĀDHYAMIKA and YOGĀCĀRA, traditions well known in their own right such as CHAN or ZEN Buddhism and the Buddhism of Tibet, but also many other schools, denominations, and movements. Key concepts include BODHISATTVA, PRAJÑĀPĀRAMITĀ, ŚŪNYATĀ, UPĀYAKAUŚALYA and TATHATĀ. (For a general view see Robinson 1982 & Williams 1989; for specific leading concepts see Dayal 1932; Pye 1978; Streng 1967.)

**Mahdī** (Arabic: 'the guided one'). In Islām, guided by ALLĀH. The term in SUNNĪ Islām is given to those religious figures who periodically appeared in Islāmic history to revive and restore the faith of the community when it had fallen into decrepitude. The term also carries millenarian and eschatological associations, as it is believed the Mahdī will return towards the end of time to establish a reign of justice on earth before the Day of Judgement. SHĪ'A Muslims hold that the Mahdī is their twelfth IMĀM who is in spiritual occultation but who will reappear to rule by divine ordinance.

**Mahdiya**. A militant reform organization founded in the Sudan by Muḥammad Aḥmad b. ʿAbdallāh (*d* 1885), the self-proclaimed MAHDĪ and KHALĪFA of the Prophet Muḥammad; his aim was to drive out foreign (Anglo-Egyptian) control over the Sudan and restore his community to the ways of the Prophet. His descendants still play an important role in the country's political affairs, one such, Sādiq al-Mahdi, becoming Prime Minister.

**Maheśvara**. *See* DAIJIZAITEN.

**maheśvara**. *See* ŚAIVISM.

**Mailman Radien**. *See* RADIEN.

**mairu**. *See* O-MAIRI.

**Maitreya**. The Sanskrit name for the Buddha who is to come, when the time is ripe, as the successor of the historical Śākyamuni Buddha. The PĀLI form of the name is Metteya.

**Maitri**. *See* UPANIṢADS.

**Maji-Maji**. A mass movement in the former colony of Tanganyika (now Tanzania) in the early 20th century which was vigorously anticolonialist, culminating in a failed revolt against the German authorities. It combined pre-existing religious ideas with political themes and proved influential in the development of consciousness about the necessity of independence from the colonial powers (Gwassa 1972).

**Majjhima Nikāya**. *See* NIKĀYA.

**makhafa** (Arabic). Fear, awe. *See* MA'RIFA.

**makrūh** (Arabic: 'hated', 'disapproved'). In Islamic law (SHARĪ'A), one of the five categories into which all human actions are classified; this category includes acts which should be avoided, though they are not subject to punishment.

**maktab** (Arabic). A school for the teaching of the QUR'ĀN at the primary level of education. They were often intended for and attended by orphans. In Egypt the *maktab* is also called a *kuttāb*.

**mākutu** (Māori). Witchcraft. The various means employed always involve KARAKIA, powerful words.

**mal de ojo** (New World Spanish). Evil eye. A power understood to be an affliction and attributed to people who have 'strong vision'. If such a person admires a child and experiences envy, the child may become ill (Ingham 1986).

**Mālikī**. *See* MADHHAB.

**Malkhut** (Hebrew: 'Kingdom'). The kabbalistic name for the last of the ten SEFIROT, which is receptive in relation to the energies of all the others. Malkhut represents the manifestation of God on the material plane, and is often identified with the SHEKHINAH.

**Malókun**. *See* OLÓKUN.

**Mamapacha**. *See* PACHAMAMA.

**mammisi** (Egyptian). The birth house: a chapel attached to Egyptian temples of the Graeco-Roman period (*c.*332 BCE–400 CE), where the god's birth took place; this, and the divine marriage, were depicted in the wall-scenes.

**Mammon** (from Aramaic, *māmōn*: 'riches'). In Christian literature, the principle of wealth-seeking elevated to usurp the honour due to God.

**mamori**. *See* O-MAMORI.

**mana**. A concept of great importance in Pacific religions. There is no equivalent in the experience and, consequently, in the vocabulary of Europeans, who split up the one word into many translations: 'authority', 'control', 'influence', 'prestige', 'power', 'psychic force', 'effectual', 'binding', 'authoritative' etc. *Mana* was made known in Europe through a letter written by the missionary R.H. Codrington to Max Müller at Oxford, published in 1878. Codrington explained *mana* as 'a force altogether distinct from physical power, which acts in all kinds of ways for good and evil, and which it is of the greatest advantage to possess or control' (Codrington 1891: 118n). There followed the publication of similar concepts elsewhere: ORENDA (Iroquis), WAKAN (Lakota), MANITOU (Algonkian), HASINA (Madagascar), *manngur* (Kabi of Queensland), MEGBE (Bambuti pygmies), *elima* (Congo), the Muslim *baraka* etc. This led to a general theory termed 'dynamism', characterized by G. van der Leeuw as 'the interpretation of the universe in terms of Power' (1938: 27). Dynamists claimed to explain the religiousness of 'primitive man', to whom life means 'Power, not Law' (Leeuw 1938: 56). *Mana* served for some time as a synonym for the general concept of 'supernatural power' and also as a minimum definition of 'the magico-religious'. Universality, however, began to crumble away when more accurate researches proved that *mana* in the Pacific is not identical with concepts of 'power' elsewhere. While the theoretical misconstruction of *mana* is a European affair, the concept continues to be of practical importance in specific regions. Codrington had discovered *mana* among Melanesians, but its source was Polynesia. The word is used in Polynesia today even by white people, who interpret it to mean 'social prestige', while Polynesians themselves continue to be aware of its religious force. Its significance has changed, however, with the coming of Christianity and colonization. What remains of its Polynesian meaning has been put into words by a New Zealand Māori: 'Mana in its double aspect of authority and power may be defined as "lawful permission delegated by the gods to their human agents and accompanied by the endowment of spiritual power to act on their behalf and in accordance with their revealed will". This delegation of authority is shown in dynamic signs or works of power' (Marsden 1975: 3). (Johansen 1954, 1958; Greschat 1980; Irwin 1984).

**manas** (Sanskrit: 'mind'). One of the categories of the SĀMKHYA system, not to be confused with 'spirit' (PURUṢA, ĀTMAN) or BUDDHI (faculty of understanding). It is close to the mediaeval *sensus communis*, i.e. the faculty which unifies sense-impressions.

**Manat**. *See* 'DAUGHTERS' OF ALLAH.

**Manda dHeiyi**. *See* MANDAEANS.

**Mandaeism**. *See* MANDAEANS.

**Mandaeans**. Gnostic baptist community of southern Iraq (especially Baghdad, Amara and Basra) and south-western Iran (Chuzistan) with a rich body of handwritten literature in Semitic (Mandaean), the main works being the *Ginza*, the *Book of John* and the *Prayerbook*. Their origin is to be found among the early Jewish baptist sects of Jordan (1st century BCE – 2nd century CE) and in Syrian GNOSTICISM. The traditional theology is characterized by the dualism of light and darkness, body and soul, and the highest god is called 'the (big) life' and sends his messengers of light, Abel, Enosh, Seth and Manda dHeiyi ('Knowledge of Life'), down to earth to enlighten and liberate the soul. The cult ceremonies are an important element, and include regular baptism (*masbuta*) in running water, and funeral rites (*massiqta*). The community has approximately 1,500 members and consists of priests (*tarmidi*) and lay members, the majority of whom are goldsmiths, silversmiths and blacksmiths. (Drower 1937; Rudolph 1978).

**maṇḍala** (Sanskrit). A marked-out area or a raised earthen platform, representing the cosmos in miniature and used as a place of purification, initiation and meditation. Indian in origin, the concept of the *maṇḍala* spread throughout East and Central Asia in the context of esoteric Buddhism. However, it also changed from being a physical place which was entered by teacher and initiand to a diagrammatic aid for meditation already occupied by buddhas and bodhisattvas with whom to identify. Shingon Buddhism (see SHINGON-SHŪ) makes use of a twofold maṇḍala consisting of the Womb Maṇḍala (*taizōkai*) and the Diamond Maṇḍala (*Kongōkai*) (Yamasaki 1988: 123–51). For the use of the maṇḍala as an area of initiation in the Tibetan tradition, see Tucci 1974. Diagrammatic maṇḍalas are also known in Indian Jainism, for which see Rawson 1973. Outside the Indian context the very concept of maṇḍala was seized on by C.G. Jung as a symbol of psychological integration and pursued thematically with the use of ingenious parallels.

**mandūb** (Arabic). Recommended or approved, an action which is not strictly obligatory but which is worthy. One of the five categories into which Islamic law (SHARĪ'A) classifies human acts.

**manes**. A generalized Roman term for ghosts; it admitted many subdivisions. *See also* LEMURIA; PARENTALIA.

**Mangai**. *See* RATANA CHURCH.

**Manichaeism**. A gnostic religion of late antiquity founded in the 3rd century CE by Mesopotamian-born Mani (in Greek Manichaios, from Aramaic Manihaiya meaning 'living Mani'). Mani (216–276/7) was raised in the context of ELKESAISM, from which religious community he was expelled. In 240 he began to spread his own teaching with journeys in Iran and India. After initial acceptance at the Persian court Mani and his followers suffered persecution under Vahram I (274–7), and Mani himself died in prison. Nevertheless, Manichaeism continued to extend its influence, becoming the state religion of the Central Asian Kingdom of the Uigurs and holding out in China at least until the 14th century. In the western world it spread through Syria, Egypt and North Africa (where the theologian Augustine (354–430) was a lay believer for ten years before being converted to Christianity). Eventually the religion disappeared, partly as a result of persecutions and partly for lack of a broad popular basis, but its influence on the BOGOMILS and the CATHARS continued to be felt in the European Middle Ages. The teaching of Mani was drawn from gnostic, Judaeo-Christian and Iranian sources and is marked by a severe DUALISM of light and darkness, spirit and matter, good and evil. Interest centres on the liberation of the soul or divine spirit from the earthly world. This imprisonment was caused by the attempt of the world of light to put the process of creation, initiated by darkness (*hyle*), into reverse. An original human being, sent into battle against darkness by God, had had to leave parts of his being in the darkness, thus leading to individually fragmented souls in need of salvation. Light-beings, or messengers of light, are charged with the salvation process, for example Seth, Enoch, Noah, Buddha, Zarathustra, Jesus and, finally, Mani himself. All of these bring knowledge (GNOSIS) about the nature of the world and the inner divinity of humankind, awaiting salvation. This knowledge leads to self-understanding promising release. In addition, a severely ascetic way of life is required which is only feasible for a minority known as the 'chosen ones' (Greek: *eklektes*; Latin: *electi*). Lay believers or 'hearers' (Greek: *Katechumenoi*; Latin: *auditores*) supported the 'chosen ones' economically (one vegetarian meal per day), but could hope not for full liberation but only for a higher rebirth, e.g. as *electi*. When all the light elements of the cosmos have been liberated and sinful souls have been purified following judgement, the world will come to an end, and darkness will be finally overcome. The leadership of the Manichaean church, with its two strata, was in the hands of a hierarchy of the *electi*, headed (after Mani's death) by an Archegos (Greek: 'leader') based in Seleukia-Ktesiphon, then in Baghdad and, from the 10th century, in Samarkand.

There was an extensive literary culture in various languages (Syriac, Persian, Greek, Coptic, Latin, Chinese, Turkish) which presented Mani's teaching in a manner adapted to the religious and cultural traditions of particular areas. However, much of this literature is preserved in fragmentary form only (Asmussen 1975).

**manistic god**. An ancestral god. The term derives from MANES.

**manitou** (Algonkian). The term (with variations) for spiritual powers in Algonkian (northern North America) languages. The name Kitche Manitou (Great Spirit), which originally stood for the collective of spiritual powers, now often refers to a HIGH GOD. *See also* TOTEM.

**manitu**. *See* MANA.

**Manjusrī**. A frequent interlocutor of the Buddha in MAHĀYĀNA sūtras, being a BODHISATTVA who is advanced in the PRAJÑĀPĀRAMITĀ, and one whose figure is therefore often to be seen at the entrance to Zen Buddhist meditation halls.

**manmukh** (Punjabi). In Sikhism, one who fails to follow the Word of the GURŪ and lives instead according to his or her own reasoning and impulses.

**manngur**. *See* MANA.

**mano-vijñāna** (Sanskrit). One of six forms of consciousness (VIJÑĀNA) corresponding to the six senses counted in MAHĀYĀNA Buddhism. This one corresponds to the world of mental perceptions itself, distorted however by the wilful intentions of the percipient subject. *See also* ĀLAYA-VIJÑĀNA.

**Manpukuji**. *See* ŌBAK-SHŪ.

**mantra** (Sanskrit). An incantational formula designed for ritual use, with or without semantic meaning, widely used in Hinduism and Buddhism. In some cases a mantra is assigned by a spiritual teacher to the disciple. However, a mantra may be non-secret and used by many. In practical religion mantras are commonly supposed to provide magical protection against calamities. On the other hand, they are also thought to carry the quintessential truth of the teaching with which, through regular use, the individual is able to identify.

**Manusmṛti** (Sanskrit: 'The Laws of Manu'). The single most important Hindu code of traditional Hindu civil and criminal law (*c.*200 BCE). Manu is identified with the sole survivor of the Great Flood in which humankind perished. The Sanskrit term for human person, *manuṣya*, means literally Manu's offspring. Manu's code associates the division of castes with the creation of the universe.

**manusya**. *See* MANUSMṚTI.

**Mao Shan Sect**. *See* SHANG-QING SECT.

**Māori religion**. The religious system of the indigenous inhabitants of New Zealand, centred on the concepts of MANA and TAPU (=taboo), which together determined the nature and limits of power. Also important were a wide range of nature and other divinities (ATUA). A cult linking current generations with ancestors was focused on the elaborately carved assembly houses. From the colonial period onward Māori religion has partly been determined by the response to western invasion and Christian missions, leading to a reformulation of Maori values (MAORITANGA) and to independent movements such as the RĀTANA CHURCH and the RINGATŪ CHURCH. (Greschat 1980; Irwin 1984; Schlang 1989)

**Māoritanga** (Māori). The Māori dimension of New Zealand culture. It comprises all those cultural elements characteristic for the Māori people as distinct from white New Zealanders. The term also denotes an attitude of pride in being of Māori descent and the attempt to increase Māori influence in all sectors of society including the churches. Because spiritual concepts like TAPU, MANA and others are central to the Māori worldview and social life, the increasing emphasis on Māoritanga is of great religious significance, even in the political or economic sphere which are usually regarded as secular. (Greschat 1980; Schlang 1989).

**maqāmāt** (Arabic: singular, maqāma). In the terminology of SUFISM, the dynamic character of the 'science of hearts' which traces the mystic's itinerary (*safar*) to ALLĀH, these are the stations or stages of the journey. The stages correspond to a similar number, varying from seven to twelve, of steps or states of the soul (*aḥwāl*; singular, *ḥāl*) denoting virtues acquired by the seeker and graces received from Allāh. The lists of stages and states vary according to individual Ṣūfīs, but almost always contain terms such as TAWBA ('repentance'), SABR ('patience', 'renunciation'), *tawakkul* ('reliance') and *rida* ('satisfaction').

**marabout**. Derived from the Arabic MURĀBIṬ, the name given, especially in North Africa, to a Muslim saint or his descendants.

**marae** (Polynesian). A place of assembly, having various functions in different parts of Polynesia. In the Society Islands it was a rectangular structure with a raised stone platform at one end and served as ceremonial centre. In pre-European New Zealand it was an open space at the centre of the village used for receiving visitors and for other social activities. Today the term denotes either the open space in front of a Māori meeting house or – more often – the whole complex of meeting house, dining hall and the surrounding area. In contemporary New Zealand society the *marae* is the focus of MĀORITANGA and is of prime importance to Māori spirituality and social life.

**maranatha** (Aramaic). A word meaning 'O Lord, come', which appears in the Aramaic original in the Greek letter of Paul to the Corinthians (*I Corinthians* 16.22) and later used in the context of eucharistic liturgy as an expression of Christian hope.

**Marcionism**. The teaching of Marcion (*d c.* 160 CE) and his followers, according to which the legalistic, yet capricious and cruel God of the OLD TESTAMENT was to be rejected in favour of the God of love revealed in the NEW TESTAMENT especially in the writings of Paul. The new revelation was believed to be effected through a Christ whose sufferings were caused by the creator god (DEMIURGE) of the Old Testament. Some relationship to GNOSTICISM and DOCETISM is thus apparent. Marcion's teaching is known only through the possibly distorting writings of Christians regarded as orthodox, he himself having been excommunicated in 144 CE. Thus, though he appears to have taught an austere morality he was accused by Hippolytus of immorality.

**Marduk**. The Sumerian god of Babylon who rose to supreme power (described mythically in ENUMA ELISH) in the late 2nd millennium. He is asserted to be a DYING-AND-RISING GOD, but this is without foundation. (Wagner 1967; 159–70; Sommerfeld 1982; Frymer-Krensky 1983; Lambert 1984).

**Maria Lionza**. A new religion in Venezuela founded by a legendary woman of the 19th century, Maria Lionza, who is now revered as a divinity. Other figures of veneration are of three types: Maria Lionza herself in association with the Virgin Mary and other Catholic saints, African spirits, and Indian spirits. Cultic activities include ecstatic and healing rituals.

**maʿrifa** (Arabic). Knowledge, a term used with particular significance in SUFISM, denoting a direct knowledge of the Divine will of ALLĀH; together with love (*mahabba*) and fear or awe (*makhafa*), these three standpoints are said to comprise between them the whole of man's subjective obligation towards Allāh.

**mariolatry**. A condemnatory term formed by analogy to IDOLATRY (*see also* BIBLIOLATRY), referring to undue adulation of Mary the mother of Jesus. *Distinguish* MARIOLOGY.

**mariology**. The systematic exposition of teaching about Mary the mother of Christ, usually referred to as the Blessed Virgin Mary in Catholic and Anglo-Catholic contexts. *Distinguish* MARIOLATRY.

**Maronites**. Members of a Christian church mainly living in Lebanon, in communion with the Roman Catholic Church but maintaining an independent hierarchy, liturgy and traditions (i.e. being one of the UNIAT CHURCHES). The name is believed by members of the church to derive from that of St Maro, who initiated a monastic tradition at the end of the 5th century.

**Mars**. A major Italian divinity with festivals in March and October. In origin Mars was an agrarian god, who only later, under Greek influence, became identified with ARES. *See also* OCTOBER HORSE.

**martyr** (from the Greek *martus*: 'witness'). Originally a person who bore witness to his faith (in Christianity) while undergoing hardships. The term was later restricted to cases when this led to death, known as BAPTISM BY BLOOD. The term is now used in various religions, notably in Islām. *See also* MASHDAD.

**martyrology**. The pious collection and elaboration of stories of Christians who have died for their faith, i.e. MARTYRS. By extension the word also designates a calendar or register of martyrs such as has been used at least since the 4th century to encourage their commemoration.

**Masada**. The Herodian palace used as the last refuge of ZEALOTS against the Romans, and which was destroyed after siege in 73 CE (Yadin 1966). *See also* JEWISH WAR.

**masbuta**. *See* MANDAEANS.

**mashhad** (Arabic: 'a place of witness'). The equivalent of the Greek *marturion*, applied to SHĪ'A Muslim shrines in particular, whether or not their occupant is believed to have died a martyr. The most famous is Mashhad, the city in north-east Iran where the tomb-shrine of the IMĀM ʿAlī Riḍā is situated.

**al-Masīḥ**. *See* 'ISĀ.

**masjid**. *See* MOSQUE.

**masjid al-Jāmiʿ**. *See* MOSQUE.

**maskilim**. *See* HASKALAH.

**Masowe Vapostori**. The Apostolic Sabbath Church of God, an African religious movement among the Shona people, founded by John Masowe in 1932. It places great emphasis upon the role that women spirit mediums play in connecting the human and divine worlds, and makes baptism the central religious ritual.

**Mass**. The central rite in the Roman Catholic Church commemorating the death and resurrection of Jesus Christ. The special feature of the rite is the act of consecration of the bread and wine by an ordained priest in terms of the doctrine of transsubstantiation. For more general features *see also* EUCHARIST. The term Mass is sometimes used in other churches such as the Church of England, but the range of doctrinal variation is greater.

**massacre of St Bartholemew**. *See* HUGUENOTS.

**massiqta**. *See* MANDAEANS.

**mastaba tomb**. The ancient Egyptians originally buried their dead in shallow pit-graves, marked by a pile of stones. By 3100 BCE they began to build tombs for the royalty and nobility, consisting of a mud-brick or stone superstructure above ground and a brick-lined subterranean burial chamber. The term in Egyptology for such burial places is 'mastaba tomb', '*mastaba*' being the Arabic word for 'bench' and the tomb's superstructure being bench-shaped. From these structures there developed the step pyramids and true pyramids for the kings, although the nobles continued to use the mastaba-tombs and the mass of people were buried in pit-graves (Reisner 1936).

As the afterlife became democratized from the Middle Kingdom (1991–1786 BCE), the use of tombs and tomb goods extended downwards to the middle-classes; rock-cut tombs in the cliffs along the Nile came to replace the mastaba tombs. In the New Kingdom (1567–1085 BCE) the kings were buried in rock-cut tombs in the Valley of the Kings at Thebes, and the courtiers and officials were interred in rock-cut tombs scattered over the neighbouring mountain-side.

Essentially, the ancient Egyptian tomb had two functions: it housed and protected the deceased's MUMMY and funerary goods, and provided a place (the tomb-chapel) where the family or funerary priest could continue to present food-offerings on behalf of the deceased. *See also* NECROPOLIS.

**Masyumi**. Abbreviation for Majlis Syuro Muslimin Indonesia ('Consultative Council of Indonesian Muslims'), founded in 1943, in 1945 established as a political party dominated by Muslim modernists, but banned in 1959 (Boland 1982).

**mataka bana**. *See* BANA.

**mate**. *See* ZEME.

**materialism**. The doctrine that only matter and its combinations exist, exemplified in the ancient world in the works of Democritus and Lucretius and more recently in those of La Mettrie, d'Holbach and their successors, as well as in much Marxism and some Indian thought. *Contrast* IDEALISM.

**matn**. *See* ISNĀD.

**matres** Latin [matrae, matronae]. Widely worshipped Celtic mother goddesses who bore various local names and usually appeared in groups of three.

**matrimony**. Marriage regarded as a sacrament and hence a partnership until death in the Roman Catholic Church and to a considerable extent also in other Christian churches.

**matsuri** (Japanese). A festival, especially in a Shintō context, and, more generally, worship. A *matsuri* is an occasion for offering prayers, thanksgiving, reports and praise to a deity or deities. It usually starts with solemn rituals, which are followed by joyous community celebrations. The rituals centre on the presentation of food offerings, the recitation of set prayers (*norito*), music, and worship, and are followed by a communal drink of rice wine. Further celebrations may include a procession with the deity, dancing, dramatic performance, sumo wrestling and feasting. *Matsuri* are closely related to the cycle of agricultural seasons, but many stress regional community identity in a historical perspective. For examples *see* GION MATSURI; KANDA MATSURI; NATSU MATSURI; SANJA MATSURI; SANNŌ MATSURI; YABUSAME.

**matsya**. *See* AVATĀRA.

**Māturīdī** (Arabic). An early school of theology in Islam, named after Abū Manṣūr al-Māturīdī (*d* 944). *See also* KALĀM.

**matzah** (Hebrew). Unleavened bread eaten by Jews at the Passover SEDER, and for the following week of Passover. *Matzah* commemorates the EXODUS from Egypt, when the Israelites did not have time to allow their bread to rise. It is described in the Passover HAGGADAH as 'the bread of affliction' or of 'poverty'. Later generations would interpret the avoidance of yeast on Passover as a purification from sin, or the inflation of ego. Thus, eating *matzah* on Passover and refraining from eating fermented foods came to represent a return to essentials.

**Māui**. The Polynesian culture hero who, among other things, fished up various islands, snared and slowed down the sun and obtained fire from the underworld. According to Māori tradition he was killed when trying to gain immortality for mankind.

**Maundy Thursday**. *See* HOLY WEEK.

**Mawlawiya** (Arabic). The ṢŪFĪ order, pantheistic in tendency, founded by Jalāl al-Dīn al-Rūmī (1207–73), with its headquarters in Konya, Turkey. Members of the brotherhood are distinguished by a white costume with a skirt which flares out during a whirling dance accompanied by music performed on reed-flutes, violins and drums. The name derives from the title given to the founder Mawlana ('Our Master'). The Turkish form of the word is *Mevlevi*.

**Mawu**. A major deity of the Ewe of Togo and Ghana and the Fon of the Dahomey kingdom (Republic of Benin). Among the Ewe it is current as a general word for God. Among the Fon it is a goddess, often referred to as a dual deity Mawu–Lisa, of whom Lisa is the male, associated with the day, and Mawu with the night (Herskovits 1933).

**Maya calendar**. *See* KATURI; KIN; LONG COUNT' SHORT COUNT; NAYEB.

**Mazdakism**. A revolutionary movement in 5th-century Iran led by Mazdak i Bamdad, who sought to overthrow the concept of landed property as the basis of society, and espoused a morality based on tolerance, love and asceticism. A dualistic cosmology based on the opposition of light and darkness was drawn from MANICHAEISM. After initially finding the support of Shah Kavad I, Mazdak and his associates were murdered in 528 and his followers violently persecuted. (Klima 1957, 1977).

**Mazu** [Ma-tsu] (Chinese: 'Grandma'). The popular name for a Chinese deity whose official designation is *Tianshang Shengmu*

[*T'ien-shang Sheng-mu*] ('Holy Mother in Heaven'). According to a widespread legend she was originally a girl born on an island off the coast of Fujian [Fukien] province in the 10th century. Because of her virtuous life and the miraculous deeds she effected she was worshipped by the populace after her death. She proved to be an exceptionally efficacious deity, which made her cult very popular in the south-eastern coastal region. The cult was officially recognized by the state and imperial titles bestowed on the goddess. She is one of the most important popular deities in south-eastern China and the guardian of sailors and fishermen.

**mbari**. Shrine houses erected by the Igbo of the Owerri area in south-western Nigeria when a deity, most often the EARTH GODDESS Ala, demands it by sending some calamity. The shrine house is decorated with wall paintings and mud sculptures on a surrounding verandah (Cole 1982).

**mbatsav**. *See* TSAV.

**M'Bona**. An important kingship cult, centred in southern Malawi, with a history of six centuries; its network of shrines and elaborate rituals has been preserved until today (Schoffeleers 1972).

**Mecca**. One of the two sacred Muslim cities (*al-ḥaramayn*) situated in western central Arabia, the other being MADINA. Mecca was the birthplace of the prophet, Muḥammad b. ʿAbdallāh, where he communicated his first revelations (*see* QUR'ĀN) to the nascent community of believers. The early history of the city is obscure, tradition ascribing the building of its important shrine, the KA'BAH, to the patriarch Ibrāhīm (Abraham). Mecca had long been associated with a sacred enclave (*ḥaram*) as a centre of pilgrimage for idol-worshippers, although small numbers of pure monotheists (*ḥanīf*; plural, *ḥunafā*) were apparently present in Mecca when Muḥammad commenced his prophetic career. Mecca has continued to be Islam's most sacred city as the site of the annual pilgrimage, the ḤĀJJ.

**Medamud**. *See* MONT.

**Medb**. A figure of Irish Celtic mythology. Originally a queen renowned for the freedom with which she chose and discarded lovers, she came to symbolize the power over Ireland and therefore every prospective king of Ireland was obliged to take her as a wife. The war goddess MACHA and Ériú, a goddess who represented Ireland itself, were also said to fulfil this function, which can be interpreted as a sacred union between the king and his country.

**Medicine Lodge**. *See* MIDEWIWIN.

**Medina**. *See* MADINA.

**megalithic religion**. The presumed practices and beliefs associated with huge prehistoric stone structures without apparent practical function such as menhirs, dolmens and stone circles. In fact menhirs are still in use to symbolize the presence of ancestral spirits among the Savara tribe of Andhra Pradesh, India (Rao 1989). Other megaliths are presumed to have a calendrical, ritual function, the pre-eminent example being Stonehenge in Wiltshire, England, although various interpretations are hotly disputed.

**megbe**. A vital force among the Pygmies of Zaire, unequally distributed in nature and the cosmos, and concentrated in the elders (Schebesta 1975).

**megbe**. *See* MANA.

**meithila-shin** (Burmese: 'woman ascetic'). In Burma there are no Buddhist nuns (*bhikkhunī*) with higher ordination, but only female lay members (*meithila-shin*) who observe the TEN PRECEPTS and who wear the monastic robe.

**Mekal**. A form of RESHEF (perhaps related to an early form of *Apollo*) worshipped in Beth Shan (Near East) in the 2nd millennium BCE. (Thompson 1970; Astour 1967: 310–14).

**Melqart**. The god of Tyre ('King of the city'), and possibly a form of MOT. He was identified with *Herakles* by the Greeks. (Lipínski 1970; Bonnet-Tsavellas 1983, 1985).

**memedi** (Javanese; Indonesian: 'frighteners'). In Java a group of spirits who often take the form of relatives and frighten or plague people, but generally do no harm (Geertz 1960a).

**Memphis**. *See* COSMOGONY; NEFERTEM; PTAH; SOKAR.

**menerik**. *See* ARCTIC HYSTERIA.

**Mēness** (Latvian: 'moon'). Baltic moon god. Like SAULE he is said to ride over the mountain of heaven or cross the sea in a boat. He is a divine warrior with an army of stars, and protector of human warriors with whom he fights side by side, just as the fertility deities Saule and DIEVS participate actively in farming. There is no evidence for a cult connected with Mēness other than particular prayers requesting his protection.

***Meng Zi*** [*Meng-tzu*] (Chinese: 'The Book of Mencius'). One of the Four Books (SI SHU), the basic Confucian texts selected by the Neo-Confucians of the Song dynasty (960–1279). It was written by Meng Ke (*c.*372–289 BCE), better known as Meng Zi ('Master Meng'), or his disciples, who was one of the principal exponents of the Confucian school in antiquity. It contains lengthy dialogues which illustrate his political and moral philosophy.

**Mennonites**. *See* ANABAPTISTS.

**menologia** (Latin). Provincial Roman rustic calendars. The two preserved menologia contain priceless information on agrarian religion. *See also* FASTI.

**menorah** (Hebrew). A candelabrum. The *menorah* of the second Temple in Jerusalem had seven branches, and is an ancient symbol of Judaism. Combining astral and arboreal symbolism the *menorah* represents the presence of Yahweh and the king in the temple. The ḤANUKKAH *menorah* has eight, plus a special SHAMMES candle which is used to kindle the others. (Yarden 1971; Meyers 1976; Barker 1987: 221–32).

**mentsch** (Yiddish: 'man'). In Judaism, the ideal of a considerate and mature human being. The adjective *mentshlikh* refers to decency and responsibility, and *mentshlikkeyt* means fitting and humane conduct. (Compare German *Mensch*, *menschlich*, *Menschlichkeit*.)

**Mercury**. An ancient Italian divinity whose appearance in Roman religion was strongly conditioned by his Greek counterpart, HERMES. For the Romans he was particularly concerned with commerce.

**merit**. The beneficial spiritual energy generated by good deeds, especially moral and religious deeds. The idea occurs characteristically among religions that teach that the spiritual path begins with basic morality, and that such 'meritorious' actions bring rewards, i.e. the fruits of merit, in this life, the next life, or both. With the emergence of the idea that the souls of the dead go either to HEAVEN or to HELL, as opposed to an older belief in a single afterlife realm where all souls go, merit and its opposite, demerit, were thought to determine the soul's destiny. The concept of a *store of merit* in heaven shows up in many religions. The accumulation of merit made on earth welcomes one, like relatives, to heaven, said ancient Persians. Jesus advised his followers to lay up a treasure in the heavens, which cannot be destroyed or lost, unlike earthly treasure (*Luke* 12.32f). Similarly, the Buddha taught that one should lay up provisions in heaven, which bring happiness and which cannot be stolen (*Udānavarga* 10.11).

Merit plays a large role in the religions originating in India (Hinduism, Buddhism, Jainism), which posit an underlying moral force (KARMA) such that good deeds (PUṆYA, 'merit') and bad deeds (*pāpa*, 'demerit') bear fruit in this or future lives. A traditional Buddhist list mentions ten means of making merit: giving, morality, meditation, respect, service, transfer of merit, thanksgiving, teaching, listening and right views. Hindus and Jains had similar lists. The ritual of transferring the merit one has made to 'all beings' provides Buddhists with a way of helping the dead. (Amore 1970; Wheel Publications 1975; Keyes 1983). *See also* PINKAMA; PUÑÑAKAMMA; PUÑÑAKKHETTA. Also, the possibility of advanced individuals transferring merit to others played an important role in the development of the Bodhisattva ideal in Mahāyāna Buddhism (Basham 1981).

In rabbinic Judaism merit was thought to

be accomplished by faith in God, obedience to the Torah, charity, hospitality, participation in rituals and circumcision, observing the sabbath and holy days, and related practices (Marmorstein 1920; Davies 1955).

Although the term is not used in the New Testament, many Christian theologians, from Tertullian onward, stressed the importance of certain good works mandatory for baptized Christians, as well as additional works done for extra merit. Salvation is by grace through faith, but Roman Catholicism taught that works of merit could greatly reduce the time spent in PURGATORY. Also, merit could be transferred to the deceased to speed them through PURGATORY – a practice similar to the Buddhist transfer of merit.

Popular conceptions of merit have been criticized from within the religious traditions. Just as the Protestant Reformation began with a strong reaction against the commercialization of INDULGENCES, which had become in effect certificates of merit, so too do modern Buddhist reformers (such as the Ven. Buddhadasa in Thailand) criticize popular practices relating to merit. In arguing that these hold people back from developing the wisdom which leads to NIRVĀṆA they appeal to a higher level of spirituality which is 'beyond both merit and demerit'.

**Mertseger**. An ancient Egyptian serpent goddess and personification of 'The Peak', the mountain on the west bank at THEBES. She received particular devotion from the royal *necropolis* workmen (*c.*1500–1100 BCE).

**Meru**. According to traditional Hindu cosmology the mountain at the centre of the world, imagined as a cone of a height of 84,000 *yojanas*, reaching 16,000 *yojanas* deep into the earth, with a diameter on top of 32,000 *yojanas* and 16,000 *yojanas* at the base. On the summit of Mount Meru the city of BRAHMĀ extends over 14,000 *yojanas*, around it are situated the city of Indra and the realms of other minor devas. The capital of ***Brahmā*** is enclosed by the river Ganges, which issues from the foot of VIṢṆU and falls here from the sky, dividing into four mighty rivers. Mount Meru plays a great role in Hindu mythology. In Bali and Eastern Java *meru* is also a name for pagoda-like CANDI.

**Meshkent**. A protective goddess of childbirth in ancient Egypt, the personification of the birth bricks on which a child was delivered.

**Mesoamerican religion**. The Native American religion of the cultural unit geographically encompassing approximately the lower two-thirds of Mexico, Guatemala, Belize, El Salvador and Honduras. The development of this unity begans with the earliest settlers from about 11,000 BCE, with transition toward agricultural village societies by 1500 BCE, when early ceremonial centres emerge. From this period until contact with European invaders (1492) a series of cultures rose to varying heights of cultural efflorescence and/or dominance, i.e. Olmec, Maya, Toltec, Zapotec, Tarascan, Huastec, Mexica (Aztec). Shared pre-Contact cultural traits include: a range of agricultural techniques such as swidden, raised field and irrigation; a focus on maize, beans and squash; stone technology, with metals (gold, silver, copper) used decoratively or as luxury materials; transportation by human bearers or canoe; social organization centred on the agricultural village, with market and ceremonial ties to larger ceremonial/civic centres. Merchants, warriors, artisans, civil servants and farmer-labourers formed basic classes controlled by aristocratic classes; architecture was of the pyramid-temple/plaza construction; art shows elaborate development of pottery, murals, sculpture, jewellery, and costume; intellectual/religious systems include calendrics, mathematics, astronomy and hieroglyphic writing systems intertwined in a complex religion involving a hierarchy of deities, a repetitively collapsing and renewing multi-layered universe, and an interdependent relationship between human and deity for the well-being of the cosmos.

'Mesoamerica' continues to be used as a viable concept in scholarly literature in reference to post-Contact colonial and contemporary peoples in a given historic matrix, although cultural traits now include impact from Spanish colonial and nationalistic influences. As such it is also acceptable to speak of Mesoamerican religion as an integral phenomenon. (Adams 1977).

**Mesopotamian religion**. Sumerian, Semitic (Amorite, Babylonian, Assyrian), Hurrian,

Kassite and other cultures contributed to a diverse pattern of belief and practice which was dominated by Sumero-Babylonian elements, but which together may be referred to as Mesopotamian religion. (Dhorme 1910, 1945; Deimel 1914; Hooke 1953; Albrektson 1967; Ringgren 1973; Jacobsen 1976; Saggs 1978).

**Messiah** (from Hebrew: *mashiakh*). Literally, an 'anointed' one, that is a king. The demise of the royal dynasty at the EXILE led to aspirations for later restoration (see the reaction to the 6th-century Zerubbabel in *Zechariah*), often combining king and high priest in a binary conception. In the centuries before the Common Era, Jews anticipated a messiah like David, who would be a successful military and political head of Israel, as well as an example of piety and devotion to God. Later, the Jewish idea of the Messiah expanded. And increasingly, the advent of the Messiah was conceptualized eschatologically, becoming a common theme in APOCALYPTIC. More than a national leader, the RABBIS anticipated a saviour figure who would end all injustice, lead the Jews back to ISRAEL, and initiate the resurrection of the dead. (Bentzen 1955; Mowinckel 1956; Barker 1987). *See also* MESSIANISM.

**messianism**. A form of ESCHATOLOGY which expects the end to be ushered in by the appearance in this world of a MESSIAH, that is, 'an anointed one' (from the Hebrew *mashiakh*, which was translated accordingly into Greek as *Christos*). In late pre-Christian Judaism there were various forms of messianic expectation, some of them including the expectation of cosmic conflict and great travail for humankind. In general, messianism is no longer a subject of wide interest in Judaism, though it surfaces from time to time. While most Christian churches affirm that the messiah (Christ) will come again, this belief is an organizing principle of faith for Adventists. In a wider sense the term messianism may be used of any belief system which focuses on salvation through a divine figure who is yet to come. (Schürer 1979: 488–554).

**Metamorphoses**. A major work by Ovid, full name Publius Ovidius Naso (43 BCE – 17 CE), a prolific poet whose amatory works caused the Emperor Augustus to banish him to Tomis on the Black Sea in 8 CE. His *Metamorphoses*, probably complete at the time of exile, recounts in 15 books a history of mythology from creation to the death of Julius Caesar. Although much of the work utilizes Greek mythologies, Ovid retells them from a Roman perspective. *See also* AUGUSTAN RELIGION. For Ovid *see also* FASTI.

**metanarrative**. In semiotic analysis, any discursive reflection upon a narrative, and more particularly the narration of the manner in which a narrative is grammatically produced. The term has been popularized by J-F Lyotard (Lyotard 1984), who uses it to refer to the 'grand narratives' about human progress which have been told since the enlightenment – for example by Hegel, Comte and Marx. These narratives have a 'meta' character because they claim to narrate the *necessary* stages in the production of a 'true humanity', thereby assigning to the contingent developments of western history a falsely universal character. *See also* NARRATIVE; POSTMODERNISM.

**metaphysics**. A branch of philosophy dealing with the most fundamental constituents of reality. It covers ONTOLOGY (i.e. accounts of what exists), the analysis of fundamental concepts like 'SUBSTANCE' and 'CAUSE', and questions about the realm of the suprasensible.

**Meter**. In ancient Greece, the mother of gods, humans, and animals. She was often worshipped with lively and ecstatic music.

**Methodism**. The pattern of church life characteristic of the Methodist Churches and deriving from the reformist practice and theology advanced by the brothers John and Charles Wesley. Institutionally it may be regarded as having been founded in 1784 with the legal incorporation of the 'Yearly Conference of the People called Methodists', but religiously it began much earlier in the 18th century as a movement of disciplined yet emotional personal piety within the Church of England. The separate administration of the sacraments began in 1795. Methodism grew very rapidly in North America, where it declared itself episcopal;

US Methodists today outnumber British Methodists by about ten to one.

**methodological agnosticism**. The provisional suspension of views concerning the existence or non-existence of God(s), intended to facilitate an understanding of religion as a socio-cultural phenomenon without reference to divine activity or theological norms. Methodological agnosticism is to be preferred to METHODOLOGICAL ATHEISM in that the latter may itself be easily confused with the maintenance of a position on a theological question.

**methodological atheism**. The provisionally held assumption that God does not exist, the purpose of which is to facilitate an understanding of religion as a socio-cultural phenomenon without reference to divine activity or theological norms. *See also* ATHEISM; METHODOLOGICAL AGNOSTICISM.

**metropolitan**. A senior bishop bearing responsibility for several episcopal sees, especially in the ORTHODOX CHURCH. The position is analogous to that of an ARCHBISHOP in the Anglican Communion.

**Mevlevi**. *See* MAWLAWIYA.

**mezuzah** (Hebrew: 'doorpost'). A box hung on the doorpost of a Jewish home, containing scriptural verses such as 'You shall love the Lord Your God with all your heart, with all your soul and with all your might . . . and these words shall be . . . upon the doorposts of your house and upon your gates.' In the Middle Ages a *mezuzah* might be inscribed as a talisman, with additional incantations, and in recent times it became fashionable for women to wear a *mezuzah* as a charm, around the neck.

**Middle Way**. In his first sermon Gautama BUDDHA taught a Middle Way between indulging and mortifying the flesh (*see* DHARMA). In later interpretation a middle way was also sought between various conceptual alternatives such as existence and non-existence (*see* MĀDHYAMIKA).

**Midewiwin**. A semi-institutional form of Anishnabe (northern North America) religion, found in its present form at least as early as the 17th century. Similar ritual complexes are found in adjacent cultures, and in English are usually termed 'Medicine Lodge'.

**Midgard**. World inhabited by human beings in Germanic pre-Christian mythology, created in the middle of GINNUNGAGAP out of the body of the first giant Ymir.

**Midgard Serpent**. The World Serpent in Germanic pre-Christian mythology which lay in the sea coiled around MIDGARD. It was one of the most feared enemies of the gods and mankind, and according to the PROSE EDDA one of the offspring of the god LOKI. At RAGNAROK the Midgard Serpent is said to flood the earth through its angry movements, before it is killed by THOR, who himself then dies from the snake's poison.

**mi'dhana**. *See* MINARET.

**Midrash** (Hebrew). The rabbis' homiletical 'interpretations' and embellishments of the Bible. Midrashic accounts of Bible stories may freely contradict one another, giving reign to the creative imagination of the RABBIS. Midrash developed both within and alongside the TALMUD, so that collections given over to rabbinic folklore are also called Midrash.

**Mihintalē**. The site of Mahinda's arrival to Sri Lanka and conversion of the Sinhalese King Devānaṃpiyatissa to Buddhism in the middle of the 3rd century BCE. Mihintalē is located about eight miles to the east of the city Anurādhapura.

**miḥrāb** (Arabic). The apsidal niche in one interior wall of a MOSQUE indicating the direction (*qibla*) of MECCA, towards which the Muslim worshipper must face while performing the prayer.

**mikkyō** (Japanese). Secret teaching. A general term for the esoteric tradition in Japanese Buddhism, common to both the Shingon and Tendai (*see* SHINGON-SHŪ; TENDAI-SHŪ).

**miko** (Japanese). A female officiant at a Shintō shrine. Roles of the *miko* include performing in ceremonial dances and assisting priests at wedding ceremonies. Historically the *miko* were mediums conveying the messages of a deity when in trance, but this function is now continued outside the system of SHRINE SHINTŌ.

**mikoshi** (Japanese). A palanquin or vehicle used to transport a deity when moving between a main Shintō shrine and a temporary shrine during a festival, when progressing through the deity's community area, or when moving to a new shrine. In a typical festival the main *mikoshi* of a shrine is borne by enthusiastic young man and may be accompanied by a procession of priests and groups of other people dressed in traditional costumes.

**milungu**. Nature-spirits in Zambia who once were spirits of the dead: this mutation is rather frequent in eastern and southern Bantu-speaking Africa (Baumann 1975a).

**Mimir**. *See* AESIR; ODIN; YGGDRASILL.

**Min**. An ancient Egyptian god of fertility and of deserts, whose cultic centre was at Coptos. Later he was associated with AMUN at THEBES. Lettuce of a special variety was offered to Min to increase his potency.

**minara**. *See* MINARET.

**minaret** (from Arabic, *mināra*). The tower of the MOSQUE from which Muslims hear the call to prayer five times a day. Perhaps more accurately called the *mi'dhana*, literally, the place from which the call to prayer (*'adhān*) is made by the *mu'adhdhin* (commonly known in English as the *muezzin*).

**minbar** (Arabic). The elevated structure of steps in a MOSQUE from which the sermon is given during the Friday prayers. The earliest extant *minbars* are hollow, wood-panelled constructions, although marble was also used in certain places.

**Mind Learning**. *See* SHINGAKU.

**Minerva**. The ancient Italian goddess of crafts, identified from an early time with the Greek goddess ATHENA.

**Mingtang** [Ming-t'ang] (Chinese: 'Hall of Light'). A building used by the Chinese emperors for various rituals, among them the cult of the Wu Di ('Five Emperors'). During the Han dynasty (206 BCE – 220 CE) it was first situated near the Taishan [T'ai-shan] mountain and connected with the FENG-SHAN Ritual. Later dynasties erected their *Mingtang* in or near the capital.

**Minotaur**. The legendary bull-headed, otherwise man-like creature to whom seven youths and seven maidens from Athens were sacrificed each year by King Minos of Crete in the LABYRINTH built for this purpose. The word 'Minotaur' itself, from Minos and *tauros* (Greek: 'bull'), may reflect the identification of a SACRAL KINGSHIP claim with a bull cult which already existed. The slaying of the Minotaur by the Athenian hero Theseus reflects in story form the eclipse of the Minoan civilization, which had thriven between 2500 and 1500 BCE.

**minyan** (Hebrew). A quorum of ten Jewish men, which is needed to recite KADDISH, read the TORAH portion, and perform other special prayers.

**miqveh** (Hebrew). A ritual bath employing naturally flowing waters. A *miqveh* is used by Jewish women to prepare to resume sexual relations with their husbands following the completion of their menstrual cycle, and by Jewish men to prepare for SABBATHS and holy days.

**Mīrabāī**. A 16th-century princess from Rājasthān, rejected by her husband's family because of her ardent devotion to KṚṢṆA, spending the rest of her life at Vṛiṇḍaban, composer of deeply felt hymns which are still popular. According to legend she did not die but bodily entered one of the *Viṣṇu*-images in Vriṇḍaban.

**miracle**. A striking event, usually in apparent violation of the laws of nature, presumed to be brought about by supernatural power in a religious context. The function of miracles is most frequently to legitimate or validate a religious teaching, institution, or leaders, and in this sense they have been common world-wide. In Christian theology the two classic forms of proof for the validity of revelation were from prophecy and from miracle. Hence the philosopher David Hume (1711–76) devoted much space to a critical analysis of the concept, concluding that the greatest miracle of all was belief in miracle. In other contexts, e.g. Buddhism, there is no debate about miracle, since it is understood that supernatural events in this category are expedients taking place on a secondary level for those who need to benefit from them.

**mi'rāj** (Arabic). Originally 'ladder', later the term used in Islamic tradition to refer to the ascension to heaven of the Prophet Muḥammad alluded to in the QUR'ĀN (17.1); the term is associated with *isrā'*, meaning the night journey made by the Prophet (whether in body or in spirit, awake or asleep is debated by theologians) from MECCA to Jerusalem, from where the ascension occurred.

**mira-mira**. Afflictive and highly contagious spirit possession in Angola, caused by spirits of unrelated dead (Baumann 1975a).

**Mishnah** (Hebrew). The rabbinic code of law which is considered 'second' only to the TORAH itself. The Mishnah consists of six sections which were compiled by Rabbi Judah Hanasi around 200 CE.

**misogi** (Japanese). The practice of using water to remove pollution and sin from body and mind. Its origin is found in the myth of the god Izanagi no mikoto, who purified himself by bathing in a stream after a journey to the land of Yomi. There is a widely practised form of austerity in which *misogi* is combined with Buddhist cold water ablutions (*mizugori*). In Shintō this is called *kessai*, and may take the form of a warm bath, splashing cold water over oneself, or washing by the seaside or by a river. At its simplest, purification by water is practised by every visitor to a Shintō shrine by washing the hands and mouth. The practices of sprinkling salt over oneself after attending a funeral, and placing small piles of salt at the entrance to restaurants are also said to be related to the concept of *misogi*.

**missal**. A liturgical book used in the Catholic Church, which, since the early Middle Ages, has contained the texts and instructions necessary for the celebration of the MASS.

**mi-tama** (Japanese). In Shintō, spirit, soul, especially a pure, lofty soul. Tama matsuri is a festival held to pray to, give thanks to, and appease the souls of the dead; Aramitama is a spirit empowered to bring life force; Nigimitama is a spirit which realizes union and harmony; Kushimitama is a spirit that causes mysterious transformations; and Sakimitama is a spirit that imparts blessings. Together, these are called the four spirits.

**Mithraeum** (Latin). A cave-like sacred place of the Mithras cult, with relief showing the god Mithras (*Mithras tauroctonus*) killing a bull. *See* MITHRAISM.

**Mithraism**. A MYSTERY RELIGION of the Roman Empire (1st – 4th centuries CE), which began in Syria in the 1st century BCE and centred around the ancient Iranian god Mithras ('Contract', 'Loyalty'). It found believers above all in the Roman army, and the Emperors Hero and Commodus were also initiated. In 307 Mithras, the 'invincible sun god' (*Sol invictus*), was pronounced God of the Empire and thus became a serious rival to Christianity. The celebration of the birth of Mithras on 25 December (solstice) was reinterpreted by the Church as the birthdate of Christ. Many churches, especially in Rome, were erected over Mithraic sites. Although there are many archaeological monuments of Mithraism from the areas of the Roman Empire (Syria, the Near East, the Balkans, Germany, Britain, but not in Egypt and Greece), usually representing Mithras killing a bull together with signs of the zodiac and other symbols, their meaning is uncertain and there is little literary documentation. It is unlikely to be an Iranian religion as there were no Iranian Mithras mysteries, but rather a Hellenistic-Roman soldiers' or men's cult which borrowed from Iranian and other oriental cults but represented an independent development in the context of the shift from official religion to private, individual longing for salvation from death and fate (*Heimarmene*). In killing the life-giving bull, Mithras acted in the name of the god AEON ('Time', *Aevum*), of Saturn, or of the sun, and was the believers' (*consacranei*: 'initiated') model and guarantor of victory and salvation. The believers, or 'brothers' (*fratres*), underwent tests and lived according to strict rules and religious hierarchy. Initiation consisted of baptism or ablution, purification, special meals, the wearing of wreaths and costumes and trials of courage, accompanied by blessings and astrological symbolism. Mithraism was interpreted philosophically in NEOPLATONISM (Porphyrius, Jamblichus). (Vermaseren 1963; Bianchi 1979; Hinnells 1975).

**Mithras**. *See* MITHRAISM.

**Mithras tauroctonus**. *See* MITHRAISM.

**mitnaggid** (Hebrew). An 'opponent' of the Ḥasidic movement (*see* ḤASIDISM).

**Mitnaggdim**. *See* ḤASIDISM.

**mitre**. *See* BISHOP.

**mitzvah** (Hebrew; plural, *mitzvot*). Technically, one of the 613 'commandments' which the RABBIS derived from the TORAH, 248 'thou shalt' commandments, and 365 'thou shalt not's'. More broadly, the *mitzvot* encompass the interpretation of these commandments by the rabbis in terms of various customs, rules and regulations. In Yiddish parlance, a *mitzvah* is thought of as any act of service to God, or a good deed done for one's neighbour. It is primarily the performance of *mitzvot*, rather than the espousal of certain formulae of belief, which defines Jewish religion.

**miya** (Japanese). One of several terms for a Shintō shrine. *Miya* (also meaning 'palace') was earlier distinguished from *yashiro*, another ancient term for shrine, but the two are now closely synonymous. *See also* JINJA.

**mizimu**. Spirits of the dead in large parts of eastern Africa, for which related terms are current in central and southern Africa. The concept is influential for the Bantu-speaking regions, where ancestral spirits are much more important than nature-spirits (Baumann 1975c: 619f). *Mizimu* act as mediators between the household, kin-group, or local community and the supreme being to guarantee rain, fertility and health. As known ancestors and relatives they have to be regularly propitiated through offerings at ancestral shrines. Masters of the ancestor cult are the heads of the social units. Occasionally the *mizimu* become guardian spirits or are reincarnated in their grandchildren (Colson 1951: 104). Important spirits of heads of large families, headmen, heroes, or kings are worshipped at sacred places like hills or trees; they can be transformed into divinities with their own priests and ritual functionaries. *See also* RYANGOMBE; M'BONA.

**Mjollnir**. *See* THOR.

**modalism**. *See* SABELLIANISM.

**modernism**. As relating to religion, a movement which held that religious beliefs and practices ought to be adapted to fit the norms of the so-called 'modern' world. Thus modernism is opposed to 'primitivism' or 'traditionalism', both of which hold that religious beliefs should adapt to conditions thought to have existed in the primitive or traditional past. Originating in Western Europe and North America, the modernist movement cut across Judaism, Protestantism and Roman Catholicism. By extension, the term has been prominently applied to recent reform movements in Theravāda Buddhist and Islamic countries. In a loose sense religious modernism is sometimes taken to be synonymous with religious libertinism. In theory, the sense of what counts as 'the modern world' is critical because at any given time the meaning of 'modern' varies with the fashions of the contemporary age. But in practice, 'modernism' refers to a particular set of tenets that were characteristic of the particular age in which the movement first came into prominence, namely Western Europe in the late 19th and early 20th centuries.

Modernism in the religious sense thus can be defined by identifying areas especially sensitive to figures classically identified as religious modernists, e.g. the Catholics Alfred Loisy, Friedrich von Hügel, Giovanni Genocchi and Antonio Fogazzaro; the Jews Salomon Reinach, Louis-Germain Lévy and James Darmesteter; the Protestants Charles Augustus Briggs and Auguste and Paul Sabatier; and the Theravāda Buddhists Anagârika Dharmapâla and K.N.

Jayatilleke. One may identify at least six theses to which most modernists have been committed:

(1) Anti-propositionalism and symbolism. Religious doctrines are not to be interpreted literally. Doctrines have no precise meaning. Rather they are to be read vaguely as tending to indicate certain states of affairs, whether internal or external to human consciousness. Doctrines are symbolic.

(2) Science. Scientific claims are, on the other hand, to be taken literally, whether these be in the human or natural sciences; religious doctrines are interpreted in concord with the claims of science – and thus inoffensive.

(3) Evolution. The world of human affairs, religion included, is a world which is constantly changing, typically in adaptive or progressive ways.

(4) Divinity. Personal divinity is only a symbol of the ultimate reality, which may be described variously, but typically in more or less pantheist, impersonal or undetermined ways.

(5) Political liberalism. Representative democracy with generous protection for sacredness of human equality and individual civil rights is the preferred form of government.

(6) Socialism. The most moral form of economic life is one in which the good of all is placed above the good of the few. (Bechert 1966–7; Poulat 1979; Reardon 1975.)

**Modimo**. The deified first ancestor of the Tswana and Sotho, the name being related to MIZIMU and wavering between the meaning of ancestral god and malevolent ghost (Baumann 1936).

**Moism**. A philosophical school in ancient China which derives its name from its founder Mo Di [Mo Ti] (*c.* 475–395 BCE). Its doctrines are transmitted in the book *Mo Zi* [*Mo-tzu*], whose philosophical content is very rich, ranging from systematic essays on political, social and religious matters to chapters on formal logic and military defence. The basic line of argument is a kind of utilitarianism which is used to support such doctrines as universal love, the existence of ghosts and spirits or the opposition to offensive war. In the famous chapters on 'Universal Love', for instance, it is argued that the origin of social and inter-state conflicts is the distinction between self and others. If all men would love others in the same way as they love themself and their own kin, there would be no conflicts between individuals or families. Likewise, the existence of spirits is grounded on the utilitarian argument that the belief in divine retribution induces people to virtuous conduct.

The Moist school was a well-organized movement which seems to have attracted a considerable following during the period of the Warring States (403–221 BCE). It was opposed to the Confucians, whose ritualism it regarded as a waste. After the founding of the Qin [Ch'in] dynasty (221 BCE) Moism disappeared as an organized school of thought, although some of its egalitarian ideas may have survived in popular Taoist movements.

**mokṣa** [mukti] (Sanskrit: 'liberation'). The last and highest of the *puruṣārthas* ('ends of life') and the focus of VEDĀNTA. While the term occurs only a few times in the UPANIṢADS, it occupies a central place in the writings of Śaṅkara and subsequent Vedāntins. A major controversy between Advaita Vedānta and other schools is the question whether *mokṣa/mukti* entails complete cessation of individuality and whether it is possible to attain *mokṣa/mukti* while still in a body (JĪVANMUKTI). Some BHAKTI-schools, especially that associated with Caitanya (GAUḌĪA-VAIṢṆAVISM) decry Vedāntic *mokṣa/mukti* as incompatible with *bhakti* and to be rejected.

**mokugyo** (Japanese). A wooden fish-shaped drum of obscure origin used in East Asian Buddhist temples.

**monarchianism**. A position in Christian doctrine ascribed to Novatian (3rd century CE), which stressed the undivided, complete sovereignty of God. As in ADOPTIONISM, SABELLIANISM and PATRIPASSIANISM, it rejected a sharp distinction between the persons of the Trinity.

**mondō** (Japanese). A dialogue exchanged between Zen monks expressing their spirituality.

**monism**. The doctrine that different realities are fundamentally one, commonly contrasted with DUALISM. It is exemplified in Spinoza's view that there is only one SUBSTANCE, and in theories seeking to break down the antithesis made between body and SOUL (or mind), e.g. MATERIALISM. Some philosophically accented forms of Indian religious thought may be described as monistic (*See* BRAHMAN; VEDĀNTA).

**monophysitism** (from Greek, *monos*: 'one'; and *physis*: 'nature'). The doctrine that Christ had one nature, namely the divine nature, rather than two complete natures, human and divine, united in one person, as the COUNCIL OF CHALCEDON (451) insisted. *Compare* TWO NATURES.

**monotheism**. Belief in a single, personal and transcendent GOD. The term is most commonly used with reference to the Jewish, Christian and Islamic traditions, having arisen to distinguish these from polytheism as found in the Near Eastern and Mediterranean cultures of antiquity. It may be used more widely, e.g. with respect to ATENISM. However, in this case the personal nature of God was not clearly conceived and thus he was not considered to be active in historical events as in the Jewish conception. Hesitation over such extension of the usage of the term may be moderated if it is recalled that from a Jewish or a Muslim point of view Christianity ceased to be monotheistic with the development of Trinitarian theology (*see* TRINITY). Seen thus, SIKHISM would be a clearer example of monotheism than Christianity.

**monotheletism** (from Greek *monos*: 'one'; and *thelein*: 'to will'). The Christian theological view that there is one single will in Christ, and not a separate human and divine will. Monotheletism (also occurring as 'monothelitism'), which was formulated and eventually rejected in the 7th century, is in principle similar to MONOPHYSITISM, in that it sought to stress the unity of Christ's person.

**monothelitism**. *See* MONOPHYSITISM.

**monstrance**. A holder for the HOST (bread or wafers consecrated during a MASS) in which the latter can be seen and venerated. Monstrances have been used in western Christianity since the Middle Ages but were rejected by most Protestant churches as implying a misleading objectification of the SACRAMENT. The monstrance is usually richly decorated and is sometimes carried by priests, bishops, or the Pope, in solemn procession.

**Mont**. In ancient Egypt, a local god of THEBES before AMUN; later, a warrior-god with centres at Tod, KARNAK, Medamud and Armant (for the cult of the sacred Buchis bull).

**Montanism**. A 2nd-century Christian sect, asserting the world's imminent end and the need for strict ethical preparedness. The movement was initiated by the prophesying activity of Montanus and two prophetesses named Prisca and Maximilla. A well-known convert to the sect, attracted by its asceticism, was the theologian Tertullian.

**Moon**. *See* GRANDMOTHER MOON.

**moral arguments for the existence of God**. Attempts to prove the existence of God through evidence of moral experience have not been common, despite the fact that the relationship between religion and morality has been a topic of intense discussion in both Eastern and Western thought from ancient times to the present. The nearest approximation in antiquity to a moral proof of the gods is found in the writings of the Chinese sage Mo Tzu (479–381 BCE), who argued for the existence of ghosts and spirits on the grounds that such beings are required in order to witness the practice of righteousness on earth, so that the virtuous can be rewarded and the wicked punished, thereby ensuring that happiness is properly distributed, in accord with the Will of Heaven (Part III, §31). Even though the Stoics had suggested that the existence of Gods might be inferred from the moral virtue exhibited in the lives of true philosophers (Dragona-Monachou 1976: 224–7), the most celebrated moral argument for God was invented only in modern times. Immanuel

Kant (1724–1804) argued in his critical writings on pure and practical reason that it is necessary to postulate the existence of God as a regulative idea in order to account adequately for our experience of the moral law and its demands (*see* CATEGORICAL IMPERATIVE). Kant's proof can be summarized as follows. It is our duty to promote the highest good (*see* SUMMUM BONUM). It must be possible to attain the highest good, since 'ought' implies 'can'. Although it must be possible for the highest good to be realized, it cannot be within our power as finite beings to bring it about. We can achieve virtue, but we cannot ensure that happiness will be added to virtue. But only if happiness is added to virtue is the highest good fully achieved. Reason demands that this must be possible and, consequently, that there must be a cause adequate to this effect. Only a rational and moral being who was creator and sustainer of the universe would have power sufficient to make happiness proportional to virtue. Therefore, it is *morally necessary* to hold that God exists. Unlike some less circumspect appeals to conscience as proof of the existence of God (e.g. John Henry Newman (1801–90) in *The Grammar of Assent*, ch. V, §1), Kant pointedly avoids claiming that the fact of God's existence can be shown by such a proof. That, according to his *Critique of Pure Reason*, would be asking more of human reason than it is capable of doing. But he does claim that the moral argument leads us to the concept of a Divine Being to whom speculative reason cannot of itself ever approach (A814–5; B842–3). And the existence of this 'God', which remains a purely regulative idea, is a necessary postulate of practical or moral reason (A634; B662). Partly because it presupposes acceptance of the Kantian theory of ethics, this particular 'proof' has never attained anywhere near the popularity of other arguments for the existence of God. Even so, the great Jewish neo-Kantian Hermann Cohen (1842–1918) regarded the moral argument as the only possible proof of God's existence (Cohen 1924: 1 44ff; cf. 284–305). Within British thought, the Kantian argument has been adapted and put to use by W. R. Sorley (1855–1935) and A.E. Taylor (1869–1945), among others. The classical expression of this type of argument remains, however, the form originally given it by Immanuel Kant. *See also* ARGUMENTS FOR THE EXISTENCE OF GOD.

**moral theology**. *See* ASCETICAL THEOLOGY.

**morality**. Either possession of a moral quality or some particular moral code. However, G.W.F. Hegel contrasted Kantian *Moralität*, meaning individual conformity to universally valid norms of conscience, with *Sittlichkeit*, or customary morality, which is inseparable from particular historical societies and the behaviour normatively expected from culturally specified social roles. *See also* ETHICS.

**morality play**. *See* MYSTERY PLAY.

**Morcha** (Punjabi: 'entrenchment'). Generally a non-violent confrontational campaign organized by the Sikh AKĀLĪ DAL against its rivals.

**Mormonism**. A religion founded in America by Joseph Smith (1805–44) as 'The Church of Jesus Christ of Latter-Day Saints', which adds the Book of Mormon to the Bible as a source of revelation. It now exists in additional forms, the largest of which is 'The Reorganized Church of the Latter Day Saints'. Smith was assassinated in 1844, but the religion had already demonstrated its staying power and was governed via the council of 12 apostles under the leadership of Brigham Young. The Church established itself in Salt Lake City in 1847. The Reorganized Church, led by Joseph Smith's son, also named Joseph, established itself in Independence, Missouri. One important Mormon ritual is vicarious baptism for the dead. The Temple in Salt Lake City permits entrance only to members who strictly adhere to Mormonism's principles. (For a general account, see Allen & Gilen 1976.)

**Morrígu**. Irish Celtic war goddess who influences battle through magic and appears as an omen to those who are to be slain.

**mortal sin**. According to Catholic teaching mortal sin is a deliberate act of sin which frustrates the saving power of God. Unlike venial sin, which is of a lesser order and does not automatically prevent the action of divine grace, it is obligatory to confess mortal sin to a priest if circumstances permit. In extreme situations, however, divine forgiveness is believed to be available where there is a genuine desire for it and an act of contrition follows.

**Mosaic law**. The LAW and COVENANT received at SINAI by Moses, legendary hero and saviour of the Israelites from Egypt. One strand (E) in the tradition sees Moses as the recipient of the revelation of the name YAHWEH (*Exodus* 3), but this is a secondary form of an older text (Wyatt 1979b). He has also been seen as an archetypal king. (Widengren 1950; Wyatt 1986a) (Nielsen 1968; Coats 1988) *See also* PENTATEUCH.

**moshav** (Hebrew). A 'co-operative' Jewish settlement in the State of Israel, in which families are responsible for their own homes and tracts of land, but farm equipment and other means of livelihood are shared jointly.

**mosque**. In Arabic MASJID, literally a place of prostration or prayer, hence the place where Muslims perform the five daily prayers and the congregational prayer on Fridays; in this latter sense the edifice is also called a *masjid al-jāmiʿ*, congregational mosque, in which the solidarity of believers is expressed in communal prayer.

**Mot** (Common Semitic). A Canaanite god of death, and an opponent of BAAL in the BAAL CYCLE, who contained but could not destroy him. Mot received no cult at UGARIT, but was worshipped as MELQART ('King of the city') at Tyre (Albright 1969: 79).

**Mother of God**. *See* THEOTOKOS; PANAGIA.

**Mount Olorunkole**. *See* SERAPHIM SOCIETY.

**Mozarabic Rite**. The form of the MASS which was current in the Iberian peninsula until the Middle Ages, taking its name from the part of Spain which came under Arabic rule. Under the Moors it survived the unificatory pressures from Rome in liturgical questions and was preserved in a few churches in Toledo even after their defeat in the 15th century. In form it is related to the Gallican Rite (*see* GALLICANISM), but its historical and theological significance lies in the very fact of its survival, along with the AMBROSIAN RITE, as an alternative form of the Mass.

**Mozi**. *See* MOISM.

**mṛtyu** (Sanskrit: 'death'). The inevitability and mysteriousness of death incites humans to reflection and speculation, plays a crucial role in the UPANIṢADS and in the VEDĀNTIC systems, whose very purpose lies in the overcoming of death and the attainment of immortality. In the context of SAṂSĀRA, repeated death (*punarmṛtyu*) appears as a particularly frightening possibility which to forestall the Upaniṣads recommend a variety of practices (*vidyās*), mostly consisting in a focusing of awareness on the deathless self (ĀTMAN), the core of the human person.

**mu** (Japanese). Nothing.

**mu'adhdhin** (Arabic). In Islām, the person who calls the faithful to prayer from the MOSQUE. *See also* MINARET.

**muʿāmalāt** (Arabic). The religious obligations which Muslims extend towards each other such as contracts between parties relating to property and marriage and towards humankind in general. *See also* ʿIBĀDĀT.

**mubāḥ** (Arabic). Permissible or allowed, referring to a wide range of human acts which are judged in Islamic law (SHARĪʿA) to be morally neutral.

**mudang** (Korean). A Korean SHAMAN, usually female. Ecstatic SHAMANISM is traditional mainly in northern and central Korea while in southern areas the role of shaman is hereditary. The ecstatic or charismatic shaman is termed *kangshinmu*. *See also* KUT. (Kim 1989).

**mudrā** (Sanskrit). Predetermined hand gestures depicted in Indian iconography and used live in Indian dance, tantric ritual and esoteric Buddhism. Originally the word meant 'seal' (and was so translated into Chinese), but metaphorically it quickly came to mean a confirmatory sign, e.g. that the earth itself bears witness to the Buddha's enlightenment, that the teaching is being set in motion, or even demonstrating fearlessness or protection. Thus as used in ritual it came to be regarded as a magically effective gesture. (Saunders 1969).

**muftī**. *See* FATWA.

**Muhājirūn** (Arabic: 'emigrants'). Those supporters of the Prophet Muḥammad who emigrated with him from MECCA to MADINA. Together with the *anṣār* ('helpers'), who were his supporters in Madina, they formed the nucleus of the nascent Muslim community.

**Muhammadiyah**. An Indonesian socio-religious organization founded in 1912 in Yogyakarta by the Kyahi Haji Ahmad Dahlan. Unlike the NAHDATUL ULAMA it was influenced by the reformist principles of the Islamic modernist (ṢALAFIYYA) movement, today working mainly in the educational and social field. (Alfian 1969; Federspiel 1970; Noer 1973; Nakamura 1976, 1979; Peacock 1978; Boland 1982).

**Muhammadiyya**. *See* MUHAMMADIYAH.

**al-Muḥarram** (Arabic). The first month of the Islamic lunar calendar. The tenth of the month, called ʿAshūrā', is observed by Sunnī Muslims as a voluntary fast day. For SHĪʿA Muslims, the day marks the anniversary of the battle of Karbalā' (680) in Iraq in which Ḥusayn b. ʿAlī, grandson of the Prophet Muḥammad, was killed; his death is remembered by pilgrimages to sacred Shīʿa shrines (MASHHAD), like Karbalā', and the performance of a passion play (*taʿziya*) commemorating and recounting his martyrdom.

**muḥtasib** (Arabic). In traditional Islām, a legal official appointed to oversee the markets as an inspector of weights and measures and price controller. He was a censor of public morals and was also empowered to demolish unsafe houses, repair foul water supplies and keep the market streets clean.

**mujtahid**. *See* IJTIHĀD.

**mukanda**. The collective initiation of boys into adult society in central Africa. Under spiritual guidance by elders and NGANGA the boys experience four to twelve months' seclusion, circumcision, and bush school in traditional lore (Baumann 1975c).

**mukti** (Sanskrit). Liberation from round of birth, death and rebirth. *See also* SAHAJ; MOKṢA.

**Mukuru**. Ancestral god of the Herero, likewise the first ancestor, the recently deceased and the current headman. Mukuru called mankind and the quadruped animals out of the sacred tree (Baumann 1936).

**Mukyōkai** (Japanese). Non-church. A loosely organized Japanese Christian movement based on Bible study and adopting a critical stance towards the historic western churches, initiated by Kanzō Uchimura. (Caldarola 1979).

**Mulenga**. The most important of the MILUNGU spirits, who eventually became a divinity responsible for rain and harvest (Baumann 1975a).

**Mulungu** [Mungu]. A widespread name for the supreme being in eastern Africa, related to U-NKHULUNKHULU and KALUNGA (Baumann 1936). Mulungu, as used by the Yao near Lake Malawi, is derived from the adjective *Kulungwa* ('old', 'great'). He is the creator of heaven and earth, an impersonal power which is immanent in the shadow-soul after death (*see* FANANY), and also the aggregate of all the dead (Hetherwick 1902: 93). Mulungu combines very typically for Bantu-speaking Africa the aspects of a far-away celestial HIGH GOD (DEUS OTIOSUS) who turns up in myth as a personified cause of existence but is scarcely worshipped in cult, a chthonic god (*see* CHTHONIC DEITIES) who rules the dead in some kind of underworld, and an ancestral god who incorporates the ancestors.

**mu'min**. *See* IMĀN.

**Mummy**. The dried and preserved body of a deceased person. Although known in various cultures throughout Asia and South America, the process of preserving a body through drying out, usually known as mummification, was of particular importance in ancient Egypt. The Egyptians wished to preserve the body in a recognizable form after death, so that the KA could identify it and use it to partake of sustenance in the tomb. The earliest burials (pit-graves in the sand) achieved this by natural and unintentional means; the heat and dryness of the sand desiccated the body tissues before decomposition occurred. However, with the building of brick-lined MASTABA TOMBS (*c.*3100 BCE) this effect was lost, and a period of trial and error followed when they looked for alternative methods of preserving the likeness of the deceased (Smith 1914). By *c.*2800 BCE the process known today as mummification had been developed for the royal family; this achieved preservation by chemical means. Later its use was extended to all those who could afford it; the bodies of the poor, still buried in shallow desert graves, continued to be naturally desiccated.

Mummification is not described in any known Egyptian sources, but the Greek historian Herodotus provides a detailed account of the process. There were three grades of mummification, which varied in cost according to the degree of elaboration. The most expensive method involved evisceration of the body: all the viscera except the heart (seat of the intellect and the emotions) and the kidneys were removed. The viscera and the body were then treated with dry natron (a carbonate of sodium found in the Wadi Natrun in the Delta), which dehydrated the tissues and prevented decomposition. These two stages were crucial; the organs were then either stored in CANOPIC JARS or packaged and replaced in the bodily cavities. Various other processes – washing, anointing and packing the body with spices – were carried out and the body was wrapped in layers of linen bandages and adorned with amulets (magical protective jewellery). In the Graeco-Roman Period (*c.*332 BCE – 2nd century CE), a portrait of the deceased, painted in his lifetime, was placed over the face of the mummy.

This type of mummification was supposed to imitate the process used for the god of the dead, OSIRIS; according to Herodotus, the process took 70 days, but modern experiments have shown that 40 days is the optimum time required to produce good results, and the remaining 30 days were probably taken up with religious rites.

'Mummy' is derived from the Persian word 'mumia', originally used for the black, bituminous substance which oozed from the 'Mummy Mountain' in Persia and was credited with medicinal properties. Because of their blackened appearance, the word was later applied to the preserved bodies of ancient Egypt and these, it was also assumed, could be used effectively as ingredients in medicines.

The embalmers were a wealthy and highly regarded group; their patron deity was ANUBIS, jackal-headed god of the cemeteries and embalming. Their skills in mummification and society's acceptance of the dissection of the human body after death contributed to the ancient Egyptians' acknowledged skills in medical diagnosis and treatment.

Today mummies provide Egyptologists and palaeopathologists with evidence of disease and living conditions (David 1979, 1986); techniques such as radiology and histo-pathology can reveal information about a range of diseases suffered by the Egyptians. The evidence remains in the skeleton (revealed by X-rays), or in the soft tissues and viscera which can be rehydrated and examined by means of light and electron microscopy.

**Mumonkan**. *See* WU MEN KUAN.

**Muṇḍaka Upaniṣad**. *See* OM, UPANIṢAD.

**Maṇḍukya Upaniṣad**. *See* UPANIṢAD.

**mundus** (Latin). A ritual pit in ancient Rome, the cover of which was lifted on 24 August, 5 October and 8 November. On those days the MANES were considered to roam the upper world.

**Mungu**. *See* MULUNGU.

**muqallid**. *See* IJTIHĀD.

**murabit**. *See* MARABOUT.

**Muratorian Canon**. A list, probably dating from the late 2nd century CE, which gives the names of the writings of the New Testament and of others not included. The list of approved writings is not identical with what later came to be the agreed canon: *Hebrews*, *James*, and *1* and *2 Peter* are not included, whereas *The Apocalypse of Peter* and *The Wisdom of Solomon* are.

**murīd** (Arabic: 'seeker'). The ṢŪFĪ neophyte or student who attaches himself to a SHAYKH in order to gain instruction and guidance in the Ṣūfī path (TARIQA).

**murshid** (Arabic). Spiritual guide, a title given to a ṢŪFĪ master, teacher or SHAYKH by his pupils.

**murtadd** (Arabic). 'One who turns back', especially from Islām; hence, an apostate. In the QUR'ĀN (16.106f) the apostate is threatened with punishment in the next world only. However, a new element appears in the Prophetic Tradition (ḤADĪTH), namely, the death penalty, although traditions vary on whether the offender should be given a chance to repent. While the law stipulated capital punishment for males, the penalty for women was imprisonment. The law, which has only infrequent historical attestations as to its use, was recently invoked against the author Salman Rushdie for his book *The Satanic Verses*.

**mūrti** (Sanskrit: 'embodiment'). Images of deities, which, after appropriate ritual, are believed to be the bodily presence of the particular God whose form they represent. Medieval texts (*vāstuśāstras*) contain specific instructions with regard to the creation of sacred images, their emblems and the *mudras* they exhibit. Only images corresponding to these specifications can be set up in a temple for worship, unless the image is a so-called *svayambhu mūrti*, i.e. an image which was not fashioned by human hand. Besides the iconic images there are also aniconic images such as the *śālagrāma*, a stone of a particular kind found in the Gandak river in Nepal which is accepted as an embodiment of VIṢṆU.

**Musar** (Hebrew). The 19th-century movement of ethical 'exhortation', self-scrutiny, and self-improvement, founded by Rabbi Israel Salanter. In many ways the Musar movement developed parallel with ḤASIDISM, but it emphasized the study of TALMUD and deep personal piety, rather than ecstatic prayer and the master–disciple relationship.

**Muses**. Ancient Greek personifications of artistic ideas and values: Calliope (epic poetry), Clio (history), Euterpe (flute), Erato (lyric poetry), Terpsichore (dance), Melpomene (tragedy), Thalia (comedy), Polyhymnia (mime) and Urania (astronomy). The Muses were daughters of Zeus who lived on Mount OLYMPUS.

**Muslim**. *See* ISLĀM.

**Muslim Brethren**. *See* AL-IKHWAN AL MUSLIMUN.

**Muspell**. *See* GINNUNGAGAP, RAGNAROK.

**musubi** (Japanese). A fundamental concept in Shintō with such meanings as 'birth', 'creation', 'becoming', 'accomplishment', 'combination', 'harmonization'. Numerous deities (KAMI) are connected with *musubi*, having names such as Takamimusubi no kami (Exalted Musubi Deity), Kamimusubi no kami (Sacred Musubi Deity), Homusubi no kami (Fire Musubi Deity), Wakamusubi (Young Musubi), Ikumusubi (Life Musubi) and Tarumusubi (Plentiful Musubi). Takamimusubi no kami and Kamimusubi no kami, together with Amenominakanushi no kami, are the three gods mentioned in the Japanese myth of creation. The *Kojiki* relates that they appeared at the beginning of the creation of heaven and earth and were the basis for the birth and growth of all things. Amenominakanushi no kami means 'God Ruling the Centre of Heaven'. Some Shintō scholars have held that all the gods of Shintō are merely manifestations of this one deity and in the movement to organize Shintō thought in the mid-19th century these three deities, together with Amaterasu Omikami, were considered to be the highest *kami*.

**Mut**. An ancient Egyptian vulture goddess, consort of AMUN and mother of KHONSU; primarily worshipped at THEBES.

**mutakallim** (Arabic). In Islām, a theologian. *See also* KALĀM.

**mutasawwif** (Arabic). Used in a general sense to denote a Muslim mystic or ṢŪFĪ, one who is an adept in TAṢAWWUF; strictly speaking, one who is on the mystical path but who has yet to reach the end.

**Muʿtazilī** (Arabic). An early school of theology in Islām. *See also* KALĀM.

**Mvidye**. The supreme being of the Luba and their neighbours in southern Zaire; a celestial HIGH GOD with ancestral aspects; and a collective name for 'the ancestors'. In this case the abode of the dead is named KALUNGA. (Vansina 1975).

**Mwari**. The supreme being in Zimbabwe, closely connected with rain and fertility and with an important rain-cult centre in the Matopo hills (von Sicard 1975).

**mwavi**. The most frequent term in Bantu languages for ordeal by poison, in East and Central Africa, as a method for detecting theft, adultery and especially witchcraft (Baumann 1975a).

**Myōō**. *See* FUDŌ MYŌŌ.

**Mysteries of Cybele**. Cult of the mother goddess Cybele (Latin: Magna Mater; Greek: Meter Megalē) of Phrygian origin, combined from the 4th century BCE with the worship of Attis. During the 2nd to 5th centuries CE both deities, as in other oriental cults, became the centre of mysteries focusing on initiation ceremonies and the hope of salvation (details are uncertain). A baptism of rebirth conducted with bull's blood is associated with the cult (TAUROBOLIUM). The worship of Cybele which appeared in Rome in 204 BCE was not yet connected with mysteries.

**Mysteries of Demeter**. *See* ELEUSINIAN MYSTERIES.

**mysterium tremendum et fascinans** (Latin: 'something unknown which is both awesome and enchanting'). In *Das Heilige* (*The Idea of the Holy*) by Rudolf Otto (1869–1937), this phrase plays the central role in his characterization of the experience of 'the Holy' or the NUMINOUS as some essentially unknowable power ('the wholly other') which 'in a strange harmony of contrasts' repulses by its dreadfulness and yet at the same time attracts by its wonderfulness (see especially chapters 4–6). *See also* HOLY.

**mystery play**. Religious dramas portraying various biblical themes from the creation to the passion of Christ. Deriving from the Middle Ages, when they had an important didactic function vis-à-vis a largely illiterate population, they have enjoyed a revival in modern times. Famous examples are the York and Chester cycles in England, and in Germany the Oberammergau Passion Play. A secondary development from the mystery plays was the morality play, in which the main emphasis was placed on the dramatization of virtues rather than biblical narrative. The most famous of these is entitled *Everyman*, a play first performed in the Netherlands.

**mystery religions**. A term of Greek origin meaning 'secret cult' accessible only to the initiated. Originally the word 'mystery' was used with specific reference to the ELEUSINIAN MYSTERIES, but in antiquity it took on a more general meaning which was gradually broadened by its use in philosophy and theology, so that it became the general expression for mysterious divine wisdom or secret teachings known only to insiders. Mystery religion has now become the technical term in religious studies for Greek and oriental secret cults of late antiquity, including Christianity, which involve initiation rites. It can also refer to other religions, e.g. Buddhism. Characteristic of mystery religions is their esoteric nature, which is maintained by initiation ceremonies (*initia* being the Latin translation of the Greek *mysteria*) and the pledge of secrecy (arcane discipline); the teaching is mainly concerned with salvation theories (rebirth, deliverance from death and suffering) and the assurance of eternal life, whereby the gods of the cult act as models and guarantors. These cults can, in association with social movements, take on revolutionary character which leads to antagonism with the official religion and social structure. Well-known examples of mystery religions in the technical sense are the ancient Greek mysteries of Demeter and Kore (Persephone) in ELEUSIS, DIONYSOS (Bacchus), ORPHEUS, and the Cabirians of Samothrace, and the oriental-Hellenistic mysteries of MITHRAS, ISIS and OSIRIS, CYBELE

(Magna Mater) and Attis, and the Phrygian god of salvation, Sabazios. Our knowledge and understanding of the cults is still very incomplete. Mystery religions flourished greatly in the Roman Empire and were open to all sections of the population. Characteristics of these cults which early Christianity adopted in the course of its assimilation to the ancient world still survive, especially in Greek Orthodox and Roman Catholic churches. (Metzger 1984; Burkert 1987; Meyer 1987)

**mystical theology**. *See* ASCETICAL THEOLOGY.

**mysticism**. One of the most commonly used, and perhaps also misused, terms in the scientific study of religion. It has its origins in a Greek word meaning 'to remain silent'. Mysticism may be defined as a heightened form of religious experience in which the subject feels the immediate presence of God or of some ultimate reality, resulting in an expansion of consciousness and in a feeling of transcending the ordinary world. A mystic may briefly lose all concept of time and space during the experience itself. Through such direct, often ecstatic, experience of the divine, new knowledge and awareness are often thought to be communicated to an individual in a way unfamiliar to him or her. Thus mystical experience seems to bring insight into the 'true nature' of the world, into the nature of God, Brahman, Unitary Consciousness, or whatever else the specific religious tradition designates as being the highest or innermost principle of existence.

The fact that intense experiences of this kind can be found in different religions and cultures has been interpreted to mean that mysticism is only partially dependent on outer cultural factors and that it reveals deep psychological structures. In recent years research in the psychology of religion has emphasized that the intense experiences of ordinary people are similar in nature to those found in great mystics. Research on mysticism has been intensive in the 20th century, some dealing with individual mystics and some attempting to explain phenomena in a wide theoretical perspective. Some theories are phenomenological or typological, the main intention being classification, but would-be explanatory theories of a psychological and sociological kind are also current. At the beginning of the 20th century, contributions to research in this area were made by, among others, William James (1902), James H. Leuba (1925), J.B. Pratt (1920), and Rudolph Otto (1917). In recent decades W.T. Stace (1960), E. Arban (1963), Ralph W. Hood (1970, 1975) and N.G. Holm (1982a) have made contributions to the field. For a classic treatment of the Christian mystics see Underhill 1916 and for a recent study of Islamic mysticism see Schimmel 1975. *See also* KABBALAH; VIA UNITIVA.

**myth**. Originally a Greek word, with the simple meaning of 'a story'. For Christian apologists and many enlightenment thinkers, a myth was a story believed by some to be true, but known in fact to be false. 'Myth' was thus contrasted with 'revelation' for Christians and 'history' for philosophers. These senses of the term still circulate, and are used when certain features of a story are singled out for emphasis, e.g. a lack of historicity. But students of religion and culture have tended to adopt the sense of myth developed by the romantic movement: myth is thus an 'important' story, or a derivative of an important story. Thanks to the romantics, the emphasis is shifted from the story in itself to the way it is regarded. 'Myth' is thus a kind of title, like 'king', which applies to an honourable story or class of stories.

These stories are said to be important for a number of reasons, but principally because they are believed and consequently because they are markedly valued, or devalued, by particular human societies or some of their members. Thus, what has the strength of myth for one human society may not be myth for another. Whether or not they are true like history or science is irrelevant from the romantic viewpoint. What matters to a story being a myth is its existential status within a particular human group. So, to understand whether a story is a myth one must inquire about how a particular society looks on its stories.

Some examples of how a society may designate certain stories as myths are the following. Myths may, first, give an account of particularly important characters (e.g. buddhas and bodhisattvas, gods and goddesses, ancestors, spirits, heroes and heroines, prophets, sages etc.). They may, secondly, recount a particularly important event (e.g. the creation or destruction of the world, or of society). Third, they may be important in events that the society values (e.g. at festivals or rituals).

Myths have often been defined as 'stories about the gods'. This may have at least two meanings: first that myths are by definition about a certain class of beings, and second that myths are essentially religious. As to the first, the contemporary study of religion rejects such a definition, because it imports the position of particular religious traditions (e.g. that gods exist) into the definition of key categories. Thus, since the idea of god or gods is only 'important' to theisms it would prejudice the question as to why atheistic religions would find certain stories important. As to the interpretation that all myths are religious, it must be replied that this too is invalid, unless the term 'religious' simply stands for the realm of 'important' – in which case the definition becomes merely tautologous. This is to say that there may be other ways stories are taken to be 'important' aside from their religious significance.

Two further points may be added. First, although myths seem to vary across the world's cultures and religions, it may be that there are cross-culturally universal myths, as argued by Jung and his followers. Second, in some societies 'myths' may be less important than other domains of culture, such as rituals, dances or architecture. (Clifford 1973; Strenski 1987). *See also* MYTHOLOGY; MYTH AND RITUAL.

**Myth and ritual school**. A movement in the interpretation of religion which emphasized the performative character of myth, especially myths of creation, their ritual setting, and the role of the king in carrying them out. There were two wings of the myth and ritual school: one in Britain, led by S.H. Hooke (influenced by Perry – *see* PAN-EGYPTIANISM) and A.M. Hocart; the other in Scandinavia, led by G. Widengren and I. Engnell.

**mythology**. Strictly speaking, the study of MYTH. However, in widespread usage the term has come to refer to any network of myths, or all myths in general. According to the influential theories of Max Muller (1823–1900) the history of religions may be largely regarded as a decline from a pure and lofty perception of the infinite towards a decadent obsession with the detailed intrigues of mythology. Andrew Lang (1844–1912), on the other hand, regarded mythology, like folklore, as a 'study of survivals' (i.e. survivals from an archaic stage in the development of human consciousness).

# N

**naas**. *See* NAASSENES.

**Naassenes**. A gnostic school of the 2nd–3rd century CE whose name derives from the concept that the snake in the Garden of Eden (Hebraic: *nahash*; Greek: *naas*) was an instrument of the benevolent god and was right to tempt Eve and Adam towards true knowledge (GNOSIS). It is also known as the Ophite school (Greek *ophis*: 'snake'). Two works quoted by the Church Father Hippolyt (2nd century), a homily and a psalm, are associated with the Naassenes.

**Nabī**. *See* RASŪL.

**Nag Hammadi**. A place in north Egypt near which 13 papyrus codices were found in 1945–6, containing 51 coptic writings, most of which were previously unknown. The majority is gnostic literature, including the *Gospel of Truth*, the *Gospel of Thomas*, the *Gospel of Philip*, the *Apocryphon of John*, the *Revelation of Adam*, the *Nature of the Archons*, the *Revelations of James*, the *Exegesis on the Soul*, the *Book of Thomas*, the *Acts of Peter and the 12 Apostles*, the *Letter of Peter to Philip*, the *Three Pillars of Seth*, the *Revelation of Peter*, the *Paraphrase of Shem*, the *Trimorphic First Thought*, and hermetic writings (Robinson 1988).

**Naglfar**. A huge ship in Germanic mythology which carries the army of the giants to the battle of RAGNAROK. It is made of dead people's nails, hence the belief that nails should be kept short to delay the ship's completion.

**nagual** [nahualtin] (Nahuatl). In Aztec culture, a sorcerer, magician, or necromancer, one who uses spells and incantations, changes shape, takes on animal disguises, and is often associated with jaguars. Since *nagual* derives from the Aztec word Nahaulli, referring to guardian spirits, the term 'nagualism' is sometimes used to refer to the identity formation characteristics of the guardian spirit complex. (Lopez Austin 1984; Ruiz de Alarcon 1984).

**nahash**. *See* NAASSENES.

**Nahdatul Ulama**. Literally, 'Awakening of the Ulama', established in Indonesia in 1926 as a political organization representing the traditionally oriented *ʿulamā*'; after its break with the MASYUMI in 1952, it became an independent political party, which since 1985 confined itself as a socio-religious association mainly to social and educational activities. (Federspiel 1970; Noer 1973; Steenbrinck 1974; Dhofier 1980; Boland 1982).

**Nām** (Sanskrit, Punjabi: 'name'). A Sikh concept of the immanence of God (*see* TEN GURŪS). In the words of Gurū Nānak, 'the self-existent God manifested himself in Nām' (GURŪ GRANTH SĀHIB 463).

**n'ama**. *See* NYAMA.

**nāma** (Sanskrit: 'name'). The name of God, of great significance in the BHAKTI traditions. The practice of *japa*, repetition of a revealed name of God, is recommended as an unfailing means to find salvation. 'Taking the Name' is seen as being equivalent to entering religious life in a serious way. 'Sins against the Name' are considered unpardonable.

**Nāmdhārī Movement**. A Sikh sectarian movement, begun in the mid-19th century by Balak Singh, which has remained popular both in the Punjab and in Sikh diaspora communities. The Nāmdhārīs (also known as Kūkās) are renowned for having introduced important social and religious reforms, particularly under the early leader, Rām Singh. They share many beliefs and practices with orthodox Sikhs but differ in their interpretation of the place of the Guru. They believe in a continuing succession of living Gurus.

**Nām Simran** (Punjabi). Sikh meditation on or repetition of the name of God (NĀM).

**Namu Amida Butsu**. *See* NENBUTSU.

**Namu Myōho Rengekyō**. The title of the Lotus Sutra as pronounced in Japanese and, with the prefix *Namu* (from Sanskrit *namaḥ*) meaning 'hail to', chanted as a religious formula to focus on this sutra. Although the origins of this formula are Chinese it was given a central importance by Nichiren (1222–28) and is therefore chanted in various sects and movements of Nichirenite inspiration (*see* NICHIREN-SHŌSHŪ; NICHIREN-SHŪ).

**Nanabozo**. *See* NANABUSH.

**Nanabush** [Nanabozo]. In Algonkian language cultures (northern North America) the TRICKSTER or culture hero (also GLOOSCAP; WISACA). His theriomorphic form is that of a rabbit. *See* THERIOMORPHIC SPIRITS.

**Nanna**. The Sumerian moon god, identified with the Babylonian divinity SIN.

**Naqshbandī** (Arabic). A brotherhood of ṢŪFĪS founded by Muḥammad b. Muḥammad Bahā' al-Dīn Naqshband (*d* 1389).

**narasinha**. *See* AVATĀRA.

**narcissism**. In the context of depth psychology, the love of oneself and the desire to gain libidinous satisfaction through one's own body. As such, it is regarded as a natural phase in the development of the small child (during the first three years of life). This period is important for the development of a sound self-esteem. If this does not occur, a narcissistic personality characterized by grandiosity and an exaggerated estimation of oneself results, which may be combined with a disposition to depression, envy, and a sense of shame. According to the 'object-relation theory', the early development of the personality is of importance in the development of narcissistic features. Religion (or religious concepts) can be the object of narcissistic PROJECTION, and can thereby become a means to gain power and influence while at the same time it can function as a mechanism of punishment. The term is drawn from the Greek mythical personage Narcissus, son of the river god Cephissus, who was enamoured of his own reflection in the waters of a spring, taking it for the image of a water NYMPH.

**narrative**. A term which has become a key focus of interest for recent Christian theology, allied to a kindred preoccupation in philosophy, history and social theory. Increasingly, these disciplines have claimed that all human thought and action have a narrative structure, which discursive thought cannot really transcend. All philosophic 'foundationalism' is here rejected, because the starting points of narratives are in a sense 'arbitrary', and always imply earlier developments not fully articulated. 'Narrativism' is similarly adverse to Cartesian or Kantian accounts of subjectivity as transcending any empirical content; instead, subjective identity is seen as constructed through the repetition and re-enactment of narrative in which the subject features as a 'character'. Theologians such as Hans Frei have pointed out how a narrativist perspective gives renewed significance to the fact of the story-form taken by so much of the Christian 'revelation'. *See also* METANARRATIVE; POSTMODERNISM.

**al-nāsikh wa'al-mansūkh** (Arabic). The doctrine of abrogation of verses in the QUR'ĀN. Muslim scholars explained certain apparent changes in the revelations to the Prophet Muḥammad as God's own work of deletion and alteration, since certain commands in scripture had only been intended for temporary application. Thus when circumstances changed, a verse was abrogated (*mansūkh*) and replaced by another (*nāsikh*).

**nat** (Burmese: 'lord'). A Burmese god. In Burmese folk religiosity there are 37 national *nats* and numerous local ones.

**National Church**. *See* GODIANISM.

**Nature of the Archons**. *See* NAG HAMMADI.

**Native American religions**. Although encompassing a rich variety of religio-ecological situations, from gathering-hunting cultures to complex civilizations with writing, as well as a larger number of language families and languages than can be found in the rest of the world, Native American religions also exhibit, with few exceptions, a number of common features. These include a general, common cosmology of a spherical universe delineated by the FOUR DIRECTIONS, FATHER SKY and EARTH MOTHER; a focus on the number FOUR and its multiples; an understanding of humans, plants, animals and deities as having familial relationships; and the ritual use of TOBACCO. Since the cataclysmic coming of Europeans (perhaps 90 per cent of the populations of many millions died of epidemic diseases) over the last 500 years, the cultures and religions have undergone varying degrees of changes and syntheses. In Meso-America native religions have become synthesized with popular Christianity. In North America the practice of native religions was deemed illegal by the Canadian and United States governments until recently.

**natsu matsuri** (Japanese). The Shintō summer festival. Since summer is the season when pestilences, insect damage to crops, and unexpected disasters such as storms and floods are most likely to occur, summer festivals characteristically are held to pray for protection against such calamities.

**natural religion**. The idea of natural religion should be distinguished both from the notion of nature worship and from the concept of natural theology. 'Nature worship' has been used to refer to an early form of religious expression that emerges from a recognition of human dependence upon and the need for winning the favour of the elemental forces in the environment which impinge upon human life. 'Natural theology', on the other hand, refers to that which can be known of God, or the gods, by inference of human reason from knowledge of the visibly natural world. Some philosophers and theologians have spoken of 'natural revelation', comprised of a knowledge of God which is always and everywhere available to all intelligent persons; they have, therefore, considered the religious response to that knowledge to be natural religion. However, 'natural religion' more clearly designates a religious response to a natural rather than a supernatural reality, a response constituted by a set of beliefs about duties which persons have with regard to the formation of community, without reference to a reality of any kind outside of or greater than the ordinary natural world visible to all. The idea of natural religion, therefore, involves a rejection of all traditional beliefs in supernatural beings, powers or states, but without denying the reality of the needs or functions that such traditional forms of religion appear to fill. Humanism is often considered to be such a natural religion.

**natural theology**. Theology in the Christian intellectual tradition which is not based on the revelation vouchsafed through the Bible (Old and New Testaments) but rather on knowledge of God derived from creation in general through the exercise of the human mind. *See also* REVELATION.

**natura naturans** (Latin: 'nature naturing'). A term used in medieval scholastic philosophy to distinguish the active, creative power of nature (that is to say, God) from the created nature of substance (that is to say, the world), which was termed *natura naturata* ('nature natured').

**Naunet**. *See* NUN.

**Navā Vidhān** (Bengali). A movement, also known as the New Dispensation Church, founded in 1879 by Keshub Chandra Sen after his split with the BRĀHMO SAMĀJ. It signalled an attempt to synthesize the various spiritual paths of East and West into one 'universal religion'. (Kopf 1979; 270).

**nave**. *See* AISLE.

**Nāyaka** (Pāli: 'Chief Monk'). In Sri Lanka, a title of a Buddhist monk who is either a

Provincial or a District Chief Monk. The Supreme Chief Monk of a monastic Order in Sri Lanka is known as *Mahānāyaka* and the Deputy Supreme Chief Monk as *Anunāyaka*.

**Nazirite**. A person under a vow to Yahweh, eschewing alcohol and impure food (*Numbers* 6.1–21). (Vaux 1965: 464–7).

**ndoki**. A widespread term, especially in Angola, Zambia, and southern Zaire, for WITCH or wizard; a person who uses inherited or acquired witchcraft as psychic force (*see* LIKUNDU) or, with the assistance of medicine (*see* WANGA) or the spirits of malevolent dead, in a covert manner against society (Baumann 1975a).

**necromancy**. The prediction of the future on the basis of communication with the dead.

**necropolis** (from Greek: 'city of the dead'). A cemetery in which provision is made for the continued welfare of the dead on the assumption of their continued existence. Clear examples are the great cemeteries of ancient Egypt, such as the Valley of the Kings and the Valley of the Queens. These were situated on the west bank of the Nile, so that the funeral procession sailed across the river from the town or village on the east bank. The Egyptians called their tombs the 'House of the Ka [the dead person's spirit]'. It was regarded as the dwelling place of the deceased and equipped with funerary furniture, clothing, jewellery, make-up and models of servants, brewers, bakers and estate-workers who would create, by means of magic, the comforts of life in the afterlife. The walls were decorated with scenes of daily life and food production, and these again were magically 'activated' at the funeral by a special ritual, to provide the deceased with a range of activities and a perpetual food supply. Inside the tomb, the mummified body (MUMMY) was encased in one or more wooden coffins, enclosed in a rectangular box either made of stone or wood (sarcophagus). The coffins and sarcophagi were decorated with scenes and funerary texts to protect the deceased and ensure his passage into the next world. The tomb provided a continuing location on earth to which the deceased could return at will and pass some time; a 'false door' carved or painted on one wall allowed the Ka to 'enter' the tomb, occupy the mummy or portrait-statue, and partake of the food-offerings, presented either as art representations or as real offerings brought by the family or priest.

**Nefertem**. A god of the ancient Egyptian city of Memphis, often represented either sitting on a lotus or wearing a lotus on his head.

**Negative Confession**. *See* WEIGHING THE HEART.

**negi** (Japanese). The senior priest of a Shintō shrine, ranking after GŪJI and *gongūji*.

**neidan** (Chinese: 'inner pill'). Usually rendered 'inner alchemy', a very complex Chinese notion of physiological refining processes aiming at immortality (*see* LONGEVITY), avoiding disease and mental disorder, transgressing the laws of crude matter etc. The meditational practices involved in the *neidan* concepts (different traditions existed and developed in various Daoist centres throughout south China) consisted of visualizing spirits within the adept's body, the controlling of 'energy routes' as the microcosmic reflection of outwardly perceived realities, the 'undoing of bonds' that limit one's mind and body.

Complementary to the 'inner alchemy' practices the 'outer alchemy' tradition must be mentioned. Generally believed to precede neidan by several centuries, 'outer alchemy' (*waidan* [*waitan*]) means the concocting of ELIXIRS, drugs of immortality, turning base metals into gold etc. It is difficult to determine exactly when such very costly alchemical practices were given up to be substituted by a 'refining of elixirs within' the body, but the idea of *neidan* in China is intimately linked with Daoist medicinal knowledge, the Five Element theory (*see* WU XING) and cosmographic notions, in short: constituents that stem from very ancient times. It is surprising, then, that the proper Chinese term *neidan* should not have been known until the 8th or 9th century. Recently specialists of Chinese history of religions and the history of science have taken up the complicated issue, e.g. Baldrian-Hussein 1988; Needham 1983: part 2, § 33.

**neitan**. *See* NEIDAN.

**Neith**. An ancient Egyptian goddess of Sais in the Nile Delta. Neith was widely worshipped as a creator-goddess, associated with weaving and warfare, and as a guardian of the dead.

**Nekhbet**. A predynastic (before 3100 BCE) vulture goddess of Upper Egypt who protected the king, with a cult-centre at Nekhen (El Kab).

**Nekhen**. *See* NEKHBET.

**nembutsu**. *See* NENBUTSU.

**nemesis**. The retribution certain to ensue upon committing evil acts, particularly involving pride or conceit. The abstract idea of nemesis, a word drawn from Greek, was in ancient Greece personified as a female deity, Nemesis.

**nemeton**. A Celtic holy place, often a sacred grove or glade, where cultic activities took place in open air.

**nenbutsu** [nembutsu] (Japanese). The meditational formula 'Namu Amida Butsu' ('Hail Amida Buddha') recited in various sects of Japanese Buddhism (especially JŌDOSHŪ, JŌDO SHINSHŪ, JI-SHŪ) in order to express faith in this mythical Buddha's saving power or 'other power' (*tariki*). Literally the term means 'thinking of the Buddha' and derives from the Chinese *nien-fo*, a translation of the Sanskrit *buddhānusmṛti*.

**nenjūgyōji** (Japanese). A cycle of annual events in the Japanese religious calendar. Every religious organization has its own table of such events, some of which overlap with public holidays.

**Neo-Confucianism**. The common Western designation for the revival of the Confucian philosophy (CONFUCIANISM) during the Song [Sung] dynasty (960–1279). There were two important schools in Neo-Confucianism, named *Li Xue* [*Li Hsüeh*] ('Study of Reason', 'Study of Principle') and *Xin Xue* [*Hsin Hsüeh*] ('Study of Mind').

The *Li Xue* school, whose outstanding representative was Zhu Xi [Chu Hsi] (1130–1200), gained political prominence when it became the only state-approved interpretation of the Confucian tradition since the Yuan dynasty (1279–1368). The philosophical synthesis of Zhu Xi, who systematized the thinking of earlier philosophers, provided a metaphysical system that finally supplanted that of Buddhism, which had dominated Chinese philosophy during the 1st millennium. Basic concepts of Zhu Xi's ontology are LI (variously translated as 'reason' or 'principle') and QI [*ch'i*] ('material force').

The nature of everything that exists depends on its *li*, while its actual form is realized through the condensation of *qi*. This applies also to the realm of anthropology. Hence, the nature of man is defined by the *li* of humanity (REN [*jen*]), which is always the same, whereas the differences between individual men are caused by their particular composition of *qi*. It is the aim of the Confucian gentleman to investigate the nature of all things in order to adapt himself to the cosmic principle TAIJI [*t'ai-chi*]. Through self-cultivation he can realize his own human nature as part of the cosmic principle and as such become a sage (SHENGREN [shengjen]).

The philosophy of Zhu Xi was based on the classical writings of Confucianism, the Five Classics (WU JING [Wu Ching]) and particularly the Four Books (SI SHU [Ssu Shu]), of which he wrote authoritative commentaries. The study of the Confucian tradition constituted the most important aspect of what was called 'the investigation of things' (*ge wu* [*Ke-wu*]), being necessary for self-cultivation.

The other main current of Neo-Confucianism, the *Xin Xue* school, paid much less attention to the study of books. Its founder Lu Xiangshan [Lu Hsiang-shan] (1139–93) maintained that self-cultivation was not to be achieved through the study of external things or books but through introspection into one's own mind (*xin*). The most important thinker of the school was Wang Yangming (1472–1529), who taught that all men possess innate knowledge of the good which has to be realized and put into practice to accomplish self-cultivation. Although his school was highly influential in private circles during the Ming dynasty (1368–1644), it never matched the position of the official *Li Xue*.

**Neoplatonism**. A development from Plato's (428–347 BCE) philosophy, current in the 2nd and 3rd centuries CE, its main representatives being Plotinus, Porphyry and Proclus. It distinguished the divine, eternal, unchanging realm and the mutable, decaying world. The former, God, the One, is unable to relate directly to the latter, it lies beyond all human experience and is knowable only by abstraction. The philosopher therefore seeks to rise from the world to God, by divesting himself of all that is spatial, temporal and changing. Then the individual, the soul, apart from its body, becomes one with the impassible One. Christian doctrines of creation, incarnation and resurrection are alien to Neoplatonism; however, Christian MONOTHEISM, and thus philosophical monotheism, are similar. (Armstrong 1967).

**Neo-Sannyas Movement**. *See* RAJNEESH MOVEMENT.

**Neo-Scholasticism**. *See* SCHOLASTICISM.

**Nephthys**. An ancient Egyptian deity, the daughter of GEB and NUT, sister of ISIS, OSIRIS and SETH (her husband); and mother of ANUBIS. Nephthys was a protector of the dead and featured in the Osiris myth.

**Neptune**. An ancient Italian water divinity, later identified with the Greek POSEIDON and hence with oceans specifically.

**Nergal**. The Assyro-Babylonian god of death and war, consort of Allatu. The Sumerian equivalent is ERESHKIGAL.

**Nerthus**. Fertility goddess worshipped in Denmark in the 1st century CE, who, according to Tacitus in *Germania*, lived on an island sanctuary and travelled among her followers in a wagon, communicating via her priest.

**neshamah** (Hebrew: 'breath'). Soul, in the sense of individualized spirit.

**Nestorianism**. The extremely influential theology of Nestorius (*d c*.451), who asserted two separate persons in Christ, human and divine, morally united through the co-operation of their two wills. It rejected any COMMUNICATIO IDIOMATUM.

**New Dispensation Church**. *See* NAVĀ VIDHĀN.

**New Testament**. The collection of works in Greek which eventually came to be agreed upon as normative or 'canonical' for the Christian Church in addition to the Bible inherited from Judaism. It consists of the four Gospels, the *Acts of the Apostles*, the epistles (letters) of various apostles, and the *Book of Revelation*. The list was not at first stable (*see*, e.g., MURATORIAN CANON), and although apostolic authorship was an important criterion it must be said that historically speaking this cannot be regarded as assuredly factual in all cases. The term 'testament' (from Latin *Testamentum*, translating the Greek *diatheke*) has also been translated into English as 'dispensation' or 'covenant' (*see* ARK). Thus, the New Testament is understood as the scriptural record of the new covenant which God has made with his people, now taken to include the whole of humankind.

**New World religions**. The indigenous, imported, and engendered religions of the Americas from the pre-Columbian period (prior to 1492) to the present. The circumstances determining these religions include the following: (1) the ecological isolation of the western hemisphere from the rest of the world for at least a dozen millennia, which led to (2) a critically different gene pool of flora and fauna, which in turn led to (3) major differences in the biophysical and cultural development of lands and peoples that (4) after the 1492 contact between hemispheres had powerful demographic consequences. These consequences were: (a) massive, almost genocidal epidemics among the indigenous populations of the New World; (b) the enslavement and importation of African peoples to replace the lost labour force of the New World; and (c) the immigration of European and Asian peoples as part of the colonization enterprise. (5) A further effect of colonization was massive ecological upheaval and transformation due to importation of Old World flora/fauna; and (6) the Christian missionary effort that, as well as suppressing non-Christian religions, was used to enhance the ideological legitimation of the exploitation of the indigenous, imported, and engendered peoples of the New World. These factors have contributed to the extinction or marginalization of some religions, to the complex adaptation of Catholic Christianity (in Latin America) and to the emergence of new movements of various kinds. *See also* NATIVE AMERICAN RELIGIONS; MESOAMERICAN RELIGION; ANDEAN RELIGIONS; AFRO-AMERICAN RELIGIONS.

**Ngai**. *See* ENKAI.

**nganga**. In large parts of Bantu-speaking Africa, a medical expert who engages in diagnosis and therapy of all kinds of illness. Apart from this he has also to deal with the social, psychological, religious and economic aspects of the diseases and has to reintegrate the patient into the divine and human order. Basically he works as a healer and herbalist, but as diseases are often thought of as having been caused by extra-human forces, he also has to act as diviner, witch-finder, or exorcist. Sometimes he even becomes a prophet. On the other hand all these functions can be divided among different experts (Baumann 1975c: 629). The *nganga* uses his power (*see* WANGA) for the benefit of society. He is the main opponent of the evil forces (*see* NDOKI; LIKUNDU) and an important spiritual guide of the people.

**ngoma**. Among the Eastern Bantu, a ritual instrument or the dances of male or female mediums in trance, through whom ancestral spirits utter prophecies (Breutz 1975).

**ngulu**. Nature-spirits in northeast Zambia. This concept is not so frequent in eastern and southern Africa (*see* MILUNGU) (Baumann 1975a).

**nibbāna**. *See* NIRVĀṆA.

**Nicaea**. *See* COUNCIL OF NICAEA.

**Nicene Creed**. *See* CREED.

**Nichiren-shōshū**. One of various Japanese Buddhist sects based on the teaching of Nichiren (1222–82) and in particular on his interpretation of the LOTUS SŪTRA. This sect is particularly important because of its connection with the SŌKA GAKKAI. (The suffix *-shōshū* means 'correct sect'.) *See also* DAISEKIJI. *Contrast* NICHIREN-SHŪ.

**Nichiren-shū**. A major sect of Japanese Buddhism based on the teaching of Nichiren (1222–82) and the LOTUS SŪTRA. *Contrast* NICHIREN-SHŌSHŪ.

**Nichts** (German). Nothing. With the definite article as *das Nichts* the concept takes on a distinctly metaphysical meaning, as in the works of Nietzsche and Heidegger and may be translated as 'nothingness' or 'non-being'.

**nien-fo**. *See* NENBUTSU.

**Niflheim**. *See* GINNUNGAGAP, HEL.

**niggun** (Hebrew; plural, *niggunim*). A 'melody', or Ḥasidic song. ḤASIDISM's principal artistic contribution (outside the field of literature) was the creation of a genre of folk songs which emphasize melody rather than lyrics. While most *niggunim* were based on the repetition of a single line of scripture (especially Psalms), a *niggun* needs no words to cast its hypnotic spell.

**nigimitama.** *See* MI-TAMA.

**Nihang** (Punjabi). Warrior Sikhs, identifiable by their dark blue clothes and weaponry, often protectors of GURDWĀRĀS in the Punjab (originally known as AKĀLĪS).

**nihil obstat**. *See* IMPRIMATUR.

**nihilism**. A despair about ultimate meaning along with a concomitant legitimation of violence in a universe where everything else is equally aleatory and self-assertive. Contemporary forms of nihilism tend to be associated with the name of Friedrich Nietzsche, who accused Christianity itself of being nihilistic, both because its asceticism denied 'life', and because its high valuation of 'truth' had led, paradoxically, to the discovery that there is no absolute truth. Nietzsche, however, suggested as an antidote a 'positive' nihilism which would embrace this circumstance not as failure, but as the liberation of the different, the time-bound and the creative, which are all to be both suffered and celebrated. Several 'postmodernist' thinkers, such as Gilles Deleuze, also adopt a related attitude (*see* POSTMODERNISM).

**Nihongi**. *See* NIHON SHOKI.

**Nihonshoki.** The Chronicles of Japan, a classical work compiled in Chinese at the imperial Japanese court in 720. Thirty volumes of narrative cover the time from the age of the gods through the reign of Empress Jito (reigned 690–97). The first half of the work contains many myths and legends, while the latter half is more historically reliable. Together with the KOJIKI, it is an important source for Shintō thought.

**nikai**. *See* NIKĀYA.

**Nikāya** (Sanskrit, Pāli: 'heap', 'group', 'assembly'). A group of Buddhist monks; a Theravāda term denoting a monastic order, a sect of the *SAṄGHA*. In Sri Lanka there are three principal monastic orders, *Syāma Nikāya* (founded 1753), *Amarapura Nikāya* (1802) and *Rāmañña Nikāya* (1864), which hold independent higher ordination (*upasampadā*) ceremonies for their novices. These *Nikāyas* are further subdivided into numerous smaller monastic orders in such a way as to constitute a complex net of monasteries. All monks trace, however, their line of pupillary succession back to the founder or small group of founders of the order concerned. Additionally, there are some monasteries which do not belong to any *Nikāya*, but are the creations of Buddhist modernists, often Europeans. In Burma and Thailand the structure of the monastic orders is similar, although the organization is not so centralized as in Sri Lanka. The Thai word is in transcription spelled *nikai*.

In the Pāli Canon, TRIPIṬAKA, the word *nikāya* has the loose meaning of group or collection, when referring to, for example, the parts of the Canon known as *Dīgha-nikāya*, *Majjhima-nikāya* etc.

**Nine Gods**. *See* COSMOGONY.

**Nimbarka**. *See* VIṢṆU.

**Nirankārī movement**. A Sikh sectarian movement begun in the early 19th century by Bābā Dayāl as a reaction to current Hindu and Sikh practice. The founder taught that God was *nirankār* ('formless') and thus could not be worshipped through incarnations and idols. He stressed the importance of the GURŪ GRANTH SĀHIB and meditation on the Name (NĀM). Like the NĀMDHARIS, the Nirankārīs revere a living gurū. *See also* SANT NIRANKARIS.

**nirmānakāya**. *See* TRIKĀYA.

**nirvāṇa** (Sanskrit: 'blowing out') [Pāli: *nibbāna*]. A Buddhist term denoting freedom from desire and the end of suffering. It is the ultimate goal of all Buddhist aspiration. It has two aspects: (1) a complete blowing out of the fires of craving, hatred and delusion, with the five aggregates (*skandha*) still existing (enlightenment during life-time), and (2) a complete blowing out of the five aggregates as well (enlightenment at the moment of decease), i.e. final *nirvāṇa* or *parinirvāṇa* (Pāli: *parinibbāna*). *Nirvāṇa* is characterized as unconditioned non-being outside the round of rebirths, a sphere of non-existence outside space and time.

*Nirvāṇa* also occurs in Hindu writings generally, e.g. in the BHAGAVADGĪTĀ, as a synonym for MOKṢA/MUKTI.

**niśān sāhib** (Punjabi). A saffron or blue flag, depicting the Sikh emblem (a two-edged sword encircled by two curved swords), commonly kept in a GURDWĀRĀ.

**Nishi Honganji**. *See* HONGANJI.

**nistar** (Yiddish). A 'hidden' TZADDIQ, who serves without his role being known to the public, or possibly even to himself.

**Nitnem** (Punjabi). The Sikh daily religious observance; the recitation at appointed times of verses from the *gutkā*, a book comprised of passages from Sikh scripture.

**niyya** *See* IMĀN.

**Njord**. Germanic god of the sea and of ships, member of the VANIR and father of FREYR and FREYJA. He was worshipped by fishing communities and seafarers.

**nkila**. Local nature-spirits, north of the river Zaire; south of the Zaire, dangerous ancestral spirits (*see* MILUNGU) who have been offended (Vansina 1975).

**nkisi**. Nature-spirits in the forest regions of central Zaire, worshipped in cult. In the savannah of southern Zaire the meaning is rather 'powerful objects', comparable to WANGA (Vansina 1975: 672f).

**nominalism**. The theory of knowledge which treats general terms as referring to similar qualities in individuals, and so denies the existence of UNIVERSALS. The term is also used of some later SCHOLASTICISM that was sceptical of METAPHYSICS and NATURAL THEOLOGY, equated morality with God's arbitrary decree, and questioned the medieval synthesis of reason and revelation. *Contrast* REALISM.

**Nommo**. The ancestral deity of the Dogon of Mali (Griaule & Dieterlen 1965).

**non-being**. Some thinkers have accorded a certain problematic reality to non-being. For Plato in *The Sophist*, 'is not' must be in some sense real, otherwise no assertion may be denied, and there can be no truth or falsity. For Hegel, 'Being' as such is empty and indeterminable, and therefore identical with 'non-being'. For Aristotle, by contrast, and most Christian thinkers, in particular Augustine and Aquinas, 'non-being' has more the heuristic value of a mathematical zero: 'creation out of nothing' means that all reality is from God; evil as privation means that something that should be present is lacking, and does not denote a substantially 'negative' quality. *See also* BEING.

In eastern religious thought, too, careful distinctions must be made. Buddhism, for example regards a fixation on either being or non-being as spiritually undesirable, leading to the wrong views of eternalism or ANNIHILATIONISM. The Mahāyāna concept of 'emptiness' should therefore not be translated 'the void', as if it were a metaphysical principle in itself; it is simply intended to defuse possible mistaken views about the permanence of being (*see* ŚŪNYATA). The Chinese (Daoist) concept *wu* (Japanese, *mu*) does in some contexts have a cosmogonic metaphysical function, as when phenomena are supposed to originate from nothingness or, in effect, non-being (MU).

**Non-Church Movement**. *See* MUKYOKAI.

**none**. *See* PRIME.

**non-returner**. *See* FOUR FRUITS.

**norito** (Japanese). Words addressed to a deity or deities in an ancient style of Japanese. A Shintō priest recites *norito* on behalf of the faithful. The style of expression is typified by the *norito* recorded in the *Engi shiki*, a book of court procedures compiled in the 10th century. *Norito* include words of praise for the gods, lists of offerings, words identifying the persons originating and pronouncing the prayer, and the subject of the prayer. During the period of STATE SHINTŌ in the Meiji period, shrine norito were standardized by the government, but these restrictions were removed after 1945.

**norns**. Female figures of Germanic mythology who had the power to predict fate. They usually appeared in groups of three (corresponding to their threefold knowledge of past, present and future). *See also* YGGDRASILL.

**noumenon**. An object of pure intellectual intuition, as opposed to an appearance to the senses. Kant made use of this notion to refer to that reality beyond or outside the framework of the phenomenal order, which is, therefore, devoid of phenomenal attributes of a spatio-temporal kind. Whatever passes through the spatio-temporal forms of sensuous (empirical) intuition and can be further organized under the categories of reason within Kant's structure of thought belongs to the phenomenal realm, but that realm does not exhaust the nature of things since more can be coherently thought than can be sensuously experienced. God, for example, is such a noumenal reality because God can be thought but not empirically experienced. *Contrast* PHENOMENON.

**novena**. A period of nine days during which special devotions are carried out, the practice being particularly current in the Roman Catholic Church.

**Nuadu** [Nuada]. King of the TUATHA DÉ DANANN, the gods of Irish Celtic mythology, who loses a hand in the first of the two legendary 'battles of Mag Tured' and, in accordance with the Irish custom that a king must be without physical or ethical failure, therefore loses his throne. The doctor god DIANCECHT replaces his hand with a silver one, after which he resumes the kingship together with the epithet 'of the silver hand'.

**Num**. The sky god of the Nentsy Samoyeds, regarded as the highest god residing in the heaven (*num*: 'sky', 'firmament'). Num was a remote god, a creator of the world, who could be contacted by the assistance of other spiritual beings (Holmberg 1927).

**Numa**. The legendary second king of Rome (8th century BCE). Although he was credited with giving Rome many religious institutions, later research has shown such attribution to be anachronistic, based on Etruscan religious influence in the 6th century BCE.

**numen** (Latin; plural, *numina*). In the earliest Roman religion, a dynamic force. Numina are often without any real names. Traditional scholarship has held that divinities evolved from them, but this view is now in disrepute. *Numen* is the official journal of the International Association for the History of Religions.

**numinous** Based on the Latin NUMEN, the term 'numinous' or 'the numinous' was used by Rudolf Otto (1869–1937) in *Das Heilige* (1917) for that 'unnamed something' which he saw as the awesome, transcendent focus of religions. He characterizes the experience of the numinous as an awareness of a MYSTERIUM TREMENDUM ET FASCINANS. Otto's work was translated into English as *The Idea of the Holy* (1923). *Compare* HOLY.

**Num-Tārem**. *See* NUM-TŪREM.

**Num-Tūrem** [Num-Tārem]. The high god of two Ob-Ugrian peoples, the Khanty and the Mansi. As the creator of the world and the lord of the heavens or the universe Num-Tūrem was originally a *deus otiosus*, a remote higher being. Christian and Islamic influences rendered him more important in everyday life and he came to be worshipped among both peoples. (Karjalainen 1921–7).

**Nun**. The watery abyss from which the earth emerged. In the Egyptian creation myths, Nun is personified as a man with a female counterpart, Naunet.

**nuncio**. A diplomat BISHOP serving as ambassador of the HOLY SEE at the Vatican to the government of a secular state. According to widely accepted protocol a nuncio is regarded as the dean of the diplomatic corps in any one country. In cases when this is not so the title is modified to 'pro-nuncio'.

**nuor-yin**. *See* YIN.

**Nut**. An ancient Egyptian sky-goddess, wife of GEB, daughter of SHU (air) and TEFNUT (moisture). Nut gave birth daily to the sun and was sometimes represented as a cow.

**Nü Wa**. In Chinese mythology, the ancestress of mankind and the sister of FU XI. She united with her brother and gave birth to men. Thereafter they decreed that unions between brothers and sisters should be forbidden and in this way regulated the institution of marriage. Nü Wa is therefore popularly worshipped as the goddess of go-betweens. According to another legend she moulded man using yellow earth.

**nyama** [n'ama]. In Mande languages, a kind of life force in living beings. As such it is often dangerous after death, in particular avenging its owner if he has been slain. Certain animals and man have a specially dangerous *nyama*. Baumann took over this word (from languages in Mali) to designate 'revenge power' of animals and humans in other parts of Africa. (Dieterlen 1941; Baumann 1950).

**Nyame** [Nyankopon]. The supreme being, sky god of the Akan of Ghana and Baule of the Ivory Coast (Nyamye) (Rattray 1923).

**Nyankopon**. *See* NYAME.

**Nyembe**. A female secret society in Gabon with rituals in bush-camps, not in the local cult-house like its male counterpart BWITI (Hirschberg 1965).

**Nyikang**. A mythic ancestor of the Shilluk kings who built up a kingdom (on the southern Nile) and created human order, which, as it is believed, has to be maintained by the kings. Nyikang is the subject of most Shilluk mythology and of the public cult (Lienhardt 1954).

**nymphaeum** (Latin). A shrine built in veneration of the nymph or NYMPHS who inhabit a distinctive natural site such as a spring or a grove.

**nymphs**. Female figures representing natural phenomena – seas, oceans, mountains, springs, pools and trees. They appear originally in ancient Greek culture, where they were regarded as daughters of Zeus, but they became a common theme in later western art. *See also* NYMPHAEUM.

**nyorai** (Japanese). The Japanese equivalent for Sanskrit Tathāgata, a title given to a Buddha, hence Shaka Nyorai (Sanskrit, Śākyamuni Tathāgata).

**Nyx**. *See* ORPHIC MYSTERIES.

**Nzambi**. A widespread name for the supreme being between Cameroun and Namibia, indicating creation through 'moulding' like other *-mbi* gods (compare KIUMBI). The frequent occurrence in western Central Africa is partly due to Christian missionaries who used it for 'God', but it is a genuine African concept that has existed at least since 1491 in the kingdom of the Congo (Baumann 1975c). Nzambi is a celestial HIGH GOD and personified cause of existence, but also a still active creator who can be directly approached in prayer by everybody. He is often seen as a counterpart to the chthonic and/or ancestral gods like KALUNGA. Invocations are made to him during first-fruit ceremonies of the Kuba of Zaire, but no groups are organized for his cult. (Vansina 1975).

# O

**oath**. The binding of a person through his or her word, guaranteed in the ancient world by the presence of gods, sometimes by animal sacrifice, and later by appeal to a sacred object such as the Holy Bible. The use of oaths implies fear of the power of the sacred, which might be thought to retaliate if the oath is broken. Although swearing (an oath) on the Bible has remained common practice as a legal act in some countries, it has also been rejected by smaller Christian groups (e.g. Quakers) on the basis of a New Testament injunction (*Matthew* 5.33–7). The oath has not figured as such in cultures (e.g. across the whole of eastern Asia) where the concept of potential divine retaliation is relatively weak.

**oath of abjuration**. The oath required of all office holders in England between 1701 and 1858 in abjuration of the claims of the PAPACY.

**Ōbaku-shū**. A Japanese Zen Buddhist sect whose head temple is Manpukuji at Uji near Kyōto. Founded in 1654, this temple was led by Chinese masters for many generations.

**Obàtálá**. [Orisha-nla]. The deity (ORISHA) who, in the Nigerian Yoruba pantheon, is next to the ultimate creator god (OLORUN). Obàtálá is the creator of men. (Idowu 1962).

**obayifo**. Among the Akan of Ghana, a witch. Witches both female and male are thought to kill relatives by sucking their blood or catching their life-soul at night and to form associations in which they feast on their victims. Similar beliefs are widely held in other parts of Africa (especially West and Central Africa) (Debrunner 1961).

**o-bon** (Japanese). A Japanese summer festival of Buddhist origin at which the spirits of departed ancestors are welcomed to feasting and dancing. Nowadays it is usually celebrated on 13, 14 and 15 July, following the solar calendar.

**occasionalism**. The doctrine put forward by Malebranche (1638–1715) that mind and body do not interact with each other, but that God so devises that their operations occur in parallel sequences.

**Ockham's razor**. The principle of ontological economy that 'entities are not to be multiplied beyond necessity', named after its formulator, William of Ockham (*c*.1285–1349).

**October Horse**. An early Roman festival of MARS on 15 October, involving dismemberment of a horse and use of the ANCILIA.

**Odin**. Germanic god of war, death, magic and wisdom; the 'All-father' and leader of the AESIR. Odin was worshipped above all as a god of battle who granted victory and gave advice and special weapons to his followers, who proved their loyalty by sacrificing their defeated enemies to him by hanging, piercing with a spear and burning. At their own death their dedication to Odin was symbolized by cremation. With his spear Gungnir, Odin was said to provoke and influence warfare. Together with the VALKYRIES he chose the warriors who were to be slain in battle and then enter VALHALLA, thus preparing an army for the gods' final battle at RAGNAROK. As well as inspiring the BERSERKS with invincible battle frenzy, Odin was believed to inspire wisdom and the gift of poetry. This he had gained by sacrificing one of his eyes to be allowed to drink from the spring of Mimir (*see* YGGDRASILL); hence one of his names was 'One-Eyed'. According to another myth he stole the mead of inspiration back from the giants and restored it to ASGARD, and he is also said to have hung from the World Tree Yggdrasill in order to obtain secret knowledge from the runes below. Odin's most valued possession was his eight-legged horse Sleipnir on which he could ride through the air and even journey to HEL. A god of similar functions was worshipped by the Germans as Wodan or Wotan and by the Anglo-Saxons as Woden (from which Wednesday is derived). All three gods were regarded as the ancestors of royal dynasties and their cult was followed by rulers and warriors (*see* THOR). (Davidson 1964).

**odu**. *See* IFÁ.

**Oduduwa**. A Yoruba ancestral divinity associated with creation.

**Odyssey**. The epic poem attributed to Homer which recounts the trials and journeys of the heroes who had fought in the Trojan War, particularly Odysseus, as they made their way home to Greece. Odysseus overcomes supernatural dangers largely by human courage, patience and cunning.

**Oecumenical Council**. *See* ECUMENICAL COUNCIL.

**Oedipus complex**. According to psychoanalytic theory, a boy's unconscious, sexually tinged love of his mother and aggression toward his father. In the realm of religion, the complex is used to explain CONVERSION experiences, for example. The Oedipus complex is presumed to develop at the age of four or five, but can in some cases remain a permanent pattern of behaviour throughout a person's life. The term is sometimes also used to describe a girl's love of her father and her aggression toward her mother, but the special term 'Electra complex' exists to describe these feelings. Great importance has been attributed to these complexes in the development of neuroses and other psychological disturbances. The idea of the 'Oedipus complex' is drawn from the life-story of the legendary prince of Thebes who unwittingly, but in fulfilment of the oracle of DELPHI, killed his own father and married his own mother.

**o-fuda** (Japanese). A wooden or paper amulet on which is written the name of a Shintō or Buddhist deity. The *o-fuda* is taken home from the shrine or temple, enshrined on the house altar (*kamidana*) and worshipped to obtain divine aid.

**Ogbóni** [Oṣugbo]. A men's secret association among the Yoruba of southwestern Nigeria. Ogboni is a cult of the earth as the source of morality and as such had great political and juridical power in the old Yoruba states (Morton-Williams 1960).

**Ogdoad**. *See* AMUN; COSMOGONY.

**Ogma**. Celtic god of eloquence and poetry in Ireland, believed to have invented the *ogham* alphabet. His Gaulish equivalent is Ogmios, whose attributes of a club and animal skin show him also to be a god of strength and led to his equation with the Roman hero HERCULES. According to the Roman author Lucian, the Gaulish Ogmios is depicted smiling with followers chained by their ears to his tongue.

**Ogmios**. *See* OGMA.

**Ogo**. *See* YURUGU.

**Ògun**. God of metal and war of the Yoruba and the Edo of Benin in Nigeria. He is considered to be one of the earliest deities, a road maker and a pioneer. (Idowu 1962; Awolalu 1979).

**Ōharae**. *See* HARAI.

**ōjō** (Japanese). Rebirth in the realm of a Buddha, used particularly with respect to rebirth in the PURE LAND of Amida (AMITĀBHA) Buddha.

**Ōjōyōshū**. A work written by the 10th-century Japanese monk Genshin, pioneering PURE LAND Buddhist teaching in its Japanese forms. The title is usually translated as 'Essentials for Attaining Birth', in which 'birth' refers to rebirth in the PURE LAND of Amida (AMITĀBHA) Buddha.

**oklad** (Russian). An ornamented and often bejewelled metal cover originally made to protect especially treasured ICONS, later made together with the icon, revealing only the face and hands of the sacred figures. The *oklad* is an extension of the *riza*, which leaves the whole body visible and which was itself an extension of the *bazma*, an ornamental metal covering for the frame only.

**Ōkuninushi no kami**. An important divinity in early Shintō mythology. Descended from Great Land Possessor of Susanoo no mikoto, Ōkuninushi no kami was persecuted by his many brothers and repeatedly exposed to danger, but was always saved by the intervention of mysterious helpers. In one legend illustrating his kindness, he is depicted saving a rabbit whose fur was torn off by crocodiles. Receiving permission to marry Susanoo no mikoto's daughter Suseribime he was designated possessor of the manifest world. There he punished evil spirits, developed the land, cured illnesses and gave medicines, removed damage caused by birds and insects, and then presented the land to Ninigi no mikoto, the grandson of Amaterasu Ōmikami. Ōkuninushi no kami is enshrined at Izumo Grand Shrine and is widely worshipped as a provider of happiness, especially marital happiness. An alternative reading of the characters for his name leads to the form Daikoku, under which designation he is one of the seven gods of fortune.

**olam** (Hebrew; plural, *olamot*). The 'world', meaning either the planet earth or the entire universe of time and space. In KABBALAH, the *olamot* refer to the specific dimensions of reality – Emanation, Creation, Formation or Action – which constitute the Four Worlds.

**Old Believers**. A sect of the Russian Orthodox Church arising from their excommunication in 1667 for not accepting liturgical reforms initiated by the patriarch Nikon. They suffered considerable persecution but also received renewed support from those who resented the modernization programme of Peter the Great. They are also commonly referred to as *Raskolniki* ('schismatics') and *Starovetsi* ('Old Believers').

**Old Catholics**. The common name given to a number of churches, notably in the Netherlands (Church of Utrecht), Germany, Austria and Switzerland, which have maintained the apostolic tradition in continuity with western Catholicism, but which for various reasons do not recognize the general jurisdiction of the Pope or the dogma of infallibility. The Old Catholic churches are in communion with each other as also with the CHURCH OF ENGLAND and other churches of the ANGLICAN COMMUNION.

**Old Testament**. The term used to describe the Hebrew BIBLE from a Christian standpoint, implying a contrastive relationship with the New Testament (or rather, NEW COVENANT), regarded as the fulfilment of the OLD COVENANT. The Old Testament has usually been held in high esteem in the Christian churches and used regularly for both liturgical and theological purposes. The radical discontinuity between Old and New Testament proposed by Marcion (*see* MARCIONISM) did not find wide acceptance. Nevertheless the term should be avoided with reference to JUDAISM, for which the Bible is the Hebrew Bible.

**Olódùmaré**. *See* OLÓRUN.

**ol-oiboni** (East Nilotic). Medical experts and diviners among the Maasai and their neighbours in Kenya and Tanzania, partly resembling NGANGA, but also functioning as rainmakers, prophets and an important institution for age-group rituals (Berntsen 1979).

**Olókun** [Malókun]. God of the sea, of fertility and wealth; a principal deity of the Edo of the Benin kingdom, also worshipped in parts of the Yoruba country of southern Nigeria (Bradbury 1957).

**ololiuhqui** (Nahuatl). Morning glory seeds used in Aztec culture in a hallucinogenic drink for oracular purposes (Ruiz de Alarcon 1984).

**Olórun** [Olódùmaré]. Lord of Heaven the HIGH GOD of the Yoruba of Nigeria. As an almighty, all-knowing creator he is set apart from the lesser gods (ORISHA) (Idowu 1962). *See also* GANDOMBLÉ.

**Olympian gods**. Greek family of deities presumed to dwell on MOUNT OLYMPUS (Greek *Olympos*). The Olympian gods are essentially celestial deities as opposed to

CHTHONIC DEITIES associated with the earth. The reigning head of the Olympian gods is ZEUS, most powerful of all the ancient Greek gods.

**Olympos**. *See* OLYMPUS.

**Olympus**. The frequent, Latin form of the ancient Greek *Olympos*, the mountain on which normally resided the celestial OLYMPIAN GODS. Mount Olympus (modern Olimbos) lies to the south of Thessaloniki.

**OM** [AUM] (Sanskrit). The *praṇava* or original mantra, usually precedes all prayers and invocations and is also used to conclude them. It has no translatable meaning; the MUṆḌAKA UPANIṢAD declares the elements of AUM as associated respectively with *jāgrita sthāna*, *svapna* and *suṣupti* and the whole of AUM as identical with *turīya*. More modern authors associate it with the vibrations that are incessantly transmitted from the atoms or with notions of creation connected with sound.

**o-mairi** (Japanese). A visit to a Shintō shrine or a Buddhist temple, including an act of reverence or prayer. The verbal noun with honorific prefix derives from *mairu* meaning 'to go up to [from a humble standpoint]'.

**o-mamori** (Japanese). A small amulet obtained from Shintō shrines or Buddhist temples in Japan and worn on the body for protection.

**Ombimbi**. A mothers' festival in Angola, where the spirit of a deceased 'mother' is transferred to a representative of her 'daughters' (Baumann 1975b: 498).

**o-mikuji** (Japanese). Divination by lots to predict good or ill fortune, to decide the order of an undertaking or to choose between alternatives. The basic procedure is to write the various possibilities or alternatives on pieces of paper or sticks of wood, place them before the deity, recite prayers over them, and then draw one. Pre-printed *o-mikuji* are sold at shrines and temples.

**omphalomancy** (from Greek *omphalos*: 'navel'). The divination of the number of children a mother will bear by counting the number of knots in an umbilical cord.

**omphalos** (Greek: 'navel'). Navel, as in the expression 'navel of the world'. *Compare* (though not connected symbolically) OMPHALOMANCY.

**once-returner**. *See* FOUR FRUITS.

**ongghot** (Mongolian). Figurines or painted figures representing the spirits of deceased shamans and shamanesses. (Heissig 1980).

**oni** (Japanese). A spirit possessing a fearful countenance, great strength and a near-human form. The image of such demons has varied with different historical periods. For example *oni* have been portrayed as visitors from far-away regions. Remnants of this belief are still recognizable in local customs observed during the New Year season, in which men dress in strange costumes and visit the homes of villagers. In general, however, the *oni* is regarded as a type of devil.

**ontological arguments for the existence of God**. The name given first by Kant (1724–1804) and used regularly since then to designate any attempt to prove from an analysis of the concept of 'the supreme being' or 'the most perfect being' the necessary existence of a being to which that concept would uniquely apply. Kant argued that all such attempts must fail: it is not possible to infer the *existence* of a supremely perfect necessary being from the *concept* of a supremely perfect necessary being, because it is never possible to infer the existence of any object from its concept and because 'existence' is not a property or a predicate, the denial of which somehow contradicts the concept of a supremely perfect necessary being. Descartes (1596–1659) had argued that existence is a 'perfection' which uniquely and necessarily belongs to God as 'a supremely perfect being' (*un être souverainement parfait*). Existence is said to belong to God in the way that 'the sum of its three angles is 180°' belongs to triangularity: '. . . from the fact that I cannot conceive God without existence, it follows that existence is inseparable from Him, and hence that He really exists. . . .' (*Meditations*, §5) Leibniz (1646–1716) argued that Descartes had succeeded in showing only that the existence of God is necessary *if possible*, without having shown that God's existence *is* possible. Leibniz allows that God, as Necessary Being, can be shown *actually* to exist if it can be shown that it is *possible* for God to exist. And that can be shown if it can be demonstrated that all positive attributes or 'perfections' can without contradiction coinhere in God. Having shown at least to his own satisfaction that this is possible, Leibniz claims thereby to have shown that God must necessarily exist. It was specifically against the proposals of Descartes and Leibniz (which he described as 'merely so much labour and effort lost') that Kant directed his critical energies. Although he restricted the designation 'ontological argument' to their proofs, others extended the term to cover the argument given by Anselm of Canterbury (1033–1109) in §2–4 of his *Proslogion* (*see* RATIO ANSELMI). Occasionally the 'ontological argument' has been attributed to Ibn Sīnā [Latin: Avicenna] (980–1037), but his proof is more properly classified as a species of COSMOLOGICAL ARGUMENT FOR THE EXISTENCE OF GOD (Davidson 1987: 214–15). If ancient precedent for the proof must be sought, it is more plausibly to be found in the musings of the Stoic philosopher Cleanthes (*c.*331–232 BCE), who argued for the existence of the gods from degrees of perfection to the necessity of a supremely perfect being, though his proof draws on empirical as well as conceptual considerations (Dragona-Monachou 1976: 92–6). There are no close parallels in classical Indian philosophy to the 'ontological arguments' as they have been developed in the West. The nearest parallel, which is fairly remote, is to be found in §3 of the *Nyāyakusumāñjali*, where Udayana (11th century CE) argues – probably against the materialists – that God cannot not exist (Potter 1977: 108ff, 574–9). Various versions of ontological arguments have been proposed – and extensively discussed – in Western religious thought in the 20th century. (See, e.g., Hick & McGill 1968; Hartshorne 1962; Plantinga 1974.) The most thorough history of all the varieties of ontological arguments and their critics is Rohls 1987. *See also* ARGUMENTS FOR THE EXISTENCE OF GOD.

**ontology**. The literal meaning of this Greek-derived term is 'knowledge of being' and hence it is taken to mean that part of metaphysics focusing on the question of what there is, i.e. the essence of things, or the nature of BEING ITSELF. *See also* ONTOLOGICAL ARGUMENTS FOR THE EXISTENCE OF GOD.

**ontotheology**. A term coined by Kant to refer to speculative enterprises, such as COSMOLOGICAL ARGUMENTS FOR THE EXISTENCE OF GOD or ONTOLOGICAL ARGUMENTS FOR THE EXISTENCE OF GOD, which he considered to be illegitimate uses of our faculty of theoretic reason. Heidegger extended the term to all METAPHYSICS, suggesting that such discourse was an illegitimate conflation of ONTOLOGY with THEOLOGY, which betrayed the integrity of both. The key element in this conflation according to him is the false treatment of BEING ITSELF as a merely objectified 'being'; much talk of 'God' treats Being as if it were an object that could be observed and manipulated. *See also* BEING.

**opele**. *See* IFÁ.

**Open Brethren**. *See* PLYMOUTH BRETHREN.

**Ophites**. *See* GNOSTICISM, NAASSENES.

**oracle**. A divine utterance which may be solicited at will on special occasions, of particular importance in ancient Greek religion. *See also* DELPHI; DIDYMA; DODONA.

**oracle bones**. The common Western designation for inscribed tortoise shells and bones of mammals which since 1899 have been unearthed in great number in northern China. They are the earliest Chinese documents, written in a script which has largely been deciphered. Most of them date from the Shang dynasty (17th century – *c.*1066 BCE) and were used for divination. They provide information about ancestor worship and other aspects of the social and religious life during the Shang dynasty.

**ordination**. A rite marking the passage from the state of layman to that of an ordained DEACON OR PRIEST in Christian churches. As a SACRAMENT it is understood to convey a special grace giving power for deacons to transmit authorized teaching and, additionally for priests, to perform the consecration during the EUCHARIST or MASS and to pronounce the forgiveness of sins. In the traditional pattern ordinations are carried out by BISHOPS (themselves priests) whose office is defined by consecration in the APOSTOLIC SUCCESSION. At the same time this pattern no longer reflects the important role apparently played by presbyters in the early Christian church if NEW TESTAMENT sources are considered. *See also* HIERARCHY.

**ordination (Buddhism)**. *See* PRAVRAJYĀ, UPASAṂPAD.

**orenda** (Iroquois). The term for sacred power in Iroquoian (North America) languages, similar to MANITOU in Algonkian languages and WAKAN in Siouan languages. *See also* MANA.

**original sin**. The belief that human beings are corporately involved in a rebellion against the will of God symbolized by the temptation and fall of Eve and Adam, who previously led innocent lives in the Garden of Eden (*Genesis* 3). This has often been understood as an inheritance transmitted at conception, but it has also been interpreted as a fundamental condition of human existence without dependence on chronological inheritance. (*See also* SIN; AUGUSTINIANISM.) In most Christian theology the one exception to the condition of original sin was considered to be Christ himself, who is believed to re-establish the right relationship between God and humankind from God's own side. Thus, Christ is regarded in Christian faith as the universally required redeemer from original sin. *See also* IMMACULATE CONCEPTION.

**original vow**. *See* HONGAN.

**óriṣà**. *See* ORISHA.

**orisha** [òriṣà] (Yoruba). Deities or gods of the Yoruba of southwestern Nigeria. The term is used for the lesser gods, excluding the HIGH GOD, OLORUN. There are innumerable *orisha*, whose conception and worship vary in different parts of the Yoruba country. *Orisha* often personify powers of nature like rivers, winds etc. or elements of human culture like metal or agriculture. Myths of origin depict them as human beings who at their death changed into deities. According to another myth they originated from the 'arch divinity' ORISA-NLA, coming into being as the scattered pieces of this god (Idowu 1962; Frobenius 1913). Orisha also play a significant role in the Afro-American religion SANTERÍA, in which the individual *orisha* are identified with Christian saints.

**Orisha-nla**. *See* OBÀTÁLÁ, ORISHA.

**Oro** [Oru]. A men's secret cult among the Yoruba of Nigeria used for law-enforcement and punishment. The name designates also the bull-roarer whose sound is the 'voice' of the Oro deity. (Frobenius 1913)

**Orphestelestes**. *See* ORPHIC MYSTERIES.

**Orphic mysteries**. A religious movement centred around the figure of Orpheus, the mythical Greek singer. Isolated evidence suggests it existed from the 6th century BCE in Greece, southern Italy and Scythia (southern Russia). The adoption of Eleusinian and Dionysian traits (Orpheus was thought to be the founder of these mysteries) has made it difficult to identify the origins and peculiarities of Orphism. It seems to have been a group of missionaries (*Orphikoi*) with their own priesthood but no sacred objects, who devoted themselves to the problem of liberating the divine soul (PSYCHE) from this world. Only fragments of their literary heritage (*hieroi logoi*) from the 3rd to 5th centuries survive. Central to their teaching is a THEOGONY and ANTHROPOGONY: Chronos (time) created the world egg from which the androgenous Phanes emerged, who gave birth to Nyx (Night) and with her begot GAIA (Earth), Uranos (Heaven) and Kronos. Kronos' son Zeus devoured Phanes and thus became the ruler of the world. With his daughter Persephone-Demeter he begot Dionysos-Zagreus, but the latter was torn to pieces and devoured by the Titans, whom Zeus subsequently destroyed with lightning. Mankind was created from their remains and therefore contains both good (Dionysian) and evil (titanic) elements. In order to liberate the divine soul from the body (*soma*) which imprisoned it like a tomb (*sema*),

Zeus begot Dionysos-Lyseus. This myth gives rise to the practices of Orphism: in order to free the soul from its bodily exile and anguished wanderings, the believers perform purification rites and follow rules of abstinence (e.g. prohibition of meat) which are disclosed to them in secret consecration ceremonies by consecration priests (*Orpheotelestes*). Believers can look forward to a happy life after death, while non-believers face Tartaros. Orphism was especially common among the lower social strata and answered a longing which was not satisfied by the official religion. Despite Plato's contempt for the Orphic mysteries, they gained philosophical recognition in NEOPLATONISM. (Kern 1922; Guthrie 1952; West 1983).

**Orphicism**. *See* ORPHIC MYSTERIES.

**Orphism**. *See* ORPHIC MYSTERIES.

**orphikoi**. *See* ORPHIC MYSTERIES.

**Orthodox Church**. A general term for the historic churches of southern and eastern Europe which are in communion with the bishopric (i.e. the see) of Constantinople (Istanbul), notably the Greek Orthodox Church and the Russian Orthodox Church. They are characterized by rich liturgical practice and the widespread devotional use of icons (*see* ICON; ICONOCLAST CONTROVERSY). The Orthodox churches may be said to share a tradition that has developed in culturally unbroken sequence since the very beginnings of Christianity. The separation between the eastern and western branches of Christianity reflects in part the long drawn-out break-up of the Roman Empire, but ecclesiastically an unwillingness on the part of the Eastern Orthodox Churches to recognize the authority of the PAPACY in Rome.

**Orthodox Judaism**. A collection of religious movements that reject the innovations of both REFORM JUDAISM and CONSERVATIVE JUDAISM. Orthodox Jews generally affirm that HALAKHAH does not change with the times, and that only a few outstanding authorities are entitled to interpret Jewish law.

**orthodoxy**. The official and normative teaching of a church, as opposed to beliefs and teachings presumed to be erroneous.

**Oru**. *See* ORO.

**Orunmila**. *See* IFÁ.

**Oschophoria**. An Athenian festival linking the ripening of fruit with the change in status of young male citizens, including dancing, singing, and a procession from the temple of DIONYSOS to the temple of ATHENA at Skira as well as athletic competitions.

**Oshún**. Yoruba goddess of water, sensuality and jealousy. In the MACUMBA religion (southern Brazil) she is identified with St Catherine.

**Osiris**. The ancient Egyptian god of fertility and vegetation, judge of the dead and king of the underworld. In mythology, he was originally a human king who brought civilization to Egypt. Plutarch's version of the myth (Griffiths 1970) relates that Osiris was murdered by his brother SETH. His wife ISIS posthumously conceived his son, HORUS; he avenged his father's death by fighting Seth. After judgement by the gods, Osiris was resurrected as god of the dead, a role linked to the annual inundation of the Nile and the regeneration of the vegetation.

With the democratization of funerary beliefs in the Middle Kingdom (*c.*1991–1786 BCE), Osiris could offer his pious followers an individual resurrection. This even applied to the poorer classes who could not afford a tomb as a posthumous dwelling (*see* MASTABA TOMB) and therefore continued to be buried in pit-graves with a few simple possessions. His main cult-centres were ABYDOS and Busiris. Together with Isis, Osiris found renewed popularity in the Hellenistic world and the Roman Empire.

**Oṣugbo**. *See* OGBONI.

**Ōtani-ha**. The branch of JŌDO SHINSHŪ which is based on the temple known as Higashi (East) Honganji in Kyōto, established in 1602 as an alternative to the Nishi (west) Honganji. Ōtani is the hereditary name of the abbots of both branches.

**Ouranos**. The ancient Greek father god who inhabits the sky. He and GAIA are the parents of the Olympian gods.

**ousia**. *See* SUBSTANCE.

**Oxford Movement**. *See* HIGH CHURCH.

**Owl**. In Native American religions, the female, night-time equivalent of EAGLE. Owl is a powerful spirit used for shamanic functioning, particularly in communicating with the dead. Under Euro-American influence, Owl is now a negative spirit in many cultures.

**Oxum**. *See* OSHÚN.

# P

**pabbajja**. *See* PRAVRAJYĀ.

**paccekabuddha.** *See* PRATYEKABUDDHA.

**pacha**. *See* HANAQPACHA.

**Pachamama** [Mamapacha]. The Quechua name in the Andean highlands of Peru and Bolivia for mother earth. Offerings to Pachamama, who is considered responsible for the fertility of cultivated land, are called in Spanish *pago a la tierra* ('payment to the earth'). A *pago a la tierra* may contain up to 50 different elements, including COCA leaves, maize seeds and spices. Special celebratory periods for Pachamama are 1–5 August, 25 December to 1 January, 24 June, and Holy Thursday and Trinity Sunday. During these times the land may not be cultivated because it is identified with the living Pachamama who is awaiting her offerings. Relations with Pachamama are concerned mainly with fertility or, negatively, with crop failure, but religious specialists also communicate with her over general questions of land use, genealogical questions and relations with the dead. The ALTOMISAYOQ can establish direct contact with her but others can divine her will only by means of coca leaves. The Pachamama cult derives from pre-conquest and even pre-Inca times, but in spite of eradication efforts by missionaries it is still practised in the rural highlands. (Mariscotti de Görlitz 1978).

**padanda**. *See* PEDANDA.

**paganism**. A term used to refer to the religion of 'the country people' (Latin: *pagani*, hence also 'pagans'), i.e. religion based on diverse local deities, regarded in the early Christian period as inimical to Christian faith. The term was therefore extended to refer to the non-Christian religion of the Roman Empire and eventually to all non-Christian religions. Since it no longer refers to anything specific, while strongly reflecting a particular religious stance, the terms 'paganism' and 'pagan' have no place in scientific literature.

**pago a la tierra**. *See* PACHAMAMA.

**pagoda**. *See* STÚPA.

**Paguyuban Ngesti Tunggal**. Literally, 'The Society for the Meditation of the Oneness', a modern, organized mystical movement with puritanical and intellectual features, founded in 1949 in Surakarta, Java. (Hadiwijono 1967; Jong 1973; Mulder 1983a).

**Paguyuban Sumarah**. Literally, 'The Society of the Self-surrenderers', a mystical movement founded in 1950 in Yogyakarta, Java, working as a kind of 'training school' for communion and unity with God through meditation. (Hadiwijono 1967; Mulder 1983a).

**Pales**. A pair of Roman shepherds' divinities, honoured at the festivities known as Parilia (21 April). Despite rustic origins, they remained popular at Rome and were connected with the city's birthday.

**Pāli** (Sanskrit, Pāli). Nowadays used as the name of a middle Indo-Aryan language, derived from Sanskrit, in which the Theravāda Buddhist Canon is preserved (*see* TRIPIṬAKA). Originally the term indicated a 'text', specifically a Buddhist scripture.

**Pali Canon**. *See* TRIPIṬAKA.

**pamangku**. *See* PEMANGKU.

**Pan**. The ancient Greek god of the countryside, symbolizing uncivilized powers of creativity and procreation, often causing panic in war as in sex.

**Panagia** (Greek: 'all-holy'). (1) Mary as the mother of God. (2) A breast-plate ICON worn by a bishop of the Orthodox Church on feast-days.

**panakawan** (Javanese; Indonesian). A clown figure of distinctive Javanese origin in WAYANG performances, accompanying and assisting the heroes of the BRATAYUDA cycle (Ras 1978).

**Panathenaia**. Ancient Greek festival celebrating the birth of Athens, when new fire was brought to the altar of ATHENA on the ACROPOLIS; many cattle were sacrificed, military might displayed, athletic competitions held, and Athena's robe presented. The birth of Athena was portrayed on the frieze of the PARTHENON.

**Pancacara**. *See* LINGAYATS.

**Pañcarātra** (Sanskrit: 'Five Nights'). An ancient VAIṢṆAVA tradition, which forms the common substratum to the theologies of RĀMĀNUJA, MADHYA, Vallabha etc. It holds that VIṢṆU is not only the creator of the universe but that the universe is Viṣṇu's own body and that for purposes of salvation Viṣṇu exists in five different forms: as *para* he is the unmanifested Supreme, as *vyūha* he divides himself into four manifestations accessible to higher beings, as *vibhava* he assumes bodily forms in animal and human *avatāras*, as *antaryāmin* he dwells in the hearts of people, as *arca* he descends into images and becomes dependent on the worship offered by humans.

**pañcaśīla** Sanskrit: 'five injunctions'). The five injunctions required of lay Buddhists namely: not to kill; not to steal; not to commit unlawful sexual intercourse; not to lie; not to consume intoxicants. *See also* ŚĪLA.

It was on the basis of this well-known notion of *pañcásila* that Sukarno built his new set of five principles, in 1945, as the basis of the Indonesian state. They are: (1) belief in the One and Only God, (2) nationalism, (3) humanism, (4) democracy in terms of general agreement by mutual deliberation, (5) social justice. (Dahm 1969, 1971; Boland 1982).

**Panchen Lama**. Originally a designation for lamas of high scholarly repute (*panchen* being short for Pandita Chen-po, meaning 'great scholar') at the Monastery of Tashilhunpo in Tibet. In 1662 the office became formalized in that a reincarnated child successor was 'discovered', and in 1728 the Panchen Lama was set up as a second temporal head in parts of Tibet (and hence a rival to the DALAI LAMA) by the emperor of China.

**pondok**. *See* PESANTREN.

**pan-Egyptianism**. A term used to describe the diffusionist views of Grafton Elliot Smith and W.J. Perry, according to which Egypt was the main source from which dominant religious and cultural themes derived. Indirectly, and particularly in association with similar assumptions about Mesopotamia, these views contributed to the appearance of the MYTH AND RITUAL SCHOOL.

**panentheism**. (from Greek, *pan* + *en* + *theos*: 'all-in-God'). A term generally used (in contrast to THEISM and PANTHEISM) to characterize a relationship between God and World in which 'God' includes all that is, without 'God' being reducible to the sum of all that is. The term was evidently coined by Karl Christian Friedrich Krause (1781–1832), but it is in recent philosophy associated mainly with the use made of it by Charles Hartshorne (*b* 1897) and those influenced by him. He also uses virtually as a synonym the phrase 'di-polar theism', by which is meant a doctrine of God that presents the divine reality as embracing (but in different senses, in order to avoid paradox) both the absolute and the relative, both the infinite and the finite, both the eternal and the temporal, both the necessary and the contingent. *See also* PROCESS PHILOSOPHY/THEOLOGY.

**pangestu**. *See* PAGUYUBAN NGESTI TUNGGAL.

**Pan Gu** [P'an Ku]. A primordial giant in Chinese cosmogonic myths. According to some accounts he arose out of the Chaos (*Hundun*) and grew for 18,000 years. After his death the different parts of his body were transformed into heaven, earth, sun, moon and the various other natural phenomena. Other myths narrate that he separated heaven and earth with a chisel and an axe. The Pan Gu mythological theme in Chinese literature seems to be of comparatively late origin and may have been adopted from non-Chinese tribes living in the south.

**Paninis Grammer**. *See* ŚAIVISM

**Pañj kakke** (Punjabi). The 'five Ks', symbols worn by all Sikhs who are members of the KHĀLSĀ: *keś* (uncut hair), *kanghā* (comb), *kirpān* (sword), *kara* (steel bangle) and *kaccha* (breeches). *See also* KEŚDHĀRĪ.

**Pañj pyāre** (Punjabi: 'Five beloved'). The first members of the KHĀLSĀ, initiated in 1699 by Gurū Gobind Singh and invested with the symbols (PAÑJ KAKKE) now worn by many Sikhs.

**paññā** (Pāli: 'wisdom') [Sanskrit: *Prajñā*]. A Theravāda term denoting primarily the full apprehension of the Four Noble Truths. *See also* BHĀVANĀ; PRAJÑĀ.

**pansala** (Sinhalese: 'abode', 'monastery'). In Sri Lanka, a monk's residential quarter, usually a house.

**Panth** (Punjabi: 'path'). The term used to refer to the Sikh community. In 1708, on his death, Gurū Gobind Singh gave temporal authority to the Sikh panth and spiritual authority to the GURŪ GRANTH SĀHIB.

**pantheism** (from Greek, *pan* ('all', 'everything') + *theos* ('god')). A modern word, evidently introduced by John Toland (1670–1722), and generally applied pejoratively to positions of which one disapproves to suggest that 'God' is reduced to another word for 'the sum of all that is'. The term is not ordinarily used as a self-description, even by those widely held to be 'pantheists'. *See also* DEUS SIVE NATURA; PANENTHEISM.

**Pantheismusstreit** (German: 'dispute about pantheism'). A many-faceted controversy in German philosophy and theology shortly after the death of Gotthold Ephraim Lessing (1729–81) over the possibility that he may have been more favourably inclined toward the PANTHEISM of Spinoza (*see* DEUS SIVE NATURA) than had been generally thought. Principal antagonists of the dispute in this narrow sense were Lessing's friend Moses Mendelssohn (1729–86) and Friedrich Heinrich Jacobi (1743–1819), who suggested that Lessing had been a Spinozist. Immanuel Kant (1724–1804) also entered the controversy, as did Johann Wolfgang Goethe (1749–1832). One consequence of it all was that Spinoza was for a time widely discussed and his influence amongst the Romantics was furthered by favourable reference to his thought in *God – Some Conversations* by Johann Gottfried von Herder (1744–1803) and in the *Speeches on Religion* by Friedrich Schleiermacher (1768–1834).

**Pantokrator** (Greek: 'ruler of all'). Christ represented as Lord over life and death.

**Pao-P'u-tzu**. *See* BAO PU ZI.

**papacy**. The office held by the POPE, i.e. the Bishop of Rome and head of the Roman Catholic Church. The term pope, or *papa* ('father'), was also used in ancient times of other leading bishops, e.g. the Bishop of Alexandria. The belief that the Bishop of Rome should be regarded as pre-eminent in the church, being the successor of St Peter, is very old in the western church, but has usually been resisted in the eastern ORTHODOX CHURCH as well as by almost all Protestants. Of the many stages in the development of the theology of the papacy, the most outstanding are without doubt the promulgation of the papal bull UNAM SANCTAM (1302), declaring the subordination of temporal (i.e. political) power to the spiritual power of the papacy, and the decision of the VATICAN COUNCIL of 1870 which stated that definitions of the pope concerning faith and morals were infallible. These assertions have given the papacy a unique position in the authority structure of the Roman Catholic Church.

**papal bull**. *See* BULL .

**Para**. *See* PAÑCARATRA.

**parable**. Generally speaking, a story that has a specific religious point to it, and is thus distinct from an allegory, in which the various details all carry separate meaning. Characteristic of the teaching activity of Jesus as narrated in the New Testament, many of the parables underwent a process of allegorization which can be discerned through comparative study of the Gospels.

**paradigm**. A system of concepts providing a framework for the interpretation of data.

**Paradise**. The primordial, idyllic home of God and man. *See also* EDEN; PARDES.

**paradox**. The simultaneous and meaningful maintenance of notions that are contradictory. In the history of Christian thought, the concept of paradox gained prominence through the writings of Kierkegaard, who identified the absolute paradox as that which thought cannot think by itself unless it was given, namely, the INCARNATION, the event in which God became human and the infinite became finite in history. The concept of paradox might be thought to be applicable in the context of MAHĀYĀNA and especially ZEN BUDDHISM as expressed in the KŌAN. In this case logically contradictory notions are not maintained, but used to lead into a spiritual freedom from the constraints of logical thought.

**Paraphrase of Shem**. *See* NAG HAMMADI.

**Pârâśurāma**. *See* AVATĀRA.

**Pardes** (Hebrew) The mystical 'garden' of Jewish hermeneutics, embracing PSHAT, the 'simple' meaning of the text, *Remez*, its 'allegorical' meaning, *Drush*, its 'interpretation' and *Sod*, its '*esoteric*' meaning. These four levels correspond with the Four Worlds of Kabbalah. The word is derived, like the Greek word *paradeisos* (PARADISE), from Persian.

**Parentalia**. A Roman festival for the dead, generally on 13–21 February. It emphasized the honour and benevolence of the dead, in contrast to LEMURIA. *See also* MANES.

**Parilia**. *See* PALES.

**parinibbāna**. *See* NIṚVĀṆA.

**parinirvāna**. *See* NIṚVÁṆA.

**paritta**. *See* PIRIT.

**parousia** (Greek). In the NEW TESTAMENT and in Christian theology, the imminent presence or appearance of Christ at the end of time.

**Parsis**. *See* ZOROASTRIANISM.

**Parthenon**. The temple of the virgin (Greek: *parthenos*), i.e. the virgin goddess ATHENA on the ACROPOLIS.

**Parvaṭi**. *See* GANEṢA.

**pasa**. *See* ŚAIVA SIDDHANTA; PASUPTAS.

**Pascal's Wager**. An argument put forward by Blaise Pascal (1623–52) in his *Pensées*, seeking to convince a man of the world that religious belief is a safer bet than doubt: if the belief turns out to be true, its adherents will have won an eternity of bliss; if false, they will merely have missed out on a few earthly pleasures.

**Passover** [Hebrew, *Pesah*]. A festival commemorating the angel of death 'passing over' the Israelite homes at the tenth plague, and the EXODUS from Egypt which followed it. As a spring festival of freedom, Passover was one of the three pilgrimage festivals at which Jews in ancient Israel would assemble at the Temple in Jerusalem. It is thought to have been an ancient spring festival which was given a new historical interpretation in the context of the Exodus tradition, the killing of the first lambs being taken as a prefigurement of the killing of the Egyptian firstborn. The festival also incorporated the New Year festival of unleavened bread, which was similarly related to the Exodus theme (*see* MATZAH). On the historical development see Segal 1963; Vaux 1965: 484–93; Kraus 1966. Passover is widely celebrated in Jewish homes, even today, by the conduct of a Passover SEDER.

**pasu**. *See* ŚAIVA SIDDHANTA, PĀŚUPTAS

**Pāśupatas**. A sect of ŚAIVAS, who worship ŚIVA as Lord (*pati*) of cattle (*paśu*). Humans are like cattle, tied by a noose (*pāsa*) which only the grace of the Lord (*pati*) can loose.

**pater noster** (Latin: 'our father'). The first two words of the Lord's Prayer, i.e. the prayer taught by Jesus himself (*Matthew* 6.9ff), in its Latin version. As a single word, the term 'Paternoster' has also been widely used as a name for this prayer.

**pati**. *See* ŚAIVA SIDDHANTA; PĀŚUPTAS.

**paticca-samutpāda**. *See* PRATĪṬYA-SAMUTPĀDA.

**pātimokkha**. *See* PRĀTIMOKṢA.

**patriarch**. Title for a senior BISHOP in the Orthodox Church. Also, a bishop of a chief episcopal see.

**patriarchal religion**. A presumed religious system reconstructed from the narratives of *Genesis* 12–50, the historical validity of which is dependent on the status accorded to the PATRIARCHS. The 'god of the fathers' is sometimes claimed as a distinctive element (Alt 1966b: 1–77) but this may have been misconstrued (Wyatt 1978). As a general term 'patriarchal religion' is also used to indicate religious structures that are dominated by male authority, especially in the Judaeo-Christian tradition.

**patriarchate**. A chief episcopal see, exercising ecclesiastical jurisdiction over adjoining territory. The COUNCIL OF NICAEA (325) recognized Rome, Alexandria and Antioch as patriarchates; the COUNCIL OF CHALCEDON (451) added Jerusalem and Constantinople.

**patriarchs**. The forebears of Israel: the ancestors (specifically Abraham, Isaac and Jacob) who anticipated the settlement in Palestine under Joshua. From a historical point of view the patriarchs are at best eponymous and legendary figures; however, the older historical treatment is now giving way to a more theological understanding of the ancient narratives, bringing out the symbolic meaning of the patriarchs. (Thompson 1974; Seters 1975; McKane 1979; Hendel 1987). *See also* PATRIARCHAL RELIGION.

**patripassianism**. A doctrine stressing the divine unity, which excluded the distinction of the divine persons of the Trinity to such an extent that it could say that the Father suffered crucifixion.

**Patristics**. The study of the teachings of the Church Fathers (Latin: *patres*) from the 2nd to the 8th centuries CE. The period may be considered to be closed with the seventh and last Ecumenical Council (Nicaea 787, dealing with the ICONOCLAST CONTROVERSY) recognized by both Eastern (Orthodox) and Western (Catholic) Christianity. During the patristic period crucial themes of Christian thought were debated and partly though diversely settled: The extent of authoritative scripture; principles of church order and liturgy; the relationship to Platonist philosophy on the one hand and to the Roman state on the other; the nature of the Trinity; the nature of Christ as human and divine (CHRISTOLOGY); the doctrine of grace. Hence the study of Patristics is essential for all later theological study, especially in an ecumenical perspective.

**patshatl**. *See* POTLATCH.

**Paulicianism**. A sect professing dualistic doctrines similar to MANICHAEISM which claimed the authority of Paul of Samosata (3rd century CE) and flourished in the 8th and 9th centuries in Armenia and Asia Minor. After expulsion to Bulgaria the Paulicians influenced the emergence of the BOGOMILS and hence later of the CATHARS (Garsoian 1967).

**pav**. *See* PINKAMA.

**pax deorum** (Latin: 'peace of the gods'). The right relationship between gods and humans to which Roman religious specialists devoted much attention.

**pedanda** (Balinese). An ordained Brahman priest of Hindu-Balinese religion, with profound knowledge of the sacred scriptures and of the various rituals, especially purificatory rites such as consecrating water (AGAMA TIRTA). (Hooykaas 1973).

**Pelagianism**. A teaching named after the British monk Pelagius (4th–5th centuries CE) which stressed that every individual should use his god-given human capacities to realize his own salvation. Original sin and the necessity of grace for good works were denied; Christ's death effected the forgiveness of sins, releasing man from evil and enabling his entry into responsible living following Christ's example.

**Pele**. Hawaiian volcano goddess, currently regarded folkloristically, but nevertheless with some awe, in view of continuing eruptions on Hawaii Island (the largest island of the Hawaiian group).

**pemangku** (Balinese). A Balinese village priest officiating at temple ceremonies and assisting the PEDANDA at various rituals, such as preparing holy water (AGAMA TIRTA). (Hooykaas 1973).

**penance**. One of the seven sacraments of the Roman Catholic Church. On the basis that Jesus gave the power to bind and loose to Peter (*Matthew* 16.19) and to all the apostles (*Matthew* 18.18). ordained priests are believed to be able to free people through the SACRAMENT of penance from sins committed after BAPTISM. Penance usually consists of a prescribed devotional activity such as saying a number of specified prayers (*see* INDULGENCE), but public penance has also included temporary EXCOMMUNICATION, fasting and almsgiving.

**penates** (Latin). Roman household tutelary divinities, often linked with the *lares*, hence the phrase 'lares and penates', meaning minor gods of daily life.

**Pentateuch** (from Greek, *pentateuchos*: 'five-volumed'). The first five books of the Hebrew Bible, traditionally ascribed to MOSES. Intense literary-critical activity led to the view, dominant for a century, that four sources, known as J,E,D and P, accounted for contradictions, doublets and theological diversity. This view has been increasingly challenged (Eissfeldt 1966; Rendtorff 1977; Whybray 1987). The dating varies but recent views tend to assign the Pentateuch to the 6th century BCE (i.e. to the period of the EXILE). This has a bearing on the meaning in that, however ancient some parts may be, the final reference is to exilic experience and reflection (Clines 1978). Narratives about the PATRIARCHS offer paradigms for ISRAEL, interspersed with LAW codes covering social and ritual prescriptions for nascent Judaism. The whole work (excluding parts of *Deuteronomy*) was intended as a parable of the whole Jewish historical experience, drawing on MYTH, folktale and legend, and highlighting various typological possibilities.

**Pentecost**. The Christian festival celebrating the descent or gift of the Holy Spirit as narrated in *Acts of the Apostles*, chapter 2. The name derives from the Greek for 'fiftieth day', since this event is believed to have taken place on the fiftieth day after the resurrection of Christ. Pentecost is also called Whitsunday.

**pentecostalism**. A general designation for Christian groups or movements in which special emphasis is placed on the activity of the Holy Spirit, as manifested especially in speaking in tongues, or GLOSSOLALIA.

**People of the Book**. In Islām, the term used of religions possessing written scripture as revelation from God. Originally this applied to Jews and Christians but was later extended to include other communities (e.g. Zoroastrians and Hindus) that fell under Muslim domination. In Arabic the expression is *ahl al-kitāb*. *See also* DHIMMĪ.

**pepo** (Swahili). An afflictive possession cult (*see* BACHWEZI) on the East African coast, caused by *pepo* ('wind') spirits (Baumann 1975a).

**perahära**. *See* DAḶADĀ MĀLIGĀVA.

**perichoresis** (Greek: 'proceeding around'). A Patristic term referring to the mutual interpenetration of the persons of the Godhead, which, while being a TRINITY, is one and indivisible: each distinct person participates fully in the other's being.

**pericope**. *See* LECTIONARY.

**Perkons**. Baltic thunder god. His name is identical with the Latvian word for thunder. Folklore represents him as a smith whose weapon is a round stone with magic power, and emphasizes his position as head of a household. In his capacity as rain-giver he is worshipped as a fertility god and harvest celebrations are held in his honour. He is also seen as a defender of justice against evil spirits.

**peripteros** (Greek). A temple with a single range of columns around it.

**per se nota**. (Latin: 'known through themselves'). A phrase used by medieval thinkers to describe propositions regarded as self-evident, e.g. that the whole is greater than the part.

**Persephone**. In ancient Greece, the daughter of DEMETER and wife of HADES, who was commemorated in the ELEUSINIAN MYSTERIES.

**persona** (Latin). As originally used of a dramatic role, and so a dramatic mask, *persona* (i.e. person) did not connote a self-conscious being. Tertullian (*c.*150-*c.*225) used *persona* to signify the distinctions in the TRINITY, speaking of three persons in one substance, and to explain unity in CHRISTOLOGY, speaking of one person with two natures. *See also* HYPOSTASIS; PROSOPON.

**pesantren** [pondok] (Indonesian). A traditional religious school roughly comparable to the Middle Eastern MADRĀSA, run by a KIYAI, emphasizing religious studies and the mediation of mystical knowledge. (Geertz 1960a; Steenbrinck 1974; Dhofier 1980).

**peta**. *See* PRETA.

**pétun**. Obsolete French for TOBACCO, derived from a Guarani (South American) term.

**peyote** (Nahuatl) [Aztec, *peyotl*]. In Meso-American Native religions, an important hallucinogenic cactus (*Lophophora williamsii* or *Lophophora lewinii*) and a major spirit. Button-shaped segments of the mescal cactus are used ritually to seek oracular visions (Ruiz de Alarcon 1984). In the post-reservation period in North America, peyote is the centre of a revitalization movement, variously synthesized with Christianity, incorporated as the Native American Church.

**peyotl**. *See* PEYOTE.

**Phanes**. *See* ORPHIC MYSTERIES.

**pharaoh**. An ancient Egyptian king. The term is derived from 'Per-aa', meaning 'Great House' (the king's residence). Each king, believed to be born of the union of the supreme god and the previous king's Great Royal Wife, could mediate between gods and mankind, and could perform religious rituals. When alive, he was believed to be the incarnation of the god HORUS; after death, every king became OSIRIS, god of the underworld. At his coronation, he received crowns imbued with special powers that enabled him to rule effectively. To mark his 30th jubilee, and subsequently at three-yearly intervals, the king celebrated the Sed festival which rejuvenated his ability to rule.

**Pharisees**. The 'sect' of RABBIS in the SECOND TEMPLE period who, unlike the Sadducees, were more concerned with the piety of the ordinary Jew than with Temple ritual. They emphasized the ritual life of the synagogue and the home, interpreting the TORAH broadly, so as to apply it to the conditions of their day. Their theology stressed eschatology, demonology and resurrection. When the Temple was destroyed in 70 CE it was the JUDAISM of the Pharisees which survived, and provided the foundation for RABBINIC JUDAISM. (Herford 1924; Manson 1938; Finkelstein 1962; Schürer 1979: 381–403).

**phenomenology of religion**. Phenomenology is a complex philosophical approach seeking to elaborate a science of phenomena in the sense of a descriptive though (in the narrow sense) non-empirical science of that which appears in consciousness. Though the concept has been used by a number of modern philosophers it is associated today primarily with Edmund Husserl (1859–1938). In the study of religion 'phenomenology' designates a 20th-century development against this background, especially as elaborated by the Dutch scholars G. van der Leeuw, C.J. Bleeker and others. Their approach entailed an exploration of the religious consciousness both in its various manifestations and in relation to an invisible ESSENCE of religion thought to be found in some way or other in all the specific religions. More recently 'phenomenology of religion' has come to be more commonly used to mean the sensitive, objective description of various religions, whether singly or in conjunction, with special consideration being given to the consciousness or self-understanding of the religious people in question, but without dependence on a normative religious or ideological viewpoint (Sharpe 1976).

**phenomenon**. Something known by means of the senses and referred to, therefore, as an appearance or object of perception. Phenomena are the product of the interaction between the world and the innate structures of the human mind through which the world is perceived. Such realities are contrasted, in the philosophy of Immanuel Kant for example, with that which can be thought but not experienced. The latter, noumenal reality, is also contrasted with phenomenal reality as essence is to appearance, so that the NOUMENON is taken to be the thing as it is in itself.

**Philae**. A sacred island near the First Cataract of the Nile, devoted to the cult of Isis. The Egyptian temples (mainly from the Graeco-Roman Period, *c.*332 BCE–3rd century CE) were removed to the neighbouring island of Agilqiyyah in a rescue project after the High Dam was built at Aswan.

**philosophical theology**. The use of philosophical reasoning in the construction, explanation and defence of a THEOLOGY, e.g. by using philosophical arguments to establish the existence of God (*see* NATURAL THEOLOGY), to deduce the main DIVINE ATTRIBUTES, and to reason about topics like IMMORTALITY and the PROBLEM OF EVIL. It is often equated with PHILOSOPHY OF RELIGION, because they both study many of the same questions. But, strictly speaking, philosophical theology is a discipline which seeks to make a positive contribution within theology, whereas philosophy of religion may be critical of any and every theology.

**philosophy of 'as if'**. *See* 'AS IF' PHILOSOPHY.

**philosophy of religion**. Philosophical thought about religion. The phrase was first used in Germany in the late 18th century for the philosophical investigation of the origin, essence and content of religion, and the critique of its value and truth. It is the latter concern which has tended to predominate in recent decades, though the term is also used sometimes to embrace PHILOSOPHICAL THEOLOGY. Thus, modern philosophy of religion is much concerned with assessing the reasons for religious belief, especially arguments for God's existence (*see* NATURAL THEOLOGY), investigating the nature of RELIGIOUS EXPERIENCE and language, and considering the philosophical problems raised by religion. These problems include the coherence of THEISM, the PROBLEM OF EVIL, MIRACLES, IMMORTALITY, and the nature and possibility of religious truth (Davies 1982).

**physico-theological arguments for the existence of god**. The term used by Kant in *Critique of Pure Reason* to designate a type of theistic argument from design in which orderliness of the universe is stressed. *See also* ARGUMENTS FOR THE EXISTENCE OF GOD.

**pietism**. A general term for devotional movements in the context of LUTHERANISM which sought to restore an emotional dimension to personal religion, especially during the 17th and 18th centuries, leading figures being Spener, Gerhardt, Francke and von Zinzendorf. Further afield, German pietism was influential on METHODISM through the person of John Wesley.

**pilgrimage**. The deliberate traversing of a route to a sacred place which lies outside one's normal habitat. Thus, the nature of pilgrimage, as distinct from visiting a holy place such as a local shrine or church, lies as much in the *way* as in the goal. It is for this reason that pilgrimage can be used metaphorically for journeys which have no clear goal at their end, e.g. for the journey of life itself. It is for this reason too that attention has been drawn to the separation of pilgrims from ordinary daily life, defined by Victor Turner in a term derived from van Gennep as 'liminality'. Symbolized by ritual preparations, special clothing and the choice of a prescribed route, this is said to give rise to a special social status experienced by the pilgrims as 'communitas' (Turner 1978). It is the importance of the way which brings out secondary characteristics of pilgrimage. Thus the way is often difficult, for merit (or at least value) is attached to completing it. Because it is difficult and worth completing, paradoxically it is made easier, by roads, airports and special trains. Again, although the way, for example to Compostela, is important in itself, not every pilgrim goes the same way; there are several ways to Compostela, and they are all *the* way to Compostela. The extreme case of the importance of the way may be found in the circulatory Buddhist pilgrimage of Japan, for here the task lies in completing the path to multiple goals, for example 33 temples of the BODHISATTVA Kannon-sama (Pye 1987), so that the goal is dispersed throughout the way. When such a pilgrimage is miniaturized so that it can be completed in one small area in an hour, or even a few minutes, we might even say that the goal is identified with the way. Although the pilgrim's path is emphasized here in order to bring out the structure of pilgrimage, the perceived goals are, of course, important in the pilgrims' consciousness. At the same time they are too varied to be caught in a simple heading: sacred mountains as in China, sacred cities (Jerusalem, Lhasa, Tenri), mausolea (Konya), the Black Stone of Mecca, places where visions and healings have been experienced such as LOURDES. Sometimes one religion displaces an older tradition at the same sacred spot (Mecca) and in other cases the sacred destinations have dual occupancy, e.g. Kataragama in Sri Lanka, or Mount Kailash in the Himalayas. *See also* ḤĀJJ.

**piṇḍapāta** (Pāli: 'alms-round'). The Buddhist monastic practice of going daily for alms, which entails going begging food from door to door every morning at about ten o'clock – a Buddhist monk must take his only meal of the day before noon.

**pinkama** (Sinhalese: 'act of merit'). In Sinhalese Buddhism there is a dichotomy *pin/pav*. *Pin* ('merit') makes for a good rebirth, *pav* ('demerit') makes for a bad rebirth. *Pin* and *pav* are considered quantifiable and transferable, i.e. merit can be acquired and it can be transferred to, for example, a dead relative. The Sinhalese villagers say that they acquire merit or demerit by keeping or breaking the Five Precepts. *Pinkama*, then, is the term used for an act of MERIT. Especially the Ten Good Deeds are acts of merit. The most typical *pinkama* in Sri Lanka are the feeding of monks (DĀNA, Sinhalese *dānē*), preaching (BAṆA) and recitation of sacred texts called PIRIT. Therefore *pinkama* is primarily a public, not a private, event. *See also* KAṬHINA.

**Pir** (Persian). The title given to a ṢŪFĪ master or SHAYKH, especially in the Indian subcontinent.

**pirit** (Sinhalese: 'protection') [Pāli: *paritta*]. A Theravāda term denoting both a collection of Buddhist texts believed to provide physical and mental protection, and the chanting of these texts to avert evil. It is a typical rite of crisis in Buddhism.

**Pistis Sophia** (Greek: 'Faith Wisdom'). A 5th-century gnostic writing in Coptic which belongs to the British Museum's *Codex Askewianus* and was first published in 1851 in Berlin. (Schmidt & MacDermot 1978).

**Pi-yen-lu**. *See* HEKIGANROKU.

**Platform Sūtra**. A Chinese work (Liu Tsu Tan Jing, i.e. Platform Sūtra of the Sixth Patriarch) containing the legend and dialogues of Hui Neng (637–712) (Japanese: Enō), who is regarded as the founder of the 'southern' school of CHAN Buddhism, from which most later schools derived (Yampolsky 1967).

**Platonic philosophy**. *See* ALEXANDRIAN THEOLOGY.

**Platonism**. The adoption and development of the philosophy of Plato (*c*.428–*c*.348 BCE) by later thinkers, which is seen in the ancient world, in much early Christian theology and in the Renaissance. Plato's central doctrine was the theory of Forms or Ideas, which are eternal transcendent realities apprehended by thought and serving as the ideal patterns of earthly realities. Hence Platonism characteristically distinguishes between an unseen eternal world, which is the true reality, and the world of changing phenomena; and it often depreciates the body (*see* DUALISM). Many Christian Platonists treated the Forms as ideas in the mind of God.

**Plato's beard**. W.V.O. Quine's phrase for the tendency to assume that if a statement is meaningful, the entities to which it refers must in some sense exist, resulting in an inflated ontology (Quine 1953). *See also* OCKHAM'S RAZOR.

**plenary indulgence**. An INDULGENCE which frees one from all of the punishment for sins committed which, according to Roman Catholic teaching, would otherwise be suffered in PURGATORY.

**pleroma** (Greek: 'fullness'). A gnostic designation for the supernatural, spiritual world, which is often represented as populated by pairs of celestial beings.

**Plymouth Brethren**. A Christian movement, so named after its foundation at Plymouth, England in 1830, which may accurately be described as millenarian and fundamentalist. A central part is played by the eucharistic service, held on Sundays without the leadership of an ordained ministry. The Plymouth Brethren largely withhold themselves from secular life. A serious split occurred in 1849 between the Open Brethren and the Exclusive Brethren, partly turning on the degree of adaptation to the world thought to be acceptable.

**pneuma** (Greek: 'spirit'). A term from Aristotelian and Stoic psychology which in gnostic texts is often used to designate the unworldly, divine spark trapped in the worldly body awaiting release. True gnostics therefore called themselves 'Pneumatics', while the simpler believers ('Church Christians') were referred to as 'Psychics', the PSYCHE (Greek: 'soul') being the lower spiritual instance in man which unlike the *pneuma* had only limited, if any, potential for salvation. At the same time *pneuma* was the regular word for spirit in early Christian teaching, as in the designation Holy Spirit (*Hagion Pneuma*).

**Pneumatics**. *See* PNEUMA.

**Polo**. *See* PORO.

**polytheism**. The belief, or, rather, the assumption that there are many gods and/or goddesses.

**pomerium** (Latin). The legal and religious boundary of a Roman town, within which the local gods of the place were venerated.

**pongyi** (Burmese). The most common Burmese term for a Buddhist monk (BHIKKHU): (i.e. he who has much merit [PUÑÑA, *see* PUṆYA] and is the means for procuring it for others).

**pontifex maximus**. The head of the Roman pontifical college of the *flamines* (*see* FLAMEN). In later periods, up to the present day, also used as an honorary title for the POPE.

**Pope**. The title used in the Roman Catholic Church for the Bishop of Rome, investing him with supreme authority in questions of faith and morals and in leadership of the HIERARCHY. The special function assigned to the Pope is based on the Roman Catholic understanding of the New Testament passage *Matthew* 16.18ff in which Peter is believed to have been given authority over the other apostles as the rock on which the church is built. Since Peter is also believed to have been the first bishop of Rome, this primacy was claimed for his successors in office. The title was also used of archbishops in other centres such as Alexandria. After the fall of the Roman Empire the popes at Rome took over the title Pontifex Maximus earlier used by Roman Emperors in their high-priestly function. At the same time any idea that spiritual leadership could be transferred to the PATRIARCHS of Constantinople, or even Moscow ('the third Rome'), was firmly rejected. In modern times the juridical position of papal (i.e. the Pope's) authority within the Roman Catholic Church has been strengthened even more (*see* INFALLIBILITY) and the claim to authority over non-Catholic Christians has hardened accordingly, in spite of progress in other aspects of inter-church relationships. *See also* HOLY SEE; PAPACY.

**Popol Vuh**. A major religious text from the Quiche Maya (Guatemalan highlands) containing materials ranging from cosmogonic myths to the events leading to the founding of the Quiche kingdom. Originally in hieroglyphic form, it was rewritten in the 16th century in a Latin alphabet adaptation and is highly significant for ethno-archaeological correlations (Tedlock 1985).

**Poro** [Polo, Purrah]. A men's association or 'secret society', widely spread in Sierra Leone and Liberia. The term occurs in various languages of these countries such as Kpelle, Gbande, Loma, Susu, Bullom and Temne, and is also widely used in francophone West Africa to designate associations of a generally similar type but with a different local name, for example among the Senufo. Initiation into the Poro gave the status of a full member of society. The initiates were secluded in the bush, where they underwent trials, training, ritual death and rebirth. Seclusion often lasted several years. Poro is a graded association in which ancestor worship is central. In former times it exercised strong political, diplomatic and juridical powers. A complementary women's association is SANDE. (Little 1965–6; Giorgi 1977).

**posadha**. *See* UPOSATHA.

**Poseidon**. The ancient Greek god of the sea, widely worshipped by sailors. The son of CRONOS and RHEA and brother of ZEUS and Posdidon, Poseidon became god of the sea when he and his brothers overthrew Cronos; however, he was also regarded as a deity of fertility by virtue of rain and rivers. *Compare* NEPTUNE.

**positionlessness**. The attainment of spiritual peace on the basis of not advancing, maintaining or defending a specific intellectual position, while making use of the inherent weakness of any such positions to liberate others from attachment to them. Such *positionlessness* is characteristic of the VIMALAKĪRTI Sūtra and of the MĀDHYAMIKA School.

**positive religion**. A term used to refer to the particular religious traditions that are empirically observable, in contradistinction to that which might be thought to be common to all religions and is available only conceptually as the essence of religion. Immanuel Kant, for example, contrasts the essence of religion as the ideal of moral behaviour with observable Christianity, its dogmas, rituals and the like, which constitute but one set of techniques, so to speak, for fulfilling one's moral (i.e. religious) obligation.

**positive theology**. Positive theology is akin to POSITIVE RELIGION in that it is based on the specific givenness of revelation in history. Such theology attempts by historical-empirical methods to gather and analyse the revelatory data from the positive sources scripture and tradition, forgoing abstract philosophical speculation.

**positivism**. The belief that all genuine human knowledge is contained within the boundaries of science. It is exemplified in Logical Positivism, developed by Rudolf Carnap and others in Vienna in the 1920s and 1930s, but is also found in earlier thinkers, e.g. Auguste Comte. Positivism has usually been understood as leaving no room for religious meaning.

**post-exilic**. Pertaining to the Jewish people in the period after the EXILE.

**postmodernism**. There are at least three important foci for the use of this word. The first is the realm of culture, where 'postmodern' artistic forms in literature, painting, music and architecture are distinguished from those of 'modernism'. Broadly speaking, postmodernism eschews modernism's technological purity, psychological introspection and lack of historical reference, in favour of eclectic and ironic historical allusion, playful use of traditional genres and plot-modes, and foregrounded artifice and ambiguity. It tends to combine a cultivated allusiveness with a greater enjoyment of popular culture than modernism was prepared to entertain.

The second is the socio-economic sphere. Here the term is associated with the decline in importance of heavy industry and the supervisory state, conjoined with the increased dominance of market economics in all areas of social life. In place of the central state's confidence in a modernist project of scientific planning and the inculcation of humane secular values, comes a market mediation of many different cultural preferences, many of them of a 'traditional' character, at least in outward appearance.

The third is the sphere of philosophy. Here the term refers to disenchantment with the 'enlightenment project', conceived as seeking the peaceful uniting of human beings on the basis of a consensus about scientific truth and rational, ethical values. On the whole, thinkers labelled 'postmodern' are those who embrace a relativizing scepticism and a concomitant cultural pluralism. For this perspective the public domain is reduced to a site of regulated and open-ended struggle, which relates to the recent social dominance of market economics. However, the term is also applied to other thinkers – often under Wittgensteinian influence – who wish to reinstate a traditional, pre-enlightenment belief and practice, but with a full 'post modern' awareness that they are espousing merely one perspective, a linguistic 'form of life' which cannot be argued for on any universal basis. *Compare* MODERNISM.

**poststructuralism**. Structuralism tends to reduce syntagmatic, temporal sequences to instances of a paradigmatic 'spatial' coding of a set of simultaneous relationships. Poststructuralism reverses this emphasis, concentrating on the way in which a particular diachronic development can modify or subvert the static inventory of a fixed synchronic system. In Saussurean linguistics, which has greatly influenced the structuralist outlook, a particular utterance, or *parole*, only has meaning in terms of its occupation of a foreordained syntactic position in relation to the totality of all other linguistic elements, which in their pre-established grammatical organization constitute the deepest level of language, or *langue*. Poststructuralism tends to reject this subordination of *parole* to *langue*, stressing that particular utterances can be creatively innovative, thereby rendering the 'total' grammatical system indeterminate and always incomplete. While the structuralist view that language organizes knowledge and constitutes subjectivity remains in place, poststructuralism sees language as an anarchic process, whose formalities are subordinate to the shifting strategies of force and desire.

The difference between the two outlooks should not, however, be exaggerated. Only certain structuralists, like Claude Lévi-Strauss, have embedded synchronic organization in a natural order which humans cannot fully penetrate and history cannot modify. Others, like Michel Serres, simply assert the dominance of different paradigms in different historical eras. Here the problem of 'paradigm shifts' already points to a preoccupation with the non-formalizable. *See also* DIFFERENCE; POSTMODERNISM; NIHILISM; STRUCTURALISM.

**Potalaka**. The mountain in southern India which is the legendary dwelling place of the bodhisattva AVALOKITEŚVARA. By extension it is also used to refer to the traditional dwelling of the DALAI LAMA in Tibet, and to other mountains where Avalokiteśvara is believed to dwell.

**potlatch** (from Nootka, *patshatl*). The major ritual of Native American cultures of the northwest coast. It is a complex ceremony of sharing material goods in conjunction with renewing spiritual and socio-political ritual relationships. These clan-sponsored ceremonies have become widely known because of the often massive and articulated masks, the elaborate costumes, the theatrical staging and the complexity of the visual symbolism of the dances, as well as the lavishness of the gifts offered the guests. Banned by the Canadian government until the second half of the 20th century, with the ritual paraphernalia being confiscated, it is now undergoing a revitalization (Walena 1981).

**poya**. *See* UPOSATHA.

**pragmatism**. A philosophical movement that emerged in late 19th-century America, associated largely with Charles S. Peirce (1839–1914), William James (1842–1910) and John Dewey (1859–1952), whose work represents a rejection of traditional philosophy. Rather than simply trying to understand the world they sought to emphasize the relevance of knowledge to practical life situations. Thus, seeing thought as primarily instrumental in character, they minimized the distinction between thought and practice. Pragmatism forms the intellectual background to William James' influential work *The Varieties of Religious Experience* (1902).

**prajñā** (Sanskrit: 'wisdom') [Pāli: *paññā*]. A Buddhist term denoting the insight into the nature of reality, especially causality (*see* PRATITYASAMUTPĀDA), tantamount to Enlightenment. It should not be confused with wisdom in a more general sense or with *Sophia* in Hellenism. *See also* PAÑÑA; PRAJÑĀ-PĀRAMITĀ.

**prajñā-pāramitā** (Sanskrit). The perfection of wisdom (*prajñā*, also translated as 'insight'), a quality cultivated by BODHISATTVAS in MAHĀYĀNA Buddhism. By means of *prajñā* bodhisattvas perceive all things in their true nature as having the quality of buddha-hood, or of being intrinsically 'empty' of discriminatory characteristics. It is the leading concept in a group of sūtras dominating the early phase of Mahāyāna Buddhism. (Conze 1958, 1960). *See also* MĀDHYAMIKA.

**Prakṛti**. *See* PURĀṆAS, SĀMKHYA.

**Prambanan** (Indonesian). A site near Yogyakarta, Central Java, well known for its ancient Javanese Hindu CANDI, a complex of temples devoted to the TRIMURTI (Stöhr & Zoetmulder 1965).

**pranava**. *See* OM.

**prapatti** (Sanskrit: 'surrender'). The highest act of BHAKTI, in which a person formally surrenders his or her self and possessions to God. In a general way the BHAGAVADGĪTĀ refers to it; it became a theological topos in RĀMĀNUJA and later Śrīvaiṣṇavism, where it is also formalized in a specific ritual.

**Prarabkarma**. *See* PUNARJANMA.

**Prārthana Samāj** (Hindi: 'Prayer Society'). Inspired by the social teachings of the BRĀHMO SAMĀJ, this group formed in 1867 in Bombay. Its most eminent leader was M. G. Ranade, whose principal concerns were the elimination of caste restrictions and improvement in the status of women and untouchables.

**Prasannapadā**. *See* MĀDHYAMIKA.

**Prasthana trayi**. *See* ĀCĀRYA.

**prasthana trayi**. *See* ĀCĀRYA.

**prātimokṣa** (Sanskrit: 'disciplinary code') [Pāli: *pātimokkha*]. The corpus of Buddhist monastic rules governing the life of the individual monk or nun. The rules, which are to be recited regularly every fortnight, are classified and arranged in the *Vinaya Piṭaka* (*see* VINAYA) by the penalty set for infringement in decreasing order of gravity.

**pratītya-samutpāda** (Sanskrit: 'arising by way of condition') [Pāli: paṭicca-samuppāda]. A Buddhist term denoting the driving forces of the round of rebirths (SAṂSĀRA) and usually translated as 'dependent origination'. The causal chain is usually presented as having the following twelve links or conditions. Through (1) ignorance are conditioned (2) the karmic formations; because of these formations consciousness (3) continues even after physical death and through consciousness are conditioned (4) the mental and physical phenomena to which (5) the six senses (including mental consciousness) belong; through the six senses are conditioned (6) the sense contacts, which involve a pleasant, an unpleasant or a neutral feeling, (7) through which is conditioned (8) thirst or desire (TṚṢṆĀ); this causes (9) clinging or attachment to the five aggregates (SKANDHA), through which is conditioned (10) becoming, the action of which produces (11) birth, the appearance of the five aggregates and internal organs; and through birth is conditioned (12) old age and death. This process continues perpetually until one attains enlightenment from this conditioned vicious circle. Enlightenment, as presented in the story of the Buddha's enlightenment, involves being fully aware of all the interconnections between the above-named factors. Though normally presented as a list of twelve, some versions, possibly older, have only nine or ten. Later interpretations, suggesting puzzlement over the precise sequence, interpreted the whole in terms of three subsequent existences or presented the twelve as a circular chain of existences.

**pratyekabodhi**. *See* BODHI.

**pratyekabuddha** (Sanskrit: 'solitarily enlightened buddha') [Pāli: *paccekabuddha*]. A buddha who has attained enlightenment independently by himself/herself and does not teach others, but lives a solitary life as a hermit. *See also* BODHI; SAMYAKSAMBUDDHA.

**pravrajyā** (Sanskrit: 'going forth' [from home to homelessness]') [Pāli: *pabbajja*]. Formal entry into the Buddhist Order as a novice (*śrāmaṇera*; Pāli: *sāmaṇera*). Nowadays known specifically as 'lower ordination' or ordination as a novice, thereby distinguishing it from the 'higher ordination' (UPASAMPAD) or ordination as a monk (BHIKṢU). Originally the two were, however, the same.

**prayascittas**. *See* TAPAS.

**Prayerbook**. *See* MANDAEANS.

**predestination**. The doctrine that, since salvation depends on the divine gift of grace, God preordains those who will be saved and hence knows in advance those who will be damned.

**presbyter**. *See* PRESBYTERIANISM.

**presbyterianism**. The general name for those churches, such as the Church of Scotland, in which the government of the church is placed in the hands of presbyters or elders; this being believed to be more clearly in accordance with the pattern documented in the New Testament than other forms of church hierarchy or government.

**Preserved Tablet**. *See* LAWḤ MAḤFŪZ.

**preta** (Sanskrit: 'gone forth', 'dead'). The 'ghost' of a person who, for whatever reason, usually because of sudden death or improperly carried out last rites, did not find liberation and is roaming the earth. There is a very rich preta-lore in India; an entire section of the *Garuḏa Purāṉa*, the 'preta kalpa' is devoted to descriptions of these ghosts, and Indian folk-literature generally abounds with ghost stories.

In the Buddhist universe, the term denotes a class of living creatures – below gods, animals and men but above demons – considered to be hideous ghosts suffering from hunger and other discomforts. Although in theory a *preta* can be the reincarnation of anyone's relation, it is in practice regarded as one's own dead relation, usually a dead parent. Rice or other food may be put out for the *preta*, who are often referred to in English as 'hungry ghosts'.

**priest**. A term used in the context of many quite different religions to designate one who mediates, usually through specialist routines such as sacrifice, between God or gods and humankind. The English word itself arose as a contraction of the term 'presbyter' (*see* PRESBYTERIANISM) current in the New Testament, but it has commonly taken on the meaning of the Greek *hiereus* and Latin *sacerdos*, which bore the wider meaning indicated above. There is a complex theology of priesthood in biblical and later Christian theology with significant divergences of interpretation. In particular, the strong identification of the ordained priesthood with the sacrifice of the mass performed by his mediation is characteristic of Catholic Christianity but rejected as unbiblical in most Protestant churches. In principle the latter usually argue, with Luther, for the priesthood of all believers. More widely, the term 'priest' is of sufficient generality to be used in the context of many religions. This is true even for Buddhism, where sacrifice is practically unknown, but where in East Asia ordained 'monks' who care for small temples specialize in rituals that link the living and the dead and thus in effect carry out a priestly activity.

**Priestly Work**. An exilic or early post-exilic composition gathering traditional tales, legal traditions and myths into a symbolic account of Jewish history from creation to the writer's time (550–400 BCE). Episodes were selected to reflect the exilic concerns of nascent Judaism (land tenure, national survival, racial purity, strict obedience to TORAH etc.). The Priestly Work (known as P; *see* PENTATEUCH) comprises *Genesis–Numbers*, *Deuteronomy* 34 and perhaps *Joshua* 13–21

(Ackroyd 1968: 63, 97). (*See also* Friedman 1981: 44–132; Clines 1978.)

**primal religion**. A classificatory term used to denote the religion associated with a tribal or clan culture while avoiding the evolutionary overtones of 'primitive'. Primal religion is particularistic, being the religion of specific peoples in specific places. It accepts, celebrates and manages the basic processes of life: conception, birth, adolescence, death; growth and harvest, hunt and capture; it seeks to avoid or counter disease, disaster and social damage. Mythologically the origin of the world (*see* COSMOGONY) is often linked to the origin of the group. Ritually the individual is transferred from one social position to another, through the various stages of life (rites of transition), until he joins the ancestors. Being related to an integrated, natural life-pattern, primal religion is typical of pre-modern and especially pre-literate societies. However, in some instances complex religious traditions, notably Hinduism, Judaism, Confucianism and Shintō, show many signs of having arisen in a process of continuous adjustment from the primal religion of the relevant ethnic group. (Turner 1969).

**primbon** (Javanese). A Javanese religious tract, mostly an instructional notebook, consulted as a kind of mystical almanac 'to co-ordinate earthly events with cosmic conditions' (Mulder 1983a) (Hadiwijono 1967).

**prime**. The psalms, prayers, readings and versicles used at the first hour of the liturgical day, i.e. at 6 a.m. in religious houses and by priests using a breviary. Similarly 'terce', 'sext' and 'none' are those of the third, the sixth and the ninth hours respectively.

**prime mover**. *See* COSMOLOGICAL ARGUMENTS FOR THE EXISTENCE OF GOD(S).

**Priscillianism**. A movement inspired by the teachings of Priscillian which had a considerable following in Italy, France and Spain from the late 4th to the early 6th centuries. Priscillian himself, for a while Bishop of Avila, was condemned to death with several followers at Bordeaux, this being the first case of capital punishment for HERESY. His teaching, described by its opponents as Manichaeist (*see* MANICHAEISM), distinguished sharply between spirit and matter and regarded the latter, along with the body, marriage, procreation and meat-eating as belonging to the realm of the devil.

**priyai** (Javanese). A member of the educated aristocratic class of Java, 'stressing the Hinduist aspects and related to the bureaucratic element' (Geertz 1960a:6). (Niel 1970; Koenjaraningrat 1971; Sutherland 1973, 1975, 1979).

**priyayi**. *See* PRIYAI.

**problem of evil**. The problem posed by the apparent incompatibility between evil in the world and the existence of an almighty and perfectly good God. An attempt to reconcile the two is known as a THEODICY. The classical starting point for consideration of the problem is the *Book of Job*, in which Job's faith is tested by various forms of suffering.

The Christian Fathers hardly treat physical evil, except in reference to demons prompting it, and as a training in patience and courage. Ignatius of Antioch (*c.*35–*c.*107), recognizing that God was especially revealed in the 'evil' of crucifixion, saw no theoretical answer to evil's existence, it being an occasion for obedience to God's trustworthy goodness. Athanasius (296–373) likewise sees persecution as a time for Christian witness and the willing facing of the death penalty as 'proof' of RESURRECTION. Irenaeus (*c.*130–200) rejected GNOSTICISM's allegation that evil was an illusion of finite, temporal existence; he attributed it to rebellion against God. Origen (*c.*185–254) equally attributed evil to abuse of freedom in a relatively stable physical order. Consequential evil is both a punishment and a disciplining back into goodness.

Modern treatments distinguish between moral and natural (or physical) evil. The most common approach to the former is the 'Free Will Defence': moral evil is regarded as the result of human freedom, a price worth paying either because freedom is an instrinsic good or because its good effects outweigh its bad ones. A popular approach to natural evil is the 'Greater Good' defence, which sees it as a necessary feature of a world which is to serve as an arena for character-building or 'soul-making'. (Hick 1978).

**procession**. A technical term in Patristic theology indicating the derivative relationship of the HOLY SPIRIT, who 'proceeds' from the Father, in contrast with the Son, who is 'begotten'. *Compare* GENERATION.

**process philosophy/theology**. In its most general sense, any system of thought that stresses 'continuum' and 'becoming' over 'substance' and 'being', or the 'dynamic' over the 'static'. In this sense, it can embrace Heraclitus (*d c.*480 BCE) and the BUDDHA (5th century BCE), F. W. J. Schelling (1775–1854) and Teilhard de Chardin (1881–1955). In its more specific sense, the term refers mainly to the intellectual systems developed by Alfred North Whitehead (1861–1947), Charles Hartshorne (*b* 1897) and by those who have been influenced by either or both of these thinkers. The theologically most influential exponent of 'process thought' remains Hartshorne, who has developed a 'di-polar theism' in an attempt to overcome the alternative of THEISM and PANTHEISM. Hartshorne has sometimes called the result PANENTHEISM, according to which God is world-inclusive, but 'God' and 'World' are not interchangeable in the Spinozan sense of DEUS SIVE NATURA. To be God, God requires *a* world, but not necessarily *this* world; to be the world, however, the world requires not simply *a* God, but *the* one and only God. Moreover, according to Hartshorne, God is 'perfect' not in the sense of unchanging, but in the sense of being unsurpassable by any other actual or possible being; God is surpassable by God alone. In this sense, God – too – is 'in process' of becoming what God is. (Whitehead 1969; Hartshorne 1948).

**projection**. In psychoanalysis, a defence mechanism through which psychological needs, feelings, and attitudes (often unconscious) are transferred on to people and objects in one's environment. Projections can also be transferred on to spiritual beings such as gods, spirits and saints. Thus, in the case of Christianity, a father image is projected on to God and a mother image is projected on to the Virgin Mary.

**projectionism**. The theory that God or gods are no more than objectifications of human wishes or needs. Most theories of projection are reflexive: some subjective wish is projected upon some other object, which can be either real or imaginary, and it in turn is then believed to act upon the original subject as if it were an independent agent. Such theories are found in Eastern and Western thought, ancient and modern. Xenophanes observed that the gods are given qualities that are properly human, and that if animals could draw gods, horses would portray them as horses and lions, as lions. In his *Confessions*, Augustine treated 'pagan' gods as projections of human desires. In the Tibetan *Book of the Dead*, the dying are instructed that the gods and devils that appear at death are merely 'dream images', projections of inner karmic forces. Such theories in modern Western thought are in the main traceable to the work of Ludwig Feuerbach (1804–72) and Karl Marx (1818–83), on the one hand, or to that of Sigmund Freud (1856–1939) and the psychoanalytic school, on the other. Some social psychologists, notably Eric Fromm (1900–80), build on both Marx and Freud. Another strand in the tradition of projectionism builds on aspects of Kantian thought as extended in the 'AS IF' PHILOSOPHY of Hans Vaihinger (1852–1933).

**Prometheus**. An ancient Greek HERO who stole fire from heaven and helped humans plan sacrifices so that they as well as the gods would benefit from the food consumed in the sacrificial meal. ZEUS regarded this as catering to the arrogance of mankind and Prometheus was chained to a rock in the Caucasus, his liver being eaten away by an eagle, until he was released by HERAKLES (Hercules).

**Promised Land**. *See* HOLY LAND.

**pro-nuncio**. *See* NUNCIO.

**proofs for the existence of God(s)**. *See* COMMON CONSENT ARGUMENTS; COSMOLOGICAL ARGUMENTS; DESIGN ARGUMENTS; FIVE WAYS; MORAL ARGUMENTS; ONTOLOGICAL ARGUMENTS; RATIO ANSELMI.

**Prose Edda**. A prose account of Germanic mythology written in the 13th century by Snorri Sturluson (1179–1241). The Prose Edda frequently refers to and incorporates older poems contained in the EDDA collection.

**prosopon**. The Greek equivalent of Latin PERSONA. For Nestorius (*d c.*451) *prosopon* signified an individual's external aspect. It thus described the union of God and man in Christ, Christ being the common *prosopon* of that which was united. *See also* NESTORIANISM.

**protestant ethic**. A term used by the sociologist Max Weber (1864–1920) to designate virtues such as diligence and thrift, understood as a religious duty and leading to economic success, which is in turn believed to be a confirmation of election by divine providence. Weber regarded this complex of Protestant beliefs and values as having contributed significantly to the development of western capitalism. Conversely he regarded its absence in other cultures such as India and China, where capitalism failed to develop rapidly in spite of the availability of relevant technological knowledge, as a negative confirmation of the thesis. More recently the argument has been modified, especially by Bellah (1957) to take account of more detailed studies of the example of Japan, where analogies to the Protestant ethic have been perceived, and correlated with the process of modernization including the development of capitalism. Weber's classic work on the subject was *The Protestant Ethic and the Rise of Capitalism*, first published in German.

**Protestantism**. The generic term for all those forms of Christianity which reject the authority of the PAPACY and regard the Bible as the central source of Christian teaching. Historically its most influential forms have been LUTHERANISM and CALVINISM, in turn leading to PRESBYTERIANISM. Churches such as the ANGLICAN COMMUNION are in principle protestant in the above sense even though not formally defined as such. Although it is the question of authority which is fundamental, this is resolved in a spectrum of positions ranging from liberal protestantism to extreme biblical fundamentalism, and in a great variety of church organization and government. At the same time these solutions are not usually sought for their own sake but in order to bring out specific aspects of Christian teaching positively, e.g. 'justification by faith alone' in Lutheranism. The shift in the focus of authority has led to an emphasis on preaching and exposition of the Bible as the Word of God, sometimes, but by no means always, with a corresponding neglect of sacramental worship.

**pseudepigrapha**. Any literature that is falsely attributed to a well-known figure. The term refers commonly, as 'the Pseudepigrapha', to post-biblical texts attributed to such partly legendary figures as Moses, Enoch, the Twelve Patriarchs, etc. *See also* APOCALYPTIC.

**pshat**. (Hebrew). The 'simple' meaning of a text, which can be described in terms of its vocabulary, grammar and syntax.

**psyche**. In ancient Greek, that part of human beings which survives the death of the body and journeys to HADES, the underground realm. The term has passed into general western usage to refer to the inner person and hence into the modern term 'psychology'.

**psychoanalysis**. A therapeutic school that has its origins in the work and research of the neurologist Sigmund Freud (1856–1939) in Vienna. Of fundamental importance is the assumption that unconscious psychological processes in the inner self and symptoms of neurosis are caused by unconscious conflicts. Other areas of psychoanalysis of particular interest are theories relating to dreaming, sexual (libidinous) instinct, and those which deal with the way in which the ego defends itself when it comes in conflict with instincts (id) and demands made by the world at large (superego).

Freud himself analysed religious phenomena from the point of view of his own school of psychoanalytical thought. He identified the ritualistic characteristics of religion as parallels to the involuntary acts of neurotics, the need for atonement as consequences of unsolved Oedipal conflicts, the emphasis of the transcendental nature of religion as illusions and daydreams, and the religious feeling of guilt as an expression of the struggle to control one's death instinct (Thanatos). Many of Freud's followers have revised his theories in different ways. The applications of the theories in the interpretation of different phenomena in the human psyche in which religious ingredients may be found are many.

**psychology of religion**. The modern psychological study of religion has developed, by and large, in parallel with the emergence of psychology as a scientific discipline (for which see Sancher 1990). The dominant theories in the psychology of religion, therefore, are the theories which have had wide currency within academic and clinical psychology, ranging from the more speculative (derived in the main from the psychoanalytic tradition) to the more empirical or even experimentalist.

In the United States, psychology of religion experienced an upsurge around the end of the 19th century. Among its foremost representatives may be mentioned G. Stanley Hall (1844–1924), E.E. Starbuck (1866–1947) and James H. Leuba (1868–1946). Subjects of special interest were conversion and mysticism. The name most widely known in the field of psychology of religion in the United States, however, is that of William James (1842–1910), whose influential Gifford Lectures were published in 1902 under the title *The Varieties of Religious Experience*. This work deals with the relation between religion and physiology, the question of the reality of the unseen world, conversion, mysticism and holiness. In particular, it proposes a typology of religious experience along psychological lines.

In Europe, the psychology of religion began to take the form of a scientific discipline just before the turn of the century. Within the 'experimental' (Dorpat) school, test subjects were requested to consider religious texts and asked to express the associations they gave rise to and to describe the pictures that were created in their minds in response to the texts. Representatives of this line of enquiry were Oswald Külpe (1862–1915), Karl Girgensohn (1875–1925) and Werner Grühn (1887–1961).

Widely influential was the more speculative school of depth psychology, which had its origins in the pioneering work of Sigmund Freund (1856–1939). The basic theme of Freud's *Totem and Taboo* and *The Future of an Illusion* is that religion serves to compensate for emotional deprivations in psychodynamic fashion. The 'analytical psychology' of Carl Jung (1875–1961) with its notions of the 'collective unconscious' and 'archetype' took more account of Asian traditions and thus contributes to what has since become known as New Age spirituality. This departure from his Freudian background is documented in *The Undiscovered Self* (1958).

While such theorizing is by no means dead, increasing attention has been paid in the meantime to the procedures and findings of psychology as 'hard science'. Argyle and Beit-Hallahmi's *The Social Psychology of Religion* (1975) provides an excellent survey of research of an empiricist and experimental variety. This is designed, for example, to explore the possible relationships and causal effects between religious affiliation and beliefs, on the one hand, and social and political views on the other (Meadow & Kahoe 1984). At the same time the theme which fascinated the pioneer William James continues to attract much interest. Thus, theories derived from the experimental mainstream are applied to account for the genesis of various kinds of religious experience, not least those associated with conversion (Batson & Ventis 1982; Proudfoot 1985). In Scandinavia, particular interest has been shown in 'role theory' (Sunden 1966; Holm 1987).

In that the psychological study of religion is bound up with the issues of mainstream psychological inquiry in general works there is much about religion in general works on psychology (e.g. Zimbardo *et al*. 1977). However, the psychological study of religion is also bound up with other disciplines and is of considerably more importance than might appear if attention is simply paid to those who address religion *as* psychologists. It is virtually impossible to find a sociological or anthropological account of religion which does not introduce psychological ingredients. Historically speaking, such contributions have not always been especially sophisticated; but the fact remains that psychological theories and assumptions have generally played crucial roles in accounts of the religious life. One only need think of the role played by anxiety and 'loneliness' in Max Weber's portrayal (1904–5) of the operation of the PROTESTANT ETHIC of work (Weber 1976). Sophisticated recourse to the psychological factor is found in the culture and personality school of American anthropology (Spindler 1980). Even more sophisticated theorizing is found in works which draw on contemporary psychological thought, for example Lawson and McCauley's *Rethinking Religion* (1990). As their subheading 'Connecting cognition & culture' serves to indicate, cognitive science is to the fore, as indeed it is in Sperber's influential *Rethinking Symbolism* (1975). Meanwhile, research on such classic topics as conversion, especially to new religious movements, continues to be developed (Robbins 1988).

Along with progress inspired by western psychological theory (see Brown 1965 for an overview), researchers are now studying the 'psychologies' embedded in religions themselves. Whether implicitly or explicitly, religions always provide accounts of human nature: what has gone wrong; how things should be; how things can be put right. Hence there have been various studies of cultural psychologies and their 'technologies' of the self, especially of small-scale societies (Lutz 1988) and eastern traditions (Collins 1982; Kippenberg *et al*. 1990). These 'indigenous' accounts (Heelas & Lock 1981) cannot be ignored in the study of how religions provide ways of making sense of what it is to be a 'person', help 'construct' emotions, and serve to influence action.

**psychostasia**. *See* WEIGHING THE HEART.

**Ptah**. A god of Memphis in ancient Egypt, patron of craftsmen and a creator-deity, associated with the dead (Holmberg 1946).

**pūjā** (Sanskrit: 'worship'). The worship of a sacred image, as done by VAIṢṆAVAS. It forms part of the religious duties of Vaiṣṇavas and is highly specified in its details. Both *pūjā* in homes and in temples has to follow a prescribed ritual so as to be effective. Since it is the central activity of temple-priests, these are called *pūjāris*. The term is also current in Buddhism, where it has the meaning of an act of veneration, typically through the placing of offerings before a Buddha image.

**pulpŏp** (Korean). The 'law' of the Buddha, i.e. Buddhadharma.

**Punarjanma** (Sanskrit). 'Rebirth' in a bodily sense, i.e. reincarnation, is a universally accepted tenet with Hindus. It is presupposed by all schools of religion whose very *raison d'être* is to provide persons with means to avoid rebirth. Rebirth is due to KARMA accumulated and not disposed of during a lifetime; the quality of existence one is reborn into depends on the *prārabdha karma* that a person has at the time of death. The overcoming of rebirth and redeath is the central theme of the UPANIṢADS.

**Punarmṛtyu**. *See* MṚTYU.

**Punjabi Suba**. A Punjabi-speaking State (*see* KHĀLISTĀN).

**punna**. *See* PŪṆYA.

**Puññakamma** (Pāli: 'merit-making', 'acquiring merit'). In Theravāda countries, a term referring to the idea that the Buddhist monks and monasteries provide a 'field of merit' (PUÑÑAKKHETTA) for the laity. By taking part in the various festivals, ceremonies and acts of veneration as well as by giving alms and gifts to the monasteries and the monks, the laity acquire merit for a better rebirth. Thus 'merit-making' has become the path of the laity.

**puññakkhetta** (Pāli: 'field of merit'). A Theravāda term denoting that the Buddhist monks and the monasteries and temples provide a 'field of merit' for the laity. This means that by meritorious deeds the laity can acquire merit for a better rebirth and thus eventually attain NIRVĀṆA. *See also* PUÑÑAKAMMA.

**puṇya** (Sanskrit) [Pāli: *puñña*]. Merit; an Indian, and especially a Buddhist term denoting both a meritorious deed and a good KARMA. Occasionally used as a term for the potential results or results of good *karma*. *See also* MERIT.

**Purāṇas** (Sanskrit: 'Ancient Books'). A large class of voluminous works, containing mythologies, laws, genealogies of kings, accounts of creation etc. originally existing only in oral traditions but at various times and in various parts of the country reduced to writing. Besides the 18 *Mahāpurāṇas* and the 18 *Upapurāṇas* (most of them associated with BRAHMA, SIVA, VIṢṆU, Devī) there are countless others, such as the *Sthālapurāṇas* or accounts associated with particular holy places. They are the most important source of religious education for the average Hindu and still very popular. Some of them, e.g. the *Viṣṇupurāṇa and the Bhāgavatam*, considered as ŚRUTI ('revelation') by some schools of VAIṢṆAVAS, have also been utilized in scholarly theological works.

**Pure Land**. The 'pure land' of a Buddha. The concept arose on the basis of the idea that every buddha, in the various cosmic periods and directions, presides over a 'Buddha-field' (*buddhakṣetra*), which, as a bodhisattva, he has to prepare and purify. The Chinese term *jing tu* first referred to this purification of Buddha-lands, but then came to mean the pure (Buddha) land as an established state, as also in Japanese (*jōdo*). While there is a strong tradition of 'seeing' the pure land of a Buddha (especially of AMITĀBHA Buddha) in the mind, there is an equally strong tradition of objective representation.

**purgative path**. *See* VIA UNITIVA.

**purgatory**. In Roman Catholic belief, a temporary place of suffering for those who will be saved at the Last Judgement but are not pure enough to enter the bliss of heaven immediately. Through suffering in purgatory the remains of sin are purged. An INDULGENCE assures the remission of some of the time which would otherwise need to be spent in purgatory.

**Purim** (Hebrew: 'lots'). The Festival of 'Lots', celebrating the day (appointed by a random draw) upon which all the Jews of the Persian Empire were to have been murdered. According to the story, the Jewish Queen Esther, encouraged by her pious uncle Mordecai, turned the favour of the Persian Emperor Ahasuerus against the anti-semitic Prime Minister, Haman. Their fortunes were reversed, so that it was the anti-semites and not the Jews who were destroyed. Because of this reversal, Purim is celebrated as a Jewish carnival festival. The *Scroll of Esther* is read in its entirety, and people rattle noise-makers whenever the name of Haman is mentioned. It is traditional to get drunk 'to the point that one does not know' the difference between cursing Mordecai and praising Haman. Like ḤANUKKAH, it is a prominent holiday though it originated long after the times of the TORAH.

**puritanism**. A term that was first applied to those who, during the reign of Elizabeth I of England, objected to liturgical practices and vestments for which there was no scriptural basis. By extension it was then applied to a wide range of reformist movements and churches in England and America that sought to draw the consequences of an unmediated reading of the Bible for Christian life, thus Presbyterians, Baptists and Quakers. This did not lead to a common puritan theology although the influence of CALVINISM was strong. Self-denial and austerity were valued in practical life as the right path for the avoidance of post-salvation sin. Reliability, diligence and thrift (no wasteful consumption) were the practical outworkings, and hence a connection has often been made with economic development, and even specifically with the rise of capitalism (*see* PROTESTANT ETHIC).

**Purrah**. *See* PORO.

**Puruṣa**. *See* PURĀṆAS.

**puruṣa** (Sanskrit). Male, with specifically religious connotations in a variety of Hindu systems of thought. The ṚGVEDA connects the creation of the world with the sacrifice of a *puruṣa*, out of whose limbs the various *varṇa* ('castes') originate. In the Sāṁkhya *puruṣa* represents the spiritual, inactive principle which in interaction with *prakṛti* ('matter', 'activity') is responsible for the evolution of the world but whose real ultimate aim is *kaivalya*, aloneness and isolation. In *Vaiṣṇavism* the title *puruṣa-*

*uttama* (Puruṣottama, 'supreme Person') is given to VIṢṆU as an honorific.

**Puruṣarthas**. *See* MOKṢA/MUKTI.

**puṣṭimārga** (Sanskrit: 'the path of increment'). A branch of the BHAKTIMĀRGA founded by Vallabha (1475–1531) is characterized by the great importance it attributes to the role of the GURŪ: salvation is promised to those who unconditionally follow the *guru*'s word.

**pylon**. *See* ISLAND OF CREATION.

**Pyŏlsang**. Korean god of smallpox, to whom devotions are paid in order to avert diseases.

**pyramid**. A monumental building in stone based on a square and tapering to a point, known in ancient Egypt and ancient Central America. In Egypt kings were buried in pyramids at certain periods (*c*.2800–2181 BCE; *c*. 1991–1786 BCE). The earliest was the Step Pyramid at Sakkara, which Imhotep designed for Zoser, but those built for Cheops, Chephren and Mycerinus at Giza are the most famous (Edwards 1987). The Greeks called these buildings *pyramis* ('wheaten cake') – hence 'pyramids', but the Egyptian name was *Mer* ('Place of Ascension'). The Egyptians believed that the pyramid provided the dead king with access to his father, the sun-god, in the sky. The pyramid was part of a complex which also included a Valley Temple (where the king's body may have been mummified), linked by a covered causeway to a Mortuary Temple (adjoining the pyramid), where the funerary rites were performed.

**Pyramid Texts**. One of the most important sources of early Egyptian belief, these spells were inscribed on the interior walls of several pyramids from the 5th Dynasty (2494–2345 BCE) onwards, to provide the king with a means of access to the celestial hereafter (Mercer 1952). Compiled by the priests of *Heliopolis*, they incorporated elements of predynastic religion (before 3100 BCE), and the cults of RE and OSIRIS. During the Middle Kingdom (1991–1786 BCE), when the idea of an afterlife for everyone became widespread, these spells were inscribed on the coffins of the nobility (*see* COFFIN TEXTS), and by the New Kingdom (1567–1085 BCE) became the basis for the Theban BOOK OF THE DEAD.

**pyx**. A small box used for carrying the HOST, i.e. bread or wafers consecrated during a MASS, to the sick. Unlike a MONSTRANCE, a pyx is not intended for displaying the Host, simply for transporting it.

# Q

**Q**. In New Testament studies, the name given to a source of tradition which, because of the close parallels which exist, is presumed to have been known to both Matthew and Luke as authors of gospels, but which was not known to Mark. The letter Q is short for the German word *Quelle*, which means source. There is no evidence for the separate existence of this source as a written document.

**qaḍā**. *See* QADAR.

**qadar** (Arabic). Decree, the word frequently accompanying *qaḍā* ('deciding') in Islamic thought to express the notion of ALLĀH'S (God's) eternal and foreordained command over all things. The conclusion of absolute predestinarianism was rejected in Islām as theologians attempted to harmonize Allāh's power with a degree of free will for his creatures and thus their assumption of responsibility for their actions which would be rewarded or punished by a compassionate, forgiving deity. *See also* KHAṬĪA, *compare* QADARIYA.

**Qadariya** (Arabic). An early Muslim group which upheld a belief in free-will, that man possessed power (QADAR) over his own actions. The name also designates a ṢŪFĪ brotherhood (ṬARĪQA) founded by the saint ʿAbd al-Qādir al-Jīlānī (1077–1166).

**qadb** (Arabic). Contraction. A term used by ṢŪFĪS in contrast with BASṬ ('expansion'). It is applied to one of the spiritual states (AḤWĀL) corresponding with the station or stage (MAQĀMĀT) of fear. ALLĀH seizes upon and contracts the heart of the mystic, inducing in him a sense of desolation, which is the state of being veiled while *bast* is the state of revelation.

**qadhf**. *See* ḤADD.

**qāḍī** [cadi, kadi] (Arabic). A Muslim religious judge acting in the SHARIʿA courts. Although in theory his competence extended to all matters of civil and criminal law, in practice the *qāḍī* resolved disputes mainly on points of family law, inheritance and on matters of pious foundations (WAQF) and the like.

**Qadiani movement**. *See* AḤMADIYA.

**Qalandariya** (Arabic). Wandering DARWĪSHES (dervishes) without fixed abode whose unconventional behaviour provoked much disapproval in the Muslim world in the 13th and 14th centuries. They practised physical mortification but were slack in their obligatory religious observances and thus held to be immoral by orthodox circles as well as by other ṢŪFĪ brotherhoods.

**qānūn** (Arabic). Customary or administrative law in Islam, recognized by royal decree. Even in the early centuries of Islam, there existed *qānūn* law alongside of the SHARĪʿA.

**qawl**. *See* IMĀN.

**Qebehsennuf**. *See* CANOPIC JAR.

**qi** (Chinese). A term translated into English as 'breath', 'pneuma' or 'configurational energy', into French as 'matière-energie' (Schipper 1982: §51). The concept of *qi* underwent great changes during Chinese history. Initially *qi* was seen as the 'substance-matter' that fills out the space between heaven (*yang* element, see YIN-YANG) and earth (*yin* element) and is also present in man's body and manifest in one's actions. However, during the Song (Sung) dynasty (960–1206) at the latest the viewpoint switched from this cosmological notion to become a philosophical question of heavenly norms and man's ethical correspondence to these *a priori* norms. In DAOISM *qi* is viewed as the vital substance that has to be nourished by certain respiratory and meditational practices. In Chinese medicine the lung is seen as the control organ of man's innate *qi*, and 'bad' *qi* in one's body means that sickness may occur. Through traditional *qi* practices (many of them of Daoist origin) the ordinary person is able to expell 'bad' *qi* from the body, and take in fresh (or 'pure') breath again, thus avoiding internal disorders of the body.

**qibla**. (Arabic). The direction which the Muslim faces for prayer, that is, towards MECCA. *See also* MIḤRĀB.

**qiyās**. *See* SHARĪ'A.

**qlippot** (Hebrew). The kabbalistic doctrine that 'shells' now obscure the spark of the infinite light of the AYN-SOF which is in everything. The religious task is to return these sparks to their source.

**Qollarrí**. *See* INKARRÍ.

**Qormustu Tngri**. The chief of a group of 33 gods (TNGRI) and sometimes even of all 99 heavenly beings in Mongolian traditional belief. The name is thought to derive from the Iranian Ahuramazda. (Heissig 1980: 49–50).

**Quadragesima**. *See* QUINQUAGESIMA.

**Quakerism**. *See* SOCIETY OF FRIENDS.

**Quakers**. *See* SOCIETY OF FRIENDS.

**Quan Zhen Sect**. The Perfect Realization Sect, one of the main streams of later monastic DAOISM. Founded by Wang Zhe (Daoist appellation: Wang Zhong Yang) in the Jin Dynasty (1115–1234) around the middle of the 12th century, the school incorporated Confucian and Buddhist thought in its doctrines, thus providing a sound, institutionalized basis for latter schools of the THREE TEACHINGS kind. In contrast to the ZHENG YI SECT members of the Quan Zhen order were not allowed to marry, had to leave their homes to live in monasteries and observed throughout rigid regulations concerning food, current duties etc. The main teachings of the founders of Quan Zhen Daoism stressed the cultivation of such basic Daoist principles as purity, simplicity, the yang-side (heavenly principle, YIN-YANG) of nature, non-action (WU WEI) and NEIDAN (inner alchemy as a form of meditation). Under Mongol rule (1206–1368) the sect enjoyed imperial protection. It split into a northern and a southern school after the death of its founder, Wang Zhe. From the northern school emerged a sub-sect called Longmen (Dragon Gate Sect), which forms the most prominent branch of monastic Daoism to date, with Bai Yun ('White Cloud Monastery') its principal monastery in Peking.

**Queen Mother of the West**. *See* XI WANG MU.

**Quetzalcoatl**. An important Mesoamerican deity, a feathered serpent having culture-hero, recurrent cosmic (corresponding to the movements of the planet Venus) and historical characteristics. It is also the title of major priests in Aztec religion.

**quietism**. Any form of religious life that adopts an outwardly passive attitude on the grounds that salvation or religious fulfilment has already occurred inwardly. Such a tendency may be documented in various religions, although the term arose in the context of Christianity. Against the background of COUNTER-REFORMATION theology quietism was positively espoused, for example, by Miguel de Molinos (*d* 1697), who regarded interior contemplation as the highest form of the religious life. Since this led to his followers abandoning outward forms of Catholic practice, such as confession and the use of rosaries, his teaching was formally condemned in 1687.

**Quimbanda**. An Afro-American religion making use of black magic and otherwise similar to MACUMBA. *See also* UMBANDA.

**Quindecimviri**. The Roman priestly custodians of the SIBYLLINE BOOKS, 15 in number.

**Quinquagesima** (Latin: 'the fiftieth'). The Sunday before the beginning of LENT (which is on Ash Wednesday), being the seventh Sunday before EASTER and hence marking a period of 50 days. By analogy the Sunday preceding (eighth before Easter) is called Sexagesima and the one before that is Septuagesima (ninth before Easter), even though the figures do not add up. Quadragesima refers to the 40 days of Lent itself and also to the first Sunday in Lent.

**Quirinus**. A deity of the Quirinal Hill in Rome. His origins predate the city and he is sometimes connected with Romulus.

**Qumran**. Ancient Jewish settlement on cliffs north-west of the Dead Sea and home of the religious community usually identified as ESSENES. Qumran was the site of important manuscript discoveries known as the DEAD SEA SCROLLS. (Vermes 1977; Schürer 1979: 555–97).

**Qur'ān** [Koran] (Arabic). The Islamic scripture. The corpus of revelations granted by ALLĀH (God) to His Messenger (RASŪL) Muḥammad through the archangel GABRIEL. The first revelation was said to have occurred in the month of RAMAḌĀN around the time of Muḥammad's 40th year (*c*.610) in a mountain cave near Mecca, in present-day Saudi Arabia. RAMAḌĀN later became marked as the sacred month of the Muslims' prescribed period of fasting. Revelations continued until just before Muḥammad's death in 632, and they were collected together in their final form, according to tradition, within a generation of his death.

In structure, the Qur'ān comprises 114 chapters, called *sūras*, arranged mainly according to length, the shortest and earliest passages of only a few verses, called *ạyas*, being placed at the end of the work. There is no chronological or thematic order. The passages which tradition assigns to the Meccan period of the prophet Muḥammad's life may be broadly distinguished from those of the later period at Madina, in which there is more legal content designed to aid in the governing of the nascent Muslim community. Running through the entire text, however, is the unifying theme of Allāh's absolutely just governance over all creation and His guidance to all mankind as to the appropriate responses to be made to ensure salvation in the afterlife. Among these, mention is made of what later became known as the FIVE PILLARS of the faith, which include the basic ritual expressions of ISLĀM. The textual style is, with minor exceptions, non-narrative, being rather epigrammatic.

Koranic passages adorn MOSQUES as a major decorative feature and they permeate classical Islamic literature as well as being sprinkled through modern speech. As a living canon for Muslims the Qur'ān is intended to be recited and listened to as much as read. Recitation either of single passages or of the whole work (which is about the same length as the New Testament) accompany both formal religious occasions and ceremonies marking the rites of passage. Certain passages are recognized as especially fitting for specific occasions and are committed to memory for the purpose. (Arberry 1964; Gatje 1976; Watt 1978; Rahman 1980).

**qutb** (Arabic). In Islām, the Pole or Axis, the great mystic saint who stands at the apex of the hierarchy of ṢŪFĪ saints that is always present in the world.

# R

**Rabbi** (Hebrew: 'my master'). An ordained authority in Jewish law, and a respected leader of the Jewish community.

**Rādhā** (Sanskrit: 'prosperity').The favourite *gopī* of KṚṢṆA. Her ardent love for *Kṛṣṇa*, disregarding all conventions and other considerations, has been celebrated in such works as the *Gītagoviṇḍa* by Jāyadeva and much later literature of GAUḌĪYA VAIṢṆAVISM. She is held up as exemplar for the *bhakta*, whose only interest ought to be Kṛṣṇa.

**Radhāsoamī Movement**. An organization founded in Agra in 1861 by Śiv Dayāl Singh. The most popular branch of the movement is now that which has its centre at Beas in the Punjab under the spiritual leadership of Mahārāĵ Caran Singh, who attracts disciples from India and the West. The movement draws on SIKHISM for some of its philosophy, though, in its emphasis on the living gurū, it is more akin to Punjābī Hindu movements (e.g. DIVINE LIGHT MISSION) or those at the interface between Hinduism and Sikhism (e.g. NĀMDHĀRĪ MOVEMENT; NIRANKĀRĪ MOVEMENT). (Mangalvadi 1977; Babb 1986).

**Radien**. 'The ruler', the head of the gods of the Saami (Lapps). Among some Saami groups the same god was called Mailman Radien (the ruler of the world) or Veralden Olmai (the man of the world). His symbol, the WORLD PILLAR, showed that he was regarded as the sustainer of the world. Radien was worshipped mainly in connection with reindeer breeding. (Holmberg 1915; Karsten 1955; Hultkrantz 1962).

**Ragnarok**. The end of the world predicted in Germanic mythology, the inevitable culmination of the hostility prevailing in the world. In the detailed account given in the *Voluspá*, a poem of the EDDA, the earth is destroyed by fire and flood and the gods with their army from VALHALLA perish in a great battle with the giants, the monsters (including the wolf Fenrir and the MIDGARD SERPENT) and the army from Muspell, the land of light and heat. After Ragnarok a few gods survive, including BALDER, who returns from HEL, and a man and a woman also remain to repopulate a new, pure earth. *See also* YGGDRASILL; HEIMDALL.

**rahbar**. (Arabic: 'leader'). A title given to a ṢŪFĪ teacher, master or saint.

**Rāhit nāmā** (Punjabi). The code of conduct of the KHĀLSĀ or Sikh order. Several versions were in use until this century, when attempts have been made to produce a commonly accepted code. This resulted in the issuing in 1950 of the Sikh Rahit Maryādā (McLeod 1984).

**raigō** (Japanese). The 'welcoming appearance' of Amida (AMITĀBHA) Buddha with attendant bodhisattvas to take a dying person to the PURE LAND. Also pronounced *raikō*, this term can refer to pictures of such an appearance, painted as an aid to the dying.

**raikō**. *See* RAIGŌ.

**rājayoga**. *See* YOGA.

**Rajneesh Movement**. Rajneesh, later known as Bhagwan, began to promulgate his ideas and practices in the mid-1960s in India, including, in 1970, his 'Dynamic Meditation'. From that time, he began to attract both Indians and Westerners into his Neo-Sannyas Movement, based from 1974 in Poona and later removed to Oregon, USA. Though formally influenced by aspects of

HINDUISM, BUDDHISM and psychotherapy, Bhagwan's philosophy is unlike any of them, providing an unusual combination of meditation, therapy techniques, devotional practices and monistic philosophy. (Mangalvadi 1977; Thompson & Heelas 1986).

**Rāma**. The hero of the *Rāmāyaṇa*, the oldest and most popular epic of India, attributed to Vālmīki. Rāma is celebrated as the ideal king, whose virtues are an inspiration for all succeeding generations. He and his wife Sītā exemplified the ideal couple. The *Rāmāyaṇa* has been retold in Indian vernaculars since the Middle Ages; the Hindī *Rāmcaritmanas* by Tulsīdās has become the most popular book ever in the whole of North India. The Rāma story continues to fascinate Indians: yearly recurring *Rāmlīlās* re-enact scenes from the *Rāmāyaṇa* and a recent television production of the *Rāmāyaṇa* became an astounding success all over India.

**Ramaḍān** (Arabic). The ninth month of the Islamic lunar calendar during which fasting (ṢAWM) is enjoined. During one night of the second half of the month there occurs the 'Night of Power' (*Laylat al-Qadar*), commemorating the advent of the first segment of Qur'anic revelation to the Prophet Muḥammad. The end of Ramaḍān is celebrated by the ʿĪD AL-FIṬR, the feast of the breaking of the fast, one of the two great festivals of the Muslim year.

**Rāmakrishna Mission**. A movement based around the inspiration of Rāmakrishna Paramahansa, the 19th-century Bengali mystic whose spiritual experience drew on *advaita vedānta*, tantra, devotion to the goddess and an appreciation of other religions. The movement was founded in 1886 after Rāmakrishna's death by his disciple, Vivekānanda, who was successful in revitalizing Hinduism in India, propagating it abroad, and passing on a knowledge of Rāmakrishna's eclectic teachings (Rolland 1930). The Mission and associated Order continue to have an impact in East and West.

**Rāmakrishna Sāradā Math** (Bengali). An organization founded in 1954 but based on the inspiration of Sāradā Devī (1853–1920), the wife of Rāmakrishna Paramahansa. It is a division of the RĀMAKRISHNA MISSION and has branches all over India, exclusively for the training of women as religious leaders.

**Ramalila**. *See* RĀMA.

**Ramana Ashram**. *See* ARUNĀCALA.

**Ramanna Nikāya**. *See* NIKĀYA.

**Rāmānuja** (1017–1137). The greatest representative of VIŚIṢṬĀDVAITA VEDĀNTA, a combination of VAIṢṆAVA religiosity and UPANIṢADIC thought. Identifying VIṢṆU with BRAHMAN, Rāmānuja polemicises against the impersonalistic VEDĀNTA of Śankara and develops a complete system of theistic Vedānta, in which image-worship and temple-ritual play as great a role as study of scripture and reflection on words. His commentary on the BRAHMASŪTRAS is called *Śrībhāṣya*, indicating the central role which ŚRĪ, the consort of Viṣṇu, plays in his thinking. His followers, a large group especially in South India, form the Śrīvaiṣṇava SAṂPRADĀYA.

**Rāmāyana**. *See* BHAKTIYOGA, RĀMA, SMṚTI.

**Rāmcaritmanas**. *See* RĀMA.

**Raskolniki**. *See* OLD BELIEVERS.

**Rastafarianism**. A new religion or religious movement in the Caribbean, especially in Jamaica, which is also known in West Africa. Rastafarians have no fixed cult or religious community. Their interpretation of the Bible is that Haile Selassi, a descendant of David, fulfilled the biblical prophecy of the advent of a black Messiah. The religion is connected with aspirations towards a reversal of racial roles in society.

**rasūl** (Arabic: 'messenger'). In Islām the designation for Muḥammad (*c*.570–632), who was called the *rasūl Allāh*, the Messenger of God, to whom was vouchsafed revelations which comprise the Islamic scripture, the QUR'ĀN. Muḥammad is also referred to as *nabī* ('prophet'), the term in practice being interchangeable with *rasūl* although some regard this latter designation the higher rank (Lings 1986).

**Rātana Church**. The largest indigenous church in New Zealand, having a membership of about 35,000, including a considerable number of whites. It was founded by Tahupōtiki Wiremu Rātana. In 1918 he received a divine revelation and was ordered to convert the Māori people to Christianity and to improve their situation. He first co-operated with representatives of all major denominations and started a faith-healing campaign, exhorting his followers to give up all superstitious beliefs and practices. But in 1925 he formed his own church after dissensions with the Catholic and the Anglican Church, particularly concerning the 'Faithful Angels', who play a significant role in the Rātana creed and who are regarded as God's workers and messengers. Rātana himself is believed to be the 'Māngai', a 'mouthpiece' of God. (McLeod 1963, 1972; Greschat 1980; Schlang 1989).

**ratio Anselmi** (Latin: 'Anselm's argument'). The name by which Anselm's proof of God in his *Proslogion* (see especially Chapters 2–4) was known in the Middle Ages. In modern times Anselm's argument is generally, though not universally (Barth 1960, Pegis 1966), classed as a type of ONTOLOGICAL ARGUMENT FOR THE EXISTENCE OF GOD, even though Kant did not explicitly include it under that rubric in his discussion of theistic proofs in his *Critique of Pure Reason*.

**rationalism**. The belief that the human reason can attain knowledge of things by looking for logical explanations for what exists and happens. More recently, the term has been used in a narrower sense, of the rejection of religious belief as irrational.

**Ratu Adil** (Indonesian: 'Righteous King'). Javanese messianic ruler, roughly comparable to the MAHDĪ, who is expected to restore social justice and cosmic order. (Hardjamardjaja 1962; Dahm 1969; Kartodirdjo 1970, 1973)

**Rauravagama**. *See* ĀGAMAS.

**Raven**. The TRICKSTER or culture hero of Native American religions of the northwest coast. Myths of Raven releasing the sun have East Asian correspondences.

**Ravidāsī Movement**. A sectarian movement, closely related to Sikhism, the members of which belong to the low caste Chamār community. The movement gives special status to Ravidās, the 15th-century poet of the SANT tradition whose verses appear in the GURŪ GRANTH SĀHIB. It was begun in the 1950s by Chamārs who had migrated to the United Kingdom, in continuation of an earlier movement set up in the Punjab in the 1920s.

**Re**. The important ancient Egyptian sun-god and creator deity, Re's solar aspects were often incorporated in other gods. His main centre was HELIOPOLIS (Perry 1925).

**realised eschatology**. *See* ESCHATOLOGY.

**realism**. In SCHOLASTICISM, the view that UNIVERSALS have a real existence (*contrast* NOMINALISM). More recently, and quite differently, the term has been used to denote belief in the reality of the external world, and confidence in the powers of the human mind to come to know it.

**real presence**. A theory of the EUCHARIST or MASS according to which the body and blood of Christ are truly present in the bread and wine of the sacrament and not merely figured or symbolized.

**Rebbe** (Yiddish). The Yiddish form of RABBI, used to acknowledge a person who not only has rabbinical ordination, but is a spiritual master. Reb is a more informal title showing affection and respect.

**recapitulation**. In Christian theology, Christ's 'summing up' of all that God intended humanity to be. Irenaeus (*c.*130–200) also saw Christ as the 'summing up' of all God's previous self-revelations.

**Rechabites**. A small, probably nomadic group in ancient Israel noted for its fierce loyalty to YAHWEH and rejection of luxurious Canaanite living (Frick 1971). Since they also abstained from wine their name was borrowed by a modern group of teetotallers.

**Reconstructionism**. The American movement established by the religious humanist Mordecai Kaplan, in response to CON-

SERVATIVE JUDAISM. Rather than a body of law, Reconstructionism conceives of Judaism as a 'civilization' which must continually adapt itself to contemporary conditions.

**reductionism**. In the philosophy of the sciences, a theory about explanation and theories. It holds that concepts and theories from one domain may change by being subsumed by or 'reduced to' those of another. Reductionism thus opposes the view that theories are *a priori* 'autonomous' and immune to subsumption by other theories. Hence, it opposes claims that particular phenomena can therefore be *explained* in their own terms.

In the philosophy of science, reductionism is subject to precise and complex, value-neutral uses. One speaks, first, either of *homogeneous* kinds of reductions, as between theories *within* the same domain of knowledge, or *inhomogeneous* kinds of reductions, as between theories *across* different domains of knowledge. Then, one may consider the *direction* of reduction. In microreduction, wholes are explained in terms of parts, e.g. if biochemistry explains cell division, microbiology is reduced to biochemistry; in macroreduction, wholes explain parts, e.g if general systems theory explains human behaviour without remainder, it reduces psychology to itself. Finally, reductions may be interpreted in at least two ways. First, reduction by *deduction* or *derivation* names a logical operation by which the theorems of one theory are logically subsumed by those of another, such as in attempts to derive mathematics from logic. Second, reduction by *replacement* is the wholesale dismissal of one theory while substituting another. Such reductions lie behind attempts to replace mentalist psychology with brain-state materialism.

In the context of the study of religion, reductionism represents a threat to the value of explanations claimed autonomous by the study of religion. It is thus a vague, pejorative and emotive term, reflecting anxiety about academic territory and the adequacy of a discipline's ability to account for a range of phenomena in its own particular way. Here, 'to reduce' roughly means 'to diminish' or 'to impoverish' the concepts and explanations peculiar to the study of religion, and 'to replace' them with views emanating from other academic fields.

Thus, it is critical to note that the issue of 'reductionism' only arises where conflicting explanations are brought into play. Left to themselves, the disciplines often ignore each other. But once the desire to establish conceptual order in favour of one theory over another is set into motion, the issue of reduction arises. For instance, psychologists might wish to establish the power of their methods of explanation over non-psychological religious explanations of mystic trance. Religious accounts of mystic trance would then be subsumed to psychological ones by first showing that religious explanations were either special cases of more inclusive psychological ones (inhomogeneous reduction by deduction or derivation) or that there were other reasons why they should be 'inhomogeneously replaced' *en bloc* by psychological ones. (Nagel 1961; Schaffer 1967; Strenski 1976).

**Reformation**. *See* CALVINISM; HUSSITES; LUTHERANISM; PROTESTANTISM.

**Reform Judaism**. A Jewish movement which began in 19th-century Germany, and endeavoured to adapt to modern conditions by emphasizing Judaism as a 'prophetic tradition' and denying the binding quality of rabbinic law.

**regression**. A defence mechanism in which, according to psychoanalysis, a temporary, or sometimes more permanent, return to infantile behaviour takes place. PRAYER, for example, has been interpreted by some as being regressive behaviour.

**Reiyūkai**. A well-established lay Buddhist organization in modern Japan which places a strong emphasis on the teachings of the LOTUS SŪTRA and on the values of family life, including the care of ancestors.

**relativism**. The idea that there is no absolute truth, but only a multiplicity of 'perspectives' which intrinsically belong to specific physical and cultural situations. Certain thinkers have in addition espoused a relativism with regard to *meaning*; not only is there no rational way of deciding between different perspectives, it is also impossible to translate one perspective into the linguistic terms of another. The two perspectives are therefore doubly 'incommensurable'. Often relativism is viewed as having nihilistic implications; however, a relativist may still positively embrace a particular perpective – though without 'reasons' that could be presumed to be clear to all. Alternatively, she or he may argue that the quest for 'truth' paradoxically miscontrues the protean and shifting character of reality. *See also* NIHILISM; POSTMODERNISM.

**religio** (Latin). A Roman term originally denoting something out of the day-to-day, whether good or evil. An interesting example of its wide range of meanings is found in Pliny the Elder's observation (1st century CE) that because the blood of a mole was considered to have curative properties, the animal was 'full of religion' (*capax religionis*). *Compare* RELIGION.

**religion**. For the purpose of dispassionate enquiry and discussion, a religion may be regarded as a system of belief and ritual with subjective depth and social extension. The adherent or exponent of a particular religion will usually prefer a more substantial definition reflecting the special nature of his or her faith or experience, but such normative definitions are likely to conflict with each other. For this reason they cannot be adopted for scientific purposes. Since many religions are evidently comparable to each other in a number of striking ways, in spite of many differences, it is appropriate to use the word 'religion' in the singular to refer collectively to the cases being considered. However, this does not mean that one single feature is necessarily of determinative significance for religion in general. Thus, the study of religion is not dependent on an essentialist definition of the subject matter. Furthermore it may be noted that the modern use of the term is not dependent on its etymology (*see* RELIGIO).

**Religiöser Menschheitsbund**. An inter-religious humanitarian association founded by Rudolf Otto and known in English as the Inter-Religious League, but now defunct.

**religious *a priori***. A concept referring to a special category of experiential religious knowledge, which, according to some thinkers, is a fundamental feature of human awareness and hence a necessary presupposition for the understanding of specific religions. It was first advanced specifically by Rudolf Otto in his work *The Idea of the Holy* (1923; German original: *Das Heilige*, 1917), drawing on Kant's theory of knowledge. However, there is a significant divergence from Kant. The latter had argued that the human mind is structured in a certain way by prior, rational categories which alone make it possible to understand information derived from the external world by the physical senses. Thus for him, *a priori* knowledge is rational. Otto instead suggested that the religious *a priori* is a non-rational faculty drawing on experience of the NUMINOUS. In fact, though using Kantian language, Otto's approach is more akin to that of Schleiermacher, who considered that all human beings share a feeling of absolute dependence, as creatures, which is furthermore the basis for understanding any specific religion. Whether or not such a view is necessary or acceptable as a presupposition in the study of religion has been widely disputed in recent years.

**religious experience**. In common usage, a state of mind or feeling regarded by the subject as being beyond ordinary explanation and as caused by the presence of God or by some other religious factor. Religious thinkers are concerned with the nature and varieties of such experience and with assessing its role within religions, whilst philosophers ask questions about its cognitive status and interpretation, and about how it may be explained (as in James 1902). *See also* MYSTICISM.

**Remez**. *See* PARDES

**Remonstrants**. *See* ARMINIANISM.

**ren** [jen] (Chinese). One of the Confucian cardinal virtues, sometimes translated as 'benevolence' or 'human-heartedness'. In the *Lun Yu* it signifies not only a virtue, but appears to be the sum of all qualities which characterize the JUNZI [*chün-tzu*] ('superior man'). In Neo-Confucianism the meaning of *ren* is further extended and includes the feeling of unity with all things.

**renunciation**. For renunciation in Buddhism, *see* AGĀRASMĀ ANAGĀRIYAN; PRAVRAJYĀ. The Buddha's abandonment of his palace in favour of asceticism and meditation is known as the Great Renunciation.

**Reorganized Church**. *See* MORMONISM.

**repetition**. A key term for poststructuralists like Jacques Derrida and Gilles Deleuze. It derives, via Heidegger, from Kierkegaard, who wrote a book which bears it as its title. Kierkegaard contrasted the 'modern' and 'Christian' idea of repetition with the ancient Platonic idea of recollection. Recollection seeks to return to an 'original', and mere copies are regarded as ontologically deficient. By contrast, repetition looks to the future and implies that a stable, recognizable entity is not present 'to begin with', but it is only isolated *through* its being repeated. Unlike the aspiration of *mimesis*, however, repetition can never be merely 'identical', because of the uniqueness of every moment in time and space. Given this fact, along with the infinite divisibility of every moment, it follows that no moment can be identified outside its recurrence, although this is also its transformation. This is precisely why it is repetition and not 'originality' which establishes identity.

From the above it will be realized that, for Kierkegaard, repetition stands in a kind of dialectical relationship to difference. However, superadded differences here establish identity, and are not themselves sublated within identity, as for Hegel. Moreover the superaddition is positive, not the outcome of a movement of negation. Thus the logic of 'repetition' comes to displace Hegelian and Marxist dialectics in the work of Deleuze and those influenced by him. *See also* DIFFERENCE.

**rephaim**. Dead kings in West Semitic religion, invoked as 'healers' or 'saviours', thus being gods in the *Royal Cult*. In the Hebrew Bible they appear as giants. (De Moor 1976; Pope 1977; Levine & de Tarragon 1984; Olmo Lete 1986).

**Requiem**. A MASS said for the dead. The name is taken from the beginning of the opening prayer, said or sung in Latin, expressing the wish that God grant eternal repose to the souls of the dead. This is followed by the KYRIE, Credo (*see* CREED), SANCTUS, BENEDICTUS and AGNUS DEI, but there is no GLORIA in a Mass said or sung for a decreased person. The text of the Agnus Dei varies from the usual in that repose for the souls of the dead is besought instead of peace on earth.

**requiescat in pace** (Latin: 'May he/she rest in peace').

**Rerum novarum**. The name given to a papal encyclical issued on 15 May 1891 which set out the social teaching of the Roman Catholic Church in broad outline as an answer to widespread calls for social justice following on the industrial revolution. It affirmed the right of private property on the one hand and the right to a just wage on the other. Depending on the point of view it has been regarded both as revolutionary and as conservative.

**reserved sacrament**. *See* TABERNACLE.

**Reshef**. The Canaanite god of pestilence (*rašpu*) worshipped in Syria and Egypt in the 2nd millennium BCE. In iconography he wears a pointed cap with streamers, and carries a spear and *ankh* sign. He resembles BAAL; both deities are identified in Egypt with SETH. He survives in the HEBREW BIBLE as personified plague. Reshef is identified in UGARIT with the Babylonian NERGAL. (Conrad 1971; van den Branden 1971; Fulco 1976; Yadin 1985).

**resurrection**. A Jewish and Christian belief in the restoration or raising of a physical person to life. Some scholars see both resurrection and 'eternal life' as beliefs of great antiquity. Most however see relatively primitive ideas of a shadowy post-death existence as surviving undeveloped down to a late period in the Ancient Near East. The Maccabaean crisis led to a change in Jewish conceptions. Resurrection initially appears in order to vindicate those who die as martyrs or to punish those surviving apostasy (*Daniel* 12.1–3); in 2 *Maccabees* 7.13f. it is a reward only. Finally it becomes a universal destiny (T.Benj.10.7–10). Three main conceptions develop: a physical resurrection (1 *Enoch* 51.1, 90.33), a spiritual one (2

*Enoch* 22.8ff., 56.2), and the discarding of the body with spiritual survival (*Wisdom* 3.1, 4 *Maccabees* 18.23). In Christianity the concept of resurrection is closely associated with the resurrection of Christ, with which believers are mystically identified even in this life. An ambivalence between a physical and a spiritual understanding of resurrection, apparent in the NEW TESTAMENT, has continued down to the present day.

**revealed religion**. A religion based on a special act or acts of God (or gods) at a particular point or points in history. Through such divine initiative the special nature and intention of God (or the gods), which would otherwise remain hidden, is disclosed. Judaism, Christianity and Islam are, each in its own way, examples of revealed religion, but so too are newer and hitherto less well-known religions such as Mormonism and Tenrikyō. *See also* REVELATION.

**revelation**. The disclosure of divine truth through the intitiative of a divine being. Although religions diverge considerably with repect to the mode or vehicle of revelation, 'revealed religions' widely share the assumption that God, and the will of God for the world, cannot be discerned by human thought alone. Thus, revelation is believed to take place through the giving of the Law to Moses, through the Prophets, through the person of Jesus Christ, the voice of the Angel Gabriel to the Prophet Muḥammad, the discovery of special writings (as in Mormonism), the appearance of visions, etc. The classic problem for all revealed religions is the relation between revealed and natural knowledge, faith and reason. This problem is analogous at the moral level to that of the relation between salvation and human effort. (*See* NATURAL THEOLOGY.) One attempt to resolve this question in the Christian tradition was by making a distinction between general and special revelation; general revelation being God's self-disclosure through creation, open to all, and special revelation occurring through the history of Israel and the work of Christ. Revealed truth *per se* is commonly believed to be preserved in special writings, which therefore take on a sacred character, e.g. Vedas, Bible, Qur'ān, Book of Mormon, and naturally enough most religious groups regard their own revelation as normative and final.

**Revelation of Adam**. *See* NAG HAMMADI.

**Revelation of Peter**. *See* NAG HAMMADI.

**Revelations of James**. *See* NAG HAMMADI.

**revivalist movement**. A reawakening of an existing religious tradition to new life after a period of ossification. Hence it commonly emphasizes adult CONVERSION and ecstatic experience. Since a revivalist movement claims to represent lost authentic tradition, it should not normally be regarded as a new religion. However, a new denomination or church may easily result on account of differences with existing ecclesiastical authorities, e.g. QUAKERISM; METHODISM; LAESTADIANISM.

**Ṛgveda**. The first of the four Vedas, the oldest and most authoritative revealed text, consisting of about 1,050 hymns addressed to various DEVAS and used in sacred rituals. Some of the hymns – which may be 3,000 and more years old – are still used at occasions like name-giving, marriage and cremation.

**Rhea**. In ancient Greece, the wife of CRONOS. She helped her children, the OLYMPIAN GODS, to liberate themselves from their father. *See also* POSEIDON; ZEUS.

**riḍā** (Arabic). Satisfaction. *See* MAQĀMĀT.

**Rifā'iyya** (Arabic). One of the early Ṣūfī brotherhoods, like the QADARIYA, with local chapters, which gradually spread throughout the Muslim world. The order takes its name from its founder, Aḥmad al-Rifā'i (*d* 1175).

**Rightly Guided Caliphs**. The four immediate successors (*singular* KHALĪFA) to the leadership of the Islamic community following the death of the Prophet Muḥammad (632), who ruled in MADINA until 661. They had each been a close companion of the Prophet and in turn were Abū Bakr, ʿUmar, ʿUthmān and ʿAlī. The last named is considered by SHĪ'A Muslims to have been the sole legitimate successor to the Prophet, the others having usurped their roles. In Arabic they are referred to as *al-khulafā' al-rāshidūn*.

**rimu**. Forest monsters in central East Africa, neglected spirits of the dead, related to GAUNAB and MODIMO (Baumann 1936).

**Ringatū Church**. An indigenous church in New Zealand which teaches and practises a Māori form of Christianity. Formally established in 1938, it was founded in 1868 by Te Kooti, who received divine messages through visions while unjustly imprisoned on the Chatham Islands. He started to instruct his fellow-prisoners, and after fleeing, fighting the government troops and being eventually pardoned in 1883 he set about forming his own church. The regular services (on the 12th of each month and on four seasonal festivals) take place in traditional meeting-houses, and combine liturgical texts, selected from the Bible by Te Kooti and rearranged according to his inspiration, with Māori patterns of worship. Central spiritual ideas and values are also expressed through the ceremony of welcome, which precedes the church meetings as all other Māori gatherings. Today the church has about 6,000 members, most of them living in the eastern part of the North Island. (Greenwood 1942; Greschat 1980; Schlang 1989).

**Rinzairoku**. Japanese title of the text containing records of the Chinese Zen master Lin-chi (Japanese, Rinzai), who died 867 CE.

**Rinzai-shū**. The Rinzai sect of Japanese Zen Buddhism, named after its Chinese founder Lin-ch'i (Japanese, Rinzai) and established in Japan in 1191, since when it has greatly flourished.

**Rinzai Zen**. *See* RINZAI-SHŪ.

**Risshōankokuron**. 'Treatise on the establishment of righteousness and the ensuring of peace in the country', written by Nichiren in 1259 as a challenge to the Buddhism of the day in Japan.

**Risshō Kōsei-kai**. An important lay Buddhist movement in modern Japan based on the teachings of the LOTUS SŪTRA. The Risshō Kōsei-kai is particularly well known for its system of counselling groups (*hōza*) and its contribution to peace activities. *See also* NAMU MYŌHŌ RENGEKYŌ.

**Riyaya** Also *lebaran* or Hari Raya (literally, 'Grand Day'); the Indonesian name for 'ĪD AL-FIṬR, the feast of breaking the fast, celebrated also by non-Muslims and thus representing the 'most syncretic of public festivals' (Geertz 1960a: 379).

**riza**. *See* OKLAD.

**rNying ma pa**. A traditional form of Tibetan Buddhism claiming the authority of Padmasambhava, a sage believed to have visited Tibet in the 8th century CE. In fact the rNying ma pa transmitted a variety of ancient Buddhist teachings and practices which were probably brought to Tibet by various intermediaries. (Snellgrove & Richardson 1980: 170ff)

**robiglia**. *See* ROGATION.

**Robigus**. The Roman NUMEN of wheat rust, with a major festival on 25 April and possibly another in July at harvest time.

**rogation** (from Latin, *rogare*: 'to ask'). A petition for the protection of crops, usually in the course of a procession round the area for which protection is sought. The main traditional day of rogation in western Christianity was 25 April, this being the day of a pre-Christian observance with similar intent called *robiglia*.

**role theory**. A field of social psychology that considers learned patterns of behaviour in a social community by means of which people relate to others in order to solicit a desired response. The roles are, therefore, always found in pairs like, for instance, parents–children, teacher–student, husband–wife, priest–layman. The term has been borrowed from the world of the theatre. Certain similarities to roles in a theatre production exist, but the differences between the two outweigh their similarities. In normal social life, we do not always have the opportunity to choose roles and we do not see them as being fictional and thus solely as roles which we act out. Within the field of the psychology of religion the Swede Hjalmar Sundén has used the term 'role' to explain religious experience. Characteristic of his role theory is that myths and legends about gods or people in sacred traditions are presumed to suggest such roles with which others then identify. In certain situations, given appropriate motivation, persons take on the roles of such traditional figures and experience the world using them as structuring patterns (Sunden 1966).

**Roman religion**. Roman religion, originally based on local land divinities and apparently without elaborate mythology in the early period, was strongly influenced by Greek models and HELLENISTIC RELIGION generally. Thus, for example, departed spirits were considered to roam below or above ground (see LEMURIA; MANES; PARENTALIA), while Vergil's *Aeneid* 6 represents a literary reworking of more complex Homeric traditions on the underworld. The political scale of the Roman Empire left it open to the incursion of cults of diverse origin (*see especially* MITHRAISM; MYSTERY RELIGIONS). Religion was however partially controlled politically and in some respects heavily mobilized, as in the emperor cult, for Roman emperors were usually voted divine honours by the Senate after their death. This cult derives from the Greek hero cult and the Hellenistic ruler-cult. Earlier scholarship viewed the cult as empty rituals designed to focus provincial loyalty, but current consensus recognizes a more substantial symbolic meaning, a way to recognize the extraordinary achievement of the Roman Empire (*see* AUGUSTAN RELIGION). Fundamental sources for knowledge of Roman religion are found in the surviving fragments of the works of Marcus Terentius Varro (116–27 BCE). Roman intellectuals such as Cicero considered that if there were to be gods then they should represent virtues rather than vices, thus celebrating the good which is within man himself (*De Legibus* II, xi). In spite of the conceptual haphazardness of Roman religion, if this be considered coextensively with the full extent of the Roman Empire, the Latin language has contributed the key terms 'sacred' (*sacer*) and 'religion' (*religio*) to all later reflection on the subject.

**Rongo** [Lono, Ro'o]. One of the major Poynesian ATUA ('gods'). The name can be translated as 'sound', but his domain is agriculture. In New Zealand he is also the lord of peace.

**rosary**. A string of beads with an established number of members used for counting prayers. A Roman Catholic rosary usually has 55 or, less commonly, 165 beads, and may be used for counting the number of times the Ave Maria is to be said while meditating on events in the life of Christ. Buddhist rosaries vary considerably but may also be used for counting simple devotional phrases such as the NENBUTSU; when 108 beads are counted they refer to the 108 human passions referred to in Buddhist teaching.

**Ro'o**. *See* RONGO.

**Rosh Hashanah** (Hebrew). The Jewish 'New Year', which marks the beginning of the lunar year in the autumn. It is said that God inscribes each person's fortune for the coming year on Rosh Hashanah, based on their conduct in the year past. It marks the opening of the Jewish High Holidays, the 'Ten Days of Repentance', during which Jews ask forgiveness of God and their fellow men, so as to set their accounts to rights before the closing of YOM KIPPUR.

**rōshi**. *See* TEISHŌ.

**Ṛṣi** (Sanskrit: 'seer'). The inspired authors of ŚRUTI, venerated as spiritual ancestors of Hindus. One group – the *saptarṣis* – is particularly famous and many later scholars derive their lineage from them, such as the Bhārgavas, responsible for the accepted MAHĀBHĀRATA version, who claim to be descendants of the Vedic *ṛṣi* Bhrigu.

**ṛta** (Sanskrit: 'rule', associated with *ṛtu*, 'season'). The lawfulness of nature which extends also to human behaviour. In the ṚGVEDA Mitra and Varuṇa are called the 'custodians of *ṛta*' who will punish transgressors. In some ways the Vedic *ṛta* foreshadows the later Hindu idea of KARMA.

**Ṛtu**. *See* ṚTA.

**ruaḥ** (Hebrew). A term meaning both 'wind' and 'spirit'.

**Rudra** (Sanskrit: 'the howler'). A Vedic DEVA who later became merged with ŚIVA, as this god's terrifying aspect. *Rudra* probably originated as a non-vedic deity, who did not receive offerings at regular sacrifices but for whom scraps of food were deposited on cross-roads, and who was implored to stay away because he was supposed to cause disease and strife. Rudra-worship later became acceptable and his followers gained equal status to other SAṀPRADĀYAS.

**Ruhanga**. A supreme being without cult in western Uganda; mediators between him and mankind are the BACHWEZI spirits (Baumann 1936).

**Ryangombe**. In Ruanda-Urundi, a *deified hero* who acts as intermediary between IMANA and the initiates of his widespread cult and secret society (Maquet 1954).

**ryōbu mandara** (Japanese). 'The two mandalas', which play a prominent part as aids to meditation in Shingon Buddhism (*see* SHINGON-SHŪ). The *taizōkai* mandara is the MANDALA of the womb world (*taizōkai*; Sanskrit, *garbhadhātu*) and the *kongōkai* mandara is the mandala of the diamond world (*kongōkai*; Sanskrit, *vajradhātu*).

**Ryobu Shintō**. Dual Shintō, a term used to refer in general to Shintō as syncretized with Buddhism, and particularly to syncretic Shintō as interpreted in Shingon Buddhism (*see* SHINGON-SHŪ).

# S

**Sabazios**. *See* MYSTERY RELIGIONS.

**Sabbatarianism**. Strict emphasis on the keeping holy of Sunday (i.e. the Christian Sabbath) as the Lord's Day, and a matter of great controversy in England and Scotland from the 16th century onwards. Key works were Nicholas Bound's *True Doctrine of the Sabbath* (1595) and James I's *Book of Sports* (1618). At its most extreme, not only leisure activities that involved payment of admission (by law in 1781) but even the use of non-religious books and music were disallowed. The struggle to maintain the distinctiveness of Sunday in Britain is continued by the Lord's Day Observance Society.

**Sabbath** [Hebrew, *Shabbat*; Yiddish, *Shabbes*]. The seventh day, of 'rest'. As God rested from the creation of the world on the seventh day, according to the account in *Genesis*, so Israel is bidden to rest from all forms of constructive work on the Sabbath, and to rejoice in the Creator (*Exodus* 20.11) or in redemption (*Deuteronomy* 5.14). It is probable that the fixing of the Sabbath on the seventh day took place at the time of the EXILE, replacing an earlier observance of uncertain frequency. Although it comes weekly, the Sabbath (falling on the modern Saturday) takes precedence over all other festivals in Judaism and is celebrated with three special meals, as well as with special prayers. (Vaux 1965: 475–83; Kraus 1966: 78–87; Andreasen 1972; Strand 1972; Carson 1982).

**śabda** (Sanskrit: 'word'). A term of great significance in Indian religions as seen in the Vedantic concept of *śabda-brahman* and the extensive *śabda* philosophy of the Indian grammarians (Bhartṛhari and others). *Śabda* also plays a great role with many *sant*-poets (e.g. Kabir), from whom Gurū Nanak took it over. In its Punjabi form, Sabd, the word refers to the word of God (*see* TEN GURŪS) revealed through Gurū Nanak and subsequent leaders and now found in the GURŪ GRANTH SĀHIB.

**Sabellianism**. The exclusion of intrinsic distinction within the divine nature by asserting Father, Son and Spirit to be different 'modes' of God's self-manifestation in the world. This modalistic understanding of the Trinity derives from the teaching of Sabellius (3rd century BCE).

**ṣabr** (Arabic). In Islamic ethico-ascetic mysticism, the term means 'renunciation;' in this, its spiritual sense, it involves renunciation in face of the natural impulses. In a physical sense, too, the word means endurance or patience, either in performing difficult tasks or in suffering ills. *See also* MAQĀMĀT.

**sacbe** (Maya: 'White way'). Raised causeway roads connecting many Classic Maya ceremonial centres externally and internally (Adams 1977).

**sacra**. *See* ARCANUM.

**sacral kingship**. The concept of kingship as either divine or, in some cases (because the king is the son or descendant of a divinity), providing unique mediation between the divinity and the general population. The concept was common in the ancient Near East (Frankfort 1948: 215–333) but has been much more widely known, for example in pre-conquest Central and South America. A clear example persisting to this day, in spite of variations in the legal context, is the Japanese *tennō* ('lord of heaven'), who is presumed to be descended from the sun goddess AMATERASU. It is evident that the religious concepts employed in such cases, whatever their variations, provide cosmic legitimation for whatever the actual power structure in fact is. In a broad sense, therefore, almost all monarchies, being arbitrary, require a mythical accompaniment.

**sacrament**. In most Christian teaching a sacrament is understood to be an outward and visible sign of an inward and spiritual grace received from God. The first tractates dealing with thc sacraments as seven in number date from the Middle Ages. However, the number seven has been established in Roman Catholic teaching as a matter of faith since the Council of Trent (1545–63), over against the Protestant view that only two sacraments were instituted by Jesus Christ himself, namely BAPTISM and the EUCHARIST. When seven are counted the additional five are CONFIRMATION, PENANCE, MATRIMONY, EXTREME UNCTION (or holy unction), and ORDINATION.

**sacramentals**. Minor symbols of the Christian faith such as the sign of the cross, use of the rosary, or the wearing of liturgical vestments symbolic of the season in the church year, but also specific acts of prayer or devotion such as grace at meals, set litanies, and prayers at the stations of the cross. In Catholic teaching such 'sacramental' acts are thought to assist the believer, but not, like the sacraments, to convey the grace of God EX OPERE OPERATO.

**sacred**. A synonym for 'holy'. 'Sacred' usually implies a distinct separation from the profane or ordinary. *See also* HUACA.

**Sacred Books of the East**. A 50-volume series of major religious works of Asia edited by Friedrich Max Müller and first published between 1856 and 1899. The translations were contributed by illustrious scholars of the day but in the light of recent advances should now be used with caution.

**sacred bundle**. In many Native American religious traditions, ritual objects, especially those with sacred power, kept wrapped in bundles. After the adoption of the horse into North American Plains cultures, as more and more objects and coverings were added, these bundles could attain a relatively large size. Tribal bundles are in the keeping of respected persons who take on considerable responsibility and often onerous personal daily ritual requirements.

**sacred heart**. The 'sacred heart' of Christ became widespread as a special object of devotion in the Roman Catholic Church in the 16th and 17th centuries, and a liturgical feast devoted to it was proclaimed in 1765. It springs from the idea that the spear plunged into Christ's body at the crucifixion laid bare his heart, which shows forth salvation for all humankind.

**sacred marriage**. The ritual use of sexual intercourse in temple and royal cults, especially in ancient Near Eastern religion. Often referred to as the *hieros gamos*. (Kramer 1969; Wyatt 1985a). *See also* GEBIRAH; BAAL CYCLE; ISHTAR.

**sacred pipe**. In Native American religions pipes are often used for the central ritual of TOBACCO smoke offerings to the spirits. There are many types of pipes, the simplest being a straight tube. Most pipes utilize a variation of the elbow shape. For the last one thousand years the most important ritual pipe in North America has been one in which the stem and bowl are separable, frequently called the sacred pipe. Specific sacred pipes figure in tribal and clan myths, as well as a few cosmogonic myths. The bowl and stem are usually made of different substances, respectively stone or clay and wood, and symbolize female and male generative energy. The bowl and stem are kept apart until used in rituals, their joining and separation signalling the beginning and end of the ritual. Only when the male stem is inserted into the female bowl is the sacred pipe considered potent, although at all times the ritual pipes are treated as sacred objects and may be found in ritual bundles.

The essential aspects of sacred pipe ritual are the same throughout North America, and can be traced back to the earliest ethnohistoric sources covering a wide area. Basically the ritual involves offering the pipe stem first to the major cosmic spirits – the Four Directions, Sky (Sun) and Earth. Both men and women participate in pipe rituals (excluding rituals that are gender specific), and both sexes may keep pipes. Sacred pipe rituals engender communion in two ways. First, the breathing in of tobacco smoke and then blowing it towards the spiritual recipient, along with offering the mouthpiece to the spirit, creates communion between the smoker and the spirit. Second, sacred pipe ritual is generally communal, the participants sitting in a circle. The lit pipe is passed in the direction of the sun's movement among the participants, each of whom offers smoke. Thus, a communion is also created among the participants of the ritual. More elaborate sacred pipe rituals involve a dance, with the bowl of the pipe often removed to avoid the possibility of the bowl falling off the stem, an event which would create a spiritually dangerous situation.

Sacred pipe bowls may be found in a variety of shapes, even within the same culture, and are most commonly made from red or black stones, the former symbolizing life, and the latter, the earth. Most ritual bowls are undecorated. Stems come in varying length up to a metre. Again, most stems on ritual pipes are plain, although some are elaborately decorated with the feathers of the eagle and other sacred birds. The eagle feathers symbolize the sending of prayers accompanying the smoke offering to the spirits.

**sacrifice**. The offering of living creatures, plants or other objects to a deity. Sacrifice has been and still is widespread all over the world. The most common central idea seems to be that of making the deity happy by providing for its needs, thus ensuring a stable relationship between the deity and the society whose needs will then also be met in correspondence. This idea can be accentuated in two ways. First, the idea of satisfying and even pacifying or propitiating a potentially wrathful deity can be emphasized; in a subjective transformation this leads to the idea of the expiation of guilt when a transgression against the wishes or commandments of the deity has occurred. Second, the idea of gratitude may be emphasized, which, when symbolized through the offerings of first fruits or a representative meat or fish offering, reinforces the loyalty of the group to its own natural social and economic processes. For sacrifice in the ancient Near East, where the concept has been explored in particular detail, see Gray 1925; Rowley 1950a; de Vaux 1965: 415–54; Kraus 1966: 112–34; Brichto 1973; Davies 1977. On human sacrifice in pre-conquest Central America see Gonzalez 1985. *See also* FENG SHAN.

**sacristy**. A room near the altar area of a church in which liturgical vessels and vestments are kept and prepared. The sacristy may also function as a vestry, where the vestments are donned, but sometimes there is an additional vestry, especially for servers and choir members.

**Ṣadaqa** (Arabic). Voluntary and spontaneous alms-giving or what would be more generally known as 'charity'. For Muslims, it is distinguished from *zakāt*, the obligatory alms payment.

**Saddharma Puṇḍarīka Sūtra**. *See* LOTUS SŪTRA.

**Sadducees**. The party of Jewish priests, merchants and aristocracy, who in Graeco-Roman times rejected the oral law of the PHARISEES and supervised Temple affairs according to the written TORAH. They were called Sadducees (probably = Zadokites) by Josephus and New Testament writers. Being conservative in their beliefs (e.g. they rejected RESURRECTION), and tending to collaborate with the Jewish state, they ceased to exist after 70 CE. (Manson 1938; Schürer 1979: 381–2, 404–14).

**sādhana**. *See* BHAKTI.

**sadhu**. *See* SAṂNYĀSIN, YOGI.

**ṣāf** (Arabic). Pure, one of the words that some scholars formerly have cited as the possible origin of the term ṢŪFĪ. Were this etymology accepted, which by and large it is not, then the word Ṣūfī would mean 'seeker after purity'.

**safar** (Arabic). Mystic's journey. *See* MAQĀMĀT.

**sage**. *See* SHENGREN.

**ṣaghā'ir** (Arabic: singular *Ṣaghīr*). In Islām, light sins. *See* KHAṬĪA.

**saḥāba** [*ashab*]. Companions of the Prophet. *See* SALAFIYA.

**Sahaj** (Sanskrit, Punjabi). Ultimate union or bliss (also referred to as MUKTI, 'liberation') achieved by process of meditating on God's name (NĀM) and living a virtuous life. Sikh teaching recognizes different stages (*khaṅd*) on the path to *Sahaj*, including duty, knowledge, endeavour, fulfilment and truth.

**sahajdhārī** (Punjabi). An uninitiated Sikh. *See also* AMRIT; AMRITDHĀRĪ.

**ṣaḥīḥ** (Arabic: 'sound'). In the classification of Prophetic traditions (ḤADĪTH) in Islām, the strongest and most reliable accounts. For this reason, the word is used of the six canonical collections of traditions, the dual sense, *ṣaḥīḥayn*, being used of the two most respected collections of Muḥammad b. Ismāʿīl al-Bukhārī (*d* 870) and Muslim b. al-Ḥajjāj (*d* 875).

**Sahlas**. *See* DEMIURGE.

**Sāī Bābā Movement**. A movement focused on the figure of Sathyā Sāī Bābā (*b* 1926), whose present home is at Praśanti Nilayam, Andhra Pradesh, and who is said to be both a reincarnation of Śirdī Sāī Bābā, a 19th-century mystic, and an incarnation of Śiva. He is renowned for his thaumaturgical powers, and has a following amongst Indians, in the subcontinent and abroad, and Westerners. (Mangalvadi 1977; Babb 1986; Sharma 1986).

**saint**. A holy person; also a person who has been canonized by ecclesiastical authority (*see* CANONIZATION). The cult of the saints is extremely complex since the particular virtues of the various saints may act both as a meditative and as a protective device. For example, the extreme humility of the Spanish San Ramón, popular in Latin America, is both a virtue to emulate and a protection against calumnies.

**Sais**. *See* NEITH.

**saisel itchi**. *See* STATE SHINTŌ.

**śaiva-āgamas**. *See* ŚRŪTI.

**Śaiva Siddhānta** (Sanskrit: 'the final truth of Śiva'). A school of ŚAIVISM founded upon the 28 Śaiva ĀGAMAS and the teachings of the 63 Nayanmars. It acknowledges three principles: *pati* (Lord), *paśu* (human person) and *pāṣa* (bondage). In order to gain freedom, four elements are necessary: *vidyā* (knowledge), *kriyā* (ritual action), YOGA (austerity) and *caryā* (a virtuous way of life). ŚIVA is the supreme reality. He is immanent in the world and appears in a human form as the GURU. Human birth is important, because only in such a birth is liberation possible. Liberation is the appearance of the hidden *śivatva* ('Śiva nature') in the soul through knowledge, when humans understand that their true nature is Śiva. Śaiva Siddhānta also accepts the possibility of JĪVANMUKTI; having achieved this a person is beyond good and evil. All activities of Śiva are ordered toward the liberation of humans, his essence is to be 'full of grace'.

**Śaivism**. The collective term for all *saṁpradāyas* of Hindus for whom Śiva is the Supreme Being, the second largest segment of Hinduism, particularly popular in South India, probably originating in prehistoric times in the mountain regions of the Himālayas. Śiva, the Great Lord (*maheśvara*) is a composite of many elements: Indus-valley cult, Vedic RUDRA worship, tribal traditions and later theological thought. The Sanskrit etymology of *Śiva* ('the benevolent one') is probably of later date; it is assumed that he was originally known by his Tamil name *śivan* ('the red one'). Organized Śiva-worshippers are mentioned already in ancient texts (Pāṇini's grammar, MAHĀBHĀRATA), Śaivism has a large number of scriptures which are known as ĀGAMAS, besides the commonly accepted Śiva PURĀṆAS.

**Sakkara**. The NECROPOLIS of Memphis, Egypt's first capital city, with tombs and funerary buildings from many periods, including the Step Pyramid and the Serapeum where the APIS bulls were buried (Lauer 1976).

**sākṣātkāra** (Sanskrit). The appearance of the deity in his or her bodily form is considered the highest reward for the BHAKTĀ and the assurance of final salvation.

**Saktas**. *See* DURGĀ.

**śakti** (Sanskrit: 'power'). Power personified either in the Goddess or in the potency inherent in a Great God. Thus, she is seen as the life-energy of ŚIVA: without her (expressed in the *i* in Śiva's name) he is inert and impotent (he is *śava*, 'a corpse'). As Great Goddess (known under the names of DURGĀ, KĀLĪ, Devī etc.) she is Supreme Being and the focus of a distinct ancient branch of Hinduism: ŚĀKTISM or Tantrism.

**Śāktism**. A branch of Hinduism characterized by its affirmation of material reality, life and enjoyment. It has two branches: right-hand and left-hand. The former is Devī-BHAKTI, loving devotional worship of the Goddess, much like BHAKTI to VIṢṆU or ŚIVA. The latter is associated with secret initiations and rituals in which the rules of conventional morality are broken so as to liberate the worshipper from all fetters that bind him or her to society and convention. The sacred books of the Śāktas are called Tantras and are considered to be revelations by the Goddess.

**Śākya**. The tribe, belonging to the KSATRIYA caste, into which Gautama BUDDHA was born, hence his appellation, ŚĀKYAMUNI.

**Śākyamuni** (Sanskrit: 'the sage of the Śākya'). A title of Gautama BUDDHA.

**salaf**. *See* SALAFIYA.

**salafiya** (Arabic: 'the (virtuous) forefathers'). Predecessors whose perfect orthodoxy, piety and religious knowledge make them worthy of being taken as models and guides. The term was early applied in Islām to refer to the exemplary witnesses of the nascent community, those Companions (*ṣaḥaba*, *aṣḥāb*) of the Prophet Muḥammad and their Successors (*tābiʿūn*), many of whom were the Companions' contemporaries. In modern Islamic reformist usage, the *salaf* can refer to the first three generations of Muslims, in contrast to the *khalaf*, or later generations under whose influence Islām became corrupted and distorted by innovation (BIDʿA). Modern reformers include, however, certain later outstanding thinkers as belonging to the Salafiya line, figures such as al-Ghazālī (*d* 1111), Ibn Taymiya (*d* 1328) and the real inaugurator of 20th-century Islamic renewal, the Egyptian scholar Muḥammad ʿAbduh (*d* 1905). Abduh's disciple, Muḥammad Rashīd Riḍā, named his movement the Salafiya (Hourani 1962).

**śalāgrama**. *See* MŪRTI.

**salamatan**. *See* SLAMETAN.

**ṣalāt** (Arabic). Prayer, one of the FIVE PILLARS of the Islamic religion.

**Salvation Army**. An evangelical Christian movement founded in England in 1865 by William Booth which combined intense preaching with a strong social concern. The Salvation Army, which with its 'General' and other 'officers' makes much use of terminology drawn from military life, is highly visible on account of the uniforms worn and the playing of its brass bands. Its social work in aid of the homeless, and those suffering from alcohol and other addictions, is of great significance in urban contexts to the present day, especially but not only in Britain and the USA. *Compare* CHURCH ARMY.

**salve regina** (Latin: 'hail [holy] queen'). An ancient hymn addressed to Mary, the mother of Christ, which is widely used in the Roman Catholic Church, so named after its opening words.

**samādhi** (from Sanskrit, *samā* ('together') and *dhi* ('mind')). (1) In Yoga, a high state of concentration. (2) In Buddhism, right effort, right mindfulness and right concentration of the eightfold path in the FOUR NOBLE TRUTHS. (3) In daily usage in India, both the death of a saintly person and the memorial built over his or her tomb, which frequently becomes a point of pilgrimage for devotees.

**saman**. *See* SHAMAN.

**sāmana**. *See* ŚRĀMANA.

**samanera**. *See* PRAVRAJYĀ.

**samanya bana**. *See* BAṆA.

**Samantabhadra**. *See* BODHISATTVA, FUGEN BOSATSU.

**Samaritans**. 'Guardians' of TORAH: the name of a Jewish group centring on the temple at Mount Gerizim, and maintaining only the PENTATEUCH as canonical. By the Christian era they had become alienated from the Jerusalem authorities. (Purvis 1968; Macdonald 1964; Coggins 1975)

**samatha bhāvana**. *See* BHĀVĀNA.

**Sāmaveda**. The second of the vedic *saṁhitās*, containing instructions on the modes and tunes in which the hymns of the *Ṛgveda* are to be recited.

**sambhogakāya**. *See* TRIKĀYA.

**saṃgīti** (Sanskrit: 'rehearsal', 'council') [Pāli: *saṅgīti*]. A Buddhist council. After the death of Gautama BUDDHA the oral tradition of Buddha's teaching was recited, collected and edited at four councils, i.e. at Rājagṛha, Vaiśalī and at two different councils at Pāṭaliputra, the last one of which according to the Theravāda tradition was held under the auspices of King Aśoka.

**saṃhitas**. *See* ATHARVAVEDA; BHAKTI; BRAHMAṆAS; SAMAVEDA; YAJURVEDA.

**Sāṁkhya**. One of the six orthodox systems of Indian religious philosophy (usually paired with YOGA) according to tradition founded by Kapila. Possibly the oldest of the philosophical schools, it has become associated with virtually all branches of Hinduism. While in its original form a non-theistic and non-vedic, dualistic system, in combination with VAIṢṆAVISM, ŚAIVISM and ŚĀKTISM it makes ĪŚVARA the creator of PURUṢA ('spirit') and *prakṛti* ('matter') and asserts its Vedic character. The most important texts are the *Sāṁkhakārikās* of Īśvarakṛṣṇa from the 3rd or 4th century CE.

**Samkhyakarikas**. *See* SĀMKHYA.

**Saṃnyāsa**. *See* ĀŚRAMA.

**saṃnyāsin** (Sanskrit: 'renouncer'). The designation of a person who has reached the last and most perfect stage (*āśrama*) in life. Ideally he/she is to be without a fixed abode, without any personal possession or attachment, exclusively concentrating on *mokṣa* (liberation). In today's usage the word *samnyāsi* sometimes is used as a synonym for *sādhu*, a person belonging to any of the numerous religious orders or otherwise distinguishing him/herself as 'religious' by a certain kind of dress, hairdo, etc.

**saṁpradāya** (Sanskrit). Often translated as 'sect'. Groups of people within Hinduism following a particular person or tradition. Most religiously active Hindus belong to one of the numerous *saṁpradāyas*, which keep forming and developing also in our time.

**saṃsāra** (Sanskrit, Pāli: 'keeping going'). A Buddhist term denoting the perpetual round of rebirths, referring specifically to being reborn, growing old, suffering (DUḤKHA) and dying. This sequence of repeated births in the world has no beginning and it can be ended only by enlightenment (BODHI). *Saṃsāra* is the unbroken chain of the psycho-physical aggregates (SKANDHA), which arise and perish from instant to instant, carried along continuingly for all eternity on the whirling wheel of lives. Of this fleeting movement, a single lifetime constitutes merely a fraction. The necessity to escape *saṃsāra* is also a major endeavour of Hindus and Jains.

**samyaksambodhi**. *See* BODHI.

**samyaksambuddha** (Sanskrit: 'fully enlightened buddha'). A Buddhist term denoting a person who, after the world has revolved, rediscovers and realizes the lost knowledge of the releasing Doctrine (DHARMA). *See also* BODHI; MAHĀKALPA; PRATYEKABUDDHA; ŚRĀVAKABUDDHA.

**samyasi**. *See* SAṂNYĀSIN.

**Sanchi**. *See* STŪPA.

**san chiao**. *See* THREE TEACHINGS.

**Sanctus** (Latin: 'holy'). A hymn derived from Jewish worship and used in the Christian EUCHARIST just before the consecration. It is one of the main pieces in the MASS as a musical composition.

**Sande** [Sandi]. A women's association widespread in Liberia and Sierra Leone, the name being current in the various languages of these countries. The association is also known under the name Bundu (or Bondo) both among some of the same ethnic groups and elsewhere. Yet another designation is the local English GREEGREE. The association is complementary and in many ways similar in ritual to the men's association PORO. (Bledsoe 1980; Holsoe 1980; MacCormack 1975).

**Sandi**. *See* SANDE.

**sandilya**. *See* BHAKTI.

**sando**. A diviner among the Senufo (Ivory Coast, Mali, Burkina-Faso). The diviners, mainly women, form a spirit-cult association known as SANDOGO (Glaze 1981).

**sandogo**. *See* SANDO.

**san gang** [san kang] (Chinese). In Confucianism, the Three Fundamental Principles, i.e. the relationship between ruler and subject, between father and son, and between husband and wife.

**Saṅgha** (Sanskrit, Pāli: 'congregation'). A Buddhist term originally denoting the community of all Buddhists: monks, nuns, laymen and laywomen. Today *Saṅgha* refers to the monastic order of ordained monks or nuns and novices.

**Sangharāja** (Pāli: 'King of the Sangha'). A title used at various times in Theravāda countries for the Supreme Monk of the local monastic orders, the SAṆGHA.

**sangiti**. *See* SAṂGITI.

**Ṣàngŏ**. *See* SHANGO.

**Sanja Matsuri**. The Shintō Festival of the Three Shrines, celebrated annually on 17 and 18 May at Asakusa Jinja in Tokyo. Asakusa Jinja was formerly called Sanja Daigongen Sha or Sanja Myojin Sha and was the tutelary shrine of Asakusa in the Edo period (1600–1868). This brilliant festival continues to draw large crowds.

**san jiao**. *See* THREE TEACHINGS .

**San-lun**. *See* MĀDHYAMIKA.

**sanmai** (Japanese). The Japanese equivalent of the Sanskrit term SAMĀDHI, meaning meditation, usually through concentrating on a particular focus, whether a natural object or a visualized bodhisattva or buddha.

**Sannō**. Literally 'Mountain King', a popular name for the Japanese deity Ōyamakui no kami, enshrined at Hie (Hiyoshi) Taisha in Shiga Prefecture and in Hie shrines throughout the country. The term originated among the Buddhist priests at Enryaku on Mount Hiei, who worshipped the god of the mountain as their tutelary deity.

**Sannō ichijitsu Shintō**. *See* TENDAI SHINTŌ.

**Sannō Matsuri**. A festival celebrated annually on 14 and 15 June at Hie Shrine in Tokyo. In the Edo period (1600–1868), while the Kanda Matsuri was the festival for the townspeople, the Sannō Matsuri was celebrated to entertain the *shogun*. As an official festival it was a ceremonial affair known for the beauty of its procession of floats and as such is still popular today. *See also* SANNŌ.

**Sanshin**. Korean mountain god, believed to influence individual destinies and hence frequently occurring in shamanic paintings (Kim 1989).

**Sanshu no Shinki** (Japanese). The three imperial regalia of Japan which symbolize the legitimacy of the imperial throne. They are (1) the mirror, called the Yata no Kagami, preserved as the manifestation of the goddess Amaterasu Ōmikami at the Grand Shrine of Ise, a replica being kept at the imperial palace; (2) the sword, called Kusanagi no Tsurugi, being a manifestation to the deity enshrined at Atsuta Grand Shrine, while again a replica is preserved at the imperial palace; (3) the jewels, called

Yasakani no Magatama, which have always been preserved in the imperial palace. According to legend, all three treasures were handed down by Amaterasu Ōmikami, and are said to symbolize the virtues of wisdom, courage and benevolence.

**Saṅskār** (Sanskrit, Punjabi). Sikh life-cycle rites, particularly name-giving, marriage, initiation (AMRIT) and cremation, all of which include the reciting of prayers and the reading of the GURŪ GRANTH SĀHIB in addition to the sharing of sweet food (KARAH PRAŚĀD) and other ritual activities. *See also* ARDĀS; HUKAM.

**Santería** (New World Spanish). A religious complex of West African derivation (primarily Yoruba mixed with Spanish Catholic) emerging in Cuban slave society and carried via emigration throughout the Caribbean, North America, Brazil and Mexico. Veneration of ancestors, establishing and maintaining relationships with deities (ORISHA in Yoruba; *Santos* in Spanish) through animal sacrifice, spirit possession and divination, serve as the central frame. Membership involves a series of often costly initiations, the primary one being the *asiento* (Spanish: 'seating'), the seating or mounting of the divinity in the initiate. (Murphy 1989; Gonzalez Wippler 1973).

**Santiago de Compostela**. *See* COMPOSTELA.

**Sāntiniketan**. In Sanskrit this means 'abode of peace'. *Śāntiniketan* was first founded by Debendranath Tagore as a traditional Indian school. It then became the site of Rabindranath Tagore's ashram and educational colony, established in the tradition of religious and cultural universalism developed by the BRĀHMO SAMĀJ. It is best known for R. Tagore's Viśva Bharatī, founded in 1921: a university for the promotion of intercultural and international activity and understanding leading to the unification of humanity (Kripalani 1971).

**Sant Nirankārīs**. A 20th-century sectarian movement, not to be confused with the earlier NIRANKĀRĪ MOVEMENT of Bābā Dayāl. This sect is seen as heretical by orthodox Sikhs and has been involved in bitter clashes with them.

**santri** (Javanese; Indonesian). A devout Muslim who tries to live in accordance with the formal rules, ethics and values of Islam; in a narrower sense, and originally, referring to a student in a PESANTREN. (Geertz 1960a; Jay 1963, 1969; Koenjaraningrat 1971).

**Sant tradition** (from Sanskrit, *sant*: 'saint', a general designation of a person dedicated to a religious life). In a special sense the term is applied to a group of founders of late medieval movements, like Gurū Nānak (*see* SIKHISM), Kabīr, and others who de-emphasized traditional forms of sectarian religiosity and stressed a common human faith and ethics.

**Sanūsiya** (Arabic). One of the most important ṢŪFĪ brotherhoods of North Africa founded by Sīdī Muḥammad ibn ʿAlī al-Sanūsī (*d* 1859). This widespread order was the spearhead of resistance to Italian imperialism in North Africa in the early 20th century.

**sanzen** (Japanese). The occasion on which a trainee Zen monk presents his current state of mind to the Zen teacher in a personal interview, especially in Rinzai Zen (*see* RINZAI-SHŪ).

**Sapta Darma** [Sapta Dharma]. Literally, 'The Seven Holy Obligations'; a mystical movement founded in 1952 in Pare, East Java, which will lead its adherents to eternal life through mystical devotion and prayer training. (Hadiwijono 1967; Mulder 1983a).

**Sapta Dharma**. *See* SAPTA DARMA.

**saptarsis**. *See* ṚṢI.

**Sarapis**. A Hellenistic-Egyptian deity resulting from the combination of OSIRIS and APIS, whose cult was introduced by Ptolemaios I (305–283 BCE) and apparently has its origin in Sinope on the Black Sea. Sarapis was identified with ZEUS, HELIOS or HADES and was represented bearing a bushel of corn on his head. The main place of worship in

Alexandria, the Sarapeion, was destroyed by Christians in 391.

**Sarasvati**. *See* BENZAITEN.

**sarcophagus**. *See* NECROPOLIS.

**Sarekat Islam**. Literally, 'Islamic Union'; an Indonesian Muslim association of nationalist character, founded in 1912 in Surakarta Java. In 1927 it was transformed into a political party and continued its work until 1973. (Djaelani 1959; Korver 1962; Niel 1970; Noer 1973; Boland 1982).

**Sarvāstivāda** (Sanskrit: 'those who teach that everything exists'). An early school of Buddhism which split off from the STHAVIRAVĀDA, and over against which early MAHĀYĀNA Buddhism took form.

**śāsana** (Sanskrit: 'teaching, instruction'). A term usually denoting the Buddhist 'church', i.e. Buddhist teachings, institutions and practices; in a general sense tantamount to Buddhism. *Buddha-śāsana* refers more specifically to the bearers of the teaching of Gautama BUDDHA, i.e. to the monastic tradition and the monks. *See also* SĀSANA REFORM.

**Sāsana reform**. The reforms of the Buddhist monastic orders in the Theravāda countries principally during the 18th and the 19th centuries. These reforms were promoted and protected by the kings: in Sri Lanka King Kīrti Śrī Rājasiṃha (1747–82), in Burma King Mindon Min (1853–78) and in Thailand King Mongkut (1851–68).

**Sa skya pa**. A school of Tibetan Buddhism dating from the 12th century CE and based on the Sa-skya monastery (founded in 1073). The school pays particular attention to a MAHĀYĀNA Buddhist tantric text known as the Hevajra Tantra.

**Satan** (Hebrew: 'adversary'). Originally any agent of YAHWEH who prevents some action (e.g. *Numbers* 22.22, 32 [verb used of angel]; *Psalms* 109.6). In *Job* 1–2 Satan is a minor deity, who serves (too enthusiastically!) as 'devil's advocate' to test Job. In later writings he is the chief of demons, who frustrates divine purposes (*2 Samuel* 24.1 with *1 Chronicles* 21.1), led a war in heaven against God (according to later interpretations of *Isaiah* 14.12ff; *2 Enoch* 29.4f; *Revelation* 12.7ff, and will be destroyed at the final divine-messianic triumph. Satan is frequently identified with the snake who tempts Eve in *Genesis* 3. *See also* BEELZEBUL; BELIAL; APOCALYPTIC. Satan has also been compared and contrasted several times with the Buddhist tempter Māra (Ling 1962; Boyd 1975).

**Sātapa Brāhmaṇa**. *See* BṚHĀDARANYAKA UPANIṢAD.

**Sātgurū** (Punjabi: 'True Gurū'). A term used in Sikh texts to refer to God. Nānak, the first of the ten spiritual leaders later known as the TEN GURŪS, who was influenced theologically by his participation in the North Indian SANT TRADITION, held that God is *nirguna*, without qualities, but also that God is present in all as the inner teacher (*saguna*), able inwardly to guide a person along the path to liberation (MUKTI). *See also* GURŪ.

**Sathyā Sāī Organization**. *See* SĀĪ BĀBĀ MOVEMENT.

**satī** (Sanskrit: 'faithful wife'). The self-immolation of widows, usually on a pyre together with, or shortly after the demise of, their husbands. *Satī*-memorials were often frequented as places of pilgrimage. Following a strong anti-*satī* movement led by Rājā Rām Mohan Roy the British East India Company outlawed *satī* in 1822 in its territories (it had been outlawed before by Muslim rulers in some parts of India). Incidents of *satī* (sometimes forced) are still reported in India even now.

**satipaṭṭhāna** (Pāli: 'establishing awareness'). The earliest form of Buddhist meditation described in the *Mahā Satipaṭṭhāna Sutta* of the Pāli Canon, rediscovered as a method by Burmese masters in the early 20th century.

**Saturn**. An ancient Roman divinity of uncertain derivation whose festival took place on 17 December. His festival, the Saturnalia, involved reversed roles for slaves and masters as well as celebration of the end of agricultural work for the year. Occasional identification with the Greek god CRONOS is not connected with the cult.

**Satyāgraha** (Sanskrit, 'truth-grasping'). The practical philosophy of M. K. Gandhi (1869–1948), which combined the two principles of non-violence (AHIMSĀ) and adherence to the Truth (*satyā*), the former being the means to the bringing about of the latter. These principles and their practical expression formed the foundation of Gandhi's ashram in Ahmedabad and the subject of *The Story of My Experiments with Truth*, and have since been a major influence on individuals and movements in India and abroad. (Sarma 1973; French & Sharma 1981).

**satyrs**. Ancient Greek spirits of wild and rustic life, attendants of DIONYSOS and also associated with PAN. Satyrs were portrayed as part animal and part divine, and excessively erotic and licentious.

**Saule**. Baltic sun goddess; also the word for sun. Folk tradition depicts her riding over the mountain of heaven in a chariot and in the evening sinking into the sea or crossing it westwards in a boat to reappear in the East in the morning. Like DIEVS she is believed to inhabit a farm on the mountain of heaven and to descend to earth, causing fields to be fertile by walking across them. The summer solstice is celebrated in her honour, with feasting and dancing round an open fire; the goddess is said to be present dancing among her worshippers. She is attributed with human emotions, crying over the loss of possessions or arguing with her daughters (*see* SAULES MEITA) or the moon god MĒNESS.

**Saules meita**. 'Daughter of the sun.' Sometimes another name for SAULE, the Baltic sun goddess, but usually refers to her daughters, a number of heavenly beings who act out courtship and marriage ceremonies in the Baltic myths, together with the *Dieva Deli*, the sons of DIEVS. They are characteristic of the important role of divine family relations in Baltic mythology.

**ṣawm** [ṣiyām] (Arabic). Fasting, one of the FIVE PILLARS of the Islamic religion, especially that which is obligatory during the lunar month of RAMAḌĀN. Fasting can also be undertaken as a voluntary act at other times throughout the year.

**scarab**. A dung-beetle, one of the most potent ancient Egyptian amulets. Made of faience, stone, metal, pottery or glass, the scarab represented a form of the sun-god at his rising, known as KHEPRI. The scarab came to have significance as the concept of coming into existence or the renewal of life, and was both worn as an adornment in life and placed between the MUMMY bandages in death, to ensure resurrection. A large version, the Heart Scarab, was placed over the heart of the mummy and was inscribed with a spell from the *Book of the Dead* to prevent the deceased's heart from witnessing against him at the day of judgement.

**scepticism** (from Greek *skepsis*: 'doubt'). The view that reason lacks the capacity to arrive at any firm conclusions. Extreme sceptics are called 'Pyrrhonists', who, following Pyrrho of Ellis (365–275 BCE), deny the possibility of certainty of knowledge by taking a position of silence or withholding judgements concerning anything. Augustine, in the 4th century, held that scepticism is self-defeating, since for one to be deceived one must first know that one exists. Descartes in the 17th century established modern philosophy by transforming scepticism into a methodological kind of doubting. In the 19th century Kierkegaard suggested that a leap was necessary in order to overcome scepticism if truth was to become a lived experience.

**schism** (from Greek, *schisma*: 'rent', 'tear'). Originally a wilful separation from the church. It did not involve doctrinal error, being a sin against love and unity and not against the faith. The claim that others are schismatic implies a corresponding claim that one's own position remains unchanged. However, from the standpoint of presumed ORTHODOXY, schism is to be regretted while HERESY is to be deplored. For an analytical study of schism in the early church see Greenslade 1953.

**Schmalkaldic Articles**. An uncompromising statement of the teachings of Martin Luther, drawn up by himself at the request of the Elector of Saxony for the General Council of Mantua in 1537. The statement was approved by a meeting of protestant political leaders and theologians. However, they also approved a conciliatory appendix by Melanchthon, which, unlike the articles themselves, made allowance for the supremacy of papal jurisdiction. *See also* SCHMALKALDIC LEAGUE.

**Schmalkaldic League**. An alliance of protestant groups including followers and political supporters of both Luther and Zwingli, formed at Schmalkalden in 1531 against the Habsburgs. *See also* SCHMALKALDIC ARTICLES.

**scholasticism**. In general, a highly elaborate, intellectualized system of religious thought based on apparently secure presuppositions; thus, it is appropriate to speak in certain contexts of Buddhist scholasticism, Muslim scholasticism, etc. In particular, as Scholasticism, the philosophy and theology pursued in the *scholae* (schools) of the medieval European universities, often distinguished by their rigorous, rationalistic character. Neo-scholasticism is the revival of this thought, particularly of the work of Thomas Aquinas, in the Roman Catholic Church in the 19th and 20th centuries. *See* THOMISM; ACCIDENTS; ARGUMENTS FOR THE EXISTENCE OF GOD; FIVE WAYS; NOMINALISM; OCKHAM'S RAZOR; PER SE NOTA; SUBSTANCE.

**Scylla**. *See* CHARYBDIS.

**Second Council of Nicaea**. *See* ICONOCLAST CONTROVERSY.

**Second Temple**. The Second Temple in Jerusalem, built after the return of the Jews from EXILE and rededicated in 516 BCE, though the rebuilding continued for over a century. Under Herod the Great the Temple was completely reconstructed but it was destroyed by the Romans in 70 CE. (Widengren 1977: 515–32).

**Sect Shintō** (Japanese: Kyōha Shintō) An official designation which was used from 1882 onwards to designate voluntary religious movements loosely connected with Shintō, with a view to separating them from State Shintō, which was considered obligatory. Since 1945 the term has no longer been relevant in a legal sense, because of the disestablishment of Shintō itself, and some of the religions in question reject it for their part. Strongly Shintoist in orientation were Shintōkyō (also Shintō Taikyō or Shintō Honkyoku), Shinrikyō, Taishakyō (related to Izumo shrine), Misogikyō and Shinshūkyō while Confucianist leanings were displayed by Shūsei Ha and Taiseikyō. Jikkōkyō and Fusōkyō regarded Mount Fuji as a centre of religious devotion and Mitake kyō focused on Mount Ontake, still a major religious centre. Of particular importance are Kurozumikyō, Konkōkyō and Tenrikyō, which are still significant religious organizations a century later.

**Sed festival**. *See* PHARAOH.

**Seder**. Literally, the 'order' of the PASSOVER service which is recited by Jewish families around the table, usually in their homes. The *Seder* is marked by the drinking of four cups of wine, and the eating of matzas, bitter herbs and other foods with ritual significance. As well as partaking of dinner, a *Seder* consists of reading the HAGGADAH and singing the blessings, prayers and songs it contains. Meant to be a joyous festival of freedom, the Passover *Seder* may include a good deal of informal discussion and improvisation, and is not always an entirely orderly event.

**Sedna**. A major Inuit (far northern North America) deity who functions as the Sea Mother. She releases the game animals essential for human survival and must be placated by SHAMANS who descend to her when she is irritated by human foibles.

**seite** [siei'di]. A sign for a sacred place among the Saami people. The seites were usually stones formed by nature, but cliffs or even mountains could also be regarded as seites. Offerings were made to seites in order to bring luck in reindeer breeding, hunting and fishing. (Holmberg 1915; Karsten 1955; Hultkrantz 1962).

**sefirot** (Hebrew; singular, *sefirah*). According to the KABBALAH, the ten 'enumerations' or emanations by which the creation is related to its source in the AYN SOF.

**seiðr**. *See* VQLVA; FREYJA; AESIR.

**Sekhmet**. An ancient Egyptian lioness goddess and consort of *Ptah*; also the Eye of RE and destroyer of mankind. She was the patroness of doctors and healing.

**selamatan**. *See* SLAMETAN.

**self**. The centre of consciousness in a person, commonly regarded as the most important factor constituting human identity and individuality. *See also* SOUL.

**self-religion**. *See* SELF-RELIGIOSITY.

**self-religiosity**. A term used to characterize the seminal teaching of the New Age of the contemporary west. The ultimate source of existence is believed to lie within – most obviously in the realm of the true self, but also in the realm of the natural at large. Whatever is elemental is the sacred; whatever derives from the artifices of modernity is the villain. Accordingly, self-religionists endeavour to liberate themselves from the contaminating effects of having been socialized/indoctrinated into the mainstream. They draw on a wide range of disciplines to discover their essence, that is, what they are by virtue of their 'original blessing'. This variety of spirituality, basically a highly optimistic form of humanism (which is spiritualized in the process), is now a well-established cultural and practical resource for those intent on manifesting their 'inherent glory' (Heelas 1992).

**Selket**. An ancient Egyptian scorpion goddess, one of four female guardians of the dead. She is known in Greek as Selkis.

**Selkis**. *See* SELKET.

**Sema**. *See* ORPHIC MYSTERIES.

**semantron**. A long bar of wood struck with a mallet in Greek Orthodox churches to summon worshippers.

**Semar**. One of the Javanese PANAKAWAN, actually superior to all gods, representing 'the realistic view of life as opposed to the idealistic' (Geertz 1960a: 277) by reminding man of doing his duties. (Brandon 1970; Magnis-Suseno 1981).

**sembahyang** (Javanese, Indonesian). The Javanese-Indonesian term for ṢALĀT, performed by all SANTRI, though 'they differ somewhat in the elaboration with which they carry out the act' (Geertz 1960a: 216).

**sendatsu** (Japanese). Originally a Buddhist term meaning 'leader' or 'guide', especially a leader of ascetic practices or pilgrimages. From the 9th century onwards the practice of visiting Shintō shrines such as Kumano and Yoshino became popular, and thus the term came to be used to refer to guides for such pilgrimages in a Shintō context.

**Senju Kannon**. In Japanese Buddhism, the thousand-armed Kannon (AVALOKITŚVARA), whose many arms and eyes (marked on the hands) symbolize compassion. In iconography 40 arms are common, standing for one thousand, which in turn stand for a limitless number of saving arms.

**sentient beings**. An expression used in Buddhist contexts, especially in MAHĀYĀNA Buddhism, to refer to all living beings in the various possible states of rebirth. Mahāyāna Buddhism posits the Buddha-hood of all living beings, at least latently, and indeed also of plants and inanimate specks of dust.

**Sephardi** (Hebrew). In contrast to ASHKENAZI, the designation of Jewish communities and culture deriving from Spain, Portugal, North Africa, the Balkans and the Levant.

**Septuagesima**. *See* QUINQUAGESIMA.

**Septuagint** (from Latin, *septuaginta*: 'seventy'). The first translation of the Hebrew Bible, made into Greek in the 3rd century BCE. The name derives from the 70 scholars who, according to legend, were said to have been working separately, for 70 days, and came up with identical translations.

**Serapeum**. *See* APIS, SAKKARA.

**Seraphim Society** [Egbe Serafu]. Any one of a wide range of religious groups with hundreds of thousands of followers in West African countries, especially Nigeria, all of which emphasize the centrality of prayer. Public confession and hymn-singing are other important aspects of worship. Though originally intended to be supplementary to the 'established' churches, the Seraphim Societies have gradually developed their own institutional forms. Annual pilgrimages to revelatory sites are encouraged, especially to Mount Olorunkole, where an angel is said to have appeared to warn people of a judgement by God. Cherubim Societies are similar to Seraphim Societies (Peel 1968).

**Serapis**. A god who combined Greek and Egyptian features, introduced into Egypt (Alexandria) under Ptolemy I (305 BCE) as a cult intended to unify Greeks and Egyptians.

**Serat Centini**. Old-Javanese didactic handbook of mystical knowledge, conceived as a cycle of tales. One of the most representative of SULUK literature. (Soebardi 1971; Rasjidi 1977).

**serdab**. *See* KA.

**Servant Songs**. Four poems in DEUTERO-ISAIAH (*Isaiah* 42.1–9, 49.1–6, 50.4–9, 52.13–53.12), drawing on royal ideological motifs as indicating divine favour to the Jewish exiles. The servant is variously identified, either individually (e.g. as Jehoiakin or a descendant) or collectively as the exiles. (The 'suffering servant' of the fourth poem is a redemptive figure, later interpreted messianically.) Christian theologians have taken the Servant Songs as prophetic references to the suffering Christ. (North 1948; Clines 1976; Whybray 1978; Wilcox & Paton-Williams 1988).

**servus servorum dei** (Latin: 'servant of the servants of God'). An epithet used in formal documents by the POPE of himself, first by Gregory the Great (*d* 604).

**Seshat**. An ancient Egyptian goddess of writing and measurement, who recorded the royal lifespan and measured out the temple plan.

**sesshin** (Japanese). An intensive training period in a Zen Buddhist monastery, e.g. one week in each month.

**Seth**. In ancient Egypt, the son of GEB and NUT and brother and murderer of OSIRIS. Identified as Typhon by the Greeks, he was represented as an unidentified, boar-like animal. Warlike and violent, Seth's colour was red. With a major role as evil-doer in the Osiris myth, Seth came to be regarded as a demon or fallen god.

**Seth**. *See* GNOSTICISM, MANDAEANS, MANICHAEISM.

**Sethians**. *See* GNOSTICISM.

**seva** (Sanskrit). *Seva* is a central term in VAIŚNAVISM, where it means worship of the image of God in the form of feeding, clothing etc, and extends to the 'service of the gurū', the representative of God. In Sikh tradition service is most commonly focused on the GURDWARA, on maintaining the premises and working in the kitchen, though a broader view of service to the community at large now often applies. It has also been taken up by various modern Hindu movements in the sense of social service (Sevāśram).

**seven deadly sins**. Seven MORTAL SINS, apparently first so listed by Pope Gregory the Great (*d* 604) – pride, covetousness, lust, envy, gluttony, anger and sloth.

**Seveners**. *See* ISMĀ'ĪLĪS.

**seven sacraments**. In medieval Christianity the number of SACRAMENTS was generally held to be seven, and this view, shared in the Orthodox churches, was formalized for the Roman Catholic Church at the Council of Trent. The seven are: BAPTISM, CONFIRMATION, MASS, ABSOLUTION, EXTREME UNCTION (i.e. anointing at the point of death), ORDINATION and MATRIMONY. Protestant churches frequently regard only BAPTISM and the communion or EUCHARIST (corresponding to the Catholic mass) as sacraments, on the grounds that these two were specifically instituted by Christ, as related in scripture.

**Seventh Day Adventists**. *See* ADVENTISTS.

**Sexagesima**. *See* QUINQUAGESIMA.

**sext**. *See* PRIME.

**Shādhiliyā** (Arabic). A ṢŪFĪ order, founded by ʿAlī al-Shādhilī (*d* 1258), which spread mainly in Egypt and North Africa.

**Shāfʿī**. *See* MADHHAB.

**shahāda** (Arabic). Literally, 'witnessing'; in the sense that the Muslim's declaration of faith is his witnessing that 'There is no God but ALLĀH and Muḥammad is His messenger (RASŪL).' To this the SHĪʿA Muslim will add 'Alī is the friend (WĀLĪ) of God.'

**Shahar and Shalem**. The Dioscuri (morning and evening manifestations of Venus) in CANAANITE RELIGION, with twinship, royal and redemptive symbolism. (Harris 1906; Fevrier 1937; Olmo Lete 1981: 427–48). *Compare* ASHTAR.

**Shahīd** (Arabic, Punjabi). Martyr; Gurū Arjan, the fifth Sikh Gurū (*see* TEN GURŪS), was the first of many Sikh martyrs.

**Shaka Nyorai**. *See* NYORAI.

**Shakers**. A small body of enthusiastic Christians so named because of their tendency to shake physically while meeting for prayer (compare the Quakers, *see* SOCIETY OF FRIENDS). The movement began in 1747 and found new strength in the late 18th century under the leadership of Ann Lee, named Mother Ann by her followers and regarded as 'the female principle in Christ'. The Shakers held property in common, were mainly celibate, and lived in separate communities of their own. In modern times their numbers, never large, have dwindled drastically.

**shaking tent**. A North American form of shamanizing with circumpolar correspondences found in northern Algonkian religions. The SHAMAN, who is bound and placed in a small structure, calls the spirits, especially TURTLE. The structure shakes as the spirits enter and their voices are heard from within. At the end of the séance, the shaman is found unbound.

**Shalom** (Hebrew: 'peace'). A greeting which is related to the Hebrew word for 'complete'. 'Shabbat Shalom' is a common SABBATH greeting.

**shaman**. An expert in reciprocal ecstatic communication between the normal and the supranormal. The term derives from the Tungus word *saman* and was originally adopted by Russians to refer to the ritual specialists of Central Asian, Siberian and Arctic peoples. The shaman's function as a mediator between the normal and the supranormal worlds is based on his relationship with helping spirits and his ability to reach the realms of the other world. The specific tasks of the shaman vary in different communities. The position of shaman was either handed down within the family (via the spirits of ancestor shamans) or acquired by incidental vocation. The so-called shaman's sickness (*see* ARCTIC HYSTERIA), which was interpreted as the call of the spirits to become a shaman, often preceded the initiation period, during which an older shaman transmitted the traditional shamanic knowledge and introduced the singing, drumming and other techniques of ecstasy to the beginner. The length of the initiation period, the number of rites and the control of the initiate's abilities varied in different cultures and depended on the position of the shaman in his community. Common features were the novice's visions, during which he experienced his initiation by the spirits and acquired his own guardian or helping spirits, which were often zoomorphic. The initiate's experience that the spirits destroy his former ego, physically dissecting or boiling it, and thereafter reassemble it, recapitulates a wider theme of death and rebirth and is connected with animal ceremonialism. (Eliade 1964; Siikala 1978; Harner 1980; Basilov 1984; Findeisen 1967). *See also* SHAMANISM.

**shamanic drum**. The drum is the most important of the SHAMAN's attributes in the Arctic and Asiatic areas. The drum is the basic means of shamanic trance technique. By drumming, the shaman gathers his helping spirits and journeys to the other world. The shaman uses his drum as his vehicle; thus the Transbaykal Evenks call the drum a boat, the Yakuts, Buryats and Soyots call it a horse and the drumstick a whip. At the same time the drum represents the helping spirits of the shaman. The membrane of the drum is made from the skin of an animal chosen by the spirits and its frame from a special shaman's tree, representing the WORLD TREE. Designs painted on the skin (e.g. among the Tatars and the Lapps) and carvings on the drum frame express the shamanic conception of cosmology and supranormal beings. (Emsheimer 1944, 1946, 1948; Lot-Falck 1961; Manker 1938–50; Harva 1938).

**shamanism**. A complex pattern of diverse rites and beliefs centring on the activities of the SHAMAN which has been primarily documented in the cultures of Northern and Central Asia. Characteristic of shamanism is a special technique of ecstasy by which the shaman transfers to an altered state of consciousness in order to contact his helping spirits and to create a rapport with the supernatural world by their mediation. Shamanistic rites were held, for example, to guarantee success in hunting, fishing or some other occupation, to protect the clan's lands, to increase and develop the family, or to bear the souls of the dead to the family underworld. The most important of the shaman's duties, and common to all branches of shamanism, were healing and prophesy. All the vital elements of shamanism were present at the séance: the shaman, his client, the audience and the shaman's assistants, spirits called on by the shaman which were symbolized in ritual objects, especially in the shaman's drum (*see* SHAMANIC DRUM) and dress. The settings for séances, shamanic requisites and ritual practices varied in different cultures and depended on the status and class of the shaman. However, the basic structure of the séance, the means of ecstasy, the concept of the spirit helpers and the part played by the audience are elements common throughout Northern and Central Asia.

Some scholars have stressed the concept of the flight of the soul as the central idea of shamanism. According to Mircea Eliade, who regarded the technique of ecstasy as the basis of shamanic ritual behaviour, the shaman specializes in a trance, during which his soul is believed to leave his body and ascend to the sky or descend to the underworld (Eliade 1964). While in some cultures the idea of the shaman's journey is replaced by or accompanied by traditional forms according to which the shaman is able to contact the spirits without leaving the body, it must be noted that the journey element alone is not sufficient as the nucleus of shamanistic ideology (see Hultkrantz 1973). The journey of the shaman, spirit possession (Findeisen 1957), the entering of the spirit into the shaman's body (e.g. in Central and Eastern Siberia) and the manifestation of spirits by ventriloquism (e.g. in Paleoasiatic areas) are functional alternatives articulating the communication between the shaman and the other world (Siikala 1978).

Because of the wide distribution of such phenomena as the journey of the soul to the other world, the concept of multiple souls as a basis of this, the invocation of helping spirits during trance, visionary trance techniques etc., the question of the geographical confines of shamanism has been open to dispute. Practices and ideas parallel to 'classical' Siberian and Arctic shamanism have been traced in North and South America, Oceania, South-east Asia and in pre-Christian Scandinavian and Finno-Ugrian cultures. At the same time the wide distribution of shamanistic phenomena and the endemicity of its basic ideas – soul flight, soul dualism, animal spirit helpers and the link with animal ceremonialism – support the view that the roots of shamanism lie in the palaeolithic hunting cultures (Lommel 1965). (See also Diószegi & Hoppál 1978; Hoppál 1983).

**Shamash**. An Assyro-Babylonian sun-god. Probably a fusion of the Semitic sun-goddess (*see* SHAPSH) with the Sumerian god UTU. He maintains cosmic justice, and according to Hammurabi's stela delegates legal powers to the king (Ringgren 1973: 56–9).

**shammash** (Hebrew) [Yiddish: *shammes*]. A beadle attending to the practical needs of a BEIT HAMIDRASH. Also, the ninth candle which is used to light the other candles on a ḤANUKKAH MENORAH.

**shammes**. *See* SHAMMASH.

**Shang Ch'ing**. *See* SHANG QING.

**Shangdi** [Shang-ti]. The name (probably meaning 'God on High') for the supreme deity of the Shang dynasty (16th century – *c*.1066 BCE). Opinions on how this deity was imagined differ. It seems to have been related to the ancestors of the Shang kings. Since the Zhou [Chou] dynasty (*c*.1066 – 221 BCE) Shangdi was equated with TIAN ('Heaven'), the highest deity of the Zhou people. In Chinese popular religion the title 'Shangdi' is given to several celestial deities, like YUHUANG.

**Shango** [Ṣàngǒ]. GOD of lightning among the Yoruba of Nigeria, who is mainly worshipped in the northern parts of the Yoruba country which belonged to the Oyo empire (Idowu 1962).

**Shangó**. *See* CHANGÓ.

**Shang-qing Sect**. An influential Daoist sect (*see* DAOISM) founded in 364 CE by a certain Yang Xi, who experienced the revelation of sacred scriptures in 31 *juan* (books, fascicles). This corpus of scriptures was continuously revised and enlarged until its widespread acceptance was secured in the fertile lower Yang-Tse region. The holy mountain of the sect is Mao Shan (one of the ten 'major cave-heavens', *see* DONGTIAN) near Nanking; thus the sect is also known as the Mao Shan Sect.

The main issue of the 'Upper Clear' (*shang qing*) adept was the cultivating of QI ('breath', 'pneuma') and a meditational method called 'keeping the spirits' (*cun shen*), which means that the gods that supervise the physiological functioning of the body as a microcosm are visualized and controlled. The highest aim was to attain the *dao* and enter into the 'Upper Clear Heaven'. The Mao Shan Sect, at first an independent religious movement, in the 12th century merged with the Daoist tradition of the 'Heavenly Master' (*see* ZHENG YI DAO). Mao Mountain until today remains a pilgrimage centre of importance for the region.

**Shang-ti**. *See* SHANGDI.

**Shan Hai Jing** [*Shan-hai Ching*] (Chinese: 'Classic of Mountains and Seas'). An ancient Chinese geographical work. Its different parts originated probably between the 5th and 1st century BCE. The book is an important source for ancient Chinese geography, mythology, popular customs and ethnography.

**Shankpanna**. *See* SHOPONA.

**Shapsh**. The West Semitic sun-goddess. She pairs with ASHERAH (as morning and evening sun) to mother the twin Venus-gods SHAHAR AND SHALEM (Caquot 1959). *Compare* SHAMASH.

**sharīʿa** (Arabic: 'pathway'). Islamic canon law. The normative path for the guidance of Muslims which comprises all of God's prescriptions for mankind. The law is based upon the QUR'ĀN, the traditions of the Prophet (HADĪTH), consensus of the community (IJMĀʿ) and, where these provide no clear guidance, analogical reasoning (*qiyās*). Covering not only the FIVE PILLARS of the faith, but also all aspects of daily life, actions are classified on a five-point scale as either obligatory (*wājib*), recommended, neutral, disapproved or forbidden (*ḥarām*). The scope of the law has in practice been greatly reduced in much of the Muslim world, largely under the impact of imported European legal systems; the remaining domain of the law lies in matters of marriage, divorce and inheritance. In some countries like Turkey, the former competence of the law has been abolished. (Coulson 1979).

**Shavuot** (Hebrew).The Festival of Weeks, which follows seven weeks after PASSOVER, commemorating the giving of the TORAH to the Children of Israel, on Mount SINAI. It is the second of the three pilgrimage festivals.

**shaykh** (Arabic: 'elder'). A title of respect bestowed upon any learned or accomplished man such as a distinguished scholar or alim. It is also a title given to a ṢŪFĪ master, teacher or saint. The term is applied too as a title for the various officials of the mosque-university al-AZHAR in Cairo.

**Shaykh al-Islam** (Arabic). An honorary title variously accorded Muslim religious scholars, theologians, mystics and jurists. In the heyday of the Ottoman Empire the title was applied especially to the Mufti of Istanbul, whose office gradually acquired religious and political importance without parallel elsewhere; the office declined in importance in the 19th century and was abolished in 1922 along with other traditional religious institutions upon the creation of the Turkish Republic.

**al-Shayṭān** (Arabic). The Islamic name for SATAN. *See also* IBLĪS.

**She** [Sheh]. The God of the Soil, who has been worshipped in China since highest antiquity. In imperial times the cult of She, usually combined with Ji [Chi], the God of the Grains, was part of the official state cult. Each administrative unit had its own local god of the soil, with Earth (Di [Ti]), which was worshipped by the emperor in person, on top of the hierarchy. In popular religion the god of the soil was called TUDI.

**Shechem**. A central Palestinian city occupied by Israelites (*Genesis* 34). An OMPHALOS site (*Judges* 9.37), where *Deuteronomy* originated. (Nielsen 1955; Wright 1965; Wright 1970).

**Shekhinah**. (Aramaic and Hebrew). The divine 'Presence', as it makes itself known in the material world. In the MIDRASH the SHEKHINAH became associated with a specifically feminine aspect of God, concerned with inter-personal relationships. It is associated in Kabbalah with the SEFIRAH of Malkhut, or the manifestation of the Kingdom of God on earth. (*See also* KABBALAT SHABBAT.) The exile of the Shekhinah is associated with the alienation of the people Israel from her relationship with God.

**Shem**. *See* GNOSTICISM.

**Shema**. (Hebrew: 'hear'). The prayer which expresses the central affirmation of Jewish faith: 'Hear O Israel the Lord our God, the Lord is one.' This quotation from *Deuteronomy* 6.4 is followed in both the morning and evening services by *Deuteronomy* 6.5–9 and two other passages from the TORAH. It is inscribed within TEFILLIN and MEZUZAHS, and has been recited by Jews – especially martyrs – upon death.

**shen** (Chinese: 'divine', 'good'). A term having a variety of significations. It may signify any kind of spiritual beings, e.g. the gods of mountains, rivers or stars, but also the spirits of deceased human beings. Many of the popularly worshipped *shen* or gods are actually deified men. Generally *shen* are spirits that belong to the sphere of YANG as opposed to GUI ('demons'), which relate to YIN. Hence, the HUN souls are regarded as *shen*, while the PO souls are GUI.

**shengren** [sheng-jen] (Chinese). Usually translated as 'Sage'. In Neo-Confucianism the term is used to denote the ideal to be reached by self-cultivation.

**Shen Nong**. In Chinese mythology, the 'Divine Husbandman', regarded as the inventor of agriculture and medicine. According to some traditions he succeeded FU XI and was followed by HUANG DI.

**Shīʿa** [*Shīʿism*]. A term derived from the Arabic expression *Shīʿat* ʿAlī ('party' or 'partisans of ʿAlī'), one of the two forms of religious expression in Islām (the other being the majority Sunnī form). Shīʿa tenets involve the acknowledgement of ʿAlī b. Abī Ṭālib, cousin and son-in-law of the Prophet Muḥammad and ʿAlī's descendants as the true leaders (IMĀMS) after the Prophet of the Muslim community. In law and theology, only minor points of difference separate the Shīʿa from the Sunnis. Shīʿa communities are significant in Iran, Iraq, Lebanon, India and Pakistan and the revolution in Iran (1978–9) rekindled Shīʿa consciousness and their role in contemporary political affairs (Jafri 1979).

**Shichi-go-san**. The Shintō 'Seven-five-three' festival, held on 15 November. A rite of passage in which five-year-old boys and three- and seven-year-old girls visit their local shrine to pray for special protection.

**Shi Jing** [*Shih Ching*] (Chinese: 'Book of Songs'). The oldest anthology of Chinese poetry. It contains 305 songs of various origin, the oldest of which go back to the early Zhou dynasty (*c.*1066–221 BCE). The songs were highly estimated by Confucius and his school, who included the *Shi Jing* in the Five Classics (WU JING).

**shikinen sengū** (Japanese). The transfer of a Shintō deity to a new shrine building after a prescribed number of years. It is likely that shrine facilities were originally rebuilt annually, at which time ceremonies were performed to renew the power of the enshrined deity. When permanent shrine buildings came to be erected, however, the transfer to a new building was carried out only once in a prescribed number of years. At Ise Shrine the transfer is performed once every 20 years: 1973 (for the 60th time), 1993, and so on. Some other shrines are rebuilt at regular intervals of, for example, 30 or 50 years. The rebuilding ensures the cleanliness and hence the purity of the wooden structure.

**Shikoku pilgrimage**. *See* JUNPAI.

**shimenawa** (Japanese). A sacred rope marking the presence of a Shintō god or the border of a sacred area. Zig-zag strips of paper, called *shide*, are hung from the rope, which is made of twisted new straw.

**shinbutsu bunri** (Japanese). The separation of Shintō and Buddhism. The Japanese Imperial Restoration of 1868 was accompanied by a movement in the Shintō world to restore the purity of everything Japanese. Hence, on 28 March 1868 the government issued an order to abolish the previous custom of amalgamating Shintō and Buddhism (*see* SHINBUTSU SHŪGŌ). As a result of this order, it was forbidden for Shintō gods to be called *bosatsu* (BODHISATTVA), for Buddhist scriptures to be read before the Shintō deities, for Buddhist priests to participate in Shintō worship services, or for shrines to have Buddhist paraphernalia within their precincts.

**shinbutsu shūgō** (Japanese).The harmonization of Shintō, the native Japanese religion, with Buddhism, which had arrived from India via China. This process of synthesis was particularly conspicuous during the Nara period. Thus, before constructing the huge statue of the Buddha at the Buddhist temple Tōdaiji in Nara (741), Emperor Shōmu first commanded the Buddhist priest Gyōki to report the plan to the goddess at Ise Shrine and to make an offering of relics of the Buddha; Buddhist scriptures were also offered to the Usa Hachiman Shrine. Syncretic practices such as building shrines on temple grounds and pagodas in shrine precincts, and reading Buddhist scriptures before Shintō deities or presenting them to shrines, all continued until the two religions were forcibly separated in the early Meiji period, from 1868 onwards (*see* SHINBUTSU BUNRI). Associated with this approach was the theory of HONJI SUIJAKU.

**shingaku**. A religious and ethical movement headed by Ishida Baigan (1685–1746). While based on Shintō (special reverence was paid to AMATERASU ŌMIKAMI), concepts borrowed from Zen Buddhism and Neo-Confucianism were used to preach everyday ethics at a popular level. The literal meaning of the term is 'Mind (or Heart) Learning'.

**shingon** (Japanese). A 'true word', i.e. a string of syllables mystically conveying truth, a MANTRA. *Compare* SHINGON-SHŪ.

**Shingon Buddhism**. *See* SHINGON-SHŪ.

**shingon-shu**. A major school of Japanese Buddhism founded by Kūkai (774–835), with a headquarters on Mount Kōya. Although there are various subsects they are hard to distinguish in practice. For common features see RYŌBU MANDARA; SHINGON; SOKUSHIN JŌBUTSU. *See also* BUZAN-HA; CHIZAN-HA.

**Shingyō**. An abbreviation for Hannya Shingyō (*see* HEART SUTRA).

**shinjin** (Japanese). True faith, especially in the context of the Japanese Buddhist school JŌDO-SHINSHŪ.

**shinnyo** (Japanese). Suchness; corresponds to Sanskrit TATHATĀ.

**shintai**. *See* GO-SHINTAI.

**Shintō**. The traditional religious practices carried on in shrines throughout Japan's history, as well as the attitudes toward life which support these practices. At the core of this religion is a reverent religious attitude which has prevailed since antiquity and which leads Japanese believers to experience the will and activity of the gods through various events of everyday life. As a community religion Shintō has no normative revelation, but through the interpretation of ancient mythology and the re-evaluation of folk ways, it has developed a loosely coherent system of religious belief. At present there are in Japan some 80,000 shrines, of which some 97 per cent belong to the Association of Shintō Shrines (JINJA HONCHŌ). Shintō in this form may also be known as SHRINE SHINTŌ. (Herbert 1967; Ono 1962; Holton 1938; Kageyama 1973).

**shirk**. *See* ALLĀH.

**Shiromanī Gurdwārā Parbandhak Committee (SGPC)**. The 'Chief Gurdwārā Management Committee', which was formed in 1920 and given official recognition in 1925 by the Punjab Government to manage Sikh GURDWĀRĀS. The SGPC has also been responsible for producing the Rahit Maryādā (*see* RAHIT NĀMĀ).

**Shitennō**. Japanese designation for the four heavenly kings who guard the four directions of the compass to protect the teaching of Buddhism and the welfare of the land. The Shitennō Temple (Shintennōji) built in 587 in (present-day) Ōsaka is named after them.

**Shiva**. *See* ŚIVA.

**Shōbogenzō**. *See* SŌTŌ-SHŪ.

**shofar** (Hebrew). A ram's horn used as a trumpet. It is blown on the Jewish New Year and at the conclusion of YOM KIPPUR.

**shoḥet**. (Hebrew). A person whose vocation it is to be a ritual slaughterer of KOSHER meat.

**Shopona** [Ṣọpọná, Shankpanna]. God of smallpox among the Yoruba of southwestern Nigeria (Idowu 1962).

**short count**. The Mayan cycle of 13 KATUN (13 × 7,200 days, or 256¼ years), each *katun* of which was named from the last day, always Ahau (day name), on which it ended (Coe 1980). *See also* LONG COUNT.

**shou yi** (Chinese: 'to maintain the One'). A key term in Chinese meditational practices. It aims at holding together the HUN and the PO souls in one's body, concentrating upon internal and external deities that regulate the physical mechanism to avoid disease and ageing. Several methods are known, most of them involving either visualizations of protective or regulative deities or practices pertaining to the 'refining' of pure QI.

**Shrine Shintō**. *See* SHINTŌ.

**Shroud of Turin** [the Holy Shroud]. A cloth believed by those who venerate it to be the very burial shroud in which the body of Christ was wrapped after the crucifixion. This belief is based on an imprint of a human body showing the STIGMATA and with a face suggesting great suffering and spiritual power. Efforts have been made to demonstrate by scientific means that the material is older than the Middle Ages, since when it can be traced historically. Others, however, take the critical view that even great age does not necessarily imply authenticity.

**Shu**. An ancient Egyptian God of the air, son of ATUM, husband of TEFNUT, and father of GEB and NUT. Shu featured in the COSMOGONY of HELIOPOLIS.

**Shugendō**. A complex of beliefs and practices originating partly in traditional Japanese mountain cults and partly in esoteric Buddhism (Tendai and Shingon Buddhism – *see* TENDAI-SHŪ; SHINGON-SHŪ). Shugendō is directed towards the achievement of supernormal powers, including the power of healing, by means of severe ascetic practices such as standing under cold waterfalls. While the interpretative tradition is dominated by Shingon Buddhism, Shugendō also shows traces of ancient SHAMANISM, for example in the wearing of animal pelts (Blacker 1975).

**Shu Jing** [*Shu Ching*] (Chinese: 'Book of Documents'). A collection of historical records dealing with the words and deeds of ancient Chinese rulers from the legendary sage kings Yao and Shun to the early Zhou dynasty (*c.*1066–221 BCE). The historical value of these documents is difficult to assess. Some texts were already recognized as forgeries in antiquity, while others are regarded by modern scholars as ancient myths transformed into history. Nevertheless, the *Shu Jing* has been highly respected by the Chinese literati, who included it in the Confucian canon of the Five Classics (WU JING).

**Shulḥan Arukh**. The 'Set Table', the Hebrew book in which Joseph Caro codified his commentary on Jewish law, the 'Beit Yosef'. Written in the 16th century, the *Shulḥan Arukh* continues to be the most influential summary of HALAKHAH for the Orthodox Jewish community (*see* ORTHODOX JUDAISM).

**Shun**. A legendary ruler of high antiquity in China. According to tradition he was selected because of his great virtue by YAO as successor. In Confucianism Shun is honoured as one of the ancient sage-kings and a paradigm of filial piety (*see* XIAO). It is doubtful whether he can be regarded as historical.

**Shushōgi**. A widely used text summarizing the teaching of Sōtō Zen Buddhism, compiled in modern times on the basis of Dōgen's more difficult *Shōbōgenzō*.

**Sibylline Books** (Sibylline Oracles). Collections of prophecies preserved at Rome on the Capitoline Hill. Tradition held that the books were the work of the Greek Sibyls, and arrived there in the 6th century BCE. They were consulted by the QUINDECIMVIRI at times of crisis. The books provided a compendium of prophetically conceived history which was freely drawn on by early Christian APOLOGISTS. *See also* AESCULAPIUS.

***Sic et Non*** (Latin: 'Yes and No'). A work by Peter Abelard (1079–1142) listing the discordant views of theologians on 150 disputed issues, as a focus of theological discussion. It greatly influenced SCHOLASTICISM's view of theology as a subject for rational debate. (Henke and Lindenkohl 1851).

**síd**. *See* TUATHA DE DANANN.

**Siddur** (Hebrew). Literally, the 'order' of Hebrew prayers. The Siddur is the Hebrew prayer book, which features daily prayers for morning, afternoon and evening services, as well as additional prayers for SABBATHS and Holy Days.

**sidra rabba**. *See* GINZA.

**siei'di**. *See* SEITE.

**Sigi**. A masquerade ceremony of the Dogon of Mali, which is part of their ancestral cult and commemorates the first human death. The feast is celebrated every 60 years over a period of eight years in sequence from village to village. The term also appears in the French form, Sigui (Griaule 1963).

**Sigui**. *See* SIGI.

**Sikh** (Punjabi: 'Disciple'). A follower of the teachings communicated by the TEN GURŪS. According to the Sikh code of conduct (*see* RAHIT NĀMĀ, a Sikh is one who believes in one true Gurū or God, the teachings laid down in the GURŪ GRANTH SĀHIB, and initiation into the faith (AMRIT). *See also* SIKHISM.

**Sikhism**. The religion of the Sikhs, originating with the teaching of Gurū Nanak (1469–1539). The leading concept, Gurū, indicates its home in the Indian religious world. At the same time a strict monotheism, the ideal of universal equality and the eventual recognition of a sacred book, the GURŪ GRANTH SĀHIB, as a permanent revelation are more reminiscent of the Islamic tradition, which was also a dominant factor in the formative period. In spite of these affinities Sikhs view their faith as a unique revelation which provides those who adhere to it with a distinctive, shared identity. Forced to take up arms at an early stage in their history, the Sikhs are renowned for their physical bravery. Nevertheless, peacefulness and love, of man and of God, are regarded as the highest values (Cole & Sambhi 1978; Cole 1984a; McLeod 1984). Apart from the 14 million Sikhs who live in India (1980), Sikhs now live in other countries, particularly those of the 'Old Commonwealth' and the USA. The United Kingdom has the largest diaspora population with around 250,000 Sikhs. (Barrett 1982; Juergensmeyer & Barrier 1979). *See also* AMRITSAR; GURDWĀRĀ; JANAM SĀKHĪS; KHALSA; SIKH; TEN GURŪS.

**śīla** (Sanskrit: 'right behaviour', 'virtue', 'morality'). The term is widely used in Hinduism, Jainism and Buddhism. *See also* PAÑCAŚĪLA.

**silsila** (Arabic: 'chain'). The chain of tradition handed down by ṢŪFĪ SHAYKHS to their pupils, comprising the teachings of a particular brotherhood. The word also applies to the chain of authorities making up the ISNĀD of a ḤADĪTH in the Islamic literature of prophetic tradition.

**Silvanus**. The Roman god of uncultivated land, considered dangerous and akin to the Greek satyrs.

**sīmā** (Pāli: 'boundary'). A Buddhist term denoting the consecrated boundary within which higher ordination (UPASAMPAD) and other (monastic) ceremonies are performed.

**simḥah** (Hebrew) [Yiddish: simkheh]. Joy or celebration. Also an occasion, such as a wedding or a circumcision, which is a cause for celebration.

**simkheh**. *See* SIMḤAH

**Simonians**. *See* GNOSTICISM.

**simony**. A term of disapproval for commercial dealings in religious services or offices, so named after Simon Magus, who attempted to buy spiritual power from the early Christian Apostles (*Acts of the Apostles* 8.18–24). In European Christianity simony was frequently perceived as a real danger, and legislated against down until modern times, in that the patronage of ecclesiastical 'livings' or 'benefices' led to the possibility of their being acquired by financial inducement.

**sin**. Transgressions against the known will of God (also referred to as 'actual sin') and the state of being separated from perfect communion with God as a result of the FALL (also referred to as ORIGINAL SIN). In general, Christian theology has followed the lead of Augustine (354–430) in understanding original sin to be universal in humankind, and has rejected the teaching of Pelagius (flourished 410 CE), who considered that sinless lives may have been led both before and after Christ.

**Sin**. The Assyro-Babylonian moon-god (equivalent to the Sumerian Su.en, NANNA), concerned primarily with kingship and fertility. (Lewy 1945–6; Jacobsen 1976: 121–7).

**Sinai**. The sacred mountain on which Moses received the DECALOGUE and COVENANT (*Exodus* 19–24). The story is composite, combining in the exilic period disparate traditions, and setting them as paradigms and parables of national history. Sinai is thematically related to ZION, with OMPHALOS symbolism. (Nicholson 1973; Levenson 1985; Wyatt 1986c).

**Singh** (Punjabi: 'Lion'). A name taken by all male members of the Sikh KHĀLSĀ.

**Singh Sabhā** (Punjabi: 'Sikh Society'). The first *sabhā* was established in 1873 in AMRITSAR for the purpose of reviving Sikh religious practices and supporting educational and literary ventures.

**Sino-critical approach**. An approach to the study of religion which entails the continuous revision of the way in which the subject is understood in the light of Chinese perspectives on religion. *Compare* AFRO-CRITICAL APPROACH; GENDER-CRITICAL APPROACH.

**Si Shu** [Ssu Shu] (Chinese). The Four Books, a collection of basic Confucian writings brought to prominence by the Song dynasty (960–1279) Neo-Confucianists. They contain the DA XUE [*Ta Hsüeh*], ZHONG YONG [*Chung Yung*], LUN YU [*Lun Yü*] and MENG ZI [*Meng-tzu*]. The name 'Si Shu' was first used by Zhu Xi (1130–1200), who wrote commentaries on all of them which became the basis of the official interpretation of Confucianism since the Yuan dynasty (1279–1368).

**Sita**. *See* RAMA.

**Śiva-Linga**. *See* LIṄGAYATS.

**Śivata**. *See* ŚAIVA SIDDHANTA.

**skandha** (Sanskrit: 'aggregate') [Pāli: *Khandha*]. A Buddhist term characterizing the human being as psycho-physical aggregates with five aspects: body, feelings, perceptions, volitions and consciousness. All five aggregates are conditioned, i.e. they arise, endure and disappear continuously until there is enlightenment (BODHI). *See also* ANĀTMAN.

**Skira**. Ancient Greek festival held at the end of the year, including a procession to Skira, when the Athenian king was symbolically killed, reflecting the exchange of roles between Athens and Eleusis as a regression to chaos prior to the re-establishment of social order and institutions; newly harvested grain was put into storage bins to mark the harvest and the reproductive capacity of seed.

**Skuld**. *See* YGGDRASILL.

**slametan** [selamatan; salamatan] (Indonesian, from Javanese (originally Arabic) *slamat/slamet*: 'blessing', 'well-being', 'harmony' etc.). As sacred communal meals of various kinds, *slametan* represent the key rituals of AGAMA KEJAWEN 'in the attempt to sustain, maintain, or redress order' (Mulder 1983a: 261). Depending on the importance of the occasion, a *slametan* consists of a dinner of several courses, which is blessed by a religious expert and served to the participants; bigger *slametan* are usually accompanied by WAYANG performances.

There are different occasions for holding a *slametan*: life crises (birth, circumcision, marriage, death etc.) and calendrical or village festivals, often in connection with the agricultural cycle, but also good or bad events in an individual's life (illness, a threat of sorcery or evil spirits etc.), and even more 'secular' occasions such as house-moving, academic graduation etc. Briefly put: 'A *slametan* can be given in response to almost any occurrence one wishes to celebrate, ameliorate, or sanctify' (Geertz 1960a: 11); it serves 'to demonstrate the desire to be *slamet* through the attempt to achieve undisturbed continuity or to redress a disturbed equilibrium'; so its purpose is 'the maintenance of existing order and the constraint of danger' (Mulder 1983b: 262). (Koenjaraningrat 1971; Jay 1969).

**Sleipnir**. *See* LOKI, ODIN.

**ślokas**. *See* BHAGAVADGĪTA.

**smṛti** (Sanskrit: 'memory'). Literature embodying (orthodox) Hindu tradition. Some such works carry the name *smṛti* (e.g. *Viṣṇusmṛti*, MANUSMṚTI); others, like the MAHABHĀRATA or *Rāmāyaṇa*, are considered to be of similar authority. The group of people calling themselves *smārtas*, followers of tradition, are usually associated with Advaita Vedānta and not necessarily 'traditionalists' in a general sense.

**Sobek**. An ancient Egyptian crocodile-god, associated with RE, and worshipped particularly at KOM OMBO, where mummified crocodiles are preserved, and in the Fayoum.

**Society of Friends**. The formalized name of the 'Friends of the Truth', a Christian sect also commonly known as 'Quakers' from their tendency to tremble physically when religiously moved (*Compare* SHAKERS). The movement was begun by the travelling seeker and preacher George Fox (1624–91), who relied on the inner voice of the Holy Spirit, thus challenging the external authority of scripture and church alike. This is reflected in the form of the Quaker 'meeting', which is liturgically unstructured except for a concluding handshake on the part of two elders, and which allows any individual participants who feel moved by the Spirit to speak aloud, with or without reference to scripture.

**Sod**. *See* PARDES.

**Sōka Gakkai**. An important lay Buddhist movement of modern Japan based on the teachings of Nichiren and of the LOTUS SŪTRA. The literal meaning of the name, Sōka Gakkai, is 'value creation society', and its full name for many years has been Nichiren Shōshū Sōka Gakkai, signifying a close relationship with the monastic tradition of NICHIREN SHŌSHŪ. *See also* DAISEKIJI; NAMU MYŌHŌ RENGEKYŌ.

**Sokar**. Hawk-headed funerary god of the ancient Egyptian city of Memphis; in the Late Period (660 BCE onwards), he was part of the composite god of the dead, PTAH-Sokar-OSIRIS. He is known in Greek as Sokaris.

**Sokaris**. *See* SOKAR

**sokushin jōbutsu** (Japanese). 'Obtaining Buddha-hood in this very body', a teaching strongly promoted by Kūkai, founder of Shingon Buddhism (*see* SHINGON-SHŪ).

**Sol** (Latin: 'sun'). Roman sun god, originally one of the INDIGITES, and ancestral divinity of the Aurelian family at Rome. His worship became particularly popular in the 3rd century CE under the influence of the emperors Elagabalus and Aurelian. The iconography influenced Christian representations of Jesus. Sol Invictus ('The Invincible Sun') was a designation for MITHRAS. *See also* ISIS CULT.

**solar temple**. *See* ISLAND OF CREATION.

**Solomon's Temple**. *See* WAILING WALL; ZION.

**Soma**. *See* ORPHIC MYSTERIES.

**soma** (Sanskrit). A word with many meanings (e.g. 'moon' etc.), the most prominent of which is that of a plant, whose juice was used in the Vedic soma-sacrifice, which plays a great role in ancient Indian ritual. The soma-plant was identified as fly agaric by W. Wasson – a theory much debated among specialists.

**sombra**. *See* SUSTO.

**Son of Heaven**. *See* TIAN.

**Sŏnangshin**. A Korean deity who guards the approach to villages and ensures safe passage for travellers.

**Sophiology**. A form of religious philosophy seeking to mediate between THEISM, incarnational theology and PANTHEISM through the concept of the female divine wisdom, Sophia, regarded as a kind of world-soul. Advanced by the Russian thinker Vladimir Solofieff (1853–1900), it was also taken up by theologian Sergius Bulgakov (1874–1944).

**sorabe** (Malagasy). 'Great writings', sacred manuscripts in the possession of the Antaimoro tribe of Madagascar. These writings are in the Malagasy language, but written in Arabic script. Since they are stored by hanging inside the roof of a hut, they require renewal from generation to generation. Those trained to copy the texts, on locally produced bark paper, are deemed to possess magical and divinatory powers and hence great authority. Power is thought to be vested in the script rather than in the wording of the *sorabe* (Mack 1986).

**soteriology** (from Greek *soter*: 'saviour'). A teaching or teachings on the subject of salvation.

**sotoba** (Japanese). A Japanese equivalent of the Indian word STŪPA, used in particular to refer to long wooden memorial tablets in Buddhist cemeteries, notched in five sections at the top and bearing appropriate inscriptions.

**Sōtō-shú**. Zen Buddhism in the lineage of the Chinese Ts'ao-tung-tsung, as established in Japan by Dōgen (1200–53). Sōtō Zen emphasizes the practice of ZAZEN as a method of realizing one's own essential Buddha-nature. The main writing of Dōgen, for centuries the essential reference work of the sect, is his *Shōbōgenzō*. The majority of the millions of registered member families of Sōtō-shū in modern Japan do not themselves practise zazen but avail themselves of funeral services performed by the temple priests. *See also* SHUSHŌGI.

**Sōto- Zen**. *See* SŌTŌ-SHŪ.

**soul**. The principle of life, reason and self-consciousness. Plato taught that the human soul is composed of reason, self-assertion and desires, whereas Augustine analysed it in terms of memory, understanding and will. Today the term is often regarded as just another way of describing the human personality or character; but many philosophers and religious thinkers have taught that the soul is an immaterial, unextended and indivisible substance which is immortal. *See also* NESHAMAH; SELF.

**speaking in tongues**. *See* GLOSSOLALIA.

**Spenta Mainyu**. *See* ZOROASTRIANISM.

**Sphinx**. The ancient Egyptian sphinx is usually male with a lion's body and the head of a god or king. The Greek word 'sphinx' may be derived from the Egyptian words meaning 'living image'.

**Spider**. In western Native American religions, a TRICKSTER or culture hero.

**spirit**. Originally a metaphor for the 'wind' or 'breath' whereby God creates and empowers living beings. The term has come to be used of immaterial entities, including the human SOUL.

**spirit possession**. A state of consciousness which is indigenously understood as a foreign spirit, demon or divinity taking hold of a particular person. The person often behaves in an unusual manner and is sometimes believed to pass on messages from the Beyond. It is often a question of ecstatic states of consciousness or trance (*see* ECSTASY). Spirit possession is often interpreted as being negative and measures are sometimes taken to free the person from possession. This is called EXORCISM. Spirit possession is common in most religions. In the case of the positive understanding of spirit possession, as in Christianity, this term is not used, but rather phrases like 'filled with the Spirit' or 'baptism in the Holy Spirit'.

**śramaṇa** (Sanskrit) [Pāli: *samaṇa*]. A pre-Buddhist term denoting a homeless wandering ascetic.

**sramanera**. *See* PRAVRAJYA.

**śravakabodhi**. *See* BODHI.

**śrāvakabuddha** (Sanskrit: 'enlightened disciple'). A BUDDHA who has attained enlightenment while being a disciple of Buddha. *See also* BODHI; SAMYAKSAMBUDDHA.

**Śrī** (Sanskrit: 'wealth', 'well-being'). A name of the Hindu Goddess, the consort of VIṢṆU, also used as a general sign of auspiciousness. In modern India it is used commonly as honorific, equal to English 'Mister' or 'Sir'.

**Śribhasya**. *See* RĀMĀNUJA.

**Śrivaiṣṇavas**. *See* AḶVĀRS.

**Śrivaiṣṇava Sampradaya**. *See* RĀMĀNUJA.

**śruti** (Sanskrit: 'hearing'). In Hinduism, a technical term for revelation and the books which contain it. All Hindus would consider the VEDA (in the wider sense, i.e. *saṁhitās*, BRĀHMAṆAS, ĀRṆYAKAS, UPANIṢADS) as *śruti*. Depending on the SAṂPRADĀYA they belong to, they would also include other works. Thus, VAIṢṆAVAS consider the VIṢṆU- and the BHĀGAVATA PURĀṆAS as *śruti*, as do Śaivas the ŚAIVA-ĀGAMAS, and ŚĀKTAS the *Tantras*. *Śruti* is used for theological proof texts in arguments.

**Stabat mater** (Latin). The short name for a medieval hymn whose subject is the sorrow of Mary beneath the cross on which Jesus was hanged. More fully the opening words are *Stabat mater dolorosa* ('His mother, sad, was standing . . .').

**stama**. *See* OM OR AUM.

**Star of David**. *See* MAGEN DAVID.

**Starovetsi**. *See* OLD BELIEVERS.

**State Shintō**. The pre-war Japanese state distinguished the religious ceremonies of the imperial court and of the shrines from those of other religions. Shrine rites and education fell under public administration, as well as shrine administration and policy. However, after the Second World War, the Occupation authorities issued an order calling for the abolition of this system, which had reached its full development in modern times after the restoration of the monarchy (Meiji Restoration, 1868). State Shintō was founded on the idea that the prosperity of the nation, the safety of the imperial house and the happiness of the people are blessings granted when human politics coincide with the will of the gods, a view expressed by the term *saisei itchi*, or unity of worship and rule. This harks back to the word (*matsuri-goto*) that was used to refer to both religious rites and government. The term *kōdō* (Imperial Way) is also used to designate this ideal conduct of politics, seeing the emperor's official worship of Amaterasu Ōmikami and the gods of heaven and earth as a fundamental condition of good government.

**stations of the cross**. A series of 14 carvings or paintings which show the sequence of incidents at the end of Christ's life, before which prayers are said, especially during LENT and in particular on Good Friday. In effect this practice amounts to a miniature pilgrimage, reflecting the traditional route of pilgrims in Jerusalem to Calvary. The 14 stations are as follows: Pilate's decision that Christ should be crucified; Christ is given the cross to carry; he falls for the first time; he meets his mother Mary; Symon of Cyrene is made to carry the cross for him; Veronica wipes the face of Christ; he falls for the second time; he meets with women of Jerusalem; he falls for the third time; his clothes are removed; he is nailed to the cross; he dies on the cross; his body is removed from the cross; his body is laid in the tomb.

**stele**. A stone slab, usually inscribed and used as a gravestone or, with a historical or religious inscription, placed in a temple.

**Sthalpuranas**. *See* PURĀṆAS.

**sthavira**. *See* THERA.

**Step Pyramid**. *See* SAKKARA.

**Sthaviravāda** (Sanskrit: '(those who teach) the doctrine of the Elders [*Sthavira*]'). An early Buddhist school, standing in opposition to MAHĀSAṂGHIKA. *See also* THERAVĀDA.

**stigmata**. The marks of suffering on the body of Christ, notably from the nails of the cross and the crown of thorns, believed to be reproduced in others through mystical identification with the suffering of Christ, first of all in the case of Francis of Assisi.

**Stoicism**. A philosophy named after the *stoa* (hall) where it originated in Athens in the 3rd century BCE. It taught that nature is pervaded by a cosmic reason, and that human virtue consists in living according to nature. Stoic ethics, but not Stoic metaphysics, were influential on Christianity.

**stotra** (Sanskrit: 'hymn'). An important category of religious literature in the Hindu tradition. Since worship is usually accompanied by the recitation of hymns to the deity thus honoured, over the centuries vast collections of *stotras* have accumulated in Sanskrit and in vernaculars. Many such collections have been printed and are widely used.

**stream-winner**. *See* FOUR FRUITS.

**structuralism**. Strictly speaking, any method in the natural, mathematical and human sciences which ignores apparent differences of content in favour of formal isomorphic resemblances between different segments of reality. Thus, for example, one might demonstrate that a similar principle of formal organization underlay the eating habits, the language, the class structure and the courtship rituals of a particular society. Such a discovery of unexpected symmetry at the formal level tends to subvert causally deterministic social theories which trace all cultural 'superstructures' to ultimate 'drives' such as sexual desire or economic ambition. In its focus on systems, structuralism also tends to be more concerned with synchronic simultaneity and the permanent 'function' of parts within a whole, rather than in temporal change. In recent years, structuralism has often informed many aspects of the study of religion, especially via the influence of social anthropology. *compare* POSTSTRUCTURALISM.

**stūpa** (Sanskrit) [Pāli: *thupa*]. A dome-shaped or bell-shaped mound, a stylized tumulus, commemorating the death of a Buddha or other enlightened person and usually containing relics. Probably from about the 1st century BCE *stūpas* were also used to contain Buddhist writings, representing, as DHARMA, the BUDDHA himself. The form of the *stūpa* developed variously, and dramatically, in South-east Asia where the dome representing the original mound was elongated with a spire, and in China, Korea and Japan, where it took on the character of a storeyed tower (pagoda). The central pillar around which all these variations were developed is of pre-Buddhist Indian origin and probably symbolized a cosmic centre. In Sri Lanka giant *stūpas* similar to that of Sanchi (India) played an important role from an early date. The Sinhalese term for *stūpa* is *dagaba* ('a relic-container'). Individual wooden funeral posts in Japan, known as SOTOBA, are also derived from the stupa, in that the deceased are expected to attain buddhahood (Dallapiccola 1980).

**sublimation**. According to psychoanalysis, a defence mechanism involving inhibited libido (life instinct) such as, for example, oral and anal desires which are satisfied through creative activities in the areas of art, literature, music, religion, science etc.

**substance**. That which exists in itself and persists throughout change, e.g. a man or a tree. As the Latin equivalent of the Greek *ousia*, the term signified a thing's essential defining characteristic. In western Christendom it gradually came to signify especially the permanent, unifed reality of God, in contrast with the differentiated divine persons of the Trinity. At the same time Christ had been defined as being 'of the same substance with the Father'. (*See also* ACCIDENTS; HOMOOUSIOS; TRANSSUBSTANTIATION.) Baruch Spinoza (1632–77) taught that there is only one substance, which is infinite and is identified with God.

**Subud**. *See* SUSILA BUDI DARMA.

**Sucellos**. Celtic god depicted above all in the Rhône valley holding or leaning on a hammer. His other attributes include sickle, club and bowl. The same figure is sometimes named SILVANUS, the Roman god of vegetation.

**Suddhādvaita Vedānta**. *See* BHAKTI.

**Sūdra**. *See* CASTE.

**suffragan bishop**. *See* BISHOP.

**Ṣūfī** (Arabic). One who has reached the end of the mystical path. *See also* SUFISM; MUTASAWWIF.

**Sufism** [Arabic: *taṣawwuf*]. Islamic mysticism. Sufism is the expression of personal piety which holds out the hope of direct contact with ALLĀH (God) in the present world but at a moment suspended in time. This may be compared but not totally contrasted with the more common form of Islamic piety, the ideal of which is the communal obedience or submission to the will of Allāh as embodied in the religious law (the SHARĪ'A), seen as preparation for the eventual salvation of both the individual and the community.

The origins of Sufism are still unclear, although multiple forces, both within and outside the community were at work at various stages of its development. The earliest Arabic sources depict Sufism proper emerging from an informal movement of ascetics in the decades following the death of the Prophet Muḥammad in 632. Indeed, the word Ṣūfī originally referred to the ascetic practice of wearing rough robes of wool (*ṣūf*).

In the two centuries between the death of Ḥasan al-Baṣrī (728) and the execution of al-Ḥallāj (922), Sufism had developed most of its characteristic features, from the former's austere piety to the ecstatic transcendentalism of the latter. The famous female mystic of Basra, Rābi'a al-Adawiya (*d* 801) contributed the ideal of love of Allāh, while the Egyptian Dhu 'I-Nun (*d c.*859) described the various stages of the Ṣūfī path. In the sense that all Ṣufīs believed in the purification of the soul they were ascetics; some, however, had come to stress the goal of ecstatic emotional experience over the process of purification. This led to friction between the Ṣūfī and the more legalist piety. It was not until the appearance of al-Ghazālī (1058–1111), legal scholar, theologian and philosopher, that Sufism was justified as true in spirit and form to mainstream Islamic faith and practice; he stressed the crucial importance of inner purification and devotion. While his solution was not without its critics, by the 13th century the basic ideas of Sufism had fully permeated Islamic thought.

Ṣūfī brotherhoods (singular, ṬARĪQA) emerged next as a force influencing and embracing the masses, certain of them developing international networks of local chapters. The brotherhoods were characterized by initiation rites, prescribed orders of ritual, a spartan existence, social obligations to the community and missionary activities which often meant political involvement. Until the 19th century they provided a kind of religious bond which enabled the Muslim community to withstand the destructive forces of both external pressures and internal political disintegration. (Nicholson 1979; Schimmel 1975; Lings 1982) *See also* BEKTASHI; MAWLAWIYA; MUTASAWWIF; NAQSHBANDI; QALANDARIYA; QUTB; SILSILA; SUHRAWARDIYA.

**suggestibility**. Receptiveness to suggestive influences (e.g. hypnotic suggestion). Two basic forms of suggestibility, primary and secondary, can be distinguished. Primary suggestibility has its roots in the so-called ideo-motor tendency, i.e. thoughts and ideas that give rise to motor responses but which lie somewhere under the threshold of consciousness. These are functions which practically all people share. Secondary suggestibility has to do with the atmosphere, anguish and fear that exist in a certain situation and which make one more vulnerable to influences from an outside source. In religious contexts (enthusiastic preaching, the threat of eternal punishment etc.) secondary suggestibility is used. In this way people can be led into experiences and behaviour which later, upon mature consideration, might be deemed to be forced and outside of the control of one's own will. The line between suggestibility and intense communication of an acceptable nature (education, entertainment, reprimanding) is somewhat difficult to draw.

**Suhrawardiya**. A ṢŪFĪ brotherhood founded by Shihāb al-Dīn al-Suhrawārdī (*d* 1234). It was one of the most prominent orders of the Muslim Middle Ages and was closely connected with the revival of the Abbasid Caliphate in Baghdad in the early 13th century.

**suijaku**. *See* HONJI-SUIJAKU.

**Sukhāvativyūha**. *See* JŌDO SANBUKYŌ.

**Sukkot** (Hebrew). The Festival of Tabernacles, at which Jews build temporary booths with thatched roofs to commemorate the sojourn of the Children of Israel for 40 years in the wilderness of SINAI. Following PASSOVER and SHAVUOT, it is the third of the three pilgrimage festivals. Also known as the Festival of Booths, it was originally an autumnal (lunar) New Year festival in Israel and Judah (*Numbers* 29.12–39 etc.) and was given a historical meaning later (*Leviticus* 23.43). (Vaux 1965: 495–506).

**sülde** (Mongolian). A protective spirit often thought to reside in the banner of a great khan, whose charisma is thereby focused. Such banners or standards were traditionally the objects of devotion and prayer after the death of the leaders with whom they were linked. A *sülde* is also regarded as a TNGRI. (Heissig 1980: 84–90).

**suluk** (Javanese). Originally, old-Javanese mystical songs attributed to the WALI SONGO; also sung by the DALANG at WAYANG performances. (Zoetmulder 1935; Soebardi 1975; Groenendael 1985).

**suman**. A generic term among the Akan/Ashanti of Ghana for charms, talismans and amulets (Rattray 1927).

**Sumarah**. *See* PAGUYUBAN SUMARAH.

**Sumeru**. The huge mountain of Hindu and Buddhist cosmology, otherwise known as MERU.

**summa** (Latin). Especially in the Middle Ages, to a comprehensive work covering all aspects of theology and philosophy. Famous examples are Aquinas' *Summa theologica* and *Summa contra gentiles*.

**summum bonum** (Latin: 'the highest good'). That good to which all other values are subordinated. The notion dominates much ethical reflection and what constitutes the highest good varies, as might be expected, in the various systems of ethics constructed in the history of Western thought. For Aristotle, for example, the highest good was happiness; for hedonists (*see* HEDONISM) it was pleasure and for Cynics it was knowledge. Some interpretations of the *summum bonum* have been purely formal, as for example in the thought of Kant. For him the highest good was to be found in the good will (defined as the will that wills the good simply because it is the good and not for the sake of the benefit that willing it might bring). In Christian thought the highest good has been seen as being in a state of harmony with God or, with the mystic strand of that tradition, union of the soul with God.

**Sun**. *See* FATHER SUN.

**Sun Dance**. The best known of the Native American rituals, although it only became widespread among those cultures which thrived on the western plains of North America after the adoption of the horse. Of especial interest to non-Native cultures has been the practice of self-torture, which has a more limited locus, especially among those cultures that spoke one of the Siouan tongues. For other cultures, it is generally known as the Thirst Dance, fasting and thirsting being the primary form of self-sacrifice.

The Sun or Thirst Dance incorporated a number of features common to rituals: a ritual of annual communal gathering, a calendrical year-renewal ritual, a hunting fertility ritual, and an individualistic vision questing ritual (*see* VISION QUEST). The ritual was generally held in early summer, when there was sufficient fresh grass to pasture the large number of horses to be found at a tribal gathering of smaller nomadic groups. It was held around the time of the summer solstice and dedicated as well to the replenishing of the bison herds.

Two features were at the heart of many of the rituals. The first was the cutting down of a tree with complex warrior rituals to serve as the centre post, the *axis mundi*, of the Sun Dance lodge. The second was the central role of women, who in many cultures (e.g. Blackfoot and Cheyenne) not only sponsored the ritual, but engaged in ceremonial intercourse with the ritual leader. Surrounding the ritual is a web of myth and symbols so rich and complex that relatively little has been recorded.

Abstinence from water and food, and the near continual dancing in the hot sun over a period of four days, combined with the self-torture found in some cultures, engendered visions pertinent to hunting and warrior success. In this century, the focus of the visions has shifted towards individual and communal revitalization, particularly in regard to overcoming the negative effects of cultural domination since the inception of reservations. With the lifting of the legal bans on the ritual in Canada and the United States in the last few decades, there has been a resurgence of participation among the youth of a number of Plains cultures. Participation has become intertribal, with many making the rounds of the Sun Dances, which now take place in various locations throughout the summer (Jorgenson 1972).

**Sunna**. [sunnah] (Arabic). See ḤADĪTH. Written as 'Sunnī', the word refers to Muslims of the mainstream community of Islām as distinct from the minority SHĪ'A expression of the faith.

**Sunnī**. *See* SUNNA.

**śūnya**. *See* ŚŪNYATĀ.

**śūnyatā** (Sanskrit). Emptiness. In MAHĀYĀNA Buddhist teaching all the factors of phenomenal existence, including psychological experience, are regarded as being in their essential nature (*svabhāva*, literally 'own-being') empty (*śūnya*).

**supererogation**. Works of supererogation are good deeds, according to Roman Catholic theology, which go beyond that which may normally be expected. The most commonly cited examples are the vows of poverty, chastity and obedience taken in most religious orders.

**sūra** (Arabic: plural, *suwar*). A chapter of the QUR'ĀN, the Muslim scripture.

**sursum corda** (Latin). The very ancient phrase addressed by the celebrant to the congregation at the beginning of the liturgy of the EUCHARIST, meaning 'Lift up your hearts!', to which is given the response 'We lift them up to the Lord!'

**Susanoo no mikoto** [Susanowo]. The younger brother of the Shintō sun-goddess Amaterasu Ōmikami. According to the mythology he was unable to contain his own great power and hence caused disturbances among the gods. Though once banished from Takama no hara (the Plain of High Heaven) he later saved a maiden from an eight-headed dragon and gained possession of the sword that is now one of the three imperial regalia (*see* SANSHU NO SHINKI). He was thus transformed into a benevolent deity and is now especially petitioned for salvation from disaster. Identified with Gozu Tennō, he is enshrined at Yasaka Jinja in Kyōto. *See also* GION MATSURI.

**Susila Budi Darma** [Susila Budhi Dharma; Subud]. A mystical movement founded in 1947 in Java as an international organization. Its name, derived from the Sanskrit terms *susila, budhi* and *dharma*, is interpreted by Muhammad Subuh, the founder of the movement, as righteous life according to the will of God (*susila*), inward power of human nature (*budhi*), and devotional receiving of the grace of the Almighty (*dharma*). Susila Budi Darma, better known under its abbreviation, Subud, 'claims to be a movement for adherents of all religions, without making its members disloyal to their own religion' (Boland 1982: 217). Unlike other TAREKAT or KEBATINAN movements (ALIRAN), Subud has some followers in Europe, the United States and elsewhere, having become known through the works of several Western authors about their personal experience with it (Bartók 1959; Hien 1963).

**susto** (New World Spanish). Fright leading to soul-loss. A frightening experience resulting from an encounter with a ghost, supernatural being, natural or supernatural event which may jar the *sombra* (shadow-soul) and cause it to leave the body or to fall asleep. Children and women are particularly susceptible. Natural events include maternal separation, weaning, bereavement, separation from loved ones, violent encounters, murders, threats by or to family members, or threats to livelihood. A combination of sadness, loss of appetite, and fitful sleep are common symptoms of *susto*. (Ingham 1986)

**susupti**. *See* OM.

**sūtra** (Sanskrit) [Pāli: suttal]. The literal meaning of *sūtra* is thread, but in Indian religious contexts it refers to an authoritative text. Late Vedic *sūtras* include *śrauta-sūtras*, *gṛhya-sūtras*, *śulva-sūtras*, intended to summarize large bodies of writings relating to public and domestic sacrifices. The later philosophical systems produced their '*sūtras*' as well, e.g. the *Yogasūtra* by Patañjali and the *Brahmasūtra* by Bādarāyana, which commanded great authority. The Buddhist *sūtras* deal with the teachings of Buddha, the Sūtra Piṭaka being the second 'basket' of the Buddhist Canon. (*See* TRIPIṬAKA).

**sutta**. *See* SŪTRA.

**Sutta Piṭaka**. *See* TRIPIṬAKA.

**svabhāva**. *See* ŚŪNYATĀ.

**svapna**. *See* OM.

**svayambhu mūrti**. *See* MŪRTI.

**Svetasvatāra**. *See* UPANIṢADS.

**Swāminārāyan Saṃpradāya** (Sanskrit, Gujarati). A Hindu movement established by Sahajānanda Swāmi (1781–1830), later known as Swāminārāyaṇ. The *saṃpradāya* is based in Gujarāt (with Gujarāti members in Africa, the UK and USA). It is a devotional movement of ascetic and lay members which accepts Swāminārāyaṇ as a manifestation of Nārāyaṇa, the supreme person (*puruṣottama*). (Williams 1984).

**Sweat Lodge**. The most common ritual to be found throughout the native cultures of the Americas, and having close links with practices found throughout the circum polar region. Native American structures for sweating vary, including rooms dug from the earth (southeast), parts of longhouses (northwest), mud-covered domes (southwest), and domes covered with skin or bark, or more recently canvas or blankets (northeast and Plains). The latter structure is essentially the traditional northern woodland dwelling.

The sweat lodge embodies a wealth of symbolism. The dark hemispherical interior of the dome-shaped structure reproduces the night sky; the symbolic doors, the FOUR DIRECTIONS. The physical entrance opens eastward for many cultures, the direction of the rising sun, the source of knowledge, of beginnings. In some cultures, the physical openings are differently orientated, but with related symbolic understanding: to the south, symbolizing life, or to the west, the direction of life's path. The floor of the structure is the surface of the EARTH MOTHER; the pit dug in its centre, her vagina. Cedar, sage and other plants used to cover the floor of the lodge are purifying plants.

Cedar represents the healing and life-giving power of nature, and is related to BEAR, the primary spirit of regeneration and healing. The willow branches often used for the structure's framework signifies growth and regeneration. The fire in which the rocks are heated represents FATHER SUN, the most potent power of the male Sky. As the female rocks become red-hot in the fire, they are transformed into Grandfathers, the male sacred persons. When they enter the lodge's pit, Earth's vagina, under the canopy of the dark night, the female Sky, cosmogony is recapitulated. As the glowing red Grandfathers are sprinkled with water, the fluid of life, hissing steam, shoots forth, surrounding the act of cosmic coition with hot vapour. The lodge dome becomes a womb in which grows the seed of new life. Both the cosmos and the participants are re-created.

Sweat lodge rituals tend to precede most other Native rituals in North America and also take place on their own. The neurophysiological effects of the ritual combined with the potent symbolism creates a mild TRANCE state among the participants and allows for direct communion and communication with the spirits. Sweat lodge functions include healing, purification and preparation for other rituals, and communal decision formation and strengthening.

The sweat house was also known in Aztec culture and is termed *temazcal* (or *temazcalli*) in Nahuatl (Viesca 1986).

**śyama**. *See* KṚṢṆA.

**Syama Nikaya**. *See* NIKĀYA.

**Syllabus of Errors** [Latin: Syllabus Errorum]. A list of 80 beliefs of variously modern, liberal and political character, declared by Pope Pius IX in 1864 to be erroneous.

**syllogism**. A traditional form of argument in which one proposition is inferred from two other propositions (the premises), which each have one term in common with the conclusion. The following is an example: 'All persons are mortal; Henry is a person; therefore, Henry is mortal.' Syllogisms are of more than one kind depending upon the kinds of propositions of which they are composed – categorical, hypothetical, disjunctive and mixed. Syllogistic logic was first developed by Aristotle whose work provided the foundation for the much more powerful developments of modern symbolic and mathematical logic. The influence of Aristotle's logic on Christian thought is particularly evident in the Middle Ages (*See* SCHOLASTICISM; THOMISM).

**symbol**. An object that stands for something more abstract or general. The cross, for example, is a symbol in Christianity representing Christ's suffering and death. Symbols usually presuppose a certain learning process in order to be fully understood. Through attachment to specific emotional experiences and models of thought, symbols acquire great importance in the creation of intense experiences and commonly have clear implications for action based on belief.

**synagogue**. A Jewish congregation or the place where it gathers for worship. Probably originating at the time of the EXILE, the Jewish synagogue flourished as a local place of worship throughout the DIASPORA and in Palestine, promoting the use of scriptures and ignoring sacrificial cult. The term itself is of Greek origin. (Schürer 1979: 417–63). *See also* BEIT HAMIDRASH; BEIT HAKNESSET.

**Synod of Dort**. *See* ARMINIANISM.

**Synod of Whitby**. *See* CELTIC CHURCH.

**Synoptic Gospels**. The three gospels of Matthew, Mark and Luke, whose narratives when viewed together (i.e. synoptically) display such striking parallels that the dependence of one upon another must be accepted. It may be regarded as satisfactorily demonstrated that Mark is the oldest of the three and was used extensively by Matthew and Luke. Matthew and Luke very probably had a second common source, designated Q, although this no longer exists separately. Matthew and Luke also have further material special to their own texts, designated M and L respectively.

# T

**Ta'aroa**. *See* TANGAROA.

**tabernacle**. A special receptacle, often richly decorated and of special material, for conserving the bread or wafers consecrated during a MASS. It is often placed on or near the main altar of a church, but large churches may have special chapels for this 'reserved sacrament'.

**Tabernacles**. *See* SUKKOT.

**Tābiʿūn**. Successors of the Companions of the Prophet. *See* SALAFIYA.

**taboo**. *See* TAPU.

**Ta-chih-tu-lun**. A substantial treatise attributed to Nāgārjuna (*see* MĀDHYAMIKA) and translated into Chinese by Kumārajīva. Well known in Japanese Buddhist circles as *Daichidoron*, the treatise deals with PRAJÑĀPĀRAMITĀ and related subjects.

**taeshin** (Korean). Ancestral spirits of shamans in Korea, often depicted iconographically in various forms such as Taeshin Mamura (Ancestral Great Spirit) or Taeshin Halmŏni (Grandmother Great Spirit).

**tafsīr** (Arabic). Explanation or commentary, in Islām especially on the QUR'ĀN; the science of interpreting scripture, particularly applied to its external, philological aspects, whereas *ta'wīl* came to mean allegorical interpretation, a method favoured by ṢŪFĪS and the SHĪ'A.

**ṭahāra** (Arabic). Ritual purity in Islām, a state which the Prophet Muḥammad declared to be half of faith, required before performance of the prayer (ṢALĀT) and other ritual acts. Purity is achieved by major ritual ablution, *ghusl*, after menstruation or coitus or minor ablution, *wuḍūʿ*, performed before worship. The corresponding states of impurity are 'major' (JANĀBA) and 'minor' (HADATH).

**tahuatinsuyu**. *See* TAWATINSUYU.

**T'ai-chi t'u**. *See* TAIJI TU.

**t'ai-hsi**. *See* TAI XI.

**taiji** [t'ai-chi] (Chinese: 'Great Ultimate'). A metaphysical concept that plays an important role in Chinese cosmology. In the YI JING the term is used to signify that which was before heaven and earth and all beings. In Neo-Confucianism *Taiji* is equated with the LI ('principle') of the universe which through the interaction of YIN and YANG produces all that exists. *See also* TAIJI TU.

**Taiji tu** (Chinese: 'Chart of the Great Ultimate'). A Chinese cosmological concept dating (in its standard form) from the 11th century CE. The chart (or diagram) is originally a mystical way to explain Daoist (*see* DAOISM) ways to IMMORTALITY through NEIDAN (inner alchemy) techniques, but was used and converted by Zhou Dunyi, who anticipated a new mainstream of Chinese philosophy (later to be called and studied as NEO-CONFUCIANISM) by fusing Daoist metaphysics and Confucian rationalism. One starting point was his Taiji-diagram, and the explanations thereof (for translation into English see Chan Wing-tsit: 1963: 463ff). *See also* TAIJI.

**taima**. *See* JINGŪ TAIMA.

**T'ai-p'ing Ching**. *See* TAIPING JING.

**Taiping Jing**. A Chinese text belonging to the school of DAOISM. At present two versions of the *Taiping Jing* are extent, both contained in the great collection of Daoist writings, the DAOZANG. The original version comprised 170 chapters, of which 57 now remain. Another shorter synopsis of the original is made up of only ten chapters and can be dated to the 19th century. The 170-chapter version was dated by Kaltenmark as belonging in parts to the Han dynasty (206 BCE–225 CE). As the title indicates, the scripture deals with the quality and the restoration of a period of 'Great Peace' (*Taiping*). The text frequently makes mention of a 'Celestial Master' who will restore peace and harmony. It is this Master (usually called 'Heavenly Master') who is viewed as the founder of the TIANSHI DAO, a Daoist sect of the 2nd century CE.

Interwoven with pieces of text on morality, the art of rulership and other matters of a more practical concern are treatises that deal with the cultivation of the body and QI ('breath', 'odem'). The very elaborate Daoist terminology in the *Taiping Jing* also includes the notions of YIN-YANG, FIVE ELEMENTS, LONGEVITY, the 'Realized Man' (*see* ZHEN REN) etc. (Kaltenmark 1979).

**Tai Shan**. Chinese holy mountain (1545 m. in height) located in Tai'an district, Shandong province. The earliest temple structures are said to date back to the Qin dynasty (221–206 BCE). Imperial sacrifices (FENG) to the mountain are mentioned frequently in the ancient Chinese classics. Tai Shan belongs to the group of five holy mountains (WU YUE) whose gods are responsible for the well-being of the empire. The god of Tai Shan is the god of destiny, the administrator of souls.

**T'ai Shan**. *See* TAI SHAN.

**Taittiriya**. *See* UPANIṢADS.

**tai xi** (Chinese: 'embryonic respiration'). Chinese meditational practice employed by Daoist adepts (*see* DAOISM). Here breath is a substitute for ordinary food, shunned by the Daoists. By holding and 'swallowing' one's breath the circulation and respiratory faculties of the body are enhanced. Consequently, the body becomes light and ethereal, transgressing ordinary laws of matter.

**taizōkai**. *See* MAṆḌALA.

**Takama-no-hara**. Plain of High Heaven. In Shintō, *ame (ama-)* is a lofty, sacred world, the home of the *amatsukami*, or heavenly gods (KAMI). While the myth of the descent of the gods from Takama-no-hara has been explained as a mythical indication of the migration of peoples from a specific geographical location, it is likely to have referred from the beginning to a higher world in a religious cosmological sense. *Compare* YOMI.

**Takfir wa'l** Hijra. *See* JAMĀ' AT AL-MUSLIMŪN.

**ṭalāq** (Arabic). In Islām, the term for divorce. Regulations on this matter are found in the Qur'ān, 2.228–32; 4.20.

**tallit** (Hebrew) [Yiddish: *tallis*]. A ritual prayer shawl, with braided fringes attached to each of its four corners. *See also* TZITZIT.

**talmid ḥakham** (Hebrew). A 'learned student', that is, a respected scholar.

**Talmud** (Hebrew).The central multi-volume work of Jewish law and learning. It was completed in the 5th century CE, and is divided between the Babylonian Talmud (the larger portion) and the Jerusalem Talmud. A typical page of Talmud will include a discussion from the MISHNAH, further discussion from the GEMARA, and commentaries from Rashi and his grandchildren.

**tama**. *See* MI-TAMA.

**tamagaki** (Japanese). A fence or wall surrounding shrine buildings or defining the boundaries of shrine precincts. The *tamagaki* may be made of wood or stone and is sometimes found in multiple layers as at Ise Shrine, where it is fourfold.

**tamagushi** (Japanese). A small branch of green leaves presented to a Shintō deity.

**Tammuz**. Assyro-Babylonian fertility god (Sumerian DUMUZI), often taken to be a typical DYING-AND-RISING GOD of vegetation. This interpretation, is, however, doubtful. Tammaz originated as a legendary king who performed SACRED MARRIAGE with ISHTAR (INANNA), and so was deified as her consort. After her descent to the nether world, he is taken down as her substitute, and not resurrected. (Moortgat 1949; Hooke 1953: 36–46; Wagner 1967: 136–58; Jacobsen 1970, 1976; 25–73; Alster 1972).

**Tāne** [Kāne]. The Polynesian ATUA ('god') of the forest and all creatures living in it. His name means 'man'. According to Māori traditions Tāne separated heaven and earth and created the first woman.

**Tangaloa**. *See* TANGAROA.

**Tangaroa** [Tangaloa, Ta'aroa, Kanaloa]. The Polynesian ATUA ('god') of the ocean and all creatures living in it. In some parts of Polynesia he was regarded as creator, and in the Society Islands he became the supreme being.

**tanha**. *See* ṬRṢṆA.

**Tannisho**. *See* JŌDO SHINSHŪ.

**Tannaim** (Hebrew). The rabbis of the MISHNAH.

**Tao**. *See* DAO-DE.

**Taoism**. *See* DAOISM.

**tao/te**. *See* DAO/DE.

**Tao Te Ching**. *See* DAO DE JING.

**Tao-tsang**. *See* DAOZANG.

**Tao-tsang Chi-yao**. *See* DAOZANG JIYAO.

**tapas** (Sanskrit: 'heat'). Penance imposed in order to counteract the effects of sinful deeds. The system of specific penances imposed for specific breaches of law resulted in extensive *prayāścittas*, codes which were used by the religious authorities throughout India for many centuries.

**tāpasa** (Pāli). An ascetic monk, a Theravāda term denoting the forest-dwelling monks. Especially in Sri Lanka there is a *tāpasa* movement consisting of hermits who consider the SAṆGHA corrupt and therefore not worth joining.

**tapu**. A concept of great importance in Polynesian religions. There is no equivalent in the experience and, consequently, in the vocabulary of Europeans, who split up the one word into various translations: 'under religious or superstitious restrictions', 'beyond one's power', 'inaccessible', 'sacred', 'ceremonial restriction, quality or condition of being subject to such restriction'. *Tapu* was made known in Europe as *taboo* by Captain James Cook in the account of his third journey to the Pacific, published in 1784. *Taboos* were soon looked for elsewhere and discovered in most parts of the world under different names. Sir James Frazer was first to discuss *taboo* as a universal phenomenon in a systematic way. Others made use of the term in interpreting the Hebrew Bible, unfolding sociologies of danger, explaining obsessional neurosis, probing into the meaning of uncleanness, etc. As an object of European scholarship the phenomenon became split up into the universal *taboo* and the Polynesian *tapu*. The first was of necessity speculative. 'It put the 19th-century student in the position of an art critic who knows nothing of the world's sculpture except the highly specialized and perfected art of Periclean Athens, and who, therefore, on the discovery of the universe of plastic art, discusses the idols of the Congo and the images of Easter Island in Praxitelean terms. Little can be thus clarified' (Steiner 1967: 142). The specific regional meaning proved to be more substantial. Polynesians see *tapu* at work as part of a system along with MANA and *noa*. *Tapu* protects *mana*, as it were, but it needs *noa* as a counter force, for *noa* takes *tapu* away again where it is no longer of use or where it has come about by accident. The power of making *tapu* (*whaka-tapu*) has many and various sources (the gods, the dead, humans and objects possessing *mana*), but only two forces are able to blot *tapu* out (*whaka-noa*), namely women and cooked food. Christianity and colonization have modified the old Polynesian understanding of *tapu*. How it is seen today was explained by a New Zealand Maori as follows: 'We may define tapu as the sacred state or condition in which a person, place or thing is set aside by dedication to the gods and thereby removed from profane use. This tapu is secured by the sanction of the gods and reinforced by the endowment with mana' (Marsden 1975: 4). (Greschat 1980; Irwin 1984; Johansen 1954, 1958; Smith 1974; Webster 1942). *See also* KAPU.

**taqiya** (Arabic: 'caution', 'fear'). In Islām, this has been described by an early authority as the action of one who, in order to escape his enemies, is compelled to profess unbelief with his tongue while his heart contradicts him. But blame does not fall upon him as God accepts what is in his heart. *Taqiya* is of special significance to SHĪ'A Muslims.

**taqlīd** (Arabic). Literally, 'cloaking in authority', in matters of religion. Thus in Islām, it means to follow the teachings of an authority, having faith in their correctness but without questioning the authority's arguments. In this sense it stands as opposite of IJTIHĀD.

**tarekat** (Indonesian). Equivalent to the Arabic term ṬARĪQA, designating in Indonesia a mystical order which, contrary to the KEBATINAN movements (ALIRAN) bears a more Islamic character. (Boland 1982; Mulder 1983a).

**Targum**. The Aramaic paraphrase/translation of the TORAH, which was begun in the 1st century CE and completed in the 4th. Rabbis of the TALMUD often cite word-plays in the Targum as a basis for their interpretations.

**tariki**. *See* NENBUTSU.

**ṭarīqa** (Arabic: 'pathway'). One of the Islamic mystic brotherhoods or ṢŪFĪ orders. The pathway is that leading to union with ALLĀH and can be known only through the instruction of a SHAYKH who has already completed the journey.

**tarmidi**. *See* MANDAEANS.

**Taṣawwuf**. *See* SUFISM.

**tasmiya**. *See* BASMALA.

**Tathāgata** (Sanskrit: 'thus gone' or 'thus come', metaphorically 'thus progressed' in reference to the enlightenment attained in Buddhism). According to the Buddhist Scriptures Gautama BUDDHA used this epithet of himself.

**tathatā** (Sanskrit). Suchness, the quality of things being just as they are in their true nature. The term occurs in MAHĀYĀNA Buddhism as a synonym for the nirvāṇa-like quality of all things when regarded in terms of their emptiness (ŚŪNYATĀ) of own-being (*svabhāva*). *See also* TATHĀGATA; SHINNYO.

**Tat tvam asi** (Sanskrit: 'that thou art'). One of the MAHĀVĀKYAS expressing the Oneness of BRAHMAN and ĀTMAN. The expression is found in the CHĀNDOGYA UPANIṢAD (VI, 8ff) as a kind of refrain in the instruction given by Uddālaka Aruṇi to his son Śvetaketu.

**Ta-tung-chen-ching**. *See* DA DONG ZHEN JING.

**Tauert**. An ancient Egyptian goddess of childbirth, worshipped particularly by women in labour and represented as an upstanding female hippopotamus. She is known in Greek as Thoueris.

**Tauḥīd**. *See* TAWḤĪD.

**Taurobolium** (Latin). A rite of initiation in which the initiate enters a hollow and is doused with the blood of a bull sacrificed above. *See also* MYSTERIES OF CYBELE.

**Ṭawāf**. *See* KA'BA.

**tawakkul** (Arabic). Reliance. *See* MAQĀMĀT.

**tawatinsuyu** [tahuatinsuyu]. The Inca Imperium, which was based on the idea that the Inca world consists of four quarters. (In Quechua *tawa* means 'four' and *suyu* means 'quarter'.) *See also* CEQUE, FOUR DIRECTIONS.

**tawba** (Arabic). Repentance. Originally the word meant 'turning toward', either as one who turns to ALLĀH with repentance, or of Allāh who turns with forgiveness to the penitent. Among Muslim mystics, the word is given a higher significance meaning a spiritual conversion marking the start of the Ṣūfī path (ṬARĪQA) so that the penitent is turned wholly towards Allāh; by them it is represented as an act of Allāh's grace. *See also* MAQĀMĀT.

**tawḥīd** [tauḥīd] (Arabic: 'unity'). The doctrine of the unity of ALLĀH (God), which is stressed in the QUR'ĀN ('There is no God but Allāh') and thus became a cardinal principle in Islamic thelogy.

**ta'wīl** (Arabic). Allegorical interpretation of the QUR'ĀN. *See* TAFSĪR.

**ta'ziya** (Arabic: 'mourning'). In SHĪ'A Islām, the performance of the passion play commemorating the martyrdom of Ḥusayn b. 'Alī, the Prophet Muḥammad's grandson. *See also* al-MUḤARRAM.

**Teaching of the Twelve Apostles**. *See* APOSTOLIC FATHERS.

**tefillin** (Hebrew). Commonly translated 'phylacteries', these are not so much amulets as a literal application of a biblical commandment. The black leather box-shaped instruments contain excerpts from Scripture (like the MEZUZAH), such as 'you shall bind them as a sign upon your hands, and they shall be as frontlets between your eyes'. Jewish men strap these on to their foreheads and their left arms – close to the heart – for daily morning prayers.

**Tefnut**. An ancient Egyptian goddess of moisture, daughter of ATUM, wife of SHU and mother of GEB and NUT. Tefnut featured in the creation myth of HELIOPOLIS.

**teishō** (Japanese). A Zen Buddhist term referring to an exposition of teaching given by a *rōshi* (a Zen master) to monks in training.

**tekke** (Turkish). A Turkish ZĀWIYA associated with the BEKTASHI and MAWLAWIYA brotherhoods, comprising individual cells, kitchens, infirmary, rooms for communal rites and lodgings for the teacher or SHAYKH.

**teleological arguments for the existence of God** (from Greek *teleios*: 'having achieved a goal, fulfilled a purpose'). Term regularly used to designate a type of theistic argument from design in which is emphasized purposiveness or goal-directedness of (usually inanimate) objects in the universe. *See also* ARGUMENTS FOR THE EXISTENCE OF GOD.

**teleology**. Interpretation of phenomena in terms of purposive or goal-directed activity, thus that branch of philosophical thought concerned with the principle of design that appears to characterize the structure of the universe. The significance of that principle is that it seems to imply the need for a different kind of explanation of the world from the straightforward causal accounts of PHENOMENA provided by the natural sciences. Purposiveness, therefore, is not just an object of explanation but rather a principle of explanation. This is particularly clear in the notion of the TELEOLOGICAL ARGUMENTS FOR THE EXISTENCE OF GOD, which maintain that if the world exhibits order, design and purposiveness it must necessarily have been the result of the purposive activity of some agent who created the world.

**Tell el Amarna**. *See* ATEN.

**Tellus**. A Roman earth goddess, often connected with CERES. *See also* ALTAR OF PEACE.

**temazcal**. *See* SWEAT LODGE.

**temenos** (Greek). An area marked off from common use either for a king, or for a god. In the latter case it may contain a temple or it may be used in a broader sense for a natural area where a god holds sway, e.g. the sea for POSEIDON. *Temenos* is also a leading Scandinavian journal of religious studies.

**temizuya** (Japanese). The structure where ablutions of hands and mouth are performed near the entrance of a Shintō shrine.

**Templars**. Medieval Christian knights who took a a vow to defend Jerusalem after it had been captured from the Muslims in 1099. They subsequently built up a half-religious, half-military organization in several European countries which lasted long after the fall of Jerusalem in 1187. They were also known as Knights Templar.

**Temple of the Tooth**. *See* DAḶADĀ MĀLIGĀVA.

**Ten Articles**. Ten articles of Christian faith promoted in England under Henry VIII in 1536 under the influence of PROTESTANTISM, but retaining various features rejected by most Protestants, such as the intercession of the saints.

**Ten Commandments**. Ten commandments considered in Jewish and Christian tradition to have been revealed to Moses by God at the summit of Mount SINAI. There are two versions of the ten commandments, one in *Exodus* 20.1–17 and one in *Deuteronomy* 5.6–18. The latter may be regarded as ethically more developed in that the injunction to rest on the Sabbath is justified by the need for rest itself rather than by imitation of God as Creator (who rested on the seventh day). The *Deuteronomy* version also no longer lists a man's wife in the same breath as his domestic property. In some Christian churches (Roman Catholic and Lutheran) the second commandment (against the manufacture of any image of God) is counted together with the first, so that the subsequent numeration is different from that current in the Orthodox, the Anglican and the Reformed churches. However, the commandments are everywhere assumed to be ten in number, and the number is sometimes made up by dividing the last commandment, against covetousness, into two parts. Interpretation commonly distinguishes between the religious duties expressed in the first four commandments (when keeping the Sabbath day holy is counted as the fourth) and the ethical duties listed in the last six. (Stamm & Andrew 1967; Nielsen 1968).

**ten fetters**. *See* ARHAT.

**Tendai Buddhism**. *See* TIAN TAI.

**Tendai Shintō** [Sannō Ichijitsu Shintō]. A synthesis between Buddhism and Shintō said to have been established by Saichō (767–822), the founder of the Tendai sect of Buddhism in Japan (*see* TENDAI-SHŪ), but actually a later development. *See also* SANNŌ.

**Tendai-shū**. The Japanese form of TIAN TAI Buddhism established in Japan by Saichō (767–822). Though strongly rivalled by Shingon Buddhism it remained important in itself and formed the cradle for the emergence of more distinctively Japanese forms of Buddhism, especially JŌDO-SHŪ, JŌDO-SHINSHŪ and NICHIREN-SHŪ.

**Ten Directions**. In Indian and Buddhist cosmology the four points of the compass with the four intermediary points (northwest etc.), the zenith (directly upwards) and the nadir (directly downwards). Together these amount to an integrative view of the cosmos. When Buddhas appear in the ten directions this means that Buddhahood is in principle omnipresent. *Compare* FOUR DIRECTIONS.

**tenga**. 'Earth' or 'land' among the Mosi (Mossi) and related peoples of Burkina-Faso and northern Ghana. The earth is regarded as sacred, a non-personified deity, the wife of the sky god Wende. (Zwernemann 1968).

**tengasoba**. 'Master of the land', 'Earth priest' among the Mosi (Mossi) of Burkina-Faso. A similar office is common among the peoples of the Volta region. The 'Earth chief' is a descendant of the supposed first settlers of a place, which gives him the right to apportion the land as well as the priesthood of the sacred earth (TENGA). As such he is also guardian of law and morals, and thus not infrequently a supreme judge. (Zwernemann 1968).

**Ten Good Deeds**. The Ten Good Deeds in Buddhism are: giving, keeping the precepts, meditating, transferring merit, rejoicing in another's merit, giving service, showing respect, teaching, listening to teaching and right beliefs. *See also* MERIT.

**Ten Gurūs**. Sikh tradition recognizes ten spiritual leaders who took the title GURŪ. These gurūs are regarded as vehicles for the divine word (SABDA; GURBĀNĪ) but not as avatars, incarnations or intercessors. Gurū Nānak was the first (1469–1539), followed by Aṅgad, Amar Dās, Rām Dās, Arjan, Hargobind, Har Rai, Har Krishan, Tegh Bahādur and Gurū Gobind Siṅgh, who died in 1708 after giving joint spiritual authority to the book GURŪ GRANTH SĀHIB and the corporate community or PANTH. (McLeod 1968; Cole 1984a).

**Ten Heavenly Stems**. *See* HEAVENLY STEMS.

**Ten Precepts**. In Buddhism, requirements that the monk/nun abstain: (1) from taking life; (2) from taking what is not given; (3) from wrong sexual conduct; (4) from telling lies; (5) from intoxicating liquors, which occasion heedlessness; (6) from eating at the wrong time, i.e. after noon; (7) from seeing dancing, music, vocal and instrumental, and shows; (8) from wearing garlands, perfumes and unguents, and from finery and adornment; (9) from high beds and big beds; (10) from accepting gold or silver, i.e. money. *See also* ŚĪLA; PAÑCAŚĪLA.

**Tentyra**. *See* DENDERA.

**teotl** (Nahuatl). A deity, god, or sacred being in Aztec culture (Karttunen 1983). *See also* TEOTLAHTOLLI.

**teotlahtolli** (Nahuatl). Divine word or doctrine in Aztec culture (Karttunen 1983). *See also* TEOTL.

**teponaztli** (Nahuatl). In Aztec culture, a split lateral log drum designed for two pitches, played with rubber-tipped sticks, which often served as bass (*contrabajo*) to the HUEHUETL, an upright drum accompanying ritual songs (Haly 1986).

**terce**. *See* PRIME.

**Teshub**. The Hurrian storm-god (Laroche 1948).

**teshuvah** (Hebrew: 'answer', 'return'). The Hebrew term for repentance. It implies both a response to the divine call and a return to one's own inner nature. It is less a negative dwelling on sins of the past than a positive 'return' to the path. 'Doing *teshuvah*' implies an outward return to ethical and religious behaviour, accompanied by an inner sense of restored wholeness.

**tetragrammaton**. A Greek word denoting the Hebrew name of God in 'four letters', namely the consonants Y,H,V (or W) and H, and commonly rendered in scholarly literature as YAHWEH. This name is generally rendered in English translations of the Bible as 'the Lord', and sometimes transliterated (incorrectly) as JEHOVAH. The correct vowel sounds are said to have been lost, and the rabbis considered it anyway forbidden to pronounce it, since the name might then be taken 'in vain'. The literal meaning of the tetragrammaton, with the future participle *y* occurring in front of the verb *hvh*, might be rendered as something like 'becoming-is' or 'unfolding-being'.

**Teutates**. Celtic god whose precise function is unknown. The etymology of the name (Irish *tuath*, Gaulish *touta*: 'tribe') suggests he is a tribal god, or perhaps the additional title for various tribal gods. He is connected with war and with the sacrifice of humans by drowning in a cauldron, and is associated with the Roman war god MARS, but also with MERCURY.

**text**. Normally a written source; but for POSTSTRUCTURALISM a technical term with a different meaning, in that for poststructuralists there is nothing 'outside the text'. The point of this axiom is not at all that written texts should be considered in isolation from their cultural and social 'contexts'; rather, it aims to collapse the absolute distinction between text and context. For all contexts turn out to be themselves 'textual', in so far as they are constructed of nothing but 'inscriptions': marks made on the ground, on bodies, in the air as sounds, or in human memory cells. 'Contexts' themselves need to be analysed in terms of their grammatical and narrative structures. At the same time, certain poststructuralists, more influenced by Michel Foucault and Gilles Deleuze than by Jacques Derrida, have been anxious to point out that context includes also a real articulation of physical forces; something which a text in fact invokes and simulates, forming itself as a 'textual body'. The principle of textuality has allowed certain theologians, working in a broadly neo-orthodox tradition, to argue that, for Christians, the world is situated within the text of the Bible, rather than the Bible being situated within the context of the world.

**textus receptus** (Latin: 'received text'). A version of the NEW TESTAMENT in Greek, based on various 16th-century editions and underlying the traditional English translation known as the AUTHORIZED VERSION. Modern critical study and modern translations make use of many variants which have strong claims to greater reliability.

**Thargelia**. Ancient Greek pre-harvest festival in which the 'first corn' was exhibited in procession after a man and a woman, chosen for their ugliness, were expulsed from the city.

**Thebes**. The capital city of Egypt during the New Kingdom (1567–1085 BCE). On the east bank of the Nile are the remains of the Temples of LUXOR and KARNAK; on the west bank are the Valley of the Kings, the Valley of the Queens, the tombs of the nobles, and the royal mortuary temples. The most famous discovery in the Valley of the Kings, the tomb of Tutankhamun, was made in 1922.

**theism**. Belief in a single personal God who is distinct from His creation, but who cares for it and manifests Himself in it. Major theistic religions are, in order of historical appearance, Judaism, Christianity and Islam.

**theistic proofs**. Traditional proofs for the existence of God in *theistic* religions. *See also* COMMON CONSENT ARGUMENTS FOR THE EXISTENCE OF GOD; COSMOLOGICAL ARGUMENTS FOR THE EXISTENCE OF GOD; DESIGN ARGUMENTS FOR THE EXISTENCE OF GOD; MORAL ARGUMENTS FOR THE EXISTENCE OF GOD; ONTOLOGICAL ARGUMENTS FOR THE EXISTENCE OF GOD; PHYSICO-THEOLOGICAL ARGUMENTS FOR THE EXISTENCE OF GOD; TELEOLOGICAL ARGUMENTS FOR THE EXISTENCE OF GOD; FIVE WAYS; RATIO ANSELMI.

**theodicy** A term coined by Leibniz in his *Theodicy* (1710) from the Greek *theos* ('god') and *dike* ('justice'). It denotes the justification of God, in response to the charge that the evils of the world are incompatible with His omnipotence and perfect goodness. *Compare* PROBLEM OF EVIL.

**Theologia Germanica**. Not a doctrine, but a 14th-century text of mystical theology, also known as *Theologia deutsch*, which had considerable influence on Martin Luther in his formative period.

**theological virtues**. *See* CARDINAL VIRTUES.

**theology**. The study of God's nature and relationship with creation, and of the ways in which He is believed to have made himself known.

**theosis** (Greek). In the theology of the ORTHODOX CHURCHES, the idea that through the salvific mediation of the church man himself is to become divine.

**Theosophical Society**. A society founded in 1875 in New York by Madame H. P. Blavatsky and Colonel H. S. Olcott. The society's leaders moved to India in 1879, where they formally established their movement based on teachings from HINDUISM, BUDDHISM and occultism (Sarma 1973). The society, particularly under the leadership of Annie Besant, assisted in the process of Hindu revitalization which took place in India in the late 19th and early 20th centuries. Theosophical lodges, distinctive for their stress on both the occult and Eastern religious thought, were opened in many countries and continue to function, though the headquarters remains in Madras.

**Theotokos** (Greek: 'of God'). A title conferred on Mary, Mother of Jesus, at the Council of Ephesus (431). The term was originally intended to emphasize the union of the TWO NATURES, human and divine, in Christ, the argument being that if Christ is truly divine in his human existence it cannot be wrong to refer to Mary as Mother of God. Nestorianism rejected this argument, asserting that a woman could not bear God; however, the title was upheld at the COUNCIL OF CHALCEDON (451). In popular religious devotion it encouraged the veneration of Mary as a contributor to the process of salvation and emphasized the divine nature of the incarnate Christ; Mary Theotokos is a popular theme in the icons of the ORTHODOX CHURCHES.

**thera** (Pāli: 'elder', 'senior monk'). A Buddhist monk (BHIKṢU) with more than ten years of monkhood from the day of his higher ordination (UPASAṂPAD). Hence THERAVĀDA, the way of the elders.

**Therapeutae**. A sanatorium attached to some Egyptian temples, where the mentally sick were treated by means of the 'Therapeutic Dream', a trance-like state in which they communed with the gods.

**Theravāda** (Pāli: 'the Doctrine of the Elders'). An early school of Buddhism that has preserved the tradition handed down in the Pāli language on which the Pali Canon, *Tipiṭaka* (*see* TRIPIṬAKA), is based.

**theriomorphic spirits**. Spirits in the form of animals; for example, in Native American religions, most major spirits, aside from the Four Directions. Sky (Zenith) and Earth (nadir), are of animal form. Any physical manifestation of the animal can represent the Spirit itself. *See also* BEAR; BISON; COYOTE; EAGLE; OWL; NATIVE AMERICAN RELIGIONS.

**Theseus**. The Athenian HERO whose cleverness and physical prowess enabled him to free Athens from the control of Minos, king of Crete, with the help of Ariadne. Theseus thereby became 'the ancestor' of Athens.

**Thesmophoria**. A pan-Greek festival sacred to DEMETER, celebrating her gift of agriculture in particular and life in general. It included pig sacrifices and a banquet, a day of fasting, obscenities against men, and the eating of pomegranates in honour of blood, death and birth. During the Thesmophoria, women left their customary seclusion to gather with each other, giving some anxiety and fear to men, although the fertility of citizen wives was also celebrated.

**thing**. *See* YGGDRASILL, TIWAZ.

**Third Rome**. An epithet for Moscow current from the 16th century onwards, which emphasized its claim to religious and political leadership on the model of Constantinople, the 'second Rome'.

**Thirst Dance**. *See* SUN DANCE.

**Thirty-nine Articles**. A statement of various aspects of Christian doctrine in 39 paragraphs first issued in 1563 by the Convocation of the CHURCH OF ENGLAND, and reflecting the doctrinal controversies of the time. The general tendency is to emphasize the primacy of 'Holy Scripture' which 'containeth all things necessary to salvation', while recognizing the functions of creeds and councils, and to steer a course between late medieval Catholicism on the one hand and Calvinism and the Anabaptists on the other hand. The Thirty-nine Articles are binding for the Church of England in modern times (since 1865) in the limited sense that its clergy are required to affirm their consistency with scripture and not to contradict them in their teaching.

**Thomism**. The thought of St Thomas Aquinas (*c*.1225–74) and of his followers. Aquinas sought to reconcile the recently rediscovered works of Aristotle with Christian theology. Hence he accepts much of ARISTOTELIANISM, e.g. that knowledge starts from sense experience, that there are four kinds of CAUSE, and that the SOUL is the form or activity of the body. He also transforms Aristotle's teaching about the Prime Mover into the claim that God's existence can be known by reason from created things. But he also taught that there are revealed truths, which are above reason (though not against it) and are accepted through faith, so that reason and faith each have their own domain. Thomism also embraces some characteristic AUGUSTINIAN positions, e.g. that evil is an absence of good. But it goes well beyond Aristotle and Augustine in its distinctive METAPHYSICS of being, which regards God as 'pure act' and as the source of all being. (Copleston 1955) *See also* ANALOGY; SCHOLASTICISM.

**Thor**. Germanic thunder god of great strength and vitality. His German predecessor was Donar, and his Anglo-Saxon equivalent Thunor. Mythology depicts him as the red-bearded son of ODIN and the Earth who had an insatiable appetite. With his hammer Mjollnir, the gods' most valued treasure, Thor defended ASGARD against the giants and his particular enemy, the MIDGARD SERPENT. He was believed to have power over the weather and the seasons, causing thunder when he drove across the sky in his goat-drawn wagon and lightning or thunderbolts when he threw his hammer. Consequently seafarers prayed to him for protection, and also for guidance. As well as being a weapon, his symbol the hammer was used to give blessings at birth, marriage and funeral ceremonies. While Odin's worshippers were to be found among kings and great warriors and he was sometimes accused of treachery (as only one side could win a battle even though both sides prayed to the war god), Thor was the benevolent god of the common people who guaranteed the security of the agricultural community (Davidson 1964).

**Thoth**. An ancient Egyptian ibis-headed moon-god, patron of scribes, god of learning, wisdom and writing. Thoth was regarded as a messenger of RE and was later identified as HERMES by the Greeks. As the scribe of OSIRIS in the Hall of Judgement, Thoth was worshipped particularly at Hermopolis Magna (Boylan 1922).

**Thoueris**. *See* TAUERT.

**Three Jewels**. *See* TRIRATNĀNI.

**Three Marks**. According to Buddhist teaching, the marks or characteristics of human existence – suffering, impermanence and no-self. *See also* ANĀTMAN.

**Three Pilgrimage Festivals**. *See* YOM TOV.

**Three Pillars of Seth**. *See* NAG HAMMADI.

**Three sacred treasures**. *See* SANSHU NO SHINKI.

**Three Teachings**. A standard phrase used to refer to the three major Chinese religions: Confucianism, Buddhism and Taoism. The phrase is a literal translation of the Chinese *san-jiao* [*san-chiao*], a term in traditional use taken up by the first Ming emperor in his short *Treatise on the Three Teachings* (*San Jiao Lun*), written between 1386 and 1384.

**thudong** (Thai: 'austere practice', 'pilgrim monk'). Monks who leave the monastery and go on foot to visit the various Buddhist shrines in Thailand. During this pilgrimage the monk observes the VINAYA rules and regulations with austerity: he eats his only meal of the day directly from his alms-bowl and sleeps at night in the open under a large umbrella-like shelter equipped with a mosquito-net, a shelter that can be folded for carrying on his back during the day.

**Thunderbirds**. In Native American religions, male spirits of thunder and lightning power, who may, varying from culture to culture, represent the West Wind and/or be represented by EAGLE.

**Thunor**. *See* THOR.

**thupa**. *See* STŪPA.

**Thyrsos staff**. *See* DIONYSIAN MYSTERIES.

**Titans**. *See* ORPHIC MYSTERIES.

**Tiahuannaco**. A place of worship in ancient Bolivia near lake Titicaca. It was built by a pre-Inca culture (*c*.400–1000 CE) exclusively for ceremonial use. Tiahuanaco is still well known, particularly for its 'gateway of the sun'.

**Tiamat** (Akkadian: 'depth'). A sea-goddess, killed and made into the world by MARDUK in ENUMA ELISH. *Compare* the West Semitic sea-god YAM.

**Tian** [T'ien] (Chinese: 'sky', 'heaven'). From early Zhou times (*c*.1066–221 BCE) the supreme deity of the Zhou people, being gradually assimilated with the SHANGDI of the Shang dynasty (16th century – *c*.1066 BCE). In the imperial state cult, worship of Tian was the prerogative of the emperor, who held the title *Tian Zi* ('Son of Heaven') because he had the Mandate of Heaven (TIAN MING). Although in early times Tian seems to have been conceived in anthropomorphic terms he was not portrayed in the imperial cult. In philosophical usage *Tian* signifies an impersonal force, which can roughly be translated as 'nature'.

**tiangan**. *See* HEAVENLY STEMS.

**Tian Ming** [T'ien-ming] (Chinese: 'Mandate of Heaven'). The religious legitimation of the imperial power of the Chinese emperors. The theory of Tian Ming originated in the early Zhou dynasty (*c*.1066–221 BCE). It maintains that Heaven (TIAN) selects a ruler because of his virtue and entrusts him and his descendants with the mandate to govern. If the dynasty looses its virtue the mandate will be withdrawn and given to a new dynasty.

**Tianshi Dao** (Chinese: 'The Way of the Heavenly Master'). The 'Heavenly Master' here is the founder of a Daoist sect (*see* DAOISM) dating back to the 2nd century CE. The sect in its beginnings was also called the Five Bushels of Rice Sect (*wu dou mi dao*). Today the 64th descendant of the founder Zhang (Dao) Ling is still actively engaged in Daoist religious life. The main god to be worshipped by the 'masters' was the sage Lao Zi [Lao Tzu], taking the DAO DE JING as the fundamental sacred scripture. Sick persons were treated as possessed by evil spirits, which were duly exorcised through incantations, charms and tallies. At first only a local religious leader with his teachings limited to Sichuan province, the 'Heavenly Master' of the fourth generation moved east to 'Dragon-Tiger Mountain' in Jinagxi province, establishing there an influential centre of Daoism. During the Yuan Dynasty (1260–1368) the sect merged with the LING BAO and the SHANG QING sects to form a Daoist alliance usually called Zheng Yi. Today this Zheng Yi tradition still exists (mainly along the southern Chinese coast and in Taiwan), but, as it is not a monastic religious tradition, accurate figures and data on its historical organization are scarce. On the history of the Tianshi Dao see Welch 1957; on the 'Heavenly Masters' themselves see Imbault-Huart 1884.

**Tian Tai** [T'ien T'ai Buddhism]. A school of Buddhism founded in China by its first patriarch Chih-I (538–97) which offers an elaborate system of doctrine and meditation which gave prominence to the LOTUS SŪTRA while seeking to be true to the MĀDHYAMIKA tradition. The teaching was transmitted to Japan as Tendai Buddhism (*see* TENDAI-SHŪ) and formed the matrix from which other distinctive Japanese sects emerged.

**Tian Zi**. *See* TIAN.

**tiara**. A high crown worn by Popes from the Middle Ages until the reign of Pope Paul VI (*d* 1978), when the practice was abandoned as excessively pompous.

**T'ien**. *See* TIAN.

**T'ien-shih tao**. *See* TIANSHI DAO.

**T'ien T'ai Buddhism**. *See* TIAN TAI.

**Tiermes**. The thunder god of the Saami (Lapps). The name Tiermes for the god manifesting himself in thunder was used by the Eastern Saami and has been related to the Ob-ugrian god of the sky, NUM-TŪREM, and the Samoyed god NUM. (Holmberg 1915; Karsten 1955; Hultkrantz 1962).

**Tijāniya**. A Ṣūfī brotherhood founded by Aḥmad b. Muḥammad b. al-Mukhtār b. Sālim al-Tijānī (*d* 1815) in Morocco with chapters also in Algeria where the order remained generally on good terms with the French colonial authorities.

**Tipiṭaka**. *See* TRIPIṬAKA.

**tiqqun** (Hebrew). Fixing, restoration, realignment. The Kabbalistic idea (*see* KABBALAH) of 'tiqqun OLAM' means reestablishing the world – within the individual as well as socially – so as to align the manifestation of SHEKHINAH with the divine source.

**Tisha be-Av** (Hebrew: 'the ninth day of the month of Av'). The Jewish day of fasting and mourning which marks the anniversary of the destruction of both of the Jerusalem Temples, as well as the defeat of the Bar Kokhbah revolt in the 2nd century CE and the expulsion of the Jews from Spain in 1492. It is also a day of looking forward to messianic redemption.

**Titans**. A race of ancient Greek gods who lost their power to ZEUS and the Olympians. Described by Hesiod, they are Oceanus, Coeus, Crius, Hyperion, Iapetos, Theia, Themis, Mnemosyne, Phoebe, Tethys, CRONOS and RHEA. *See also* ORPHIC MYSTERIES.

**Tiwaz**. Early pre-Christian Germanic god of battle and justice, associated with the 'thing', the council of the gods.

**tlazolli** (Nahuatl). In Aztec culture, filth, garbage, things that are worn out, 'matter out of place' (Burkhart 1989).

**tngri** (Mongolian). Heavenly beings invoked in Mongolian folk religion and SHAMANISM. The *tngri* are said to number 99, but although many can be named, this appears to be a symbolic number. *See also* QORMUSTA TNGRI; SÜLDE.

**Tobacco**. The ritual use of tobacco is unique to and ubiquitous in Native American religions. Tobacco is a sacred plant featured in many cosmogonic myths and, for many cultures, is the primary offering to spirits. In North America, tobacco offerings are central to virtually all rituals.

The cultivation of tobacco is considered a sacred task different from all other types of horticulture, all aspects of which are sacred. For example, it is usually cultivated by males, while in non-agricultural cultures, horticulture is generally an activity of females. Some cultures that are not otherwise horticultural exclusively cultivate tobacco. Cultures too far north for the growing of tobacco use various substitutes either alone or mixed with tobacco.

Tobacco may be offered to spirits in a number of ways, the primary means being placing it on the ground, on water, or on other sacred entities or symbols. Secondary methods involve burning it in a fire to create a smoke offering. Tertiary methods use various types of smoking apparatus, which allows for communion between the smoker and the spiritual recipients. These methods include cigarettes with a maize husk wrapper, cigars and various types of pipes (*see* SACRED PIPE).
Tobacco may also be chewed, ingested as a liquid infusion, ground up as snuff (often inhaled with a forked pipette, for which the Carib word is the basis for 'tobacco'), and as enemas. Ingestion as well as very large cigars in Meso-America and South America are used to engender trance for shamanistic purposes. (Wilbert 1987).

**Tod**. *See* MONT.

**Tome of Leo**. A doctrinal statement which was adopted by the COUNCIL OF CHALCEDON (451) as authoritative teaching on the manner of the INCARNATION of God in Christ. The title arises from its author, Pope Leo I, who had sent it as a letter to the Patriarch of Constantinople, Flavian, in advance of the council. Its strength lies in the balanced phrasing, which preserves the identity of the divine and human natures in the one person of Jesus Christ. On this basis it seemed possible to conceive of a communication between the two aspects (COMMUNICATIO IDIOMATUM) so that the action of God and man in the life of one person became comprehensible. This view was contradicted by MONOPHYSITISM, which argued that Christ had a single nature, namely the divine, in a human person.

**tonalli** (Nahuatl). A person's date of birth in the Aztec TONALPOHUALLI, designating a kind of animate force or soul which gives that person his or her characteristic strength, vigour, vitality or 'heat', and fate. (Lopez Austin, 1984; Ingham 1986).

**tonalpohualli** (Nahuatl). A 260-day Aztec ritual calendar of 13 months of repeating sequences of 20 day-signs or TONALLI associated with numerical coefficients running from 1 to 13. The *tonalpohualli* is thought to be based on the period of human gestation and was used as a divinatory almanac. Referred to by Maya scholars by the term *tzolkin* (Burkhart 1989).

**Tooth Temple**. *See* DAḶADĀ MĀLIGĀVA.

**Torah** (Hebrew: 'instruction', 'revelation'). The Five Books of Moses (*See* PENTATEUCH) which open the Hebrew Bible. The rabbis added a notion of 'oral Torah' to that of 'written Torah', considering their own interpretations, embellishments and expansions of the Torah to have been revealed orally at Mount Sinai, though of course they were not written down until later. Thus, the study of Torah is a central feature of Jewish life, encompassing the various works of rabbinic literature structured as commentary on the Torah. (Schürer 1979: 314–80) *See also* MISHNAH; TALMUD.

**Tore**. A mythical TRICKSTER hero of the Azande (*see* KAGGEN); the neighbouring Pygmies in Zaire worship him as 'The Forest' and ruler of the game (Evans-Pritchard 1967).

**torii** (Japanese). A symbolic gateway erected at the entrance to the sacred precincts of a Shintō shrine, separating the inner area from the profane world surrounding it. Several *torii* may be erected along the avenue of approach.

**Tossafot** (Hebrew). 'Additional' commentaries to the TALMUD, supplied by Rashi's grandchildren, and others.

**totem**. In Native American Algonkian cultures, *dodem* (commonly written 'totem') means 'clan', and many of the clans, though far from all, were named after animals. For these reasons the word totem has passed into English and other languages to mean something similar to 'badge' or 'insignia'. 19th-century anthropologists may have confused this term for the clan name with MANITOU, the term for spirits, including guardian spirits, and thus associated *totem* with the ritual prohibitions that may ensue from these relationships. Traditionally, however, there was no prohibition against eating the clan insignia in cases where it was edible.

**traducianism**. The teaching that each person's human soul is not newly created, but is generated by the parents' union. Augustine (354–436) employed it to explain the passage of ORIGINAL SIN. *Contrast* CREATIONISM.

**trance**. *See* ECSTASY.

**transcendence**. Going beyond or surpassing; most commonly used of the way in which God is believed to exist beyond and independent of the world (*see* IMMANENCE). In other contexts transcendence is understood as the surpassing of ordinary experience from within the world. *See also* TRANSCENDENTALISM.

**transcendentalism**. In general, a quality that is best described as surpassing ordinary experience. This meaning is clearly evident, for example, in Kant's theory of knowledge in which it is argued that there are innate structures of the mind that 'filter' and 'interpret' all empirical experience and therefore constitute a kind of knowledge of the world prior to our having any experience of the world. More specifically, transcendentalism refers to a particular system of thought in 19th-century America associated primarily with Ralph Waldo Emerson (1803–82) and Henry David Thoreau (1817–1862). Though primarily a 'New World' philosophy influenced by New England Puritanism and European romantic idealism it was also shaped by Platonic and Oriental influences. It is essentially a moral philosophy or philosophy of life based on a extreme optimism with respect to the potentialities of human nature. It also relies heavily on intuition and relates the inner life of persons to the course of nature in a kind of mystical PANTHEISM. Together with an intense individualism it also strongly emphasizes freedom of conscience, self-reliance and political democracy. *See also* TRANSCENDENCE.

**Transcendental Meditation**. A meditation technique brought by Maharishi Mahesh Yogi to the West in 1958 after first attempting to teach it in South India. By 1970 it had become popular with young Westerners and during the decade that followed was the focus for the development of a substantial organization (Maharishi International University) and World Plan. The meditation is generally offered to initiates in the context of modern scientific analysis and a concern for health and well-being, though its roots lie in the Indian philosophy of *advaita vedānta*. (Mangalvadi 1977).

**transfiguration**. The temporary vision of Jesus in glory, together with Moses and Elija who represented the law and the prophets, enjoyed by the disciples, Peter, James and John (*Matthew* 17; *Mark* 9; *Luke* 9). The transfiguration is celebrated as a liturgical feast in the Orthodox and the Roman Catholic churches.

**transpersonal psychology**. A movement in psychology which emphasizes dimensions in human personhood considered to transcend the bounds of the individual psyche. Transpersonal psychology seeks not only to provide a richly complex view of human experience and potential but also an integrative standpoint for the philosophical evaluation of religion and culture. For examples of this approach see Wilber 1983 and Washburn 1988, and for an appraisal see Kelly 1992.

**transsubstantiation**. In Roman Catholic theology, the change from one substance into another, and in particular the changing of the substance of bread into the body of Christ and that of wine into the blood of Christ through the act of consecration during the MASS. This teaching is based on the

Aristotelian distinction between SUBSTANCE and ACCIDENTS, and in the case of transsubstantiation the accidents, that is, the evident physical characteristics, remain unchanged. However, the change is regarded not as a temporary metaphor, but as definitive. Therefore, in distinction to most Protestant practice, the consecrated bread is conserved for veneration or for later distribution outside the normal framework of the Mass. *See also* MONSTRANCE; PYX; TABERNACLE.

**Trappists**. A particularly strict branch of the Cistercian Order inaugurated in 1664 at La Trappe in Normandy. They observe absolute silence and vegetarianism, sleep in a common dormitory and spend several hours daily on liturgy.

**treyf** (Yiddish; from Hebrew, *treyfah*: 'ripped apart'). Food, or anything else, that is not KOSHER.

**trickster**. A general term for superhuman beings with an ambivalent disposition who trick humans, usually causing discomfort but sometimes bringing good. Viewed theoretically a trickster figure is a mythological device for rendering capricious aspects of existence comprehensible and to some extent acceptable. Thus many Native American myths of re-creation (after the deluge) and of the inception of culture feature thereomorphic culture heroes who, among other things, teach proper behaviour through ribald, humorous myths. Examples of this are COYOTE, GLOOSCAP, NANABUSH, RAVEN and SPIDER. Trickster figures are found in many cultures, other examples being the divinities Ogo among the Dogon (central Mali) and Esu among the Yoruba (western Nigeria). *See also* ANANSE, LEGBA, KAGGEN, LOKI and TORE. (Radin 1972; Pelton 1980; Grotanelli 1983).

**Tridentine theology**. The theology of the Council of Trent (Concilium Tridentinum), held from 1545 to 1563. The Council of Trent was the main rallying point for the COUNTER-REFORMATION, the response of the Roman Catholic Church to the challenge of PROTESTANTISM. Tridentine theology is noted for bringing in various disciplinary reforms, such as the establishment of seminaries for training the priesthood, and at the same time taking a clear stance against Protestant theology on matters such as church authority and the doctrine of the MASS.

**trikāya** (Sanskrit). The three bodies (*kāya*), i.e. of the Buddha. In its most common form the teaching of the three bodies of the Buddha refers to the following: *dharmakāya*, i.e. the Dharma-body, the Buddha as an inexpressible principle of all existence; *sambhogakāya*, the body of bliss, in which a buddha displays a brilliant celestial presence (imitated in iconography); and *nirmānakāya*, the transformation body in which a buddha appears in earthly form as a teacher of humankind. The doctrine is not characteristic of early MAHĀYĀNA Buddhism in any systematic form, and the first recognizable account appears in the LANKĀVATĀRA SŪTRA, though with slightly different terminology.

**Trimorphic First Thoughts**. *See* NAG HAMMADI.

**trimūrti**. *See* BRAHMĀ.

**Trinity**. The Christian concept of God as three persons in one substance, Father, Son and HOLY SPIRIT, functionally distinguishable but indivisible in their essential being. The doctrine of the Trinity was initially formulated over a period of some three centuries. Decisive progress was made by Tertullian (*c.*163–*c.*225) and Augustine (354–430), who led western theology in asserting 'one SUBSTANCE and three persons', one permanent reality of god and three co-equal, divine persons (*see* PERSONA). Meanwhile, in Alexandria, Origen (*c.*185–253) taught that the son was eternally begotten but secondary in relation to the eternally creative Father; a more distinct form of subordinationism was found in ARIANISM, condemned as heretical at the COUNCIL OF NICEA (325). Even so, eastern theologians were reluctant to accept western formulations, being influenced by Origen, SABELLIANISM, Arian emperors and misunderstandings of the term HOMOOUSIOS. The COUNCIL OF CONSTANTINOPLE (381) recognized the full, co-equal divinity of Father, Son and Spirit. According to this, divine unity was based on the unbegotten Father, whence the Son was begotten and the Holy Spirit proceeded (*see* PROCESSION). Thus, the persons were distinguished, but not divided as they would be in TRITHEISM. In spite of the heated controversies and sophisticated distinctions it should not be overlooked that most theologians regard the nature of the Trinity as a mystery which transcends human comprehension, as indeed the three persons are described in the (western) Athanasian Creed: 'The Father incomprehensible (*immensus*), the Son incomprehensible, and the Holy Spirit incomprehensible. . . . As also there are not three incomprehensibles, nor three uncreated: but one uncreated, and one incomprehensible.' On the other hand, the development of Trinitarian teaching is understandable as the attempt to speak of the activity of the transcendent divine creator, the Father, within the created world, incorporating salvation through the Son and sanctification through the Holy Spirit. (Rowlinson 1928; Prestige 1964).

**Tripiṭaka** (Sanskrit: 'three baskets') [Pāli: Tipiṭaka]. The earliest settled scriptural corpus of the Buddhists in three main sections. The three main sections of the Pāli Canon, being the authoritative writings of THERAVĀDA Buddhism, are the *Vinaya Piṭaka* (books of discipline), the *Sutta Piṭaka* (dialogues of the Buddha and various collections of narrative and doctrine) and the *Abhidhamma Piṭaka* (books of doctrinal analysis and controversy). In Sanskrit these are known as the *Vinaya Piṭaka*, the *Sūtra Piṭaka* and the *Abhidharma Piṭaka* respectively, but there are wide variations in content and not all parts are extant for all of the historical schools of Buddhism. The canon of the Sarvāstivāda School, for example, an important tradition within ancient Buddhism, largely agrees with the Pāli collections as far as the *Vinaya* and *Sūtra Piṭakas* are concerned but differs widely when it comes to the *Abhidharma Piṭaka*. The threefold division is superficially maintained in the massive Chinese Buddhist Canon, but the works that fall into the treatise section (equivalent to *Abhidharma*) are extremely extensive and diverse.

**triratnāni** (Sanskrit: 'three jewels'). A Buddhist term denoting the BUDDHA, the DHARMA and the SAṆGHA, which are regarded as constitutive of Buddhism.

**tritheism**. An extreme form of Trinitarian teaching which asserts three distinct substances pertaining to the three persons of the Trinity. The term has been mainly used for denunciatory purposes, from the standpoint of church authorities.

**Trito-Isaiah**. The designation for an early post-exilic, anonymous prophet (or possibly prophets) whose writing is incorporated in the later chapters of *Isaiah*. The prophet faced the problem of disillusionment as high expectations were dissipated and internal wrangling took place between those Jews returning from EXILE and those who had remained behind in JUDAH ('the people of the land'). A universal cult was proclaimed (*Isaiah* 56) in opposition to those of a more particularist tendency, though the latter finally triumphed. (Barker 1987: 201–20) *See also* DEUTERO-ISAIAH.

**trõ** (plural, *trõwo*). Lesser deities of the Ewe of Togo and eastern Ghana, similar to the VODU of the Fon (Spieth 1911).

**tṛṣṇā** (Sanskrit: 'thirst', 'desire'). Though used more widely in Indian texts, *tṛṣṇa* took on particular importance as a Buddhist term denoting an impassioned reaction to what has been felt. It indicates that desire or craving which leads to continued existence (*see* FOUR NOBLE TRUTHS). Further analysis distinguished between (1) a thirst for sense pleasure, (2) a thirst for existence, and (3) a thirst for annihilation.

**tryefah**. *See* TREYF.

**tsafi** (Hausa). FETISH, magic. The term is used by the Hausa (northern Nigeria, Niger) and in the areas where Hausa is a lingua franca to designate any non-Muslim, non-Christian cult, ritual or ritual object. Hence, like 'fetish', it is descriptively inexact.

**Tsaghan Ebügen**. *See* WHITE OLD MAN.

**Ts'an-T'ung-Chi**. *See* CAN TONG QI.

**Ts'ao-tung-tsung**. *See* SŌTŌ-SHŪ.

**tsav**. Among the Tiv of Nigeria a power which every elder as well as any energetic, successful person is considered to possess. It is considered necessary for the prosperity of the community, but the Tiv are more concerned with fear of its nefarious use by the *mbatsav* (a type of witch, male or female), who are thought to feast on human flesh, a belief in which is widespread in Africa (*see* OBAYIFO). *Tsav* is thought to exist physically in the chest of its owner and was looked for in post-mortem examinations (like the central African LIKUNDU). (East 1965; Bohannan 1969).

**Tsui-Goab**. Supreme being and mythical hero of the Hottentots; the first ancestor with demiurgical quality, who became the personification of rain (Hirschberg 1975: 401).

**tsumi** (Japanese). In ordinary usage, essentially the same meaning as the English 'sin'. In ancient Shintō, however, error, sickness and disaster were also called *tsumi*, which thus formed a most comprehensive concept. A distinction was made between *amatsu-tsumi* (heavenly sins) and *kunitsutsumi* (terrestrial sins). *Amatsu-tsumi* were those committed by the god Susanoo no mikoto in heaven, including such destructive acts as harming agriculture. *Kunitsu-tsumi* included the inflicting of injury or death, immodest actions, killing of domestic animals, using magic, leprosy, the falling of lightning, and damage done by harmful birds. This list indicates that the occurrence of evil was often understood as being caused by something beyond man's control; evil, including even moral and criminal offences committed by humans, was considered to be caused by evil spirits which intruded from the land of the dead (YOMI). As a result, salvation from *tsumi* was considered possible by HARAE, namely, by purification, the removal of impediments, and the expulsion of the evil spirits. Thus harae, the return to a normal condition, was repeated day and night as a preparation to divine worship. The performance of the ritual indicated an acceptance of responsibility for the restoration of a normal good state, and in this sense the concept of *tsumi* and attendant actions are still current in modern times.

**Tū** [Kū]. One of the major ATUA ('gods'), widely known throughout Polynesia. His main function is that of a war god. In New Zealand he is also regarded as a prototype of man.

**Tuatha Dé Danann**. In Irish Celtic mythology a race of gods who invaded Ireland and defeated the then ruling evil spirits, the FOMORIANS, in the 'Second Battle of Mag Tured'. However, they were later conquered by Christian invaders, the Milesians, and retired to live underground in 'fairy mounds' or the *síd*. Their name means 'tribes of the goddess Danu'.

**Tudi** [T'u-ti]. In Chinese religion, the local earth god, popularly called Tudi Gong [Kung] ('Master Earth'). Every residential area, be it in the coutryside or in town, had its own Tudi, who protects its residents but also controls them. In the spiritual hierarchy he is responsible to CHENGHUANG, or the City God. Historically Tudi is considered the same as *She*, the God of the Soil.

**tung t'ien**. *See* DONGTIAN.

**Tun Huang**. *See* DUN HUANG.

**turiya**. *See* OM.

**Turtle**. A major Native American spirit that is central to many re-creation myths; whence arises a common Native term for North America itself – Turtle Island. Turtle is a spirit important to the SHAKING TENT ritual.

**Tutankhamun**. *See* THEBES.

**tuyul** (Javanese). Javanese familiar spirits, 'children who are not human beings' (Geertz 1960a: 16), helping their owner to become rich by stealing objects from other people.

**Twelve Patriarchs**. Eponymous ancestors of the tribes of Israel. *Testaments of the Twelve Patriarchs* are pseudepigraphical deathbed speeches (*see* PSEUDEPIGRAPHA) to their descendants, anticipating the messianic age. Fragments were found at QUMRAN and fuller versions survive in Greek. *See also* APOCALYPTIC.

**Twelve Terrestrial Branches**. *See* HEAVENLY STEMS.

**Twelver Shīʿa**. The name given to the main body of SHĪʿA Muslims who hold that twelve IMĀMS were the legitimate successors to the headship of the Islamic community following the death of the Prophet Muḥammad, the last of whom went into spiritual occultation in the late 9th century. In Arabic the community is called the *Ithnāʿ Ashariya* ('the Twelvers'). *See also* ISMĀʿĪLĪ.

**Two Clement**. *See* APOSTOLIC FATHERS.

**two natures**. The teaching, first explicitly advanced by Gregory of Nazianzus (329–89), that in Christ two natures are conjoined in one person, the Son, forming a unity but distinguishable in thought. This teaching countered APOLLINARIANISM, from Apollinarius (*c*.310–*c*.390), who taught that Christ had 'one incarnate nature of the divine word'. (Kelly, 1972: 280–309) *See also* MONOPHYSITISM.

**Tyche**. A female figure of ancient Greece representing fate or chance. Lacking mythology and worship, Tyche became a goddess in Hellenistic times.

**tyiwara** [chiwara]. Among the Bambara (Bamana) of Mali, a mask costume with a head-piece in the form of an antelope. It is also the name of the initiatory association which performs the *tyiwara* masquerades at an annual festival. The association, which is open to men and women, is dedicated to rituals of agriculture and food, relating also to the cosmic forces of sun and earth which bring forth crops. According to myth the divine *tyiwara* taught the ancestors the skills of agriculture. (Zahan 1980).

**Typhon**. *See* SETH.

**Tyr**. Pre-Christian Germanic god of battle and justice who gave his name to Tuesday. In the PROSE EDDA he is said to have sacrificed one of his hands in order for the dangerous wolf Fenrir to be successfully bound.

**tzaddiq** (Hebrew; plural, *tzaddiqim*). Literally, a 'righteous' or just individual; The idea developed in rabbinic Judaism that the world is sustained because of the merit of a certain number of *tzaddiqim*; eventually, Jewish tradition fixes their number at 36 (Scholem 1971). In a parallel tradition, the figure of the *tzaddiq* comes to represent not only an ethical ideal, but also the archetypal figure of the Jewish holy man who bridges heaven and earth. This spiritual characterization of the *tzaddiq*, who fulfils for rabbinical Judaism the kind of function that had earlier been served by the prophet and priest, is based upon an interpretation of *Proverbs* 10.25 as 'the *tzaddiq* is the foundation of the universe'. *See also* NISTAR.

**tzaddiqim**. *See* ḤASIDISM.

**tzedaqah**. The Hebrew word for charity, it derives from the root *tzedeq* ('justice'). The Jewish notion of charitably helping one's neighbour is based not only on a sense of generosity, but also of justice. It is considered an obligation as well as a privilege to give *tzedaqah*. The wealth of the rich is demonstrated by the *tzedaqah* they give; but as a matter of human dignity, it is expected that even the poor will give *tzedaqah*.

**tzedeq**. *See* TZEDAQAH.

**tzimtzum** (Hebrew). A kabbalistic doctrine set forth in the teachings of Isaac Luria and his school in the 16th century. *Tzimtzum* is the 'contraction' which the infinite light of the AYN-SOF imposed upon itself, so as to allow an empty space to remain in which creation might take place.

**tzitzit** (Hebrew). The braided 'fringes' on the four corners of a TALLIT, which represent the 'four corners of the world' and which are knotted so as to correspond, numerically, with the name of God. Also, a poncho-like undershirt worn by men, which has these fringes attached to its four corners.

**Tziyyon**. *See* ZION.

**Tzolkin**. *See* TONALPOHUALLI.

**tzu-jan**. *See* ZIRAN.

# U

**uayeb** (Maya). The last unlucky five days of the year in the Maya solar calendar or 'Vague Year' (Coe 1980).

**Übermensch** (German). A notion central to the philosophy of the 19th-century philosopher Friedrich Nietzsche. Nietzsche found Christianity's stress on love, pity and other such virtues to be weaknesses rather than strengths and so reacted negatively to the Christian religion. In opposition to it he maintained that the individual should not simply accept the world as he or she finds it but rather that one should set out to restructure it in accordance with one's own will. Only then, according to Nietzsche, is real value created. His philosophy, therefore, is a kind of justification of the rights of the creative individual whom Nietzsche dubs the *Übermensch* or superior person. Some echoes of this notion can be found in the works of modern philosophers and especially in non-western thinkers like Mohammed Iqbal and Aurobindo Ghose.

**ubusuna no kami** (Japanese). In Shintō, the tutelary deity of one's birthplace. A newly born child is taken for a first visit to the shrine of this deity, who is believed to protect the person throughout life. People who move to other areas later still return to their native homes to participate in festivals for their *ubusuna no kami* and consider themselves an *ubuko* or parishioner of that deity.

**Udāsī** (Punjabi). Ascetic Sikh followers of Śrī Chand, son of Gurū Nānak.

**Ugarit**. An important Bronze Age site on the coast of Syria. Documents in seven languages testify to its commercial, cultural and political importance. The tablets from Ugarit have transformed our knowledge of CANAANITE RELIGION and West Semitic languages (including Hebrew). As well as numerous ritual texts, legal documents and letters, mythological texts (e.g. the BAAL CYCLE, the gracious gods) and epic tales (AQHAT, KERET) have been found. The chief deities of Ugarit (ANAT, ASHERAH, ASTARTE, BAAL, DAGAN, EL, RESHEF) were distributed widely from Egypt to Mesopotamia, thus present in early ISRAELITE RELIGION, and influenced early religious developments in Greece. (Gray 1965; Jacob & Cazelles 1979; Craigie 1983; Curtis 1985).

**ujigami** (Japanese). Originally the ancestral deity of a clan or family, the *ujigami* later came to be viewed as the tutelary deity of a geographical area such as a village. *See also* UJIKO.

**ujiko** (Japanese). A member of a Shintō shrine community living within the geographical area of the shrine. While the term originally referred to any member of a clan claiming a common ancestral god or UJIGAMI, the meaning of the word *ujigami* changed in time from being a lineage to a territorial concept, and the term *ujiko* thus also came to refer to anyone who was born and lived in the area under the tutelage of the deity.

**ukhupacha**. *See* HANAQPACHA.

**ulamā**. *See* ULEMĀ.

**ulemā** ['ulama'] (Arabic). Learned interpreters of Islamic teaching and law.

**Ull**. Early Germanic god of unclear function, but whose name occurs in many Norwegian and Swedish place names. He is known as 'god of the shield' and is said to have crossed the sea on a magic bone.

**ultramontanism**. *See* GALLICANISM.

**Umbanda**. An Afro-American religion in southern Brazil derived from the religion of Africans (especially Bantu) but now also with many white adherents. The Africa-derived ancestor cult is an important feature which has also been extended to cover Brazilian-Indian ancestors. Umbanda has taken over cultic elements from CANDOMBLÉ, but recently Candomblé and MACUMBA have been increasingly displaced by Umbanda.

**umma** (Arabic). Community or nation. The term refers particularly to the universal Islamic community.

**ʿUmra** (Arabic). In Islām, the 'little pilgrimage' to MECCA which may be performed at times other than in the season of the annual pilgrimage (ḤAJJ).

**uMvelinqangi**. Lord of the sky and creator of the earth, originally the independent HIGH GOD of the Zulu, but displaced by UNKULUNKULU and is now mostly his epithet (Baumann 1936).

**una sancta**. *See* UNAM SANCTAM.

**Unam sanctam**. The title of a papal BULL (taken from its opening words) issued by Pope Boniface VIII in 1302, emphasizing the function of 'one holy [*unam sanctam*] catholic and apostolic church' in alone vouchsafing salvation, and the position of the POPE himself as the head of this church, to which both spiritual and temporal powers should be subject. The bull was directed against Philip IV of France.

**unction**. Anointment with oil. As a religious rite it is performed (1) at the coronation of a king or queen, (2) at baptism and confirmation in the Roman Catholic and Orthodox churches, and (3) for the sick, in which case it may be called EXTREME UNCTION or holy unction.

**underworld**. The religions of the ancient Near East had a negative view of death and its aftermath. The dead survived in a dim, dreary underworld, whose gods were to be feared (MOT in Canaan, NERGAL and his consort ERESHKIGAL in Mesopotamia). This was the early conception in Israelite religion too, in spite of attempts to prove the opposite. Important ancestors and kings were invoked beyond the grave. The dead received offerings through libation pipes set into the ceilings of burial chambers, and if the appropriate funerary rites were not performed, it was feared that they would harm the living. (Saggs 1978). *See also* ADAPA; HADES; HELL; GILGAMESH; REPHAIM.

**Uniat churches**. A large number of churches in Egypt, western Asia and eastern Europe which retain an independent tradition in liturgical practice and canon law, but which for a variety of historical reasons are 'in communion' with the Roman Catholic Church. The use of liturgical languages other than Latinis a less notable difference now than in previous decades and centuries, since the vernacular is now used generally. The most obvious differences are the practice of receiving communion in both kinds and allowing a married priesthood. The term derives via Polish from the Latin *unio* meaning union. The largest such church is the Ukrainian.

**Unitarianism**. A movement of western religious thought marked by belief in the oneness of God and the manhood of Christ, or, in other words, by the rejection of the doctrines of the Trinity and the incarnation. Unitarianism was known, but later persecuted, in Poland and Hungary in the 16th century, in England from the 17th century and in the USA from the 18th century onwards. As an organized denomination Unitarians have usually held services centred on the Bible in their chapels, and in many cases there has been a close relationship with Presbyterianism and Congregationalism. In the long run free reign given to reason and to conscience has led to an increasingly loose pattern of belief and practice.

**unitive path**. *See* VIA UNITIVA.

**unitive way**. *See* VIA UNITIVA.

**universalism**. Specifically, a term that has been used of later Hebrew prophets such as Isaiah, Hosea and Micah, who proclaimed that God's purposes extended to other nations besides the people of Israel. More widely, it is used in Christian theology for the belief that not just a chosen few but all people will be saved ultimately (*see* APOCATASTASIS). Such belief has usually been regarded as unorthodox or at least controversial in the context of Christian theology, but in many religious systems it is taken for granted. In MAHĀYĀNA Buddhism, for example, the inherent, though unperceived Buddha-nature of all living beings is presupposed, so that *nirvaṇa* is also regarded as their ultimate state without exception.

**universals**. That to which general terms apply, according to realist thinkers (*see* REALISM), e.g. 'redness' and 'beauty'.

**uNkulunkhulu**. *See* UNKULUNKULU.

**uNkulunkulu** [uNkulunkhulu]. Deified ancestor of the Zulu of Natal, the 'Very Old', created by UMVELINQANGI, whom he has displaced as supreme being. Emerging from a split reed as partly male and partly female, uNkulunkulu then procreated mankind. A cult relating to him is carried out by the headman or his sister or daughter on behalf of the community as a whole, but he is supposed to be invoked only in circumstances of communal danger such as drought or epidemic, when a black ox is sacrificed (Breutz 1975: 451). Although uNkulunkulu assisted in creation by naming all the things on earth, he is without independent creative potential, and hence he is not a HIGH GOD in the full sense. That he has been so regarded is due mainly to external missionary influence. In fact it is more appropriate to regard him as an ancestral god. (Baumann 1936: 25).

**Unleavened Bread**. An ancient Jewish New Year feast, in which a break was made from the previous year by refraining from the use of old leaven in new loaves. It was incorporated at an early date into PASSOVER.

**Upaniṣads**. The last part of the VEDA, also called VEDĀNTA ('the end of the Veda'), the basic text for the many schools of *Vedānta* philosophy. The word *upaniṣad* is usually explained as 'sitting close by', i.e. an esoteric teaching to be kept secret. The traditional number of Upaniṣads is 108; however, only 15 are referred to by the classical Vedāntins, among them the BṚHADĀRYANĀKA, the *Chāndogya*, the *Aitareya*, the *Taittirīya*, the *Īsá*, the *Kena*, the *Kaṭha*, the *Praśna*, the *Muṇḍaka*, the *Māṇḍukya*, the *Kauśītakī*, the *Maitrī* and the *Śvetāsvatāra Upaniṣad*. Apart from the information about authorship given in the Upaniṣads themselves nothing certain is known. They are dated variously from between 4000 to 600 BCE. They are unequal in length and content. Some are compendia of certain schools, others are without noticeable denominational affiliation. They propound a number of VIDYĀS, techniques through which one is to reach awareness of an unchanging and undying reality.

**Upapurāṇas**. *See* PURĀṆAS.

**upāsaka** (Sanskrit and Pāli). A Buddhist layman who observes the Five, Eight or TEN PRECEPTS.

**upasaṃpad** (Sanskrit: 'higher ordination'). A Buddhist term for the 'full ordination' of a monk or nun. It follows the 'lower ordination' (PRAVRAJYĀ) and the minimum age for it is 20.

**upasampadā**. *See* UPASAṂPAD.

**upāsikā** (Sanskrit and Pāli) A Buddhist laywoman who observes the Five, Eight or TEN PRECEPTS.

**upāya** (Sanskrit). Means, devices or stratagems. According to the teaching of MAHĀYĀNA Buddhism these were devised by buddhas and bodhisattvas to aid living beings. The Chinese equivalent, *fang-bien*, ordinarily signifies 'means' but in Buddhist contexts implies means such as buddhas devise in accordance with their soteriological skill, hence 'skilful means'. The Japanese equivalent, *hōben*, only bears this meaning. *See also* UPĀYAKAUŚALYA.

**upāyakauśalya** (Sanskrit). Skilfulness in means (UPĀYA), that is, the ability of a bodhisattva or a buddha, in MAHĀYĀNA Buddhism, to devise skilful modes of teaching which will lead sentient beings into the Buddhist path. The term is of central importance in the LOTUS SUTRA and the Teaching of Vimalakīrti (Pye 1978).

**uposatha** (Pāli). The quarter-month day of the lunar calendar. On the *uposatha* of the new and full moon the monks are supposed to recite the monastic rules, PRĀTIMOKṢA.

**urabon**. *See* O-BON.

**Uraeus**. The cobra worn on the king's brow in ancient Egypt, representing the divine daughter of RE, who spat venom at the king's enemies.

**Uranos**. *See* ORPHIC MYSTERIES.

**Urbi et Orbi**. The blessing given by the Pope on special festive occasions such as Easter or Christmas to 'the city [*urbi*] of Rome and to the whole world [*orbi*]'.

**Urd**. *See* YGGDRASILL.

**urim and thummim**. Artefacts of uncertain nature used for DIVINATION in Israelite religion up to the time of the Exile. Whatever they were (headless arrows have been suggested), they were used to decide between alternatives. Since the meanings of the Hebrew words *urim* and *thummim* were unknown, they have passed into English in untranslated form.

**Urmonotheismus** (German).The theory, advanced by Wilhelm Schmidt (1868–1954), that there was once a universally held belief in one God which later became overlaid or lost in the course of diverse cultural developments. The celestial '*high god*' perceived in many parts of the world was presumed to document this theory, which thus had a clear function for Christian theology in linking the observed diversity of religions to the concept of natural theology. From a historical point of view however the theory must be regarded as in principle speculative. This is because it is not possible to document satisfactorily either the universality of such belief or the historical sequence of its alleged decay. (The German prefix *Ur* means 'original' or 'primal'.)

**ushabti**. The small, mummiform figure made of mud, clay, wood, wax or faience which was placed in the tomb from the Middle Kingdom (1991–1786 BCE) onwards in Ancient Egypt. Sets of *ushabti* (up to 400) were put in tombs to undertake agricultural labours on behalf of the deceased in the next world; they are often shown with agricultural tools in their hands. They also carry an inscription from the BOOK OF THE DEAD (Chapter 6), which ensured that they would work for the deceased when called upon ('ushabti' means 'answerer'). The origin of ushabti coincides with the rise in popularity of OSIRIS, who promised his followers existence after death in his kingdom.

**Usūl al-fiqh**. *See* FIQH.

**utgard**. Realm of the giants, adversaries of the gods and men, in Germanic pre-Christian mythology.

**utilitarianism**. The theory that actions are right or good only in so far as they further the happiness of the greatest number of people. The theory is associated particularly with the philosophy of John Stuart Mill (1806–73).

**uTixo**. Supreme being among the Xhosa in southern Africa. An equivalent of the Hottentot deity TSUI-GOAB, uTixo also resembles UNKULUNKULU of the neighbouring Zulu. In conception, however, uTixo has two aspects, being partly a celestial (sky or thunderstorm) god and partly an ancestral god. (Breutz 1975: 451).

**Uto**. The Sumerian sun god, identified with the Babylonian SHAMASH.

**al-ʿUzza**. *See* 'DAUGHTERS' OF ALLAH.

# V

**Vairocana**. A mythical Buddha also known as Mahāvairocana Tathāgata, or in Japanese Dainichi Nyorai, and of central importance in Shingon Buddhism (*see* SHINGON-SHŪ). Vairocana figures in a 7th-century sūtra, now extant only in Chinese and Tibetan versions, and known in Shingon Buddhism as the *Dainichikyō*.

**Vaiśna**. *See* SĀMKHYA.

**Vaiṣṇavism**. The largest section of Hinduism, the community of the followers of VIṢṆU. Its origin is pre-Christian. It contains a great number of SAṀPRADĀYAS with their own particularities as regards worship and rules of life. It is a flourishing religious tradition which has also developed in some of its branches a missionary movement outside India, such as the International Society for Krishna Consciousness (HARE KRISHNA MOVEMENT) a branch of (Neo) Gauḍīya-Vaiṣṇavism.

**Vaiśya**. *See* CASTE.

**vajradhātu**. *See* RYŌBU MANDARA.

**Valentinianism**. The most prominent school of Christian GNOSTICISM in the 2nd – 3rd centuries, founded by the Alexandrian Valentinus around 138–158 in Rome. Both his own writings and those of the differing 'Italian' and 'Oriental' schools formed by his followers survive only in fragments, some of them among the NAG HAMMADI texts. A characteristic Valentinian concept is that of the *pleroma* peopled by 15 pairs of abstract beings, including Christ and the Holy Spirit.

**Valhalla**. ODIN'S 'hall of the slain' in ASGARD, the kingdom of the Germanic gods, inhabited by the dead warriors chosen by Odin and the VALKYRIES to fall in battle and join the army ready to fight for the gods at RAGNAROK. They would feast on pork and mead (made of the milk of the hart which feeds on YGGDRASILL) each night and go back into battle each day. These warriors were rulers or famous heroes and it was considered an honour to be chosen. Valhalla was possibly also open to women who died a violent death (usually by burning), either as a sacrifice to Odin or as an act of loyalty to a dead husband or betrothed (see Davidson, 1964: ch. 6). The myths usually depict Valhalla as a place of luxury with a roof of shields, but it is also a feared symbol of the grave.

**Valkyries**. Literally 'choosers of the slain' – female spirits who in Germanic pre-Christian mythology served the war god ODIN and were connected with battle in various ways. They decided the course of battle and imposed the 'war-fetters', which made warriors powerless. They chose the warriors who were to be slain for Odin, led them to his hall, VALHALLA, and waited on them there. They were also associated with Odin's ravens, who feasted on the dead after a battle, and in Old Norse literature they appeared in dreams as omens of war.

**Vallabha**. *See* BHAKTI; PAÑCARĀTRA; PUSTIMARGA; VIṢṆU.

**Valley of the Kings**. *See* MASTABA TOMB; NECROPOLIS; THEBES.

**Valley of the Queens**. *See* NECROPOLIS; THEBES.

**vānaprastya**. *See* AŚRAMA.

**Vanir**. A race of gods in Germanic mythology who brought peace and fertility to mankind. These gods were closely connected with the earth and the sea, and their cult laid great importance on the veneration of dead ancestors. The Vanir were at war with the other race of gods, the AESIR, with whom they finally reached a truce.

**Varaha**. *See* AVATĀRA.

**Varṇa**. *See* CASTE; PURĀṆAS.

**Varunabhakti**. *See* BHAKTI.

**vas** (Sinhalese: 'rains'). A Buddhist term originally denoting the three-month monsoon period in north-east India, during which Gautama BUDDHA told monks to desist from their wanderings and stay in a rain retreat settlement, i.e. monastery (*ārāma*). The Sinhalese monks still observe *vas*, although the period is not climatically as distinct in Sri Lanka as it is in north-east India.

**vassa**. *See* VAS.

**vastusastras**. *See* MURTI.

**vates**. *See* FAITH.

**Vatican**. In a narrow sense, the name of the residence of the Pope in Rome; but in a broader sense, the central complex of authority structures in the Roman Catholic Church. Vatican was originally the name of one of the seven hills on which Rome was built. According to tradition, it is also where the apostle Peter is buried.

**Vatican Council**. The First Vatican Council was convened in Rome during 1869–70 by Pope Pius IX. As well as differentiating Christian belief from pantheism, materialism and atheism, the most notable result was the declaration of the infallibility of the Pope when speaking *ex cathedra*, i.e. in discharge of his papal functions, on questions of faith or morals. The Second Vatican Council was called by Pope John XXIII during 1962–5, and is generally considered to have strengthened liberalizing tendencies within the Roman Catholic Church. A practical decision of great importance was the abolition of Latin as the common liturgical language of the church. The council also created theological openings to other religious faiths.

**Vaudois**. *See* WALDENSIANS.

**Veda** (Sanskrit: 'knowledge'). The corpus of Hindu scriptures. In the broad sense, it comprises *saṃhitās*, BRĀHMAṆAS, *āraṇyakas* and UPANIṢADS. In the second, it is restricted to the *saṃhitās*, the four collections of ṚG, SĀMA, YAJUR and ATHARVAVEDA. The most important of these is the ṚGVEDA.

**Vedānta** (Sanskrit: 'End of Veda'). Both The UPANIṢADS and the system of philosophy built on them. Vedānta, which has ten main branches, most of which are still flourishing, is the best known and most typical philosophy of Hinduism.

**Vedantasutra**. *See* BRAHMASŪTRA.

**Vedantasutrabhasyas**. *See* ĀTMAN.

**Vendidad**. *See* ZOROASTRIANISM.

**Veṇhu**. *See* VISṆU.

**venial sin**. *See* MORTAL SIN.

**Venus**. An ancient Italian goddess of non-Roman origins, devoted to agrarian fertility. Greek influence identified her with APHRODITE in the 3rd century BCE, but the full range of mythology associated with Aphrodite was not transferred.

**Veralden Olmai**. *See* RADIEN.

**Verdandi**. *See* YGGDRASILL.

**verification**. The process of showing that something is true, e.g. through sense-experience. The Logical Positivists (*see* POSITIVISM) claimed that propositions that are unverifiable (e.g. those of METAPHYSICS and THEOLOGY) are meaningless. *Contrast* FALSIFICATION.

**Verstehen** (German: 'understanding'). A term associated with the work of Wilhem Dilthey, the 19th-century German philosopher. He considered that whereas the natural sciences were characterized by 'explanation', in the sense of the establishing of positive causal laws, the human sciences primarily had the goal of *Verstehen*, or understanding. Scientific accuracy is here attained not by finding exact laws, but by empathetic penetration of particular human cultures in terms of the subjective beliefs and intentions of the human beings who created them. It is to be noted that while Dilthey's programme was 'humanistic', it remained also 'scientific' in a would-be rigorous sense. *See also* HERMENEUTICS; HERMENEUTIC CIRCLE.

**Vesak** (Sinhalese). The full-moon day in May on which the birth, enlightenment and the death of the Buddha are celebrated.

**Vesta**. The Roman hearth goddess, equivalent to Greek HESTIA. Her shrine at Rome contained the sacred fire, which could not be extinguished. She was served by six Vestal Virgins, who followed many archaic taboos during their period of service.

**Vestal Virgins**. *See* VESTA.

**via dolorosa** (Latin: 'mournful way'). The path taken by Christ from the pronouncement of sentence by Pontius Pilate to the place of crucifixion. *See also* STATIONS OF THE CROSS.

**via illuminativa**. *See* VIA UNITIVA.

**via media** (Latin: 'middle way'). A reference to ANGLICANISM as a balanced form of Christianity between Catholicism and Nonconformity. The term was used particularly in the 19th-century Oxford Movement.

**via purgativa**. *See* VIA UNITIVA.

**via unitiva** (Latin: 'unitive path'). The way of union with God, which in Christian mystical writings such as those of St Teresa and St John of the Cross is regarded as the crowning stage of mystical experience. It follows the purgative path (*via purgativa*) and the illuminative path (*via illuminativa*). The first of these is intended to eradicate sin, especially habitual sin, and the second leads away from attachment to that which is creaturely by giving illumination about the spiritual.

**Vibhava**. *See* AVATĀRA, PAÑCARĀTRA.

**vidya**. *See* AVIDYĀ, ŚAIVA SIDDHANTA.

**vidyas**. *See* MṚTYU, UPANIṢADS.

**vihāra** (Sanskrit, Pāli). A Buddhist monastery or nunnery. In the Pāli Canon, *Tipiṭaka*, three different terms are used to denote three types of monasteries, namely, *vihāra*, located in or near a town, *āraññā-vihāra*, located in the forest, and *dūra-vihāra*, hermitage, remote dwelling.

**vijñāna** (Sanskrit). Consciousness, a technical term in Buddhism, the Pāli form being *viññana*, normally listed as the sixth of the six senses. *See also* VIJÑĀNAVĀDA.

**Vijñānavāda** (Sanskrit). A general designation for the Yogācāra and related schools of thought in MAHĀYĀNA Buddhism which stress the primacy of consciousness (VIJÑĀNA). Vijñānavāda has sometimes been referred to as 'Buddhist idealism', but this may be misleading as the term 'idealism' itself can mean different things. An early statement of the Vijñānavāda approach is found in the LAṆKĀVATĀRA SŪTRA, but it is primarily associated with Asanga (*c*.315–90) and Vasubandhu (*c*.400–480, if the theory of a younger Vasubandhu, not the brother of Asaṇga, is followed). The works of these authors define what came to be known as the Yogācāra School. This was the main counterpoint to the MĀDHYAMIKA School in the development of Mahāyāna Buddhist thought, although there was no enmity or controversy between the two and indeed they may be regarded as in principle consistent with each other (May 1971).

**Vimalakīrti**. A legendary figure whose dialogues and magical feats are celebrated in an early and influential MAHĀYĀNA Buddhist work entitled *The Teaching of Vimalakīrti*. Vimalakīrti is a BODHISATTVA whose teaching is guided by the twin principles of PRAJNĀPĀRAMITĀ (perfection of insight) and UPĀYAKAUŚALYA (skilfulness in means), concerning which matters he has an edifiying dialogue with the bodhisattva MAÑJUŚRĪ.

(For the text see Lamotte 1962; Thurman 1976.) *See also* POSITIONLESSNESS.

**vinaya** (Sanskrit, Pāli). Discipline, the rule of the Buddhist monastic order; also the scripture containing that Rule, *Vinaya Piṭaka*, the first 'basket' of the Buddhist Canon, TRIPIṬAKA.

**viññāna**. *See* VIJÑĀNA.

**vipassanā**. *See* BHĀVANĀ.

**vipassanā-bhāvanā**. *See* BHĀVANĀ.

**vipasyanā-bhāvanā**. *See* BHĀVANĀ.

**Viracocha** [Wiraqocha]. In ancient Peru, the highest divinity who created all supernatural beings and man. Myths describe his journey from TIAHUANACO along the Vilcanota river to Cuzco and Ecuador. He was worshipped in different places in the form of certain *huaca* and in the Coricancha Temple in Cuzco (Rowe, 1975).

**Vira-Saivas.** *See* LIṆGAYATS.

**Virgin Birth**. A technical term in Christian theology to express the belief that Mary became pregnant with Jesus by the power of the HOLY SPIRIT alone and without human sexual intercourse. In the New Testament a basis for this belief is found in the relatively late infancy narratives of the Gospels of Matthew and Luke, the former (*Matthew* 1.28) making reference to prophecy in *Isaiah* 7.14. The original intention of this text is not quite clear since both the Hebrew term *'almā* and its Greek translation, *parthenos*, can mean either a virgin in a physical sense or a young woman ready for marriage. On the other hand, many famous persons in the Hellenistic world, such as Plato or Alexander the Great, as well as kings in other civilizations, have had both a human and a divine origin ascribed to them. Some modern writers regard this as the mythological expression of a common human desire to imagine a saviour who comes from an uncontaminated holy realm (e.g. Drewermann 1984–5). Notwithstanding the mythological features, Christian theologians, especially in the Roman Catholic and Orthodox churches, have frequently asserted the biological nature of Mary's virginity (e.g. in the Lateran Council of 649). This can even take the form of requiring belief in the virginity of Mary after the birth of Jesus as well as before. Since she could therefore not have had any other children, brothers of Jesus have to be reinterpreted as cousins. Moreover, since she would have had no sexual intercourse with her legitimate human husband, Joseph, the designation 'josephine marriage' has arisen for a marriage which, by vow, has excluded sexual practice. The doctrine of the virgin birth was undoubtedly the main starting point for the growth of the cult of the Virgin Mary which credits her with immense supernatural power. The virginity of Mary is also mentioned in the Qur'ān, and is consequently part of Muslim faith.

**Vishnu**. *See* VIṢṆU.

**vision quest**. In most Native American religions it is essential for individuals to gain a guardian spirit in order to function successfully for the benefit of their community. This is known as vision quest or vision questing, and is achieved in North America through fasting, running, performing the SUN DANCE and other trials which tend to engender ecstatic experiences, whereas in Meso-America and South America hallucinogenic substances are generally used for the same purpose. Vision questing through extended running, sometimes incorporating pilgrimage features, is a common aspect of both female and male puberty rituals in southwestern Native North American religions. In northern Native North American religions, however, the primary means of vision questing is by a ritual fast, usually four days in length, although fasts of seven and eight or more days also are undertaken. In these cultures, puberty rituals involve a major fast during which neither food nor water is taken and the person remains within a very small, secluded area.

**visions**. Religious experiences which often relate to the sense of sight, but sometimes to other senses. Visions commonly contain descriptions of other worlds (gods, spirits, angels etc.) but often also make forecasts for this world (prophecies). They not uncommonly have eschatological and apocalyptic features. Visions are common elements in most religions. They have gained special significance in the spiritual life of American Indians. In explaining visions, factors such as traditions and learning, depth psychological factors and the typologies of personality psychology have been adduced. Visions have often be characterized as HALLUCINATIONS or ILLUSIONS. Unlike these, however, visions normally have a clear social and religious background in a specific environment and become, therefore, meaningful for the individual him/herself and often for the group around this person. In a religious perspective visions may be regarded as having a spiritual as well as a social function. In some contexts, but only if the wider religious tradition allows, a vision may lead to the establishment of a new cult or pilgrimage centre, as in visions of Mary (*see*, for example, LOURDES).

**Viśiṣṭādvaita** (Sanskrit: 'qualified non-duality'). One of the ten systems of VEDĀNTA, whose major representative is RĀMĀNUJA (1017–1727).

**Visitation of Our Lady**. A Roman Catholic Church feast (2 July), dating from the Middle Ages, which celebrates the visit paid by Mary, the mother of Jesus, to Elizabeth, as related in the first chapter of the *Gospel of Luke*. Elizabeth is there said to be the cousin of Mary and the mother of John the Baptist, so that the birth of the forerunner of Jesus is correlated with his own.

**Viṣṇu** (Sanskrit: 'the all-pervader', possibly from an original Tamil name *veṇhu*, 'the blue one'). The most universally worshipped deity of Hinduism. In the VEDA introduced as Upendra, i.e. the younger brother of Indra, he came to prominence during the age of the early PURĀṆAS (4th to 5th centuries CE). The *Viṣṇupurāṇa*, one of the oldest and most important, is one of the major scriptures of VAIṢṆAVISM. From the 10th century onwards, the AVATĀRAS ('descents') of VIṢṆU become more prominent, especially RĀMA and KṚṢṆA, the chief figures of the popular RĀMĀYAṆA and *Bhāgavata Purāṇa*. An extensive systematic theology developed within Vaiṣṇavism, first on the basis of SĀṀKHYA and then VEDĀNTA. Some of the greatest Vedāntins (RĀMĀNUJA, Madhva, Vallabha, Nimbārka) were *Vaiṣṇavas* with a large following. Vaiṣṇavism is characterized by extensive and minutely regulated worship of images and by intense emotional devotion. Popular saints and singers like the ĀLVĀRS in South India or the *bhaktas* of medieval Mahārāṣṭra propagated the devotion to Viṣṇu in many parts of India.

**Viṣṇubhakti**. *See* LINGAM.

**Viṣṇudasa**. *See* MĀDHVA.

**Viṣṇupurāṇa**. *See* PURĀṆAS, VIṢṆU.

**Viṣṇusmṛti**. *See* SMṚTI.

**Viśva Bharatī** (Bengali). *See* ŚANTINIKETAN.

**Viśva Hindu Pariṣad** (Hindi). An organization convened in India in 1964 with the purpose of protecting Hindu society from alien ideologies and sponsoring HINDUISM at home and abroad by opening temples and libraries. Many Hindu organizations abroad are affiliated. The 'VHP' is also associated with the Rastria Svaymansevak Sangh (RSS), and organized the recent takeover of the site of Ayodhya.

**vita** (Latin: 'life'). The life, e.g. of a SAINT, told in legendary or iconographic form. In icons the vita is usually portrayed in a series of panels around the central image.

**vodu** [voḍḍ]. Deities of the pantheon of the Fon of Dahomey (Republic of Benin). Derived from the concept of *vodu* are the VOODOO cults of the descendants of slaves in the Caribbean and Brazil. (Herskovits 1933).

**Volcanalia**. *See* VULCAN.

**Volkskirche**. *See* BARMEN DECLARATION.

**Voluspá**. *See* VǪLVA, RAGNAROK.

**vǫlva**. Germanic term for seeress. The *vǫlva* practised *seiðr*, the magic connected with FREYJA, a goddess of the VANIR. During her ritual performances the *vǫlva* reached a state of ecstasy in which she foretold the future and cast spells. In Germanic mythology *vǫlva* are sometimes consulted by the gods, e.g. in the Edda poem *Vǫluspá* ('Soothsaying of the *vǫlva*'), which describes the beginning and end of the world and takes the form of a *vǫlva* revealing her knowledge to ODIN. (Davidson 1964)

**Voodoo** [Wodu, Vodo]. An Afro-American religion introduced to Haiti and the Dominican Republic by slaves from Dahomey (now Benin), West Africa. During the cult performances the medium is inspired or, literally, 'mounted', by a LOA. The purpose of the rituals is to heal sicknesses and to solve daily problems. An important part of the rituals is the sacrifice of animals, usually hens but also sheep. Voodoo has strong similarities with SANTERÍA. *See also* VODU.

**votive mass**. A MASS dedicated to a special, symbolic occasion which marks a transition for those concerned in it such as a wedding, a funeral, the election of a Pope, or the establishment of peace after conflict. It may also be celebrated without reference to specific living persons in devotion to the Passion of Christ, to the consecrated HOST, or to the Virgin Mary.

**vrata** (Sanskrit: 'vow'). A term used to generically describe festivals in honour of a deity and practices undertaken by individuals in pursuit of specific objectives. Jaina ascetics have given the name *mahāvrata*, or 'great vow', to their central commitments of non-violence, truth, respect for others' property, celibacy and non-attachment. In Hinduism, *vratas* more commonly are ritual sequences undertaken to accomplish a mundane goal. Such *vratas* are a central feature of women's religious practice. They usually entail ritual bathing, fasting and/or eating special foods, reading or reciting stories about exemplary figures, and honouring specified deities; their goals may include attracting a suitable husband, or preserving the health and prosperity of sons, husbands and brothers.

**vrndavan**. *See* LĪLA.

**Vṛtra** (Sanskrit: 'the enveloper'). The name of the most powerful ASURA (demon) in the ṚGVEDA, whose defeat is described as Indra's greatest deed. Variously interpreted as monsoon-cloud, as water-reservoir etc., Vṛtra is probably a symbol for the powers that obstructed the progression of Vedic religion on the Indian subcontinent.

**Vulcan**. An ancient Italian fire god, worshipped for prevention of fires. He had little of the mythology of his Greek counterpart HEPHAISTOS. He was worshipped at the Volcanalia (23 August). Because of the destructive nature of fire, his temple had to stand outside a city's boundaries.

**Vulgate** (from Latin, *editio vulgata*: 'common edition'). The Latin version of the Christian Bible completed by Jerome in approximately 404 CE which came into common use in western Christendom.

**Vyasa**. *See* GAṆEṢA.

**Vyuha**. *See* PAÑCARĀTRA.

# W

**waca**. *See* HUACA.

**Wadjet**. Predynastic (before 3100 BCE) cobra goddess of Lower Egypt who protected the king; her cult-centre was at Dep. She is also known as Edjo, or in Greek as Buto.

**Wahegurū** [Vahigurū] (Punjabi: 'Wonderful Lord'). A word used in Sikh meditational chanting and salutations, most notably in the phrase 'Wahegurūjī ka Khālsā, Wahegurūjī ki fateh' ('Hail to the Gurū's khālsā, hail to the Gurū's victory'). *See also* NĀM SIMRAN.

**Wahhābiya**. An Islamic reform movement originating with Muḥammad b. ʿAbd al-Wahhāb (1703–92) in Arabia and aimed at eradicating idolatrous accretions such as saint worship and other innovations (BIDʿA) in popular religion; his campaign was directed as well against what he perceived as the moral laxity of Islamic society of his day. He condemned the authority (TAQLĪD) of the medieval schools, recognizing only that of the QUR'ĀN and the Prophetic tradition (*see* ḤADĪTH) and denounced allegorical interpretation (TA'WĪL) of scripture. His doctrines, which were inspired by the famous Ḥanbalī (*see* MADHHAB) scholar Ibn Taymiya (*d* 1328), and puritanical reforming zeal became the driving forces behind the expanding political influence of the Saudi family and the founding of their kingdom in the early 20th century. Wahhābī ideas have also made their influence felt in India and West Africa. (Mortimer 1982).

**waidan**. *See* NEIDAN.

**Wailing Wall**. Actually a retaining wall surrounding the Temple Mount in Jerusalem, it is considered to be the last remnant of the western wall of the Temple of Solomon. Over the centuries following the destruction of the SECOND TEMPLE in 70 CE, generations of Jews have come to pray and cry at the Wailing Wall. Since it returned to Jewish control in the Six Day War in 1967, it has been renamed the 'Western Wall'. It is now surrounded by a large paved plaza, where Jews come to pray and celebrate and still, sometimes, to cry.

**waitan**. *See* NEIDAN.

**wājib** (Arabic). Obligatory. *See also* SHARĪʿA, FARḌ.

**wakamiya**. *See* GO-BUNREI.

**wakan** [wakanda] (Sioux). The term for spiritual powers in Sioux languages (western North America). *See also* WAKAN TANKA; MANA.

**Wakan Tanka**. 'Great Spirit' in Sioux languages (western North America), originally standing for spiritual powers collectively but in recent times rather for a HIGH GOD. *See also* WAKAN.

**Waldenses**. *See* WALDENSIANS.

**Waldensians**. A small Protestant group which originally began as a reformist movement in medieval France as a result of the life of Peter Waldo (*d* 1217), after whom the name arises (also Waldenses or Vaudois). Waldo was a merchant of Lyon who gave his wealth to the poor and took up a life of mendicant preaching. He and his followers came under a ban by the church authorities, with the result that they appointed their own ministers and, though persecuted, spread further in southern France and northern Italy. Even after the Reformation, which led to their constitution as a fully ordered Protestant church with a married priesthood and public worship, further persecution was suffered in the 17th century in France. The membership is now mainly Italian.

**wālī** (Arabic: plural, *awliyā'*). A Muslim mystic, one to whom the esoteric knowledge of the mystic path (ṬARĪQA) is given and who possesses the power of miracles (*karamāt*) and of blessing (*baraka*). Muslims believe there to be a hierarchy of saints always living in the world culminating in a principal saint called the Pole or Axis (QUTB).

**wali songo** [wali sanga] (Javanese, Indonesian). Literally, 'Nine Saints', who, according to traditional Javanese historiography, are considered to have introduced Islam into Java in the 14th – 16th centuries (Stöhr & Zoetmulder 1965).

**wanga**. A term current in Central Bantu languages to denote the spiritual power of persons such as NGANGA, great hunters and blacksmiths, or of the objects owned and manipulated by them, but also by anti-social forces.

**Waqa**. The supreme being in Ethiopia and northern Kenya. Strongly affected by Islam and Christianity, the formerly dualistic image (sky and earth) is now dominated by the monotheistic concept of a celestial god. (Haberland 1963: 561ff).

**waqf** (Arabic: 'pious endowment'). In Islām, money or property placed in trust, the income from which can be used for charitable purposes to benefit the community as a whole. Such purposes would include the building and maintanance of MOSQUES, schools and hospitals.

**wasan** (Japanese). A song of praise composed in Japanese to extol a buddha or bodhisattva or a historical patriarch. Jōdo *Wasan* is the name of a particularly famous set of such hymns composed by Shinran (*see* JŌDO SHINSHŪ).

**wat** (Thai: 'monastery'). A Buddhist monastic community in Thailand. *See also* VIHĀRA.

**Watchtower Bible and Tract Society**. An organization whose members are otherwise known as Jehovah's Witnesses.

The society was founded in the USA by C.T. Russell (1852–1916) and further developed by J.F. Rutherford (1869–1941). The magazine *The Watchtower* is widely distributed by the society's missionaries. Its teaching, based on a fundamentalist yet idiosyncratic view of Christian scripture, stresses the second coming of Christ (originally predicted by Rutherford for 1914) and the establishment of the kingdom of God on this earth. Jehovah's Witnesses refuse to take part in most forms of political organization and are therefore pacifist.

**wayang** (Javanese; Indonesian). In the strict sense, a puppet of the Javanese shadow play; as a collective term also designating various forms of Javanese and Balinese puppet shows, or the performance itself. Alongside *wayang golek* (performed with rod puppets), *wayang wong* or *orang* (dance drama, replacing puppets by human actors), and many other variants, *wayang kulit* represents the most popular form of *wayang*. Performed by the DALANG, who moves flat leather figures in front of a lamp projecting the shadows on a screen, *wayang kulit* is entertainment and drama as well as ritual event, often accompanying a SLAMETAN or similar occurrences such as circumcision, wedding and so forth.

Many stories of the *wayang* are taken from the classical *wayang purwa* ('original', 'foremost', 'earlier') repertoire, which derives its material mainly from Javanese versions of Indian epics, especially the RĀMĀYANA and MAHĀBHĀRATA (BRATAYUDA) cycles. Though it would be wrong to consider every *wayang* performance commonly a religious act (Stöhr & Zoetmulder 1965: 309), it is reasonably clear that *wayang* is an integral part of AGAMA KEJAWEN: 'seen as the projection of cosmic conditions on earth' (Mulder 1983a: 32), *wayang* demonstrates its significance not only where it is performed at purification ceremonies or protective rites, etc., but also by its influence on the secular and political everyday life of many Indonesians. (Kats 1923; Anderson 1965; Dahm 1969; Brandon 1970).

**wedjat eye**. The sacred falcon's Eye of HORUS, symbolizing completeness and wellbeing; frequently used as an amulet in ancient Egypt.

**Wee Frees**. A minority remnant of United Presbyterians who refused to join with the Free Church of Scotland when the United Free Church of Scotland was formed in 1900.

**Weighing the Heart**. The Egyptian day of judgement included the weighing of the deceased's heart as he recited the Negative Confession (declaring himself innocent of 42 sins) before OSIRIS and the divine judges. If he was blameless, his heart would balance the feather of truth (*see* MAAT), he would be declared 'justified', and his body and soul would be reunited and pass on to the kingdom of Osiris. If found guilty, however, his heart would be devoured by a fearsome animal and his eternal existence would be doomed.

This scene, included in Chapter 125 of the BOOK OF THE DEAD, is depicted in papyri and on tomb walls. The idea also occurs in Greek as *psychostasia*, e.g. as the title of a play by Aeschylus in which the lives of Achilles and Memnon are weighed against each other.

**wei shu**. *See* CHENWEI.

**Wenchang** [Wen-ch'ang]. Usually called the Chinese god of literature. His official name is Wenchang Di Jun [Ti-chün] ('Emperor Lord Wenchang'). He is popularly understood as a deified scholar named Zhang Ya, who lived during the Tang dynasty. Originally, however, Wenchang was the name of a group of stars, and some legends still show references to the worship of stars. The cult of Wenchang was especially popular among the literati.

**Wende**. *See* TENGA.

**Wenmiao** [Wen-miao] (Chinese: 'Temple of Literature'). Since the Ming dynasty (1368–1644) the name of the temple for Confucius and other sages of the Confucian tradition. Usually every administrative unit in imperial China had its own temple of Confucius.

**Wepwawet**. Jackal-headed funerary god of ancient Egypt with important centres at ABYDOS and Assiut; known as the 'Opener of the Ways'.

**Wesak**. *See* VESAK.

**Western Wall.** *See* WAILING WALL.

**Westminster Confession**. A revision of the THIRTY-NINE ARTICLES which was approved by parliament at Westminster in England in 1648 only to be abandoned later in that country. Having also been approved in Edinburgh, the Westminster Confession became the main doctrinal reference point of the presbyterian Church of Scotland. Two 'Westminster' catechisms were composed at the same time, which, together with the Westminster Confession, have been influential in Congregationalist and Baptist as well as in Presbyterian churches.

**WFB**. *See* WORLD FELLOWSHIP OF BUDDHISTS.

**whaka-noa**. *See* TAPU.

**whaka-tapu**. *See* TAPU.

**White Old Man**. A deity of both earth and water known in Mongolian as Tsaghan Ebügen ('white old man'). Pre-Buddhist in origin, he was later presented as commissioned to oversee morality by the Buddha himself. Tsaghan Ebügen has white hair, beard and clothes, and appears leaning on a staff surmounted by a dragon's head. (Heissig 1980: 76–81).

**Whitsunday**. *See* PENTECOST.

**Wilāyat al-Faqīh** [Persian, *Vilayat-i Faqih*] (Arabic: 'guardianship of the jurisconsult'). In SHĪ'A Islām, a notion which, although having a long history in Shī'a jurisprudence, became closely identified with the political outlook of Iran's late religious leader Ayatullāh Ruḥullāh Khumaynī (*d* 1989). The novel twist he gave to this concept was that a FAQĪH should not just be one among many top-ranking officials in the state apparatus but its supreme judge and guardian (Enayat 1983).

**windigo**. In northern Algonkian religions (North America), an evil, cannibalistic spirit that may possess individuals, especially in the depth of winter. Such persons, also called *windigo*, became a danger to their community.

**Wisaca**. The Cree (northern North American) culture-hero on TRICKSTER. *See also* NANABUSH.

**wisdom literature**. Egyptian texts with moral teaching that were particularly popular in the Old Kingdom (2686–2181 BCE) and the Middle Kingdom (1991–1786 BCE) (Simpson 1972). Usually couched in terms of advice given by a sage to his pupils or a father to his son, they provide an unparalleled insight into the ethics and morals of ancient Egypt. They offer pragmatic instruction in wisdom and good behaviour, appropriate to Egypt's structured and hierarchical society. Intended for the teaching of those who would become the leaders and officials, the texts are remarkable for their emphasis on fair-mindedness and clemency. They were copied as schoolboy exercises, not only because of the virtue of their content but also to act as models of literary excellence. Wisdom was regarded in the Hebrew Bible as characteristic of deity (*Genesis* 3.5) and a mark of true kingship (*1 Kings* 3.28). As prophetic conceptions of YAHWEH developed, however, royal wisdom was increasingly criticized (Whybray 1965). Wisdom books were a literary genre of international character (McKane 1979), biblical examples being *Ecclesiastes* and *Proverbs*. (Blenkinsopp 1983).

**witch**. A human being, either male or female, who is believed to cause physical, psychological or spiritual harm to other humans or living beings by means undetectable to the naked eye. Witches thus contrast with ordinary human sources of harm in that they employ extraordinary means thought to be occult or supernatural such as magic or spells; since they remain fully human, they likewise contrast with those thought to cause harm who are not human, such as demons, gods, ancestors or other spirits. Belief in witches seems common to many of the world's cultures, although they tend to be found most prominently in cultures where human conflict tends to be uncontrolled. Typically, witches are discovered by being *accused* of doing harm, whereupon they either confess or deny the accusation. But accusation – and thus strife and suspicion – remain essential features of the phenomenon. Thus, although witches are common in African (e.g. *see* OBAYIFO) and European societies, they are rarely found in China.

The uneven distribution of witches across world cultures is only one of the reasons for thinking that the phenomenon has specific sociological causes. Another is that certain classes of individual tend to be selected for accusation as witches or select themselves as witches by confessing. These are persons who are special candidates for exclusion or for alienating themselves from society. At least in Western Europe, those accused of being witches have disproportionately tended to be those people excluded from power in the ordinary world, yet toward whom a remnant of obligation was felt. Since these people inspired uncomfortable feelings of guilt, they were accused of some wrongdoing – an act of witchcraft – which in turn would sanction their retaliatory exclusion from the community. Likewise, people resentful of their exclusion from power might arrogate witchcraft powers to themselves in order to inspire the respect of the community which had excluded them. Thus, during the 17th century, Essex witch-crazes and in Salem, Massachusetts, elderly, often indigent, women were prime candidates for accusation as well as willing volunteers of confessions about their responsibility for acts of suspected witchcraft. Apparently, the rise of economic individualism relaxed the bonds of community responsibility for the poor at this time, and led to the rise of indigence among the population. At the same time, guilt afflicted many of society's members whose consciences were still governed partly by the older morality of responsibility and neighbourliness on the one hand, but increasingly by the new morality of individualism. When the poor would curse for refusing charity, it would be natural to think that subsequent misfortune resulted from transgressing the old morality, and that it had been caused by the indigent poor – in effect by a 'witch'.

There is no evidence that witches in Western Europe or America represent the survivals of pre-Christian religions. (Important treatments are Evans-Pritchard 1937;

Thomas 1971; Douglas 1970.) *See also* BRUJO.

**Wodan**. *See* ODIN.

**Woden**. *See* ODIN.

**Wolfenbüttel Fragments**. Seven extracts from a longer work by H.S. Reimarus (1694–1768) which, being published under this title by G.E. Lessing shortly after his death, contributed to the modern development of biblical criticism.

**Womb Maṇḍala**. *See* MAṆḌALA.

**Workings of Creation**. *See* KABBALAH.

**Workings of the Chariot**. *See* KABBALAH.

**World Buddhist Sangha Council**. An international organization of Buddhist monks and nuns founded in Colombo in 1966.

**World Congress of Faiths**. An inter-religious association based on a series of congresses and strongly supported in recent years by the RISSHŌ KOSEI-KAI, a Japanese lay Buddhist movement.

**World Council of Churches**. The World Council of Churches is the main focus of the modern ecumenical movement, having been founded in Amsterdam in 1948 on the basis of earlier conferences, on 'Life and Work' and on 'Faith and Order', which had taken place in 1937. Numerous Churches have joined it as a 'fellowship of Churches which accept our Lord Jesus Christ as Lord and Saviour'. However the Roman Catholic Church is still not a member at the time of writing.

**World Fellowship of Buddhists (WFB)**. A world-wide union of Buddhists founded in Colombo in 1950, where the first Buddhist World Conference was held later the same year. The Sinhalese Buddhologist G.P. Malalasekere (1899–1973) was the first president.

**World's Parliament of Religions**. An inter-religious conference held in Chicago in 1893, which for the first time brought a wide range of religious leaders together from both Asia and the western world.

**world pillar**. A cosmic pillar which supports the sky and links the earth. The idea is found in the archaic cosmological tradition of many cultural areas. North Asian and Arctic peoples imagined the sky as a tent and the Pole star as a pillar, 'nail' or 'hole' in its centre. The world pillar was symbolized either by the poles that support the dwelling and were considered as sacred, or by separate stakes connected to ritual activities. As an axis of the world the cosmic pillar is parallel to the WORLD TREE. (Holmberg 1922–3; Harva 1938; Karjalainen 1921–7; Eliade 1958).

**World Serpent**. *See* MIDGARD SERPENT.

**world tree**. A tree that connects the sky, earth and underworld in the centre of the world. The concept is one of the most widespread cosmological ideas. The cosmic tree becomes a tree of life when related to the ideas of fertility and immortality. In the Eurasian cultural area there is a parallel in the so-called SHAMAN's tree used by shamans ascending to the upper world or descending to lower levels of the cosmos. The tree played a central part in shamanic initiation and replicas or symbols of it were used as ritual objects (*see* SHAMANIC DRUM). (Holmberg 1922–3; Harva 1938; Eliade 1958). *See also* YGGDRASILL.

**Wotan**. *See* ODIN.

**Wounded Knee.** *See* GHOST DANCE.

**wu chang** (Chinese: 'five constants'). In Confucianism, the Five Cardinal Virtues, which since Dong Zhongshu [Tung Chung-shu] (*c*.179–*c*.104 BCE) are listed as REN [*jen*] ('benevolence'), *yi* [*i*] ('righteousness'), LI ['rules of propriety', 'etiquette'], *zhi* [*chih*] ('wisdom') and *xin* [*hsin*] ('trustworthiness').

**Wu-Chen-P'ian**. *See* WU ZHEN PIAN.

**Wu Ching**. *See* WU JING.

**Wu Di** [Wu Ti] (Chinese: 'Five Emperors'). A collective name for five celestial gods ruling the four directions and the centre. Their cult was first instituted in the 3rd century BCE by the First Emperor of the Qin [Chʿin] dynasty.

**Wuḍūʿ**. *See* ṬAHĀRA.

**wu hsing**. *See* WU XING.

**Wu Jing** [Wu Ching] (Chinese: 'Five Classics'). Five scriptures which since the Former Han dynasty (206 BCE – 23 CE) were regarded as canonical by the Confucian literati. They included the SHI JING [*Shih Ching*] ('Book of Songs'), the SHU JING [*Shu Ching*] ('Book of Documents'), the LI JI [*Li Chi*] ('Book of Ritual'), YI JING [*I Ching*] ('Book of Changes') and the CHUNQIU [Chʿun-ch'iu] ('Spring and Autumn Annals') with its three commentaries.

**wu lun** (Chinese: 'five personal relationships'). In Confucianism, relationships that define the correct behaviour in a given situation. These are the relations between (1) father and son, (2) ruler and subject, (3) husband and wife, (4) elder and younger generation, and (5) between friends.

**Wu men kuan**. An influential writing in the CHAN tradition of Buddhism, being a collection of anecdotes illustrating such themes as the buddha-nature of all beings, sudden englightenment and non-dualism. The title includes the name of its author, Wu-men (1183–1260), i.e. 'gateless' and means literally 'the gateless barrier'. It is also widely known, because of its influence in ZEN Buddhism, by the Japanese pronunciation of the title, *Mumonkan*. (Blyth 1966; Shibayama 1974).

**wuqūf** [waqfa] (Arabic). Literally 'halt'. *See also* 'ARAFAT.

**Württemberg Confession**. A statement of protestant Christian faith drawn up by the reformer Johann Brenz in 1552, adopting a mainly Lutheran position in conciliatory form for use at the Council of Trent (*see*. TRIDENTINE THEOLOGY), where it was, however, rejected.

**Wu Ti**. *See* WU DI.

**wu wei** (Chinese). Not (taking) action, non-action, *laisser faire*; a Chinese Daoist concept (*see* DAOISM) of far-reaching implications. In general it is understood in the sense of 'let things spontaneously develop out of themselves, according to their innate nature', thus rejecting the idea of education as a tool for moral instruction that is so prominent in CONFUCIANISM. In the book *Lao Tzu* [Laozi] (chap. 3) the concept of non-action is developed along political lines. The sage (i.e. the emperor) does not interfere by wilful executive action but yet everything is well regulated. (Loy 1985).

**wu yue** (Chinese). The five sacred state-cult mountains of China: Mount Tai (present Shandong Province), Mount Heng (Hunan Province), Mount Hua (Shaanxi Province), Mount Heng (written with a different character; Shanxi Province), and Mount Song (Henan Province). For Mounts Hua and Heng (in Hunan) alternatives existed in pre-Christian times (possibly also for Mount Heng in Shanxi, the exact location of the 'original' one being open to debate). However, the 'set of five' given above is considered to be the orthodox series. In the course of history the gods of these mountains (but also of other mountains such as the four holy Buddhist mountains, the five Guardian-Mountains etc.) were given titles like court officials. Emperors had mountain temples constructed, modelled after the palace in the capital, to perform imperial sacrifices (FENG SHAN), asking for protection from heaven and renewing their heavenly mandate as the 'sons of heaven'. The five state-cult mountains are now adorned with both Daoist and Buddhist temples. (Mullikan & Hotchkis 1973) *See also* TAI SHAN; WU YUE ZHEN XING TU.

**Wu Yue Zhen Xing Tu** (Chinese: 'Chart of the True Form of the Five Sacred Mountains'). A sacred magico-geographical scripture of DAOISM, sometimes also called or closely associated with the 'Text of the Three Kings' (*San Huang Wen*). The scripture is a graphic representation of the real shape of a mountain, thus everybody who comes to possess the text is said to be able to command the mountain god or gods. This in turn means that evil may be effectively warded off, that armies have to retreat and that opponents will find their deserved end. On the other hand, only the ethically most qualified are allowed (by the mountain spirit) to find this powerful chart (in the deepest recesses of the mountain), so that its use will be a benevolent one for mankind. The date of this talismanic writing is not certain but the *Wu Yue Zhen Xing Tu* is already mentioned in a 4th-century Daoist historical text, a fact that points to the antiquity of the belief in the control of natural powers through charts, charms and talismans.

**wu yüeh**. *See* WU YUE.

**wu yüeh chen hsing t'u**. *See* WU YUE ZHEN XING TU.

**Wu Zhen Pian**. An important scripture on Daoist NEIDAN practices (see DAOISM), compiled by Zhang Ziyang and dated 1075 CE. Formally the work is composed in rhymes of various patterns. Its main objective is to show that whoever wants to attain immortality (*see* LONGEVITY) has to practice 'inner alchemy' (*see* NEIDAN), i.e. create the Golden Drug of immortality within one's body through physiological refining processes controlled by meditation and visualization. The agents of refinement stressed by the Wu Zhen Pian are the 'Three Precious' i.e. essence (*jing*), breath (QI) and spirit (*shen*). As one is processed to react with the other, thus ultimately to reach the state of 'emptiness' (*xü*) that symbolizes the unity with heaven and earth, the adept transgresses the world of the profane but still has to cultivate his or her 'character' (*Xing*). The last 32 poems, songs and miscellenia reflect the CHAN influence on the Wu Zhen Pian's theoretical foundations. A number of commentaries have been compiled over the centuries, most of them included in the DAOZANG and the DAOZANG JIYAO.

# X

**Xango**. *See* CHANGÓ.

**xenolalia**. *See* GLOSSOLALIA.

**Xiang Er Zhu**. A commentary on the DAO DE JING, allegedly written by the 'Heavenly Master' Zhang (Dao-) Ling, the founder of the TIANSHI DAO (Heavenly Master Sect) of early Chinese DAOISM. The commentary, interwoven with the original Dao De Jing, was found by Sir Aurel Stein at the Dunhuang Caves in former Chinese Turkestan (now Xinjiang Province) and is now in the British Museum. It comprises 34½ chapters of the original 81-chapter Dao De Jing (chapters 3 to 37, formed as one body of text, not subdivided). As one of the oldest commentaries of the *Dao De Jing* the *Xiang Er Zhu* is of importance for the study of the transmission of ideas associated with this Daoist classic. According to Isabelle Robinet (Robinet 1977: 45) the *Xiang Er* commentator deforms the original meaning of the *Dao De Jing* in order to make an interpretation possible that puts the reader on guard against heterodox doctrines.

**xiao** [hsiao] (Chinese: 'filial piety', 'filiality'). A basic notion of Confucian ethics, signifying the complete obedience and support due to the parents. Confucius defined it as follows: 'When [the parents] are alive, serve them according to *li* ['propriety']. When they die, bury them according to *li* and sacrifice to them according to *li*' (*Lun Yu*, II, 5). The duty of *xiao* includes ancestor worship and the procreation of sons. In the *Xiao Jing* [*Hsiao Ching*] ('Book of Filial Piety') *xiao* is declared the root of all virtues: 'Filial piety begins with the serving of our parents, continues with the serving of our ruler, and is completed with the establishing of our own character.' In this way, *xiao* can be interpreted not only as the basis of the family but also as the foundation of social order.

**Xiao Jing**. *See* XIAO.

**Xi Wang Mu** (Chinese: 'Queen Mother of the West'). A Chinese mythological fairy queen residing either on KUN LUN mountain or on Jade Mountain. According to old myths she is an authority on LONGEVITY and administers a garden with peach-trees (peaches are a symbol of immortality). In classical Chinese sources Xi Wang Mu is described as resembling 'a human, with the tail of a leopard and the teeth of a tiger'. She is in charge of calamities and the five kinds of disaster that might befall the empire. As an authority on matters concerning immortality, Xi Wang Mu was incorporated into the Daoist legends (*see* DAOISM) on the qualities of the *dao* and its personification. (Cahill 1985–6).

# Y

**yabusame** (Japanese). Horseback archery, in which a rider draws and shoots blunt arrows as his horse races past three square wooden targets, performed originally by warriors at shrines for the purpose of divining the outcome of the year's harvest. The Tsurugaoka Hachimangu Yabusame festival in Kamakura is a famous example.

**Yahweh**. Also written without the vowels as YHWH (*see* TETRAGRAMMATON). The chief, and later the only god of ISRAEL and JUDAH. Perhaps in origin a local form of EL (Cross 1973: 73). The meaning of the name remains obscure, but see TETRAGRAMMATON and the discussion in Murtonen 1952. Yahweh is generally characterized as 'the god who acts in history', that is, in ELECTION, EXODUS and the land-apportionment of Palestine. In succeeding centuries the use of the name declined, most likely because of the increasing growth of more abstract monotheistic thought and the consciousness of the fact that the name expresses God's holy character. In Hebraic thought, a name was considered to express the inner character or identity of its bearer. By the late Hellenistic period, as a way of preserving it from sacrilege, its use was forbidden except by the high priest in the temple for blessings and prayers, and the substitute ADONAI ('My Lord') was employed on other occasions. But in the Middle Ages, Christianity combined the vowels in 'Adonai' with the four consonants in the tetragrammaton to produce the name JEHOVAH, usually rendered in English as 'Lord'. (Labuschagne 1966; Lang 1983; Ollenburger 1987).

**Yahweh-Alone Party**. An inelegant term denoting an exclusivist movement in JUDAH and Israel promoting the YAHWEH-cult. *See also* JOSIAH'S REFORM. (M. Smith 1987; Lang 1983: 13–59).

***Yajurveda***. One of the four Vedas (*saṁhitās*), dealing with ritual. There are various recensions (a so-called white and a black *Yajurveda*).

**Yajña**. *See* ĀGAMAS, AGNI.

**Yajñas**. *See* BRAHMANAS.

**yakkha**. *See* YAKṢA.

**yakṣa** (Sanskrit: 'demi-gods') [Pāli: *yakkha*]. In Buddhist Scriptures a term denoting supernatural beings of religious and moral status close to that of man. A distinction is made between morally neutral deities living in trees or on mountains and malevolent demons who frequent cemeteries and lure lonely travellers to sudden death. *Yakṣas* are important in Hindu lore from early on, an example being Yakṣa Kubera, the god of wealth.

**Yam**. A West Semitic sea-god representing chaos and killed by the creator god (BAAL or YAHWEH). Comparable to the Akkadian sea-goddess TIAMAT. *See* BAAL CYCLE; DRAGON.

**Yama** [Yamarāga]. In Hinduism, the Lord of the realm of the dead. According to legend he was a son of BRAHMĀ and the first mortal to die. He was put in charge of the netherworld. His servants scour the earth for victims. The practices of the BHAKTIMĀRGA are designed to escape from their clutches. Yama became especially important in popular Chinese religion as Yen-lo, although his office was related to the Buddhist hells; he plays a similar but lesser role in Japan as Emma-Ō.

**yamabushi**. *See* SHUGENDO.

**Yāmarāja**. *See* YĀMA.

**yamas-niyamas**. *See* AHIṀSĀ.

**Yam Suf** (Hebrew). A term commonly translated as 'Red Sea' or 'Sea of Reeds', through which Israel passed dry-shod at the EXODUS. Better construed as 'Sea of extinction' (Montgomery 1938; Batto 1983), Yam Suf is identified as the chaos DRAGON, vanquished by YAHWEH, in many poetical passages (e.g. *Exodus* 15; *Psalms* 74; see Day 1985; Kloos 1986), and cosmologically positioned in opposition to JERUSALEM (Wyatt 1987).

**yang**. *See* YIN-YANG.

**Yao**. A legendary ruler of high antiquity in China. In the *Shu Jing* Chinese history begins with Yao who was a lord of great virtue. Because he considered his own son unworthy he selected SHUN to succeed him on the throne. In Confucianism Yao is a paradigm for the sage, an ideal to be reached by self-cultivation. Modern historians doubt whether Yao and Shun can be regarded as historical.

**yashiro** (Japanese). One of several terms for a Shintō shrine. The character used to write it is also pronounced *-sha*, which becomes *-ja* in the word JINJA, the most general term for a Shintō shrine in modern Japanese. *See also* MIYA.

**Yashts**. *See* ZOROASTRIANISM.

**Yasna**. *See* ZOROASTRIANISM.

**Yawm al-dīn** *See* ĀKHIRA.

**Yawm al-qiyāma**. *See* ĀKHIRA.

**yebola**. Dance-groups of a spirit possession cult in northern Zaire, originally intended as therapy, today also presented as 'folklore' (Hulstaert 1975: 732).

**Yellow Court**. *See* HUANG TING JING.

**Yellow Emperor**. *See* HUANG-LAO DOCTRINE.

**Yen-lo**. *See* YĀMA.

**Yeshivah** (Yiddish: 'place of sitting'). An academy of TALMUD studies. A *yeshivah* 'bokher' is a 'youth' who studies at a *yeshivah*.

**Yesod** (Hebrew) Foundation. The ninth of the ten SEFIROT, in which all of the higher energies are gathered and channelled into manifestation in MALKHUT. Yesod is associated with the male principle, and also with the figure of the *Tzaddiq*.

**Yetzer** (Hebrew: 'inclination'). In Pharisaic thought (*see* PHARISEES), two opposing tendencies influencing and reinforcing moral decisions (*Test. Asher* 1.5–5.4).

**Yggdrasill**. The WORLD TREE of Germanic mythology; centre of creation and sacred place where the gods held their council, the 'thing'. Yggdrasill is described as a great ash, which has three roots, one stretching into ASGARD, the realm of the gods, one into the world of the giants and the third into the land of cold and death. Under the first root is the Well of Urd guarded by the three NORNS, Urd, Verdandi and Skuld, who predicted human fate; under the second root is the Spring of Wisdom guarded by Mimir (*see* AESIR, ODIN). Although Yggdrasill is constantly gnawed at by serpents and harts, it is evergreen and stands firm; when it shakes RAGNAROK is nigh. The name probably means 'horse of Ygg [i.e. Odin]' and can be explained by the story of Odin hanging (metaphorically riding) on the tree to gain wisdom (*see* ODIN). The tree formed a link between the different worlds, symbolized by a squirrel running up and down to carry hostile messages between the serpent at the bottom and the all-seeing eagle at the top; hence seeresses (VQLVA) and seers often used the vantage point of a seat in a tree in their rituals for communicating with the other world.

**YHWH** . *See* TETRAGRAMMATON, YAHWEH.

**Yid** (Yiddish). A Jew. *Yiddishkeit* means all aspects of 'Jewishness'.

**Yi Ching**. *See* YI JING.

**Yi Jing** [*I Ching*] (Chinese: 'Book of Changes'). One of the most influential Chinese scriptures. Although it was included by the Confucians in their canon of the Five Classics (WU JING) it does not belong exclusively to the Confucian tradition but was equally esteemed by the Daoists and the popular religion. The *Yi Jing* as it is known today is a very complex book. Its origin was probably an ancient manual of divination centring on the symbols of the *Ba Gua* [*Pa Kua*], or Eight Trigrams, which were developed into 64 hexagrams. During the Zhou dynasty (*c.*1066–221 BCE) several other texts were added as explanations and commentaries, which are attributed to various sages, among them Confucius. Throughout Chinese history the *Yi Jing* has been respected as a book which reveals the principles of the cosmos, containing the deepest mysteries of man and nature. Unfortunately, its symbols and language are very difficult to understand, giving room to different interpretations. Nevertheless, the symbolism of the *Yi Jing* had a lasting influence on the Chinese conceptualization of the universe. Its use in divination or analysis of events is effected by the selection of one of the hexagrams by means of 50 yarrow sticks or three coins. The standard current English translation is that by James Legge, first published in 1899 in the Sacred Books of the East, but some regard Richard Wilhelm's *I Ging: das Buch der Wandlungen* as the best translation into a European language.

**yin**. Among the Tallensi of northern Ghana, destiny. Shrines are erected to the destiny of individuals, usually men, which is presumed to have been chosen before birth. In cases of misfortune one tries to influence the prenatal 'spoken destiny', *nuor-yin*. (Forde 1954).

**yin-yang** (Chinese). The Chinese concept of a cyclical duality that stands for the material agents of heaven and earth, the sources of all creations. *Yin* and *yang* are already mentioned in the first commentaries to the Book of Changes, the YI JING. According to traditional beliefs *yin* and *yang* are catalytic forces that generate the feelings and passions in man (i.e. his vital mental powers), whereas in nature they are responsible for the weather and the seasons (i.e. the outward living conditions that man depends on in his work with nature). Both microcosmic and macrocosmic aspects of the *yin-yang* notion are basically of the same 'quality', so that man is able to influence the generative process that makes his life 'livable' through proper moral conduct. Harmonizing one's own inner cyclical forces (by nourishing the breath; *see* QI) enhances human control over outward conditions. The material aspects of *yin-yang* are represented by the five elements (*see* WU XING): wood, water, fire, earth and metal. The rotation of these elements as temporarily active agents combined with the rising and the decaying of the *yin* or *yang* forces constitute an endless creation of the 'myriads of things'. It is this endless creation that man is a part of and that he should not counteract for fear of harming himself by upsetting the natural 'way' of heaven and earth. (*see dao* in DAO-DE) On the workings of *yin-yang* see Maspero 1981.

**YMBA**. *See* YOUNG MEN'S BUDDHIST ASSOCIATION.

**Ymir**. *See* MIDGARD.

**yoga** (Sanskrit: 'yoking'). A term with many meanings. In its most generic sense it is synonymous with 'path', 'practice', 'religion' (*karmayoga*, BHAKTIYOGA, *jñānayoga* etc.). In its specific sense it designates a set of exercises practised either with the aim of physical benefits (*haṭhayoga*) or spiritual emancipation (*rājayoga*). The latter were brought into a system by Patanjali (3rd or 4th century) in his well-known *Yogasūtras*.

**Yogācāra**. *See* VIJÑĀNAVĀDA.

**Yogasūtras**. *See* YOGA.

**yogi**. A practitioner of YOGA. The term is often used generically for an ascetic or religious, similar to *saṃnyāsin* or *sādhu*.

**yomi**. In Shintō, the world where evil, unhappiness, destruction and curses originate. Whereas TAKAMA-NO-HARA is the ideal world of the gods, Yomi is the nether world, inhabited by evil spirits and regarded as a place of death.

**Yom Kippur** (Hebrew). The Day of Atonement, a day of fasting and prayer which concludes the Jewish High Holidays. At this time, it is said, God seals the Book of Life, which is inscribed at ROSH HASHANAH. Yom Kippur is the Jewish holiday most widely observed by Jews, and is considered the most solemn day of the year.

**Yom Tov** (Hebrew). A holy day. One of the High Holy Days or the Three Pilgrimage Festivals (PASSOVER, SHAVUOT and SUKKOT).

**Yongshin**. Korean name for the dragon god who rules the sea and is therefore responsible for maritime safety and a successful catch of fish.

**yoni**. *See* LIṆGAM.

**Yoshida Shintō**. One of the academic schools of Shintō, founded by Yoshida Kanetomo (1435–1511). Yoshida explained Shintō as the original source of Confucianism, Buddhism and Taoism.

**Yoshino**. *See* SENDATSU.

**Young Men's Buddhist Association (YMBA)**. An organization founded by C.S. Dissanayake in Colombo in 1898, a convert from Roman Catholicism, and modelled on the Young Men's Christian Association. In 1906 the YMBA was founded in Rangoon, Burma. *See also* ALL-CEYLON BHIKKHU CONGRESS.

**Young Men's Christian Association (YMCA)**. An organization founded in 1844 by George Williams as a fellowship based on prayer and Bible reading. The YMCA has specialized in providing training programmes and social amenities of various kinds, including safe lodging hostels, especially in large cities.

**Young Women's Christian Association (YWCA)**. An organization founded on the model of the YOUNG MEN'S CHRISTIAN ASSOCIATION in 1855. The World Young Women's Christian Association was formed in 1894.

**yoyanas**. *See* MERU.

**Yu** [Yü]. Also Da Yu [Ta Yü] ('Yu the Great'). A semihistorical Chinese emperor. According to tradition he was appointed by SHUN to control the great floods, a task he accomplished after nine years' labour. He succeeded Shun as emperor and became the founder of the Xia [Xia] dynasty (21st – century – 16th century BCE.

**Yuhuang** [Yü-huang] (Chinese: 'Jade Emperor'). The supreme deity of the Chinese popular pantheon. As a celestial deity he may be regarded as the popular form of TIAN ('Heaven'). In contrast to the latter, however, *Yuhuang* is represented anthropomorphically as a divine emperor who rules the universe, governing the hierarchy of gods as well as controlling the fate of men. Belief in and cult of the Jade Emperor emerged during the Tang dynasty (618–906).

**Yün-ch'i-ch'i-ch'ian** *See* YÜNQI QIQIAN.

**Yünqi qiqian**. A repository of Daoist sacred scriptures in 122 sections (*juan*) compiled by Zhang Junfang during the years 1004–1007. The work is a collection (mostly of abstracts) of texts dealing with all kinds of Daoist worship, meditation, medicine, NEIDAN practices, charms, spirit and immortality (*see* LONGEVITY) cults. Its value is derived from the fact that it lists the essentials of Chinese DAOISM before the 11th century and includes otherwise lost works of importance for the study of religious history in China.

**Yurugu**. The fox, *Vulpes pallidus*, who in divination foretells the future among the Dogon of Mali. Diviners interpret the footprints left by foxes who come to eat food offerings placed on divining 'tables' traced in the sand. In the Dogon creation myth Yurugu (also known as Ogo) was a rebel against the supreme God, AMMA, and brought disorder and death into the world; he is the representative of the wilderness. (Griaule & Dieterlen 1965).

**yuwipi**. A Lakota (Sioux, North America) ceremony of healing and divination similar to the Algonkian SHAKING TENT ritual. Today it takes place inside darkened modern rooms with the SHAMAN tied up in a blanket with his hands and feet bound; at the end of the ceremony the shaman is found unbound, thereby proving his power.

# Z

**Zabūr** (Arabic). The term in Islām for the Psalms of David. (Qur'ān 4.163).

**zāhid** (Arabic; plural, *zuhadā'*). A Muslim ascetic.

**Ẓāhir**. *See* BĀṬIN.

**zakāt** (Arabic). One of the five pillars in Islām, the alms-tax paid 'in the way of God', funds allocated for the general welfare of the Muslim community contributed by every believer as an obligatory religious duty. The word *zakāt* is also rendered as 'purification tax' as it combines both the senses of the '*virtue*' of charity and '*gift*'. *See also* ṢADAQA.

**Zamzam** (Arabic). The sacred well of MECCA associated in Islamic tradition with the story of Abraham, the well being opened by an angel to save Hagar and her son Ismail from dying of thirst in the desert.

**Zanahary**. The supreme being, creator of heaven, earth, and mankind in Madagascar; ancestors are mediators between him and the people (Schomerus-Gernböck 1975: 804). This traditional divinity is not usually identified with the creator god of Christianity, known in Malagasy as 'fragment lord' (ADRIAMANITRA).

**Zao Jun** [Tsao Chün] (Chinese: 'Lord of the Stove'). A god (often called 'Kitchen God' in English) that can be traced back to antiquity, who plays an important role in Chinese popular beliefs. Each household has its own Kitchen God who is a kind of spiritual custodian and arbiter of the length of life. He records the deeds of the family members and reports them during his visit to heaven at the end of each year to YUHUANG ('Jade Emperor').

**Zār**. An afflictive spirit possession cult in Ethiopia, Sudan and Somalia, mainly frequented by women and the poor (Lewis 1971).

**zāwiya** (Arabic). An abode for a teaching SHAYKH who gathered pupils around him. The name applies to the headquarters of a ṢŪFĪ brotherhood in North Africa. In Turkey and Iran the corresponding terms are TEKKE and KHANQAH respectively.

**zazen** (Japanese: 'Seated meditation'). Meditation in the lotus position with legs crossed and hands precisely positioned. The correct position is maintained with the help of a small round cushion.

**Zealots**. A movement of Jewish nationalists who, as documented by the historian Josephus, resisted the Roman occupation of Israel in the 1st century CE and brought on the destruction of Jerusalem and the Temple in the year 70. The designation of one of the 12 apostles, Simon, as 'the zealot' (*Luke* 6.15) may or may not imply that he was a member of this party, whose existence is not otherwise certainly demonstrated for the lifetime of Jesus.

**Zeme**. Baltic earth goddess; also the Latvian word for earth. Her Lithuanian name is Zemyana. The earth goddess grants life and fertility but also brings death. She is venerated in many cultic rites connected with childbirth and the harvest. She is also called *Zemes māte*, 'earth mother', and many other *mātes* or 'mothers' of various natural or social phenomena exist in folk tradition as independent functions of Zeme, e.g. 'field mother' (*Lauku māte*), 'hot-bath mother' (*Pirts māte*), 'graveyard mother' (*Kapu māte*). The goddesses SAULE and LAIMA are also known as *Saules māte* and *Laimas māte* respectively.

**Zemyana**. *See* ZEME.

**Zen** (Japanese). The equivalent of the Chinese word CHAN, itself derived from Sanskrit DHYĀNA meaning 'meditation', and nowadays often referring to the teaching and practice of Zen Budhism. *See also* RINZAI-SHŪ; SŌTŌ-SHŪ.

**zendō** (Japanese). A meditation hall, especially in Zen Buddhism.

**Zeus**. Ancient Greek god, son of CRONOS and RHEA, king of the OLYMPIAN GODS and father of humans and other gods. In the maintenance of customs and laws and as head of a patriarchal family of gods and humans, his judgement was considered just and his power greater than that of any other; his preeminent symbols are lightening and the thunderbolt. *Compare* JUPITER.

**zhen ren**. A term designating the 'Perfect, Realized One', the highest ideal and attainment a practicing Daoist strives to reach and to be. A *zhen ren* is perceived as embodying the principles of ZIRAN ('Nature'), spontaneity of thought and action, thus comprehending the *dao* of Heaven and Earth.

**Zhong Yong** [*Chung Yung*] (Chinese: 'Doctrine of the Mean'). A Confucian text, which, like the DA XUE, was originally a chapter of the LI JI, but was given special prominence by the Song [Sung] dynasty Neo-Confucianists, who selected it as one of the Four Books (SI SHU). According to tradition the ZHONG YONG was written by Zi Si [Tzu Ssu], the grandson of Confucius. It deals with moral self-cultivation and the ordering of society.

**Zhuang Zi**. A Chinese philosopher presumably of the 4th century BCE, and hence the name of the book usually ascribed to him. The work is a difficult case – applied literary criticism points to various authors over a lengthy period of time (Paper 1977). The extant version contains 33 chapters, but it is generally believed that the first commentator (Guo Xiang, *d* 312 CE) skipped and excluded quite a few of the original chapters. Thus, the text as it has come down to us reflects a number of authors' thoughts and constitutes a 'collection of various Daoist writings' (Feng Youlan 1948). The text is rhymed throughout (but translated into prose by Giles 1926, and others). Together with the *Dao De Jing* it forms the basis of Chinese metaphysics, but it is much more than that: it reflects the overall intellectual climate of its time, stressing epistemological and metaphysical, but also practical problems of life. That a work so complex and intellectually diverse should be labelled a 'book for times of world decline' is still all too common, but of late scholars like Chang T. T. (Chang 1983) and Chin P. W. (Chin 1978) have brought out the intellectual background of the work and the person(s) involved with its compilation, trying to bring to light the whole range of thinking represented in the text.

**ziggurat**. Staged temples in Mesopotamia, symbolizing the OMPHALOS (navel as a symbol of cosmic orientation). This type of building was parodied in the Tower of Babel story (*Genesis* 11.1–9). (Dhorme 1945: 178–97).

**zinā'** (Arabic). In Islām the term meaning both fornication and adultery, that is, illicit sexual relations between persons not in a state of legal matrimony or concubinage. The penalties prescribed are flogging and stoning, although the evidence of four witnesses is required to establish guilt.

**zindīq** (Arabic: plural, *zanādiqa*). The term used in Islamic law to describe the heretic whose teaching is a threat to the community, a crime liable to capital punishment.

**Zion**. (from Hebrew, *tziyyon*: 'excellence', 'the ideal'). Mount Zion refers specifically to high land at JERUSALEM, regarded in ancient Israel as the dwelling-place of YAHWEH, then becoming the site of Solomon's Temple and the SECOND TEMPLE, thereafter remaining a focus of national Jewish identity. Zion in general refers both to the physical location of the HOLY LAND and to the aspiration of the Jewish people to be gathered there and live in harmony with God among the nations.

**Zionism**. The modern social and political movement founded by Theodore Herzl towards the end of the 19th century. Zionism has sought to promote the establishment and support of a Jewish State in Palestine, which would serve as the homeland for the Jews of the world.

**Zionist Churches**. The Zionist Church (unrelated to Jewish ZIONISM) was established by John Dowie (1847–1907) in Zion City, Illinois, USA, but developed in creative new ways in a southern African setting by African religious groups, being particularly successful among the Zulu and Swazi peoples. The connections of these African Zionist churches to the original church are now extremely tenuous. Zionists place great emphasis upon spiritual insight, spiritual possession and healing (broadly conceived) and frequently testify to the power of the Holy Spirit in their lives. Their religious message is closely tied to a political message and their complex perspective has provided a powerful context for resistance against the colonial power of the South African government and its apartheid policies. (Sundkler 1961).

**ziran** (Chinese: 'self-so'). A key concept of DAOISM, a fundamental spontaneity that is the (unconscious) *leitmotiv* of the realized man (*see* ZHEN REN). Already in the Daoist text DAO DE JING the term *ziran* is used for something that is or comes naturally: to speak little (chap. 23); the *dao* (*see* DAO-DE) models itself after 'it-so-being' (or 'nature', chap. 25); Thus *dao* is something that is so through a spontaneous, unconscious quality, the undifferentiated 'will' of Heaven and Earth that can be adopted and cultivated as a mode of action only by the most determined persons, i.e. the refined Daoist.

**Zohar** (Hebrew: 'Splendour', 'Enlightenment'). A book that is the single most important and influential work of KABBALAH. Written in a peculiar Aramaic and attributed to Rabbi Shimon bar Yoḥai of 2nd-century Palestine, the Zohar presents itself as mystical MIDRASH on the TORAH. It first appeared in 13th-century Spain at the hand of Moshe de Leon, whom many scholars today take to be its author.

**Zoroastrianism**. Ancient Persian religion named after its founder Zoroaster (reputed to have lived *c.*1000 BCE) and surviving today as the religion of the Parsis in India (especially Bombay), Pakistan, Britain and elsewhere. Teaching is based on the *Avesta*, the collective name for various texts such as the *Yasna*, the *Yashts* and the *Vendidad*. The *Yasna* ('sacrifice') includes the GĀTHĀS ('verses'), which are presumed to stem from Zoroaster himself, though the texts were gathered in written form in the 4th or 5th century CE. Zoroastrianism is known for its strong emphasis on ethical and ritual purity, for its fire ceremony during which the *Yasna* is recited and *haoma* (a plant juice) is consumed. Doctrinally, the cosmos is understood in terms of ethical DUALISM, more specifically, as a struggle between the good spirit Spenta Mainyu and the evil spirit Angra Mainyu and correspondingly as an ethical struggle in human experience. Over all there rules Ahura Mazdā, God himself, the creator, and in this sense Zoroastrianism is monotheistic (*see* MONOTHEISM). (See Boyce 1975, 1982, 1984).

**Zostrianos**. *See* GNOSTICISM.

**zuhd** (Arabic). Abstinence, first from sin, then from all perishable things by detachment of the heart and, among Muslim mystics, the virtue of complete asceticism or the renunciation of all that is created.

# Bibliography

Aberbach, M. and Smolar, L. (1967). Aaron, Jeroboam and the golden calves. *Journal of Biblical Literature*, **86**, 129–40.

Abelard, P. (1851). Sic et Non. In Henke and Lindenkohl (1851).

Abercrombie, N. and Warde, A. (1992). *Social Change in Contemporary Britain*. Cambridge.

Abimbola, W. (1976). *Ifá: an Exposition of Ifá Literary Corpus*. Ibadan.

Achtemeier, P.J. (1978). *Society of Biblical Literature Seminar Papers*, **13**, Chico.

Ackroyd, P.R. (1968). *Exile and Restoration*. London.

Adams, R.E.W. (1977). *Prehistoric Mesoamerica*. Boston.

Ahlström, G.W. (1963). *Aspects of Syncretism in Israelite Religion*. Horae Soderblomianae, 5. Lund.

— (1984). The travels of the ark: a religio-political composition. *Journal of Near Eastern Studies*, **43**, 141–9.

Ahmad, A. (1967). *Islamic Modernism in India and Pakistan, 1857–1964*. London.

—(1969). *An Intellectual History of Islam in India*. Edinburgh.

Akkeren, P. van (1970). *Sri and Christ: a Study of the Indigenous Church in East Java*. London.

Albrektson, B. (1967). *History and the Gods*. Lund.

Albright, W.F. (1969). *Archeology and the Religion of Israel*. Garden City.

Alexander, P.S. (1977). The historical setting and the Hebrew Book of Enoch. *Journal of Jewish Studies*, **26**, 156–80.

Alfian (1969). *Islamic Modernism in Indonesian Politics: the Muhammadiyah Movement during the Dutch Colonial Period, 1912–1942*. Madison.

Allen, J.B. and Gilen, M.L. (1976). *The Story of the Latter Day Saints*. Salt Lake City.

Allen, T.G. (1960). *The Egyptian Book of the Dead: Documents in the Oriental Institute Museum at the University of Chicago*. Chicago.

Allport, G.W. (1950). *The Individual and his Religion: a Psychological Interpretation*. New York.

Alster, B. (1972). *Dumuzi's Dream*. Mesopotamia, 1. Copenhagen.

Alt, A. (1966a). *Essays in Old Testament History and Religion*. Oxford.

— (1966b). The god of the fathers. In Alt (1966a), 1–77.

Ammermann, N. (1987). *Bible Believers: Fundamentalism in the Modern World*. New Brunswick.

Amore, R.E. (1970). *The Concept and Practice of Doing Merit in Early Theravada Buddhism*. Ann Arbor.

Anderson, B.R.O'G. (1965). *Mythology and the Tolerance of the Javanese*. Ithaca.

— (1972). The idea of power in Javanese culture. In Holt (1972), 1–69.

Andreasen, N.-E.A. (1972). *The Old Testament Sabbath: a Traditio-historical Investigation*. SBL Dissertation Series, 7. Missoula.

— (1983). The role of the Queen-Mother in Israelite society. *Catholic Biblical Quarterly*, **45**, 179–94.

Andrew, M.E.: *see* Stamm & Andrew 1967.

Anselm of Canterbury (1965). *Proslogion*. Oxford.

Antes, P. (1985). *Christentum: eine Einführung*. Stuttgart.

Arberry, A.J. (1964). *The Koran Interpreted*. Oxford.

Arbman, E. (1963). *Ecstasy or Religious Trance*. Uppsala.

Argyle, M. and Beit-Hallahmi, B. (1975). *The Social Psychology of Religion*. London.

Arinze, F.A. (1970). *Sacrifice in Igbo Religion*. Ibadan.

Aristotle (1924). *Metaphysics*. Oxford.

Armstrong, A.H. (ed.) (1967). *The Cambridge History of Later Greek and Early Medieval Philosophy*. Cambridge.

Asmussen, J.B. (1975) *Manichaean Literature*. New York.

Astour, M.C. (1967). *Hellenosemitica*. Leiden.

Attridge, H.W. and Oden, R.A. (1976). *The Syrian Goddess (De Dea Syria) Attributed to Lucian*. SBL Texts and Translations, 9. Missoula.

Augustine (1983). *Confessions*. Hodder Christian Classics. London.

Awolalu, J.O. (1979). *Yoruba Beliefs and Sacrificial Rites*. London.

Babb, L. (1986). *Redemptive Encounters: Three*

*Modern Hindu Styles in the Hindu Tradition*. Berkeley.
Bailey, L.R. (1971). The golden calf. *Hebrew Union College Annual*, **42**, 97–115.
Baldrian-Hussein, F. (1988). Inner alchemy: notes on the origin and use of the word *neidan*. *Cahiers d'Extrême-Asie*, **4**.
Barabas, A.M. (1987). *Utopias Indias: Movimientos socioreligiosos en México*. Mexico City.
Barker, M. (1987). *The Older Testament*. London.
— (1988). *The Lost Prophet*. London.
Barrelet, M.-T. (1955). Les déesses armées et ailées. *Syria*, **32**, 222–60.
Barrera Vasquez, A. and Rendon, S. (1948). *El libro de los libros de Chilam Balam*. Mexico City.
Barrett, D. (ed.) (1982). *World Christian Encyclopedia*. Oxford.
Barrick, W.B. (1975). The funerary character of High Places in ancient Palestine: a reassessment. *Vetus Testamentum*, **25**, 565–95.
Barth, K. (1960). *Anselm: Fides quaerens intellectum*. London.
Bartók, E. (1959). *Worth Living for*. London.
Bary, W.T. de (1960). *Sources of Chinese Tradition*. New York.
Bascom, W. (1969). *Ifa Divination: Communication between Gods and Men in West Africa*. Bloomington.
Basham, A.L. (1981). The evolution of the concept of the bodhisattva. In Kawamura (1981).
Basilov, V.N. (1984). *Izbranniki duhov*. Moscow.
Batson, C.D. and Ventis, W.Z. (1982). *The Religious Experience: a Social-psychological Perspective*. Oxford.
Batto, B.F. (1983). The Reed Sea: *Requiescat in pace*. *Journal of Biblical Literature*, **102**, 27–35.
Baumann, H. (1928). Likundu: die Sektion der Zauberkraft. *Zeitschrift für Ethnologie*, **60**, 73–93.
— (1936). *Schöpfung und Urzeit des Menschen im Mythus der afrikanischen Völker*. Berlin.
— (1950). Nyama, die Rachemacht: über einige mana-artige Vorstellungen in Afrika. *Paideuma*, **4**, 191–230.
— (ed.) (1975a). *Die Völker Afrikas und ihre traditionellen Kulturen*, 1. Wiesbaden.
— (1975b). Die Südwest-Bantu-Provinz. In Baumann (1975a), 473–512.
— (1975c). Die Sambesi-Angola-Provinz. In Baumann (1975a), 513–648.
Beattie, J.H.M. (1966). *Bunyoro: an African Kingdom*. New York.
Bechert, H. (1966–7). *Buddhismus, Staat und Gesellschaft in den Ländern des Theravada-Buddhismus*, 2 vols. Frankfurt.
Beckford, J. (1986). *New Religious Movements and Rapid Social Change*. Beverly Hills.
Bellah, R. (1957). *Tokugawa Religion*. Toronto.
Bentzen, A. (1949). King ideology – 'Urmensch' – 'Troonsbestijgingsfeest'. *Studia Theologica*, **3**, 143–59.
— (1955). *King and Messiah*. London.
Bergson, H. (1911). *Creative Evolution*. London.
Bernhardt, K.-H. (1955–6). Anmerkungen zur Interpretation des KRT-Textes von Ras Schamra-Ugarit. *Wissenschaftliche Zeitschrift der Ernst Moritz Arndt-Universität Greifswald*, **5**, 102–21.
Berntsen, J.L. (1979). Maasai age-sets and prophetic leadership: 1850–1910. *Africa*, **49**, 134–46.
Besmer, F.E. (1983). *Horses, Musicians and Gods: the Hausa Cult of Possession-trance*. South Hadley.
Beyerlin, W. (1961). *Origins and History of the Oldest Sinaitic Traditions*. Oxford.
Bianchi, U. (1976). *The Greek Mysteries*. Leiden.
— (ed.) (1979). *Mysteriae Mithrae*. Leiden.
Bimson, J.J. (1978). *Redating the Exodus and Conquest*. JSOT Supplements, 5. Sheffield.
Binder, L. (1960). Islamic tradition and politics: the Kijaji and the alim. *Comparitive Studies in Society and History*, **2**, 250–56.
Black, J.A. (1981). The New Year ceremonies in ancient Babylon: 'taking Bel by the hand', a cultic picnic. *Religion*, **11**, 39–59.
Black, M., Vanderkam, J. and Neugebauer, D. (1985), *The Book of Enoch or 1 Enoch*. Leiden.
Blacker, C. (1975). *The Catalpa Bow: a Study of Shamanistic Practices in Japan*. London.
Blacker, C. and Loewe, M. (eds) (1975). *Ancient Cosmologies*. London.
Bledsoe, C.H. (1980). Stratification and Sande politics. *Ethnologische Zeitschrift Zürich*, **1**, 143–9.
Bleek, D. (1923). *The Mantis and his Friends*. Cape Town.
Blenkinsopp, J. (1988). Second Isaiah – prophet of universalism. *Journal for the Study of the Old Testament*, **41**, 83–103.
Block, D.I. (1984). 'Israel' – 'Sons of Israel': a study of Hebrew eponymic usage. *Studies in Religion*, **13**, 301–26.
Blyth, R.H. (1966). *Mumonkan*. Tokyo.
Bohannan, P. and Bohannan, L. (1969). *A Source Notebook on Tiv Religion*, 2: *Tsav*. New Haven.
Bokenkamp, S. (1983). Sources of the Lingbao-scriptures. In Strickmann (1983), 450–58.
Boland, B.J. (1982). *The Struggle of Islam in Modern Indonesia*. The Hague.
Bonhoeffer, D. (ed. Bethge, E., trans. Bowden, J. *et al.*) (1971). *Letters and Papers from Prison: the Enlarged Edition*. London.
Bonnet-Tzavellas, C. (1983). Le dieu Melqart en Phénicie et dans le bassin méditerranéen: culte national et official. *Studia Phoenicia*, **1–2**, 195–207.
— (1985). Malqart, Bes et l'Héraclès Dactyle de Crète. *Studia Phoenicia*, **3**, 231–40.

Born, K. (1975). Nordkongo und Gabun: der Westen. In Baumann (1975a), 685–721.
Boston, J.S. (1977). *Ikenga Figures among the North-West Igbo and the Igala*. London.
Boyce, M. (1975–1982). *A History of Zoroastrianism* 2 vols. Leiden.
— (1984). *Textual Sources for the Study of Zoroastrianism*. Manchester.
Boyd, J.W. (1975). *Satan and Māra: Christian and Buddhist Symbols of Evil*. Leiden.
Boylan, T. (1922). *Thoth, the Hermes of Egypt*. London.
Bradbury, R.E. (1957). *The Benin Kingdom and the Edo-Speaking Peoples of South-western Nigeria*. Ethnographic Survey of Africa: Western Africa, 13. London.
Brandão, C.R. (1986). *Os Deuses do povo: um estudo sobre a religião popular*. São Paulo.
Branden, A. van den (1971). 'Reseph' nella Bibbia. *Bibbia e Oriente*, **13**, 211–16.
Brandon, J.R. (1970). *On Thrones of God: Three Javanese Shadow Plays*. Cambridge.
Breutz, P.-L. (1975). Die Südost-Bantu. In Baumann (1975a), 409–56.
Brichto, H.C. (1973). Kin, cult, land and afterlife – a biblical complex. *Hebrew Union College Annual*, **44**, 1–54.
Brown, L.B. (1965). *Advances in the Psychology of Religion*. Oxford.
Brueggemann, W., (1972). From dust to kingship. *Zeitschrift für die Alttestamentliche Wissenschaft*, **84**, 1–18.
Bultmann, R. (trans. Beasley-Murray, G.R. *et al.*) (1971). *The Gospel of John: a Commentary*. Oxford.
Burkert, W. (1987). *Ancient Mystery Cults*. Cambridge.
Burkhart, L.M. (1989). *The Slippery Earth*. Tucson.
Burrell, D. (1973). *Analogy and Philosophical Language*. New Haven.
Cahill, S. (1985–6). Reflections of a metal mother: an introduction to the biography of Hsi Wang Mu by the T'ang Taoist Tu Kuang-t'ing. *Journal of Chinese Religions*, **13–14**, 127–42.
Caldarola, C. (1979). *Christianity: the Japanese Way*. Leiden.
Calverley, A.M. (1933). *The Temple of King Sethos I at Abydos*. 4 vols. London.
Campbell, A.G. (1979). Yahweh and the ark: a case study in narrative. *Journal of Biblical Literature*, **98**, 31–43.
Caquot, A. (1959). La Divinité solaire ougaritique. *Syria*, **36**, 90–101.
— (1979–80). Horon: revue critique et données nouvelles. *Les Annales Archéologiques Arabes Syriens*, **29–30**, 173–80.
Carson, D. (ed.) (1982). *From Sabbath to Lord's Day*. Grand Rapids.
Cassirer, Ernst (1951). *The Philosophy of the Enlightenment*. Princeton, New Jersey.
Cavaignac, P. (1950). *Les Hittites*. L'Orient ancien illustré, 3. Paris.
Cazelles, H.: *see* Jacob & Cazelles 1979.
Chadwick, H. (1966). *Early Christian Thought and the Classical Tradition*. Oxford.
— (1986). *Augustine*. Oxford.
Chakraborti, H. (1973). *Asceticism in Ancient India in Brahmanical, Buddhist, Jaina, and Ajivika Societies, from the Earliest Times to the Period of Sankaracharya*. Calcutta.
Chan, Wing-tsit (1963). *Sourcebook in Chinese Philosophy*. Princeton.
Chang, Tsung-Tung (1983). *Metaphysik, Erkenntnis und praktische Philosophie in Chuang-tzu*. Frankfurt.
Charles, R.H. (1913). *The Apocrypha and Pseudepigrapha of the Old Testament*. 2 vols. Oxford.
Charlesworth, J.H. (ed.) (1983). *The Old Testament Pseudepigrapha, 1: Apocalyptic Literature and Testaments*. London.
Chavannes, E. (1910). *Le Tai Chan*. Paris.
Chicago University, Oriental Institute (1936). *Epigraphical and Architectural Survey*. Chicago.
Chin, P.W. (1978). *A Study of the Chuang-Tzu: Text, Authorship and Philosophy*. Wisconsin.
Cicero (1979). *On the Nature of the Gods*. Loeb Classical Library, 268. London.
Clifford, J. (1972). *Person and Myth*. Bloomington.
Clines, D.J.A. (1976). *I, he, we and they: a Literary Approach to Isaiah 53*. JSOT Supplements, 1. Sheffield.
— (1978). *The Theme of the Pentateuch*. JSOT Supplements, 10. Sheffield.
Coakley, S. (1988). *Christ without Absolutes*. Oxford.
Coats, G.W. (1988). *Moses: Heroic Man, Man of God*. JSOT Supplements, 57. Sheffield.
Codrington, R.H. (1891). *The Melanesians*. Oxford.
Coe, M.D. (1980). *The Maya*. London.
Coedès, G. (1963). *Angkor: an Introduction*. Oxford.
Coggins, R.J. (1975). *Jews and Samaritans*. Oxford.
Cohen, A.A. and Medes-Flohr, P. (eds) (1987). *Contemporary Jewish Religious Thought: Original Essays on Critical Concepts, Movements and Beliefs*. New York.
Cohen, H. (ed. Strauss, B.) (1924). *Jüdische Schriften*, 3 vols. Berlin.
Cole, H.M. (1982). *Mbari: Art and Life among the Owerri Igbo*. Bloomington.
Cole, W.O. (1982). *The Guru in Sikhism*. London.
— (1984a). *Sikhism and its Indian Context, 1469–1708*. London.
— (1984b). Materials for the study of Sikhism: a survey of some recent publications. *Religion*,

**14,** 193–8.
Cole, W.O. and Sambhi, P.S. (1978). *The Sikhs: their Religious Beliefs and Practices*. Library of Beliefs and Practices. London.
Collins, J.J. (1978). Methodological issues in the study of 1 Enoch. In Achtemeier (1978), 315–22.
— (1984). *The Apocalyptic Imagination*. New York.
Collins, S. (1982). *Selfless Persons*. Cambridge.
Colson, E. (1951). The Plateau Tonga of Northern Rhodesia. In Colson & Gluckman (1951), 90–115.
Colson, E. and Gluckman, M. (eds) (1951). *Seven tribes of British Central Africa*. London.
Commissie voor het Adatrecht (ed.) (1910-55). *Adatrachtbundels*, 1–45. The Hague.
Conrad, D. (1971). Der Gott Reschef. *Zeitschrift für die Alttestamentliche Wissenschaft*, **83**, 157–83.
Conze, E. (1958). *Buddhist Wisdom Books*. London.
— (1960). *The Prajnaparamita Literature*. The Hague.
Copleston, F.C. (1955). *Aquinas*. Harmondsworth.
Coulson, N.J. (1979). *A History of Islamic Law*. Edinburgh
Craig, W.L. (1979). *The Kalām Cosmological Argument*. London.
— (1980). *The Cosmological Argument from Plato to Leibniz*. London.
Craigie, P.C. (1983). *Ugarit and the New Testament*. Grand Rapids.
Creel, H.G. (1970). *What is Taoism?* Chicago.
Cross, F.M. (1973). *Canaanite Myth and Hebrew Epic*. Cambridge, Massachusetts.
Curtis, A. (1985). *Ugarit (Ras Shamra)*. Cities of the Biblical World. Cambridge.
Cusanus, N. (ed. Hopkins, J.) (1985). *Of Learned Ignorance*. Minneapolis.
Czaplick, M.A. (1914). *Aboriginal Siberia: a Study in Social Anthropology*. Oxford.
Daftary, F. (1990). *The Ismailis: their History and Development*. Cambridge.
Dahlgren, B. (ed.) (1987). *Historia de la religion en Mesoamérica y áreas afines I Coloquio*. Mexico City.
Dahm, B. (1969). *Sukarno and the Struggle for Indonesian Independence*. Ithaca.
— (1971). *History of Indonesia in the Twentieth Century*. New York.
Dallapiccola, A.D. (1980). *The Stūpa: its Religious, Historical and Architectural Significance*. Wiesbaden.
Danell, G.A. (1946). *Studies in the Name Israel in the Old Testament*. Uppsala.
Danto, A. and Morgenbesser, S. (eds) (1961). *The Philosophy of Science*. New York.
David, A.R. (ed.) (1979). *The Manchester Mummy Project: Multidisciplinary Research on Ancient Egyptian Mummified Remains*. Manchester.
— (1981). *A Guide to Religious Ritual at Abydos*. Warminster.
— (1982). *The Ancient Egyptians: Religious Beliefs and Practices*. London.
— (ed.) (1986). *Science in Egyptology: the Proceedings of the 1979 and 1984 Symposia*. Manchester.
Davidson, H.R.E. (1964). *Gods and Myths of Northern Europe*. Harmondsworth.
Davidson, H.A. (1987). *Proofs for Eternity, Creation and the Existence of God in Mediaeval Islamic and Jewish Philosophy*. New York.
Davies, B. (1982). *An Introduction to the Philosophy of Religion*. Oxford.
Davies, D. (1977). An interpretation of sacrifice in Leviticus. *Zeitschrift für die Alttestamentliche Wissenschaft*, **89**, 387–99.
Davies, N. de G. (1903–8). *The Rock Tombs of el Amarna*. 6 vols. London.
Davies, W.D. (1955). *Paul and Rabbinic Judaism*. London.
Dawkins, R. (1986). *The Blind Watchmaker*. Harlow.
Dawson, R. (1981). *Confucius*. Oxford.
Day, J. (1985). *God's Conflict with the Dragon and the Sea*. Cambridge University Oriental Publications, 35. Cambridge.
— (1986). Asherah in the Hebrew Bible and northwest Semitic literature. *Journal of Biblical Literature*, **105**, 385–408.
Debrunner, H.W. (1961). *Witchcraft in Ghana*. Accra.
Debus, J. (1967). *Sie Sünde Jeroboams*. Forschungen zur Religion und Literatur des Alten und Neuen Testaments, 93. Göttingen.
De Groot, J.J.M. (1892). *The Religious System of China*. Leiden.
Deimel, A. (1914). *Pantheon Babylonicum*. Rome.
Deleuze, G. (1990a). *Difference and Repetition*. London.
— (1990b). *The Logic of Meaning*. London.
Deleuze, G. and Guattari, F. (1988). *A Thousand Plateaus*. London.
Derrida, J. (1976). *Of Grammatology*. London.
Descartes, R. (1960a). *A Discourse on Method*. London.
— (1960b). *Meditations*. The Library of Liberal Arts. Indianapolis.
Dhofier, Z. (1980). *The Pesantren Tradition: a Study of the Role of the Kyai in the Maintenance of the Traditional Ideology of Islam in Java*. Canberra.
Dhorme, E. (1910). *La religion assyro-babylonienne*. Paris.
— (1945). *Les religions de Babylonie et d'Assyrie*. Mana, 1. Paris. [Bound with Dussaud 1945].
Dieterlen, G. (1941). *Les âmes des Dogons*. Paris.

— (1951). *Essai sur la religion Bambara*. Paris.
Dijk, C. van (1981). *Rebellion under the Banner of Islam*. Verhandelingen van het Koninklijke Instituut voor Taal-, Land- en Volkenkunde, 94. The Hague.
Dikshit, T.R.C. (1966). *The Samnyāsa Upaniṣads, with the Commentary of Sri Upaniṣad-Brahmayogin*. Madras.
Dilthey, W. (1957–1970). *Gesammelte Schriften*. Stuttgart, Göttingen.
Dion, P.-E. (1976). Les deux principales formes de l'angélologie de l'Ancien Testament dans leur cadre oriental. *Science et Esprit*, **28**, 65–82.
Diószegi, V. and Hoppál, M. (eds.) (1978). *Shamanism in Siberia*. Budapest.
Djaelani, T. (1959). *The Sarekat Islam Movement: its Contribution to Indonesian Nationalism*. Montreal.
Donner, H. (1973). Hier sind deine Götter, Israel. In Gese & Rüger (1973), 45–50.
Douglas, M. (ed.) (1970). *Witchcraft, Confessions and Accusations*. London.
Dragona-Monachou, M. (1976). *The Stoic Arguments for the Existence and the Providence of the Gods*. Athens.
Drewal, H.J. and Drewal, M.T. (1983). *Gęlędę: Art and Female Power among the Yoruba*. Bloomington.
Drewermann, E. (1984–5). *Tiefenpsychologie und Exegese*. 2 vols. Olten.
Drower, E.S. (1961; 1st edn. 1937). *The Mandaeans of Iraq and Iran*. Oxford.
Dull, J. (1966). *A Historical Introduction to the Apocryphical Texts of the Han Dynasty*. Seattle.
Dumarcay, J. (1978). *Borobudur*. Kuala Lumpur.
Dumont, L. (1980). *Homo Hierarchicus: the Caste System and its Implications*. Chicago.
Dus, J. (1968). Die Stierbilder von Bethel und Dan und das Problem der 'Moseschar'. *Annali dell'Istituto Orientale di Nápoli*, **18**, 105–37.
Dussaud, R. (1945). *Les religions des Hittites et des Hourrites, des Pheniciens et des Syriens*. Mana, 1. Paris [Bound with Dhorme 1945].
Duvernoy, J. (1979). *Le Catharisme*. Toulouse.
East, R. (ed.) (1965). *Akiga's Story*. London.
Edwards, I.E.S. (1987). *The Pyramids of Egypt*. Harmondsworth.
Eissfeldt, O. (1966). *The Old Testament: an Introduction*. Oxford.
Eliade, M. (1951). *Le Chamanisme et les techniques archaïques de l'extase*. Paris.
— (1958). *Patterns in Comparative Religion*. London.
— (1964). *Shamanism: Archaic Technique of Ecstacy*. London.
Ellis, M. de J. (ed.) (1977). *Essays on the Ancient Near East in Memory of J.J. Finkelstein*. Memoirs of the Connecticut Academy of Art and Sciences, 19. Hamden.
Emsheimer, E. (1944). Zur Ideologie der lappischen Zaubertrommel. *Ethnos*, **9**.
— (1946). Schamanentrommel und Trommelbaum. *Ethnos*, **4**.
— (1948). Eine sibirische Parallele zur lappischen Zaubertrommel?. *Ethnos*, **12**.
Enayat, H. (1982). *Modern Islamic Political Thought*. London.
— (1983). Iran: Khumayni's concept of guardianship of the jurisconsulat. In Piscatori (1983), 160–80.
*Encyclopedia of Islam*: *see* Houtsma *et al*. 1987.
Evans-Pritchard, E.E. (1937). *Witchcraft, Oracles and Magic among the Azande*. Oxford.
— (1956). *Nuer Religion*. Oxford.
— (1967). *The Zande Trickster*. London.
Fackenheim, E. (1987). *What is Judaism?* New York.
Fariss, N.M. (1984). *Maya Society under Colonial Rule*. Princeton.
Faulkner, R.O. (1973–8). *The Ancient Egyptian Coffin Texts*. 3 vols. Warminster.
Federspiel, H.M. (1970). *Persatuan Islam: Islamic Reform in Twentieth Century Indonesia*. Ithaca.
Feng, Y. (1948). *A Short History of Chinese Philosophy*. New York.
Fernandez, J.W. (1982). *Buriti: an Ethnography of the Religious Imagination in Africa*. Princeton.
Feuchtwang, S. (1974). *An Anthropological Analysis of Chinese Geomancy*. Collection Connaissance de l'Asie, 1. Vientiane.
Février, J.G. (1937). Un aspect du dioscurisme chez les anciens Sémites. *Journal Asiatique*, **229**, 293–9.
Fichte, J.G. (1845–6). *Johann Gottlieb Fichtes sämtliche Werke*. 8 vols. Berlin.
Findeisen, H. (1957). *Schamanentum, dargestellt am Beispiel der Besessenheitspriester nordeurasiatischer Völker*. Stuttgart.
— (1967). Die 'Schamanenkrankheit' als Initiation. *Abhandlungen und Aufsätze aus dem Institut für Menschen-und Menschheitskunde*, **45**.
Finet, A. (ed.) (1970). *Actes de la XVIIe rencontre assyriologique internationale*. Brussels.
Finkelstein, L. (1962). *The Pharisees*. 2 vols. Philadelphia.
Fishbane, M.A. (1987). *Judaism: Revelation and Traditions*. New York.
Flew, A. (1955). Theology and Falsification. In Flew & MacIntyre (1955). 96–130.
Flew, A. and MacIntyre, A. (eds) (1955). *New Essays in Philosophical Theology*. London.
Foerster, W. (1974). *Gnosis*. Oxford.
Fokken, H. (1916). Gottesanschauungen und religiöse Überlieferungen der Masai. *Archiv für Anthropologie*, **43**, N.F. **15**, 237–52.
Forde, D. (ed.) (1954). *African Worlds: Studies in the Cosmological Ideas and Social Values of African Peoples*. London.
Foucault, M. (1970). *The Order of Things*. London.

Fox, M.V. (1974). The sign of the covenant. *Revue Biblique*, **81**, 557–96.

Frankfort, H. and Pendlebury, J.D.S. (1933). *The City of Akhenaten*. London.

Frankfort, H.A. (1948). *Kingship and the Gods*. Chicago.

Frei, H. (1974). *The Eclipse of Biblical Narrative*. New Haven.

Fremantle, F. and Trungpa, C. (translators) (1975). *The Tibetan Book of the Dead*. Berkeley.

French, H.W. and Sharma, A. (1981). *Religious Ferment in Modern India*. New York.

Freud, S. (1913). *Totem and Taboo*. London.

— (1961). *Civilization and its Discontents*. New York.

— (1964). *The Future of an Illusion*. Garden City.

Frey, E. (1986). *The Kris*. Singapore.

Frick, F.S. (1971). The Rechabites reconsidered. *Journal of Biblical Literature*, **90**, 279–87.

Friedman, R.E. (1981). *The Exile and Biblical Narrative*. Harvard Semitic Monographs, 22. Chico.

Frobenius, L. (1913). *The Voice of Africa*, 1. London.

Frymer-Krensky, T. (1983). The attributes of Marduk: the so-called 'Marduk ordeal text'. *Journal of the American Oriental Society*, **103**, 131–41.

Fulco, W.J. (1976). *The Canaanite God Rešep*. American Oriental Series, 8. New Haven.

Fung, Yu-lan (1952). *A History of Chinese Philosophy*. Princeton.

Garsoian, N.G. (1967). *The Paulicianism Heresy*. The Hague.

Gaster, T.H. (1950). *Thespis*. New York.

Gaston, L.L. (1962). Beelzebul. *Theologische Zeitschrift*, **18**, 247–55.

Gatje, H. (1976). *The Qur'an and its Exegesis: Selected Texts with classical and Modern Muslim Interpretations*. London.

Geertz, C. (1960a). *The Religion of Java*. Glencoe.

— (1960b). The Javanese Kijaji: the changing role of a cultural broker. *Comparative Studies in Society and History*, **2**, 228–49.

— (1971). *Islam Observed*. Chicago.

— (1973). *The Interpretation of Cultures: Selected Essays*. New York.

Geertz, H. (1961). *The Javanese Family: a Study of Kinship and Socialization*. Glencoe.

— (1967). Indonesian cultures and communities. In McVey (1967), 24–96.

Gerlach, L.P. and Hine, V.H. (1970). *People, Power, Change: Movements of Social Transformation*. Indianapolis.

Gese, H. H. and Rüger, H.P. (eds) (1973). *Wort und Geschichte* [K. Elliger *Festschrift*]. Alter Orient und Altes Testament, 18. Kevelaer.

Gibson, J.C.L. (1978). *Canaanite Myths and Legends*. Edinburgh.

Giles, H.A. (1926). *Chuang Tzŭ: Taoist Philosopher and Chinese Mystic*. London.

Gilhus, I.S. (1985). *The Nature of the Archons*. Studies in Oriental Religions, 12. Wiesbaden.

Giorgi, G. (1977). *La società segreta del Poro*. Bologna.

Glaze, A.J. (1981). *Art and Death in a Senufo Village*. Bloomington.

Gonzales, J.L. (1989). *El Huanca y la Cruz*. Lima.

Gonzáles Martínez, J.L. (1987). *La religion popular en el Peru: informe y diagnóstico*. Lusco.

Gonzalez, Y.T. (1985). *El sacrificio humano entre los Mexicos*. Mexico City.

Gonzalez-Wippler, M. (1973). *Santería*. New York.

Grabbe, L.L. (1976). The seasonal pattern and the Bacal cycle. *Ugarit-Forschungen*, **8**, 57–63.

Gray, J. (1949). The desert god 'A$\underline{t}$tr in the literature and religion of Canaan. *Journal of Near Eastern Studies*, **8**, 72–83.

— (1964). *The KRT Text in the Literature of Ras Shamra*. Leiden.

— (1965). *The Legacy of Canaan*. Leiden.

Greenberg, J.H. (1946). *The Influence of Islam on a Sudanese Religion*. New York.

Greene, W.C. (1944). *Moira: Fate, Good and Evil in Greek Thought*. Cambridge, Massachusetts.

Greenslade, S.L. (1953). *Schism in the Early Church*. London.

Greenwood, W. (1942). *The Upraised Hand or the Spiritual Significance of the Rise of the Ringatu Faith*. Polynesian Society Memoir, 21. Wellington.

Greschat, H.-J. (1980). *Mana and Tapu: die Religion der Maori auf Neuseeland*. Berlin.

Griaule, M. (1963). *Masques Dogons*. Travaux et Mémoires de l'Institut d'Ethnologie, 33. Paris.

Griaule, M. and Dieterlen, G. (1965). *Le renard pâle*. Travaux et Mémoires de l'Institut d'Ethnologie, 72. Paris.

Griffiths, J.G. (1970). *Plutarch: De Iside et Osiride*. Cardiff.

— (1976). *Apuleius: The Isis-book*. Leiden.

Grintz, J.M. (1977). Some observations on the 'High Place' in the history of Israel. *Vetus Testamentum*, **27**, 111–13.

Groenendael, V.M.C. van (1985). *The Dalang behind the Wayang*. Verhandelingen van het Koninklijke Instituut voor Taal-, Land- en Volkenkunde, 114. Leiden.

Grotanelli, C. (1983). Tricksters, scapegoats, champions, saviors. *History of Religions*, **23/2**: 117–39.

Grout, D.J. (1973). *A History of Western Music*. London.

Grunebaum, G.E. von (1976). *Muhammadan Festivals*. London.

Guthrie, W.K.C. (1952). *Orpheus and Greek Religion*. London.

Gwassa, C.G.K. (1972). Kinjikitile and the ideology of Maji Maji. In Ranger & Kimambo (1972), 202–17.
Haar, B. ter (1948). *Adat Law in Indonesia* (1939). New York.
Haberland, E. (1963). *Galla Süd-Äthiopiens*. Stuttgart.
Hadiwijono, H. (1967). *Man in the Present Javanese Mysticism*. Baarn.
Hair, P.E.H. (1967). An ethnolinguistic inventory of the Upper Guinea Coast before 1700. *African Language Review*, **6**, 32–70.
Haliburton, G.M. (1971). *The Prophet Harris*. London.
Haly, R. (1986). Poetics of the Aztecs. *New Scholar*, **10**, 85–133.
Hammarshaimb, E. (1949). The Immanuel sign. *Studia Theologica*, **3**, 124–42.
Hanson, P.D. (1975). *The Dawn of Apolcalyptic*. Philadelphia.
— (ed.) (1983). *Visionaries and their Apocalypses*. London.
Harbans Singh (1969). *Guru Nanak and the Origins of the Sikh Faith*. Bombay.
Hardjamardjaja, A.M. (1962). *Javanese Popular Belief in the Coming of Ratu Adil, Righteous Prince*. Rome.
Harnack, A. von (1924). *Marcion* Leipzig.
— (1986). *What is Christianity?* Fortress Texts in Modern Theology. Philadelphia.
Harner, M. (1980). *The Way of the Shamans: a Guide to Power and Healing*. San Francisco.
Harris, J.R. (1906). *The Cult of the Heavenly Twins*. Cambridge.
Hartshorne, C. (1948). *The Divine Relativity: a Social Conception of God*. New Haven.
— (1962). *The Logic of Perfection*. Lasalle.
Harva [Holmberg], U. (1938). *Die religiösen Vorstellungen der altäischen Völker*, FF Communications, 125. Helsinki.
Hayes, J.H. and Miller, J.M. (eds) (1977). *Israelite and Judaean History*. London.
Healey, J.G. (1977). The underworld character of the god Dagan. *Journal of Northwest Semitic Languages*, **5**, 43–51.
Heelas, P. (1992). The sacralisation of the self and New Age capitalism. In Abercrombie & Warde (1992), 139–66.
Heelas, P. and Lock, A. (1981). *Indigenous Psychologies*. London.
Hegel, G.W.F. (1977). *The Phenomenology of Spirit*. London.
Heidegger, M. (1962). *Being and Time*. London.
Heidel, A. (1942). *The Babylonian Genesis*. Chicago.
— (1946), *The Gilgamesh Epic and Old Testament Parallels*. Chicago.
Heimpel, W. (1982). A catalog of Near Eastern Venus deities. *Syro-Mesopotamian Studies*, **4**, 9–22.
Heine-Geldern, R. (1963). *Conceptions of State and Kingship in South East Asia*. Ithaca.
Heissig, W. (1980). *The Religions of Mongolia*. London.
Hendel, R.S. (1987). *The Epic of the Patriarch*. Harvard Semitic Monographs, 42. Atlanta.
Hengel, M. (1974). *Judaism and Hellenism*. 2 vols. London.
Henke, E.L.T. and Lindenkohl, G.S. (1851). *Abelard: Sie et non*. Marburg.
Henricks, R.G. (1979). The Ma Wang Dui manuscripts of the Lao-Tzu and the problem of dating the text. *Chinese Culture*, **20/2** 7–15.
Herbert, J. (1967). *Shinto: the Fountainhead of Japan*. London.
Herder, J.G. von (trans. Buarkhardt, F.H.) (1940). *God – Some Conversations*. Indianapolis.
Herford, R.T. (1924). *The Pharisees*. London.
Herskovits, M.J. and Herskovits, F.S. (1933). An outline of Dahomean religious belief. *Memoires of the American Anthropological Association*, **41**.
Hesiod. (trans. Evelyn-White, H.G.) (1964). *The Homeric Hymns and Homeria*. Loeb Classical Library, 57. London.
Hetherwick, A. (1902). Some animistic beliefs among the Yaos of British Central Africa. *Journal of the Royal Anthropological Institute of Great Britain and Ireland*, **32**, 89–95.
Hick, J. (1976). *Death and Eternal Life*. London.
— (1978). *Evil and the God of Love*. London.
Hick, J. and McGill, A. (eds) (1968). *The Many-faced Argument*. London.
Hien, G. van (1963). *What is Subud?* London.
Hinnells, J.R. (1975). *Mithraic Studies*. Manchester.
— (1985). *Persian Mythology*. London.
Hirschberg, W. (1965). *Wörterbuch der Völkerkunde*. Stuttgart.
— (1967). Gedanken zum Wesen und zur Verbreitund des Fanany-Glaubens-komplexes in Afrika. *Paideuma*, **13**, 1–19.
— (1975). Khoisan sprechende Völker Südafrikas. In Baumann (1975a), 383–408.
Hodgson, M. (1974). *The Venture of Islam*. 3 vols. Chicago.
Hoffner, H.A. (ed.) (1973). *0rient and Occident* [C.H. Gordon *Festschrift*]. Alter Orient und Altes Testament, 22. Kevelaer.
Holleman, J.F. (1981). *Van Vollenhoven on Indonesian adat law: selections from Het adatrecht van Nederlandsch-Indië*. Translation Series, 20. The Hague.
Holm, N.G. (1987). *Scandinavian Psychology of Religion*. Religionsvetenskapliga Skrifter, 15. Åbo.
— (1982a). Mysticism and intense experiences. *Journal for the Scientific Study of Religion*, **21**, 268–76.
— (ed.) (1982b). *Religious Ecstasy*. Scripta Instituti Donneriani Aboensis, 9. Stockholm.

Holmberg, S. (1946). *The God Ptah*. Lund.
Holmberg, H. (1915). *Lappalaisten uskonto*. Porvoo.
—— (1922–3). Der Baum des Lebens. *Annales Academiae Scientiarum Fennicae*, **B/16**.
—— (1927). *The Mythology of All Races*, 4: *Finno-Ugric, Siberian*. Boston.
Holsoe, S.E. (1980). Notes on the Vai Sande Society in Liberia. *Ethnologische Zeitschrift Zürich*, **1**, 97–111.
Holt, C. (1972). *Culture and Politics in Indonesia*. Ithaca.
Holton, D.L. (1938). *The National Faith of Japan*. London.
Hood, R.W (1970). Religious orientation and the report of religious experience. *Journal for the Scientific Study of Religion*, **9**, 285–91.
—— (1975). The construction and preliminary validation of measure of reported mystical experience. *Journal for the Scientific Study of Religion*, **14**, 29–41.
Hooke, S.H. (1953) *Babylonian and Assyrian Religion*. London.
Hooykaas, C. (1964). *Agama Tirtha*. Verhandelingen der Koninklijke Nederlandse Akademie van Wetenschappen, Afd. Letterkunde, Nieuwe Reeks, 70/4. Amsterdam.
—— (1973). *Religion in Bali*. Iconography of Religions, 13/10. Leiden.
—— (1974). *Cosmogony and creation in Balinese Tradition*. Bibliotheca Indonesica, 9. The Hague.
—— (1977). *A Balinese Temple Festival*. Bibliotheca Indonesica, 15. The Hague.
Hoppál, M. (ed.) (1983). *Shamanism in Eurasia*. 2 vols. Göttingen.
Hourani, A. (1962). *Arabic Thought in the Liberal Age, 1788–1979*. London.
Houtsma, M.T., Arnold, T.W., Basset, S.R. and Hautmann, R. (eds) (1987). *Encyclopedia of Islam*. Leiden.
Hulstaert, G. (1975). Nordkongo und Gabun: der Zentrale Teil. In Baumann (1975a), 722–46.
Hultkrantz, A. (1962). Die Religion der Lappen. In Paulson *et al*. (1962). 283–303.
—— (1973). A definition of shamanism. *Temenos*, **9**, 25–37.
Humbert, P. (1940). *Études sur le récit du Paradis et de la Chute dans la Genèse*. Neuchâtel.
Hume, D. (1976). *Dialogues Concerning Natural Religion*. Oxford.
Hunter, J. (1987). *Evangelicalism: the Coming Generation*. Chicago.
Idel, M. (1988). *Kabbalah: New Perspectives*. New Haven.
Idowu, E.B. (1962). *Olódùmare: God in Yoruba Belief*. London.
Imbault-Huart, C. (1884). La légende du premier pape des Taoistes et l'histoire de la famille pontificale de Tchang. *Journal Asiatique*, **Nov–Dec 1884**, 391–461.
Ingham, J.M. (1986). *Mary, Michael and Lucifer: Folk Catholicism in Central Mexico*. Austin.
Irwin, J. (1984). *An Introduction to Maori Religion*. Bedford Park.
Isaac, E. (1964). Circumcision as a covenant rite. *Anthropos*, **59**, 444–56.
Istituto per la Cività Tenicia e Punica (1984). *Adonis: Relazioni del Colloquio in Roma 22–23 Maggio 1981*. Collezioni di Studi Tenici, 18. Rome.
Jacob, E. and Cazelles, H. (1979). Ras Shamra. *Dictionnaire de la Bible*, supplement **9**, cols. 1124–466. Paris.
Jacobsen, T. (1968). The battle between Mardurk and Tiamat. *Journal of the American Oriental Society*, **88**, 104–8.
—— (1970). Toward the image of Tammuz. In Moran (1970), 73–103.
—— (1976). *The Treasures of darkness*. New Haven.
Jafri, S.H.M. (1979). *Origins and Early Development of Shi'a Islam*. London.
James, W. (1902). *The Varieties of Religious Experience*. New York.
Jay, R.R. (1963). *Religion and Politics in Rural Central Java*. New Haven.
—— (1969). *Javanese Villagers, Social Relations in Rural Modjokuto*. Cambridge.
Jeremias, G. (1971). Lade uns Zion. In Wolff (1971), 183–98.
Jesudason, S. (1937). *Ashrams, Ancient and Modern: their Aims and Ideals*. Vellore.
Jochim, C. (1986). *Chinese Religions: a Cultural Perspective*. Englewood Cliffs.
Johansen, J.P. (1954). *The Maori and his Religion in its Non-ritualistic Aspects*. Copenhagen.
—— (1958). *Studies in Maori Rites and Myths*. Copenhagen.
Jonas, H. (1970). *The Gnostic Religion*. Boston.
Jones, K. (1976). *Arya Dharm: Hindu Consciousness in 19th-century Punjab*. Berkeley.
Jong, S. de (1973). *Een Javaanse Levenshouding*. Wageningen.
Jorgenson, J.G. (1972). *The Sun Dance Religion: Power for the Powerless*. Chicago.
Juergensmeyer, M. and Barrier, N.G. (1979). *Sikh Studies: Comparative Perspectives on a Changing Tradition*. Berkeley Religious Studies Series. Berkeley.
Jung, C.G. (1953–79). *Collected Works*. 20 vols. Princeton.
—— (1958). *The Undiscovered Self*. London.
Kageyama, H. (1973). *The Arts of Shinto*. New York.
Kaltenmark, M. (1953). *Le Lie-sien tchouan – Biographies Légendaires*. Peking.
—— (1969). *Lao Tzu and Taoism*. Stanford.
—— (1979). The ideology of the T'ai-P'ing ching. In Welch & Seidel (1979), 19–52.
Kant, I. (1929). *Critique of Pure Reason*. New York.

— (1949a). *Critique of Practical Reason*. Chicago.

— (1949b). *Foundations of the Metaphysics of Morals*. Chicago.

— (1960). *Religion within the Limits of Reason Alone*. La Salle.

— (1973). *Critique of Judgement*. London.

Kapelrud, A.S. (1952). *Baal in the Ras Shamra Texts*. Copenhagen.

— (1969). *The Violent Goddess*. Oslo.

Karjalainen, K.F. (1921–7). *Die Religion der Jugra-Völker*. 3 vols. FF Communications, 41, 44, 63. Helsinki.

Karsten, R. (1955). *The Religion of the Samek*. Leiden.

Kartodirdjo, S. (1970). *Religious Movements of Java in the 19th and 20th Centuries*. Yogyakarta.

— (1973). *Protest Movements in Rural Java: a Study of Agrarian Unrest in the 19th and 20th Centuries*. Singapore.

Karttunen, F. (1983). *An Analytical Dictionary of Nahuatl*. Austin.

Kats, J. (1923). *Het Javaansche Tooneel*, 1: *Wayang Purwa*. Weltevreden.

Kauffman Doig, F. (1986). Los dioses andinos: hacia una caraterizacion de la religiosidad andina fundamente en testimonios arqueologicos y en mitos. *Vida y espiritualidad* [Lima], **3**, 1–16.

Kawamura, L.S. (ed.) (1981). *The Bodhisattva Doctrine in Buddhism*. Waterloo, Ontario.

Kelly, J.N.D. (1972). *Early Christian Creeds*. London.

Kelly, S. (1992). The prodigal soul: religious studies and the advent of transpersonal psychology. In Klostermaier & Hurtado (1992), 429–41.

Kempers, A.J.B. (1973). *Borobudur*. The Hague.

— (1979). *Monumental Bali*. The Hague.

Kennedy, H. (1986). *The Prophet and the Age of the Caliphates*. London.

Kepel, G. (1985). *The Prophet and Pharaoh*. London.

Kern, O. (1922). *Orphicorum fragmenta*. Berlin.

Keyes, C.F. and Daniel, V.E. (1983). *Karma: an Anthropological Inquiry*. Berkeley.

Kim, T. (1989). *Paintings of Shaman Gods of Korea*. Seoul.

King, M. (ed.) (1975). *Te Ao Hurihuri*. Wellington.

Kippenberg, H., Kuiper, U. and Sanders, A. (eds) (1990). *Concepts of Person in Religion and Thought*. Berlin.

Kippenberg, H.G. (ed.) (1984). *Struggles of Gods*. Berlin.

Klass, M. (1980). *Caste: the Emergence of the South Asian Social System*. Philadelphia.

Klima, O. (1957). *Mazdak*. Prague.

— (1977). *Beiträge zur Geschichte des Mazdakismus*. Prague.

Kloos, C. (1986). *YHWH's Combat with the Sea*. Leiden.

Klostermaier, K. and Hurtado, L. (eds) (1992). *Religious Studies: Issues, Prospects and Proposals*. Atlanta.

Knibb, M.A. (1978). *The Ethiopic Book of Enoch*. Oxford.

Knott, K. (1986). *My Sweet Lord: the Hare Krishna Movement*. New Religious Movements Series. Wellingborough.

Koch, K. (1972). *The Rediscovery of Apocalyptic*. Studies in Biblical Theology, 2/22. London.

Koentjaraningrat (1971). The Javanese of South Central Java. In Murdock (1971), 88–115.

Kopf, D. (1979). *The Brahmo Samaj and the Shaping of the Modern Indian Mind*. Princeton.

Kort, A. and Morschauer, S. (eds) (1985). *Biblical and Related Studies Presented to Samuel Iwry*. Winona Lake.

Korver, A.P.E. (1962). *Sarekat Islam, 1912–1916*. Amsterdam.

Kramer, S.N. (1969). *The Sacred Marriage Rite*. Bloomington.

— : see also Wolkstein & Kramer 1984.

Kraus, H.-J. (1966). *Worship in Israel*. Oxford.

Kripalani, K. (1971) *Tagore: a Life*. Delhi.

Kuhn, H.B. (1948). The angelology of the non-canonical Jewish apocalypses. *Journal of Biblical Literature*, **67**, 217–32.

Labat, R. (1935). *Le poème babylonien de la création*. Paris.

Labuschagne, C.J. (1966). *The Incomparability of Yahweh*. Pretoria Oriental Series, 5. Leiden.

Lambert, M.D. (1977). *Mediaeval Heresy*. London.

Lambert, W.G. (1984). Studies in Marduk. *Bulletin of the School of Oriental and African Studies*, **47**, 1–9.

Lambert, W.G. and Millard, A.R. (1969). *Atra-Hasis*. Oxford.

Lamotte, E. (1962). *L'enseignement de Vimalakirti*. Louvain.

Lang, B. (1983). *Monotheism and the Prophetic Minority*. The Social World of Biblical Antiquity Series, l, Sheffield.

Langdon, S. (1923). *The Babylonian Epic of Creation*. Oxford.

de Lange, N. (1987). *Judaism*. Oxford.

Langton, N. and Langton, B. (1940–41). The cat in ancient Egypt. *Annales du Service des Antiquités de l'Égypte*, **40**, 993–6.

Laroche, E. (1948). Teššub, Ḫebat et leur cour. *Journal of Cuneiform Studies*, **2**, 113–36.

— (1968a). Le 'panthéon' hourrite de Ras Shamra. *Ugaritica*, **5**, 518–27.

— (1968b). Notes sur le panthéon hourrite de Ras Shamra. *Journal of the American Oriental Society*, **88**, 148–50.

Lauer, J.P. (1976). *Saqqara: the Royal Cemetery of Memphis: Excavations and Discoveries since 1850*. London.

Lavan, S. (1974). *The Ahmadiyah Movement: a History and Perspective*. Delhi.

Lawson, E.T. (1984). *Religions of Africa*. San

Francisco.
Lawson, E.T. and McCauley, R. (1990). *Rethinking Religion*. Cambridge.
Leclant, J. and Clerk, G. (1972–4). *Inventaire bibliographique des Isiaca*. Leiden.
Leeuw, G. van der (1938). *Religion in Essence and Manifestation*. London.
Legge, J. (trans.) (1899). *I Ging*. Sacred Books of the East. Oxford.
Lessius, L. (1977). *On the Providence of God and the Immortality of the Soul* (1631). English Recusant Literature, 1558–1640, 349. London.
Leuba, J.H. (1925). *The Psychology of Religious Mysticism*. New York.
Levenson, J. (1985). *Sinai and Zion: an Entry into the Jewish Bible*. New Voices in Biblical Studies. Minneapolis.
Levine, B. and de Tarragon, J.-M. (1984). Dead kings and Rephaim: the patrons of the Ugaritic dynasty. *Journal of the American Oriental Society*, **104**, 649–59.
Lewis, I.M. (1971). *Ecstatic Religion*. London.
Lewis, N. (1988). *The Missionaries: God against the Indians*. London.
Lewy, J. (1945–6). The late Assyro-Babylonian cult of the moon and its culmination in the time of Nabonidus. *Hebrew Union College Annual*, **19**, 405–89.
L'Heureux, C.E. (1979). *Rank among the Canaanite Gods*. Harvard Semitic Monographs, 21. Missoula.
Lienhardt, G. (1954). The Shilluk of the Upper Nile. In Forde (1954), 138–63.
— (1961). *Divinity and Experience: the Religion of the Dinka*. Oxford.
Lieu, S.N.S. (1985). *Manichaeism in the Later Roman Empire and Medieval China*. Manchester.
Lin Yu Tang (1948). *The Wisdom of Laotse*. New York.
Lindblom, J. (1959). *A Study in the Immanuel Section in Isaiah (Is vii.l–ix.6)*. Lund.
Ling, T.O. (1962). *Buddhism and the Mythology of Evil*. London.
Lings, M. (1982). *What is Sufism?* London.
— (1986). *Muhammad*. London.
Lipínski, E. (1970). La fête de l'ensévelissement et de la resurrection de Melqart. In Finet (1970), 30–58.
— (1972). The goddess A̱tirat in ancient Arabia, in Babylon, and in Ugarit. *Orientalia Lovaniensia Periodica*, **3**, 101–19.
— (1973). Eshmun, 'Healer'. *Annali dell'Istituto Orientale di Nápoli*, **33**, 161–83.
Little, K.L. (1965–6). The political function of the Poro. *Africa*, **35**, 349–65; **36**, 62–71.
Lommel, A. (1965). *Die Welt der frühen Jäger, Medizin-männer, Schamanen, Künstler*. Munich.
Lopez Austin, A. (1984). *Luerpo humano e ideologia*, 2 vols. Mexico City.
Lot-Falck, E. (1961). L'animation du tambour. *Journal asiatique*, **249**.
Loy, D. (1985). Wei Wu-wei: nondual action. *Philosophy East and West*, **35/1**, 73–86.
Lutz, C. (1988). *Unnatural Emotions*. Chicago.
Lyotard, J.-F. (1984). *The Postmodern Condition*. London.
McCarthy, D.J. (1965). Covenant: the present state of enquiry. *Catholic Biblical Quarterly*, **27**, 217–40.
McClelland, E.M. (1982). *The Cult of Ifá among the Yoruba*. London.
Mac Cormack, C.P. (1975). Sande women and political power in Sierra Leone. *West African Journal of Sociology and Political Science*, **1**, 42–50.
MacDonald, J. (1964). *The Theology of the Samaritans*. London.
Mack, J. (1986). *Madagascar: Island of the Ancestors*. London.
McKane, W. (1979). *Studies in the Patriarchal Narratives*. Edinburgh.
Mackie, J.L. (1982). *The Miracle of Theism: Arguments for and against the Existence of God*. Oxford.
McLeod, W.H. (1968). *Guru Nanak and the Sikh Religion*. Oxford.
— (1976). *The Evolution of the Sikh Community: Five Essays*. Oxford.
— (1980). *The B40 Janam Sakhi*. Amritsar.
— (1984). *Textual Sources for the Study of Sikhism*. Textual Sources for the Study of Religion. Manchester.
Macquarrie, J. (1973). *Existentialism*. Harmondsworth
MacQueen, J.G. (1986). *The Hittites and their Contemporaries in Asia Minor*. London.
McVey, R.T. (1967). *Indonesia*. New Haven.
Magnis-Suseno, F. (1981). *Javanische Weisheit und Ethik: Studien zu einer östlichen Moral*. Munich.
Makarim, S. (1974). *The Druze Faith*. New York.
Mangalvadi, V. (l977). *The World of Gurus*. Delhi.
Manker, E. (1938). *Die lappische Zaubertrommel*, 1: *Die Trommel als Enkmal materialer Kultur*. Acta Lapponica, 1. Stockholm.
— (1950). *Die lappische Zaubertrommel*, 2: *Die Trommel als Urkunde geistigen Lebens*. Acta Lapponica, 6. Stockholm.
Mansel, H. (1859). *The Limits of Religious Thought* London.
Manson, T.W. (1938). Sadduceee and Pharisee: the origin and significance of the names. *Bulletin of the John Rylands Library*, **22**, 144–59.
Maquet, J.J. (1954). The Kingdom of Ruanda. In Forde (1954), 164–89.
Marcos, S. (1987). Curing and cosmology. *Development*: *Journal of the Society for International Development*, **1**, 20–25.

Mariscotti de Görlitz, A.M. (1978). *Pachamama Santa Tierra*. Berlin.
Marmorstein, A. (1920). *The Doctrine of Merits in Old Rabbinical Literature*. London.
Marsden, M. (1975). God, man and universe: a Maori view. In King (1975), 190–219.
Martin, L.H. (1987). *Hellenistic Religions: an Introduction*. New York.
Martin, M.-L. (1975). *Kimbangu: an African Prophet and his Church*. Oxford.
Maspero, H. (1981). *Taoism and Chinese Religion*. Amherst.
Maupoil, B. (1943). La géomancie à l'ancienne Côte des Esclaves. *Travaux et Mémoires de l'Institut d'Ethnologie*, **42**.
May, J. (1971). La philosophie bouddhique idéaliste. *Asiatic Studies*, **25**.
Mayes, A.D.H. (1977). Approaches to the problem of historical reconstruction. In Hayes & Miller (1977), 297–308.
Mbiti, J.S. (1969). *African Religions and Philosophy*. London.
Mbon, F.M. (1988). Brotherhood thanatology. *Archives de Sciences Sociales des Religions*, **65/1**, 161–71.
Meadow, M. and Kahoe, R. (1984). *Psychology of Religion: Religion in Individual Lives*. New York.
Mendenhall, G.E. (1954). Covenant forms in Israelite tradition. *Biblical Archeologist*, **17**, 50–76.
Mercer, S.A.B. (1942). *Horus, Royal God of Egypt*. Grafton.
— (1952). *The Pyramid Texts in Translation and Commentary*. New York.
Merrill, A.L. (1968). The house of Keret. *Svensk Exegetisk Årsbok*, **33**, 5–17.
Metcalf, B.D. (1982). *Islamic Revival in British India: Deoband, 1860–1900*. Princeton.
Metzger, B.M. (1984). A classified bibliography of the Graeco-Roman mystery religions. In Temporini & Haase (1984), 1259–423.
Metzger, M. (1970). Himmlische und irdische Wohnstatt Jahwes. *Ugarit-Forschungen*, **2**, 139–58.
Meyer, M.W. (1987). *The Ancient Mysteries: a Sourcebook*. San Francisco.
Meyers, C. (1976). *The Tabernacle Menorah*. Missoula.
Meynell, H. (1982). *The Intelligible Universe: a Cosmological Argument*. London.
Millard, A.R.: *see* Lambert & Millard 1969.
Molin, G. (1954). Die Stellung der Gebira im Staate Judah. *Thologische Zeitung*, **10**,161–75.
Montalbano, F.J. (1951). Canaanite Dagon: origin, nature. *Catholic Biblical Quarterly*, **13**, 381–97.
Montgomery, J.A. (1938). *Yam Sup* ('the Red Sea') = *Ultimum Mare? Journal of the American Oriental Society*, **58**, 131–2.
De Moor, J.C. (1971). *The Seasonal Pattern in the Ugaritic Myth of Ba'lu According to the version of Ilumilku*. Alter Orient und Altes Testament, 16. Kevelaer.
— (1976). Rāpi'ūma–Rephaîm. *Zeitschrift für die Alttestamentlicher Wissenschaft*, **88**, 323–45.
— (1987). *An Anthology of Religious Texts from Ugarit*. Nisaba, 16. Leiden.
Moortgat, A. (1949). *Tammuz*. Berlin.
Moran, W.L. (ed.) (1970). *Toward the Image of Tammuz and Other Essays*. Cambridge, Massachusetts.
Morgan, R. and Pye, M. (eds) (1977). *Ernst Troeltsch: Writings on Theology and Religion*. London.
Mortimer, E. (1982). *Faith and Power*. London.
Morton-Williams, P. (1960). The Yoruba Ogboni cult in Oyo. *Africa: Journal of the International African Institute*, **30**, 362–75.
Motzki, H. (1975). Ein Beitrag zum Problem des Stierkultes in der Religionsgeschichte Israels. *Vetus Testamentum*, **25**, 470–86.
Mowinckel, S. (1948). Urmensch und 'Königsideologie'. *Studia Theologica*, **2**, 71–89.
— (1956). *He that Cometh*. Oxford.
Mulder, N. (1983a). *Mysticism and Everyday Life in Contemporary Java*. Singapore.
— (1983b). Abangan Javanese religious thought and practice. *Bijdragen tot de Taal-, Land- en Volkenkunde*, **139**, 260–67
Mullikan, M.A. and Hotchkis, A.M. (1973) *The Nine Sacred Mountains of China*. Hong Kong.
Murdock, G.P. (1971). *Social Structure in Southeast Asia*. Chicago.
Murphy, J.M. (1989). *Santeria: an African Religion in America*. Boston.
Murtonen, A. (1952). *A Philological and Literary Treatise on the Old Testament Divine Names* אל, אלוה, אלהים, *and* יהוה. Helsinki.
Nagel, E. (1961). The meaning of reduction in the natural sciences. In Danto & Morgenbesser (1961). 117–37.
Nakamura, M. (1976). *The Crescent Arises over the Banyan Tree: a Study of the Muhammadiyah Movement in a Central Javanese Town*. Canberra.
— (1979). *The Reformist Ideology of Muhammadiyya*. Canberra.
Needham, J. (1983). *Science and Civilization in China*, **5**. Cambridge.
Nelson, H.H. (1944). The significance of the temple in the ancient Near East, 1: The Egyptian temple with particular reference to the Theban temples of the Empire period. *Biblical Archaeologist*, **7**, 44–53.
Nelson, R.D. (1981). *The Double Redaction of the Deuteronomistic History*. JSOT Supplements 18. Sheffield.
Neugebauer, O.: *see* Black *et al*. (1985).
Newman, J.H. (1870). *An Essay in Aid of a Grammar of Assent*. London.

Nicholson, E.W. (1973). *Exodus and Sinai in History and Tradition*. Oxford.

Nicholson, R.A. (1979). *Studies in Islamic Mysticism* (1921). Cambridge.

Niel, R. van (1970). *The Emergence of the Modern Indonesian Elite*. The Hague.

Nielsen, E. (1955). *Schechem: a Traditio-historical Investigation*. Copenhagen.

— (1968). *The Ten Commandments in Recent Perspective*. Studies in Biblical Theology, 2/7. London.

Nietzsche, F. (1974). *The Genealogy of Morals*. New York.

Nilsson, M.P. (1985). *The Dionysiac Mysteries of the Hellenistic and Roman Age*. Lund.

Nock, A.D. and Festugiere, A.J. (1954). *Corpus Hermeticum*. Paris.

Noer, D. (1973). *The Modernist Muslim Movement in Indonesia, 1900–1942*. London.

North, C.R. (1948). *The Suffering Servant in Deutero-Isiah*. Oxford.

Noth, M. (1930). *Das System der zwölf Stämme Israel*. Beiträge zur Wissenschaft vom Alten und Neuen Testament, 4/1. Stuttgart.

— (1981). *The Deuteronomistic History*. JSOT Supplements, 15. Sheffield.

Och, B. (1988). The Garden of Eden: from creation to covenant. *Judaism*, **37**, 143–56.

Oded, B. (1977). Judah and the exile. In Hayes & Miller (1977), 438–88.

Oden, R.A.: *see* Attridge & Oden 1976.

Ohlmarks, A. (1939). *Studien zum Problem des Schamanismus*. Lund.

Oldenburg, U. (1969). *The Conflict between Baal and El in Canaanite Religion*. Leiden.

Ollenburger, B.C. (1987). *Zion: the City of the Great King*. JSOT Supplements, 41. Sheffield.

Olmo Lete, G. del (1981). *Mitos y leyendas de Canaan*. Fuentes de la Sciencia Biblica, 1. Madrid.

— (1986). The 'divine' names of the Ugaritic kings. *Ugarit-Forschungen*, **18**, 83–95.

Ono, S. (1962). *Shinto: the Kami Way*. Tokyo.

Onunwa, U. (1989). Godianism: from a local black protest to a quest for world peace. *Journal of Dharma*, **14/1**, 48–61.

Ossio, A.J.M. (ed.) (1973). *Ideología mesiánica del mundo Andino*. Lima.

Otto, E. (1966). *Egyptian Art and the Cults of Osiris and Amun*. London.

Otto, R. (1917). *Das Heilige*. Stuttgart.

— (1923). *The Idea of the Holy*. New York.

Overmyer, D.L. (1976). *Folk Buddhist Religion*. Cambridge, Massachusetts.

— (1986). *Religions of China*. San Francisco.

Paley, W. (1802). *Natural Theology*. London.

Pallis, S.A. (1926). *The Babylonian Akitu Festival*. Copenhagen.

Paper, J. (1977). Dating the Chuang-tzu by analysis of philosophical terms. *Chinese Culture*, **18/4**, 33–40.

— (1988). *Offering Smoke, the Sacred Pipe and Native American Tradition*. Moscow, Idaho.

Parker, S.B. (1977). The historical composition of KRT and the cult of El. *Zeitschrift für die Alttestamentlicher Wissenschaft*, **89**, 161–75.

Pascal, B. (1973). *Pensées*. Everyman Library. London.

Patai, R. (1965). The goddess Asherah. *Journal of Near Eastern Studies*, **24**, 37–52.

Paton-Williams, D.: *see* Wilcox & Paton-Williams 1988.

Paulson, I., Hultkrantz, A. and Jettmar, K. (eds) (1962). *Die Religionen Nordeurasiens und der amerikanischen Arktis*. Die Religionen der Menschheit. Stuttgart.

Peacock, J. (1978). *Purifying the Faith: the Muhammadijah Movement in Indonesian Islam*. The Kiste and Ogan Social Change Series in Anthropology. Menlo Park.

Pease, G.Y.F. (1973). *El Dios Creador Andino*. Lima.

Peel, J.D.Y. (1968). *Aladura: Religious Movement among the Yoruba*. Oxford.

Pegis, A.G. (1966). St Anselm and the argument of the *Proslogion*. *Mediaeval Studies*, **28**, 228–67.

Pelton, R.D. (1980). *The Trickster in West Africa*. Berkeley.

Perry, W.J. (1925). The cult of the sun and the cult of the dead in Egypt. *Journal of Egyptian Archaeology*, **11**, 191–200.

Peterson, D.L. and Woodward, M. (1977). Northwest Semitic religion, a study of relational structures. *Ugarit-Forschungen*, **9**, 233–48.

Pettigrew, J. (1975). *Robber Noblemen*. London.

Piscatori, J. (ed.) (1983). *Islam in the Political Process*. Cambridge.

Plantinga, A. (1974). *The Nature of Necessity*. Clarendon Library of Logic and Philosophy. Oxford.

Plato (trans. Jowett, B.) (1953a). *The Dialogues of Plato*. Oxford.

— (1953b). *Euthyphro*. In Plato (1953a), vol. **1**, 303–27.

— (1953c). *Laws*. In Plato (1953a), vol. **4**, 189–544.

— (1953d). *The Sophist*. In Plato (1953a), vol. **3**, 321–428.

Pope, M.H. (1955). *El in the Ugaritic Texts*. Leiden.

— (1977). Notes on the Rephaim texts from Ugarit. In Ellis (1977), 163–82.

Popper, K.R. (1959). *The Logic of Scientific Discovery*. London.

Porten, B. (1968). *Archives from Elephantine*. Berkeley.

Potter, K.H. (ed.) (1977). *Encyclopedia of Indian Philosophies*, 2: *Indian Metaphysics and Epistemology: the Tradition of Nyāya-Vaiśesika up to Gaṅgeśa*. Princeton.

Poulat, E. (1979). *Histoire, dogme et critique dans*

*la crise moderniste*. Paris.
Pratt, J.B. (1920). *The Religious Consciousness: a Psychological Study*. New York.
Prestige, G.L. (1964). *God in Patristic Thought*. London.
Pritchard, J.B. (1969). *Ancient Near Eastern Tests Relating to the Old Testament*. Princeton.
Proudfoot, W. (1985). *Religious Experience*. Berkeley.
Provan, I.W. (1988). *Hezekiah and the Books of Kings*. Beihefte zur Zeitschrift für die Alttestamentliche Wissenschaft, 172. Berlin.
Przywara, E. (1946). *Polarity*. London.
Purvis, J.D. (1968). *The Samaritan Pentateuch and the Origin of the Samaritan Sect*. Harvard Semitic Monographs, 2. Cambridge, Massachusetts.
Pye, M. (1978). *Skilful Means: a Concept in Mahayana Buddhism*. London.
— (1987). *O-meguri, Pilgerfahrt in Japan*. Schriften der Universitatsbibliothek Marburg, 31. Marburg.
— (1989). *Marburg Revisited, Institutions and Strategies in the Study of Religion*, Marburg.
Quezada, N. (1989). *Enfermedad y maleficio*. Mexico City.
Quine, W. van O. (1953). *From a Logical Point of View*. Cambridge, Massachusetts.
Radin, P. (1956, 1972). *The Trickster, a Study in American Indian Mythology*. New York.
Rahman, F. (1979). *Islam*. Chicago.
— (1980). *Major Themes of the Qur'an*. Chicago.
Raittila, P. (1976). *Lestadiolaisuus 1860 luvulla*. Helsinki.
Ralston, H. (1987). *Christian Ashrams: a New Religious Movement in Contemporary India*. Lewiston.
Ranger, T.O. and Kimambo, I. (eds) (1972). *The Historical Study of African Religion*. London.
Rao, S.K. (1989). Megalithic religion among the Savara of Srikakulam District, South India. *The Eastern Anthropologist*, **43**, 289–94.
Ras, J.J. (1978). De Clownfiguren in de Wayang. *Bijdragen tot de Taal-, Land- en Volkenkunde*, **134**, 451–65.
Rasjidi, H.M. (1977). *Documents pour servir à l'histoire de l'Islam à Java*. Publications de l'École Française d'Extrême-Orient, 112. Paris.
Rattray, R.S. (1923). *Ashanti*. Oxford.
— (1927). *Religion and Art in Ashanti*. Oxford.
— (1930). *Akan-Ashanti Folktales*. Oxford.
Rawson, P. (1973). *Tantra, the Indian Cult of Ecstasy*. London.
Reardon, B. (1975). *Liberalism and Tradition*. Cambridge.
Reisner, G.A. (1936). *The Development of the Egyptian Tomb down to the Accession of Cheops*. Cambridge.
Rendtorff, R. (1977). The 'Yahwist' as theologian? The dilemma of pentateuchal criticism. *Journal for the Study of the Old Testament*, **3**, 2–10.
Richard, A. (1956). *Chisungu*. London.
Ringgren, H. (1973). *Religions of the Ancient Near East*. London.
Robbins, T. (1988). *Cults, Converts and Charisma*. London.
Roberts, J.J.M. (1973). The Davidic origin of the Zion tradition. *Journal of Biblical Literature*, **92**, 329–44.
Robinet, I. (1977). *Les commentaires du Tao To King jusqu'au VIIe siècle*. Paris.
— (1983). Le Ta-tung chen-ching: son authenticité et sa place dans les textes du shang-ch'ing ching. In Strickmann (1983), 394–433.
Robinson, F. (1988). *Varieties of South Asian Islam*. Research Papers in Ethnic Relations, 8. Warwick.
Robinson, J.M. (ed.) (1988). *The Nag Hammadi Library in English*. San Francisco.
Robinson, R.H. (1982). *The Buddhist Religion: a Historical Introduction*. The Religious Life of Man. Belmont.
Rodinson, M. (1974). *Muhammad*. Harmondsworth.
Rohls, J. (1987). *Theologie und Metaphysik: der ontologische Gottesbeweis und Kritiker*. Gütersloh.
Rolland, R. (1930). *Prophets of the New India*. London.
Rowe, W.L. (1975). *The Cosmological Argument*. Princeton.
Rowland, C. (1982). *The Open Heaven*. London.
Rowley, H.H. (1950). *From Joseph to Joshua*. Oxford.
— (1967). *Worship in Ancient Israel*. London.
Rowlinson, A.E.J. (ed.) (1928). *Essays on the Trinity and Incarnation*. London.
Rudolph, K. (1978). *Mandaeism*. Leiden.
— (1984). *Gnosis*. Edinburgh.
Ruiz de Alarcon, H. (trans. Andrews, J.R. and Hassig, R.) (1984). *Treatise on the Heathen Superstitions*, Civilization of the American Indian Series. Norman.
Saggs, H.W.F. (1978). *The Encounter with the Divine in Mesopotamia and Israel*. London.
Sancher, R. (1990). *Pioneers of Psychology*. New York.
Sarma, D.S. (1973). *Hinduism through the Ages*. Bombay.
Sasson, J.M. (1973). The worship of the golden calf. In Hoffner (1973), 151–9.
Saunders, E.D. (1960). *Mudrā, a Study of Symbolic Gestures in Japanese Buddhist Sculpture*. New York.
Saussure, F. de (1985). *Course in General Linguistics*. Oxford.
Savory, R.M. (ed.) (1976). *Introduction to Islamic Civilization*. Cambridge.
Schäfer, P. (1977). The Hellenistic and Macca-

baean periods. In Hayes & Miller (1977). 539–604.

Schaffer, K. (1967). Approaches to reduction. *Philosophy of Science*, **34**, 122–42.

Schapera, I. (1930). *The Khoisan Peoples of South Africa*. London.

Schebesta, P. (1975). Die Urwald-Pygmäen. In Baumann (1975a), 775–84.

Schimmel, A. (1975). *The Mystical Dimensions of Islam*. Chapel Hill.

Schipper, K.M. (1982). *Le corps taoiste*. Paris.

Schlang, S. (1989). *Religiöse Aspekte von Maoritanga*. Mundus Reihe Ethnologie, 30. Bonn.

Schleiermacher, F. (1987). *Speeches on Religion*. Cambridge.

Schmidt, C. and MacDermot, V. (1978). *Pistis Sophia*. Nag Hammadi Studies, 9. Leiden.

Schmökel, H. (1928). *Der Gott Dagan*. Leipzig.

Schoffeleers, M. (1972). The history and political role of the M'Bona cult among the Mang'anja. In Ranger and Kitambo (1972), 73–94.

Scholem, G. (1946). *Major Trends in Jewish Mysticism*. New York.

— (1971). *The Messianic Idea in Judaism*. New York.

Schomerus-Gernböck, L. (1975). Madagaskar. In Baumann (1975a), 785–815.

Schur, I. (1937). *Wesen und Bedeutung der Beschneidung im Licht der alttestamentlichen Quellen und der Völkerkunde*. Helsingfors.

Schürer, E. (1973). *The History of the Jewish People in the Age of Jesus Christ*. Edinburgh.

— (1979). *The History of the Jewish People in the Time of Jesus Christ*. Edinburgh.

Segal, J.B. (1963). *The Hebrew Passover*. London.

Seidel, A. (1983). Imperial treasures and Taoist sacraments: Taoist roots in the Apocrypha. In Strickmann (1983), 291–371.

Seiwert, H. (1985). *Volksreligion und nationale Tradition in Taiwan*. Stuttgart.

Seters, J. van (1975). *Abraham in History and Tradition*. New Haven.

Shackle, C. (1984). *The Sikhs*. Minority Rights Group Report, 65. London.

Sharma, A. (1986). New Hindu religious movements in India. In Beckford (1986), 220–39.

Sharpe, E.J. (1976). *Comparative Religion: a History*. London.

Shibayama, A. (1974). *Zen Comments on the Mumonkan*. New York.

Sicard, H. von (1975). Das Gebiet zwischen Sambesi und Limpopo. In Baumann (1975a), 457–72.

Siikala, A.-L. (1978). *The Rite Technique of the Siberian Shaman*. FF Communications, 220. Helsinki.

Simpson, W.K. *et al*. (1972). *The Literature of Ancient Egypt: an Anthology of Stories, Instructions and Poetry*. London.

Sivin, N. (1978). On the word 'Taoist' as a source of perplexity. *History of Religions*, **17**, 303–330.

Skinner, S. (1982). *The Living Earth Manual of Fengshui: Chinese Geomancy*. London.

Smallwood, E.M. (1976). *The Jews under Roman Rule*. Studies in Judaism in Late Antiquity, 20. Leiden.

Smith, D.H. (1973). *Confucius*. London.

Smith, E.W (1961). *African Ideas of God*. London.

Smith, G.E. (1914). Egyptian mummies. *Journal of Egyptian Archaeology*, **1**, 189–206.

Smith, J. (1974). *Tapu Removal in Maori Religion*. Wellington.

Smith, M. (1987). *Palestinian Parties and Politics that Shaped the Old Testament*. London.

Smith, M.S. (1986). Interpreting the Baal cycle. *Ugarit-Forschungen*, **18**, 313–39.

Smith, S.P. (1913–15). *The Lore of the Wharewananga*. Polynesian Society Memoir, **3–4**, New Plymouth.

Smolar, L.: *see* Aberbach & Smolar 1967.

Snellgrove, D. and Richardson, H. (1980). *A Cultural History of Tibet*. Boulder.

Snouck-Hurgronje, C. (1893–4). *De Atjèhers*. 2 vols. Batavia.

Soebardi, S. (1971). Santri religious elements as reflected in the Book of Tjentini. *Bijdragen tot de Taal-, Land- en Volkenkunde*, **127**, 331–49.

— (1975). *The Book of Cabolèk*. Bibliotheca Indonesica, 10. The Hague.

Soggin, J.A. (1975). *Old Testament and Oriental Studies*. Biblia et Orientalia, 29. Rome.

Soloman, R.C. (1972). *From Rationalism to Existentialism*. New York.

Solomon, N. (1991). *Judaism and World Religions*, London.

Sommerfeld, W. (1982). *Der Aufstieg Marduks*. Alter Orient und Altes Testament, 213. Kevelaer.

Sparks, H.F.D. (ed.) (1984). *The Apocryphal Old Testament*. Oxford.

Sperber, D. (1975). *Rethinking Symbolism*. Cambridge.

Spieth, J. (1911). *Die Religion der Eweer in Süd-Togo*. Göttingen.

Spindler, G. (1980). *The Making of Psychological Anthropology*. Berkeley.

Stace, W.T. (1960). *Mysticism and Philosophy*. Philadelphia.

Stamm, J.J. and Andrew, M.E. (1967). *The Ten Commandments in Recent Research*. Studies in Biblical Theology, 2/2. London.

Starbuck, E.D. (1901). *The Psychology of Religion: an Empirical Study of the Growth of Religious Consciousness*.

Stead, G.S. (1977). *Divine Substance*. Oxford.

Steenbrinck, K.A. (1974). *Pesantren, Madrasah, Sekolah: recente ontwikkelingen in Indonesisch Islamonderricht*. Meppel.

Steiner, F. (1967). *Taboo*. Harmondsworth.

Stöhr, W. (1976). *Die altindonesischen Reli-*

*gionen*. Leiden.
Stöhr, W. and Zoetmulder, P.J. (1965). *Die Religionen Indonesiens*. Die Religionen der Menschheit, 5/1. Stuttgart.
Stowasser, B. (ed.) (1987). *The Islamic Impulse*. London.
Strand, K. (ed.) (1982). *The Sabbath in Scripture and History*. Washington.
Strenski, I. (1976). Reductionism and structural anthropology. *Inquiry*, **19**, 73–89.
— (1987). *Four Theories of Myth in Twentieth-century History*. London.
Strickmann, M. (1983). *Tantric and Taoist Studies*, 2. Brussels.
Strieder, P. (1966). *Deutsche Malerei der Dürerzeit (Die Blauen Bücher)*. Königstein im Taunus.
Stuehlmuller, C. (1970). *Creative Redemption in Deutero-Isaiah*. Rome.
Stutterheim, W.F. (1926). Oost-Java en de hemelberg. *Djawa*, **6**, 333–49.
Sundén, H. (1966). *Die Religion und die Rollen*. Berlin.
Sundkler, B.G.M. (1961). *Bantu Prophets in South Africa*. Oxford.
Surgy, A. de (1981). *La géomancie et le cult d'Afa chez les Evhé du littoral*. Publications Orientalistes de France.
Suter, D.W. (1979). *Tradition and Composition in the Parables of Enoch*. SBL Dissertation Series, 47. Missoula.
Sutherland, H.A. (1973). *Pangreh Pradja: Java's Indigenous Administrative Corps and its Role in the Last Decades of Dutch Colonial Rule*. New Haven.
— (1975). The Priyai. *Indonesia*, **19**, April, 57–77.
— (1979). *The Making of a Bureaucratic Elite*. Singapore.
Suzuki, D.T. (trans.) (1968). *The Lankavatara Sutra*. London.
Swellengrebel, J.L. (1960). *Bali: Studies in Life, Thought, and Ritual*. The Hague.
— (1969). *Bali: Further Studies in Life, Thought, and Ritual*. The Hague.
Swinburne, R.G. (1977). *The Coherence of Theism*. Oxford.
— (1979). *The Existence of God*. Oxford.
Talbot, P.A. (1969). *The Peoples of Southern Nigeria*, Plymouth.
Tarragon, J.-M. de: *see* Levine & Tarragon 1984.
Tcherikover, V. (1961). *Hellenistic civilization and the Jews*. Philadelphia.
Tedlock, D. (trans.) (1985). *Popul Vuh*. New York.
Temporini, H. and Haase, W. (eds) (1984). *Aufstieg und Niedergang der rom. Welt*, 2. Berlin.
Tennant, F.R. (1903). *The Sources Of the Doctrine of the Fall and Original Sin*. Cambridge.
Terrien, S. (1970). The omphalos myth and Hebrew religion. *Vetus Testamentum*, **20**, 315–38.
Thomas, E.J. (1927). *The Life of the Buddha*. London.
Thomas, K. (1971). *Religion and the Decline of Magic*. New York.
Thomas Aquinas (1964). *Summa theologiae*. London.
— (trans. Pegis, A.C.) (1975). *Summa contra gentiles,* 4 vols. Notre Dame.
Thompson, H.O. (1970). *Mekal: the God of Beth Shan*. Leiden.
Thompson, J. and Heelas, P. (1986). *The Way of the Heart: the Rajneesh Movement*. New Religious Movements Series. Wellingborough.
Thompson, L.G. (1973). *The Chinese Way in Religion*. The Religious Life of Man Series. Encino.
— (1969). *Chinese Religion: an Introduction*. The Religious Life of Man Series. Belmont.
Thompson, T.L. (1974). *The Historicity of the Patriarchal Narratives*. Beihefte zur Zeitschrift für die Alttestamentliche Wissenschaft, 133. Berlin.
Thureau-Dangin, F. (1921). *Rituels accadiens*. Paris.
Thurman, R.A. (1976). *The Holy Teaching of Vimalakirti*. London.
Tremearne, A.J.N. (1914). *The Ban of the Bori: Demons and Demon Dancing in West and North Africa*. London.
Tucci, G. (1961). *The Theory and Practice of the Mandala: with Special Reference to the Psychology of the Unconscious*. London.
Tully, M. and Jacob, S. (1985). *Amritsar: Mrs Gandhi's Last Battle*. London.
Turner, V. (1969). *The Ritual Process*. London.
Turner, V. and Turner, E. (1978). *Image and Pilgrimage in Christian Culture*. Oxford.
Tyloch, W. (ed.) (1990). *Studies on Religions in the Context of Social Sciences: Methodological and Theoretical Relations*. Warsaw.
Underhill, E. (1916). *Mysticism*. London.
Ustorf, W. (1975). *Afrikanische Initiative: das aktive Leiden des Propheten Simon Kimbangu*. Frankfurt.
Utrecht, E. (1975). The Javanese dukun and his role in social unrest. *Cultures et Développement*, **7/2**, 319–35.
Vaihinger, H. (1924). *The Philosophy of 'as if'*. New York.
Vanderkam, J.: *see* Black *et al*. 1985.
Van Driel, G. (1969). *The cult of Aššur*. Assen.
Vansina, J. (1975). Südkongo. In Baumann (1975a), 649–84.
Vanstiphout, H.L.J. (1984). Inanna/Ishtar as a figure of controversy. In Kippenberg (1984), 225–38.
Vaux, R. de (1961). Les chérubins et l'arche de l'alliance, les sphinx gardiens et les trônes divins dans l'ancien orient. *Mémoires de l'Université*

St-Joseph, **38**, 93–124.
— (1965). *Ancient Israel*. London.
— (1969). Sur l'origine Kénite ou Madianite du Yahwisme. *Eretz Israel*, **9**, 28–32.
— (1971). La thèse de l'amphictyonie Israélite. *Harvard Theological Review*, **64**, 415–36.
— (1978). *The Early History of Israel*, 1. London.
Vermaseren, J. (1963). *Mithras, the Secret God*. London.
Vermes, G. (1977). *The Dead Sea Scrolls: Qumran in Perspective*. London.
— (1968). *The Dead Sea Scrolls in English*. Harmondsworth.
Vermeylen, J. (1985). L'affaire du veau d'or (Ex 32–34). Zeitschrift für die Alttestamentliche Wissenschaft, **97**, 1–23.
Viesca, C. (1986). *Medicina prehispanica de México*. Mexico City.
Vollenhoven, C. van (1928). *De ontdekking van het adatrecht*. Leiden.
Vriezen, T.C. (1967). *The Religion of Ancient Israel*. London.
Wagner, G. (1967). *Pauline Baptism and the Pagan Mysteries*. Edinburgh.
Wainwright, G.A. (1934). Some aspects of Amun. *Journal of Egyptian Archaeology*, **20**, 139–53.
Walena, S. (1981). *Feasting with Cannibals: an Essay on Kwakintl Cosmology*. Princeton.
Wallace, A.F.C. (1969). *The Death and Rebirth of the Seneca*. New York.
Wallis, R. (1977). *The Road to Total Freedom: a Sociological Analysis of Scientology*. New York.
Ward, K. (1989). '0bedient rebels' – the relationship between the early 'Balokole' and the church of Uganda: the Mukono crisis of 1941. *Journal of Religion in Africa*, **19**, 194–227.
Ware, J. (1966). *Alchemy, Medicine and Religion in the China of AD 320: the Nei P'ien of Ko Hung*. Cambridge, Massachusetts.
Warne, R.R. (1990). Elaine Pagels' *Adam, Eve and the Serpent*: reactions and responses. *Laval Théologique et Philosophique*, **Feb 1990**.
Washburn, M. (1988). *The Ego and the Dynamic Ground: a Transpersonal Theory of Human Development*. Albany.
Watt, W.M. (1973). *The Formative Period of Islamic Thought*. Edinburgh.
— (1978). *Bell's Introduction of the Qur'an*. Edinburgh.
Weber, M. (1976). *The Protestant Ethic and the Spirit of Capitalism*. London.
Webster, H. (1942). *Taboo: a Sociological Study*. Stanford.
Welch, H. (1957). *Taoism: the Parting of the Way*. Boston.
Welch, H. and Seidel, A. (1979). *Facets of Taoism*. New Haven.
Wescott, J. (1962). The sculpture and myths of Eshu-Elegba. Africa, **32/4**, 336–53.
West, M.L. (1983). *The Orphic Poems*. Oxford.
Wheel Publications (1975). *Kamma and its Fruits*. Kandy.
Whitehead, A.N. (1969). *Process and Reality: an Essay in Cosmology*. New York.
Whybray, R.N. (1978). *Thanksgiving for a Liberated Prophet*. JSOT Supplements, 4. Sheffield.
— (1987). *The Making of the Pentateuch*. JSOT Supplements, 53. Sheffield.
Widengren. G. (1950). The ascension of the apostle and the heavenly book. *Uppsala Universitets Årskrift*: 7.
— (1977). The Persian period. In Hayes & Miller (1977), 489–538.
Wilber, K. (1983). *Up from Eden: a Transpersonal View of Human Development*. Boulder.
Wilbert, J. (1987). *Tobacco and Shamanism in South America*. New Haven.
Wilcox, P. and Paton-Williams, D. (1988). The servant songs in Deutero-Isaiah. *Journal for the Study of the Old Testament*, **42**, 79–102.
Wilhelm, R. (1956). *I Ging: das Buch der Wandlungen*. Düsseldorf.
Williams, P. (1989). *Mahayana Buddhism: the Doctrinal Foundations*. London.
Williams, R. (1984). *A New Face of Hinduism: the Swaminarayan Religion*. Cambridge.
Wilson, R.M. (1964). *The Gnostic Problem*. London.
Wolf, A.P. (ed.) (1974). *Religion and Ritual in Chinese Society*. Stanford.
Wolff, H.W. (ed.) (1971). *Probleme biblische Theologie* [G. von Rad *Festschrift*]. Munich.
Wolkenstein, D. and Kramer, S.N. (1984). *Inanna, Queen of Heaven and Earth*. London.
Woodward, M.: *see* Peterson & Woodward 1977.
Wright, G.E. (1965). *Schechem*. New York.
Wright, G.R.H. (1970). The mythology of pre-Israelite Shechem. *Vetus Testamentum*, **20**, 75–82.
Wyatt, N. (1978). The problem of the 'god of the fathers'. Zeitschrift für die Alttestamentliche Wissenschaft, **90**, 101–4.
— (1979a). Some observations on the idea of history among the West Semitic peoples. *Ugarit-Forschungen*, **11**, 825–32.
— (1979b). The development of the tradition in Exodus 3. *Zeitschrift für die Alttestamentliche Wissenschaft*, **91**, 437–42.
— (1980). The relationship of the deities Dagan and Hadad. *Ugarit-Forschungen*, **12**, 375–9.
— (1983). The stela of the seated god from Ugarit. *Ugarit-Forschungen*, **15**, 271–7.
— (1984). The 'Anat stela from Ugarit and its ramifications. *Ugarit-Forschungen*, **16**, 327–37.
— (1985). 'Araunah the Jebusite' and the throne of David. *Studia Theologica*, **39**, 39–53.
— (1986a). The hollow crown: ambivalent elements in West Semitic royal ideology. *Ugarit-*

*Forschungen*, **18**, 421–36.
— (1986b). The AB cycle and kingship in Ugaritic thought. *Cosmos*, **2**, 135–42.
— (1986c). The significance of the burning bush. *Vetus Testamentum*, **36**, 361–5.
— (1987). Who killed the dragon? *Aula Orientalis*, **5**, 185–98.
— (1988). The source of the Ugarit myth of the conflict of Ba'al and Yam. *Ugarit-Forschungen*, **20**, 375–85.
Xenophon (1979). *Memorabilia*. Loeb Classical Library, 168. London.
Yadin, Y. (1966). *Masada*. London.
— (1985). New gleanings on Resheph from Ugarit. In Kort and Morschauer (1985), 259–74.
Yamasaki, T. (1988). *Shingon, Japanese Esoteric Buddhism*. Boston.
Yampolsky, P. (1967). *The Platform Sutra of the Sixth Patriarch*. New York.
Yang, C.K. (1967). *Religion in Chinese Society*. Berkeley.
Yarden, L. (1971). *The Tree of Light*. London.
Yu-lan, Fung (1952). *A History of Chinese Philosophy*. Princeton.
Zahan, D. (1974). *The Bambara*. Iconography of Religions, 7/2. Leiden.
— (1980). *Antilopes du soleil: arts et rites agraires d'Afrique noire*. Vienna.
Zijl, P.J. van (1972). *Baal*. Alter Orient und Altes Testament, 10. Kevelaer.
Zimbardo, P. Ebbesen, E and Maslach, C. (1977). *Influencing Attitudes and Changing Behavior*. Reading, Massachusetts.
Zoetmulder, P.J. (1935). *Pantheisme en monisme in de Javaansche Soeloek-litteratuur*. Nijmegen.
Zwernemann, J. (1968). *Die Erde in Vorstellungswelt und Kulturpraktiken der sudanishen Völker*. Berlin.